JN399452

Grandpa Was a Soldier

TO.

Grandpa was a Soldier

First published on October 30, 2025.

Author: Moon Young-il
Publisher: Yang Moon-gyu
Design : Jang Young-do, Ahn So-ra

SIWAESEI Publishing
Registration Number: 319-2005-000014
Address: 107-1, Sangga-dong, 159 Chunghyeon-ro, Jochiwon-eup,
Sejong Special Self-Governing City (30021)
Main Phone: (1982)044-863-7652
Fax: 0505-116-7653
Mobile Phone: (1982)10-5355-7565
Email: sie2005@naver.com
Supplied by: Korea Publishers Cooperative
Orders: (1982)02-716-5616
Fax: (1982)031-944-8234~6

ISBN 979-11-91914-93-1 (03810)

Grandpa Was a Soldier

SIWAESEI

My Personal History

Career

Feb.1999-Present	: Adviser to the Korea Research Institute for Strategy
	: Leader, Study Meeting of Korean National Security Strategy Thought History
Mar.1997-Feb.1999	: Invitation Professor in national security and military strategy, the Korea National Defense University
May.1994-Aug.1996	: Visiting Scholar in military science, Ball State University, U.S.A, Return to my home Korea(1996)
Oct.1988-Mar.1993	: Vice-Chairman the National security Council and The National Emergency Planning Board, Republic of Korea
Dec.1987-Oct.1988	: Deputy Commander in Chief, 1st Field Army
Jul.1986-Dec.1987	: Corps Commander, 1st Army Corps
Jul.1984-Jul.1986	: Deputy Chief of Staff for Operation Education and Training - (G-3), Army H.Q, Seoul
Jan.1983-Jul.1984	: Commander, 8th Infantry Division
May.1981-Jan.1983	: Commander, 7th Airborne Special Warfare Brigade
May.1980-May1981	: Chief of Staff and Chief Instructor, Army War College
Oct.1979-May.1980	: Military Professor, the National Defense University
	: Chief of Military Assistance Inquiry Group to Morocco
Nov.1977-Oct.1979	: Regiment Commander, Recruit Training Center
Feb.1977-Nov.1977	: National Security Study Cores, National defense University
Sep.1975-Feb.1977	: Assistant Chief of Staff(G-2) - Special Warfare Command H.Q
Mar.1974-Sep.1975	: Division G-4, Capital Mechanized Infantry Division
Jun.1972-Mar.1974	: Battalion Commander, Capital Mechanized Infantry Division
	: Activation (24. Oct.1972)-the 2nd Mechanized Infantry battalion (the 106 troop)
Sep.1970-Jun.1972	: Instructor, the Korean Army War college

Jan.1969-Sep.1970	: Combine Forces course: Führung Academy der Bundesware (War College) -West Germany
Nov.1967-Jan.1969	: Special Warfare officer, Special Warfare Agency-Army H.Q
Oct.1966-Nov.1967	: Military History Officer, the Korean Tiger Division to Vietnam
Sep.1965-Oct.1966	: Counterespionage Operation Officer, the 5th Division H.Q
Oct.1964-Sep.1965	: Instructor, the 107 R.O.T.C-Yeunsai University
	: Officer Advanced Course-Kwangju Army Infantry School
May.1962-Oct.1964	: Instructor, Ranger & Guerrilla School-Army Infantry School
	: Marriage (22. Apr), Birth (27. May. 63) of 1st son, Jung-un
Jan.1962-May.1962	: Unconventional Warfare Course, Special Warfare School-John F. Kennedy Center, N.C, U.S.A.
Jun.1958-Jan.1962	: Company Commander, Battalion S-3, platoon Leader
	: Commissioned (16. Jun. 1958) as 2nd Lt, Korea military

Academy

Jul.1954-Jun.1958	: Cadet, Korea Military Academy-Hwarangdae, Taeneung
May.1935-Jul.1954	: Dongnae High School, Busan Normal (middle) School, Dongnae Primary School
9th May.1935	: My (your grandfather) Birthday! Dongnae, Busan Korea

Education

MA in 'Human Resource Management', Chunbuk National University, 1983
BA in 'General Science', Korean Military Academy, 1958

Honor

Gukseon Medal, Order of National Security Merit, from president of R.O.K, 1993
Cheonsu Medal, Order of National Security Merit, from president of R.O.K, 1988
Legion of Merit (Degree of Officer), from President of U.S.A, 1989
Honorary Citizenship : Fayetteville, NC and Muncie, IN of U.S.A
Pistol (cal 45) Champion: Championship, 1960- R.O.K Army

Publication

* The History of Thoughts on American National Security strategy (in korean), Seoul Korea, 1999, 582 pages, ISBN : 89-7312-117-0
* The History of Thoughts on Korean National Security Strategy (ancient & Medieval Periods) (in korean), Seul Korea, 2007, 791 pages, ISBN : 978-89-87647-40-193900
* The History of Thoughts on Korean National Security Strategy (modern periods) (in korean), Seoul Korea, 2018, 703 pages, ISBN : 979-11-6222-615(93910)
* The Korean National Security Strategy Thoughts History (Present periods) (in korean), in progress
* The Korean National Security Strategy thoughts (Future periods) (in Korean), in progress

Gen. Moon Young Il's Oral History of His Military Life Long, May.2016. Modern Korean Oral History Material Office of Korean Central Research Institute, Dictation (Seoul Univercity Geujang-gag, Prof. Kim Do Min)

Essay

『Asia-Pacific Collective Security System Plan』 (in Korean), 1977
『Arms Control, Disarmament & Security』 (in Korean), 1988
.... and Various articles on national security and strategy.

Foreword

During my time as a cadet at the Korea Military Academy (KMA) and later as a young, commissioned officer in the 1950s and 1960s, I felt disheartened to see many senior generals taking up positions in ordinary companies as presidents or advisors after their military service. Some even entered politics as assembly members upon retiring as generals. This trend led me to resolve that, upon my own retirement, I would dedicate my life to writing memoirs and autobiographies, staying true to my identity as a military serviceperson. Over the years, I came to understand why they made such choices, but I still believed that individuals like Admiral Yi Sun-sin, who achieved great feats worthy of historical record, should document their accomplishments through memoirs. As a general who served in a time of peace, I hesitated to write my own autobiography, considering my life to be that of an ordinary serviceperson. However, in 2015, when I was nearly 80 years old, Professor Kim from the Kyujanggak Institute for Korean Studies at Seoul National University approached me. He was responsible for the "Section on Modern Military History of the Armed Forces of Korea" in a project to publish the "Modern Korean Oral History Data Sheet" by The Academy of Korean Studies. He told me, "Someone recommended you, General," and asked me to share my military history, from my cadet years to my service in the Tiger Division dispatched to Vietnam. I initially responded that my military career was ordinary, but he explained that he was collecting oral records from individuals to piece together a comprehensive history of Korea's armed forces. Thus, I began recounting my experiences, speaking for three to four hours a day, over 20 sessions, while Professor Kim recorded everything. This resulted in the creation of the original and revised versions of the "Recorded Copy of General Moon Yeong-Il's Oral Descriptions." I received ten copies of these, along with a DVD of the recordings and the publication rights. Professor Kim encouraged me, saying, "If you write an autobiography based on these records, it will make a wonderful book for future generations." Every time I saw the 'Recorded Copy' on my bookshelf, alongside the 'card folder' containing the records, I felt compelled to write my autobiography. My primary motivation was to ensure that my only grandson, who had settled in the United States, and his descendants, understood their roots before they sought them out. I wanted them to appreciate Korea, the homeland of their grandfather, who dedicated his life to the country, striving to combat evil and uphold righteousness. I hoped they would always do their best for both Korea and the United States, their home country. In recent times, there has been a growing disconnect between people and their understanding of the military, with some even intentionally disparaging it. I decided to write this autobiography to offer insights into my career as a Korean military serviceperson, albeit an ordinary one, and to provide a glimpse into the military history of Korea's Armed Forces over half a century, from the 1950s to the 1990s. I aimed to create a narrative that would serve as a puzzle piece in the broader history of Korea's military during my era, a permanent record alongside the 'Recorded Copy.' I also hoped that teenagers aspiring to join the military, cadets (especially those at KMA in Taereung), and soldiers and officers of all ranks in long-term service would learn valuable lessons and gain wisdom from past mistakes by reading about my life-a life dedicated to the country, striving to combat evil and uphold righteousness. As I completed this autobiography, my grandson, Jun Ho, visited to share news of his marriage to Kate, his best friend and girlfriend since middle and high school in the United States. It was one of the most joyful moments of my life, filling my heart with happiness. I pray that God's blessings and grace will always be with Jun Ho and Kate. Finally, as I publish this autobiography about the life of a serviceperson, I extend my gratitude to my family and my wife, who have been by my side throughout my life. To my wife, who married me when I was a young, poor First Lieutenant fresh out of KMA, endured the hardships of a military family, and celebrated our diamond anniversary, our 60th anniversary, I say, "I would marry you all over again if given the chance."

From Ilsan, Gyeonggi-do, Seoul Korea on Autumn, 2025

Table of Contents

My Personal History 04

Preface 07

Part 1 : Dreaming of Becoming a Great Man

Chapter 1: Grandpa's Childhood

1. **Grandpa's hometown, your place of origin** 25
   Dongnae, Busan, Republic of Korea, my hometown and a good place to live in with a long history of traditions/ Grandpa's father, who lived with a pioneering spirit and studied new learnings/ My mother's lifelong dedication to our family is a story of resilience.

2. **The Japanese Colonial Era and Liberation (1935-1948)** 29
   My birth, marked by mother's auspicious dream and my childhood/ Entering elementary school through an exam/ Our serviceman principal boasted, 'the Military Academy and Nrmal School'/ School life at the end of the war/ Developing lifelong habits/ Learning 'Hangul' from my mother / Life in Dongnae, Busan, post-liberation/ A battle with a class bully after becoming class president

3. **Busan Normal School and the Dream of Greatness (1948~1950)** 34
   Entering Busan Normal School/ The establishment of the Republic of Korea through the May 10th Election./ The post-liberation era of cattle-drawn carriage in Busan/ Reading about the United States and great figures at the U.S. Information Service/ Dreaming of becoming a great man/ Almost becoming my teacher's adopted son

4. **The Korean War and the Call to KMA (1950-1954)** 37
   The outbreak of Korean War on June 25th and the beginning of temporary tent school The desperate evacuation from the Masan line

commissioned as second lieutenant in Republic of Korea Army/ My Korea Military Academy (KMA) class ring symbolizes my eternal commitment to the nation, akin to a wedding ring/ At KMA, I learned invaluable lessons and developed key characteristics : studying military history, adhering to rules, treating everyone equally, rewarding and punishing fairly, understanding the true meaning of civilian control, practicing modesty and mutual respect, using honorifics, fostering autonomy, self-reliance, and embodying loyalty and devotion/ I struggled with socializing due to my abstinence from drinking and singing, yet I was full of pioneering spirit, eager to create something from nothing/ I kept 'A Father's Prayer' by General Douglas MacArthur close to my heart

Part 2. Dreaming of Becoming a Commander (General), a Hero

Chapter 3: Early Years After Being Commissioned, Serving as a Platoon Leader and Company Commander on the Central and Western Frontlines (1958-1961)

1. Officer Basic Course (OBC) at Sangmudae Army Infantry School 77

2. Proudly Becoming the Platoon Leader of the 1st Regiment of the Capital Infantry Division (October 1958) 78

The Infantry Badge of the 1st Regiment: A Symbol of Tradition and Honor/ The Mighty Platoon Leader on the Central Front/ The Environment and Daily Life of Our Platoon (and Its Leader), Sharing Joyful and Sorrowful Moments with My Subordinates/ A small unit under Gukmangbong Peak and working as its platoon leader Officers and soldiers in front units had much more work during winter. Especially when it snowed, we had to clear the training ground of snow every day, every hour, as soon as it fell. Additionally, to keep the communication roads between bases accessible at all times, we had to constantly remove snow from the tactical roads or supply routes within our region. Snowfall was frequent and heavy in the front during winter, forming part of our daily routine, training, and military life in a front unit. As mentioned, front platoon leaders spent most of the year fulfilling duties as officers of the week for the companies.

3. The 1st Regiment Combat Team (RCT) went to the frontline of Imjingang River, Munsan 81

Second Lieutenant Moon stands on the western frontline of Imjingang

River, Moonsan/ Hardwood battle position built in the late era of the Korean War/ Seongdong-ri, a front line village where villagers were returnig from evacuation/ We planned to reinforce the defensive position at the riverside downstream of the Imjingang River/ An emergency drill (Defcon-2) truly made me feel “cold and hungry.”/ We participated in a Winter Field Training Exercise (FTX. ‘ICE CAP) and an Army Training Test (ATT) with live ammunition/ Army Training Test (ATT) (with live ammunition) of the infantry/ We built the first new barracks with cement bricks in the history of ROK Armed Forces/ We (KMA Graduate and I) refused to vote in the Electoral Fraud of March 15th and promised myself to maintain ‘military neutrality.’/ Our battalion won the tactics and techniques competition against other battalions. Korean War era in Seongdong-ri, a frontline village where villagers were returning from evacuation/ We planned to reinforce the defensive position at the riverside downstream of the Imjingang River/ An emergency drill (Defcon-2) truly made us feel 'cold and hungry'/ We participated in a Winter Field Training Exercise (FTX-ICE CAP) and an Army Training Test (ATT) with live ammunition/ We built the first new barracks with cement bricks in the history of the ROK Armed Forces/ I refused to vote in the Electoral Fraud of March 15th and promised myself to maintain 'military neutrality'/ Our regiment won the tactics and techniques competition against other battalions.

4. Company commander of Combet out post (COP), Army Champion of pistol shooting in 1960. 92

I returned to the central front and experienced the April 19th Revolution./ I became the best pistol shooter in an Army competition against divisions./ AS the company commander of COP in Cheorwon near Backma-goji (the Southern Limit Line of DMZ)/ Joint Shooting Competition between ROK Army and the Eighth United States Army— I came in first for rapid fire./ I fell in love with a charming young lady and worked as the operation officer(S-3) of the GOP battalion under the new concep of FEBA, while going on dates/ The long-awaited <Military Revolution of May 16> and <Colon Report> occurred. / I entered ‘The Army Shooting Competition’ against other divisions and the ‘Joint Shooting Competition between the Korean Army and U.S. Eighth Army’ in 1961

Chapter 4: Studying Abroad in the United States, Getting Married, Drill Instructor for ‘Dongbok Night Owls,’ Guerrilla & Ranger School, and Instructor for Yonsei

University's ROTC (1961-1966)

1. Studying Abroad in the United States, Attending J.F. Kennedy Center, Fort Bragg, NC 103

A door to studying abroad in the United States opened for me/ I got engaged before departing./ On my way to the U.S. I witnessed post-war Tokyo, Japen/ I traveled past Hawaii and arrived in beautiful San Francisco, and I feel wonder./ Then journeyed across the U.S. continent (North) by train, passing through Chicago and arriving in Washington D.C./ Finally, we reached the J.F.Kennedy Center/ There, I learned about the philosophy and concept of special warfare at the American Special Warfare School/ I witnessed strict discrimination against African-Americans in southern U.S. regions/ Americans have a profound love for their flag./ I took a field trip to New York and West Point/ After completing my studies in U.S., I embarked on a road trip in the southern U.S. and Mexico, visited the Marine Corps base in San Diego, sang 'Arizona cowboy'./ The knowledge and determination I gained during my time studying abroad became the guiding pathfinders of my life.

2. Marriage and Life as a Newlywed in Gwangju, Establishing the <Dongbok (Night Owl) Guerrilla Training School>, and Serving as a Drill Instructor 126

I worked as a guerrilla drill instructor at Gwangju Infantry School and I got married and began my life as a newlywed in Gwangju/ I helped establish the <Dongbok(Night Owl) Guerrilla Training School> and lived as a drill instructor/ I volunteered for airborne tactics training(parachute) and completed it as the 15th recruit/ We made a demonstration to the Chief of Staff of the Korean Army/ my eldest son, Jeong-Eon, was born while I was instructing a drill in mountains/ I shared stories of my life as a newlywed and wonderful people I me/ I joined <Hanahoe>, an elite group in the Army

3. Educational Company Commander for the 2nd Recruit of Korean ROTC, hospitalized in the Army Hospital, Working as instructor for the 107th ROTC of Yeonsei University 136

As the company commander responsible for educating officers for the Officer Basic Course (OBC) of ROTC/ It was the sorrowful cause of matter, I lost my Parent early/ I faced and overcame significant hardships/ I recovered from the ICU of the Capital Army Hospital and lived as an instructor for the 107th ROTC of Yeonsei University/ I let my boys pick themselves up/ My second child, Seong-eon, was born/ We moved our own house, one of the national housing complex, Hwagok-dong

4. Back to the Front, Division S-3 for Counter-Espionage at Gukmang-bong peak, everyone in my compay volunteered to Vietnam 142
Back at the front as Division Operations Officer (S-3) for counter-espionage and a company commander/ Everyone in the company volunteered to go to Vietnam with the company commander.

Chapter 5: Serving in the Vietnam War as the Military History Officer for the Tiger Division

1. The Tiger Division's Encampment in Quy Nhon, Vietnam 145
The Historical Context of (Free democracy) Vietnam's Defeat/ Korea's Military Assistance to Vietnam/ The Tiger Division camped ut in Quy Nhon, middle Vietnam

2. The Document of Military History of the ROK Armed Forces' Expedition to Vietnam was recorded as one of the greatest exemplary Military Histories of the ROK Armed Forces 148
Professor Capt. Hong Seong-Tae at KMA organized the 'Department of Military History' for the first time in the ROK Armed Forces, his achievement and detailed battle reports were significant/ I mineded 'Tigers Are On There Way' to the battlefield in Vietnam, leaving my family in Korea/ I spread military 'lessens-learned' y inspecting battlefields

3. Experiencing the scene of operations, OP. Tiger, The 8th · Honggildong · Ojakyo 150
OP. Tiger and OP. 8th began/ OP Ojakgyo (Bridge of Crows and Magpies); March 1967-May 1967/ OP Hong Gil-dong (July 1967-August 1967), the TCP of the division was attacked/ Joined the search operation in Viet Cong's territory

4. The truth of the Vietnam War in the 1960s, and trivia about the ROK Army and the U.S. Army 156
President Kennedy's passionate involvement and Secretary of Defense McNamara's regrets/ Material War in Vietnam by the U.S., a Wealthy Country/ The U.S. Armed Forces Won Tactically, but Lost Strategically/ The ROK Armed Forces' strategies and operations in the Vietnam

War/ Wins and losses on the battlefield are common occurrences. War involves attack and defense, success and failure, achievements and losses. As the saying goes, "Wins and losses on the battlefield happen all the time." Here are some regretful losses I experienced and witnessed. One day, a battalion commander from the armor regiment, my senior from the Korean Military Academy, was ambushed by the Viet Cong while patrolling a company base near An Khe Pass on Route 19, heading to Pleiku. Despite fighting back fiercely, he was killed. A company in the same regiment mistakenly shot and killed three women near a banana orchard, mistaking them for Viet Cong. They were, in fact, local residents. A few days later, the Viet Cong ambushed a reconnaissance squad securing a supply route, resulting in the brutal killing or wounding of the entire squad and the loss of all equipment, including handheld transceivers./ Psychology on the battlefield: Perhaps 'Bbongjjak' music (Trot), the Arirang magazine, and cigarettes were our only joys./ Why Vietnam and the U.S. were defeated and collapsed, – "Saigon Dep Lam" -/ Goodbye, the battlefields of Vietnam! Return to Korea (October 13th-23rd, 1967)

Chapter 6: Studying Abroad at Führungsakademie der Bundeswehr, and an instructor at Korean Army college (1969-1971)

1. **Studying Abroad at Führungsakademie der Bundeswehr** 164
The Purpose of Studying Abroad at Führungsakademie der Bundeswehr and Preparation involved traveling to Europe through Japan and Arctic, eventually reaching West Germany/ Journey to West Germany via the Arctic/ Language School in Euskirchen and My Days There/ A Trip to Holland (Netherlands)/ A Trip to Explore the United Kingdom and Belgium

2. **Visiting the staff of the Brigade, the 23rd Mountain Brigade (Gebirgs Brigade) affiliated with the 1st Mountain Division** 175
The 23rd Gebirgs Brigade (Mountain Brigade) was stationed in the Alps, nicknamed "Edelweiss Brigade"/ General Situations of the West German Armed Forces on Its 10th Anniversary of Rebuilding: Rebuilt as a NATO Ally from a Defeated Country/ Visiting and Observing Field Training for Mechanized Company and Mountain Infantry Battalion/ Exploring the Beautiful Scenery of the Alps Around the Base

Chapter 7: The Establishment of the 102nd Mechanized Infantry Battalion (Oct 24th.1972), and the Capital Mechanized Infantry Division (Mar 22nd.1973)

1. Commander of the 1st Battalion, 98th Regiment, 32nd Division (April 1972) 203
We assumed armored personnel carriers (APC, M113) and prepared to establish <Rainbow Troop>

2. The 102nd Mechanized Infantry Battalion of the Army (The 1660th Troop of the Army) was Established (October 24th, 1972): 204
Acquisition of armored vehicles and preparations for the creation of the Rainbow Unit/ Strengthening Combat Power and Reorganizing the Infantry Battalion to a Mechanized Infantry Battalion/ Establishing and developing the 102nd Mechanized Infantry Battalion (The 1660th Troop of the Army), <The Rainbow Troop>

3. Establishment of the Capital Mechanized Infantry Division (CMID) (March 22nd, 1973) 206
Transition from the 32nd Infantry Division to <Capital Mechanized Infantry Division>/ Inheriting the Traditions of the Honorable "1st Battalion of the 1st Regiment of Capital Infantry Division"- "Tiger Division"/ The Outcome of the Combat Commandment Inspection: 'Happy and Sad'

4. Serving as Military Logistics Staff (G-4) of the Division, the 1st World Oil Crisis and Its Influence 208
I managed the unit and overcame hepatitis a while on duty/ Defcon-3 was issued, and all Armed Forces were checked for defense readiness condition

Chapter 8: Working as the commander of the rear and staff, a professor, foreign inspection, the Chief of Military Assistance Investigation Commission (March 1975-May 1981)

1. Work in the rear after a long time of frontline activity, G-2 Special Warfare Command (Information Office) 211
Director of G-2 Special Warfare Command Information Office/ I was part of the entourage for the annual 'Asia Special Warfare Commander Meeting, 1975' in the USA

2. I engaged in diplomacy with neutral countries 214
I served as the Chief of the <Military Assistance Investigation Commission to Morocco>/ This involved addressing Morocco's request for military assistance, outlining the missions and structure of the Investigation Commission/ Conducting local investigations in Morocco / Reporting the findings upon returning to Korea

3. Studying at Korea National Defense University Graduate School - Public opinion poll on ROK Armed Forces' nuclear armament, inspecting in the U.S., and my graduation thesis 218
The process of studying at Korea National Defense University (KNDU) Graduate School/ My graduation thesis: "Collective Security in the Pacific Rim, and Planning a Triangular Security among Korea, the U.S., and Japan"

4. Regiment Commander of Nonsan Training Centor, a Directer of KNDU, Incident of President Park, Chief of Military Assistance Investigation Commission to Saudi Arabia, 221
I got a new job, the Regiment commander of Nonsan Training Center, so I will be 'the cream of the crop'/ The historical events occurred, <10.26 Incident> and the related <12.12 Incident> ad related <Gwangju Incident>/ As well as counter measures to the 'Second World Oil Crisis', I was there

5. I became the Chief of Staff and Head Professor at the Republic of Korea Army College (July 1980 - November 1981) and was promoted to general (January 1st, 1981). 227
/ Chief of Staff at ROK Army College:/ I became a general (January 1st, 1981) and aspired to be a battlefield commander and hero:/ Being the Head Professor at ROK Army College, an opportunity to renovate the education system:

Part 3. Dreaming of Becoming a 'Commandant General', a 'Hero'

Chapter 9: Commander of Upper Units of the Army, Deputy Chief of Staff of Operations at the Army Headquarters (Dangun era 4314-4321, AD 1981-1988)

1. Commander of the 7th Airborne Special Warfare Brigade (November 1981-January 1983) 253

Missions, Composition, and Capabilities of the Unit/ Education, Training, and Operations of the Unit/ Creative Effort to Improve the Mission-Oriented Unit

2. Commander of the 8th Infantry Division of the Army (January 1983-July 1984) 256
The Missions of the 8th Division and the Authority of the Division Commander/ The Missions of the 8th Division and Its Commander's Motto of Duty/ The Troop's Field Maneuver Exercise and Demonstration; Participation in the Field Training Exercise for the T/S Combined Forces Command of 1984/ In March 1984, I participated in the Field Maneuver Exercise for the Team Spirit (T/S) of 1984, with the presence of the President and the U.S. Army's Chief of Staff.

3. As Deputy Chief of Staff of Operations (G-3) at the Army Headquarters, the Army's Strategy, operations, education, training, organization, and equipment (1984~1986) 261
I held a position that all Army generals aspire to. It is a role of great importance and honor, and I felt privileged and deeply responsible to have been selected among many qualified generals. Military personnel, whether commanders or staff, are generally granted a degree of authority to fulfill their missions. The Staff of Operations, the Army's key and highest staff, is endowed with general authority, though it can be misused within its scope. The Deputy Chief of Staff of Operations of the ROK Army serves and assists the Army's Chief of Staff. Using the authority granted, the Deputy Chief must design and plan education and training for the Army in both wartime and peacetime, conduct this training, improve equipment and weapons, and manage domestic emergency operations during peacetime. Unfortunately, the authority to command operations in wartime is vested in the ROK-US Combined Forces Command and executed through the "Joint Chief of Staff." I hope for the swift realization of "true self-reliant national defense," strengthening the ROK-US alliance./ In preparing strategies and operations, particularly against North Korea's "Invasion plan to South in 5 to 7 days," which included biological and chemical warfare, the Army had already moved some mobilized divisions slightly north since 1980. After conducting numerous war games to prepare for chemical warfare, it became apparent that transporting weapons from the U.S. mainland in an emergency (taking two to three days) posed a challenge. Therefore, we needed to replace them with binary options and urgently begin research on chemical warfare attack and defense strategies. Additionally, the use of the Hyunmoo Missile in actual combat was

considered./ Development of Education and Training, and Organization of the Army, and Establishment of Central Military School for ROTC Cadets (November 1985)/ Developing the Army's Equipment and Armament

4. Commander of the 1st Corps of the ROK Army (July 1986-January 1988) 266
As my term as Chief of Staff of Operations was ending, I was appointed as a corps commander./ The History of the 1st Corps and Its Commander's Immediate Duties Under the Current Situation/ Assistance for the 1986 Asian Games and preparation for the 1988 Seoul Olympics/ Tactical discussion for the corps and the guideline for "Charging for three days at the beginning of war and having a decisive battle" (annihilation)/ False report on Kim Il-sung's death/ Participation in Field Training (Maneuver) Exercise for the Team Spirit of 1987 with the 1st Corps of the U.S. Army/ A soldier's claim: The military must not be subordinated usually to politics, but politics must be subordinated to the military depending on the situation for victory in war.

Part 4. An Old Soldier Serves National Security Until the End

Chapter 10: I Abandoned My Dream of Becoming "The Generalissimo" and Voluntarily Retired as an Old Soldier

1. The 13th Presidential Election and Upholding the Armed Forces' Neutrality and Right to Free Vote 297
President Chun Doo-Hwan's Call and a Private Meeting at the Blue House/ Upholding the Armed Forces' Neutrality and Individual Rights to Free Vote

2. I Abandoned My Dream of Becoming "Generalissimo" and Voluntarily Retired as an Old Soldie 298
Starting New Work as Vice Commander of the 1st Field Army/ "Thank God, I Have Done My Duty"

Chapter 11: An Old Soldier Serves the Nation, Focusing on National Security

1. Vice Chairman of the National Security Council and Emergency Planning Committee (October 1988-March 1993) 300
The nation called upon this old soldier once more./ I attended vice ministers' meetings and cabinet meetings, fulfilling my duties as Vice Chairman.

2. In May 1994, I became a visiting scholar at the Department of Military Science at Ball State University, Indiana, U.S.A. 303
I became a visiting scholar at the university's Military Science Department, ROTC./ My focus was on studying "security strategy thought history of the United States," along with American history, and I diligently worked on writing about it./ I experienced many new advantages in the U.S.

3. Visiting Professor at KNDU and Establishment of the Research Center for Security Strategy Thought History of the Republic of Korea 308
Becoming a Visiting Professor at KNDU (the first recruit) as an Experienced Expert/ Publishing "A Security Strategy Thought History of the United States of America"/ Establishment of "The Institute of Korea National Security Strategy Thought History" (Cyber and Private)

Afterword: "To Jun Ho, my grandson, and his descendants"

1. My children's success and their current situations 331
2. Jun Ho, my grandson, was born into my son's new family 332
3. Korea's 5,000-year history and traditions, and its relationship with the United States 332
4. A message to Jun Ho, my beloved grandson, and his descendants, from me, your grandpa 334

Part 1

Dreaming of Becoming a Great Man

Chapter 1

Grandpa's Childhood

1. Grandpa's hometown, your place of origin

♦ Dongnae, Busan, Republic of Korea, my hometown and a good place to live in with a long history of traditions

I, your grandpa, was born in Bokcheon-dong, Dongnae-eup, Dongnae-gun, Busan, Republic of Korea, in May 9th, 1935, as the second son among the six children of Moon Man-Jun and Park Gap-A, the pioneers of new culture and civilization. That neighborhood's name has now changed to Bokcheon-dong, Dongnae-gu, Busan Metropolitan City.

Dongnae, which is my hometown, thus your place of origin, as you're my descendants, is located at the southeastern end of the Korean Peninsula and has grown to become the traditional key city of Gyeongsangnam-do in Korean history. Therefore, earlier in the history than Busan (Busanjin), Dongnaeseong Fortress—2 to 4 kilometers (1.2 to 2.4 miles) in diameter, built for defense mostly against pirates from the south and barbarians from the north—was built and it was developed into Dongnaebu (It's similar to a metropolitan city of present days).

But this is what the residents of Dongnae and Dongnaeseong Fortress are most proud of. During the Japanese Invasion of Korea in 1592, the Japanese troops armed themselves with modern rifles and carried out a surprise attack, landed in Busan, and marched upward toward Seoul. But under the leadership of Commander Song Sang-Hyeon, who was the local commander, the residents, the armed forces, and the governmental organization joined forces, battled fiercely against the Japanese troops with bows and spears for two days and successfully defended the area from them. This battle is recorded as an early defense battle, which resulted in stopping the Japanese troops' march toward north in Pyongyang.

In the end, Commander Song died in battle with his staff at the command post, keeping his loyal words, "It's easy to fight and die, but it is difficult to let them pass." This has become a proud historical lesson, and it still remains in the middle of Dongnae in the form of Songgongdang (Memorial Hall).

In geographic terms, Dongnae is located at the middle and downstream of Suyeonggang River, which rises in Cheonseongsan Mountain (922), the end of Baekdudaegan Mountain Range, and flows between the range of Geumjeongsan Mountain (19802) in the west and Jangsan Mountain (634, Haeundae, Busan) in the east, reaching Suyeongman Bay in the end. Therefore, it was a beautiful and plentiful nature-friendly city that served as the water supply not only for Dongnae but also for the city of Busan for a long time (before Nakdonggang River was developed). There is Gajisan Mountain Provincial Park to its north, and it has the famous Geumjeongsan Mountain (Fortress) to its west. So, it has Dongnae Hot Springs, Haeundae Hot Springs, Haeundae Beach, and it also had Suyeong Beach in the past, which was known to be a beautiful beach with fine sand. As represented by the relic museum in Hwaksudae, Bokcheon-dong, this city has long history and traditions from the Three Han States Era (300 B.C.-300 A.D.), the Neolithic Age of the Korean Peninsula, to the Three Kingdoms Era (18 B.C.-660 A.D.).

♦ Grandpa's father, who lived with a pioneering spirit and studied new learnings

My father was born in 1900 as the third son of a farmer, who's been farming for generations, in a neighborhood of water purification plant in Myeongjang-dong, which is 2 kilometers (1.2 miles) away northeast from Dongnae-eup. He was creative and adventurous (pioneering) by nature, so he was fascinated by new learnings, which was introduced to Korea with foreign power, rather than farming. So, he was attending a Confucian school in Myeongryun-dong, which was in downtown Dongnae-eup. And when Myeongryun Academy, the root of new learnings, was established there, he entered the academy immediately to study.

When it was time to inherit the fortune, he let his two older brothers inherit the farmland. His plan was to receive his share in cash and move to downtown Dongnae-eup. And finally, as soon as he got married, he left the farming village and stopped working on farms and moved to downtown Dongnae-eup with his wife and mother-in-law. To put it in words young people, use these days, he did it blindly (?). And he nested in a corner of Bokcheon-dong, which is right next to Myeongryun-dong.

That place was somewhere in between Dongnae Girls' Middle School and Dongnae-gu Office, with a small stream running along that path. To the northwest of this stream, toward the southbound hill leading to Myeongryun-dong, were the grand "99-section houses" with tiled roofs, home to the local wealthy and aristocrats, near Myeongryun Local School. On the southeast side of the stream, which was about 10 meters (32 feet) wide with a 3-meter (9.8 feet) wide trail, lay a neighborhood of modest 3-section straw houses, even smaller than three sections, where farmers and pioneers like my family resided. Our home was a 'Choga' house, constructed with straw and supported by clay bricks, built by my father himself. It included my maternal grandmother's room, which was 3 square meters (4 square yards), and our room, where my parents, three siblings, and I lived, measuring 6 square meters (7 square yards). At that time, I had an older brother, an older sister, and a younger sister. The kitchen, also 3 square meters (4 square yards), contained two small iron pots, rice bowls on the cooking fireplace, a wooden poker on the earth floor, and piles of pine needles and dried twigs for kindling. Just outside was a Jangdokdae, a terrace for large ceramic sauce jars, about 6 square meters (7 square yards) wide. On bright full moon nights, my mother would place a bowl of pure water and rub her hands, making a wish. During this period, my father attended an academy for new learnings and literature—not an old village school, but Myeongryun School, a modern institution like Pai Chai School in Seoul—to complete his primary education. He then left the family in the care of my mother and grandmother and ventured to Japan with nothing but his pioneering spirit. There, he learned to drive a streetcar—a job as mystical then as being a drone operator is today—out of scientific curiosity and necessity, and it became his lifelong career. He returned just before the Liberation on August 15, 1945, and began working as a streetcar driver on the route between Dongdaesin-dong, Busan, and Dongnae Hot Springs. He continued this work for many years after Liberation, eventually being promoted to supervisor before retiring. After retirement, he hand-wove fishing nets using a bamboo netting needle and made weights by melting lead. He often went to Suyeonggang River or Oncheoncheon Stream to fish. I fondly remember a day spent with him, following Oncheoncheon Stream to Suyeongman Bay, as he cast the net and I collected the fish in a bucket.

♦ My mother's lifelong dedication to our family is a story of resilience.

Before her marriage, she was born into an aristocratic family that owned a grand mansion with tiled roofs by the Suyeonggang River, with a beautiful view and extensive farmland. It was located 1 kilometer (0.6 miles) northeast, over the mountain behind my father's birthplace, Okbongsan Mountain (now Myeongjang Park), which stands 250 meters (19820 feet) above sea level. Born in 1902 as the second of four sisters, she grew up as a kindhearted noble lady, attended by about ten household servants. However, by the time she married, societal changes had abolished the servant system, and her family's wealth was declining. She married a pioneer of new culture and civilization, moved to downtown Dongnae-eup, and began a challenging life she had never known. When my father pursued his studies and went to Japan, my grandmother started selling silk at the market to support our family. When she became too old, my mother took over the business, selling textiles at Dongnae Market on irregular market days to sustain us. This work was arduous and demanding.

My earliest memories, around 1940 when I was about five, include my mother selling textiles at Dongnae Market, which had a designated spot with a roof requiring tax payment, about 9 square meters (10 square yards) wide, three days a week. For the other four days, she traveled to local five-day periodic markets, Haeundae Market, Gupo Market, and Beomil-dong (Busan) Market. She carried a heavy bundle of silk on her head, made by rolling about 10 yards of silk on six to seven wooden planks, each 90 centimeters (35 inches) long, 20 centimeters (7.8 inches) wide, and 2 centimeters (0.78 inches) thick. With this bundle, she traveled by train and streetcar, and to reach Gupo Market, she walked rough mountain trails, crossing Mandeokgogae Hill, either alone or with other peddlers.

The journey between Dongnae and Gupo Market required crossing Mandeokgogae Hill, about 500 meters (0.31 miles) above sea level, located in the central saddle of the Geumjeong Mountain Range. Even on the curved mountain trail, the steep parts had a slope angle of 30 degrees, and sometimes she had to cross a deep waterway in a valley. The trail was rough, through a thick forest, 6 kilometers (3.7 miles) in a straight line and 8 kilometers (4.9 miles) on foot, making it a five-hour round trip for a middle-aged woman carrying a heavy bundle. Although there were no tigers, the Rocky Mountains and deep valleys were home to a few leopard cats. As a child, I would often meet my mother coming downhill as I went to greet her with my older sister, walking uphill on Mandeokgogae Hill. My maternal grandmother and parents endured these hardships and saved money diligently.

Finally, in 1943, they purchased a house they had long dreamed of. It had a large front yard, over 30 square meters (4010 square yards), a daecheongmaru (semi-outdoor living room) about 10 square meters (12 square yards) wide, tap water—a rarity at the time as few houses had wells, let alone a water supply system—a cement jangdokdae, and a well-grown persimmon tree in the yard. This house was in Suan-dong, where we moved. There, my younger brother (Hwa-ung), a "Liberation baby" born in 1945, and my younger sister (Mal-nam, meaning "last Moon") were born, creating a large family of nine. I can only imagine the sense of achievement and happiness my parents felt. Yet, I remember them saying on moving day that their next goal was to own a mansion with tiled roofs. Their wish came true, thanks to my older brother's early technical labor and my older sister's early marriage, when they moved to a splendid house in the neighborhood with tiled roofs, on a new street equipped with a well and a water supply system. The period of suffering during the Japanese Colonial Era and the effervescence and confusion of liberation (1935-1948) was marked by the allure of "Military academy and normal school."

2. The Japanese Colonial Era and Liberation (1935-1948)

♦ My birth, marked by mother's auspicious dream and my childhood

The night my mother gave birth to me was significant, as it was the sacred night of April 7th by the lunar calendar, just hours from Buddha's Birthday (April 8th). She had a dream of "a handsome rooster with a big cockscomb standing on our roof, lifting his head and crowing loudly." With this auspicious dream, she named me Yeong-Il, meaning "smart and successful," reflecting the hopes of past generations for their children to escape hardship and have a promising future. My older brother was named Bong-il, with "Bong" meaning "to serve," as he was the firstborn son expected to serve our parents and family.

My earliest childhood memories begin around age five, two to three years before elementary school. My daily routine involved playing outside with neighborhood friends. Grand 99-section mansions, as large as 'whales,' were centered around Myeongryun-dong, about 10 meters (32 feet) away, including the road in front of my house and the stream, to the northwest. Many of these houses were empty and abandoned, as the aristocrats had lost much of their power by then. I enjoyed playing hide-and-seek there. In summer, there was a railroad bridge for streetcars at the corner of the road from Dongnae to Busan, spanning Oncheoncheon Stream, a sizable stream (over 100 meters, or 109 yards wide) flowing from Dongnae Hot Springs (Geumjeongsan Mountain). I sometimes played on that railroad, diving into the river from a height of 7 to 8 meters (22 to 26 feet) when a streetcar approached. Occasionally, I hid behind a bridge pier, watching the streetcar's underside pass by and listening to its noise. I was a mischievous boy, engaging in many risky antics. Nonetheless, Oncheoncheon Stream was a refuge, playground, and natural learning spot for the mischievous children of Dongnae in summer.

From time to time, I would travel to Suyeong Beach, located 10 kilometers (6 miles) from downtown Dongnae-eup. Suyeong Beach was nestled between what are now known as Gwanganli Beach and Haeundae Beach. It once served as a rough airfield and was the only airfield for fighter aircraft at the Nakdonggang River's bridgehead during the Korean War. Sadly, a large apartment complex now occupies the site. Once, I took a 5-won coin from the money my parents worked hard to earn—something I did only once in my life—and took a train with friends to Haeundae Beach for some fun. When I returned home that night, my parents scolded me. On another occasion, my relatives noticed how I led a group of mischievous children in Dongnae and jokingly compared me to a 'Korean Hitler,' implying I was the 'boss' of the local kids. Despite this, even after starting school, I would throw my school bag in the semi-outdoor living room and play with friends until evening. Yet, I still managed to receive an Excellent Student Award for getting all A's in school.

♦ Entering elementary school through an exam

In 1942, I entered Dongnae Naesung Elementary School, known as Dongnae the 1st Public Elementary (National) School during the Japanese Colonial Era. The school is still located in Dongnae-gu, Busan. At that time, we had to take an entrance exam, which meant some children, though a minority, couldn't attend school. Some of my neighborhood friends couldn't go to school due to financial constraints. I still remember my mother advising me, "If they ask what Mom's job is, just say I sew at home," on the day of the interview. This was because selling items at a market was viewed as somewhat awkward compared to agriculture, industry, and commerce. After I started school, for the next four years until the Liberation in 1945, all school activities and classes were conducted in Japanese, under Japanese rule. By then, Korea had been colonized by Japan for 30 years.

The Empire of Japan not only acted as a watchdog for powerful imperialistic countries but also became one of the three nations establishing military fascism alongside Germany and Italy. This provoked the Allies, including the United States, to start the Pacific War on December 8, 1942, and Japan was waging an extensive war of aggression from the Pacific to Southeast Asia and the South Pacific. By 1941, the Empire of Japan was in its death throes, ordering the re-incarceration of Korean independence activists (the so-called Preventive Incarceration Order on Ideological Criminals) and discontinuing Korean language education in elementary schools, forcing them to teach Japanese. Whenever students spoke Korean at school, Japanese teachers would punish them immediately. Schools employed many Japanese teachers, and a captain in office carrying long swords became principals. Every morning, we had an assembly in the playground where we were made to bow 90 degrees toward the imperial palace in Tokyo, Japan, and chant "The Oath of Subjects of the Imperial Nation" before the principal's speech.

♦ Our serviceman principal boasted, 'the Military Academy and Nrmal School'

One day, our serviceman principal boasted, "In Japan, the military academy (shikan gakko) and the normal school (shiang gakko) are the best." The idea of "the best schools" was tempting, and since both names sounded similar, I began to admire these institutions, albeit vaguely. I didn't know what they were like, but as I grew older, I made connections with these schools I once admired. This made me realize that a teacher's words in childhood, regardless of who they are, hold value and can influence you later in life.

♦ School life at the end of the war

By the end of the Pacific War, I could easily sense the Allies' attacks. Bomb shelters were dug not only on the hill behind my school but also in the yards of all households for use during bombings. When an emergency alarm sounded at school, we would fold the cozy cushions from our chairs, place them on our heads, grab the hardtacks provided, and head to the bomb shelter. Inside, I watched the American B-29 long-range strike bombers with amazement and anxiety as they flew across the sky, flickering like a flock of swallows. After I got married, my wife (your grandma) shared a story. She walked to school from Samrye, near Jeonju, Jeollanam-do. One day, an American B-29 bomber suddenly bombed a railroad bridge about 100 meters (328 feet) from her. She covered her eyes and ears and lay flat on the ground as thought, avoiding injury, but the incident traumatized her for life. During wartime, commodities were scarce, and students in the southern regions often went to school barefoot, even when the dropwort garden was covered in thin ice. This led to the installation of a 'foot-washing tub (ashi araiba)' at the entrance of the classroom passageway.

♦ Developing lifelong habits

Despite the challenges, elementary school provided basic education. I started doing National Gymnastics in morning assemblies and have continued this routine for 80 years to warm up and check my condition. This lifelong habit is one of my secrets to maintaining my health. In 2nd grade, the school provided lunch, consisting of rice balls and pickled radish. Students took turns distributing food, eating together in one classroom with a Japanese homeroom teacher. She emphasized, "You must chew food thoroughly. Chew one spoonful 19 times on the left and 19 times on the right before swallowing." This became a habit, causing me to eat more slowly than others, especially after stomach cancer surgery in my 60s. While on leave from the Army, a relative noted, "First Lieutenant Moon's corpsmen are lucky. They don't have to rush meals because their commander eats slowly." She had seen soldiers unable to finish meals when ordered to "resume and go" during the Korean War, thinking it was due to a fast-eating commander. Troop actions aren't controlled by a commander's eating habits, but her observation brings a smile to my face.

In 4th grade, after the Liberation, during a physical education class, our Korean homeroom teacher had us move desks to the sides and walk straight with parallel feet along the wooden floor grains. Perhaps that's why I still walk straight without out-toeing at nearly 90 years old. These elementary school lessons became lifelong habits. Beyond habits, school taught ethics, morality, patriotism, and dreams for the future. Elementary school is foundational for education.

The Empire of Japan tried to enforce the idea that "Japan and Joseon (Korea) are one" and "All subjects must serve the Empire." Students were made to bow east (toward the imperial palace) and chant "The Oath of Subjects of the Imperial Nation" every morning. They also visited a Jinja (Japanese shrine) in Geumjeongsan Mountain weekly for worship. Once, a friend spoke Korean in class, and his female homeroom teacher harshly punished him by smashing his head on a blackboard. Witnessing this, my Korean spirit rose, and hostility toward the teacher and the Japanese grew. This was my school life until liberation (then called emancipation). I wasn't a perfect student but was always creative, active, and energetic. I received the 2nd place award—given to one student per class—for good grades but mischievous behavior in 1st and 2nd grade. The 1st place award went to well-mannered students with good grades, and the 3rd place award was for perfect attendance. I received a 3rd place award in 3rd grade and tried to rip it, but my Japanese homeroom teacher caught me and punished me with detention.

♦ Learning 'Hangul' from my mother

On August 15th, National Liberation Day, I learned Hangul from my mother using a fireplace poker in the kitchen.

When Korea was liberated in August of the year I entered the 4th grade, my Japanese homeroom teacher returned to Japan, and we were assigned a new Korean teacher, Mr. Seong. As soon as he took over, he appointed me as class president, similar to class presidents today. I believe his intention was to swiftly eliminate all remnants of Japanese influence.

On the evening of Liberation Day, August 15, 1945, I sat close to my mother as she prepared dinner. My mother, an intelligent woman, used the charred tip of a wooden fireplace poker to write Hangul on the earthen floor while tending the fire. She wrote the Korean alphabet: "Ga Na Da Ra Ma Ba Sa A Ja Cha Ka Ta Pa Ha" and the vowels "A and Ya, Eo and Yeo, O and Yo, U and Yu, Eu and I, · (A), and changes (ㅏ이ㅑ, ㅓ이ㅕ, ㅗ이ㅛ, ㅜ이ㅠ, ㅡㅣ·(아), 헨 땡이)." At that time, Hangul still included the character · (Arae a). I read these aloud to learn them. Thanks to this, I quickly became the top student in Hangul class, which was designed for those who couldn't read or recognize Hangul.

The following year, I delivered the valedictory speech at graduation on behalf of all students, and the year after that, I gave the response speech for the graduates. All of this was due to the "first Hangul class" my mother gave me in the kitchen.

Although she was a textile seller and sometimes a peddler, she came from an aristocratic family and retained her intelligence and grace. Her teachings instilled in me the knowledge and modesty that guided me throughout my life.

♦ Life in Dongnae, Busan, post-liberation

In the days following liberation, I was curious about the changes in Busan. At 10 years old and in 4th grade, I walked the new road between Busan and Dongnae, a journey of about 12 kilometers (7 miles) as the crow flies, but likely 15 kilometers (9 miles) on foot. I reached the Choryang Streetcar Stop after a long day of walking. It was a hot summer day, so I jumped into the river from Sebyeonggyo Bridge, the only bridge over Oncheoncheon Stream leading to Busan, fully clothed. Emerging soaked but refreshed, I continued my journey past Seomyeon and Busanjin to Choryang. My stamina and persistence in walking six hours under the August sun without lunch perhaps foreshadowed my future at the Korea Military Academy eight years later. As night fell, I decided to return home and waited at Choryang Station for a streetcar back to Dongnae. Suddenly, I heard two to three loud booms, each a few minutes apart, shaking the ground and shattering windows. A massive mushroom-shaped pillar of fire rose from the sea, near what is now the 3rd Wharf. As the Japanese evacuated, they destroyed large oil tanks in Jeokgi to prevent Koreans from using the oil stored there.

The day after liberation, a pile of rice was set on fire in the plaza by the southern entrance of Dongnae Market, possibly by a departing Japanese officer. This rice, from the grain ration storage, was precious. If Koreans set the fire, it might have been an act of spite or a misguided celebration of liberation. With the rice ration cut off, those without food salvaged the burnt rice, washing it repeatedly to remove the burnt smell before cooking and eating it.

♦ A battle with a class bully after becoming class president

As class president, I faced challenges, including dealing with two bullies. One was as big as a gorilla, nearly twice our size, and the other, though smaller, was still strong and thick-boned. The larger bully often harasses classmates but backs down when confronted by united peers. The smaller bully used his strength to intimidate others. After the larger bully transferred to school, the remaining bully continued his menacing behavior. My classmates urged me to confront him, despite our familial connection. Foolishly, we agreed to a duel on the hill behind our school, now known as Haksudae, surrounded by about 50 classmates. The bully was incredibly strong, and after a few punches, he overpowered me. As he strangled me, my vision blurred, but I refused to surrender. Realizing my peril, my classmates intervened, pushing him away and saving me. Such incidents were part of being class president, and I was often brave—or perhaps simple-minded—throughout my life.

3. Busan Normal School and the Dream of Greatness (1948~1950)

♦ Entering Busan Normal School

In 1948, the Republic of Korea was established, and I pursued my dream of becoming a great man. After liberation, I was in 4th grade and became class president. By the end of 5th grade, Mr. Yoon Ui-Tae, my homeroom teacher, encouraged me to take a grade-skipping exam for Dongnae Middle School, but I failed due to insufficient preparation. In 6th grade, Mr. Yoon recommended me to Busan Normal School, founded in July 1946 in Dongdaesin-dong, Busan. It was on par with other normal schools in Korea, such as those in Jinju, Jeonju, Gongju, Daegu, and Cheongju. My parents proudly celebrated my acceptance into Busan Normal School, which was gaining a reputation for excellence.

The school offered lower tuition, which pleased them. I was proud to attend this "normal school," familiar to me from the Japanese Colonial Era. The faculty, educated in the United States, were not only academically competent but also embraced democratic, advanced, and modern educational philosophies. The principal, Dr. Yoon In-gu, later became the president of Yonsei University. The vice principal, Mr. Gum Su-hyeon, was a patriotic musician who changed his family name from Kim to Gum after liberation. The music teacher, Mr. Yoon I-sang, became famous for "Symphony Fantasy No. 1, 'Korea,'" though he later aligned with North Korea. My homeroom teacher, Ms. Bang Deok-su, taught English and was the wife of Principal Yoon. She introduced me to Park Seh-jik, an upperclassman and 2nd place winner of the "Student English Speech Competition." Park later became a lieutenant general, mayor of Seoul, and chairman of the 1988 Seoul Olympics organizing committee. Our acquaintance continued from our military careers to retirement and beyond.

♦ The establishment of the Republic of Korea through the May 10th Election.

I first encountered the motto for the May 10th Election on a poster on the side wall of the Busan United States Information Service (USIS). The original USIS was located right next to where the Busan Lotte Department Store stands today. This was a General Election for The People, meant to elect assembly members. It marked the first time in Korea's 5,000-year history that both men and women could vote. My homeroom teacher at the time, who taught history, explained why it was called "the establishment of the government of the Republic of Korea" instead of "the establishment of the Republic of Korea." He said, "The word 'government' signifies an executive branch with separation of powers, but it also means 'a nation.' The President is the leader of the executive branch and the representative of the nation. Therefore, the establishment of the government of the Republic of Korea means the establishment of the Republic of Korea (Dai Han Min Guk-Han guk)." I still remember his explanation vividly.

♦ The post-liberation era of cattle-drawn carriage in Busan

During the Vacant Era after Liberation, in the age of cattle-drawn carriages in Busan, transportation for common people during the late Japanese Colonization Era included trains, streetcars, and the occasional taxi, rickshaw, and truck—these trucks were powered by wood-fired engines. In Dongnae, cattle-drawn carriages were the most common form of transportation. After liberation, trains and streetcars were so overcrowded that they didn't follow fixed schedules; they departed whenever they were ready. A few automobiles abandoned by the U.S. Army were around—like "three-quarters" (3/4, coverless trucks), "GMC" cargo trucks, and buses made by modifying "shop vans" (weapon repair vehicles)—but they weren't widely used. Instead, carriages reminiscent of those in American Western films appeared and became public transportation. Cattle-drawn carriages continued to transport cargo and people between the countryside and downtown Dongnae.

♦ Reading about the United States and great figures at the U.S. Information Service

Reading about the United States and notable figures at the United States Information Service was a significant part of my life. Mr. Gum Su-hyeon, our vice principal—renowned in Korean education and music—often remarked, "In the United States, they've finished educating people with ethics and morality, and now they're educating cats," to inspire our ethical and scholarly spirits. Each time he said this, I admired the United States even more.

Fortunately, the USIS was housed in a majestic building on a street in Daecheong-dong, conveniently along my 30-minute walk from the Main Busan Station to my school. While waiting for the train home, I would stop by a bookstore to read books for free and explore the USIS library, which was well-equipped with air conditioning and heating. At USIS, I read high-quality textbooks for American students, various magazines—including one called "Hope," which introduced the United States in Hangul—and watched entertaining films about the United States. I learned about American history, particularly the Wild West period, its governmental system with separation of powers, and the abundant lives of its citizens. This sparked my interest in the United States, an affluent country, and fueled my dream of studying there in the future.

♦ Dreaming of becoming a great man

I dreamed of becoming a great man. I often read American and Japanese books about notable figures from the United States—Korean biographies were published later, as Korea's economy and humanities developed. I was especially drawn to the stories of great American men like George Washington, Abraham Lincoln, John D. Rockefeller, and Andrew Carnegie, who embodied success. Occasionally, I read "Julius Caesar" and "Plutarch's Lives," which deeply moved me. My passion for history was ignited by the revolutionary spirits and successes of great men like General Ataturk Kemal Pasha, who revived Turkey; General Gamal Abdel Nasser, an Egyptian nationalist who liberated Egypt from colonization and wielded power during the Cold War; and President Ramon Magsaysay, who rebuilt the Philippines, which seemed more advanced than Korea at the time

I also absorbed mottos and encouragements like "Boys be ambitious, Boy Ambition!" and valuable advice such as "Human beings learn 'high' and achieve 'medium,' and learn 'medium' and achieve 'low.' So, if you have ambition, always seek the best in the world!" from "Sonyeon" (Korean for 'Boy') and "Shonen" (Japanese for 'Boy'), youth magazines that I cherished. These mottos were etched in my heart, and I aspired to become a great man. Inspired by the teachings of General (President) Washington's honesty from childhood, President Lincoln's honesty and sincerity—he volunteered to work to pay off a debt for a rain-soaked book he borrowed—and "Life Lessons" from Dale Carnegie, I dreamed of becoming a revolutionary who could revive the nation and a leader of society and mankind.

♦ Almost becoming my teacher's adopted son

Almost becoming my teacher's adopted son was a pivotal moment in my life. My family was poor, and I never tasted beef or pork until I entered the Military Academy. I didn't even know about Korean Chinese restaurants or the common dish jjajangmyeon (black bean noodles). Despite eating barley rice from a bamboo basket hanging on a roof corner, I still had three meals a day. However, when I attended normal school in Busan, the kimchi juice from my lunchbox would leak and soak into my books, causing a stench. As a result, I stopped bringing lunch to school and spent lunchtime playing in the playground, skipping meals. Granny Bang Deok-su, my homeroom teacher, and Principal Yoon In-gu, her husband, had no children. My mother later told me that Ms. Bang, believing my family was too poor to afford lunch, invited my mother to school to discuss adopting me as her son. However, my mother humbly declined the offer.

On Lunar New Year after liberation, my parents received some beef head from a "group saving for meat" with their neighbors in the countryside. They boiled it in a large pot, made it into jelly, and we ate it for about a month, thinking it was beef. My father grilled a few strands of beef intestines over a furnace, laying out a newspaper underneath, and enjoyed them with a few shots of soju. But no one in our family complained. I believed we weren't as poor as President Lincoln, a great American man, was in his childhood. I only tried to follow his life philosophy, led by honesty, even in poverty.

4. The Korean War and the Call to KMA (1950~1954)

♦ The outbreak of Korean War on June 25th and the beginning of temporary tent school

During the era of North Korea's Invasion of South Korea on June 25th and the Korean War, Busan Bridgehead and Korea Military Academy called me (1950-1954). The North Korea's Invasion of South Korea on June 25th and the Korean War broke out, marking the beginning of temporary tent school days. June 25th, 1950, was a holiday. My next-door neighbors were highly educated elders who listened to AM radio broadcasts on a high-class radio (with 5 vacuum tubes), which was rare at that time. That morning, they listened intently to a repetitive broadcast, visibly nervous. I listened closely too, and it was propaganda from the North Korean Puppet State (as we called it then), falsely claiming, "The South Korean Puppet State's armed forces invaded north by 2 kilometers (1.2 miles), therefore, our brave North Korean People's Army are fighting back and now marching south."

At dawn that day, the North Korean Puppet State, spearheading the International Communist Revolution Movement instigated by Joseph Stalin of the Soviet Union, ordered its armed forces to invade South Korea across the entire 38th Parallel for the "communist unification of the Korean Peninsula." On my way home from school (Busan Normal School), refugees from Seoul were already on the streets two to three days after the war broke out. They filled all the streets of residential areas in Daecheong-dong, Toseong-dong, Daesin-dong, and beyond, starting the next day. My school was on a street and was sturdy, so about ten days later (early July), the U.S. Army began to station there. We evacuated to the neighboring Toseong Elementary School, carrying our chairs and desks. After that, we built a temporary tent school with a military tent for 24 people, provided by the U.S. Army, on a hill in Ami-dong. From then until the truce, not only did schools evacuated from Seoul at every level, but also native schools in Busan gave their facilities to the military, and we experienced the "era of temporary tent schools."

A total of 16 countries fought in the Korean War until early 1954. The countries that dispatched their armed forces included the United States, Canada, Colombia, Australia, New Zealand, The Philippines, Thailand, South Africa, Ethiopia, United Kingdom, Belgium, France, Greece, Luxembourg, and The Netherlands. These countries dispatched one battalion (about 1,200 people), the minimum military power demanded by the UN, or more. The total Allied Forces that fought in the Korean War until 1953 numbered 341,000 people, including Americans. Additionally, according to the UN's resolution, its member states and international organizations began providing all kinds of aid. Five nations (Sweden, India, Denmark, Norway, and Italy) provided medical aid with hospitals, hospital ships, and more. Forty member states, one non-member state (Italy), and nine specialized agencies of the UN participated in providing food and civilian relief.

♦ The desperate evacuation from the Masan line of the Busan Bridgehead

In late July, as the Busan Bridgehead was being established, intense battles raged along the Nakdong River line. One evening, after school, I was waiting for a train to take me home. I sat on a hill near the Main Busan Station, watching military trains come and go. Suddenly, a six-car casualty evacuation train pulled into the platform. Even before it came to a complete stop, stretchers carrying soldiers and casualties, all covered in blood, were hurriedly unloaded from every platform and through shattered windows. They were rushed to the evacuation hospital near Yeongdo Bridge and the UN Command's hospital ship anchored offshore. These were casualties from the U.S. Army, recently injured or killed in the fierce battles at Masan, less than an hour from the Main Station, and the Nakdong River battlefield.

Naturally, no one was there to welcome this gruesome scene, except for "Geum Dal-Rae of Daegu," a locally infamous middle-aged woman. Dressed in a white Hanbok skirt and Jeogori, she danced around, exposing herself. I couldn't tell if she was performing a shamanistic ritual to comfort the souls of the fallen, but it was another horrific moment of war that I witnessed. In this terrible war, U.S. Army soldiers were injured or killed in battle. Koreans are forever grateful for the United States' support, and we can never forget the sacrifices of soldiers from all the nations that fought in the war.

♦ Witnessing the U.S. Army's capabilities at the Suyeong Aerodrome contruction site

School was temporarily closed, serving as a summer break. Everyone was struggling financially, so most students took part-time jobs. A small aerodrome at Suyeong Beach, Dongnae, was being hastily converted into an emergency airfield, capable of handling smaller transport and jet fighter aircraft. I worked as a laborer there to earn money, even though I was only 14 and in my second year of middle school. I worked both day and night for over ten days. Initially, I carried soil, sand, and gravel on my shoulders. Later, I transported iron plates for the runway using a pole to shoulder them to their destination. Around 2:00 a.m., I was scolded for dozing off due to exhaustion. Despite the hard labor, a combat aerodrome was completed in about ten days, showcasing the capability of the United States. I later learned in my military history class at KMA that this efficiency allowed them to outpace Japan, which took one to three months to build a small aerodrome, and win the Pacific War.

Reflecting on it now, although the work was grueling even for adults, I didn't find it too tiring at the time. I would have a quick dinner and rest after my daytime shift, then start my night shift immediately. To be chosen as a laborer each day, I would stretch my shoulders and try to appear confident and strong, though I hid my face under a straw hat. I was always anxious about not being selected for work, which was quite stressful. It's a joke, but maybe that's why I developed three rows of wrinkles on my forehead early on.

After the Suyeong Aerodrome runway was completed, people and ammunition were transported by air and sea. The sandy beach of Suyeong Aerodrome, once Korea's best leisure beach, became a hub where large transport ships offloaded onto amphibious transport ships. Ammunition was loaded onto freight cars at Suyeong Train Station and sent to the front. Reserve ammunition was unloaded at nearby Haeundae Train Station and transported directly to the Nakdong River line or to temporary storage on land. A labor market formed around this process.

♦ Seeing a jet fighter aircraft's destrution at a part-time job site with U.S. Army

While transitioning from my part-time job at the Suyeong Aerodrome construction site to the ammunition freight platform at Haeundae Station, I briefly worked as a houseboy for a U.S. anti-aircraft unit. This unit protected the aerodrome from enemy air attacks. My main goal was to learn English. The anti-aircraft guns were positioned at the western end of the northernmost part of Suyeong Aerodrome, just 50 meters from the runway's end. They protected Australian propeller fighter aircraft that took off hourly and Navy jet fighters from aircraft carriers, newly invented and joining the battle. The anti-aircraft guns were also tasked with shooting down enemy aircraft during raids. The new dark slate gray jet fighters always took off in pairs, rocketing into the sky near the runway's end, possibly because the runway was too short for them. One day, one of the two jets failed to take-off, crashing into a levee about 5 meters high. It caught fire and exploded with its ammunition. A fire engine arrived, but there was no time to rescue the pilot, and they couldn't approach due to flying bullets and explosions. Within ten minutes, the aircraft was reduced to ashes, leaving no trace of the pilot. The other jet circled for about five minutes before heading to the battlefield. I can only imagine the surviving pilot's feelings. That place was a battlefield, and I witnessed the horrors of war less than 50 meters away, lying on the ground to avoid bullets and explosions.

♦ Transporting ammunition at Haeundae Station

I, your grandpa, took another part-time job in Haeundae with my schoolmates, commuting on foot from downtown Dongnae through Suyeong. This job involved carrying boxes of small ammunition of various calibers, especially 105-millimeter shells in boxes or 155-millimeter shells, nicknamed “half-gallon bottles,” from freight cars to a truck 100 meters away. The 155-millimeter shells weighed about 47 kilograms, and the 105-millimeter shells weighed around 20 kilograms for two shots per box. They were heavy, and when I carried the 155-millimeter shells, I felt like I was sinking into the ground, possibly because I weighed only 53 kilograms, an average weight for middle school students at the time.

Despite the difficulty, the UN Command’s Busan Bridgehead logistic supply base was completed, enabling the successful UN Command counterattack in September, including the Incheon Landing Operation and the breakthrough of the Nakdong River line. However, people in the rear endured poverty during wartime. My family wasn’t in dire straits, so I worked part-time during the summer break when school was closed. My employer from the Korean side gave me a paper slip as payment, which I could only cash a week later at a payment spot in Jeonju. They deducted 30 to 40 percent from the original amount. I saved about 20 days’ worth of slips and cashed them all at once. With that money, I bought five pears from an orchard and a concise English dictionary, which was in Japanese at the time, leaving me with no cash to take home. This exploitation of labor by capitalists, as communists called it, was common in Korea’s wartime labor industry, though hard to imagine today.

♦ The first memorial ceremony at Dongnae High School

On June 25th, 1951, exactly one year after the Korean War began with North Korea’s invasion, the first Memorial Ceremony was held at Dongnae High School (then called “Army Cadet School”), attended by President Rhee Syng-Man. The ceremony honored the souls of Korean Armed Forces and UN Command service members who fought and died in battle over the past year, with President Rhee consoling their families in person. Some surviving families cried out, “Bring my son back!" unable to contain their grief. As a middle school student, I realized that war is a miserable thing, and the loss of a family member can sometimes overshadow patriotism. Yet, I felt I needed to adopt a more mature mindset about the divine sacrifices for the nation and its people, like the parents of soldiers in advanced nations. I also worked part-time at a rubber shoe factory before returning to normal school.

♦ Working part-time at a rubber shoe factory

As I mentioned before, I had to leave school during my second and third years when the North Korean Puppet State invaded the South, leading to the outbreak of the Korean War in 1950. This lasted until the summer and fall of that year when the Busan Bridgehead was established. During this time, I worked at Suyeong Aerodrome and Haeundae Train Station, handling logistics during the war, and I was paid for my efforts. In the winter of that same year, I found work at a small, reclaimed rubber shoe factory near the Dongnae Oncheojang hot springs, which was run by an individual and had fewer than ten employees. When the factory ceased operations in the spring of 1951, I returned to Busan Normal School.

♦ Transferring from Busan Normal School to Dongnae High School, studying by day and working by night

Despite the ongoing war, President Rhee Syng-Man prioritized education, even exempting college students from military service. Our school converted a shrine, once used by the Empire of Japan and later abandoned, into a teacher's office on the hill behind Toseong-dong by Amicheon Stream. They cleared the surrounding yard and field to set up tent classrooms. The U.S. Army, being well-resourced and generous, provided thousands of military tents, mostly accommodating 24 people, to schools in Busan, including local and evacuated ones, as well as to the burgeoning Christian churches. This allowed classes to continue uninterrupted.

I transferred from Busan Normal School to Dongnae High School, studying during the day and working at night. Although I only had a few months between returning to school and entering high school, I was fortunate to be guided by Ms. Bang Deok-su during my last semester of the third year at Busan Normal School. However, the school system changed during the war, merging the middle school curriculum with the normal school, allowing me to graduate as part of the first class of this annexed middle school, despite missing almost the entire third-year semester. I took entrance exams for both Busan Normal School and Dongnae High School and was accepted to both without difficulty. Due to my family's circumstances, including my older brother's military enlistment and our worsening financial situation, commuting to Busan became challenging. Therefore, I chose Dongnae High School, only 300 meters from my home.

To support myself, I took a part-time job as a night duty worker and security guard at International Children's Relief, usually run by European medical staff. The sign for "Annex Ewha Womans University Medical Center" still remained, although it had returned to Seoul. This was in a temporary two-story wooden building at Gukje Market. After school each day, around 3:00 p.m., I would head straight to Busan, a journey of over an hour and a half. I left my school bag in the night duty room, a small corner room on the second floor, then went downstairs to receive the medical center's key. My duties included cleaning the already tidy medical center, filling the water tank for the next day, patrolling the building, and guarding it. Frequent power outages occurred due to the unreliable electricity system. This job took significant time away from my studies, but I continued until near the end of high school when I had to quit to prepare for college entrance exams.

♦ A trip to temporarily recovered Seoul

During a lull in the war around the current Military Demarcation Line, South Korea's evacuated government returned to Seoul under President Rhee Syng-Man's special measure, even before the armistice was validated. Curious about Seoul, I decided to visit during wartime. I stayed for a few days at Moon Dental Clinic on Wonhyo-ro 2-ga, run by a distant brother-in-law, a dentist who had recently returned to Seoul after being a refugee in Busan. I spent my limited time exploring downtown Seoul, including Taepyeong-ro (now Sejong-ro), Jong-ro, Eulji-ro, and Yongsan, using streetcars and walking. The Seoul I saw was almost completely destroyed and recently recovered. People, perhaps under psychological pressure from the possibility of another enemy occupation, were busy repairing walls and ceilings for survivors and temporarily fixing shops selling necessities. Only the chatter and laughter of schoolgirls on their way home from school offered hope amidst the devastation. Standing in the middle of Sejongdae-ro, possibly where King Sejong's statue now stands, I looked around the empty ruins and promised myself to become a "great man who works to revive this nation." Thus, I achieved the first part of my "dream of Seoul," which I had cherished for a long time.

♦ Applying to and being accepted by Korea Military Academy

In early 1953, the "additional 3rd recruitment exam for KMA" was announced. What intrigued me was that KMA was moving to Seoul, and graduates would have the chance to study abroad in the United States. I took the exam as a second-year student, not yet in my graduating year. After passing the written exam, I went to the

5th Replacement Depot in Daegu for a final health check and interview. When the KMA president asked why I was applying, I replied, "I want to become a military official and reform the corruption in the military and society." In hindsight, I might have disqualified myself with that answer, and I did fail. Later, in October, the regular "4th recruitment for KMA" was announced with the same details. I applied as a third-year high school student and passed without difficulty.

At Jinhae KMA, most buildings, especially the cadet brigade's, were Quonset huts, common for rear units of the Armed Forces of Korea until the mid-late 1980s. We future students used the cafeteria after the cadets. A cadet training to become a logistics officer gave a short speech before meals, reminding us to be thankful for the farmers who grew the grains we were about to eat. His words touched me. The meal quality was described as "average for the current middle class of Korea," but it wasn't very good. Given my family's financial situation, I wasn't used to such meals, so I didn't think much of it. However, my upperclassmen told me they were starving at that time. The accepted students were announced the day after the interview, and we were immediately measured for tailored clothes, including ceremonial and full-dress uniforms. I never imagined having clothes tailored just for me, and it delighted me.

I returned home with a happy heart but couldn't give up on my entrance exam to Seoul National University. Whether I would actually attend was a decision for later. I asked my close friend Lee Yong-u, who was submitting his application to SNU, to get an application form for me. He had evacuated from Japan in 1942 and settled in our neighborhood. His family was wealthy, and his older brother was already attending SNU's medical school. Lee graduated from SNU's law school but couldn't take the high-rank law official exam due to military service, so he inherited his father's business and remained a low-rank official. However, his sons are now high-ranking judges as of 2021.

I applied to SNU, choosing the "Department of Political and Diplomatic Science" as my first and second choices and the "Department of History" as my third. My exam-taker number was "69," the same as for the Busan Normal School's second recruitment, which I took as a sign of good luck. I chose that department because politicians and diplomats were seen as heroes who saved their nations, and there was a rumor that it was more promising than law school, making it worth trying.

I couldn't go to Seoul to take the exam when all my colleagues did. My mother was against it because it was clear our family couldn't afford the tuition and living expenses in Seoul if I got accepted. Honestly, I should have realized this before she did. Of course, I felt a bit sad about not being able to try for SNU, but I understood the situation. I accepted it as my destiny to attend KMA, so I gave up my trip to Seoul for the SNU entrance. In fact, most students applying to KMA were financially struggling at that time.

♦ Heading to Seoul and KMA to pursue my dream of greatness

Finally, I was going to Seoul, the city I had always yearned for, to study. This was more exciting to me than thinking of it as my enlistment in the military. A week before my departure, my mother gave me some travel money, encouraging me to sightsee in Seoul since she couldn't send me to Seoul National University. I took a train to Seoul about a week before school started. There weren't many trains from Busan Main Station to Seoul each day, and the journey took all day, including delays. On the day I left for Seoul, my mother, older sister, and younger sister (who later became a pharmacist) came to see me off. My mother handed me a bag with a few boiled eggs and potatoes. I stood on the observation platform at the back of the train, waving to my mother and sisters until they were out of sight. As I waved, I promised myself not to return home until I achieved my goals. I resolved that while I might not make my parents happy with money, I would become a great man and honor them.

I will never forget the moment I left Busan Main Station, seeing my mother and family, feeling my mother's love and emotions. Those memories kept me moving forward whenever challenges arose. I spent the day on the train, snacking on eggs and potatoes, which were scarce at the time. Through the train window, I saw red mountains, ruined cities and villages, straw huts unchanged for thousands of years, and landscapes drenched in poverty—quite different from the romanticized images of fertile rice paddies and chimney smoke.

After a day-long journey, I arrived at Seoul Station in the evening. As soon as I got off the train, I was overwhelmed by the bustling plaza of Seoul Main Station, which had avoided bombings. It was crowded with merchants and touts offering services like inns, restaurants, jobs, and entertainment. I followed a tout who seemed trustworthy to an inn across from the station, where the Daewoo Building now stands. I checked in, carrying only a small briefcase, and tried to sleep in this faraway city, thinking about the future. However, that evening, June 23rd, a massive fire broke out behind the inn, reducing Namdaemun Market to ashes. This market was a vital shopping area for Seoulites during the city's restoration. I went outside to watch the fire from Seoul Station Plaza, optimistically interpreting it as a welcoming celebration for me, a country boy new to Seoul.

On my first night in Seoul, I planned to meet my friends Lee Yong-u and Lee In-gil, who attended SNU's law school, and explore the demolished city the next day. I fell asleep with a calm attitude, despite the burning fire behind me. The following day, I witnessed Seoul's restoration efforts as citizens salvaged bricks and household items from the rubble in Jong-ro and Eulji-ro. I walked through Seoul Station, Namdaemun, Taepyeong-ro, Jong-ro 5-ga, Dongsung-dong, and reached Myeongryun-dong, where Lee Yong-u's boarding house was. SNU's College of Liberal Arts and Sciences was then a red brick building surrounded by marronnier trees, located where Marronnier Park is today. Lee Yong-u's boarding house was in a typical area for such accommodations, north of the university's headquarters. He shared a small studio room with Kim Gyu-sik, another law student who later became president and chief of Lotte Samgang Food Company.

For the next few days, I had lunch at their place (though these boarding houses charged extra for guests), attended a law school class at the College of Arts and Sciences, and explored the city. Although I can't recall the class content, it didn't seem much different from high school. I spent the remaining days visiting Jong-ro and Eulji-ro, climbing Namsan Mountain to view the devastated city, and helping at Moon Dental Clinic on Wonhyo-ro 2-ga, where I had visited a year earlier. The family there had cleared debris and covered walls and ceilings with newspaper and textbook pages.

On June 30th, I bid farewell to my friends Lee Yong-u and Lee In-gil and set off for Taereung KMA, or Korea Military Academy, the first step on my path as a soldier. I transferred between streetcars, buses, and trains from Seoul to Taereung, trying to contain my excitement.

Throughout this journey, I held onto several guiding principles and dreams:

- I once aspired to be the "king of magazines" because of my love for them.
- As I left my hometown, I promised myself not to return until I achieved my goals.
- I kept General Nam Yi's poem in my heart, reminding myself of the importance of ambition and striving for greatness.
- I believed in the saying, "Human beings learn 'high' and achieve 'medium,' so always seek the best in the world."
- I practiced the virtues of sacrifice, service, and kindness, striving to live modestly.
- I considered myself a giver, not a taker.
- I valued equality, treating everyone with respect and honorifics, except for close family and certain exceptions.
- I cherished the idea that "a man's words are as valuable as gold" and avoided excessive talking.
- I admired President Lincoln's values of poverty, honesty, diligence, and credibility.
- I followed George Washington's principles of justice, honesty, and fairness, keeping business separate from pleasure.
- I held onto my mother's "sacred story of my birth" and the belief that I should not easily submit to others.
- In high school, I considered taking high-rank law exams and studied relevant books and magazines.
- I read extensively about Roman history, particularly Julius Caesar.
- I learned about revolution and renovation from Ataturk Kemal Pasha's biography. These principles and aspirations guided me as I embarked on my journey, determined to become a great man and honor my family.

I have read a wide variety of books, but the ones that stand out most in my memory are "Strait is the Gate" by Andre Gide, "A History of England" and "A History of France" by Andre Maurois, "The Necklace" by Guy de Maupassant, and "Madame Bovary" by an unknown author. I attempted to read "Faust" by Goethe and "The Divine Comedy" by Dante—books that everyone tries to read at least once—but I set them aside after the first few pages.

I had a deep love for magazines and once dreamed of becoming the "king of magazines." I enjoyed Japanese publications like "Bungeishunju," "Chuokoron," "Sekai," and "Shonen," as well as Korean ones such as "Sonyeon," "Heemang," "Arirang," and "Kyunghyang." I also read "Reader's Digest" and "America's Hope" (USIS). Initially, I read the Japanese versions of "Reader's Digest" and later compared them with the Korean editions to explore different themes. As for "TIME" and "NEWSWEEK," I only managed to read the first few pages of news articles after taking English reading classes, and even then, I understood only half of the content. The photographs in "LIFE" and "Geography" captivated me, so I continued reading them, and my younger sister collected them after I entered KMA.

I have a valvular heart disease in my left atrium, which could disqualify me from the physical examination required to become a commissioned officer. I have always kept a quote by Dr. Paik Nak-jun (George Paik) in mind: "The most disappointing current environment of Korea is hope and chance for young Koreans." I have adhered to my own pride, tenacity, and "pioneer's spirit."

My academic abilities, based on textbooks, were halved due to the impact of the Korean War and having to work at a young age. This decline was particularly noticeable in natural sciences, including mathematics. Regarding humility and modesty, I always thought, "Tigers rule the mountains, and teachers rule the schools..." However, at that time, I didn't realize that excessive humility could be detrimental. I understood the importance of mercy, sympathy, and good deeds and knew I should practice them, but my financial situation limited me. I could only assist those in need with kindness and a spirit of sacrifice and service.

Chapter 2

My Days as a Cadet at Hwarangdae Korea Military Academy

(Dangun 4287-4291) (AD 1954-1958)

1. Entering School and Basic Military Training (June 30th-August 31st, 1954)

♦ Korea Military Academy and its Motto: "Wisdom·Virtue·Valor"

In 1951, during wartime, President Rhee Syng-Man and Gen. J.A. Van Fleet, the commander of the UN Command at the time, made a "great and brave decision" to establish the Korea Military Academy with a standard four-year curriculum in Jinhae in October. This was deemed necessary to enhance the education of all commissioned officers in the Armed Forces of Korea and to train elite officers. KMA's motto is "Wisdom·Virtue·Valor," defined as follows: Wisdom is the ability to discern and make judgments, allowing service members to recognize their missions and understand their duty in managing military force. Virtue fosters unity and combat power through love and understanding based on benevolence and faith. Valor enables steadfast action, doing the right thing in any danger, and taking responsibility.

The curriculum was modeled after West Point Academy, the American military academy. It embraced democracy, focusing on natural sciences and the Thayer System, the educational achievement system of the American military academy. Cadets were tested through daily systems, chapter tests, and final exams, maintaining the strictest academic standards among Korean educational institutions even during wartime. The first regular recruit cadets entered the academy in January 1952. The second recruit followed in August of the same year due to changes in the national educational system. The third recruit entered in July

1953, just before the armistice. In 1954, when the capital was restored to Seoul, KMA moved from Jinhae and settled in "Taereung," or "Hwarangdae" as it is known today. When the fourth regular recruit, my class, took an oath to enter the academy on July 1st, 1954, the four-year education system of KMA and the cadet brigade were fully organized. The educational system was nationally recognized, allowing graduates to earn a Bachelor of Science degree and be appointed as second lieutenants in the Army. The graduation and appointment of the first regular class of KMA took place on October 4th, 1955. Since then, the Korea Military Academy has gracefully paralleled the military history of Korea and the history of its Armed Forces.

- * "The Long Long Gray Line!" -

♦ Entering the Academy as "The 4th Regular Class" and the Ceremony (July 1st, 1954)

On the morning of June 30th, 1954, I registered my entrance at the outdoor registration office in "The 2nd Training Ground of KMA" in the northeast corner of the academy, as it lacked the impressive main gate it has now. Below is "The Oath to Enter the Academy" that I wrote and submitted:

1. Be loyal to the Republic of Korea.
2. Be absolutely obedient to your superiors, follow their orders, and strictly adhere to the academy's regulations.
3. Ensure there will be no troublesome aftermath regarding personal matters.
4. Be willing to accept any punishment for violating the aforementioned rules.

After registration, I proceeded to Academy Building A, located on the hill above the 2nd Training Ground (Training Ground B), where I received an array of unfamiliar government-provided items necessary to transform into a cadet and begin my life as one. These included items such as an inner support for the helmet, chinstrap for the helmet, bandolier, water canteen, water canteen pouch, towel, dress shoes, boots, shoe polish, tooth powder, and toothbrush. As I received each item, I had to loudly chant their names. Naturally, being a military base, they tossed the items to me, and I caught them without dropping any. The entire situation was both wondrous and baffling. All these items, from underwear to sleeveless undershirts and socks, were made in the U.S.A.

Carrying all these items in the wondrous duffle bag, now mine, I was escorted to the soldier's quarters (the dormitory) area for the cadet brigade, located on flat land opposite the classroom hill. The soldier's quarters consisted of Quonset huts (half-moon-shaped tents with tin roofs used by the U.S. Army as temporary shelters), each about 40 meters (131 feet) long and 30 meters (98 feet) wide. Five huts were lined up horizontally (one company), with eight vertical lines (eight companies) in total. The new cadets' unit comprises two companies and eight sections, with each Quonset housing two squads (about nine people per squad).

Upon entering my assigned Quonset, I found no air conditioning or boiler. Metal beds lined the aisle in the middle (about 1 meter wide, or 3 feet wide), and two squads were separated by lockers (also used as wardrobes) in the middle. As I searched for my spot, name tags with my name and number caught my eye. For the first time in my life, I walked to a bed and a locker, or wardrobe, with my name on them. I repeatedly looked at them, deeply touched that KMA, the government, and the cadet brigade recognized the existence of me, "Moon Yeong-Il." I felt satisfied with their treatment, proud of my existence, and profoundly grateful to them (the nation and the Armed Forces). My number was "704," signifying that I was the 704th person to enter KMA, as the first recruit's first person was number 1. The fourth recruits started from number 651, and I was the 54th among the 259 new recruits based on scores. This number represented me throughout my four years as a cadet and would remain my number for eternity unless KMA ceased to exist in the cadet numbers of the four-year regular courses. During my cadet years, I always identified myself as "Yes, sir! Number 704! Moon Yeong-Il!"

Opening my locker with my name on it, I found the summer cadet suits and full-dress uniforms I had fitted for in Jinhae. A cap, casual summer outfit, sweat suit, and olive-colored "long towel" made in the U.S.A. were neatly folded and organized as if sliced with a machine. To be honest, I was simply touched again, unaware that I would be required to keep them organized starting that evening.

Finally, at 10:00 a.m. on July 1st, 1954, 259 KMA cadets in full dress uniforms gathered in the 2nd training ground. For the first time in our recruit and the history of the regular military academy since its establishment, we held the "historical entrance ceremony" along with "the oath of a serviceperson" at the training ground of Taereung KMA.

♦ How a Lion Cub is Dropped from a Cliff and Trained to Survive

As fourth-class cadets, we began our journey at Taereung KMA, embarking on a regular four-year course. Our initial step was to undergo two months of basic military training during the summer. At KMA, education and training are divided into academic education during regular semesters and military training for two months. New cadets receive this training right after the entrance ceremony in their freshman year, known as "basic military training." This summer training aims to prepare cadets physically and mentally to become soldiers and provides foundational education in tactics. The training involves repetitive practice of simple principles to instill them into our bodies and minds, developing them into habits.

The training was split into two one-month courses. The first month took place on campus, utilizing the barracks, classrooms, and training grounds. The second month was conducted off-campus, in areas such as Seoul and the southeast Gyeonggi-do region, from the forests of Taereung to Namhansanseong Fortress. The on-campus training was led entirely by cadet assistant instructors, who were carefully selected third-year cadets. The second part of the training was known as "self-governed life." A self-governing squad-commanding cadet, appointed by the cadet assistant instructor, represented the squad for the remaining month and led the self-governing life in the barracks. Although the cadet assistant instructor remained present, the section commander, a fourth-year student, directed and commanded the self-governing squad-commanding cadets.

I was once chosen to be a self-governing squad-commanding cadet, leading general training for a month and performing additional duties. It was a challenging time, but I felt proud to have been selected. The most rewarding aspect was meeting Cadet Park Jeong-Gi, a classmate from an adjacent squad who also served as a self-governing squad-commanding cadet. We became lifelong friends. Before the training began, the cadet assistant instructor delivered a speech to the new cadets: "Lions push their cubs off a high cliff and only raise those that survive. This basic military training will present you with trials to overcome, much like those lion cubs. If you fall behind, you will never join others in this proud formation. If you overcome this, the gates of glory will open for you." His words both calmed and inspired us.

We were trained in several areas: how to salute to demonstrate our loyalty and determination to the nation as service members; how to properly wear uniforms to be battle-ready in everyday life; how to walk at a 90-degree angle to reject falsehood and hypocrisy, extinguish the wrong, and bring the right to life; and how to eat with dignity as future commissioned officers and commanders, including practicing the "Gentleman, International Standard" by eating at a 90-degree angle. We also learned to organize our lockers to maintain a mindset of "always at war" and develop a habit of meticulous and perfect defense readiness. This contributed to deductions in barrack life points and affected academic grades, so everything had to be perfectly aligned, even if it meant using saliva to achieve it. We were often criticized during morning and evening roll calls, and it was sometimes used as an excuse to punish us intentionally.

We were also trained in maintaining other items and military supplies. We used U.S.-made shoe polish and "BRASSO" to shine dress shoes and decorative buckles for full dress uniforms, much like shoeshine boys. These rules controlled individuals' thoughts and behaviors, established mutual cooperation and camaraderie among the members of the military barracks community, and pursued the "Gentleman, International Standard." Personal hygiene was emphasized as a personal responsibility, and our hygiene was checked by making us remove our underwear during weekend yard ground roll calls. Along with group hygiene, the barracks were cleaned daily and on weekends. The cadets' restroom, which we called the "toilet," was a squat toilet located on a hill south of the barracks area. It was housed in a wooden building that provided some protection from wind and rain, and we cleaned its wooden floor and surrounding area daily.

♦ Running everywhere, everyday

Life in the barracks during basic military training had no concept of "at ease." Once we completed an action inside or outside the barracks, we waited for the next task or moved on to the next action. There were no breaks, and we had no time to read books or idle away. Once we stepped outside, even for one step, we had to walk at a 90-degree angle, which was as challenging as moving our spoons at a 90-degree angle to eat in the cafeteria. We had to run after taking three steps or more, meaning we had to trot or run straight to distant toilets or lavatories. However, when the lights went out at 10:00 p.m., silence fell, and we enjoyed a moment of freedom as we lay down. We took time to catch our breath, rest, write letters, do laundry, and lose track of time on weekends, from Saturday afternoons to Sunday morning roll calls. When the cadet assistant instructor generously called a holiday morning roll call a "sleeping roll call," it brought me immense joy, although some instructors took it away from us a few times initially.

♦ Training under the scorching sun

The military training ground was not in the forests of Taereung but on a nearby bare land without a single blade of grass. It was scorching in July and August, with ground temperatures reaching 35 degrees Celsius (95 degrees Fahrenheit). During basic military training, we had to suspend our intelligence to think about the academy's motto, "Wisdom, Virtue, Valor," and keep its meanings in mind. We simply counted every minute and second to perform actions like "attention," "salute," "walk at 90 degrees," "eat at 90 degrees," "close-order drill," "16 motions, rifle to your right shoulder," "36 directions, go forward," and sang the academy's song or military songs. We trained precisely for 50 minutes with 10-minute breaks in between, drinking water from ice-filled water bags, eating salt, and drinking more water, all while covered in sweat. There were no trees to provide shade around the training ground, so we sought refuge under the small shrubs during breaks, like ostriches burying their faces in the ground in an emergency.

The bayonet fighting exercise was a particularly grueling part of the training. Bayonet exercise is a skill used when facing enemies at the end of a battle, involving the use of a bayonet—a combination of a rifle and a dagger—to attack an enemy in one blow. The goal is to become proficient in using rifles and daggers like swinging a stick. An M1 Garand weighs about 5 kilograms (11 pounds), and with a bayonet attached, it weighs about 7 kilograms (15 pounds). We had to hold it with both hands, stretch it out, swing it below, above, and sideways, move our bodies, dodge enemy bayonets, and stab the enemy with our bayonets. In summary, it was a form of martial arts. Performing these basic movements at high speed and repeating the swinging and stabbing actions turned this training into a significant challenge, yet it played a crucial role in developing the service members' mentality. It was also often used by upperclassmen cadets to discipline lowerclassmen.

In August, the second part of basic military training began. This did not mean we started studying military science or conducting research. It included some indoor education, shooting training at a temporary shooting ground in Taereung to prepare us for instructing troop members after commissioning, various disciplinary training, and research on rules. The final physical training, individual battle training per squad, served as the culmination. It combined outdoor running at different levels with individual battle training in the forests of Taereung, followed by marching training at different levels.

♦ General marching trainig, exploring Namhansanseong Fortress, and lerning about the Manchu Invasion of 1636

The last general training, which marked the finale of basic military training, involved a fully armed march at Namhansanseong Fortress for one night and two days, covering an actual distance of 40 kilometers (25 miles), along with history lessons. We exited the main gate of the academy, headed south past Handok Pharmaceutical (Pfizer)—the surrounding view included Handok Pharmaceutical, Mang-u Train Station to the east, Cheongryang-ri Hygiene Hospital to the west, Jungryang-cheon Stream flowing north and south, and wide-open rice paddies and fields—continued south, changed direction to southeast around Achasan Mountain, and crossed the Hangang River via Gwangjin-gyo Bridge, the second sidewalk bridge over the Hangang River, constructed in 1936.

After passing through Jamsil and Songpa, we hiked to Namhansanseong Fortress, entering through the "South Gate." Namhansanseong Fortress was one of the three key military strongholds established around Hanyang, the former name of Seoul during the Joseon Dynasty, for its defense. Traditionally, Ganghwa-do Island served as the main base, using the strait as a natural barrier. Namhansanseong Fortress was the second base, offering strong defensive capabilities and survival conditions due to its fortress walls. The third base was Bukhansanseong Fortress, characterized by its deep valleys that posed geographic challenges to invaders. The northeastern area of Namhansanseong Fortress was open land suitable for farming, making it ideal for sustaining a prolonged stay at the fortress. At that time, I, your grandpa, surveyed Namhansanseong Fortress and gazed at the Hangang River to the north. I thought this place could historically and geographically serve as the cradle of military education in the Republic of Korea. Therefore, I considered it a suitable location to relocate the Korea Military Academy (KMA) from Taereung.

During the Manchu Invasion of 1636, Emperor Hong Taiji of the Qing Dynasty led a formidable force of 120,000 soldiers to attack Joseon, aiming to secure his rear before conquering the Ming Dynasty. They overran all regions of Joseon, including Ganghwa-do Island, where the prince and key royal family members had sought refuge. Eventually, the main forces surrounded Namhansanseong Fortress, settling near Tancheon—now Songpa Street—directly below the fortress, and pressured King Injo to surrender. The Qing forces blocked external reinforcements and severed connections between the inside and outside of the fortress, attempting a long-term siege by cutting off food supplies while maintaining a daily siege on the mountain top. Despite efforts from backup forces across the country to connect with or reinforce the fortress, they were uncoordinated and ineffective, ultimately being thwarted or defeated by the Qing troops. The Joseon forces within the fortress, numbering 13,000 soldiers, held out for 43 days in fierce defense. However, when the prince who had fled to Ganghwa-do surrendered and was taken hostage, rescuing him became impossible. With food supplies dwindling, King Injo had no choice but to endure national and personal humiliation and surrender. He prostrated himself before Emperor Hong Taiji at Samjeondo—a rice paddy near Garak Market in 1954—and surrendered by bowing deeply three times and touching his head to the ground nine times.

We studied this historical event at Namhansanseong Fortress, conducted a field study, descended the mountain along the trail, and visited the Samjeondo Monument. Confronted with the national humiliation commemorated by the monument, I vowed to dedicate myself to national defense, ensuring that no country would ever invade my nation again. We camped on a hill in Songpa on a rainy and windy afternoon and returned to the academy the following day along the same path. This marked the conclusion of our basic military training. As we marched through the main gate, the academy's military band played the song, "Hurray, hurray! Our heroes are back..." The music resonated in the skies of Taereung, and all the commissioned officers at the academy greeted us with enthusiastic applause. This was the end of our basic military training and our return to the academy. The "Song of Victory" played by the military band still echoes in my ears. Reflecting on the past two months, I realized that I had overcome challenges by reminding myself, "This is loyalty to the nation," during the extremely difficult training. This finale marked the completion of the basic military training for cadets, an experience I will never forget. The naive young man I was two months prior had transformed into a robust cadet.

2. Academic Life and Life in Barracks During a General Semester as a Freshman (September 1954-June 1955)

♦ Living with '3 Restrictions', Studying Military Science, Literature, and Natural Science Simultaneously

The sophomores, juniors, and seniors arrived at the end of August, having concluded their time in Jinhae and relocated to Hwarangdae, Taereung, Seoul. I'm certain they were more excited than we freshmen were, especially with the academy now offering a complete four-year course as a regular Korea Military Academy. Their excitement must have been heightened by leaving behind the challenging days in Jinhae, characterized by cold and hunger, to start anew. KMA is primarily a military base before being a school, with everything structured in a military fashion. The academy comprises headquarters, a department of professors, a cadet brigade, and a service support group. The cadet brigade, the core of cadet life, was the department of discipline, led by a brigadier general as the brigade commander, a lieutenant colonel as the vice commander, discipline officers for the eight cadet companies (one major per company), and a department of physical education headed by a major with several specialized instructors. They disciplined and supported the cadet regiment, a self-governed organization of cadets. The cadet regiment consisted of two battalions and eight companies, with a regimental commander cadet, four staff cadets, two battalion commander cadets, and eight company commander cadets appointed to serve at the headquarters for one year. Each company was divided into two sections, each section into two barracks, and each barrack into four squads. A squad typically had eight to nine members, including one to two junior cadets as squad commanders, two sophomore cadets, and three to four freshman cadets. Senior cadets resided in separate, independent self-governed barracks. Although daily routines were up to each cadet, missions and responsibilities required living as a group of two squads with a hierarchical system. Freshmen were tasked with cleaning indoors, nighttime outdoor lookouts, and miscellaneous duties like handling supplies.

Life at KMA's cadet brigade adhered to the "honor system" and the "3 Restrictions of KMA," strict rules designed to train cadets into leaders. The "honor system" emphasized honesty, prohibiting cheating and lying, with severe consequences for violations, including expulsion. The "3 Restrictions" prohibited relationships with women, marriage, drinking, and smoking both on and off campus. Violations led to the "Honor Committee," a self-governed cadet organization, and proven infractions resulted in expulsion without exception. This system was essential for training young men to become exemplary leaders in the nation and society. However, I never heard of anyone being punished under this rule during my time as a cadet, and none in my class faced such consequences. In essence, KMA was a place of learning and training, where everyone adhered to the rules, which became virtues for commanders at all levels after graduation.

♦ Playing Rugby on the School Rugby Team and Studying General Academics Simultaneously

One day, a confident junior upperclassman approached me in the barracks area and asked, "You, young cadet. Are you good at playing table tennis?" "Ah, no, sir, I am not," I replied truthfully, having never played table tennis before. He then said, "Ah, I knew it. Come to the rugby team tomorrow!" I had helped my mother carry bundles of fabric to the market, which perhaps made me appear as strong as a sports player. Thus, after a brief three-minute interview on the barracks streets, I was selected for KMA's rugby team. Sports players at KMA were often chosen randomly from the freshmen, underwent rigorous training, and participated in off-campus games one to three times a year. Consequently, I was assigned to the newly organized 4th barrack of the 6th company of the cadet brigade, known as "the barracks for the academy's rugby team." In 1954, I became a rugby player for KMA and balanced my academic and barracks life—living with players from freshmen to juniors in one barrack—while training for future games between the three military academies, as there were few adult teams in Korea at the time.

Although a freshman cadet's life in the barracks during a general semester may seem straightforward, it was a story of "deep and serious joy, sorrow, love, and hate." My freshman year from 1954 to 1955 was particularly intense. To convey the experience, perhaps the best way is to share a few stories from that year. As the lowest rank in a squad, freshman cadets had to be extremely cautious while fulfilling numerous challenging tasks. It was always "Old boy first" in all matters, but when it came to hard work, it was invariably "juniors' duty."

On the other hand, since we slept in adjacent beds, seniors and juniors stayed together. We juniors were sometimes bothered by the upperclassmen, but at the same time, they guided and encouraged us like brothers. We grew attached to each other and formed friendships, which gave us more advantages during our military careers. To be honest, the only difficult parts of a junior's life were cleaning indoors and outdoors, distributing supplies, and being polite to superiors.

♦ A Cadet's daily routine

A cadet's daily routine was the same for everyone during a general semester. Our day always started at 6:00 a.m. with the bugle wake-up call, which sounded like "Forceful, forceful!" We woke up as if electrified, folded our blankets and mattresses, picked up our boots, sneakers, face-washing bowls, and "Boston Bags" for vacation from under the metal beds, placed them on top to clean the floor, and ran to the training ground, each battalion separately, 500 meters away from the barracks, as if in a race, to start the morning assembly. The assembly included a headcount, singing the national anthem, Aegukga, all the way to the 4th verse, and bowing individually toward our hometowns to our parents and siblings. After the morning roll call, we trotted back, went to the lavatory, hurriedly made our beds like 'Tofu' cuts, cleaned the floor, organized our shoes, and then assembled for breakfast. We marched to the large cadet mess hall, returned, and prepared to march to the academic building.

At 7:40, all cadets of the regiment assembled in front of quarters to march to the academic building. We sang the academy's song and military songs as we marched to our classrooms and were dismissed to attend classes. Classes started precisely at 8 o'clock. Each class lasted 60 minutes, with 50 minutes for the actual class and ten minutes for a break and moving to the next class. We returned to the barracks at 11:50, assembled for lunch, and had lunch together at 12:00. We went back to the barracks, returned to the classroom, and afternoon classes began at 1:00. Classes were dismissed at 3:00 p.m. All cadets had time to study or have a free moment until dinner at 6:00 p.m. However, student athletes, especially rugby and soccer players who had to compete in the 3 Military Academies Competition every year, practiced at the training ground from 3:00 to 5:00. Night classes were from 7:00 to 9:00 p.m. The evening roll call was at 9:30 p.m., and lights went out at 10:00 p.m., marking the end of the day. Classes or academic courses began in September, similar to the American system. The first semester ended in late December, and we went on winter vacation. The second semester began in January and ended in mid-June. Then we had a ten-day summer vacation and went on summer military training for two months during July and August. Freshmen received basic military training at Taereung KMA. Sophomores went on a training tour to major combat arms departments, including infantry, artillery, tank, communications, and military engineering. Juniors went on a field training tour, visiting all military academies of the Army, Navy, Marine Corps, and Air Force. Seniors practiced working as platoon leaders in frontline units during summer training.

The academic level was very advanced, almost identical to the curriculum of West Point Academy in the U.S. Moreover, it was just after the Korean War, so many renowned professors from universities in Seoul, including SNU, were invited and treated with the respect of Army captains. They taught the first cadets of Korea to take four-year courses with care and effort and were even stricter on patriotism and military rules than the disciplinary officers of the cadet brigade. In economics, we learned about Keynes and Samuelson, "The Wealth of Nations" by Adam Smith, macroeconomics, microeconomics, and more. We also studied comparative government in political science, humanities, and metrology, as well as practical training. In my architecture class, I did practical training by calculating "I-beams" while visiting the site for designing and producing the damaged piers of The 1st Hanganggyo Bridge, which was detonated during wartime. In my ordnance science class, I disassembled and reassembled not only general ordnance but also a military vehicle engine. One of my classmates, who later became an engineering professor, led the production of Korean automobile engines and became a leader in that academic field. The academy applied the "daily system," a unique system from the American military academy. Out of 50 minutes of actual class, 40 minutes were for lecture and discussion, and the remaining ten minutes were for a quiz. Due to the honor system, cheating and lying were never forgiven. The professor would distribute the quiz sheets and leave, and the cadets would take the quiz for ten minutes. When the class president announced, "The quiz is over. Everyone leave," we all put our pencils down and exited the classroom. The class president collected the quizzes and turned them in to the professor. This system was perfect, and I never heard of any classmate violating it and getting expelled during my four years at KMA.

♦ The General's Class

Homeroom classes were organized into 12 homerooms with 20 students per grade, divided into six homerooms each in Group A and B. Assignments to homeroom classes were based on grades, from Homeroom 1 to Homeroom 6, on a monthly basis. At the beginning of my freshman year, everyone was assigned to homeroom classes based on their entrance grades, and I, your grandpa, was assigned to Homeroom 1 for many subjects. Homeroom 1 was for potential "top grade students" (around two per year), but Homeroom 6 was legendarily called "The General's Class" with comfort and encouragement. It turned out to be true decades later, as many cadets from Homeroom 6 became generals. I, your grandpa, spent a lot of time studying military science classes, so I was assigned to "The General's Class" in natural sciences a few times. At the end of every month, the professors' department posted a notice on its bulletin board with grades per subject, new homeroom assignments based on those grades, and the report card of grades at the end of the academic year was mailed to parents in the hometowns. Freshmen had to maintain a 90-degree posture even in front of this bulletin board, and if their posture was poor while looking at it, they were targeted by sophomores and had to receive special training.

When Kim Bok-Dong, a senior and section commander for summertime training, said, "It's not manly to stare at a report card," I thought he was right and stayed away from the bulletin board. However, about 60 cadets failed their grades at the end of the first semester after taking the general final exam. They couldn't go on vacation with others and had to stay at the academy, study for three days, and take the so-called "additional exam." As a result, about 50 of them ended up with insufficient grades and were expelled immediately. When my sophomore year started, the academy continued to eliminate cadets with insufficient grades. Out of the 251 cadets who entered the academy with my class, only 179 remained by the time we graduated and were commissioned, meaning 35% were eliminated. Most were eliminated after the first final exam of the freshman year. The education at KMA was truly rule-based, honest, and strict.

♦ Training as a rugby player

Being trained as a rugby player for the school's rugby team presented a conflict between non-academic training and the burdens of learning. I was accepted to KMA with relatively good grades, so I was assigned to high-level classes like Homeroom 1. I became careless as most subjects were just extensions of high school subjects at the beginning of my academic year, and I didn't try my best on the daily system because I thought it was just a quiz about memorizing things in a limited time, and its result was not impressive. Especially, while everyone focused on studying during free time (3–5 p.m.), I had to spend that time doing rigorous rugby training every day. This not only limited my study time but also accumulated physical fatigue, ultimately causing my grades to drop. As I mentioned, I was selected by an upperclassman rugby player to join in a hurry, assigned to the athlete's barracks, and started playing rugby without much time to think about it. But that doesn't mean I was forced into it. The truth is, it was a lucky and honorable occurrence. So I sacrificed my free time to study and did my best to practice and train for it.

My position was a scrum forward left wing, which made me number 1. When I went to the training ground at 3:00 p.m., training started with light running and warm-ups. Then I practiced dashes, passes, front or rear tackles against opponents holding the ball, holding the ball to my chest while lying on my back to avoid losing it, how to kick the ball over the crossbar, catching the ball and dashing to touch the goal line or the rear of the H Bar, and doing a Try by holding the ball with my entire body or toward the center Try.

The training was specific to each position, and as the number 1 scrum forward, my role was to engage with the opposing team's scrum players, overpower them, push forward, or dig my spikes into the ground to hold my position and avoid being pushed back. I also had to execute a complete scrum spin to the side by maneuvering the ball between my feet. Every day, I completed the training with a strong sense of duty, unity, and pressure from the assistant coach. Perhaps this was why I often found myself dozing off during two-hour night classes due to sheer exhaustion. This routine cost me at least four hours of free time each day compared to my fellow cadets. Additionally, my interests lay in the humanities, particularly in reading books on political science, sociology, and history. As a result, I had to take extra exams in physics and math for my freshman final exams and the first semester of my sophomore year. Ultimately, it was disappointing, but I had to make the decision to give up playing rugby for the school during my sophomore year.

For context, I was unaware at the time that I had valvular heart disease in my left atrium. This condition involves the malfunctioning of the four cardiac valves that regulate blood flow between the atria and ventricles, leading to irregular blood flow or reflux. I'm uncertain whether it was congenital or acquired, but I suspect it had been with me long before I entered the Korean Military Academy (KMA). It was likely undetectable with the simplified physical examinations for military enlistment at that time. Although I usually don't feel symptoms, they include: 1. Shortness of breath when my heart is overworked, which can worsen to difficulty in breathing; 2. Fatigue and dizziness due to disrupted blood circulation; 3. Coughing, sputum, and chest pain. This chronic illness has caused me significant trouble.

♦ My first vacation as a freshman (Dec 23rd, 1954~Jan 2nd 1955)

My first vacation during my freshman year (December 23rd, 1954 - January 2nd, 1955) was one of the happiest and most joyful periods of my life. It was the first time I returned home after leaving in late June and living as a freshman cadet for my first semester until late December at the strict KMA, a military base far from home, without a single day off to go outside. I was eager to see my parents and siblings, having realized my deep love for them during my time away. The ten-day vacation allowed me to escape the regimented life of the barracks and spend Christmas and New Year with my family and friends in my beloved hometown. I was particularly eager to be good to my parents, so I embarked on this vacation with hope and joy in my heart.

All cadets boarded a special train arranged by the government, as general trains at the time were overcrowded, with passengers lying in corridors or on luggage shelves on the Busan-Seoul route. We were seated according to our destinations, with a special car reserved for freshman cadets. The train departed from Hwarangdae Station and connected to the back of general trains at Seoul Station. The train to my hometown left Seoul Station around sunset, traveling overnight to arrive at Busan Main Station the next morning. We sang military songs, popular songs, and all kinds of songs throughout the night, even bidding farewell to fellow cadets at different stations. We continued singing until we reached Busan Main Station, where the Busan natives disembarked, without getting any sleep. This was how eagerly I anticipated the vacation.

However, upon arriving home and greeting my parents, I forgot my initial intention of being good to them. Instead, I spent my days having fun with friends, continually postponing time with my parents. Before I knew it, my vacation was over. When it was time to return to the academy, I felt deep regret for not spending more time with my parents. I promised myself to make it up to them next time and returned to the academy with sadness and disappointment, unlike my joyful journey home.

♦ The unforgettable 'Namsan Easter Worship of 1955'

The unforgettable 'Namsan Easter Worship of 1955' was another memorable experience. During my freshman year, we went on several field trips to major historical sites, including Taereung, Namhansanseong Fortress, Donggureung (Nine Royal Tombs of the East), and battlefields in Ganghwa-do, where we stayed overnight at Jeondeungsa Temple. These trips were both educational and meaningful. However, the most memorable event was the Korea-U.S.A "Easter Worship" for civilians held in Namsan Park in the spring of 1955. While I forgot many details, I vividly remember the freshness and serenity of Namsan Central Park and the trumpet solo performance by a soldier from the Eighth United States Army's military band. The music resonated throughout the park, creating a wondrous atmosphere that deeply touched me. Even now, recalling that moment evokes the same wondrous feeling.

3. Upperclassman Cadet Years (1955~1957)

♦ President Rhee Syng-Man's rebuilding of regular military academies and his affection for them

My years as an upperclassman cadet were marked by significant events. President Rhee Syng-Man, regarded as the father of the Republic of Korea, sought U.S. support in 1952 to bolster Korean Armed Forces' military power during the Korean War. He sent Korean military officials to study at U.S. military academies and resumed regular military academies in Korea, establishing high-class military educational organizations like the Military Staff College to train elite military officials. In October 1951, KMA resumed as a regular academy with four-year courses, transitioning from a temporary school in Jinhae to Hwarangdae, Taereung, in July 1954, where it remains active today.

President Rhee, passionate about education, held Bachelor's, Master's, and Doctorate degrees from prestigious U.S. universities, a rarity even in American society at the time. He believed academic education was essential for national restoration and advancement. Consequently, he exempted college students from military service during wartime and encouraged studying abroad, particularly in the United States, even if it was illegal. President Rhee was deeply invested in KMA, desiring Korea's own armed forces and KMA to educate key military officials. He supported them with Gen. J.A. Van Fleet of the US Army, then commander of the

UN Command. President Rhee frequently visited KMA, bringing VIP guests from foreign countries to witness cadet parades and showcase the academy's progress. He even invited Korean immigrants from Hawaii, a base for his independence movement, to tour KMA and fulfill their lifelong dream of seeing Korea's Armed Forces. Whenever he visited KMA and addressed the cadets, President Rhee encouraged us to become great commanders of the Armed Forces and national leaders, expressing his hopes for Korea's military future.

♦ A parade in Seoul celebrating President Rhee's birthday, memories of March 26th

A particularly memorable event was the military city parade in downtown Seoul on March 26th, 1955, President Rhee's birthday. Cadets from the Army, Navy, and Air Force academies participated. The units trained together for two months at Yeouido Aerodrome, where Yeouido now stands, rehearsing for the parade. Cadets joined the rehearsal weekly in February, traveling from Taereung to Hannam-dong by uncovered truck. Despite the cold winter weather, we wore metal helmets without earmuffs, sat in four rows on the truck, and maintained a straight posture, holding the cargo box with one hand and an M1 rifle with the other, demonstrating the cadets' unwavering dignity in snow, rain, and wind. This resulted in frostbite on our ears, hands, and feet, with some suffering long-term effects. Yet, we never blamed President Rhee. We took immense pride in participating in the parade.

On March 26th, the day of the parade, all units lined up from the entrance of the Seoul Plaza Hotel, in front of Seoul's current City Hall, to Seoul Station, with KMA at the front of the parade. We waited for our start at 10:00. The weather was cloudy, and sleet fell intermittently, making us worry that the parade we had rehearsed so diligently might be ruined. But, amazingly, as 10:00 approached, the weather turned sunny. This reminded me of President Rhee Syng-Man, whom I regarded as a commander-in-chief appointed by heaven. This weather phenomenon repeated almost every year thereafter, and I always remembered to rely on this weather pattern throughout my military career.

It proved particularly effective when I participated as a corps commander in the Korea-US Team Spirit Field Maneuver Exercise in March 1987. On March 26th, 1987, the "helicopter assault operation" was part of the final attack operation of the field exercise. The commander of the allied forces, having heard a weather forecast predicting snow and rain starting the day before, asked me if we should cancel it, expressing extreme concern. I stood firm, believing in "March 26th, President Rhee Syng-Man's birthday," and told him to "go for it," explaining my reasoning. They smiled, laughed, and believed me. As expected, by 11:00, the time to start the attack, the cloudy sky cleared, allowing us to prepare for the attack and execute the artillery fire and helicopter assault operation as planned. The attack continued successfully, enabling us to surround the enemies and secure victory, providing a wonderful conclusion to that year's "Team Spirit."

♦ Education and training at the School of Combat Arms at Sangmudae (Gwangju, Jeollanamdo)

After returning from our summer vacation, we took a train to Sangmudae Base in Gwangju for education and training at the Army's five combat arms schools. Gwangju housed these schools, with the control center named "The Army Combat Arms Education & Training Command" at Sangmudae, except for the military engineering school in Gimhae. It controlled the infantry, artillery, armor, communication schools, and other support units. Traveling on the exclusive train along the southwest line, the cadets were moved by the sight of the southeastern plains they had heard about. The vast plains, especially Mangyeong Plains, with the horizon in the distance, made me stand tall, and the swaying green rice leaves filling the plain brought me contentment.

The first part of the two-month course was an educational course on infantry science. Starting with the M1 rifle, the personal weapon for infantry soldiers, we learned theories and shooting skills for medium firearms like the 60-millimeter mortar and 3.5-inch antitank rocket, and large firearms like the 81-millimeter mortar and 56-millimeter antitank rifle, which all commissioned officers must know. We also learned how to apply them in tactics and how to command small units (platoons, companies, and battalions) as commanders and staff to carry out practices. We studied commanding theories and tactics at the battalion commander level and practiced them. Then we learned about tank structures and techniques, and tactical knowledge at Armor school. At the artillery school, we learned how to induce bombshells, measure the range of fire, calculate actual shooting, and execute actual fire. At the communication school, we learned about communication command devices for the infantry and their use, as well as combat unit communication. The final part of the education and training was a field trip to witness a "Demonstration of infantry-armor & artillery combined arms operation" at a wide flatland practice ground in 'Bihack' country.

♦ The cadet's intellectual leanings towards Proletarian ideals

In November 1959, a Colon Report titled "The U.S.A.'s Policy on Asia" was submitted to a U.S. Senate sub-committee to provide "suggestions on policy on Korea." The report's key point was, "The Armed Forces of Korea have a very low chance of carrying out a coup d'état, but it's inevitable." It highlighted this possibility while evaluating and anticipating Korea, stating, "In Korea, talented individuals from poor families enter military academies due to tuition issues, as college education at military academies is funded by the government, and they are being trained to become young, commissioned officers who may develop 'tendencies as intelligent Proletarians.' However, they harbor anger toward privileged government officials and politicians, and their anger has the potential to explode. This was true, as starting with my recruit, the 4th regular class of KMA (entered in 1954), over 90% graduated from high school that year, unlike the upperclassmen before them. They became cadets after competing at a rate of 1 out of 25 or higher, with some being students at Seoul National University's law and medical schools, and Korea University's law school.

Moreover, the 6th class (entered in 1956) included new cadets from Kyunggi High School and Seoul High School, the top high schools in Korea at the time, with 30 students from each school. I heard that Principal Kim In-gyu, who was the principal of both schools consecutively, visited KMA to experience it firsthand and encouraged his students, saying, "KMA is the most promising college in the Republic of Korea." However, the cadets at KMA at that time exhibited Proletarian thoughts and behavior, especially during their temporary term in school—they were molded into embodiments of devotion to the Republic of Korea after commissioning and starting their military careers. Perhaps this was considered loyalty to the nation, extinguishing the wrong and bringing the right to life.

4. Commissioning as a Second Lieutenant

♦ The honorable day I graduated and was commissioned as second lieutenant in the Republic of Korea Army

I was commissioned as a second lieutenant in the Republic of Korea Army as soon as I graduated with a Bachelor of Science degree. We, the 4th class, who were lion cubs pushed off the cliff on July 1st, 1954, were trained with "Wisdom, Virtue, Valor" in body and soul, completing the extremely challenging physical and mental education and training, which are hard to describe in words. Finally, on June 16th, 1958, we acquired our Bachelor of Science degrees and were honorably commissioned as confident second lieutenants in the Republic of Korea Army. As I had promised to 'give them honor rather than wealth,' I was able to bring my mother to the graduation, although my father was unwell, and I felt infinitely happy. Now, I, your son, honor you, my parents, for being commissioned as a second lieutenant in the Republic of Korea Army.

♦ I honor my parents as I am commissioned as second lieutenant in Republic of Korea Army

I was commissioned as a second lieutenant in the Republic of Korea Army as soon as I graduated with a Bachelor of Science degree. We, the 4th class, who were lion cubs pushed off the cliff on July 1st, 1954, were trained with "Wisdom, Virtue, Valor" in body and soul, completing the extremely challenging physical and mental education and training, which are hard to describe in words. Finally, on June 16th, 1958, we acquired our Bachelor of Science degrees and were honorably commissioned as confident second lieutenants in the Republic of Korea Army. As I had promised to 'give them honor rather than wealth,' I felt infinitely happy. Now, I, your son, honor you, my parents, for being commissioned as a second lieutenant in the Republic of Korea Army.

♦ My Korea Military Academy (KMA) class ring symbolizes my eternal commitment to the nation, akin to a wedding ring

KMA has a tradition of giving a 'Graduation Ring' to graduates since the 1st class graduated in 1955, and we, too, received gold class rings thanks to the care and effort of our lowerclassmen to celebrate our graduation. The rings are given on graduation day. When each graduate passed under the giant imitation gold ring, a lowerclassman from the 5th class (just one year below us) placed the ring on the graduate's left ring finger. This ring is our wedding ring with our nation, symbolizing our eternal love. Made of real gold, it shines constantly, representing the maintenance of unchanging dignity anywhere, anytime, along with the crimson ruby sparkling in the middle, symbolizing eternal loyalty and passion. As we keep this ring for life, it serves as a symbol of pride as KMA graduates. I have many stories connected to this ring, but I will share just one.

When I was a visiting scholar in the military science department for ROTC at an American university, I became a member of the Society for Military History and attended an event in Washington D.C. It involved meeting Soviet Union spies secretly, field trips, indoor discussions, and more. During a visit to the CIA headquarters, part of the schedule, an American gentleman noticed my ring (similar to the class ring of American military academies) and approached me. "Is that the graduation ring of the Korean military academy? What are you?" He said he graduated from the American military academy in 1953 and fought in the Korean War as soon as he was commissioned. He fought in the Iron Triangle, near where Korea's 3rd Infantry Division (nicknamed the skeleton troop) is now, and lost his graduation ring during a battle near Namgang when the war went into armistice. I treated him with respect, as he was more experienced than me by five years, and thanked him for fighting in the Korean War. He shared a story that interested us both as military academy graduates. "We, the military academy graduates, use our rings to communicate with each other at commissioned officer meetings and so on. We do that by knocking under the desk with our rings." This made us, two military academy graduates from Korea and the United States, grow closer as we expressed our empathy and familiarity.

♦ At KMA, I learned invaluable lessons and developed key characteristics : studying military history, adhering to rules, treating everyone equally, rewarding and punishing fairly, understanding the true meaning of civilian control, practicing modesty and mutual respect, using honorifics, fostering autonomy, self-reliance, and embodying loyalty and devotion

What I learned at KMA invaluable lessens and my characteristics include studying military history. Since my school days, I have always excelled in history. My grades in history never fell below 95 points throughout elementary, middle, and high school. This early aptitude led me to delve into works like "A Cultural History of the World" by H.G. Wells and "A Study of History" by Arnold J. Toynbee. At KMA, I expanded my knowledge by reading "On War" by General Carl von Clausewitz, "Humans and Ideas on History" by Toynbee, and works like "Why Do They Choose Socialism" and "Ideas of Society" by Iwanami Bunko. I was particularly engrossed in "Textbook of Military History" and "Atlas of Military History" from the American military academy, as well as "The Harper Encyclopedia of Military History." These books were my constant companions, not just during my academic years but whenever I had free time. Although I had to take a few extra exams, I largely ignored natural science subjects in favor of liberal arts and military science, focusing especially on military history. This foundation became invaluable in my military career and in my later studies on "Korean National Security Strategy Thought."

I believe in following rules and principles, treating everyone equally, and distinguishing between public and private matters. While these ideals are easier said than done, given the complexities of personal matters, loyalty, and legal issues, I chose to live by my conscience and the virtues I hold dear. Although I am not a perfect example, I adhere to what I believe is "right," which I define as "rules and principles." I trusted that others would share my values, particularly my colleagues and subordinates, allowing them to act without my direct intervention. As a public figure and military commander, it is crucial to be just and fair, treating everyone equally and distinguishing between public and private matters. On the battlefield, everyone must unite and demonstrate full combat power, which is why relationships and rewards must be fair and equal. Punishments must also be fair and strict to maintain military discipline, while commanders must bear infinite responsibility.

Regarding civilian control, I have observed that Korean politicians often look down on the military, despite their outward friendliness. General Carl von Clausewitz stated in "On War" that military affairs should belong to politics, as "war is the continuation of politics by other means." However, I believe that politics and military affairs are interconnected, and sometimes politics must align with military strategy for ultimate victory. True civilian control means that decisions about military operations and rules are made by a congress elected by the people, as exemplified by Winston Churchill's approval of naval plans during World War I.

I value modesty, mutual respect, and the use of honorifics. It bothers me when strangers speak informally to me, especially if it's due to age. I believe in equality among all people, regardless of age or gender, and I use honorifics with everyone, except for close family members. While this might seem overly humble in the military, where hierarchy is important, I believe in treating others as I wish to be treated. This is a principle I have remained steadfast about throughout my life.

I have developed a strong sense of autonomy, self-reliance, and independence, thanks to the teachings of my homeroom teacher, Ms. Bang Deok-su. As an adult and military commander, I have learned to live independently, relying on my own judgment and not seeking unnecessary advice. I will continue to uphold these values, using my staff's opinions as a reference but ultimately making my own decisions. I will not align myself with powerful societal figures, and I will live within my means, helping others only as much as I can afford.

True loyalty, in my view, is a virtue that all humans should uphold. It does not mean blind obedience to a leader or group, especially in wrongdoing. I respect the Army, the Korean people, truth, reason, and humanity, and I will remain loyal to these principles. I will maintain relationships based on justice, virtue, and principles, without compromising my conscience or the Constitution.

♦ I struggled with socializing due to my abstinence from drinking and singing, yet I was full of pioneering spirit, eager to create something from nothing

I acknowledge some limitations that may affect my military career. I have a valvular heart disease and cannot handle alcohol well, which affects my ability to socialize. Additionally, I lack talent in music and dance, which are often part of social gatherings. Despite these challenges, I believe my ability to make comprehensive judgments is stronger than my analytical skills, which will be advantageous in battle.

I possess a strong "pioneering spirit," inherited from my father, which drives me to create something from nothing. I will not be confined by given conditions or duties but will strive to execute my creative spirit and pursue meaningful endeavors, even after fulfilling my responsibilities.

♦ I kept 'A Father's Prayer' by General Douglas MacArthur close to my heart

I was keeping General MacArthur's Prayer close to my heart as I celebrated the honor of graduating as the 4th regular recruit at KMA and being commissioned.

The Song of KMA (1951)
- Lyrics by Gong Jung-in, composed by Kim Sun-ae

Verse 1
The waters of the East Sea swirl around my beautiful country,
where evergreen wisdom grows endlessly.
We overcome all obstacles at this academy,
The flame of KMA, as firm as iron,
Will blaze strongly through harsh history.

Verse 2
With five thousand years of Asadal's spirit, the
undying spirit soars through the sky,
Spreading tales along with the wind.
The spirit of KMA never gives up,
and it will never vanish.

Chorus
Ah! How smart and valiant!
It never changes!
Everyone sings in unison,
KMA, everyone sings their name.

Keeping 'A Father's Prayer by General Douglas MacArthur' in my heart

A Father's Prayer by General Douglas MacArthur (May 1952)

Build me a son, O Lord, who will be strong enough to know when he is weak, and brave enough to face himself when he is afraid; one who will be proud and unbending in honest defeat, and humble and gentle in victory. Build me a son whose wishes will not replace deeds; a son who will know Thee, and that to know himself is the foundation stone of knowledge. Lead him, I pray, not in the path of ease and comfort, but under the stress and spur of difficulties and challenges. Here let him learn to stand up in the storm; here let him learn compassion for those who fail. Build me a son whose heart will be clear, whose goal will be high, a son who will master himself before he seeks to master other men, one who will reach into the future, yet never forget the past. And after all these things are his, add, I pray, enough of a sense of humor, so that he may always be serious, yet never take himself too seriously. Give him humility, so that he may always remember the simplicity of true greatness, the open mind of true wisdom, and the meekness of true strength. Then I, his father, will dare to whisper, "I have not lived in vain!"

During my middl, high school and cadet days 1946~1958

1951, Ms. Bang Deok-su's class at Busan Normal School, at the church next to the temporary building in Ami-dong.

1953, In front of Dongnae High School's second temporary building.

My aspiration when I was attending Dongnae High School.

1954, The barracks of the cadet brigade at KMA in Taeneung.

1954, As KMA's representative rugby player with my classmates of 1954, me, Park Jeong-Gi, Sin U-Sik, and Kim Ji-jong, with Bulamsam Mountain in the background.

July to August 1954, The basic military training for the 1954 class of KMA.

My first vacation in 1954 was the happiest moment.

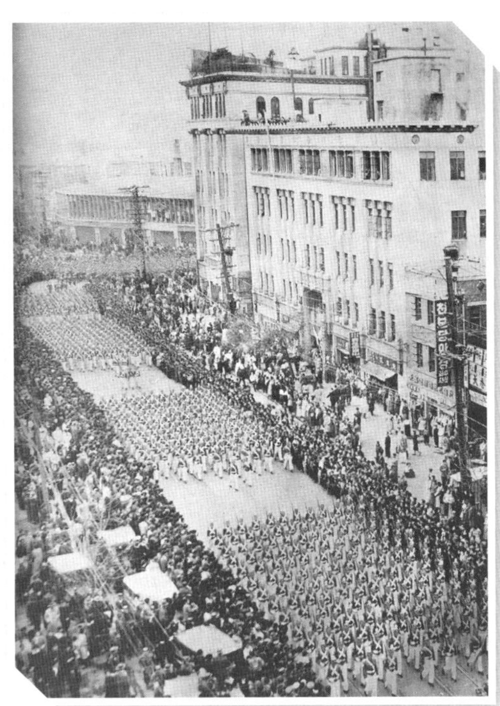

A parade to celebrate President Rhee Syng-Man's birthday in downtown Seoul every year from 1954 to 1958.

1958, A moment with my close friends Park Jeong-Gi and Park Dong-Hyeok before we were commissioned.

958, With Cadet Park Jeong-Gi, my classmate and my close friend.

文 英 一

文將軍으로 通했다 그의 泰然自若한 모숀과 悠悠한 거름거리는 그를 、또다른 닠네임으로 부르게 하였으나 나중에 戰史를 熱心히 하자 前者가 더 어울렸다 그의戰史冊은 自己가 아니면 判讀을 못할만큼 언더라인과 註釋으로 범벅이 되어있었고 戰史가 없는 날에도 *Atlas*는 如前히 그의 옆구리에 끼어있었다 무던한 친구로서 基礎軍事訓練의 그 어려운 고비에도 使役을 도맡아 나갔고 自己 整頓은 버려둔채 남의 寢具를 매만저주는 雅量과 犧牲心을 간직한 그였다

1958, An introduction of me in the yearbook, commented by Park Don-seo, my classmate

Part 2

Dreaming of Becoming a Commander (General), a Hero

Chapter 3

Early Years After Being Commissioned, Serving as a Platoon Leader and Company Commander on the Central and Western Frontlines (1958-1961)

1. Officer Basic Course (OBC) at Sangmudae Army Infantry School

Graduates from military academies are initially assigned to one of five combat arms branches upon commissioning. Unlike graduates from the 3rd military academy and ROTC, who can apply for all military occupational specialties (MOS), KMA graduates are mainly appointed to the combat arms branches, which include infantry, artillery, armor, engineering, and communication. These branches are in the front line with the most challenging duties, requiring personnel ready to risk their lives. Among these, infantry is the most demanding specialty, often chosen by ambitious officers. I, too, chose infantry as my path. Upon graduation, KMA officers select their MOS and attend the OBC for 16 weeks. My classmates and I entered the infantry OBC in Sangmudae, Gwangju, after our graduation vacation. The training included leadership and command practice, weapon and equipment usage, battalion tactics, and both indoor and outdoor exercises. Although theoretical, the training was different from KMA's education, focusing more on practical outdoor activities. Weekends were spent in Seoul or with family, allowing us to approach training with a light heart and enjoy time in Sinchon or downtown Gwangju after daily routines.

2. Proudly Becoming the Platoon Leader of the 1st Regiment of the Capital Infantry Division (October 1958)

♦ The Infantry Badge of the 1st Regiment: A Symbol of Tradition and Honor

Not long after the Korean War armistice, the Capital Division was renowned for its honor and tradition, particularly the 1st Regiment's remarkable war merit. I aspired to become the 1st platoon leader of the 1st company, 1st battalion, 1st regiment of the Capital Division. Assignments were based on service number order, and I was placed in the 1st regiment, aligning closely with my wish. This assignment marked the honorable start of my service, filled with pride. Two of us, including my classmate Lee Seung-ju, joined this regiment. Though we had no KMA seniors, the infantry badge with a prominent "1" in the center was a source of pride for all commissioned officers.

♦ The Mighty Platoon Leader on the Central Front

Finally, the day arrived. After passing through the First ROK Army's replacement depot in Wonju, I was assigned as the platoon leader of the 3rd Platoon, 11th Company, 3rd Battalion, 1st Regiment of the Capital Division, a reserve division of the 5th Corps (October 1958). Our unit was stationed under Gukmangbong Peak in Idong-myeon, Pocheon-gun, near the village of Simjae-ri. The 1st regiment was strategically located along the road between Il-dong and I-dong, dominating the rear approach from Pyeonggang (North Korean territory) to Seoul. Despite the armistice, it was still wartime, and frontline and rear units rotated every two years. The Capital Division was stationed in the rear as a reserve division for the 5th Corps. When divisions switched between front and rear, it felt like an entire corpse was moving, as families and merchants followed. At that time, General Han Sin, known for his bravery during the Korean War, commanded the Capital Division, while Colonel Kim Yeong-Hwan, respected for his military knowledge and battle proficiency, led the regiment. Upon my appointment, our platoon was tasked with training new recruits for local adaptation, and I served as an instructor for a month. The front bases were experienced units, so additional training was required for new recruits from the rear, especially from Nonsan Training Center. I became the "mighty leader" for a month, responsible for the training curriculum and its completion. I trained them as family, with strictness, kindness, and generosity, allowing them to interact with me informally. When they were assigned to different units after the training completion ceremony, I experienced the bittersweet feeling of "sending my students to faraway places." Later, whenever I visited other places, they were delighted to see me, like meeting old friends.

♦ The Environment and Daily Life of Our Platoon (and Its Leader), Sharing Joyful and Sorrowful Moments with My Subordinates

Our unit, a battalion of the division in reserve of the 5th Corps, was assembled within one fence. The company's leading members included the commander (captain), the predecessor platoon leader (a first lieutenant at the weapons platoon), myself, and Second Lieutenant Choi, a general commissioned officer. After a month of training for military strength and adaptation, new recruits were appointed to our platoon. The first sergeant, Staff Sergeant Kim from KLO, was a serious anti-communist from north of the 38th Parallel (mostly Hwanghae-do). He had served as a "contacting agent for the Korean liaison office," supporting U.S. Army espionage operations along the Yellow Sea coast. Despite his age (over 30), he was given a service number before serving in the military post-armistice. The squad leaders, recruited from nearby companies, were competent and hardworking.

Our platoon was filled with technicians. The current law mandates that only high school graduates or those with higher education can serve in the military, but back then, every male in the Republic of Korea was required to enlist. At that time, even a high school diploma was considered a high level of education, so like many other platoons, ours had numerous technicians who only had an elementary school diploma. Some members were illiterate, and a few even had intellectual disabilities, though they were rare. We had an "expert tobacco leaf dryer" from Chungcheong-do. "Mr. Ma" in our platoon was skilled at making women's purses in Myeong-dong, Seoul, and "Mr. Kim," a kindhearted man who resembled a bear, was a barber. Later in life, I was passing by a barber shop in an alley in Cheonho-dong when he ran out, shouting, "Platoon Leader Moon!" and we reconnected. We also had a high school graduate who was a talented writer; he was responsible for reading letters aloud and writing them for the illiterate members.

There was also someone who was illiterate and slightly intellectually disabled, so he was always a sentry who stayed behind, or a so-called "Advisor" in our platoon—we compared him to U.S. Army advisors, with whom we had communication issues. Still, this "Advisor" was very mature when he had someone else write letters to his home, always starting with, "Ahem, hear me, my dearest younger brother~." They were trained to respond, "Yes, sir! I will correct it, sir!" whenever a superior pointed something out during inspections. Despite this, they were naive subordinates who obeyed orders without complaint, making them easy to command. However, soon after, a higher academic criterion for new recruits was announced, causing concern among the commanders.

The barracks were built with clay brick walls and straw roofs, but they had Russian-style fireplaces (Peachyka) installed inside, providing shelter from the bitter cold of Cheorwon. As mentioned, our company had a technician in drying tobacco leaves from Chungcheongbuk-do who was responsible for the coal-burning fireplaces in the barracks of two companies, exempting him from other duties like education, training, and lookout, thus keeping the entire company warm during winter.

The battalion had a BOQ, but it was literally a hut, so fragile it could collapse if kicked. It had clay walls and a straw roof, with five individual rooms requiring us to lower our heads to enter. The rooms were separated by walls of bush clover stems with newspaper as wallpaper, allowing us to hear others breathing in adjacent rooms. The floor was made by placing clay on the lids of drum cans, so whenever a bonfire was made, the rooms filled with smoke pungent enough to drive badgers out of their holes, posing a fire hazard. But after a tiring day, I wasn't aware if my blanket was burning or if my room was covered in soot. I woke up with dark soot inside my nostrils, and thinking about what it did to my lungs gives me chills now. Only Lee Seung-ju, my Academy classmate, and I, both KMA graduates, slept in those rooms.

The front units of the Army operated a system called the "office of weekly duty," serving as a substitute for the commander after a general daily routine. Everyone was required to do nighttime duties for three to four days in a row, dividing the week in half. The senior predecessor was exempt from this duty, so the remaining two platoon leaders—usually a battalion in a reserve division, with the first sergeant serving as a substitute for one platoon leader—switched shifts. If one platoon leader went on leave, the remaining one had to work from dawn until the next day, making it extremely difficult for platoon leaders in normal units to take leave or vacation, especially new KMA officers.

This meant they stayed physically and mentally with their platoon members through both joyful and sorrowful moments. That's why platoon members viewed their platoon leader as a "mighty leader" and always sided with them in conflicts with the company commander. I've heard that during wartime, if a company commander scolded a platoon leader in front of his platoon, the members would immediately hand their gun to the platoon leader to confront the commander.

♦ A small unit under Gukmangbong Peak and working as its platoon leader Officers and soldiers in front units had much more work during winter. Especially when it snowed, we had to clear the training ground of snow every day, every hour, as soon as it fell. Additionally, to keep the communication roads between bases accessible at all times, we had to constantly remove snow from the tactical roads or supply routes within our region. Snowfall was frequent and heavy in the front during winter, forming part of our daily routine, training, and military life in a front unit. As mentioned, front platoon leaders spent most of the year fulfilling duties as officers of the week for the companies.

I never skipped nighttime patrol, even in heavy snow. It took about two hours to patrol all the tents in the company, the ammunition depot, and the main and rear entrances. The sentries for the barracks worked inside, with their primary duty being to defend against invaders. Their secondary duty was to be prepared for emergencies, maintain communication, and check on their fellow soldiers' health whenever possible. Therefore, all visitors, including the company commander or weekly duty officer, were required to provide the password. Weekly duty officers had to confirm this every time during patrols. Walking outside was difficult when snow piled up overnight, but we patrolled up to the outside sentry posts, especially the ammunition depot, which was a bit far away, before returning to the company headquarters to continue working, half-asleep. Of course, the combat uniform got wet, and my military boots were completely soaked. Since Korean-made military boots weren't supplied yet, I personally bought "walkers" made in the U.S.A. from the market. I dried them on the iron plate of the Russian-style fireplace, but sometimes left them too long, causing them to shrink like grilled squid, which was a big problem.

3. The 1st Regiment Combat Team (RCT) went to the frontline of Imjingang River, Munsan

♦ Second Lieutenant Moon stands on the western frontline of Imjingang River, Moonsan

Around June 1959, the 1st Regiment of the Capital Division formed the regiment combat team (RCT, including one artillery battalion and reinforcement with supply units) and prepared to relieve the Korean Marine Corps brigade attached to the 1st Cavalry Division of the 1st U.S. Corps, which was in charge of lines in Munsan, Paju, and Imjingang River. As a result, I was transferred as a platoon leader of a frontline battalion. However, my platoon members signed a petition saying, "You shouldn't leave." Such behavior isn't tolerated in the military, so I tried my best to stop and calm them. For the first time in my life, I said goodbye to my platoon members with deep sorrow and regret. Only platoon leaders can form such deep bonds with their members in the military, I believe.

I still remember the platoon members from that time, including "The (so-called) Advisor who stayed behind," the guitar maker, the handmade purse maker, the gemstone cutter, the hairy barber, and others. About ten years later, I was passing by a barber shop near Fizzy Water Village in Cheonho-dong to meet a relative when a hairy young man ran out and said, "Oh, Platoon Leader Moon, I am so happy to see you again." I recognized him as the hairy barber from our platoon and was delighted to see him.

Finally, our RCT departed from Pocheon, Gangwon-do, marching to Geumchon,

Gyeonggi-do. Our company marched overnight toward Tanhyeon, arriving in Daedong-ri. Our platoon passed a spot in Seongdong-ri, now Heyri Art Village, and reached a hill north of the country village at midnight. The three rifle squads moved to the front, co-located on the riverbank of Imjingang River at the frontline. "Second Lieutenant Moon," the platoon leader of the Marine Corps unit we were relieving, briefed me on the unit's situation, and I immediately began my duties. Second Lieutenant Moon of the Marine Corps was pleased to see me because we shared the same family name, and he kindly explained the current situation in detail. As they withdrew, he shouted to the village below (now 'Provence Town'), "Hey, Yeong-ja! Second Lieutenant Moon of the Army is here! Good luck with him!" and descended to the assembly area, laughing. I wished Second Lieutenant Moon of the Marine Corps and his platoon good luck for guarding the line here.

♦ Hardwood battle position built in the late era of the Korean War

The following day, I surveyed the platoon's position. The bunker at the platoon headquarters, which housed the platoon leader, messenger, first sergeant, guiding specialist, administration specialist, and weapon squad, was constructed using ten rectangular hardwood pieces, each 20 meters long and 50 centimeters thick, woven together to form a roof. The roof's edge was buried in the ground facing the enemy, slightly elevated and supported with hardwood to allow rainwater to flow off. The front part had ample space for everyone to enter and exit, though we had to bend forward to do so. A natural clay wall with a gap large enough for passage blocked the front. This structure provided adequate shelter from most enemy artillery fire even a direct hit from a 155-millimeter shell and retained the atmosphere of the Korean War. The three squad positions at the front were similarly constructed.

Imagine, one company had about 20 such bunkers, and a battalion had more than 60. Counting them from just one corps on the western front must have been substantial. Consider the logistics and methods used to supply these bunkers until they were built. This demonstrated the United States' capability and the U.S. Army's prowess in war, which was the ultimate combat power during the Korean War, convincing President Rhee Syng-Man that we could advance north.

The three front squads were stationed on a hill over 10 meters high, overlooking the Imjingang River, and they managed the waterfront riverside position for precise nighttime surveillance. Fearless large fish would leap from the water during the 10-meter tide difference, becoming a plentiful feast for our platoon members. The platoon leader had to patrol the Imjingang River's riverside almost daily along the combat trenches, which were shoulder-height. In some trenches, snakes coiled on the ground, blocking the path with open mouths, forcing me to avoid them. The platoon's communication trench stretched about 1.5 kilometers and was well-constructed, thanks to the high-quality soil.

♦ Seongdong-ri, a front line village where villagers were returnig from evacuation

Seongdong-ri, a frontline village where villagers were returning from war evacuation, lay south of the platoon headquarters tent, beyond the military supply route. This route was a restricted area for civilians. Behind it, to the south, was a village of about 30 houses in Seongdong-ri, covering roughly 20,000 square meters, which our platoon was responsible for. As villagers from the front were allowed to return, they came back from war refuge, one or two households at a time. We set up a temporary sentry post south of the village to monitor civilians entering and leaving. These villagers were frontline civilians whose lives were intertwined with ours. Returning empty-handed, they struggled like those in the rear, particularly in finding firewood for winter. The nearby area was a battlefield, a wild zone with few dead trees. Nevertheless, they needed them, so they often dug out dead or tall, skinny trees, even in the snow. I wondered if it was a coincidence. Our first platoon's sergeant would sometimes climb the hill in front of our headquarters to gaze across the Imjingang River and sigh deeply. He could see the place where he and his relatives had crossed the river before the war, his hometown village in Imhan- myeon, Gaepung-gun, North Korea. It was a heartbreaking tragedy caused by the North Korean regime.

The North Korean Army north of the Imjingang River had conscripted the "People's Organization for the Nation" from across the country to build combat trenches on the opposite riverside and establish a "War Village"—now known as the "Propaganda Village," visible from the Unification Observatory on Odusan Mountain. This village consisted of five-to-six-story apartments, still present today. We could observe their activities without binoculars, witnessing their slave-like routines. At 6:00 a.m., they awoke to an alarm, had roll call, began work, paused for lunch, and stopped working at 6:00 p.m. They seemed to boost morale by playing ball games like volleyball during breaks. At night, while in bed, I could hear North Korean troops working with shovels and pickaxes. The noise was sometimes so loud that I suspected they were digging a tunnel, but given their scale and daytime activities, I doubted they could tunnel under the Imjingang River.

♦ We planned to reinforce the defensive position at the riverside downstream of the Imjingang River

Since 1980, they have been monitoring the riverbank closely, excavating hundreds of deep wells at 4-to-5-meter intervals. I would sometimes sit on a hill by the riverbank, contemplating how to defend the Imjingang River while patrolling the front position. The river, in front of Tanhyeon-myeon, spanned about 3 kilometers at high tide. If the enemy crossed it on motorboats traveling at 10 kilometers per hour, they could reach us in 20 to 30 minutes. At low tide, the river's width decreased to less than 100 meters, exposing a mudflat in the middle, allowing them to crawl across on thin tin plates, though walking was difficult. We needed to be prepared from the second landing point of the first waterfront, but only with prior warning. I believed we needed obstacles on our riverbank, such as walls or aquatic barriers, to ensure defense, like the coastal defense position in Normandy. However, I missed the chance to suggest it, and it remained just an idea.

♦ An emergency drill (Defcon-2) truly made me feel "cold and hungry."

After six months as the leader of a combat outpost on the Imjingang Riverbank, we rotated duties in December, as was customary during wartime. Our battalion became a reserve battalion of the RCT and moved to the reserve battalion assembly area under Wollongsan Mountain. I gained invaluable experience as a combat platoon leader, which was the luckiest moment in my military career. It began with the emergency drill on the move in the combat position, the Defcon-2 Drill, conducted monthly without prior notice. The 1st RCT, our RCT, was attached to the 1st Cavalry Division of the 1st U.S. Corps, responsible for the far western front around the armistice. They conducted "emergency drill on move in the combat position during battle by the corps without prior notice" monthly. In December, the Imjingang Riverbank was engulfed in extreme cold, with temperatures below negative 20 degrees Celsius.

One day, the drill began around 3:00 a.m., with wind chills below negative 30 degrees Celsius. Fully equipped, the entire battalion immediately occupied a defense position near Wollongsan Mountain. Cold set in 30 minutes after occupation. Despite wearing all supplied undergarments, I couldn't move from my spot, standing on snow and ice, unable to sit. My only heat source was my body. All combatants below the battalion commander endured from 3:00 a.m. to 9:00 a.m. in the freezing cold, with sweat from the rush freezing inside. Hunger set in at 6:00. I truly understood the extreme and harsh conditions of the Battle of the Chosin Reservoir during the Korean War. Service members are destined to face such situations repeatedly, but the "cold and hungry" feelings I experienced then were profound. I'll share stories of other drills, but the U.S. Army—especially the 1st Cavalry Division of the 1st U.S. Corps—conducted their drills with utmost integrity, reaffirming the U.S. Cavalry Division's pride.

♦ We participated in a Winter Field Training Exercise (FTX. 'ICE CAP) and an Army Training Test (ATT) with live ammunition

In January 1960, the 1st U.S. Corps maintained combat readiness as if in an actual battle, preparing for sudden armistice changes. Besides the Defcon-2 drill, we conducted a field training exercise for the corps. The COP (western Munsan) and GOP (eastern Munsan) conducted local exercises. Reserve troops at all levels (battalions and higher) followed current operations, so our battalion withdrew to the 1st reserve line in the rear, preparing to launch a counterattack immediately.

During the coldest days of the year—possibly even below -20 degrees Celsius (-4 degrees Fahrenheit)—our battalion left the base. It was the period between 'Sohan' and 'Daehan' on the lunar calendar when we arrived at a location just below the virtual counterattack line, known as 'Ilsan' (now the northwest region of Jeongbalsan Mountain). There, we prepared a field trench with 'peachyka' for the platoon's overnight bivouac in the extreme cold. Before departing, we had been trained to set up field camps for winter bivouacking. We were instructed to dig at least 1 meter (3.2 feet) into the ground, build a chimney for the 'peachyka' in one corner, lay poncho raincoats on the bottom to block the cold, and construct an A-shaped tent to shield against rain and wind, keeping it warm inside.

However, this was under non-combat conditions at the assembly area, allowing us extra time and resources. In practice, we managed to dig only 10 to 20 centimeters (3.9 to 7.8 inches) into the frozen ground, with an additional 30 centimeters (11.8 inches) beyond that. The extreme cold made it impossible to dig deeper, so we mimicked the trench-building process for field camping. We spent our first night there in combat uniforms, which was neither comfortable nor warm. It was a sweaty, hard, and time-consuming task on that cold winter night, and things didn't go as planned. It felt like a battle in itself.

Breakfast the next morning consisted of rice and soup, served by truck. The food had grown cold and frozen on the way due to the extreme cold, but we ate it from our mess tins. After breakfast, our platoon was deployed on the LD (line of departure, counterattack) alongside an adjacent platoon. We marched about 10 kilometers (6 miles) over 10 hours, attacking and occupying heights, and engaging in cross-country battle until we reached a flatland at night. I believe it was in the middle of what is now Unjeong New Town in Paju, Gyoha-eup.

The night was pitch black, with no light except starlight, forcing us to feel our way around to secure a flat area for trench-building. Despite the extreme cold, digging even to knee depth with shovels was difficult. Exhausted and facing temperatures below -20 degrees Celsius (-4 degrees Fahrenheit) with a wind chill below -30 degrees Celsius (-22 degrees Fahrenheit), everyone wanted to lie down quickly. After minimal digging, we spread rice straw from a nearby paddy on the ground, covered ourselves with poncho raincoats and A-shaped tent pieces, and the entire platoon lay downside by side to sleep. Having a sentry on lookout was challenging but essential for combat.

The next morning, we hurried to depart at 6:00 a.m., but breakfast was late, so we ate frozen rice balls and drank cold soup while standing. We followed orders down the unpaved road—all roads, including national highways, were unpaved then. After sunrise, I looked back to see our bivouac area was an empty corner of a community cemetery. Upon reaching the road, we boarded five U.S. Army APCs, one squad per vehicle, with U.S. soldiers inside. On that frigid day, we stood on the APC's outer platform, pursuing the enemy at a slow 5 kilometers (3.1 miles) per hour, enduring a winter gale with a wind chill of -30 degrees Celsius (-22 degrees Fahrenheit), feeling our noses and ears freeze.

After advancing about 5 kilometers (3.1 miles), we disembarked to navigate obstacles in Gongneungcheon Stream, likely due to a demolished bridge, and began crossing. Reconnaissance indicated the stream was frozen thick enough for both foot and vehicle passage. Our company crossed the stream on ice, using smoke bombs (shells) from military engineers to obscure the enemy's view. At that time, Gongneungcheon Stream lacked levees, with a sandy beach and mudflat stretching 1 kilometer (0.6 miles) on both sides and a middle width of about 100 meters (109 yards). Once across, our platoon was ordered to attack Wollong Heights (Wollongsan Mountain), Height 255, and the mountain behind our battalion's station. We formed an attack formation at the southernmost line (the mountain's base edge). The slope was about 40 to 50 degrees from our position to the middle of the heights and 70 to 80 degrees from the middle to the peak. As the attack began, though my heart was racing, we crawled up the steep heights on all fours, moving at a walking pace due to rocks, pine branches, and gravel rolling down with each step. Upon reaching the 5th ridge, I used all my strength to continue climbing with a panel man, and we finally occupied the peak, reorganizing for defense.

Afterward, we became part of the reserve battalion, supporting the 1st Infantry Division. However, the cold struck again as the sun set, and my undergarments remained wet. It seemed better to be an attack troop and move quickly. Standing as a reserve unit in the extreme cold was incredibly challenging. When night fell, we moved to a new assembly point, 1 kilometer (0.6 miles) ahead. We felt our way around, unable to dig a field trench, but found a man-made cave large enough for the entire platoon. This stroke of luck allowed us to spend the night without being covered in frost.

The next day, our platoon was tasked with pursuing the retreating enemy to the Imjingang River, delivering a coup de grâce, marking the grand finale of <FTX-ICE CAP>. We departed early, with all platoon members splitting into groups to ride three waiting tanks. We charged the Imjingang Riverbank near Ogeum-ri, Paju, to deliver the final blow. It felt incredible to command the vanguard, the privilege of service and the glory of command. "Follow me!" was the real deal. Yet, I can't forget riding a frozen iron vehicle in -20 degrees Celsius (-4 degrees Fahrenheit), charging through the cold air by the Imjingang River with a wind chill of -30 degrees Celsius (-22 degrees Fahrenheit), my body and face battered by the icy gale.

♦ Army Training Test (ATT) (with live ammunition) of the infantry

The combat readiness of the 1st U.S. Corps, responsible for the western line since the war, involved relentless drills. As a reserve battalion for the regiment, in early March, still cold, we rode trucks to the Nightmare Training Ground assembly area, a general U.S. Army training site (mostly), now 'Yeou-gogae Hill' in the 'Sanjung-hosu Lake' area, for the battalion test. According to the manual, platoon leaders first set up A-shaped tents for camping. However, as mentioned, the Korean Army was still under-resourced, lacking enough A-tents for the platoon—one group had three people—so we constructed a temporary tent for the entire platoon. We broke wood nearby, built an arch-shaped framework, and covered it with A-shaped tent pieces and poncho raincoats.

The next day, we moved to the training ground, primarily used for infantry, AFV, artillery, air-land joint training, or Korea-U.S. Alliance combined operations demonstrations, and began the defense training test. I received the defense order from the company commander and went to my platoon, already at the assembly area led by the first sergeant. I ordered the platoon defense OP plan, and we deployed to the defense position immediately. Everything followed the set scenario afterward. The aggressor forces (opposing force) attacked, and our platoon executed the defense procedure, then withdrew by order to occupy a new defense position.

After the defense test, we returned to our bivouac area. Communication between companies and platoons during defense was wired (the battalion signaler laid the line). The next day, I received the attack order. After starting, the battalion's right front platoon was to occupy the 1st target heights ahead, turn 90 degrees left, and attack the battalion's final target. By order, my platoon occupied the line of departure and conducted the attack. This drill used live fire, simulating a real battle, with virtual air-to-ground fire and artillery fire.

When the colored flare was fired to signal the time of attack, everyone rushed out of their positions. My platoon members loaded their M1 rifles with live ammunition, unlocked the safety, and bravely advanced, running and crawling toward the first target height in bounds. Throughout the process, dozens of 81-millimeter mortars fired by the heavy weapons company exploded on the final target height. As the platoon leader, I held an M1 Carbine in my left hand and a handheld transceiver for platoon leaders in my right, which was as heavy as the M1 Carbine. The long antenna shook, almost like a baton. However, when it came to the geographic features visible from the ground, jumping, or crawling, it was challenging to make judgments based on the features I saw when I received the order or at the line of departure. Consequently, the platoon formed a charging formation at the farthest line of the first target height (a misjudgment), and everyone fired to prepare for a charge all at once. Then, the company commander pointed out over the transceiver that it was an interim target, and the first target was the height right after it. I ordered them to cease fire immediately, but no one could hear my voice over the noise of simultaneous firing. I had to dodge bullets, move forward, turn around, and order them to stop firing with my voice and hand gestures.

We then moved past that height and advanced toward the next bound. We successfully seized the first target, the major target of attack for my platoon. We turned 90 degrees to the left without delay, as planned, and advanced as the right front platoon of the battalion to attack the final target. First, I called the bazooka section of the weapon squad and fired twice for preparation toward the height over 300 meters (328 yards) high. This bazooka was the same model Major General William F. Dean, commander of the 24th Division of the U.S. Army, used to fire at a North Korean tank in Daejeon during the Korean War. This meant the rocket artillery was an old model, about to be discarded. It had serious recoil each time it was fired and emitted gas, damaging the gunner's face. The gunners had to risk facial damage, covering their faces with handkerchief masks, and fired with daring attitudes. Thankfully, our rocket section's gunner trusted me, his platoon leader, and completed his mission bravely.

With the rocket artillery's explosion of the target point as the signal, our platoon left the second attack departure position of the company and advanced down to the enemy's area in the valley ahead. As soon as we arrived at the farthest line, we advanced in bounds under cover from each squad to quickly cross the valley and reach the base line of the mountain, the final target height. Upon arrival, we climbed the steep height with a slope of 40 to 50 degrees without delay. We attempted to advance in bounds, but it was difficult to climb the steep height under enemy fire, even at full throttle. Nonetheless, we tried. I assumed that supporting fire from the upper unit was protecting our advance. We reached the line of fire coordination. I requested and signaled for lift fire on the sixth or seventh ridge, and the platoon made an assault volley at the enemy line. We then charged to the peak, standing with all the energy we could muster. With a panel man at the front, we crawled on all fours to climb it—just like when we attacked the heights of Wollongsan Mountain for FTX-ICE CAP—unaware that we were running out of breath. Panting to catch our breath, we finally occupied the peak.

My platoon began organizing defenses to prepare for the enemy's counterattack, without even a moment to celebrate. The next day, we received excellent grades for the ATT we had taken, and we were cleaning our bivouacking area to withdraw. Then, a few women came and charged at each other, pushing and pulling the straw rice bags we had placed at the bottom of the tent, which were their capital for business. It was the peak of "Yeou-gogae Hill," where a few dozen slash-and-burn farmer families and dozens of so-called "American Princesses" lived. These women earned money through prostitution for U.S. Army soldiers who came to take tests at the unit, highlighting their poverty. That was the first time I came face to face with the pitiful and vain aspects of life, and I still cannot forget that scene and my feelings from witnessing it.

♦ We built the first new barracks with cement bricks in the history of ROK Armed Forces

In the spring of 1960, our reserve battalion of the 1st RCT under Wollong-san Mountain in Munsan built the first new barracks with cement bricks and tin roofs using cement provided by the U.S. Army. This was the first case for the ROK Armed Forces after the Korean War. At that time, the barracks of the front units were still temporary, and the units remained in them. For example, the western region, where the U.S. Army was in charge, had hardwood bunkers for the frontline and temporary barracks with wooden walls and tin Quonsets for the rear area where the regiment was stationed.

Most rear units in regions under Korean Army control had temporary barracks with clay brick walls and straw roofs. Additionally, units shifted at the division level every year, and regiment-level units of the front division had to move every six months, taking equipment inside the barracks with them. Staying in those barracks was inconvenient.

Each company in the battalion sent one platoon to produce cement bricks to build barracks for their companies and for extra purposes. In our company, our platoon once again served as a multi-talented example—most platoon leaders from KMA were multi-talented commanders. They were sent to the center line for drills, to the COP frontline when assigned to the front, and demonstrated all kinds of work. Despite the difficulty of these tasks, they completed their work with responsibility and pride and were assigned to make cement. About 5 kilometers (3.1 miles) away from the unit's garrison, Munsancheon Stream flowed into the Imjingang River. We set up the platoon's bivouacking area at the riverbank under the levee, and once supplied with a handmade brick maker, we got to work immediately. We split our duties: Group 1 managed the bivouacking area and cooked meals; Group 2 collected and sifted sand; Group 3 made bricks and managed the cement; and Group 4 managed the bricks we made, soaking them in water for a week, sun-drying them, and storing them.

After initial trials and errors, we mastered the manufacturing skills and began mass production. The cement, made in the U.S.A., was supposed to make 20 bricks per bag. Sometimes we were asked to make 23 bricks, but that was part of a supply competition, so we persisted in making 20 bricks from time to time. That was about 60 years ago, so I am not clear about the actual numbers, but we produced about 100 bricks per day, totaling 2,000 bricks over 20 days. However, due to negligence of hygiene in the process, many platoon members, including myself, suffered from water-borne illness (dysentery). I considered it an experience. We overcame it with the power of youth and the perfect unity of the platoon leaders, completing the mission. After returning to our base, new rectangular single barracks for each company were built simultaneously by all battalions.

♦ We (KMA Graduate and I) refused to vote in the Electoral Fraud of March 15th and promised myself to maintain 'military neutrality.'

March 15, 1960, was the day of the "Electoral Fraud of March 15," one of the most shameful days in the history of the Republic of Korea. Our unit's polling station was set up at the RCT headquarters in Geumchon. I met with Second Lieutenant Im Seung-Hae, my junior alumnus (the 5th class of KMA) and a platoon leader at an adjacent company, in front of the stove in the office next to the polling station, and we made our final decision. He burned the vote notices in the stove, and I went to the polling station to observe the scene. The regiment's dispatch security organization conducted secret education for platoon leaders to prepare for the election (electoral fraud) one month before the day. They instructed us to categorize platoon members into A, B, C, D, and E, and strictly educate and supervise them to vote "Yes" 100%.

I considered my platoon to be one with me, united in the strongest bond in my military life, and I was with them through life, death, pain, and joy. The security men were telling me to deny "Universal, Equal, Direct, and Confidential" voting, the four principles of the election stated in the Constitution, and to categorize my platoon members to monitor and supervise them instead of treating them as one, forcing them to participate in the electoral fraud by the cabals of "The Liberty Party." But I could never do that to my platoon members. So, I didn't show any of that, and I emphasized the four principles of the election and voting stated in the Constitution, especially the "Confidential" part. The KMA graduates (company-grade officers like platoon leaders or company commanders) at that time all thought the same, so they either went on vacation voluntarily or intentionally, or withdrew voluntarily (burned the vote notice in a stove, etc.). Of course, General Park Chung-Hee, who later became Presid et, said that he burned his too.

I picked up the ballot at the solemn polling station, which seemed burdened by the weight of deception, and headed to the voting booth. To my surprise, it was none other than our company commander who was there. Wearing a helmet with a master sergeant's insignia, he collected the ballots from all company members as they arrived, marking the votes himself. When the ballots were taken to the box, two individuals seated there unfolded each paper to verify it before placing it into the ballot box themselves. This blatant electoral fraud and its process left an indelible mark on my memory, and I resolved repeatedly, "Electoral fraud in the military must never happen again." Later, during the "Vote for Reformation Constitution" when I was a battalion commander, and the "Presidential Election for the 6th Republic" when I was a corps commander, I adhered strictly to my beliefs, my conscience, and the Constitution, without regard for the consequences. I will share more detailed accounts of these events when I reach that part of my story.

♦ Our battalion won the tactics and techniques competition against other battalions.

Regarding the regiment's tactics and techniques competition against other battalions, the Armed Forces at that time were relentless, constantly engaging in various drills, shifting front and rear units, and competing against other units in tactics, sports, shooting, and more. The 1st RCT hosted a tactics and techniques competition against other battalions. As usual, the infantry platoon leaders from KMA were formidable, so I was assigned to operate a 60-millimeter mortar, a heavy weapon for the infantry company. I undertook additional study on the 60-millimeter M2 mortar, focusing on the gun barrel, panel, support, balance beam, scope, and firing within 2 kilometers (1.24 miles), and learned the tactics of straight alignment and adjusting the balance beam, scope, and balance line to ensure accuracy. I practiced repeatedly with the mortar team until I was proficient and ready for the test. The M2 mortars we used were old models from World War II and the Korean War, but they were still functional. Each mortar team consisted of a gunner, deputy gunner, and two ammunition bearers. The competition followed a specific order:

1. The entire artillery section ran from the waiting line to set up the mortar, while Ammunition Bearer 2 moved forward to install the balance beam.
2. The gunner inserted the scope and adjusted the settings.
3. Using the scope, the gunner aimed at the target by aligning the balance beam with the left side of the reticle.
4. The gunner shouted, "Ready to fire."

The judge then checked the reticle's aim and declared, "You passed!" Rankings were determined by evaluating the team's cooperation, proficiency, total duration, and other factors. Our team emerged victorious, earning the title of the best team in the regiment and significantly contributing to the battalion's success.

Here are the lessons I learned: To succeed in a tactical test or competition, 1. Share emotions and stay alert with your teammates, always being present with them. 2. Encourage the participants, provide them with whatever you have, like hardtacks or instant ramen, and offer comfort. 3. The coach or training instructor must push the team to exceed their goals, break records, and participate with competitive spirit, willingness, and passion, while also supporting and defending the players. These principles lead to victory. I applied for these lessons throughout my military career.

4. Company commander of Combet out post (COP), Army Champion of pistol shooting in 1960.

♦ I returned to the central front and experienced the April 19th Revolution.

In early April 1960, our 1st Regiment returned to the Capital Division and relocated to a new post in Nogok-ri, Pocheon-gun, near the corps headquarters. Shortly thereafter, the April 19th Revolution occurred. We, the regular KMA graduates, were eager to eliminate corruption at lower levels, but despite the passage of time, there was little change in the nation or society. However, the atmosphere around our post shifted temporarily.

There was a "shooting ground of heavy weapon and field exercise ground for companies and battalions," known as "Nightmare," typically used by the U.S. Army at the peak of Yeou-gogae Hill in the mountains behind our post. To facilitate the U.S. Army's frequent access to this training ground, we constructed a military road from the road adjacent to Yeongpyeong-cheon Stream in the south, straight to the peak of Yeou-gogae Hill, naming it "Unam Road" after then-President Rhee Syng-Man's other name. This road was often congested with U.S. Army vehicles, armored units, and tanks heading to the Army Training Test (ATT) ground. Consequently, the so-called American Princesses began conducting business there. After the April 19th Revolution, they were expelled, but returned individually about a month later, marking the only change in the area. It had no impact on the military's internal system, leaving us disappointed and prompting us to seek further change.

♦ I became the best pistol shooter in an Army competition against divisions.

In the Army shooting competition against other divisions, I became the best pistol shooter. The ROK Army continuously held sports, tactics, and shooting competitions to maintain combat readiness under the armistice. Officers at the Capital Division were the Army's elite, assigned based on commissioning grades or division ranks, making them a distinguished group. The commissioned officers of the 1st Regiment were particularly proud, consistently leading in division competitions with scores surpassing those of two other regiments combined. The Capital Division consistently ranked at the top in Army-wide competitions.

In particular, their shooting competition tradition was unmatched by other divisions. This "tradition of the division," fostering morale and unity, translated into combat power on the battlefield. In spring 1960, the Army-wide shooting competition against other divisions, hosted by the 5th Corps, took place at the corps shooting ground in Il-dong. Each division formed shooting teams well in advance, undergoing separate shooting practices. Large-caliber rifle shooting was excluded from the competition, focusing instead on small-caliber weapons, including pistols. First sergeants contributed to our division's success by rigorously training the team each year. “Hey, listen up. We won last year with a 00-second difference, but this record isn't good enough anymore. You have to shorten it by three seconds. Now, get to the repetitive practice!” they would say, striving to reach their goals and maintain them. Consequently, shooters used half of the year's live ammunition allocation for training, raising doubts about whether these competitions truly enhanced combat power. As a result, the competitions were discontinued ten years later. However, they had their merits, as many elite service members could lead battles effectively.

As usual, our Capital Division won in every category, including pistol shooting for commissioned officers. I scored 92% in the pistol shooting competition, earning the title of the best pistol shooter in the Army and contributing to the division's victory. However, there were a couple of incidents. One occurred during the pistol shooting competition. Our team comprised five shooters: two first lieutenants, including myself, two captains, and one major. All of us were experienced competitors with 92% accuracy in practice, but it seemed like they took tranquilizers the day before the competition to calm their nerves. This “doping” issue is common in the Olympics. Consequently, on competition day, they lacked clarity and underperformed. Unaware of this, I exceeded my practice performance and won.

The other episode was about a pistol shooting match, possibly a friendly one, involving commanders, division commanders, and higher-ranking officers. This event served as the grand finale of the competition. The commander of the 5th Corps, to which our division belonged, was filled with triumphant pride due to the results. Eager to showcase his skills, he entered the shooting ground ahead of everyone else and borrowed the pistol of the best shooter—my pistol. My pistol was customized to suit me, with a particularly sensitive firing mechanism, which could lead to mistakes if the shooter was unaware of it. As I anticipated, our Corps Commander ended up with the lowest score in the match and remarked, “It’s the person, not the gun, that creates the result.” My teammates and I laughed, feeling a bit sorry for him, and I retrieved my pistol.

♦ AS the company commander of COP in Cheorwon near Backma-goji (the Southern Limit Line of DMZ)

I was reassigned from my position as platoon leader upon returning from the division’s shooting team. I was also appointed as an operations officer at the 2nd Battalion. The Battalion Commander, Lieutenant Colonel Lee Sang-ik, was a distinguished figure—formerly the G-1 staff of the Division under General Hanshin, later serving as secretary to Minister Han Sin of Home Affairs, and eventually becoming an assemblyman in Chungcheong-do. He was a highly educated man with a kind and noble personality, admired by all. The Battalion Executive Officer was Major Choi Sang-hwa, a general commissioned officer with a giant stature and a wonderful personality. The battalion headquarters was always filled with kindness, symbolizing unity within the battalion. This period was fortunate for me, as I was fully trusted by my superiors and could serve them loyally without any reservations.

At that time, I was serving as an S-3 (operations officer) in the battalion and was tasked with organizing a regimental demonstration on defense in chemical warfare. While other companies hesitated, I embraced the challenge with the spirit of a proud KMA graduate. I planned and commanded the demonstration, showcasing how to operate in the wilderness under chemical warfare conditions and how to use gas masks and kits to all officers and soldiers in the regiment. As a result, I received compliments from the regimental commander, Colonel Kim Yeong-hwan, a 5th recruit of KMA, and encouragement from the battalion commander, which brought me joy in serving at the front.

When it was nearly time to move to the frontline, Lee Chan-u, my upperclassman from the 3rd class of KMA, resigned from frontline service to become an instructor at KMA and recommended me as his successor. Consequently, I became the company commander of the 5th Company, 2nd Battalion, 1st Regiment. The Capital Division had many experienced commissioned officers, including captains, so there must have been a significant reason for giving me this opportunity. Our battalion was assigned to the front combat outpost (COP) of the general outpost (GOP) regiment by the Military Demarcation Line and relocated to Dokseodang Village, at the front in Dongsong-ri, Cheorwon, Gangwon-do. At that time, the Civilian Control Line began from Sintan-ri (Station) above Daegwang-ri, prohibiting civilians from residing north of that line. Our company advanced further toward the front, establishing headquarters at Samjamae-goji Heights, about 2 kilometers (1.24 miles) south of the front, adjacent to the Southern Limit Line of the Korean Demilitarized Zone (DMZ).

The area of vigilance operation for the company spanned about 5 kilometers (3.1 miles), from Yeokgok-cheon Stream below Baengma-goji to Woljeong-ri Station on its right. This was the operational environment. The ridges of Height 500 to the north, far beyond the 4-kilometer (2.48-mile) wide DMZ, were blocked by walls preventing us from advancing north. On the northern part of the DMZ, the North Korean Puppet State disregarded the Korean Armistice Agreement, having already forward-stationed its battalion headquarters and subordinate troops with heavy weapons, and was constructing combat trenches and installing electric fences. The DMZ area for us and our allies south of the Military Demarcation Line only had stakes marking the line, without any metal fences or defense walls at that time. We operated a Patrol and Monitoring Team for the DMZ (MP) that patrolled the area and monitored enemy movements, in accordance with the Korean Armistice

Agreement. This unit was the size of a reinforced rifle platoon in one spot. The North Korean Puppet State, our adversary, was equipped with a battalion-level troop and heavy weapons and equipment. It only had a GP (Guard Post) serving as a dorm for resting and sleeping during patrols and as an outpost. They maintained communication and coordination with patrol teams on both the left and right, cooperating with our platoon right in their rear. The GP in front of our company was at Wanggwan-goji Heights, where my KMA junior from the 5th class was stationed, ensuring smooth cooperation.

The COP Company's wartime mission begins with a foremost detachment. When the enemy attacks, they withdraw while maintaining enemy contact, reporting immediately to the platoon outpost. The platoon outpost confirms the situation, reports to the company, and withdraws while maintaining enemy contact. The company outpost reports to the battalion and either engages the enemy or withdraws to the company while maintaining enemy contact, based on orders from higher command. The COP Company proceeds to a pre-designated combat readiness point, monitors the enemy, and engages in combat as ordered by the battalion or according to the battalion's combat SOP. In peacetime, a GOP stationed at the Southern Limit Line conducts ambush operations, changing locations daily and withdrawing before sunrise as ordered by the company (outpost) commander. It also conducts patrols in the DMZ. The COP Company commander had a jeep for mobile patrolling, given the wide area of responsibility. With that jeep, I patrolled the area, monitored the enemy, and diligently fulfilled my duties at the COP. Simultaneously, I took the opportunity to visit Baengma-goji, renowned for over 20 battles to seize the heights just before the armistice. During patrols, I contemplated tactical uses for Yeokgokcheon Stream, observed the Cheorwon Building of the Worker's Party of North Korea, now a skeletal structure, and reflected on the tragic moments of the Korean War as I passed Woljeong-ri Station.

I patrolled my platoons area almost daily. One platoon, led by Second Lieutenant Ok, a diligent general commissioned officer, had cultivated a vegetable garden within a few months and proudly showcased it. As expected, he later became the Quartermaster General due to his diligence.

♦ Joint Shooting Competition between ROK Army and the Eighth United States Army—I came in first for rapid fire.

About three months into my COP duties in Korea's central line of Cheorwon, I had become proficient with the geography, daily responsibilities, and wartime operations under the kind and appropriate guidance of Battalion Commander Lee Sang-ik and Battalion Executive Officer Choi Sang-hwa. Unexpectedly, I was ordered to compete in the joint shooting competition between the ROK Army and the U.S. Eighth Army, having qualified as a pistol shooter for the Army. My battalion commander, visibly saddened, encouraged me by saying, "Don't worry about things here and do a good job at the competition." It felt irresponsible and saddening to leave my company and its members behind for a month while they carried out important missions, but it was an order I had to follow.

Upon arriving in Seoul for the competition, preparations for the Joint Shooting Competition between the ROK Army and the Eighth United States Army were underway. Our Korean army team consisted of Korea's National Shooting Team, led by a major, already settled in Taereung, and three new shooters (one captain and two first lieutenants) representing the ROK Army. The Korean Army pistol shooting team set up tents on a hill east of Jangchungdan Park, which was an empty lot at the time, later the site for Seoul Tower Hotel, and now the location of Banyantree Seoul Hotel. We camped there for about a month, including the training and event periods.

The shooting competition was held at a pistol shooting ground for the U.S. Army, located on the ridge above where Namsan Tunnels 2 and 3 are now, with a view of the Eighth U.S. Army headquarters to the south. The competition included 50-meter (54-yard) pistol slow fire, 25-meter (27-yard) slow fire and time-limited fire, and 10-meter (10-yard) rapid fire. Shooters were categorized into masters (previous prize winners), experts (those who competed two or more times), and new shooters (first-time competitors), with me being a new shooter that year.

Surprisingly, the shooting controller for the competition was a first sergeant (sergeant first class), as we had expected a field officer to oversee such a significant event. However, he had resigned as a major and re-enlisted, and his experience made him proficient and confident during the competition. Despite the competition being between shooters from the Korean Army and the U.S. Army stationed in Korea, specifically the Eighth U.S. Army, he managed everything smoothly. This demonstrated the strong self-governance and independence of the U.S. Army and Americans.

There are certain memories that remain vivid in my mind, highlighting the stark differences between the United States and Korea at that time. One such memory involves the pistols used by both the Korean and U.S. Armies. Both armies used the same model, the .45 caliber pistol, manufactured by the American company Colt. However, during shooting competitions, there was a significant disparity in the quality and functionality of the pistols used by the two armies.

American shooters carried their pistols in individual cases, each meticulously maintained with adjustable front and rear sights. They often owned two to three pistols, each engraved with their names or initials on the ivory grips, and all were newly manufactured. These pistols had adjustable sights, allowing them to be fine-tuned for optimal performance during practice and competitions. In stark contrast, our situation was quite dire. The Korean Army shooters used pistols that had been in service since World War II. Although they were the same model as those used by the U.S. Army, they were worn out from use in the Korean War. These pistols were.

still used in combat, and their sights were fixed, making them less adaptable for competition.

The national athletes from the Taereung National Training Center would sometimes request new slides from the arsenal to ensure their sights were not overly worn. Before competitions, they employed a primitive method: visiting a blacksmith to attach additional iron to the sights, then filing them down to create a larger front sight. They would test and adjust repeatedly until they achieved the desired configuration. This routine involved days of grinding and test shooting. Some Army shooters followed this method, but I chose not to. Instead, I adapted to the pistol as it was. My pistol, used by current commanders, had seen action in both World War II and the Korean War. Its front sight was worn and shiny, reflecting sunlight. I used a lighter to blacken it, following the field manual, to reduce glare during competitions. The U.S. Army used special competition ammunition, a limited edition produced for that year, which was shiny and marked "60. match" on the cartridge base. They even used this ammunition for practice, giving them a significant advantage over Korean shooters, who had to make do with whatever ammunition was available, often leftovers from the Korean War or basic training loads. This placed us at a clear disadvantage against the U.S. Army.

The competitions were diverse and well-organized, reflecting the U.S. Army's resources and structured approach. Shooters were categorized into three groups: new shooters, experts, and masters, based on their experience and achievements. The events included 50-meter slow fire, 25-meter slow fire and timed fire, and 10-meter rapid fire, with prizes awarded in each category. The winners received trophies and medals, and there were even souvenirs to commemorate the event. This setup allowed shooters to fully demonstrate their skills and enjoy the sport.

In contrast, the Korean Army's competitions were far less organized. There was only one 25-meter slow fire event with ten bullets, and the winner received a certificate of merit. During matches, shooters supported each other quietly, and results considered both individual and group scores. Some participants even brought their unit's flag and displayed unusual symbols, adding to the spectacle.

The U.S. Army's competitions included amenities like snack breaks, with a PX vehicle providing doughnuts, coffee, and ice cream to help shooters relax and recharge. Some Korean shooters, aware of this tradition, brought a few dollars to partake. Witnessing this abundance for the first time, I vowed to strive for similar conditions in our army.

When the competition ended, I emerged victorious in the 10-meter rapid fire as a new shooter, earning a trophy that still sits in my study. I also won a silver medal in the 25-meter timed fire and a bronze in slow fire, finishing 5th among new shooters overall. The national shooters, categorized as masters, performed admirably against the U.S. Army, despite the disadvantages. I was proud of them and believed they had the potential to become future Olympic athletes. Although they invited me to join the national team, my commitment as a KMA graduate and frontline soldier made it difficult. Instead, a general officer took my place, and I returned to my company at the front.

Upon my return, I found that many of my colleagues had moved on to new positions. Lieutenant Colonel Lee Sang-ik, the battalion commander, had transferred to the division staff, and Colonel Kim Yeong-hwan, the regimental commander, had been promoted. Despite these changes, my lowerclassman, First Lieutenant Im Seung-hae, was commanding the reserve company, which eased the transition back to frontline life.

♦ I fell in love with a charming young lady and worked as the operation officer(S-3) of the GOP battalion under the new concep of FEBA, while going on dates

During my time at the Korea Military Academy, I often stayed at my brother's house in Yongsan when on leave. It was there that I met Park Jin-yeong, a charming young woman who was studying English & English literature at Ewha Womans University. She was the niece of my brother's wife and stayed at the house as a boarder. I encountered her occasionally during my visits, and each time, I was struck by her elegance and kindness. After my commission, I saw her in a new light during a leave to Seoul. Her genuine demeanor and thoughtful nature captivated me, and I found myself falling for her.

During my service in Munsan, I met her a few times whenever I was on leave. Our paths crossed again when I participated in a joint shooting competition between the Korean Army and the U.S. Army. With each encounter, my affection for her grew. I confided in the elder brother's wife about my feelings. In February 1961, after returning to my unit as the commander of the reserve company, I attended her university graduation by the elder brother's wife invitation. This gave me the opportunity to congratulate her and meet her parents, who seemed to be wonderful people.

During this period, I was working as the operations officer of the COP battalion under the FEBA (Forward Edge of Battle Area) new concept. In late February 1961, the Korean Army, in collaboration with the U.S. Army, introduced new strategies for tactical nuclear weapons at the front. This led to a reassignment of troops near the Military Demarcation Line and a restructuring of frontline positions. Previously, the frontline was a straight line under the Main Line of Resistance (MLR) concept. However, the new strategy involved forming "strong points for final defense" and connecting these points to create a U-shaped frontline, designed to lure the enemy into a trap. If the enemy advanced and fell into this area, a tactical nuclear weapon would be deployed to annihilate them, followed by a counterattack.

I was appointed as the operations officer for the 1st Battalion of the 1st Regiment to oversee the troop movements to the new operational area. In March of that year, under the moonlit night, we moved from 'Baengma-goji' to 'Eulji Strong Point' in 'Dongmak-ri.' Our regiment established the FEBA line, extending even to the depths of Jipo-ri. We spent several months constructing positions, including the regimental observation post and command office, combat trenches, and more.

During this time, whenever I had leave to visit Seoul, I would stop by Moon Dental Clinic to see her, and we would go on romantic dates. When her letters, which substituted for our dates, arrived at the front, Major Lee, our regiment's S-2 and a victim of the "Military Hair Loss Soap Incident," would excitedly notify me and ensure I received them promptly. He was a kind-hearted man who treated me generously. Once, "Miss Yeong" visited me in Front Line Cheorwon, Major Lee, upon realizing this, warmly welcomed her and urged me to meet her, even sending his jeep to pick me up.

My fellow company commanders, who were close to me, often gave me advice about marriage, half-seriously suggesting that I should be authoritative to maintain peace in the family. Despite their tone, I knew they genuinely cared for me. Thanks to these supportive superiors, my military life was neither unfamiliar nor lonely. I am grateful for their trust and kindness.

Thanks to Major Lee's encouragement, I took a brief leave from the front and went to Munhye-ri. She traveled all the way to this small village, which, despite its humble appearance, was home to many service families. Our simple date at a 'yeonggye baeksuk' restaurant, sharing a meal and conversation, was more memorable than a year's worth of dates in Seoul. Her effort to visit me in such a remote place deepened my affection for her.

To reach Munhye-ri from Seoul, she had to take an intercity bus from "Cheongnyang-ri" or "Miari-gogae" to "Uncheon," a journey of four to five hours. From there, she waited for a local bus to Munhye-ri and navigated her way to the regiment's headquarters. Her determination to see me despite the arduous journey made me love her even more.

♦ The long-awaited <Military Revolution of May 16> and <Colon Report> occurred.

During the late stage of Rhee Syng-Man's presidency, Korea was in political and economic turmoil. The 'Liberty Party' sought permanent power, and corruption was rampant. The Colon Report, submitted to a U.S. Senate sub-committee in November 1959, highlighted Korea's dependency on U.S. aid and the societal chaos. It suggested the possibility of a military coup, noting that young officers from military academies, frustrated with the privileged government officials, might lead such a movement.

On May 16, 1961, General Park Chung-Hee and 23 other leaders led a coup with 3,600 soldiers, occupying key locations with minimal resistance. The coup leaders announced martial law through KBS, and President Yoon Po-sun, acknowledging the situation, emphasized a peaceful resolution. The coup leaders sought support from KMA cadets, knowing their involvement would secure public trust. Captain Chun Doo-Hwan, a KMA alumnus, succeeded in rallying the cadets, leading to a historic parade in Seoul on May 18th. This demonstration of support from the trusted KMA cadets helped the public accept the revolution, bringing peace to the nation.

The underlying reason why the KMA cadets participated in a revolutionary demonstration, led by their regular seniors, stems from a deep-seated desire to combat corruption and irrationality within the older generation of officers. As I previously mentioned, the KMA cadets enrolled in the regular four-year course system (1st to 4th class) were driven by a reformative spirit, encapsulated in the motto, "Destroying evil and showing righteousness." When the 1st class was commissioned, they initiated reforms in the supply system from various positions, succeeding in advancing the "supply fight" from the front to the rear. During the graduation ceremony for the 2nd class, nearly all of the 1st class returned to KMA. After the official ceremony, senior officers (1st & 2nd class) and the cadets still in school gathered separately to sing the academy's song and cheering songs, chanting together under the banner of "Eliminate corruption and correct the wrong." This event occurred annually at graduation, creating an unstoppable wave of reform within the military. Initial unit officers from KMA further fueled this reform movement wherever they went. The Military Revolution of May 16th emerged amidst this climate. Consequently, all MA graduates, including the 1st class officers of the Alumni Association working in Seoul, responded to the revolution and persuaded the KMA cadets to join. The unity among regular KMA graduates, grounded in their devotion to the nation and the principle of "Destroying evil and showing righteousness," was more substantial than it appeared.

The 'Pledge of Revolution', broadcast on KBS at 4:30 a.m. on May 16th, outlined the following objectives:

1. Establish anti-communism as the foremost permanent state policy and reorganize and strengthen the anti-communist system.
2. Adhere strictly to the UN Charter, honor international treaties with dedication, and strengthen and expand the alliance with the United States for the cause of liberty.
3. Eradicate corruption and old evils entirely, and reform the decadent morals and spirit of the Korean people.
4. Immediately address national poverty, where people are literally starving, and focus on rebuilding an autonomous economy.
5. Enhance proficiency in combating communism to achieve national unification.
6. Return to our original duties after transferring power to the next political party once the aforementioned goals are accomplished.

"A new and powerful history is being created in our nation. Our nation demands unity, patience, courage, and progress. Long live the Republic of Korea! Long live the uprising armed forces!" The revolution's motto was "Demolish indirect aggression and complete the mission of revolution!" The revolution's goal was not merely about a group of young, dissatisfied commissioned officers executing a coup d'état to resolve internal military issues like promotions or treatment improvements. These young officers, in their 30s, had learned about and experienced democracy in its homeland more than any other group in Korea. They resolved to save a nation in extreme poverty and on the brink of communism. They utilized all their resources—military force and collective power—to execute the revolution, which ultimately succeeded. The early ideas on revolution strategy, or national security strategy, they wanted to communicate to Korea and the world through their pledge of revolution, were rooted in Park Chung-Hee's vision of saving the nation, the loyalty and devotion of commissioned officers committed to anti-corruption and reform, and the principle of "Destroying evil and showing righteousness" upheld by regular commissioned officers from KMA and the KMA cadets.

♦ I entered 'The Army Shooting Competition' against other divisions and the 'Joint Shooting Competition between the Korean Army and U.S. Eighth Army' in 1961

In July 1961, I participated in the "Army shooting competition against other divisions" at the 2nd Corps, an annual event. I had the honor of being selected as the division's pistol shooter. The division's shooting team was already formed and training at the division's shooting ground. Our pistol team consisted of one major, who was the team captain and a shooter, and four commissioned officer shooters, including myself. We assembled ten days before the competition, moved to the 2nd Corps, and set up camp near "Araesaembat Village," close to the shooting ground. We practiced in "Wi-saembat," a village deep in the mountains but not far from Chuncheon. Villagers, both elders and children, occasionally watched us practice. During mealtimes, we gathered firewood to cook rice and "doenjang-guk" (soybean paste soup) with ingredients we brought in mess tins. The villagers offered us potatoes, their local specialty, in exchange for some of our rice (a mix of 30% barley and 70% rice).

I was curious about their obsession with rice and realized that the "story of Gangwon-do" was still relevant there. It meant that even then, villagers considered someone who could consume 16kg (35 pounds) of rice in a lifetime fortunate. When a young woman married, her groom's family was expected to give her at least one big bag of rice (1980 kg, or 176 pounds), while a widow remarrying received a bag of barley. This tradition highlighted the poverty that plagued Korea at the time and was a key reason for the Military Revolution of May 16th. Our Capital Division won the Army shooting competition with scores far exceeding other divisions, and we returned to a warm welcome from everyone at the base, including the division commander.

Soon after, I was ordered to participate in the Joint Shooting Competition between the Korean Army and the U.S. Army for the second consecutive year. This year's competition, held at the Munsan Shooting Ground for the U.S. Army in September 1961, was larger in scale, featuring rifle (M1 Garand and Carbine) and pistol competitions simultaneously. The Army selected top shooters from each division to form the Army shooting team, aiming to select national shooters for the Armed Forces. At that time, civilians were not allowed to become professional shooters in the Republic of Korea. The pistol matches were similar to the previous year's competition. Despite challenging conditions, our team members achieved over 90% individually in the 50-meter (54-yard) slow fire. Having won prizes in the previous year's competition, I competed as an expert this year. First Lieutenant Min, First Lieutenant Kang, and I, all KMA graduates, gave our best effort.

However, we used pistols that had seen service in World War II and the Korean War, still carried by current battalion and regiment commanders of the U.S. and Korean Armies. These pistols, housed in leather holsters, were too worn out for shooting competitions. In contrast, U.S. Army shooters carried two to three of their favorite pistols in briefcases for safekeeping. Nonetheless, our national shooters worked hard to adjust the rear and front sights to match the U.S. Army's standards by welding, grinding, test shooting, and regrinding. Yet, "competition" was not the right term for this situation. Consequently, bronze medals and a 5th overall rank were the best results we could achieve.

The competition was significant, with one company from the U.S. Army serving as a supporting troop. Although I had seen many U.S. Army soldiers, it was my first time witnessing an entire troop in action. They moved in unison under their company commander's orders, appearing more disciplined than most Korean Army companies. However, upon closer inspection, everyone in that company had grown beards. This was unexpected, as I had heard that American men and U.S. Army soldiers shaved daily as part of being gentlemen. I stopped one soldier to inquire, and he explained that their company commander had ordered it. The company commander's order? I had believed that Americans and the U.S. Army lived with true liberty, yet they were completely obedient to their commander's orders. I witnessed a new and unexpected side of the U.S. Army.

Chapter 4

Studying Abroad in the United States, Getting Married, Drill Instructor for 'Dongbok Night Owls,' Guerrilla & Ranger School, and Instructor for Yonsei University's ROTC (1961-1966)

1. Studying Abroad in the United States, Attending J.F. Kennedy Center, Fort Bragg, NC

♦ A door to studying abroad in the United States opened for me

During the Korean War, nearly all commissioned officers studied abroad at OBCs, OACs, or Army universities in the United States to enhance the quality of the Armed Forces. Around 1960, additional courses were introduced: "Missile" for artillery, "Special Warfare" for infantry—Psychological Warfare, Unconventional Warfare, Counterinsurgency Warfare—and Ranger (Commando unit/agents) for infantry. In spring 1961, Park Jeong-Gi, my classmate and close friend, who was already married, took the artillery missile course. Kim Jin-Gyu, another classmate, completed that course too and settled as an instructor at the Artillery School in Gwangju. Their stories about the United States were entertaining, but I was more intrigued by the process of studying abroad.

I applied for the "Unconventional Warfare Course" as part of the recruitment process for officers studying abroad. I took a short vacation to Seoul and stayed at the Moon Dental Clinic. During my stay, I spent about ten days at the library of SNU's College of Arts and Sciences, reading English books and preparing for the examination required for studying abroad. I then took tests in military science (commander & staff) and English, which is now known as the TOEFL test. At that time, we referred to it as the 'adjutant general's corps test,' likely because it was supervised by the Staff of the adjutant general's corps. Finally, I had an interview with a U.S. Army officer.

A humorous incident occurred during the final interview. The chief interviewer, a U.S. Army major, asked about my age, my commissioning, my family, and my current duties. When I mentioned that I was working on the frontline, he inquired, "What does North Korean propaganda broadcast to the South over the DMZ say these days?" I smiled and replied without hesitation, "American go home!"—something I would say honestly to close friends. They burst into laughter and asked, "So then, what do you think?" I responded emphatically, "You are our friend!" They laughed joyfully again, and the major said, "Good, I recommend you!" After another moment of shared laughter, I passed the interview. Later, I learned that my interview results were even better than those of the general interpretation officers, who were my competitors.

Thus, I concluded my three years and three months on the frontline (as a platoon leader, operations officer, and company commander) in a meaningful and fruitful way, and I finally had the opportunity to study abroad in the United States—a long-held dream since middle school and the reason I applied to KMA. Although it was for a short period, I was thrilled to achieve it, believing in the verse, "Ask, and it will be given to you."

♦ I got engaged before departing.

Before departing to study abroad, I got engaged, thanks to my elder brother's wife. I often stayed at my brother-in-law's house in Seoul, as I had no other family in Korea. My brother's wife trusted and liked me. She was Miss Yeong's aunt and had been observing the progression of my relationship with Miss Yeong. When I was about to study abroad, she asked about my feelings and proposed, "Marry my older sister's daughter, in other words, my niece." I immediately agreed with a thankful and delighted heart. However, I explained that I couldn't marry immediately due to financial constraints and planned to save my paychecks for about a year after returning from the United States to afford a long-term lease on a house. She assured me, "I'll keep that for you, but just get married as soon as possible."

I visited my family in Busan and informed my parents about the situation. I told them, "She's the eldest daughter of a family in Jeonju that runs an orchard, graduated from Jeonju Normal School, and just graduated from Ewha Womans University with an English major, the best university in Seoul. I truly love this young lady, and I believe she will be good to both of you too. My dentist brother's wife introduced me to her and asked me to marry her." Initially, my parents hesitated because she was from Jeolla-do, a region not favored by people from Gyeongsang-do at the time, but they soon agreed, saying that brother Moon (the dentist) in Seoul had already told them about her.

My older sister, who was financially successful at the time, promised to cover the lease deposit for our new house—I think it was 100,000 won then, equivalent to 10 million won ($60,000) today (2025)—and wedding gifts. I returned to Seoul and informed her. She suggested we get engaged first due to my busy schedule and financial situation and buy a pair of watches we liked as wedding gifts. So, we got engaged verbally, and I left for the United States to study abroad with hope and excitement.

♦ On my way to the U.S. I witnessed post-war Tokyo, Japen

On January 14th, 1962, I finally departed for the United States to fulfill my dream. Miss Yeong, my fiancée and future bride, came to Gimpo Airport alone with a valuable gift to congratulate me on my journey. Her presence was heartwarming and loving, and I was grateful. I traveled with Captain Han O-gyeong, my senior from the 3rd class of KMA. I had known him since my cadet days; he was a kind and sociable upperclassman with many friends. I was fortunate to have him as a companion throughout our journey, sharing both hardships and joyful moments like battle buddies.

As we were traveling to the United States with support from the U.S. Army, we went to the U.S. Army's office (in a Quonset building) at Gimpo Airport, which served both Korean civil aviation and the U.S. Army, to receive 15 copies of the same document along with our passports. We then boarded a U.S. Army twin-engine C-46 Commando with soldiers seemingly on vacation to Japan. Although it lacked the thrill of a jet aircraft, I was deeply moved seeing my beloved Miss Yeong waving from the sendoff platform. Back then, Gimpo Airport had a sendoff platform on the roof of the 3rd floor where people could wave at departing and arriving passengers.

Looking down from the sky, Seoul was still in a state of devastation from the war. As the twin-engine plane flew higher, I saw the disorderly and curvy rice paddies in Gimpo and 5,000-year-old straw hut houses shaped like the Hangul letters "ㄱ, ㄴ, and ㅁ" below me, reflecting Korea's desperate need for a "revival of Korean people," echoing the motto of the Military Revolution of May 16th. The U.S. Army propeller plane flew for about four hours, crossing the Korea Strait, and soon I saw Japan's west coast below me. My first impression of Japan was of green mountains, forests, flatlands, well-organized rice paddies, fields, and villages with neatly decorated houses with roof tiles, unfolding like a panorama. It was a stark contrast to the ruined and demolished landscapes of Korea, which I had just left, prompting me to ponder my responsibilities toward my nation.

We landed at Tachikawa Airfield for the U.S. Army in Tokyo, Japan's capital. We were taken to the Visiting Officer's Quarters (VOQ) near the airfield, a U.S. Army dormitory about an hour from downtown Tokyo. It has since become a base for Japan Self-Defense Forces and the famous Showa Memorial Park. I took a long-awaited warm shower, which relieved my fatigue and rejuvenated me, offering comfort and warmth I hadn't experienced in Korea.

The next day, we woke early, changed into casual clothes, hurried outside, and had our shoes shined by a Japanese shoeshine boy. At that time, Japan had many shoeshine boys and Geishas. We asked for directions to a bus stop and took a bus to downtown Tokyo. Japanese buses had female conductors then, similar to Korea, and they were very kind and diligent, wearing armbands to signify their role and carrying red flags. They efficiently managed passenger traffic, echoing the conductors in Korea.

We disembarked near 6th Chuo-dori Avenue in the Ginza District and met a Japanese college student introduced by my classmate Kim Jin-Gyu. She took us on a tour of downtown Tokyo, including theaters. Despite the war it initiated, Japan in January 1961, especially downtown Tokyo, had been severely damaged by U.S. Army bombings. Fifteen years post-war, downtown Tokyo was gradually returning to peace through temporary restoration.

One memorable place the student took us was "Ye Lai Xiang," a theater in "Yuraku-cho," reminiscent of old Myeongdong streets in Seoul. The theater, a three-story structure, featured singers making entrances as the central front stage moved up and down to the 3rd floor. It was a renowned and high-quality theater in Japan at the time. More famous was the female singer "Li Xiang Lan (Yamaguchi Yoshiko)," known for the song "Ye Lai Xiang," celebrated in Japan for its poignant lyrics. The theater was named after this popular song. Although I wasn't particularly fond of music, her sorrowful song, performed as the stage ascended and descended, was quite memorable and remains vivid in my memory.

During that period in Japan, a young female singer named Misora Hibari was soothing the nation with her songs following the "Unconditional Surrender of August 15th." She was at the height of her fame. Young Korean commissioned officers who traveled to the United States during the Korean War often stopped in Japan, purchasing "doughnut LP records"—a format from the LP era, roughly the size of today's CDs—and brought them back to Korea, making her popular there as well. Her song "Come on My House, Come On!" especially resonated, capturing the essence of Japan's circumstances at the time. A classmate who visited after my term mentioned being entertained by geishas, and he was so impressed by their quality that he offered them $30, a significant amount for us back then. He recounted how the geishas explained that U.S. dollars contributed to national savings and aided Japan's recovery, leaving him impressed by their patriotism.

At that time, adult Japanese men and women on the subway were shorter than us Koreans, with the tops of their heads reaching below my chin. Standing up, I could see everyone in several cars ahead and behind. It was my first trip abroad, my first encounter with the Japanese people, and my first visit to Tokyo, the capital. Japan was already becoming organized and revitalized. I appreciated the kindness of a young lady who selflessly guided us with care. On the street, I met a woman and urgently needed a restroom. She graciously let me use the traditional style restroom in her home. Although our stay was brief, we toured Tokyo, observing the situation, thanks to the friendly guidance of a female college student. We concluded our first visit to Tokyo with hopes of returning and then headed to the United Statest.

♦ I traveled past Hawaii and arrived in beautiful San Francisco, and I feel wonder.

We flew from Tokyo to Hawaii on a C-130 Hercules military aircraft, a long-distance flight. Departing from Tachikawa Air Base at night, we flew over Tokyo for about 30 minutes before reaching the Pacific Ocean. The city was larger, wider, and brighter than Seoul, which was still recovering and dark at night. I had heard that during the Korean War, it took my predecessors 15 to 16 days to cross the Pacific by military transport ship. However, years later, we traveled on a four-engine propeller aircraft, reaching Hawaii in about 15 hours. On our return three months later, we flew even faster on a civil charter jet, highlighting the progress of civilization.

As we approached Hawaii, an entirely new landscape unfolded before my eyes. Though it was a set of islands, flying at a lower altitude revealed beautiful, well-organized farmlands. Near Honolulu International Airport, the view was even more stunning, with a deep blue sea and tall palm trees lining the streets. Seeing the world-renowned tropical scenery and the exotic Western-style houses and roads made me wonder, "When will Korea be like this?" My first impression of the United States was unforgettable, though I was disappointed not to explore Hawaii due to a lengthy airport delay. I promised myself to return for a proper tour in the future.

We departed Hawaii for the U.S. mainland, flying over the seemingly endless Pacific Ocean until we arrived at San Francisco, the gateway to the United States through the Pacific and a world-famous city. A duty officer met us and drove us to Fort Mason. I had finally realized my dream of studying abroad in the United States, even if only for a short time, and it was free. I was deeply moved. Fort Mason, an overseas replacement depot for the Army with a long history, processed the immigration of Korean officers who previously traveled by transport ship and now by military aircraft.

At the fort's immigration office, I submitted 15 copies of my documents. A middle-aged female office worker, seemingly expecting us, warmly welcomed us. She reviewed the documents and quickly processed us. She suggested we stay at a downtown hotel for the night and then move to 'Mrs. Ko's house' the next day to rest until we received further travel orders. We chose the YMCA Hotel, familiar to us, and spent our first night in the United States there. However, adjusting to the country and its society led to many memorable experiences.

After being assigned our room, we attempted to use the elevator, but we were unfamiliar with its operation. Seoul had only one six-story building with an elevator, and this was our first time using one. We pressed various buttons, causing the elevator to ascend and descend without stopping at our floor. Eventually, the front desk staff noticed our predicament and helped us reach our floor. We learned to operate the elevator through observation and practice.

Later, I left my room with a towel to shower, only to realize I had locked myself out. I had to go to the front desk for assistance to unlock the door. Such an incident, amusing by today's standards, occurred on our first day in the United States. I realized I should have sought advice from someone with prior U.S. experience, but I had chosen to learn through direct experience, so I couldn't blame anyone else.

The next day, Mrs. Ko, a Korean American woman, picked us up and took us to her home. Many Korean officers studying in the U.S. stayed with her, as she was recommended by those who came before us. Her home provided a language barrier-free environment for newcomers who weren't yet fluent in English. An intellectual woman, Mrs. Ko graduated from Ewha Womans University in Korea, married a U.S. Navy officer and settled near a Navy base in San Francisco. Her husband, a commander, was stationed in Germany, and she worked part-time assisting Korean service members new to the U.S. Her affordable accommodations offered Korean food, and we trusted her as a fellow Korean, making it easy to learn the basics of American life.

Her house, a typical terraced structure on a San Francisco hillside, had limited rooms, so our group of five or six stayed in the living room. Despite this, we felt no inconvenience and spent our early days in the United States there. San Francisco, renowned for its beautiful harbor, was a stark contrast to the underdeveloped mountain villages where we had served in Korea. Everything we saw was magnificent, amazing, and charming. I'll share just a few of the many first impressions I had of San Francisco and the United States, impressions that remain vivid to this day.

The tour began with an unforgettable first impression at the Golden Gate Bridge. This iconic structure stretches approximately 2.7 kilometers (1.67 miles) and rises 67 meters (73 yards) above the water, allowing most cruise ships to pass beneath it. The bridge is supported by two piers—one on land and the other slightly offshore, giving the impression that the entire bridge is held up by this single pier. Its arch design allows ships to enjoy an unobstructed view. If I were to compare its length and location to Korean geography, it would be akin to a structure between Gunsan and Janghang Port, about 3 kilometers (1.86 miles) long and tall enough for cruise ships to pass under, with only two piers at the ends and none in the middle to obstruct the view.

We began our walk on the bridge from the park on the south side, passing through an automatic gate similar to the subway gates in Korea today. It was our first encounter with such a system, and it was quite fascinating. As we walked, I was immediately struck by the massive main span cables drooping from the piers on both sides. Up close, these cables were astonishingly thick, with a diameter of more than 1 meter (1 yard). As we continued, we reached the pier on our side, a colossal mass of steel I-beams rising from the sea, supporting the structure above. This steel construction was so immense that even eight large men stretching their arms side by side couldn't encircle it. I was deeply impressed by the Americans' ability to construct such a monumental steel structure in the 1930s, which reinforced my perception of the United States as an advanced and powerful nation.

As we turned to leave, I noticed a man sitting comfortably on an I-beam railing, engaged in some sort of work. After we exited, I learned he was a painter, tasked with painting the bridge in "international orange," a color chosen for its visibility at sea. It takes him a year to paint from one end to the other, and two years for a round trip. This realization made me appreciate the unseen efforts behind such grand structures and offered insight into the intricacies of human society.

San Francisco Bay is home to two major bridges: the Bay Bridge and the Golden Gate Bridge. The Bay Bridge, like the Golden Gate, is a suspension bridge with a six-lane, two-level structure. Although it spans a grand 14 kilometers (198.6 miles), the Golden Gate Bridge has captured all the attention. I had always considered the Hangang Railway Bridge and Hangangdaegyo Bridge in Korea to be masterpieces, but these American bridges left me in awe of the United States' grandeur and might.

We also strolled through the Marina District, home to a yacht marina, where numerous luxurious yachts and motorboats were anchored. A beach lay before it, where Western women in bikinis lounged on beach beds, towels, or grass, sunbathing. At that time, Korean women wouldn't dare wear such attire, feeling embarrassed even in one-piece swimsuits and hesitant to lie down in public spaces. Observing these people leisurely enjoying their yachts and sunbathing on this serene beach made me ponder, "What is life?" While Koreans seemed to live to eat, these people appeared to eat to enjoy life. I wondered when such a lifestyle would be possible for Koreans.

I recalled a saying by Mr. Gum Su-hyeon, the vice principal of my school, "In the United States, they have completed educating people with ethics and morality, and now they're educating cats." This visit made his words resonate with me. Whenever I spotted a ship flying the Taegeukgi, the national flag of the Republic of Korea, even if it was a modest cargo ship amidst the foreign vessels in the marina, I felt a surge of patriotism. People often say that traveling abroad makes one a patriot, and I finally understood that sentiment.

In downtown San Francisco, we encountered a broad ten-lane road, likely the main street, with wide sidewalks where people strolled leisurely, some appearing to be tourists. As we walked, a young couple passed us with joyful, light steps. They were so charming that I watched them until we were about 10 meters (10 yards) apart. Then, the lovely lady glanced back and winked at me. It was a delightful moment, and I returned the gesture, not because I naively thought she fancied me, but because it was customary for people to greet each other with a "Hi, good morning," or even a wink, despite the bustling street. This atmosphere was enchanting, and the citizens of San Francisco seemed as romantic as their city.

As we continued our walk, we spotted a shop with a large ice cream sign and decided to go inside. I requested, "Hello, ice cream, please," and the employee asked, "What kind?" I was taken aback, as in Korea at the time, we only had one flavor of "ice cake," and most people had never heard of ice cream. The employee, realizing my confusion, pointed to the images in front of us. I finally said, "Yes, that," but he asked another question, "For here or to go out?" Although I didn't understand the words, we gestured to indicate we wanted it to go. He then asked how many people would be eating it and packed it accordingly. These experiences were so novel and unfamiliar to us young Korean officers.

We also learned about the concepts of downtown and uptown. Downtown is the hub of daily activities, where people work and live during the day, leaving at night to rest in uptown, a residential area usually located on higher ground. The next day, they return to downtown for work. This new world was astonishing. The buildings, constructed with bricks or granite, were well-designed, and the neighborhoods were convenient, organized, and beautiful. Parks with lush greenery were abundant, where people relaxed, young people ran, some strolled or read books, and couples walked together. It was all so magnificent and charming.

♦ Then journeyed across the U.S. continent (North) by train, passing through Chicago and arriving in Washington D.C.

A few days later, we received orders for a train trip across the northern U.S. continent, a rare and fortunate opportunity. We planned to revisit the beautiful and welcoming harbor of San Francisco on our return journey. Captain Han and I boarded the Union Pacific's Pullman sleeper car from San Francisco to Chicago. Our sleeping car, equipped with two vertically arranged beds, a lavatory with a three-sided mirror, and a large window for sightseeing, was serviced daily like a hotel. Leaning against the window in the corridor, we enjoyed the view from the luxurious Pullman car, which included sightseeing, dining, and sleeping cars with expansive windows. This opulent long-distance train journeyed non-stop for five days and nights to Chicago.

I have always had a pioneering spirit and a love for travel, so this luxurious train journey across the U.S. continent at a young age was a stroke of luck. The train departed from San Francisco Station, traversing the Sierra Nevada Mountain Range and the vast, seemingly endless Nevada desert, reminiscent of scenes from Western movies. It was my first time witnessing such a landscape. The train then entered Utah, crossing the Great Salt Lake, which lay in the middle of the desert. The crossing took about two hours at a slightly reduced speed, and the lake truly lived up to its name as a "great Salt Lake."

The train stopped once a day, I believe. Regardless, as it traveled continuously day and night without halting, I was captivated by the vast desert and the grand scenery, spending hours each day watching it after waking up. I enjoyed meal services in the dining car, where I was treated to restaurant-quality menus daily. Most of the staff cleaning or serving in the dining car were African-Americans. Despite repeating this routine for several days, everything felt new and unfamiliar to me, so although I tried to learn to read the menus each time, I never quite got used to it. We also couldn't get accustomed to the cheese frequently served in the dining car, so we often exchanged it for other side dishes with a kind gentleman who frequently sat across from us and dined with us.

Two days into the trip, the train stopped at Laramie Station in Wyoming. Seeing it made me incredibly happy, as if I had encountered a friend in the middle of the desert. This was because Western movies were very popular in Korea at the time, and one of them was “The Man from Laramie.” I absolutely loved that movie—it’s a Western about a man from Laramie, a captain and commissioned officer of the AFV, avenging the death of his younger brother, who was also a commissioned officer of the AFV. It’s a story of brave, just, and invincible gunmen of the Wild West era, conveying the message that everything turns out all right in the end. That’s why seeing the name Laramie made me so happy. I got off the train to look around and found a 30-minute laundry service. At that time, everyone traveled with a personal iron, so I took the opportunity to change my shirt by having the old one cleaned there.

Afterward, the train passed through Omaha, Nebraska, and Iowa over the next few days, eventually entering Illinois and arriving at West Chicago Station, our intermediate destination. We then continued past Chicago and arrived in Washington D.C., the capital. Downtown Chicago was covered in thick snow, as it was winter. We took a taxi to East Chicago Station hurriedly, so we didn't have the chance to explore the famous city. We just hoped to return someday. We transferred to a train bound for Washington D.C., traveling east all night, passing by Lake Michigan and Lake Erie, which are as large as the land of South Korea. We traversed the Appalachian Mountains, renowned for their geographical and historical significance in the United States, and arrived at Union Station in Washington D.C., the capital of the United States, the next morning.

With three hours until our next transfer, we took a taxi tour. The first stop was the Washington Monument. From a distance, it appeared as a simple pointy tower, but up close, it was a grand structure. Standing 170 meters (185 yards) tall, it had an elevator for ascending and a spiral staircase for descending. Its peak had windows offering views of downtown Washington D.C. from every direction, and windows for those walking down. This monument was completed in 1886 to honor General George Washington, the first President of the United States. It was the tallest building in the world until the Eiffel Tower in France was constructed a few years later. I heard that the materials for this monument were brought from Egypt, Africa, through Europe. Nearby, a few elderly gentlemen were begging for alms, which surprised me. I thought, "Wow, they have beggars in this wealthy country too?"

Next, we visited the Lincoln Monument, which was well-known to Koreans. Standing before the gigantic statue was an emotional experience for me. I had read many biographies in my youth, but I admired President Lincoln the most, making him my role model. He was a great man who lived with honesty and diligence despite his poverty-stricken childhood and later freed slaves by declaring the Emancipation Proclamation. Standing before his giant, snow-white statue was deeply moving. We also walked past the grand Capitol, listening to the docent's explanations. We visited the Smithsonian museums as well, marveling at the history and actual objects of aircraft and space development at the National Air and Space Museum and being overwhelmed by the exhibition of North American dinosaurs from the Jurassic era. We heard there were more monuments commemorating U.S. Presidents nearby, but we decided to visit them if we ever returned.

We then went to see the White House—Korea's Presidential residence is called the Blue House, named after this place—the residence of the President of the United States. It looked so pure, graceful, and beautiful. However, the President's residence was located on a street, easily visible to citizens and tourists. I thought this was a bold urban planning choice and a symbol of American democracy. Knowing we were military personnel, we were taken to Arlington Cemetery in the suburbs. Korea had a National Cemetery in Dongjak-dong at the time, but I never imagined such a grand, majestic, and beautiful cemetery existed, and it was open for tourism, even allowing foreigners to visit. There was a section called the "Korean War Memorial," where U.S. Army soldiers who fought in the Korean War and died in battle rested in peace. It had a post guarding the entire memorial area and an altar for holding memorial ceremonies. They held a simple, meaningful, and visually pleasing honor guard event at short intervals. Two honor guard soldiers cross-marched, 50 meters (54 yards) apart, turned around, and cross-marched again, replacing patrolling and security duties for the entire area. I also learned they held flower-offering events on Memorial Day or when a VIP visited.

It was nearly time for our train transfer, so we returned to the train station. I realized that this train station was in the middle of downtown, making it perfect for a tour of downtown Washington D.C. Washington D.C. was truly a planned city, not one that naturally formed. It was beautiful and grand, creating American history while showcasing it. It was also the center of American politics and perfectly suited to be the center of international politics today. To me, this city symbolized a completely new world, and I couldn't help but be impressed by it.

♦ Finally, we reached the J.F.Kennedy Center

Finally, we arrived at the J.F. Kennedy Center. We transferred to a coach car with chair seats instead of sleeping cars with beds. The train arrived in Fayetteville, the old capital of North Carolina, located 500 kilometers (310 miles) south of Washington D.C. We passed through long and beautiful grasslands, lush primeval forests, and modern cities on our way there. Whenever we passed Richmond or Portsmouth, familiar places I had studied in American history and military history, I observed them carefully. We arrived in Fayetteville, our destination, in the evening. The school's staff duty officer took us to the V.O.Q of the Special Warfare School at the John F. Kennedy Center, Ft. Bragg, N.C. It was a dormitory for trainees rather than simple visitor accommodations. It housed two people per building, with doors to the bathroom on both sides and the bathroom in the middle. It also had a bedroom with a closet for each individual on one side and a study area (with a desk, bookshelf, and living room) separated by a thin wall. Of course, the beds, desk, chairs, and all household appliances in the living room were in traditional American style. "Ah, finally, I'm in the United States to study abroad," I thought. Then I truly felt it.

Before I delve into my days of studying abroad in the military here, let me introduce the J.F. Kennedy Center and Fort Bragg, N.C. When the Cold War after World War II was at its peak, Nikita Khrushchev, the first secretary of the Soviet Union, claimed peaceful coexistence and détente outwardly, but secretly reinforced nuclear weapons and propagated the so-called "Anti-war, anti-nuclear, and peace" movement through half-hearted communists worldwide, masquerading as peace. Simultaneously, he actively pursued a strategy to infiltrate third-world countries, particularly in South America, Africa, and Southeast Asia, to incite insurgency and communize them. This was a strategy of indirect communization of the world, avoiding nuclear war while actively supporting wars of national liberation. Ultimately, he built a nuclear missile base in Cuba, right in front of the U.S., to directly threaten the U.S. President Kennedy, who emerged with the motto of "New Frontier Spirits," overcame the Berlin Crisis of 1961—East Germany built a wall along the border with East Berlin and East Germany, creating a commotion—and made a blockade to cut off West Berlin. Through local airlift operations and breakthrough operations on land, he battled the Soviet Union in Cuba in 1962, destroying their willingness to invade. President Kennedy also addressed the so-called Missile Gap, established Mutual Assured Destruction (MAD), and activated the three-pronged missile system (Triad).

Simultaneously, efforts were made to address "the strategy and tactics for the liberation of Third World countries." Following General Maxwell Taylor's advice, the "Flexible Response Strategy" was established, integrating both political and military strategies, along with the concept of "Counterinsurgency Operations." Based on these strategies, the Special Warfare Center was set up in Fort Bragg, North Carolina, and the Special Warfare Forces, known as the "Green Berets," were formed. This is how the United States aimed to disseminate these strategic concepts to allied countries, forming a united front under U.S. leadership.

General Maxwell Taylor, a former commander of the 101st Airborne Division, led the Normandy landings, served as the principal of the United States Military Academy, fought in the Korean War as a commander in the Eighth Army, was the Chief of Staff of the Army, Chairman of the Joint Chiefs of Staff, U.S. ambassador to Vietnam, and author of "The Uncertain Trumpet." He was also a theorist on unconventional warfare. Fort Bragg, slightly larger than Seoul, originated as Camp Bragg during the Civil War and expanded through World Wars I and II. It has become the central hub for new strategic concepts and the home of Special Operations Forces, including the 82nd Airborne Division, the Special Warfare Center, and the Green Berets. The base has grown into a large city encompassing four communities, including military personnel, civilian living areas for their families, and households, necessitating the construction of a major freeway through the base.

♦ There, I learned about the philosophy and concept of special warfare at the American Special Warfare School

At the Special Warfare School, the philosophy and theory of special warfare were taught, focusing on three major subjects: psychological warfare, unconventional warfare, and counterinsurgency operations. Officers from allied nations learned through indoor debates, case studies, and outdoor demonstrations, visiting the 82nd Airborne Division and the 7th Special Forces Group to observe their operations. Special warfare is often defined as irregular or unconventional warfare, but more accurately, it refers to "war by special methods" distinct from regular or conventional warfare. The three educational subjects are psychological warfare, unconventional warfare, and counterinsurgency operations.

Psychological warfare is a crucial strategic and tactical area in special warfare, and the course is aptly named the "psychological warfare course." Its significance is widely recognized, requiring no further explanation. Unconventional warfare involves a new definition of warfare, blending politics and military force, and employing measures outside the conventional laws of war. A demonstration by a Special Warfare Unit team, typically composed of 12 members with diverse expertise, illustrates this. Each member must speak the language of the country to which they are deployed. The demonstration highlighted a team's infiltration into anti-government areas to form and command guerrilla units, sometimes engaging in political maneuvering, assassination, and abduction, while undergoing survival training in extreme conditions.

Counterinsurgency warfare, another component of special warfare, focuses on suppressing and subduing insurgencies or violent rebellions, particularly in Third World countries. It involves pre-incident measures addressing political, social, and environmental issues, incident measures for subduing insurgencies with minimal casualties, and post-incident stability operations. These tasks are challenging due to varying local conditions, which is why the U.S. Army struggled to achieve success in the Vietnam War and guerrilla battles in South America, Africa, and other regions, despite extensive training and support.

During my time at the American Special Warfare School, I experienced life as a nationalist. Whenever I introduced myself, I emphasized "KoRea" with a strong accent, earning recognition from instructors for my strong sense of nationalism, which they considered a positive trait. My class included officers from 11 countries and various branches of the U.S. military, with ranks ranging from colonels to first lieutenants. Although the three-month course limited my ability to befriend officers from different countries, I was satisfied with the curriculum, student management, and dining facilities.

I formed a close friendship with Major A. Rafie from the Jordanian Armed Forces, who worked in the crown prince's secretarial office. Despite missing a chance to meet in Korea, we communicated using body language and shared jokes about the U.S. providing support to other countries but receiving complaints in return. Another friend was Captain J.E. Hennegan of the U.S. Marine Corps, with whom I traveled across the southern U.S. before returning to Korea.

In class, I observed unexpected behavior from U.S. Marine Corps officers, who exhibited a relaxed and sometimes disrespectful demeanor, such as putting their feet on desks. While this didn't disrupt the class, I questioned whether such behavior was appropriate for Marine Corps officers, even in a culture valuing liberty.

During outdoor practice, I witnessed demonstrations of counterinsurgency tactics, including curfews, guarding key locations, and using suppression equipment. Forces advanced with rifles and bayonets, charging and dispersing mobs. On field trips, only Korean and Vietnamese officers wore American combat uniforms, prompting me to hope for Korea's rapid development and independent defense capabilities.

We often attended gatherings at the U.S. Armed Forces officer's club or played Bingo on weekends. Young American service members, especially Marine Corps officers, socialized with nursing officers at local hospitals and enjoyed dance parties. The American officer's mess hall on the base offered an abundance of food.

After leaving Korea, everything felt new to us, and we relied heavily on our instincts, especially when it came to meals. On our first day, we were taken to the officer's mess hall, and I recalled an old story about a "mute course" from around 1950. As we entered, holding unfamiliar food trays, we lined up at the egg station. When it was my turn, the cook asked what I wanted. I hesitated, not understanding his words. Sensing my confusion, he smiled and explained by drawing shapes and showing me things. Americans, including service members, typically eat two eggs for breakfast. He gestured like a woman's breasts and said, "breasts," then "sunrise," and finally mimed mixing and said, "scramble." I opted for "two fried eggs," which I was familiar with, and he cooked them on the stainless-steel griddle right away. The next day, I started ordering scrambled eggs, having learned the words.

Honestly, I had never eaten eggs cooked so freshly before.

With eggs on my tray, I moved to the bread section, overwhelmed by the variety: sliced bread, baguettes, French toast, and more. A toaster sat next to the sliced bread. Nearby were sausages, ham, and fresh vegetable salad. For beverages, there was an array of juices, including orange juice, milk, dispensers for Coca-Cola, Pepsi, light coffee, rich coffee, and black tea. Israeli oranges were offered for dessert, but I was too full to eat them immediately. They looked too good to eat without savoring, so I often took them to my room to enjoy slowly. Back then, all these foods were new to me, but now I know their names and enjoy them. The American breakfast was quite different from the Mediterranean breakfast, even in cost. Many Korean proverbs say, "as you wish," or "as you like," and I finally understood their meaning. Everything in the United States was high-quality and abundant. Lunch was even more lavish, comparable to a full-course restaurant meal, including steak. It was evident how the U.S. treated its service members, especially commissioned officers, with special care. Breakfast cost three dollars, lunch seven, and dinner five. Despite their fanciness, I didn't find them expensive. However, with a monthly salary of about 600 dollars, it was barely enough. Some Korean officers bought Korean food ingredients from a store selling daily necessities, other than those at the PX, and cooked rice and soup at the BOQ to satisfy their tastes and save money. Occasionally, the smell bothered foreign officers, leading to warnings. We also had access to the PX, where I bought essentials like Skin Bracer and Dial soap, which became lifelong necessities, as well as commodities and leisure items like cigarettes. The PX and the store systems of the U.S. Armed Forces were something our ROK Armed Forces had to adapt to. The PX was categorized into three areas based on duty location danger levels. Area 1, for battlefields like Korea, offered prices close to raw material costs, meaning everything was tax-free. Area 2, for rear areas like Japan, had slightly higher prices. Area 3, for soldiers in America, was duty-free. American service members were well-paid, and the government treated them generously, reflecting the state's respect for them.

Western customs were unfamiliar to me at the time. Though I had heard about them, like the story of "The Blind Men and the Elephant," Western culture and customs were amusing. Now, in Korea as of 2025, we live similarly. One custom was "ladies first," where a man would pull and push a chair for a woman, both inside and outside the house. This started in the Wild West era, when women were scarce. There was also the custom of a wife dressing her husband for work and undressing him when he returned. An American colonel with a long career was my sponsor. He lived with his wife and young grandson and often invited me to his home. He once took me to Norfolk, a naval base city, to see the sea and eat seafood. We frequently had gatherings at the "Officer's party hall" on weekends. The colonel dressed with his wife's assistance, who brought him clothes and shoes. He would drive the car from the garage, park it at the porch, open the door for his wife, and then drive to the party. Upon arrival, he would open the door for her, park the car, and return to escort her inside, where he would pull out her chair. After the party, he would retrieve her belongings, bring the car around, and open the door for her again. At home, she would open the door for him, take off his clothes and hat, and hang them up. This process seemed practical but looked like "women are superior to men," which was the opposite of Korean norms. Some Koreans would boast to American friends, "In Korea, men are treated like kings at home and outside." We never imagined the world would change as it has.

A Japanese American officer from Hawaii in our class was very kind and often gave us kimchi in small glass bottles, costing six dollars each. We ate it gratefully, realizing kimchi could be mass-produced and commercialized. When we craved kimchi, we used hot sauce on vegetables, which tasted like a distant relative of kimchi but not quite the same.

I observed American younger officers with interest. They were diligent, thrifty, and good to their parents, much like us. Most officers in my class were captains, including one who invited me to his home. He earned about 3,000 dollars monthly in weekly payments. He spent 700 dollars on a 30-year housing loan, 500 on insurance, 1,000 on living expenses, and sent 300 to his parents monthly—a good American son. Despite his salary, he didn't seem wealthier than us. After his daily routine, he attended parties and clubs, went to bed late, and hurriedly got ready for work in the morning, having only bread and milk for breakfast. His wife drove him to work, and he had additional breakfast during a coffee break with doughnuts or toast and coffee. After work, his wife picked him up, and they spent evenings with family, attending dance parties, club activities, and official receptions. I wondered when Koreans would own cars and enjoy life with family, promising myself to contribute to national improvement.

One more thing surprised me: the size of pinecones and corn. The pine trees were thick and well-grown, with cones about ten times bigger than Korean ones. The corn was five to six times larger than Korean corn. Everything seemed big, thick, and plentiful. The weather felt like experiencing four seasons in one day. There was also strict discrimination against African Americans.

♦ I witnessed strict discrimination against African-Americans in southern U.S. regions

North Carolina, a southern state in the U.S., was marked by significant discrimination and segregation against African Americans, even during my time there. Fayetteville, a city near the fort, had been home to a major official slave market a century before the Civil War. Although slavery had been abolished, racial discrimination persisted. European Americans entered theaters through the front door, while African Americans were relegated to a side entrance. Seating was segregated, naturally. On buses, about 80% of the seats were occupied by

European Americans, leaving only a few seats at the back for African Americans. Train stations were divided into two separate waiting rooms under one roof. This segregation might have reflected the population ratio, but it was stark, even to my eyes. Consequently, the school advised foreigners, particularly Asians, to wear military uniforms when going on leave to avoid discrimination and to be treated with respect, often addressed as "Yes, sir." This advice proved truet.

♦ Americans have a profound love for their flag.

Americans have a profound love for their flag, which symbolizes their nation. People of all ages, both military personnel and civilians, seemed to cherish the national flag deeply. Many homes, offices, and stores in downtown areas displayed the Star-Spangled Banner even on weekdays, not just on holidays, despite not being government buildings. One day, as I was about to cross the freeway on the base after studying, I heard the 5 o'clock cannon salute and horns signaling the lowering of the flag. I stopped and saluted the Star-Spangled Banner on the training ground across from me. All the cars speeding by came to a halt, and most drivers got out, stood, and saluted in the same direction. In the United States, people pledge allegiance to the Star-Spangled Banner from kindergarten. They play and sing the national anthem and display the flag not only at national events but also at civilian events, such as competitions. Everywhere I went, I felt the power and presence of this great nation.

♦ I took a field trip to New York and West Point

During the middle of the semester in February, we embarked on a field trip to New York and West Point (the United States Military Academy, USMA) under the school's guidance. We flew to New York, took a bus to West Point, located on the northern bank of the Hudson River, to visit the USMA, a place with a long history and a close connection to us as KMA graduates. Situated at a strategic point on the Hudson River, this historically significant site served as an important military station during the French and Indian War and the American Revolutionary War. Established in 1802, USMA is the symbol of the U.S. Army, designed to educate and train talented individuals, particularly engineer officers, for building the U.S. After various events, including the Civil War, it evolved into its current form. Most of the academy's buildings are stone masterpieces of military engineering, resembling U.S. Army fortresses and reflecting the emphasis placed on their establishment. These grand and sturdy buildings, boasting a long history and traditions, inspired trust in USMA and the U.S. Army.

USMA's motto is "Duty, Honor, Country," while KMA's motto is "Wisdom,

Virtue, Valor," reflecting its role in educating and training talented individuals in a Confucian country. However, upon seeing USMA's motto after my commissioning, it seemed a more realistic and suitable lesson for commanders, especially company-grade officers who must lead troops. As I walked past the faculty department, I observed cadets moving with controlled and ordered movements, perhaps checking their final exam results before returning to their barracks. Watching them move reminded me of our days as cadets in Hwarangdae, and it filled me with happiness and familiarity.

USMA's library, also a memorial hall, featured the declaration "Give me liberty, or give me death!" and the iconic American patriotic poster "I want you for U.S. Army." These elements strengthened my impression of the United States. After exploring, I met a young Western woman who was a teacher at an elementary school in rural Connecticut. She had brought her students on a field trip. When I mentioned we were from Korea, she was surprised and asked how we managed to come from such a distant country. At that time, overseas travel was considered a rare opportunity, even for Americans. We had lunch with the cadets in the mess hall, observing their routines and recalling my days at KMA. The cadets entered the mess hall, formed a giant V-shaped position, and sat upright. Helpers, likely soldiers, placed food on the tables for the squads. A lowerclassman, the cadet in charge that day, would shout, "Delicious soup is served!" and pass the plate to the upperclassman. After a few rounds, the regimental commander cadet on the balcony would announce, "Attention! Start meal!" and everyone would begin eating. As they finished, the commander made announcements about the afternoon schedule before ordering, "The meal is over! Exit!" This system, based on the USMA's, evoked emotions as it reminded me of our dining experiences at KMA.

The movie "The Long Gray Line" depicts a master sergeant retiring after a lifetime at USMA, with cadets bidding farewell by marching past him. This endless parade of cadets, demonstrating justice, duty, and loyalty, continues year after year, serving the nation and its people. I witnessed this essence at West Point. Afterward, we took a bus on a slippery country road due to heavy snow, eventually arriving in New York, the world's greatest commercial city. We disembarked at Times Square and explored the main street. Being at the heart of New York, a place we had only heard of or seen in pictures, was exhilarating. Walking amidst towering skyscrapers, some over 60 to 70 stories high, was awe-inspiring. Like country boys in the city, we craned our necks to see the tops of these buildings but soon gave up, simply marveling at every moment. The famous Yellow Cabs were well-organized and fascinating to watch.

Next, we visited 5th Avenue in Manhattan and entered the iconic Empire State Building, a landmark I had longed to see. In 1962, it was still the tallest and most famous building in the world, completed in 1931 during the Great Depression. Standing 102 stories tall and 381 meters high, it was a true skyscraper. We took an elevator to the 86th floor, then another to the 16-story observatory and broadcasting antenna. The view from the observatory was breathtaking, with an endless horizon in every direction and a vast forest of buildings below. This sight inspired me to dedicate myself to rebuilding and developing our nation. I finally understood why my senior officers, who visited in the 1950s, said it almost changed their life philosophy. Before 1950, Korea had only a few six-story Japanese department stores, which were destroyed during the Korean War. Even in the 2020s, President Trump promised North Korea's leader that he would help them develop like the Empire State Building if they pursued nuclear disarmament. This context helps explain the profound impact this visit had on us as commissioned officers. I visited New York three more times in my life, each time returning to the observatory to relive those past emotions.

♦ After completing my studies in U.S., I embarked on a road trip in the southern U.S. and Mexico, visited the Marine Corps base in San Diego, sang 'Arizona cowboy'.

I am grateful to the United States and God for the opportunity to experience various aspects of the U.S., to expand my worldview, and to acquire diverse knowledge, even though my stay was brief, lasting only three months. After completing my short course of study, it was time to return to Korea. Captain Hennegan of the U.S. Marine Corps mentioned that he was driving back to his base in San Diego, California. Captain Han and I were fortunate to join him on a road trip across the southern United States.

Our journey began with a two-day visit to Washington, D.C. During this second visit, we met Major Park Bo-hi, the executive officer at the Defense Attaché of the Republic of Korea in the U.S. He introduced us to some Koreans living in Washington, D.C. and updated us on the high-ranking generals who had defected following the May 16th Coup d'État. Some of these generals were eager to meet us, and we had the chance to speak with them. The U.S. government had granted these Korean generals' political asylum, honoring the connections formed during the Korean War and considering future relations with Korea. These men, labeled as "men of anti-revolution," had been in exile in the U.S. for about a year. They were curious about the military, social, and political climate in Korea, so they were willing to meet with us, even though we were only company-grade officers studying abroad, not government agents. Eventually, many of these generals returned to Korea and cooperated with the military government.

Major Park Bo-hi was a kind and sociable man who spoke English fluently. I want to briefly introduce him because he later became quite famous. He was a captain and an M1 rifle instructor when I attended the infantry school in Sangmudae, Gwangju, for summer military training during my sophomore year as a KMA cadet. Although the M1 rifle was a basic infantry weapon, his engaging explanations made him the best instructor in our eyes. As I mentioned earlier, he was an army officer during the Korean War and a member of the second cadet recruit of KMA. He safely guided entertainers who came to perform for soldiers when the 3rd Corps of the ROK Army withdrew from Sangjinburi during the war. Perhaps due to this experience, after his Defense Attaché duty, he founded The Little Angels, an art company with Korean orphans as members, with support from Mr. Moon Sun-myung of the Unification Church. The Little Angels toured 16 countries that participated in the war, earning praise and popularity. They eventually became a children's choir representing Korea, enhancing the country's global reputation. Later, he assisted Moon Sun-myung in promoting the Unification Church worldwide.

During our stay in Washington, D.C., we explored many places we hadn't visited before, guided by a charming female college student who worked part-time at the Embassy of the Republic of Korea. One day, we visited 12th Street, Virginia—a residential area for impoverished African Americans near Washington, D.C.—and realized that even Washington, D.C., and capitalism had their darker sides.

After our second visit to Washington, D.C., we reunited with Captain Hennegan and embarked on the next phase of our cross-continental road trip. We traveled south from Washington, D.C., through North Carolina, further south to Columbia, South Carolina, and then turned west, arriving in Atlanta, Georgia. The journey covered approximately 1,500 kilometers (932 miles) and took about 15 hours. To put it in perspective, it was like traveling from Busan through Sinuiju, North Korea, to Shenyang, China, in a day. As soon as we left Washington, D.C., we encountered 16-lane freeways, with eight lanes on each side. Cloverleaf interchanges were dynamically constructed throughout. Unmanned toll gates had yellow baskets where we tossed coins to pass. Many of the photos I took in the U.S. were of these impressive freeways. While these pictures may seem mundane to Koreans in 2024, back in 1962, they were awe-inspiring. The Gyeongbu Expressway, Korea's first freeway, was built ten years later with great difficulty, even requiring foreign loans. Any officer who didn't dream of building similar freeways in Korea after seeing them in the U.S. was not truly a Korean officer.

We stayed at a VOQ (Visiting Officer's Quarters) on a military base near Atlanta, woke up early the next day, and visited the Atlanta Cyclorama, a museum about the Civil War. It featured a massive indoor panorama of a battlefield, as large as a soccer field. The panorama depicted a famous battle during the Civil War when General William Tecumseh Sherman's Union Army charged through enemy territory, infiltrated deep into the Confederate rear, and won a critical battle in Atlanta in 1864. General Sherman is revered in American military history for his strategy of "charging into enemy territory, being merciless, complete annihilation, and striking the enemy's rear." The story of this battle was already well-known, but the cyclorama deeply moved me, especially since I had been studying military history. It reminded me of a similar war museum I visited in Western Germany, dedicated to the decisive Battle of Waterloo.

Next, we visited Stone Mountain, located not far from Atlanta. Atlanta is a basin-like great plain, offering distant views. Stone Mountain Park was beautifully formed around a majestic stone mountain. Equestrian sculptures of three Confederate heroes—President Davis, General Lee, and General Jackson—were carved in relief on one side of the mountain. Three sculptors worked on it for 60 years. It is as impressive as Mount Rushmore, with its sculpted faces of four great men in South Dakota. We enjoyed the view, including downtown Atlanta, from the top of the stone mountain, explored the old battlefield, and then continued on our journey along the southern freeway, feeling like we were in the movie "Gone With The Wind."

As we traveled through the Appalachian Mountains, the first obstacle in pioneering the Wild West, we passed through Alabama and entered Mississippi, a state with vast grasslands. We crossed the mighty Mississippi River, a river steeped in stories from the Wild West era, flowing vertically through the North American continent. After a brief passage through Louisiana, covering about 300 kilometers (186 miles) in a straight line, we finally arrived in Texas, known for its vast grasslands, cowboys, and "Bonanza." We passed through Dallas, a city that would later become infamous for the assassination of President Kennedy. We spent a night at the VOQ of Carswell U.S. Air Force Base near Fort Worth.

On our way, we encountered a section of road with a sign that read, "Speed checked by radar." My American friend warned, "If we exceed the speed limit here, the police will catch us immediately." We weren't trying to test it, but the speed limit on American freeways at the time was usually 60 miles per hour. When we inadvertently drove at 70 miles per hour, the siren blared, and the police pursued us. They signaled us to pull over, and a police officer approached our car. I expected him to greet us politely and let us go, considering we were officers in uniform, but that wasn't the case. He asked for the driver's license, issued a ticket without much discussion, and kindly instructed us to pay the fine at a nearby bank before continuing our journey. The fine was seven dollars per mile, totaling 70 dollars. It was a significant amount for us travelers, and we felt it was unfair, but we split the cost among the three of us and continued on our way. The United States is strict about enforcing laws, especially traffic regulations.

Texas, with its cowboys, oil-rich cities like El Paso, and proximity to Mexican cities, was our next destination. Even back then, Texas cowboys were renowned. I learned this later when I studied American history. During the first pioneering of the Wild West, around 1890, they traversed vast grasslands where over 40 million buffalo roamed, providing a vital resource for Native Americans. This discovery during the second pioneering of the Wild West was dubbed the "Second Windfall of American History" and even referred to as the "Bonanza," due to another massive buffalo herd. The cowboys who drove these buffalo north to Chicago became emblematic of Texas. According to the history book I read, these buffalo herds contributed significantly to the relatively large skeletal structure of Europeans. It was indeed a significant bonanza.

We journeyed west across Texas's historic grasslands and eventually reached El Paso, a city on the Mexican border, home to many American millionaires at the time. Captain Han and I stayed at Fort Bliss, an Army base. Our American friend, Captain Hennegan, stayed with a woman he knew—a wealthy woman, the wife of a U.S. Navy commander, who lived with her daughter and owned a substantial amount of oil. We enjoyed a local tour for three nights and four days. At that time, El Paso produced the best oil in Texas, both in quality and quantity, leading to financial prosperity for its residents. For instance, the Navy commander's wife, who often invited us, would take her 14-year-old daughter to an airfield whenever the weather was nice. They would push a Cessna 172, a light aircraft, from her personal hangar, board it, and take to the skies. We joined them the next day, with five of us aboard the Cessna 172. Her daughter, who was 15 in Korean age but appeared more mature, piloted the aircraft as we flew over the surrounding areas, including the skies above New Mexico, for about an hour. I must admit, I was quite nervous during the flight. However, it was common for households there to own not only two or three cars but also one or two light aircraft like the Cessna 172. Casual flights were simply part of life for El Paso's citizens, making it difficult to gauge their true wealth.

Every night, dance parties were held at a local hall, where men and women mingled. We witnessed the extravagant lifestyles of oil millionaires, which Asians might describe as extreme extravagance, with a hint of exaggeration. We attended these dance parties with the Navy commander's wife every night. Although I couldn't dance, I spent time with them often, and her neighbors were fascinated by us Korean officers. I befriended many of them, especially the middle-aged folks, and they continued to send us cards even after I returned to Korea. One card featured a humorous drawing of an old but robust hen looking at a frail, elderly rooster with pity. I didn't understand it when I was young, but now I realize it was a reflection of their life story and a moment in that neighborhood.

El Paso was a city divided by the Rio Grande River, much like how Seoul is divided by the Hangang River. When the Republic of Texas was established in 1888, the city was split into two countries. The northern part grew in population, with the U.S. Border Patrol and oil-seeking pioneers and became the prosperous city of El Paso. Meanwhile, the southern part, called Ciudad Juarez, remained a traditional Mexican city. The north turned into a paradise, while the south became a place of poverty. One day, we crossed the border checkpoint—Americans and tourists passed easily, but Mexicans faced strict inspections—and visited the Mexican city on the south side of the river. At red lights, children would run to the car, gesturing to clean windows and begging for money. In restaurants, mariachi singers wearing sombreros and carrying guitars would serenade us until we tipped them. Tourists, mostly Americans, enjoyed singing along, tipping, and requesting encores. Artists would approach, offering to draw our portraits, which we occasionally accepted. Prostitution, both legal and illegal, was evident on the streets. I heard Americans would visit this city to partake in these customs, as prostitution was illegal in the United States. During Prohibition, heavy drinkers joined the military to drink legally, while gangsters ran moonshine operations. Even today, Americans tend to abstain from alcohol. However, one thing I vividly remember from Mexico was the stark economic inequality. I saw luxurious mansions gleaming in gold alongside people living in holes dug into nearby hills. It was a stark reminder of the worst state of capitalism, explaining why South America leaned left politically.

After leaving El Paso, a city of organized abundance and friendliness, we headed along the desert road of New Mexico toward the U.S. Marine Corps base in San Diego. After traveling 300 kilometers (186 miles) in a straight line from New Mexico, we entered Arizona. Riding on the desert freeway, a straight road even after two to three hours, with the Rocky Mountains ahead, made me feel like "a coach riding through the wilds, a cowboy riding through the wilderness," as the lyrics of a popular song went. We sang "Arizona Cowboy" and relished the desert journey. We passed through Navajo Nation, where Native Americans ran a tourism office and souvenir shop. As we approached, the exotic Monument Valley stood alone in the red wilderness. We stopped to admire the breathtaking view, thinking it was too magnificent for just the three of us to witness. Ghost towns dotted the area, devoid of people but rich in history. We ventured further and found Western movie sets, where actors performed for tourists. Navajo Nation was established to protect and monitor the remaining Navajo people after the Wild West era, allowing them to return to their ancestral lands. Navajo Nation itself is as large as South Korea, and there are numerous reservations for each Native American tribe in the United States. I could only imagine the size and power of their tribes before European colonization.

We entered Tucson National Park, a frequent setting for Western movies, where the eastern part of Saguaro National Park unfolded. It was April, the season of blooming flowers. In Korea, large cacti are rare, usually the size of a fist, and cactus flowers bloom once every 100 years. But here, giant pillar-like cacti, some towering several times taller than a human, stood alongside prickly pear cacti. It felt like a place filled with rare wonders. I heard the Grand Canyon lay just north of there, but we decided to visit it another time.

We arrived in Yuma, the last city in Arizona, about 250 kilometers (155 miles) from San Diego. Unexpectedly, we visited a jail in Yuma's suburbs. I thought our American friend wanted to show us that even such places existed in the U.S., but it turned out to be a famous tourist attraction from Arizona's Wild West era. From what I recall, the jail was still operational at the time, and we even saw an inmate complaining to a guard. I heard it's now purely a tourist attraction as of 2020.

After enjoying the final moments of our drive, we traveled through California's beautiful green lands and finally reached San Diego, the endpoint of our southern road trip. Captain Hennegan's home and workplace, the Marine Corps base, were located there. We toured the base and spotted a road named Korea Street with a 24-mile speed limit, which delighted us as a symbol of the deep connection between the U.S. Marine Corps and Korea. We passed that street and visited Captain Hennegan's house on the base, where we met his wife, had tea, and discussed our journey and Korea. His wife was very kind, and I'm sure they were thrilled to be reunited.

Our final destination was Fort Mason in San Francisco, but we decided to make stops in Los Angeles and Santa Barbara along the way. Our American friend kindly drove us to Long Beach, LA, where we witnessed a breathtaking sunset, marking the grand finale of our journey. We bid him farewell with heavy hearts. Long Beach was aptly named, stretching beautifully along the Pacific Ocean, which added a layer of significance for me.

The realization of my dream to study in the U.S., along with the knowledge and determination I gained, became guiding forces in my life. Back in the magnificent San Francisco, we aimed to conclude our cross-country journey with a flourish. We chose the iconic Greyhound Bus, a long-distance bus service, to reach San Francisco, our final stop. This bus was more convenient and affordable than trains or planes, making it popular among both Americans and international travelers. It offered a more comfortable and enjoyable experience, traveling over 500 kilometers (310 miles) on the freeway without any turbulence. Equipped with a lavatory and seats that converted into beds for overnight trips, it also stopped at major cities, allowing passengers to disembark, explore, and catch the next bus. Operating 24/7, it only required a driver change every eight hours and occasional maintenance, enabling it to traverse the U.S. in about ten days. It was a testament to the advanced nature of the United States.

From the bus, I admired the Pacific Ocean to the left and the Sierra Nevada and Coast Mountains, branches of the Rocky Mountains, to the right. Reflecting on my experiences in the U.S., my initial impression was of the vast, well-organized farmlands seen from the skies over Hawaii. The country struck me as refreshing, majestic, and beautiful. San Francisco, in particular, was an organized, vibrant city where people lived freely and happily. It inspired me to think about how we Koreans could transition from “living to eat” to “eating to live.”

♦ The knowledge and determination I gained during my time studying abroad became the guiding pathfinders of my life.

The United States appeared as a vast, abundant land where a non-stop train journey could take a week to cross. Its monumental structures, like the Golden Gate Bridge and Empire State Building, and its well-organized cities connected by freeways, seemed part of a new world beyond our reach at the time. This impression was profound enough to challenge my life philosophy, prompting a promise to myself: "We should live great lives too." Later, after visiting Europe, I became convinced that Korea could become an advanced country like the U.S. by following Europe's developmental path. My experiences in the U.S. led me to trust the country and its people. During our journey on the Union Pacific railway to J.F. Kennedy Center, we Korean officers were treated with the utmost respect. Our travel expenses, including personal calls and additional costs, were reimbursed without question. Despite the prevailing racial biases against non-Europeans, we were assigned dormitory rooms with American officers as roommates and had access to the PX and other facilities. The U.S. covered all our expenses, making the administration seamless and welcoming.

I wrote letters to Korea from San Francisco and replies awaited me at Kennedy Center. Correspondence continued smoothly, with letters reaching me at Fort Mason. The mutual respect and trust among American officers extended to us, the foreign officers, particularly the Koreans.

Upon returning to Korea, I calculated my travel expenses in San Francisco and stayed briefly at Mrs. Ko's house before departing the U.S. By then, advancements in aviation allowed American service members to travel overseas via jet airliners. While we had arrived on a military transport aircraft, we left on a Flying Tigers civilian charter flight. Our journey took us through the U.S. Air Force base on Wake Island, where we briefly experienced the native Pacific culture, before crossing the West Pacific Ocean to Gimpo Airport. As we approached Seoul, my heart raced with anticipation of reuniting with my fiancée, Miss Yeong. I eagerly watched the landscape below, noting Korea's rivers, mountains, and the flatlands of Gimpo with their rice paddies and straw huts. Even then, I fervently wished for Korea's rebuilding and reform through the Military Revolution of May 16th. Simultaneously, I hoped for another opportunity to visit the United States.

2. Marriage and Life as a Newlywed in Gwangju, Establishing the <Dongbok (Night Owl) Guerrilla Training School>, and Serving as a Drill Instructor

♦ I worked as a guerrilla drill instructor at Gwangju Infantry School and I got married and began my life as a newlywed in Gwangju

Upon returning from the United States, I was assigned as a drill instructor at Gwangju Infantry School, a position I had desired. Meanwhile, our wedding date was set shortly after my assignment. We followed the traditional wedding process, with my elder brother delivering a letter with my birth details to my future father-in-law in Jeonju, signifying acceptance of the marriage. My future father-in-law also visited my family in Dongnae to express gratitude and set the wedding date. As the day approached, we held a ceremony to deliver wedding gifts from the groom's family to the bride's in Jeonju, a custom in Gyeongsang-do. My classmates from the Korea Military Academy in Gwangju, including Park Jeong-Gi, Kim Jong-Tae, Sin U-Sik, Jang Gi-Ha, and Lee Seung-Ju, volunteered to assist. We traveled by train from Gwangju to Iri, stayed overnight at an inn, and continued to Jeonju the next day.

Upon reaching Taepyeong-ro, near my bride's house, First Lieutenant Kim carried the Samsonite luggage I brought from the U.S., acting as a mute porter. The luggage contained wedding gifts, including silk fabric my mother had saved, high heels, and opera gloves. First Lieutenant Park Jeong-Gi played the role of a dealer, while the others acted as groomsmen. I followed behind, maintaining an air of indifference while communicating with them through glances. As we approached the bride's house, they loudly announced their arrival, drawing attention from the neighborhood. My bride's family came out, offering money to invite them inside. After a playful exchange, they accepted more money and delivered the gifts, declaring the performance complete.

The schedule was demanding, spanning one night and two days, but it was a cherished tradition, and my friend gave it their all and had a great time. My future father-in-law, a generous man known for his mood swings, was in high spirits and treated us to a grand Jeonju-style feast to reward my friends for their hard work. He even arranged for us to take taxis from Jeonju to Sangmudae, Gwangju—a long journey of about 100 kilometers on unpaved country roads—and provided us with enough money for a celebration upon our return. This joyful pre-wedding event remains a cherished memory, and I am deeply grateful to my classmates who worked so hard for it.

Not long after, thanks to my elder-brother's (who was a dentist in Seoul) wife, we held our wedding at the "Oegyo-Hoegwan (Diplomatic Hall)" in an alley in Sogong-dong, right next to Moon Dental Clinic. My mother, older brother, and relatives traveled to Seoul for the wedding. Unfortunately, my father couldn't attend due to mobility issues. Thankfully, the elder brother of my lifelong friend Lee Yong-u, who graduated from SNU's medical school and had a clinic in Seoul, was able to attend. About ten of my professors and classmates from KMA, including my close friends Park Don-Seo and Cha Ho-Sun, also came. Of course, my dear friend Park Jeong-Gi and others, including First Lieutenant Min Byeong-don, a younger alumnus, were there to congratulate me. I want to take this opportunity to thank all of them once more.

For our honeymoon, we went to Onyang Hot Springs, a popular destination at the time. It was spring, and the flowers were in bloom, making me feel wonderful and hopeful about our future, which I believed would be filled with blessings. I felt warmth in my heart. However, as soon as we returned from our honeymoon, my bride had to go straight to my family's house. We were destined to live far apart, so my family thought it was necessary for her to spend a few months with her in-laws to understand the family dynamics, which made sense. We decided to move into our new house later, so my wife had to live with her in-laws without me being there for her.

Thanks to my older sister's efforts, my family's house had a similar environment to my in-laws' house in Jeonju, with a giwa roof, tap water, and a well inside the house. Still, she had to live with her grandmother-in-law, parents-in-law, and three younger siblings-in-law. My mother sold textiles at markets, making the environment challenging for her in many ways. The local culture and customs were entirely different from those in Jeonju, so my bride must have struggled both physically and mentally. After about three months, she was finally free from her in-laws, and we began our life as newlyweds in Gwangju.

Fortunately, my wife's uncle, a kind and sociable man, worked at the Gwangju Branch of KEPCO. With his genuine kindness, we were able to move into a western-style house under a bamboo forest in Yangnim-dong, Gwangju. It was a clean and neat one-story house, and we rented a section of it on a long-term lease to start our life there. For household appliances during our three years in Gwangju, we brought an aluminum briefcase from my KMA graduation, a military duffle bag, and bedding—my wife had lovingly embroidered the bedding, including my favorite pillow, which I still use today and took with me to Vietnam. We also had a foldable acrylic dining table for two, silver spoons and chopsticks from our wedding, a toaster I received as a gift, and two apple boxes covered in newspaper, which we used as a makeshift closet.

Our life as newlyweds began with kindness, but I, the groom, had to live at Dongbok Guerrilla Training School, three hours away from downtown Gwangju due to the transportation situation at the time. Each training course lasted four weeks, so I could only come home for two to three days a month. This meant that, despite being newlyweds, my wife was left alone, and I still feel sorry for her for that.

♦ I helped establish the <Dongbok(Night Owl) Guerrilla Training School> and lived as a drill instructor

The establishment of the Dongbok Night Owl Guerrilla Training School marked the beginning of my life as a drill instructor. When I arrived at the army infantry school in Gwangju, Jeolla-do, Captain Jang Gi-o, a senior from the 2nd class, was waiting for me. He had completed the same U.S. Army Special Warfare Course as I had, as well as the Ranger course at the U.S. Army's infantry commando unit. He had just been appointed as a drill instructor at the guerrilla department of the infantry school. He drafted a plan to establish a new combined course of ranger and guerrilla warfare. To establish the course, we conducted reconnaissance throughout the Jeollanam-do area to find suitable training grounds, as chosen by Captain Jang

Gi-o, the dean of the guerrilla department.

The conditions we considered included physical training grounds inside and outside the barracks, a large rocky mountain for rope climbing, a stream for hasty river crossing training, and a mountain-and-field area for wide-range external reconnaissance. We also considered historical routes used by armed North Korean spies. Based on our findings, the headquarters of the school was located by Dongbokcheon Stream, Dongbok, Doksang-ri, Dongbok-myeon, Hoasun-gun. We selected a wide and plentiful reservoir and stream, Jebibawi Rock for mountain training, avenues of approach from Gwang-yang-man Bay (a maritime invasion area for communist guerrillas) to Mudeungsan Mountain, and the entire Jirisan Mountain (Nogodan area), where communist guerrillas were most active.

Captain Jang Gi-o and his five co-instructors, including myself, set off from Sangmudae Infantry School with a tent for 24 people and a bulldozer. We crossed downtown Gwangju, went over Neoritjae, Hwasun, and arrived at the riverbank of Dongbok. We settled there, established the headquarters for the guerrilla training school, and planned the curriculum. Under the guidance of Dean (Major) Jang Gi-o, we completed our preparations for training.

The Dongbok Night Owl Guerrilla Training School began its training in outdoor tent barracks in the summer of 1962. Initially, participation was voluntary, but it soon became mandatory for professional officers. Commissioned officers wishing to serve long-term were required to take the course. Each class consisted of 50 top-level first lieutenants and captains. The four-week course was rigorous, and many officers struggled to keep up. The course became known as the "deadly Night Owl guerrilla training course" at the infantry school, and the term "Night Owl" is still revered by those who completed their military service.

Night owls are nocturnal, living in the wilderness with sharp and keen senses, and they intimidate their enemies with their calls. They embodied the spirit we aimed to instill in our trainees. Thus, we chose the night owl as the symbol for our trainees and made them chant its name. The goal was to help trainees overcome the rigorous training with courage and instill in them the spirit of the Korean commando, or guerrilla spirit. The ROK Army could then proudly say it had the Night Owl course, akin to the U.S. Army's Ranger course. The term "Night Owl" became a symbol of the Army, and those in the military or who had served would nod knowingly upon hearing it. We had the trainees chant "Night Owl!" from the moment they entered until they completed the course. One drawback was that it was difficult to match the chant's rhythm to running exercises. Nevertheless, we had them chant it during challenging training sessions, adding weight and seriousness to the experience.

During winter reconnaissance missions, I faced physical challenges even more demanding than in summer. I couldn't walk, rest, or return at will. I had to move with the trainees, following their plans, skills, and abilities, which left me physically exhausted. Even in Jeollanam-do, winter temperatures often dropped to around negative 10 degrees Celsius (14 degrees Fahrenheit). One winter night, the countryside was pitch dark, and we could only make out the mountains and fields by starlight on clear nights. It was a frigid, snowy night, and we ascended straight up to our target height. The march continued through fields and forests, trudging through snow that reached our ankles.

Sweat began to form on my upper body beneath the thick clothes I wore to withstand the cold. My head and neck were wrapped in a winter hat and a thick scarf, making it troublesome to remove my gloves to wipe the sweat, so I just kept going. Meanwhile, my thick woolen socks were soaked in sweat inside my shoes as I trudged up and down the heights. The outer leather of my shoes was constantly wet from the snow. In other words, I was both freezing and overheating, completing my missions in a condition that could easily make me sick. "Training like actual battle" was no easy feat, and testing human will was equally challenging. I endured it solely with the "power of my youth."

♦ I volunteered for airborne tactics training(parachute) and completed it as the 15th recruit

In early 1963, my fellow drill instructors—Sin U-sik, Jang Gi-ha, and I—volunteered for parachute training with the 1st Airborne Special Forces Brigade, considered a very difficult drill, during the winter maintenance period. We received permission and joined as the 15th recruit in February. We believed that if we, the instructors, could overcome this challenging drill and carry out Night Owl guerrilla training at Dongbok Guerrilla Training School, the training we provided would be the most difficult in the ROK Armed Forces. Those who completed the course would be honored, and we would be proud to train them.

At that time, the 1st Airborne Special Forces Brigade was located in Osoe-ri, Gimpo, Seoul, near Gimpo Airport. It was renowned for its valor and dignity as Korea's first airborne special warfare forces unit, and its four-week airborne tactics drill was infamous. The first two weeks of training involved repetitive physical exercises for airborne agents. The third week focused on jump and landing tactics on the ground. Finally, in the fourth week, we boarded a transport aircraft and jumped from the skies above the Hangang River. Completing four jumps during the day and one at night, a total of five, earned us a parachute badge and certificate, marking the completion of the course.

Once we entered the training course, we were subjected to strict training (50 minutes of training followed by a 10-minute break) during the scheduled routine, with free time afterward. However, we were too exhausted to take leave. During the first week, we mostly did PT warm-ups and Level 1 speed running for 3 kilometers (1.86 miles). The second week involved training to fall from a mock platform and Level 2 high-speed running for 6 kilometers (3.72 miles). In the third week, we practiced jumping from a 10-meter (10 yards) tall mock tower, controlling the parachute while falling, and Level 3 long-distance running for 12 kilometers (7.45 miles), which also served as training for leaving the site.

I was prepared for this rigorous training, but my chronic illness (valvular heart disease in my left atrium) posed difficulties during the long-distance running on Gimpo Highway. We left the unit, entered Gimpo Highway, and ran on the moderately sloped road. My chest felt suffocating, so I fell behind and ran according to my heartbeat. The row turned at the northeast corner of Gimpo Airport and headed toward Bupyeong with the fence to our right, then entered the road in front of the unit in Osoe-ri. A crowd of women came out to whistle and cheer us on, genuinely encouraging us with their applause, which strangely gave me the last bit of strength. I passed the final fitness test of 12-kilometer (7.45-mile) running because I didn't fall behind by 100 meters (109 yards) or more from the row.

Commissioned officer trainees had free time after the weekday routine, but I was too tired to take leave, and my entire family was in Gwangju, so I had no need to. The February weather in Gimpo—an open terrain at the time—was harsh, and everyone caught a cold from repeatedly sweating during the day and staying outside, but we overcame it with the power of youth. Our only respite was visiting a public bathhouse in downtown Gimpo on weekends. We went on leave together every weekend, soaking in a hot tub for 30 minutes to warm and thaw our bodies with happiness. Afterward, we would sleep on the floor for more than two hours, leaving us feeling light and refreshed. It was a rare type of training and a moment of happiness.

I endured the monotonous and exhausting physical training and jump skill training. Finally, the real jump practice course in the fourth week arrived. Each person jumped with a single equipment setup for the first attempt. We boarded a C-46, an ROK Air Force transport aircraft, at Gimpo Airport and flew from west to east over the Hangang Sidewalk Bridge (The 1st Hangang-daegyo Bridge). As we flew above the blue waters of the Hangang River with the aircraft's middle door open, I felt "extreme anxiety" from takeoff until I jumped toward the river, a feeling that persisted every time despite multiple jumps. As we approached the Hangang River, the jump master ordered us to stand, hook the loop, and conduct mutual gear checks. Standing in front of the open door, starting with the person at the front of the row, we awaited the jump master's command to "Jump!" At that moment, I thought, "I'm doomed," and jumped, subconsciously counting "Ten thousand! Twenty thousand! Thirty thousand! Forty thousand!" Miraculously, at "Twenty thousand," I felt my body rocketing in the air and automatically exclaimed, "I'm alive!" I checked the open parachute above my head. Within just 60 seconds, I experienced the most thrilling "relief" of being alive and floating in the air, drawing closer to the ground. I steered the parachute toward Namsan with all my might to avoid the blue waters of the Hangang River. I immediately detached a rifle from my belt, letting it drop tied to the strap. As the ground rose toward me, I used the falling technique of rolling sideways as learned, lifted my body, and ran toward the parachute that was just touching the ground. I weakened the parachute wind from its back, quickly retrieved it, and ran toward the tactical area, leaving the site immediately.

The sandy beach of the Hangang River, between the current 1st Hangang-daegyo Bridge and Banpo-daegyo Bridge—south of the tracks of the Gyeong-ui Line, where Hangang River Park and famous apartment complexes now stand—served as the main landing ground. Though rare, some trainees had their parachutes stuck on Hangang-daegyo Bridge, and one was taken by the wind due to a short delay, flying to Seobing-go Station of the Gyeong-ui Line, where a train was approaching and stopped. Occasionally, they fell into puddles formed by sand excavation. Sentries were always on standby to assist them, preventing falling accidents during training.

We took weekly parachute falling tests four times. Two tests were conducted with a single equipment setup, and the other two with a full equipment setup. The skills were the same as the simple equipment setup. We prepared the full equipment all night for the jump. Moreover, when we flew over the Hangang River at night, we faced strong winds with the aircraft's door open, between the stars above and the dark waters of the Hangang River below, immediately jumping out toward the sky with our lives dependent on that loop. I forgot about it until I boarded the aircraft, busy following the procedure. But when the aircraft flew into the air and reached the skies above the dark (due to Seoul's nighttime curfew) Hangang River, I felt that "extreme anxiety." Since it was done as a group, I jumped after the person in front of me, half out of subconsciousness. Then I thought, "Ah, I'm alive, this is my world," steering the parachute away from the Hangang River. When the sandy beach rose toward me and touched my feet, I used the falling technique to roll and get up. All this happened in 60 seconds. But this time, when I got up, I was right next to a puddle. I was about to slip and fall into it, but I ran with all my might, folded my parachute, and was about to head toward the assembly point. Then a special warfare soldier from the U.S. Army—one team was dispatched to the Korean special forces unit—ran to me, stopped me, opened a bottle of Johnny Walker, poured the whisky into the cap, handed it to me, and said, "Well done, well done! Congratulations!" He congratulated me for landing safely, completing the training successfully, and acquiring qualification as a parachute agent. I was thrilled to be alive in that fatal moment, succeeding in my first nighttime jump, and couldn't fully appreciate the small sip of whisky and his congratulatory words at that moment. I am still thankful to that American special warfare agent. I would come to be thankful to the U.S. Armed Forces many times throughout my life.

We returned to our Night Owl school with pride and dignity filling our hearts. We even decided to compare and see if the Marine Corps training was harder or if our Night Owl training was more challenging. Later, one or two agents from the Marine Corps school entered our school and underwent training, and they somehow approved of our curriculum as they left.

♦ We made a demonstration to the Chief of Staff of the Korean Army

In the spring of 1963, the Night Owl training course became a mandatory requirement for cadet officers to be commissioned, following a demonstration to the Chief of Staff of the Korean Army. Chief of Staff Kim Jong-o and the Chief of the U.S. Military Advisory Group, a major general, visited our school, likely at the invitation of Principal Lee Se-ho. They received explanations about our Night Owl training course at the Dongbok Guerrilla Training School and watched a demonstration of the rappelling training in front of the massive Jebi-bawi Rock. Although we couldn't showcase the entire course, Lieutenant Jang Gi-ha, my classmate, demonstrated the hasty river crossing training using a pulley in an ideal environment for such training. His impressive skills as "the chief of physical education at KMA" earned him applause and compliments.

The second demonstration took place at Jebi-bawi Rock, where Jang Gi-o, the chief of education, and Sin U-sik, my classmate, rappelled up and down the dangerous, enormous rock. They successfully demonstrated rescue rappelling for the injured using a litter, which included rope climbing, rope rappelling, and rescue rappelling. The American advisor praised us by whistling continuously, clapping loudly, and cheering as if watching a show. While the praise was gratifying, what followed was concerning. The ROK Army's Chief of Staff issued a special order: "Starting this moment, all cadets of combat arms must complete the four-week 'Night Owl training course' before commissioning." Although this seemed generally appropriate, we drill instructors, who aimed to showcase the best training in the ROK Armed Forces, faced a dilemma. Consequently, from the 180th class onward, officer cadets underwent the Dongbok Guerrilla Training during the final four weeks of their course. When we identified those who fell short of the criteria, the principal of the Infantry School remarked, "Wouldn't it be unfair if they failed just because they ran out of strength during the last four weeks, despite doing well for a year?" His point was valid, so we had to comply, albeit reluctantly. We, the drill instructors, decided to temper some of our enthusiasm for this reason, but we still strived to maintain the training's quality.

After stabilizing the system and curriculum of the ROK Army's "infantry school's guerrilla training school," we transferred our duties as drill instructors to our KMA juniors, who had completed the U.S. Army's ranger or special warfare courses. My classmate drill instructors and I returned to the main campus and became instructors of tactics. As older instructors, I was responsible for individual combat and infiltration drills. I recalled the excellent teaching methods and speeches of the instructors from my cadet days to comfort the cadets enduring hardships, focusing on individual combat skills. I ensured they could take timely breaks during the infiltration drill and played music to soothe their bodies and minds. I trained the 183rd to 187th class cadets at the infantry school and was recognized as the best instructort.

♦ my eldest son, Jeong-Eon, was born while I was instructing a drill in mountains

During one of these drills, I was in the mountains of Nam-myeon, Hwasun-gun, following the Night Owls' reconnaissance process. A police officer from Hwasun Police Station approached me with news: "The guerrilla training school contacted us. First Lieutenant, your son is born. You must go home now." I was grateful for his effort to deliver the message, despite the distance and our movement. People were kind in those days. I hurried down the mountains, transferring between trucks and buses, almost running, and arrived home by evening. Our elderly landlady, the mother of a teacher at Jungang Elementary School, welcomed me and recounted the events. I barely listened, eager to see my family. Inside, I found my healthy baby and my wife, exhausted yet happy. It was the most humane and loving moment of my life. I felt sorry, sympathetic, and grateful to my wife for enduring the pain alone in such inadequate conditions. I comforted her, saying, "You went through so much," and was deeply moved to see my child.

♦ I shared stories of my life as a newlywed and wonderful people I met

After over a year of newlywed life in Gwangju, I felt guilty for visiting my wife only every three to four days and leaving her alone for over a month. Freed from isolation at Dongbok Guerrilla Training School, I returned to Sangmudae Infantry School as a tactics instructor. During this time, our first home in Yangnim-dong, which was cozy and comfortable, was sold, forcing us to move to a rented room under a railroad near Chosun University in Seoseok-dong. The long-term lease prices had risen, so we lived on a monthly rent with the money we had. Our first son, Jeong-eon, was born there. The rumors about the room were true. Trains passed frequently, and the engineer blew the whistle at the middle-aged ladies living under the railroad. We joked about it. In summer, rainstorms battered the paper-covered door, soaking the room. We placed our baby on a swing to sleep. Our landlady installed a wind-and-rain blocker, but it was ineffective. The environment was unsuitable for raising a baby, so we moved to another rented room nearby, though it was sad. Our household items included an aluminum briefcase from my KMA graduation, a foldable Formica table for two, two apple boxes covered in newspaper, blankets, and kitchen appliances for two. Despite this, our newlywed life was happy. My close friend Park Jeong-Gi, who completed a missile course in the U.S., his family, Kim Jin-Gyu, who took the same course, and his family, and Mr. Song (Eon-jong), my wife's younger sister's husband, who had just passed a high-ranking law official exam and was assigned to the Office of Jeollanam-do, all lived in Seoseok-dong. We shared joyful and sorrowful moments, helping each other daily, and lived joyfully in Gwangju for three years. Reflecting on it now, I made many good memories.

Financially, we struggled at times. As lower-grade officers starting our independent lives, we were practically penniless, but we had decent backgrounds. Park Jeong-Gi was the son of the Daegu Stationmaster, Kim Jin-Gyu's family was upper class, my wife's family ran an orchard, and my elder sister was wealthy. Though independent, we received some parental help to pay the rent and manage three meals a day. We often held house parties to eat and talk, living with hope and ambition. However, the government was financially strained after the May 16th Military Revolution, paying most commissioned officers with "Annam Rice" from U.S. aid—Indica rice from Vietnam, produced in California—and a little cash. When my wife's family in Jeonju heard, they sent us Korean rice they grew, which we cooked and ate, trading "Annam Rice" for side dishest.

♦ I joined <Hanahoe>, an elite group in the Army

One day, my classmate and close friend Park Jeong-Gi, an instructor at the artillery school, approached me secretly. He spoke of a society called "Hanahoe," a social group of like-minded KMA graduates aiming to improve the Army, support each other, and share military life's joys and sorrows. The group, led by Chun Doo-Hwan (later President of Korea), was forming up to the 4th class, with about ten members from each year's recruits. Park wanted to recommend me and another from Sangmudae to join.

He also informed me that Min Byeong-don, our junior from the 5th class, had said, "If Mr. Moon joins, I'll join too." Hearing this, I felt an even stronger sense of loyalty from Byeong-don Min. Naturally, I was ready to accept anything Park Jeong-Gi offered me, as it was a group of respectable classmates, seniors, and juniors. Although I didn't like a few of my classmates, I had no reason to hesitate. Thus, I joined Hanahoe, where I exchanged influence with its members throughout my military career. However, there were no special group activities until I joined. After the group was formed, each class group held monthly house parties to eat and converse. Chun Doo-Hwan, our leader, often participated to strengthen our friendship and camaraderie. We didn't engage in political activities until the "December 12th Incident," which wasn't directly related to Hanahoe, but we supported each other in social connections, promotions, and position assignments. There was no monopoly or exclusion in promotions or assignments. My wife and I remained close friends with Park Jeong-Gi and his wife, maintaining our friendship throughout our lives.

3. Educational Company Commander for the 2nd Recruit of Korean ROTC, hospitalized in the Army Hospital, Working as instructor for the 107th ROTC of Yeonsei University

♦ As the company commander responsible for educating officers for the Officer Basic Course (OBC) of ROTC

In the spring of 1963, many of my classmates were selected as company commanders for the Officer Basic Course (OBC) training for the 2nd infantry ROTC recruit. Captain Lee Jong-gu, with whom I maintained a connection during my military career, also became a company commander like me. I commanded the 13th Company, with barracks near a temporary aerodrome in Sangmudae. The section commanders, equivalent to platoon leaders, were four juniors from the 8th KMA recruit, and a first lieutenant served as the company executive officer, handling administration. This course primarily trained trainees in company-level and platoon-level tactics, staff work, and leadership methods. The OBC course for ROTC had two purposes: the original "Officer Basic Course" and "officer basic training." The university's military science department couldn't provide full officer basic training, so this course supplemented their lack of experience in barracks life. Although commissioned as officers, they had to undergo "final training" to learn the basics of being officers.

Hence, company and section commanders were mostly KMA graduates. Our company, located next to a temporary aerodrome, allowed us to teach any subject, including discipline through double training, in a wide area at any time. Officers from our company later reminisced that the course was quite challenging. One of my memories is of the final course: a 12-kilometer (7.45-mile) round-trip run to Songjeong-ri Train Station. I personally commanded it, recalling an incident where younger cadets died during summer basic military training in my junior year. We ran, adjusting speed, singing military songs, and clapping. Everyone completed the course with pride. Afterward, I permitted a party, as the course was tough with no leave or parties for four weeks. Despite limitations on food and drink, they ended up having a big party, singing, playing percussion with tableware, and visiting all barracks. KMA doesn't have such a culture, and I had never seen such a drinking culture before. Korean college students' drinking culture was truly loud and flashy, potentially dangerous.

Another incident occurred two days before the course completion ceremony. They applied for leave, and I permitted it, making them promise to return on time. However, as the ceremony approached, they returned one by one. We hurriedly let them into the ceremony, but one or two officers couldn't enter and received their certificates outside. The transportation between Seoul, Gwangju, and Songjeong-ri Train Station was difficult, especially for first-timers. Fundamentally, Korean college culture is too carefree to be changed by one or two days of military education.

♦ It was the sorrowful cause of matter, I lost my Parent early

In late May 1964, my elder sister and mother visited us in Gwangju for my son Jeong-eon's first birthday celebration. It was my mother's second visit to Gwangju. During her first visit, we lived in a European-style house in Yangnin-dong, but now we rented a room monthly. She visited for Jeong-eon's birthday but couldn't relax, as she organized the party, gave Jeong-eon a gold necklace with a lucky key pendant, congratulated him, and set and cleaned feast tables for about five groups of my KMA alumni. She worked throughout her visit without resting in the narrow room.

Before they returned home, my sister mentioned taking a plane, but I couldn't afford it, so I sent them back by train. I felt like a bad and undutiful son. Transportation was inconvenient, with few trains running daily on long-distance routes, and trains and buses were always crowded. On nighttime slow trains, passengers even sat on luggage shelves, especially on the Jeolla-do line. The train trip from Gwangju to Busan, via Songjeong-ri and Daejeon, took over 12 hours, and you were lucky to get a seat. When they got home, my parents heated the room to relax my mother, but misfortune struck that night. I believe they're now at peace in heaven under God's care, and I share this story to express my regret for being undutiful to my parents at that time.

♦ I faced and overcame significant hardships

After the designated provision period, the company prepared to educate new special official cadets (judge advocates, accountants, military chaplains, military monks, etc.). We (the company advisor and the driver) were going to Nonsan Training Center to pick up the cadets and planned to stop in Jeonju to see my family, wife, and son—my family was staying with my wife's family there. I prepared two large Mudeungsan watermelons for them. On the morning of departure, I went to the well in the lodging house to wash my face. Holding my toothbrush in one hand, I opened the well's two-part lid with the other, but one part fell into the well due to my carelessness. I should have thought, "Oops, why today?" but I was too busy to dwell on it.

We took the school-provided jeep and set off. Approaching Jeongeup Village, we entered a hill with curvy roads. Suddenly, a bus rushed down from the opposite side toward Gwangju. Trying to dodge it, our jeep slipped on the unpaved gravel road and rolled into a rice paddy about 1 meter (1 yard) below. I was seriously injured. At that moment, my vision turned yellow, and I was half-unconscious. My beloved wife and Jeong-eon appeared before my eyes. I've never experienced such an illusion in my life. After a few hours, other service members—officers heading to Sangmudae in Gwangju—rescued us and took us to the 77th Field Hospital of the Consolidated Combat Branch School. I thank God that the driver and company executive officer returned safely with minor injuries, and I'm grateful to the officers who discovered us and managed the accident.

I was taken to the 77th Army Field Hospital in Gwangju for emergency treatment. My injury was severe, and I was on the verge of death, receiving sub-morphine injections. My wife, shocked, hurriedly came with her father from Jeonju. I felt deeply sorry for her. We were about to start our family life, and there I was, lying in bed in a serious condition. It was an absurd sight for her. My wife cared for me with all her might, never leaving my side, in a poorly equipped patient ward. The Army field hospital in Gwangju couldn't continue my treatment, so I was transferred to Seoul's Capital Army Hospital (now Armed Forces Capital Hospital).

Thanks to God's blessings, I didn't suffer from fatal pain and began a stable life as a seriously ill patient. They discovered a simple fracture in my right hip bone, but the golden hour was missed. About six weeks later, my left leg was shortened by 2.5 centimeters (0.98 inches) as a result.

Despite the challenges I faced, the greatest concern everyone had for me was whether my "torn 5-millimeter (0.19 inches) thick ureter"—essentially a tube as thin as a matchstick—would heal naturally. If it didn't, I would lose a kidney, and my military career would be over. I found myself at another critical juncture in my life, where luck seemed to play a more significant role than medical intervention. After a month in the hospital, the "testing ink" continued to leak from my ureter, prompting the doctors to schedule surgery. They informed me of the date and rushed to prepare. However, on the night before the operation, a doctor conducting a final checkup exclaimed with a mix of seriousness and joy, slapping his knees, "It finally healed." Another doctor confirmed, "This is a miracle. You don't need surgery, and you can continue your military career." Once again, fate had seen me through a difficult time. What is a miracle, and what is fate? To me, they are manifestations of God's will, and I like to believe they stem from the protection of my late parents and the wisdom and love of my cherished family.

During my hospitalization, my wife came to Seoul with Jeong-eon to care for me. Her younger brothers were also in Seoul at the time, all exceptionally bright and talented. Park Eun-o, the eldest, had skipped grades in Jeonju and was attending Seoul Gyeonggi Middle School. Park Do-hyeon and Park Jin-seob, the second and third brothers, had also moved from Jeonju and were enrolled at Gyeongbok Middle School. We needed someone to look after them, so we secured a long-term lease on a house in Donggyo-dong, where they could stay with my family. My wife became the landlady and sponsor, and we hired a housekeeper, but she still faced hardships as a homemaker. I felt even more remorseful considering our financial struggles during my hospitalizationt.

♦ I recovered from the ICU of the Capital Army Hospital and lived as an instructor for the 107th ROTC of Yeonsei University

After overcoming these early life challenges, I was transferred to the Reserve Officer's Training Corps (the 107th ROTC) at Yonsei University. The ROTC at Yonsei was led by a colonel and included three captains and two administrative soldiers as instructors. It was housed on the first floor and basement of the College of Theology, west of Underwood's statue. We had no major issues with personnel, facilities, or our relationship with the university, but I recall a few notable episodes.

One such incident occurred when the dynamics between students, the ROTC, the university, and the broader political climate were intertwined. A year before my transfer, the "1963 Incident" had rocked the campus. Students had besieged soldiers who entered the campus during protests against the "normalization of relations between Korea and Japan," even seizing a soldier's gun before returning it. The atmosphere among students was tense, but I focused on rules, anti-communism, and national defense in my classes, regardless of the prevailing mood. I imagine students at Yonsei, particularly those sympathetic to communism, found my lectures awkward. However, I was unwavering, guided by the principles of correcting wrongs, national defense, and anti-communism I learned at KMA.

One day, a student I had grown closer to expressed concern, saying, "There are communists on campus, especially among commerce majors. They're active from time to time. You should be cautious when discussing 'anti-communism' in class." I shared his words openly in class, urging students to embrace anti-communism, though I didn't know any individuals personally to single out. Many student council presidents from prestigious universities, including SNU, were enrolled in the ROTC course. Both the government and universities viewed the ROTC positively, as it effectively restrained leaders of anti-government protests through military-style discipline and an emphasis on national security.

The path from Yonsei University's main gate to Underwood's statue was long and winding. A baseball field, soccer field, and grassy plaza lined the central path, providing ample space for outdoor military training. Initially, ROTC trainees were unfamiliar with this type of training, feeling self-conscious about female students witnessing their disciplinary exercises. However, these experiences soon became amusing anecdotes, and the trainees grew more adept. They particularly enjoyed the 'basic act drill,' the 36-direction march, and bayonet exercises I taught them. Even the female students' council became interested and interviewed us.

During the June 3rd Incident in 1964, the government declared martial law to suppress student protests against the Korea-Japan Summit. Military troops and police were deployed to universities to quell sit-ins and street protests. Despite this, students continued to resist, leading to repeated government crackdowns and attempts at persuasion. At Yonsei, major student groups resorted to hunger strikes near Underwood's statue when protests became difficult. The ROTC Department, where I worked, was located in the College of Theology building, just 100 meters from the statue, allowing me to observe their activities during work hours and night duty.

I witnessed what was dubbed the "hunger strike show by Yonsei University students," widely reported in Seoul newspapers. It appeared that ten representatives took turns sitting, standing, or lying around the statue, drinking milk instead of water, and engaging in discussions. When journalists arrived, they distributed brochures, read them aloud, and gestured to emphasize their points. After the journalists left, they rested. I suspect these journalists were their seniors or supporters. In the evening, female students brought meals, and the group switched with the next shift. They portrayed this "hunger strike by Yonsei University students on campus" in a romanticized manner in the media, while also leading on-campus protests. They attempted to march toward Sinchon Rotary and downtown, but were often stopped by police at the front gate.

One day, the demonstration group broke through the police line at Sinchon Rotary, passed Ewha Womans University, climbed Ahyeon Hill, and reached the three-way intersection at Seodaemun-Sinchon-Mapo. They aimed to head toward Seodaemun Station, but the police, anticipating their move, surrounded them at Ahyeon Three-way Intersection. The police quickly dispersed the protesters and arrested their leader. I had followed the group from the university, observing our ROTC students from the ROTC commander's jeep parked on a road toward Mapo. As expected, I saw students being chased and surrounded by police. Many ROTC students recognized me and the jeep, running toward me for refuge. I hid them and, once the situation calmed, helped them escape through a back alley. The remaining demonstrators retreated to Sinchon Rotary, with most seeking refuge at Ewha Womans University, despite it not being their school. They held a large protest on Ewha's playground, seemingly to impress the students there, but dispersed when they received no response. Most of these students were not seasoned protesters; they were more interested in the experience and the opportunity to boast to Ewha students, who tended to look down on Yonsei students at the timet.

♦ I let my boys pick themselves up

I, your grandpa, have always been a traditional Korean man, which meant I was often indifferent to my family and strict with my children. In Korea, professionals often work far from home, leading lives quite different from civilians. Consequently, I rarely had the time to focus on my family or show them the deep interest they deserved, particularly my children. This resulted in a weaker attachment to them compared to civilians. My life philosophy dictated that I let my boys pick themselves up, dust off their clothes, and keep moving even when they stumbled. I encouraged them to go outside alone and play with local kids in the alley, fostering independence and pioneering spirits, though it meant our bond didn't grow deeper.

Jeong-eon, my eldest son, loved playing outside from a young age, and everyone adored him. Local kids his age were especially fond of him, and a middle-aged lady who ran a shop on the street called him a “VIP customer” because whenever he took something for free, his mother would pay for it later. An old gentleman, a keeper of a large house, also liked Jeong-eon very much. Like me, he enjoyed adventures. Watching him, just a bit older than a toddler, crawl up a narrow cement wall and walk along it was nerve-wracking but also delightful because of his daring nature.

Our house was in an alley just behind northern Sinchon-ro, less than 100 meters from Donggyo-dong Three-way Intersection. Sometimes, he would ride on his mother's back to Sinchon Market, about 1 kilometer away, following the alley and crossing the back alley on the hill of Changcheon Three-way Intersection. One day, while his mother stepped out briefly, this toddler embarked on a daring journey to “find his mother by walking thousands of miles”—actually just 1 kilometer—all by himself. When he went missing, his mother and the neighbors were shocked and anxious. Meanwhile, he reached Sinchon Market, looking for his mother, covered in sweat. The stall owner they frequented noticed him and, realizing he was alone and lost, left her stall in someone else's care to bring him home. They met my wife on her way to find him, and we were truly grateful to that kind stall owner. The people living in the back alleys of Sinchon and Donggyo-dong were so kind at that time.

♦ My second child, Seong-eon, was born

Around 1965, we had another reason to celebrate: the birth of our second son, Seong-eon. Unlike with our first child, we were prepared, and his mother gave birth at Korea Hospital, a well-known hospital in downtown Seoul. Despite being born prematurely due to my overworking to secure a new house, he thankfully didn't need an incubator. From birth, he was an adorable and smart child, loved by his uncles, his mother's brothers, who lived with us. As he grew, he became smarter, and his uncles would test him from time to time. When we took our two sons out or on the bus, the locals in Hwagok-dong doted on him.

♦ We moved our own house, one of the national housing complex, Hwagok-dong

In 1965, construction began on the 'national housing' in Hwagok-dong, a large-scale village. We applied immediately and were fortunate to secure a house. It was the 59-square-yard home I had wanted, with a square-shaped yard on a 316-square-yard plot within a larger 383-square-yard land. I visited the construction site almost every weekend, inspecting it. Seeing the well-constructed prototype houses with reinforced concrete, I trusted the process and eagerly awaited our move-in day. In spring 1966, the first "national housing complex" in the Gangseo area of Seoul was completed, and we moved into our dainty and beautiful house. Although modest by today's standards, it was a significant achievement then. My financially successful older sister in Busan supported us with the house's cost, about 120,000 won at the time. Since then, we no longer needed to live in leased or rented homes. I believe fewer than ten of my KMA classmates owned their homes, even if just a small room, as military officials struggled to make ends meet.

The main road entering the housing complex in Hwagok-dong was only 8 meters wide, which would seem inadequate by today's standards, but it appeared vast back then. While I worked at the front, in Vietnam, and studied in Germany, my wife used her knowledge and wisdom to install wonderful block fences and iron gates and planted two cedar trees to commemorate our move. These trees were later designated as commemorative trees for Hwagok-dong's creation during its changes in the 2000s. She planted grass in the large yard, making our house the most beautiful in the 395,368-square-yard housing complex. Grass wasn't sold as a product then, so she asked a local male house cleaner to gather some from a nearby field. She planted it in rows with gaps, maintaining it to cover the yard in grass. Her efforts fulfilled my dream of having a European-style house with grass.

4. Back to the Front, Division S-3 for Counter-Espionage at Gukmang-bong peak, everyone in my compay volunteered to Vietnam

♦ Back at the front as Division Operations Officer (S-3) for counter-espionage and a company commander

During this time, I completed the Officer Advanced Course (OAC) at Gwangju Infantry School with excellent grades and returned to the main body. In spring 1966, I was transferred to the front, an opportunity to build my career. I reported to the division commander and requested to work in operations chiefs of staff, leading to my appointment as the operations officer (S-3), chief of staff of the division (G-3). The G-3 already had an experienced chief of operations, so I became the "operations officer for counter-espionage" for the division. North Korea was sending numerous spies and armed reconnaissance units to both front and rear to communize South Korea, emphasizing the importance of counter-espionage operations.

The 5th Division, a reserve division of the 5th Corps, was responsible for the central front and counter-espionage operations in the rear area. Troops were stationed on major invasion routes in the mountains, such as Gwangdeoksan

Mountain, Baekunsan Mountain, Domachibong Peak, Domachigogae Hill, Gukmangbong Peak, Gangssibong Peak, Ottugigogae Hill, and Seoul. Operations were carried out from Domachijae (Domachigogae Hill) to Route 124 (now National Route 75), Jeokmok-ri, Gapyeong, and Ottugigogae Hill's road from Jeokmok-ri to Gapyeongcheon Stream, or in the opposite direction. When enemy infiltration was reported, operations were conducted in a tiled troop placement across all areas without limits on period or mobilization until the enemy was neutralized. Counter-espionage squads were stationed at important points to search and reconnoiter during the day and conduct ambush operations at night. A standard operating procedure (SOP) was set to take immediate action (shoot enemies or capture them alive) and report afterward in emergencies.

As the division's operations officer for counter-espionage, I frequently drove a jeep to inspect and patrol the area, making decisions, suggestions, and carrying out operations. Major patrol routes included Yi-dong, Domachigogae Hill, Gwangdeokgogae Hill, Caramel Hill (Kim Il-sung Hill), Route 372, National Route 75 (formerly Route 124), Jeokmok-ri (a forest of red pine trees, as "jeokmok" means "red trees"), along Gapyeongcheon Stream to Ottugigogae Hill road or Domachigogae Hill road, returning to Il-dong or Yi-dong, or in the opposite direction. We found armed spies in this area, shooting or capturing them alive from 1964 to 1966.

A ridiculous episode occurred during this period, now a humorous lesson. It's called, "Platoon Leader! Shall I shoot him or not?" During a night operation with tile-shaped individual placement in the lockdown area, a spy appeared. Suddenly, a soldier couldn't decide whether to shoot, indicating insufficient training or ambiguous orders, and urgently asked the platoon leader. Such hesitation could allow the spy to escape and the operation to fail, highlighting the need for clear instructions and training.

♦ Everyone in the company volunteered to go to Vietnam with the company commander.

Following the Military Revolution of May 16th, Korea was among the poorest nations, with only a few third-world countries being worse off. Consequently, many Koreans aspired to go abroad. After the revolution, there was a strong desire among Koreans to study overseas, earn money in foreign lands, or simply gain international experience. Many college students applied for jobs as coal miners in West Germany, a position that was highly regarded. Female students who wished to attend college often applied to become nurses. They were eager to work in West Germany, an advanced nation, even if it meant taking on roles as coal miners or nurses, to earn money and pursue studies abroad.

During this period, changes in the human resources environment led to my transfer from the division's S-3 to a company commander position within the regiment. Just a month after my appointment as company commander in September 1966, I was ordered to join the second rotation of personnel being dispatched to Vietnam, a task I willingly volunteered for. The first group of troops, sent in 1965, was due to return after a year, necessitating their replacement. Many of my classmates had applied to be company commanders for the first dispatch and were already serving there. I believed that regular KMA graduates, especially combat arms officers, should have battle experience. Therefore, I decided to encourage my company's members, including myself, to apply for deployment to Vietnam.

I gathered all company members and presented the opportunity, emphasizing that it was not an order. I told them, "As men, you have the chance to go overseas, expand your knowledge, and demonstrate loyalty to the nation. As soldiers, you can also support your family financially, at least enough to buy a bull. The risk of loss or damage over a year is no different here than there." I also informed them that I would be applying as well. To my offer, every member of the company agreed to apply, expressing their willingness to go if they could serve under my command. Their commitment was genuine, with the phrase "with the company commander" being crucial.

Unfortunately, the first rotation was only a partial switch, meaning the entire troop couldn't be replaced at once; instead, replacements were made individually. Consequently, all applicants, including myself, were dispatched separately, preventing me from leading my company into Vietnam. I decided to depart first, asking for their understanding and promising to reunite on the battlefield in Vietnam. I bid them farewell, sincerely praying for their safety, success in battle, and safe return to Korea.

Captain Hong Seong-Tae, a military history officer for the Tiger Division in Vietnam and my KMA classmate, reached out to me. He expressed his desire to serve as an infantry combat company commander and asked me to succeed him. The timing seemed perfect.

Chapter 5

Serving in the Vietnam War as the Military History Officer for the Tiger Division

1. The Tiger Division's Encampment in Quy Nhon, Vietnam

♦ The Historical Context of (Free democracy) Vietnam's Defeat

Before delving into my experiences in the Vietnam War, it's essential to understand why Vietnam was ultimately defeated and collapsed, unlike Korea, and the international political circumstances that led to the ROK Armed Forces' involvement. Vietnam, also known as "Annam," was famous for its unique "Annam Rice," cultivated in a three-crop system. Geographically, Vietnam stretches vertically from south to north along the eastern coast of a Southeast Asian peninsula, bordering China to the north and Laos and Cambodia to the west. Unlike Korea, Vietnam's population comprises various ethnic groups. The Viets, who inhabit the plains, make up 90% of the population, while the remaining 10% are primarily mountain people from 53 different ethnic groups. These mountain people, driven to the rocky highlands by invasions, continue to lead primitive lives, harboring resentment towards the plains' inhabitants. Most narratives about Vietnam focus on the plains' people.

In terms of religion, the majority of Vietnamese are Buddhists (60%), followed by Catholics (20%), with the remaining 20% adhering to other faiths. Around 690 B.C., during Korea's Three Kingdoms Era, Vietnam established its first kingdom, only to be conquered by Chinese forces. In 938, Vietnam regained independence, successfully repelling continuous invasions by Chinese and Mongolian troops. However, around 1400, the nation split into northern and southern kingdoms along the 17th Parallel, a division reminiscent of Korea's Cheongcheongang River Line.

The two kingdoms eventually unified in the 1700s. Yet, in 1858, during Europe's colonial expansion in Asia, France invaded Vietnam. By 1885, the Bao Dai dynasty had become a puppet state, turning Vietnam into a French colony. In 1940, Japan invaded, and Vietnam became a dual colony under weakened Vichy France and Japan. After World War II, Vietnam was liberated from colonial rule, but unlike Korea, it failed to dismantle the Japanese system or implement land reforms. France, regaining strength, reasserted control.

Under the influence of international communism, Ho Chi Minh established a Vietnamese independence movement in the northern region in May 1941, akin to Korea's Provisional Government during the Japanese Colonial Era. This movement formed anti-French and anti-Japanese fronts, created "liberated zones," and prepared for a nationwide uprising. Ho Chi Minh emerged as a symbol of national liberation, similar to Korea's Rhee Syng-Man or Kim Koo. Following Japan's surrender on August 15th, 1945, Ho Chi Minh's forces established the Democratic Republic of Vietnam in Hanoi, with support from China and temporarily the United States, launching a nationwide independence movement and war against the returning French colonial power and the Bao Dai Puppet State. They achieved victory at the Battle of Dien Bien Phu in 1954, securing the regions north of the 17th Parallel and paving the way for unification two years later.

However, in 1955, Ngo Dinh Diem, backed by the United States, established the "Republic of Vietnam" in the south, implementing a nepotistic dictatorship. His corrupt rule and failure to reform the land alienated the populace. Consequently, southern communists, or Viet Cong (VC), formed the National Liberation Front for South Vietnam in 1960, integrating regional self-defense forces and launching an armed struggle to overthrow the government. Simultaneously, three regiments of the People's Army of Vietnam (North Vietnam, NV) infiltrated the south, connecting with the Viet Cong underground. The People's Army of Vietnam commander was already directing Viet Cong units in the central region.

Meanwhile, the United States sought to strengthen the Vietnamese front, fearing a "domino effect of communization" in Asia. In 1961, while I was studying at the Special Warfare School in the United States, President Kennedy established the Special Warfare Command and the U.S. Military Assistance Command in Vietnam (U.S. MAC.V) to support the Vietnamese government politically, militarily, and economically. Subsequently, he requested assistance from 25 allied nations to support the U.S. and Vietnamese government in May 1964.

♦ Korea's Military Assistance to Vietnam

Since 1962, the Korean government had analyzed President Kennedy's firm "anti-communism strategy," international political dynamics, and Korea's political situation, concluding that dispatching ROK Armed Forces to Vietnam was inevitable. Secretly, they contacted the United States and Vietnamese governments to prepare a military assistance strategy. Eventually, President Johnson of the United States officially requested military assistance from Korea. The Korean government outlined the reasons and national benefits for military assistance as follows:

1. It was necessary to support the Republic of Vietnam, a free ally indirectly influencing Korea's national defense.
2. It was a gesture of gratitude for the assistance from allied nations during the Korean War, fulfilling an ethical obligation to combat communism together.
3. The United States, Korea's ally, had made a request.
4. The Vietnamese government had made a request.
5. It aligned with the spirit of "maintaining international peace and renouncing all aggressive wars" as stated in Article 4 of the Constitution.

Undoubtedly, the Korean government also considered the economic benefits of participating in Vietnam's post-war reconstruction, the potential to earn dollars through combat duty allowances, and the opportunity to enhance Korea's military capabilities by deploying two divisions.

Thus, the government dispatched the 1st Mobile Army Surgical Hospital to Vung Tau and the Taekwondo Instructor Unit to military academies and infantry schools of the Army and Navy as the first dispatch in September 1964. Subsequently, the ROK Military Assistance Command (The Dove Division), comprising mixed brigades from each armed force, a military engineer battalion, a transport vehicle company, Marine Corps and Air Force companies, the Navy transport unit (LST), and the pre-dispatched 1st Mobile Army Surgical Hospital and Taekwondo Instructor Unit, along with a security battalion, were sent as the second dispatch in March 1965.

The third deployment involved a comprehensive support team with combat units. The Tiger Division (Capital Division) and the 2nd Regiment of the Marine Corps (newly established Blue Dragon Division) were selected and dispatched to Quy Nhon in Binh Dinh in the central region and Cam Ranh Bay in the southern region, respectively. The following year, the 9th Division of the Army (White Horse Division) was sent to Ninh Hoa, just south of the Tiger Division's location.

♦ The Tiger Division camped ut in Quy Nhon, middle Vietnam

The Tiger Division set up camp in Quy Nhon, Vietnam. Positioned in Quy Nhon, Binh Dinh, in central Vietnam in October 1965, the Tiger Division received a tactical area of responsibility (TAOR) of 1,200 square kilometers (296,526 acres) from the U.S. Army and the Vietnamese Army. They occupied strategic points with combat companies and established a circular defense line, which served as the tactical base for the company. The division's command center also set up an independent defensive position by securing major central points. Simultaneously, all units conducted pacification operations to eliminate Viet Cong forces and carried out psychological operations targeting both the Viet Cong and local residents within the TAORs. During my assignment from October 1965 to November 1966, combat operations commenced as soon as the Tiger Division settled in. Records indicate that company-level operations occurred hourly and daily, with 30 battalion-level operations, 12 regiment-level operations, and three division-level operations taking place.

2. The Document of Military History of the ROK Armed Forces' Expedition to Vietnam was recorded as one of the greatest exemplary Military Histories of the ROK Armed Forces

♦ Professor Capt. Hong Seong-Tae at KMA organized the 'Department of Military History' for the first time in the ROK Armed Forces, his achievement and detailed battle reports were significant

The military history of the ROK Armed Forces' expedition to Vietnam is documented as one of the most exemplary in ROK Armed Forces history. Professor Hong Seong-Tae (Captain) at the Korea Military Academy (KMA) established the 'Department of Military History' for the first time in the ROK Armed Forces. After KMA in Taereung opened, military history education primarily relied on translated American military academy textbooks, which focused on European and American military history. Even the Korean War was taught using American records, resulting in principles and lessons tailored for foreign armed forces. Many records of Korea's ancient military history and the Korean War's military history were either nonexistent or unorganized, making them unsuitable as textbooks. I earnestly hoped that the ROK Armed Forces would establish and maintain a "Department of Military History" at the division level, not just during wartime but at all times. Captain Hong Seong-Tae, a military history professor at KMA during the organization of expedition troops to Vietnam, proposed the idea to Army Headquarters and successfully established a "Department of Military History" within the G-3 of a Division. He was subsequently dispatched to Vietnam to oversee the Tiger Division's Department of Military History.

♦ I mineded 'Tigers Are On There Way' to the battlefield in Vietnam, leaving my family in Korea

Responding to Captain Hong Seong-Tae's request, I was hastily assigned to the 2nd Group to replace the 1st deployment in November 1966. I bypassed the training center for Vietnam deployment in Oeum-ri, near Chuncheon, and joined the main contingent of the 2nd Group, who were about to depart from Chuncheon Train Station. Many Chuncheon citizens and students gathered at the station to bid us farewell. Our train stopped at Cheongnyang-ni Station in Seoul, where representatives of Seoul's citizens, along with my family—my beloved wife and two sons—joined the crowd to see us off. I had to explain and persuade my wife for a long time about going to the battlefield, and I felt deep sorrow thinking about how my family might feel until my safe return. However, this was the duty, responsibility, and fate of a military serviceperson. As we said our goodbyes at Cheongnyang-ni Station, my wife handed me a crocodile skin wallet as a talisman. In that moment, emotions and thoughts of leaving my family behind for the battlefield surged within me. That wallet remained in my pocket, never placed elsewhere, until it was worn out and unusable. As the train departed, I silently prayed, "Please let my wife and children be well for the next year without worrying about me."

The train journeyed through the southern part of the Korean peninsula, and we finally arrived at Busan Main Station, where we transferred to an American cruise ship (about 20,000 tons) at the 3rd Harbor. Busan citizens also gathered to send us off, including my elder brother, who ran a business in Busan and came to see me off with his trust in his brother. I felt that warriors heading to the battlefield should be sent off by their families and the nation. We departed the 3rd Harbor with the ship's horn sounding. As the waves of the Taegeukgi, the national flag, waved by the crowd and my brother at the harbor faded from view, I was once again overcome with emotion. After a week-long voyage, we arrived in Quy Nhon, Binh Dinh, in central Vietnam in November 1965, and I reported for duty with the Tiger Division.

The farewell song "Tigers are on their way," heard at Chuncheon Station, Cheongnyangni Station, and Busan Harbor, resonated with us:

(1) You protected the nation for unification in liberty and are now selected in the name of our nation.
The Tiger Division, Tiger Warriors, though the lands and skies of Vietnam are far away, we are one and we will follow you, we are one and we will follow you.

(2) You grew your strength for unification in liberty, so you can go anywhere for the nation.
The Tiger Division, Tiger Warriors, once you're under the skies of divided Vietnam, show them the mighty spirits of Hwarangdo.

(3) The hearts of those who leave and those who stay came together as one for Korea.
The Tiger Division, Tiger Warriors, no enemies are different wherever Taegeukgi flies.
You will defeat, fight, and win, and let your names be known. You will defeat, fight, and win, and let your names be known.

♦ I spread military 'lessens-learned' y inspecting battlefields

One of my responsibilities as the division's chief military history officer was to document and disseminate lessons learned from battles. This involved analyzing military history records, on-site observations, reports, and verbal accounts, often relying on one or two military officers assigned to the department. In cases of 'contingency conflict' or accidental actions, which occurred frequently, we quickly visited the site to assess the situation, evaluate it, and derive military lessons. I made it a priority to visit scenes of conflict to observe, listen, and make decisions. On occasion, I arrived at sites raided by the Viet Cong before others and analyzed the scene alone, putting myself in danger. During operation meetings at the division or operations command post, I observed everything carefully, though some subordinate commanders misunderstood my presence. This was my daily routine. I attended the daily situation briefing at the division's situation room with the division commander each morning to understand the day's operations. I then loaded a box of the U.S. Army's C-Ration onto a jeep and went on patrol with an armed driver, often around the operating regiment command center and major points. I ventured into the battlefield, relying on luck.

Sometimes I passed through downtown Quy Nhon, but mostly I traveled through sparsely populated villages, mountains, and lands. I drove for hours, covering dozens of kilometers to reach destinations, and occasionally visited multiple spots in one day. While I usually returned to the division in the evening, I sometimes spent nights at field command posts. For division operations, I stayed at the front's tactical command post for several days, attending operation meetings and situation rooms, and observing the battlefield. After the situation concluded, I sent a military history officer to different operation scenes and wrote the first draft of the military history record in the Department of Military History's Quonset hut. Once the draft was completed, the first sergeant prepared to type it on a Hangul typewriter. However, the typewriter often broke down, so I used blue carbon copy paper with candle wax on a metal plate and handwrote each letter with a carbon copy pen. I frequently lost track of time and stayed up all night during this process.

3. Experiencing the scene of operations, OP. Tiger, The 8th · Honggildong · Ojakyo

♦ OP. Tiger and OP. 8th began

Experiencing the scenes of operations, OP Maengho (Tiger), the 8th OP Hong Gil-dong, and OP Ojakgyo (The Bridge of Crows and Magpies) was an integral part of my role. The ROK Armed Forces in Vietnam devised and executed a strategy for the Vietnam War known as the "counter-guerrilla operation." This operation aimed to expand control from specific points to lines, and then from lines to entire areas. The ultimate goal was to completely dominate the initially assigned Tactical Area of Responsibility (TAOR) through this "surface operation." Initially, we fortified each company post at key locations within the TAOR. Each company then patrolled its surrounding area to assert control through intimidating fire, forced reconnaissance, or covert reconnaissance (company-level operations). Following this, we conducted operations to clear and control the areas between company bases (battalion-level operations) and then between battalion bases (regiment-level operations). We continued to expand operations within the TAOR to completely clear enemy strongholds and extend the controllable area as part of division-level operations.

When I joined, our Tiger Division was engaged in "OP Tiger, The 5th and The 6th," division-level operations that significantly expanded our TAOR northward by 1,400 square kilometers (345,947 acres). The next phase involved moving southward, which meant that our division would soon conduct operations to connect with the "White Horse Division" (the 9th Division in the Tuy Hoa area) as it expanded northward. This expansion southward was named "OP Tiger, the 8th." According to military history records, one key point for our forces was "Deo Cu Mong," a ridge located on the route to Song Cau, a coastal village south of Quy Nhon along National Route 1. It was about 40 kilometers (24 miles) in a straight line, or 60 kilometers (37 miles) by road from Quy Nhon, and was already a significant site in Vietnamese history. In the 15th century, Vietnam was divided into two dynasties, north and south, with Deo Cu Mong serving as a central point akin to Korea's Panmunjom. It continued to play this role until "OP Tiger, the 8th" after 1965.

After the Tiger Division received the TAOR, these areas were technically under Vietnamese administration but were "Vietnam during the day, Viet Cong territory at night." Deo Cu Mong was the sole meeting point on the border with the southern region (Song Cau) controlled by the Viet Cong, effectively a liberated zone. Therefore, the Tiger Division opened a market on this ridge to facilitate trade between the north and south, drawing from Korea's historical experience of division. This allowed minimal communication between neighbors in a divided country and provided us with intelligence on the enemy region in the south. Aware of this, I often visited the ridge to observe the market activities after my assignment.

When the operation began, the plan was as follows: The main target was Song Cau, south of Deo Cu Mong. There was no specific line of departure (LD); instead, each unit had helicopter platforms, and the time of departure (H-hour) was when the first helicopters took off. The initial operation control line was formed by connecting the landing zones (LZ) of each unit, effectively besieging the target area. Units were transported to nearby heights by U.S. Army helicopters (UH-1H, carrying nine armed soldiers) and landed there. If defoliants failed to clear landing points, rope repelling was used for quick landings. The units then moved through the jungle to reach downtown Song Cau (actually a small village) and clear Viet Cong hideouts. As they descended, they tightened the siege (the "rabbit-herding tactic") and subdued the Viet Cong herded into the plains, securing the area. They then initiated pacification operations to establish a new administrative body and stabilize public sentiment, transferring sovereignty (especially administrative rights) to the Vietnamese government as soon as feasible.

The D-Day and H-Hour were set for 10:30 on January 3, 1967. I traveled to Deo Cu Mong early at dawn, as National Route 1 was the only road to the operation area. It was the sole assembly area on the ridge and the critical point where the front TCP was located. I observed the battle unfold as merchants from Song Cau walked to Deo Cu Mong Market, setting up stalls to trade with merchants from Quy Nhon, despite the Viet Cong blocking paths to National Route 1. A rainstorm had persisted all night and continued at 35 knots that day. At 10:30, about 150 merchants from both north and south were detained. Simultaneously, dozens of shells bombarded downtown Song Cau, and the combat arms troop (including the division's reconnaissance company) advanced south along the left coastline, firing rifles. Numerous helicopters filled the sky. Merchants from Song Cau were terrified, crying and moaning at the sight, as the area and its residents were thrust from peace into war.

Division Commander Yu Byeong-Hyeon established mobile TCPs for the division at the 26th Regiment's TCP on Deo Cu Mong, fully supporting the 26th Regiment's commander in operations. He occasionally flew over the battlefield in a helicopter (not a special command helicopter) to observe and then returned to command the operation. On the second day, I advanced 2 kilometers (1.2 miles) south along National Route 1 with an agent from the reconnaissance company. The following day, I entered Chanh Loc, a village in Song Cau seized by our forces, with the 26th Regiment's commander and a bodyguard soldier from the 2nd Company. "National Route 1" was severed in 50-meter (54-yard) sections, and refugees wandered the village with their belongings, resembling flood victims.

On the fifth day, I rode an armored vehicle with the division commander along the repaired National Route 1. We entered the center of Song Cau after overcoming armed resistance, where residents welcomed us. We immediately discussed future administration with resident representatives, surrounded by the local populace. The division commander encouraged them to elect a new administrative leader (possibly at the governor level) and establish local autonomy. Although the order was maintained by our commander's directive during wartime, he promised to restore autonomous administration post-battle, as the ROK Armed Forces did not intend to impose prolonged military rule. Grateful for the ROK Armed Forces' unexpected actions, the residents quickly moved to elect a new leader. However, hidden Viet Cong shot the candidates (two individuals), causing prolonged struggles.

In the middle of Song Cau's Armed Forces, a plaza covered in palm tree jungle housed a concentration camp for refugees and the "Hamlet" area on one side, and a camp for 400 to 500 prisoners of war, many of whom were female, on the other. Distinguishing real Viet Cong captured in battle from semi-Viet Cong merely wandering around was challenging. Thus, we initially detained them in concentration camps and later interrogated them to gather battle intelligence and identify genuine Viet Cong. Real prisoners were then transferred to the governmental army. Surprisingly, more real prisoners emerged from the refugee camp, highlighting the Viet Cong's skill at concealing their identities. The civilians were naive, so when we offered money for guns, they surrendered two to three guns each, allowing us to collect hundreds of weapons swiftly.

By February 1, "OP Tiger, the 8th" concluded, and stabilization operations commenced. We released residents from the "Hamlet" concentration camp and transferred 480 sorted prisoners of war to the Vietnamese Armed Forces. Ah, that Deo Cu Mong! That ridge held legend, tragedy, sadness, and hope. I'm sure it will be remembered as a legend alongside the Tiger Division's story. When the operation ended, my only task was to sit at a desk in a Quonset hut in the tropical area and document military history. I completed the record in one and a half months, by mid-April. Two 10-centimeter (3.9-inch) ballpoint pens were exhausted, and the carbon copy pen's tip became too dull to use.

♦ OP Ojakgyo (Bridge of Crows and Magpies); March 1967-May 1967

Following OP Tiger, OP Ojakgyo (The Bridge of Crows and Magpies) was conducted from March to May of the same year, as planned by the ROK Armed Forces' command center in Vietnam. This operation aimed to truly implement the "expansion of surface" strategy, a hallmark of the ROK Armed Forces' counter-guerrilla operations. Through this operation, the Tiger Division (Capital Division) and the White Horse Division (The 9th Division) expanded their TAORs southward and northward, respectively, ultimately connecting with each other.

The area of operation was along the coastal road of National Route 1, stretching from Song Cau, under the Tiger Division, to Tuy Hoa, under the White Horse Division. This was a corps-level operation supported by not only the U.S. Army's helicopter unit but also the Navy and the Air Force. As a result of the operation, the two divisions of the ROK Armed Forces connected these regions, recovering and stabilizing 400 kilometers (248 miles) of National Route 1. The TAOR, under the Vietnamese government's administration and military regions, expanded by 6,800 square kilometers (1.68 million acres, about three times the size of Jeju Island) and was securely obtained. I was focused on documenting OP Tiger, the 8th, so I entrusted the record-keeping of this operation to Noh Yeong-han, a junior alumnus from the 16th class of KMA. Our Department of Military History consisted of one captain, one first lieutenant, and one first sergeant working under me.

♦ OP Hong Gil-dong (July 1967-August 1967), the TCP of the division was attacked

The command of the ROK Armed Forces in Vietnam aimed to prepare for the Vietnamese government's Presidential election, eliminate remaining enemies (including one regular regiment of the People's Army of Vietnam) within the expanded TAOR, and conduct stabilization operations. The Tiger Division and the White Horse Division were particularly focused on clearing out remaining enemies in the areas occupied by OP Ojakgyo. This operation, named 'OP Hong Gil-dong,' was conducted with assistance from the U.S. Army's artillery, helicopter unit, and the U.S. Air Force's strategic bombardment (Arc Light), among others. Our Tiger Division also aimed to expand the placement of the 26th Regiment and secure stabilization in the expanded regions. Anticipating close combat with North Vietnam's regular army (People's Army of Vietnam), we reinforced our war preparations. The division's command center installed a tactical combat post (TAC. CP) at the front, advancing to the area of the 26th Regiment's headquarters in the southern part of the Division. The 'Arc Light Bombardment' by B-52 strategic bombers of the U.S. Air Force targeted the enemy's area before the operation began.

Three formations of B-52 strategic bombers per sortie, each loaded with 108 bombs, took off from bases in the Pacific Ocean (usually Guam), crossed the Pacific, and dropped 100 tons of bombs on target areas where Vietnamese enemies were concentrated, annihilating 1.6 square kilometers (395 acres) immediately. By 1967, 1,200 sorties had been flown, and more than 1 million tons of bombs, twice the amount used during the Korean War, had been expended. I witnessed areas with dozens of giant craters, 10 meters deep and 10 meters long, resembling the aftermath of the Iri Station explosion in Korea. However, the Soviet Union's fleet, positioned along the route, informed North Vietnam of the bombers, who then alerted the Viet Cong, resulting in minimal casualties. A Viet Cong commander later confessed that the deafening noise, the formation of giant craters, and the psychological pressure from the fear of raids significantly impacted the Viet Cong's morale.

I went to the helicopter pickup zone, cleared by defoliant, early at dawn before the departure time of 07:15, when the attacking unit would land in the operational area. As we waited for the helicopters, officers and soldiers gathered in squads, playing a hopping game to relax and boost their spirits. On the evening of the 15th, about a week into the operation without spotting the enemy's main forces—they either fled or hid in tunnels—all TCP agents, except those on night duty, gathered to watch an American movie screened for military personnel before public release to boost morale. Suddenly, a noise erupted, "Bang! Clank!" A shell landed 150 meters (164 yards) away. Initially, I thought the bombardment was distant, but another shell soon followed. We dispersed, and most of us, including the Chief of Staff, ran into a nearby trench. The division commander remained in a command vehicle.

Shells flew overhead, "Swoosh! Whoosh!" with another "Bang! Clank!" behind us. It seemed the enemy targeted the officers' barracks and command center. I counted 12 shells! The enemy's 82-millimeter mortar bombs targeted the officers' barracks, and the 57-millimeter recoilless rifle aimed at the movie audience, but they narrowly missed, flying 10 meters overhead. Thankfully, we suffered no major damage, but one classmate was lightly injured by shell fragments while showering and was hospitalized. The regimental commander promptly ordered the reserve unit, the regiment's headquarters company, to search and clear the firing spot on the hill opposite us, leaving a guard group behind. The enemy had already fled, so the main force withdrew after reconnaissance, leaving one squad armed with Claymore mines to guard the area.

Around 23:00, an accident occurred with an explosion. An inexperienced agent from the headquarters company, tasked with guarding the spot, mistakenly installed a Claymore mine in the wrong direction and accidentally triggered it, causing it to explode toward the squad, resulting in six deaths and three injuries. A 'Dust Off' rescue helicopter quickly transported them. The "ta ta ta ta" sound of the Dust Off helicopter's rotor blades (UH-1H) traumatized me for life, along with that situation.

♦ Joined the search operation in Viet Cong's territory

On July 18th, I joined a search operation in a valley under 'Ba Mountain' with the reconnaissance company and G-2 (Lt. Colonel, the division's intelligence staff). As we navigated the rugged path through dense jungle, it was evident this was a Viet Cong base and battleground. A Vietnamese conical hat lay next to a skull on the ground. Personal trenches and misfired booby traps were scattered throughout. After three hours of trekking, wiping sweat, and scanning our surroundings, we reached the peak and found a hut and cultivated land. We conducted a close combat search and, finding no resistance, thoroughly searched, burned the house, and moved on. I picked a pineapple as big as a Korean melon from a garden, peeled it with a knife, and savored its fresh taste—unforgettable. As darkness fell around 18:30, I parted from the company and returned to the helicopter.

On the 21st, I joined another jungle reconnaissance operation with G-2, accompanied by the 12th Company, 3rd Battalion of the Armored Regiment (in name only, not armored), and followed two POWs from North Vietnam as they led us to their battalion's headquarters. After three hours of cautious jungle navigation, we arrived to find the battalion had vacated three days prior, leaving only traces. The site had a small training ground, medical facilities, the battalion commander's room, communication facilities, and a large well. It seemed they fled when the rainbow-colored blades of Hong Gil-dong flashed. We got lost on the way back and called for an O-1, but the prisoners guided us safely back.

4. The truth of the Vietnam War in the 1960s, and trivia about the ROK Army and the U.S. Army

♦ President Kennedy's passionate involvement and Secretary of Defense McNamara's regrets

As detailed in the chapter on studying in the United States, President Kennedy recognized the deception of Khrushchev's "Peaceful Coexistence Theory" and established the concept of "Special Warfare" in the early 1960s, involving political conspiracy battles, and was deeply involved in the Vietnam War. According to the novel 'Green Beret,' he deployed Green Beret troops in cities, though I couldn't confirm this. He recruited mountain people (Mountaineers)—native Vietnamese who took refuge in the mountains from invaders—who disliked the plains-dwelling Vietnamese. They were stationed in mountain areas along the border (on the southbound route for the North Vietnamese Army, at border surveillance spots with Cambodia), known as the "Ho Chi Minh Route." The Green Beret established bases there to observe and block North Vietnamese Army infiltration, known as the Civilian Irregular Defense Group (CIDG).

Robert McNamara, the Secretary of Defense during the Kennedy and Johnson administrations, once asserted the "scientific," or quantification, of war. This included the Planning, Programming, Budgeting System (PPBS) theory, which gained popularity in international politics for a time. He conducted a "War Game" around 1968, which suggested that the Vietnam War had effectively ended in 1966 with a U.S. victory. However, McNamara later expressed skepticism about this theory as the reality became increasingly unfavorable. In his 1995 memoir, he admitted to regretting the Vietnam War, acknowledging his misjudgment of the Vietnamese people's resolve.

♦ Material War in Vietnam by the U.S., a Wealthy Country

As I have mentioned, and as evidenced by the "Arc Light Bombardment" or Carpet Bombing, the United States is likely the only country capable of deploying unimaginably vast quantities of materials in wars and battles. A supply sergeant from the first ROK Army dispatch to Vietnam visited a U.S. Army supply depot and submitted a requisition for 435 items. The U.S. serviceperson in charge smiled, added two to three zeros to the order, and loaded boxes of supplies onto the vehicle. The ROK Army was initially impressed by the abundant U.S. support and soon developed a habit of applying for and receiving supplies in this manner, assuming it was standard practice. They requested items like canteens, shovels, and bandoliers lost or damaged in battle, treating them as expendable supplies. After each battle, they would apply for replacements and receive them. They also received a seemingly endless supply of C-Rations, the combat food, consuming them readily. By the 1970s, records showed that the ROK Army had used seven years' worth of C-Rations in just three years.

After battles, each platoon received a "consolation set," a large box filled with personal preference items such as cigarettes, coffee cookies, canned food, and bulk chocolate. The U.S. Army provided the ROK Army with both American C-Rations and Korean rice, ensuring more than enough food. The division's command center even traded Korean rice for vegetables at local Vietnamese markets to supply the officers' mess hall. Soldiers would joke, "The officers get vegetables while we get nothing but meat," a popular phrase at the time.

On December 25, 1966, Christmas Day, each unit received numerous gift boxes and paper Christmas trees. An L-19 liaison airplane flew over the ROK Army base, playing "White Christmas" to lift spirits amidst the tropical warfare. Combat duty allowances were paid to all ROK Army officers and soldiers, varying by rank. Captains received $150 per month. If they spent $30 locally and sent the remaining $120 to their families in Korea, the savings could amount to 300,000 won in a year—enough to buy a 49-square-meter national house in the suburbs of Seoul. Soldiers from farming villages could even afford to buy bulls. Combat units were paid in Vietnamese currency (about $100 per month) for pacification operations, which company commanders used to engage with local residents.

Additionally, compensatory payments are made to those physically disabled by defoliants, ranging from 700,000 to 1.5 million won ($600 to $1300) monthly, benefiting both veterans and their families. I, too, suffer from ischemic heart disease due to defoliant exposure and receive this allowance. The U.S. is likely the only country capable of such support, both now and in the future.

I often visited U.S. Army gas stations near the road to refuel my vehicle, always receiving a warm welcome and unlimited gasoline. Before heading to the battlefield, I would leave with a box of six American C-Rations, ensuring plenty of food for my driver and me. A cozy "officer's club" was established at the division's command center, offering free spirits, coffee, and soft drinks like lemon-lime soda, all supported by the U.S. Army.

U.S. Army bases operated PXs (convenience stores) in each region, selling everything from necessities to luxury goods duty-free. American service members could order items for delivery to their homes or as they transferred to rear areas. The PXs stocked everything from color TVs and Japanese-made appliances to French cosmetics like Chanel No. 5. The U.S. imported Japanese goods to boost Japan's economy and democratize the country, granting special tariff privileges. Consequently, PXs were filled with Japanese products. ROK Army troops also operated PXs, though some items like household appliances were restricted, while French cosmetics were always available.

♦ The U.S. Armed Forces Won Tactically, but Lost Strategically

The U.S. Armed Forces and its personnel were excellent, brave, and optimistic, often exceeding their formal responsibilities. They were superior to the North Vietnamese Army and Viet Cong, equipped with reconnaissance and satellite photos, helicopters, M-16 rifles, and Arc Light Bombardment. Commandos flew low over enemy areas, standing on helicopter platforms to search and eliminate enemies. Pilots completed missions despite enemy fire and rainstorms. Fire support officers, usually majors, would relax at the officer's club but were always ready to fulfill their duties promptly.

The U.S. Armed Forces' tactics and personnel were exemplary, but the national and military strategies failed in Vietnam. Like Japan's failed "strategy of dots and lines" in China, the U.S. relied on material and maneuver warfare, focusing on capturing key points without securing lines or surfaces. They believed annihilating enemy forces would ensure victory, but this approach was ineffective in guerrilla warfare, especially in the jungle.

U.S. intelligence, though accurate, took three days to process and deliver to combat units, allowing enemies to escape. The U.S. Armed Forces' reliance on strategic bombardment and key strikes proved ineffective in guerrilla warfare, as demonstrated again during the 2022 withdrawal from Afghanistan.

In Vietnam, the U.S. Armed Forces, with ample air and firepower, established bases in strategic areas, gathering intelligence and conducting reconnaissance. They deployed strike units via helicopters for "Search & Destroy" missions, believing enemy forces would weaken with each defeat. However, this approach was ineffective against guerrilla tactics, as enemies quickly evacuated within two to three days.

♦ The ROK Armed Forces' strategies and operations in the Vietnam War

The ROK Armed Forces had a fundamentally different approach to strategy, partly due to a lack of resources for maneuver warfare. Their philosophy was, "Victory in battle is achieved when an infantry soldier stands their ground until the end." Even in areas under Vietnamese government control, the ROK Armed Forces sought tactical areas of responsibility (TAOR), focusing on surface operations. After securing an area with military force, we conducted pacification operations on the residents (counter-insurgency) to prevent guerrilla forces from regaining control and to expand our territory incrementally. However, this strategy required deploying more military power and restoring the combat capabilities of the Vietnamese Armed Forces to achieve a decisive victory in the Vietnam War, which we were unable to fully accomplish.

In Vietnam, the ROK Armed Forces employed the 'Oppress and Knead

Operation' and the 'Rabbit-herding Operation (Hammerhead-Anvil OP)' both tactically and strategically. In division-level operations, a large military force would simultaneously besiege the enemy in the jungle using helicopters and ground maneuvers, executing the Hammer and Anvil tactic to conclude the operation. The besieging forces would then tighten the encirclement, driving the enemy toward the anvil. We would return to previously passed areas to search for and eliminate enemies hiding in underground tunnels or fields, conducting thorough mop-up operations. Occasionally, by order of the division commander, General Yu Byeong-Hyeon, all landed troops would first secure the surroundings and delay the rabbit-herding siege operation for a few days, despite subordinate commanders' concerns about losing the encircled enemies. The division commander's intention seemed to be to minimize our losses in less intense battles—possibly a discreet request from President Park Chung-Hee—and allow the enemy to evacuate or run into the encirclement on their own, rather than hastily tightening the siege. After maintaining the situation for a while, we would advance all at once, driving the enemies toward the plains.

♦ **Wins and losses on the battlefield are common occurrences. War involves attack and defense, success and failure, achievements and losses. As the saying goes, "Wins and losses on the battlefield happen all the time." Here are some regretful losses I experienced and witnessed. One day, a battalion commander from the armor regiment, my senior from the Korean Military Academy, was ambushed by the Viet Cong while patrolling a company base near An Khe Pass on Route 19, heading to Pleiku. Despite fighting back fiercely, he was killed. A company in the same regiment mistakenly shot and killed three women near a banana orchard, mistaking them for Viet Cong. They were, in fact, local residents. A few days later, the Viet Cong ambushed a reconnaissance squad securing a supply route, resulting in the brutal killing or wounding of the entire squad and the loss of all equipment, including handheld transceivers.**

This was the worst incident in the Tiger Division's history in Vietnam. I quickly assessed the situation and disseminated the lessons learned. The division held a military court trial, severely punishing the company commander and sending him back to Korea. Additionally, the 2nd company of the 26th regiment was raided by the Viet Cong at their base due to negligence in guard duty, resulting in 11 deaths and 22 injuries, along with the loss of weapons and C-Rations. This was a disgraceful day for the Tiger Division. The following day, a platoon from the 1st regiment, considered the best, fell into a Viet Cong ambush, leading to another disaster with one officer and 18 soldiers killed (three wounded). Some combat agents from a main regiment were also killed or wounded during the Hong Gil-dong Operation. The 5th Company was attacked during lunch, resulting in five deaths and six injuries. Tragically, the platoon leader was killed just three days after arriving in Vietnam, deeply affecting his comrades. There was also an incident where a 4.2-inch mortar battery was miscalculated, firing at the wrong angle and killing an entire squad. Major Kim from the division's command center died in a helicopter accident while en route to the U.S. Army base in Pleiku to purchase gifts shortly before returning to Korea.

♦ Psychology on the battlefield: Perhaps 'Bbongjjak' music (Trot), the Arirang magazine, and cigarettes were our only joys.

War philosopher Clausewitz once said, "War is a horrendous thing." A Korean War veteran remarked, "I cannot speak of the situations in battle, so don't even ask me about that." This is true, as describing the battlefield and the psychological phenomena that occur is incredibly challenging. (From my Vietnam War diary) I received information about an ambush where five Viet Cong officials, including a finance officer, were killed. The next day, I visited the scene with the G-2 officer by helicopter, hoping to gather important information. Upon landing, the stench of rotting corpses filled the air, reminding us of the battlefield even before we saw them. Five Viet Cong corpses lay side by side, with our combat agents on guard. One of the corpses was female, reportedly the highest-ranking official. Thanks to the company commander's guidance, I understood the combat situation based on prior information. I received documents taken from the scene for analysis to aid future operations. As I turned away, soldiers were handling the corpses, some searching the woman's body. The U.S. Army had various ways to boost morale, including visits from popular actors and actresses and early movie releases on the battlefield. Korea lacked such traditions, but we had "consolation performances" at military bases. Famous Korean singers visited at least once or twice a year. On one occasion, 'Patti Kim' and lyricist 'Gil Ok-yun' performed. However, Patti Kim's performance, featuring English songs and self-promotion, did not resonate with our troops, leading to boos and demands for her to leave. In contrast, when popular "Bbongjjak" genre singers like Lee Mi-ja, Hyun-mi, and Kim Serena performed, the atmosphere was electric, with soldiers singing and dancing enthusiastically. This stark difference highlighted the homesickness and "psychology on the battlefield." Often, the Arirang magazine, popular Korean songs, and cigarettes were our only sources of joy.

♦ Why Vietnam and the U.S. were defeated and collapsed, – "Saigon Dep Lam" -

In the summer of 1967, an American journalist visited my Quonset office and inquired about my perspective on the Vietnam War. Without hesitation, I responded, "Vietnam will be defeated and collapse within five minutes if the U.S. Armed Forces withdraw." On the morning of April 30th, 1975, when the last U.S. helicopter departed and the United States completed its withdrawal, the Vietnamese government surrendered unconditionally just two hours later, at 10:00 AM. This marked one of the rare defeats in U.S. military history. The root causes of this defeat lay in the American politicians' "misjudgment of national interests and misguided strategic choices." Key terms that defined U.S. defense strategies at the time included Kissinger's "Realpolitik," "Détente," Nixon's "Balance of Power," and the "China Card," among others. These beliefs led the United States to allow politics to overshadow military strategy once again, as it had during the Korean War. The U.S. pursued flawed national strategies, effectively agreeing to an armistice with communist North Vietnam under the guise of a "peace agreement," which forced the U.S. Armed Forces, despite their tactical superiority, to endure defeat.

Of course, the United States was not solely to blame. Vietnam itself bore responsibility for the direct causes of its defeat. A look at Vietnamese history reveals that when French imperialists invaded Vietnam during the early days of European colonial expansion in Asia, they turned the feudal Bao Dai dynasty into a puppet state. In response, nationalists launched a tenacious resistance movement for independence. Unlike Korea's Provisional Government, Vietnam was governed by international communism, particularly Ho Chi Minh's party, which received support from the Chinese Communist Party. When the French imperialists and Emperor Bao Dai attempted to maintain control over Vietnam after World War II, Ho Chi Minh's party, with backing from the Chinese Communist Party, took control of the north of the 17th Parallel. The Communist International Movement and national independence activists in South Vietnam (Viet Cong) joined forces to overthrow the colonial system and achieve independence, sparking the Vietnam War. Consequently, public sentiment in Vietnam largely supported Ho Chi Minh, and the national independence movement continued to grow fervently.

Just before my year-long assignment in Vietnam ended in 1967, I visited Saigon, the city celebrated in the song "Saigon Dep Lam (Beautiful Saigon)," which had been popular since 1965. Saigon was the traditional capital of Vietnam and the capital of the Republic of Vietnam at the time. I embarked on a "consolation trip" for three nights and four days, staying in a hotel for the Allies with strict security at night and exploring the city during the day. Since the ROK Armed Forces Command Center was also located there, I spent time alone in familiar surroundings, dining in Cho-Lon (Big Market), a street inhabited by Chinese-Vietnamese residents. During my brief visit to Saigon in 1967, amidst wartime, I witnessed deep social inequality and the resulting conflicts. This prompted me to reflect on the "cause of revolt by the people," or "Rising Expectations," a concept I had learned at the Kennedy Center in the United States a few years earlier.

Most citizens walked, with only a few using old motorcycles for transportation. In stark contrast, the ruling class enjoyed the luxury of riding in French cars, with even women driving them—a sight unimaginable in Korea at the time—through downtown. Additionally, the hotel where I stayed, comparable to a four-star hotel in Korea today, was teeming with prostitute day and night, who slept in the corridors. These scenes highlighted the extreme social inequality and class disparities. Furthermore, about 90% of farming villages were still under the tenant farming system, with most farmers cruelly exploited by local millionaires, reminiscent of the feudal era. For instance, tenant farmers' children tended the cattle of wealthy landlords to make a living. If a cow died or was injured, the child would be forced to stay in the field overnight, enduring mosquito bites. Vietnamese mosquitoes were strong enough to pierce through a military blanket, making it a severe violation of human rights. This was both communist propaganda and a reflection of the actual social conditions. The newly established "Republic of Vietnam" retained "the old colonial system" and was plagued by worsening corruption. Even as a foreign Army captain, I could foresee Vietnam's defeat and collapse.

The Republic of Korea, my homeland, faced a similar situation at the time of liberation but emerged as a democratic nation after the end of imperialism and a brief period of U.S. military rule. Under President Rhee Syng-Man's leadership, Korea abolished tenant farming through land reform, "ended its status as Japan's colony," and adopted a modified capitalist political system. This ensured stability without popular revolt, even when North Korea invaded and the Korean War erupted.

♦ Goodbye, the battlefields of Vietnam! Return to Korea (October 13th-23rd, 1967)

Human destinies are determined by fate. My comrades (mostly officers and soldiers, majors and below) and I completed our year-long combat assistance duties in Vietnam. We were replaced by additional combat agents from Korea, participated in a reporting ceremony to return home, accompanied by a military chaplain's prayer, and safely boarded the "Barret," an 18,000-ton ship chartered by the U.S. Armed Forces, bound for Korea. The ship departed Quy Nhon, the battlefield of "victory and tragedy" for the Tiger Division, and sailed slowly north along the coast. It stopped at Nha Trang the next day to pick up Marine Corps agents returning to their countries. On the 15th, it continued its northward journey, leaving the tense battlefields of Vietnam behind, and what an emotional voyage it was. "Goodbye, Vietnam of tragedy!"

However, as soon as the ship set sail, we encountered a typhoon named "Color" on the Pacific Ocean. The transport ship followed the typhoon, enduring 20-foot waves (6 meters high) and "yawing," a motion similar to pitching, as it cruised slowly at about 7.5 knots. After 24 hours, two-thirds of the soldiers and half of the officers were incapacitated by seasickness. The cafeteria, filled with plentiful and delicious food, remained empty for several days. Fortunately, I was unaffected, but I couldn't help but feel anxious as I observed the repetitive views of the sea and sky, experiencing a typhoon at sea for the first time. I watched the sailors' actions and realized that even a large ship seemed like a powerless tiny boat in a typhoon. I saw a ship about 300 to 400 meters away, a few hundred tons in size, struggling in the typhoon's grip, appearing and disappearing on the waves. It looked so fragile and pitiful that I couldn't bear to watch.

On the 22nd, about four days later, I received my final order for a 24-hour duty, calculated the final number of people, and discussed the Vietnam War with the ship's captain on my last day aboard. At 08:00 on the 23rd, we arrived at the harbor of Busan, where I had departed Korea a year earlier, and returned safely, welcomed by citizens, family, and friends. I returned from the battlefield alive, and although I did not receive any Order of Merit for military exploits, I confidently embraced my family, especially my wife, to comfort them for the physical and mental hardships they had endured. It was a deeply emotional moment.

Chapter 6

Studying Abroad at Führungsakademie der Bundeswehr, and an instructor at Korean Army college (1969-1971)

1. Studying Abroad at Führungsakademie der Bundeswehr

♦ The Purpose of Studying Abroad at Führungsakademie der Bundeswehr and Preparation involved traveling to Europe through Japan and Arctic, eventually reaching West Germany

After returning to Korea from the Vietnam War, I worked at the Special Warfare Office of HQ-ROKA (Headquarters of the ROK Army). During that period, West Germany was considered a model of national and societal revival in Korea, having achieved the "Miracle on the Rhine." Moreover, Korean coal miners and nurses were dispatched to West Germany, and President Park Chung-Hee visited them to offer consolation and encouragement, making West Germany a symbol of national revival among Koreans. It was also a country of interest for military personnel, especially strategists. I aspired to learn about the following: the military and political strategies that led to victory in the Franco-Prussian War and Austro-Prussian War; military success and political defeat in World War I and World War II; the philosophy of war by the great Clausewitz; Blitzkrieg and armored corps tactics by Rommel and Guderian; the "Generalstab" (German General Staff) that shocked Allied strategists during the war and faced war crime trials; "The Schlieffen Plan"; and the German Armed Forces, which left such a historical legacy.

As a cadet eager to learn about these topics, I also aimed to observe and study the relationship between NATO in Western Europe and the West German Armed Forces, among other things, to understand the relationship between Korea's "self-reliant defense theory," a hot topic in national defense strategy, and the "Pacific Rim Security Organization" being designed by the United States, our ally. Additionally, I sought to experience and observe European culture and civilization, which was considered the leader of modern civilization compared to American culture, which seemed distant and challenging to approach, and to identify research topics that could contribute to Korea's future development.

Studying abroad for the Republic of Korea Armed Forces at overseas military universities and similar institutions was primarily in the United States, which covered all expenses. However, three years prior to this period, the program expanded to include Canada and Germany. Following the Military Revolution of May 16th, Korea's national GDP began to rise, and the system changed so that Korea covered living expenses while the host country covered educational expenses for service members studying abroad. Despite this, married service members were not permitted to bring their spouses due to financial constraints. At that time, studying in Germany was not well-known and seemed to offer no special advantages, so few applied. In 1970, the third year of recruitment, one armor branch officer, one infantry officer, and one Marine Corps officer were selected for the staff college course for field officers.

I was the sole candidate from the infantry. Additionally, two captains were recruited for the Military Branch School (MBS) and two for the military academy in Germany, aside from the staff college course. Preparing to study in Germany under those conditions was unfamiliar. Although I had studied German briefly in high school, it still felt foreign to me. Eventually, I took a written test and had a simple interview at the German Embassy in Korea without any competition, and I was instructed to depart immediately. I owe a great deal of gratitude to Professor Min Byeong-don at the Korea Military Academy (KMA), a junior and close friend who had studied in Germany for language education, for his assistance throughout the process. I remain thankful for his help. However, it was heartbreaking to leave my family for one year and eight months, just a year after returning from the Vietnam battlefield. I embarked on this journey with the hope of learning new things, but I felt deeply sorry for my wife, who had to stay in Korea with our children and manage the family alone. I promised myself to compensate for her hardships by succeeding and improving.

♦ Journey to West Germany via the Arctic

I was scheduled to depart by the start date of the language school in West Germany, but the national budget for the New Year had not been approved by the National Assembly. Consequently, I was able to leave on January 3rd, 1969, using the previous year's exclusive budget. Accompanying me were two KMA cadets, for whom I was responsible to the Defense Attaché Office at the Korean Embassy in Germany. Both were sophomores at KMA: Kim Gwan-Jin from Seoul High School, who later became the Minister of National Defense and Chief of the Office of National Security, and Park Heung-Hwan from Kyunggi High School, who later became a corps commander. We remembered the Chief of Staff's advice, "Be safe and healthy, and achieve your goals," as we reported to Army headquarters and departed from Gimpo Airport on a Korean Air DC-9 aircraft. My family and close classmates came to see us off, and Professor Min Byeong-don and his wife accompanied my family, for which I was very grateful. Saying goodbye to my family on the sendoff platform—located on the rooftop of the airport building next to the runway—as I stood on the airplane's step car was both a responsible and emotional moment, knowing I would be away for one and a half years once again.

Two hours after departure, we arrived at Haneda International Airport in Tokyo, Japan, where we stayed for one night and day. We toured downtown the next day on a five-dollar, six-and-a-half-hour package. Tokyo Tower, built for the upcoming World EXPO and modeled after the Eiffel Tower in France, was particularly memorable.

They boasted it was two feet taller than the Eiffel Tower, though smaller in size. The next day, we visited Meiji Jingu, a site Koreans associate with the Japanese Colonization Era. It was early in the New Year, and many Japanese people, especially women, wore traditional kimonos, similar to Korea's Hanbok, as they made wishes and tossed coins into a large metal basket. The path to the shrine, about 20 meters wide and 1 kilometer long, was crowded with people of all ages making New Year wishes. Every country has its unique customs, and Japan brought its people together through this tradition. We also witnessed the Japanese "culture natural pearls," showcasing their technology, which amazed and entertained tourists. As night fell, we explored the "streets at night," filled with vibrant colors, the scent of street women, liquor, dance, gambling, and rip-offs. Japan's society has long condoned such places, using them to attract tourists and generate revenue, especially the "dollar boxes" for U.S. Army personnel after the war, a hub for "geisha diplomacy." Despite this, I wasn't as impressed as when I first saw the views from Gimpo Airport or when I arrived at Narita Airport in Japan eight years ago en route to the United States. The Military Revolution of May 16th and the national revival under the 3rd Republic of Park Chung-Hee had transformed Korea, making Tokyo's views less unfamiliar. Even looking down at Gimpo's tin roofs, once filled with straw roofs, wasn't as emotional.

At dawn the next day, we departed Japan on SAS, a Swedish airline, heading to Anchorage, Alaska. The plane flew through a heavy rainstorm with thunder and lightning, causing anxiety. After a brief stop in Anchorage, we continued our journey. The sun set three to four hours after leaving Tokyo at dawn, and we flew toward the Arctic, witnessing a phenomenon akin to a "rich aurora borealis" for an extended period. At dawn, we passed the North Pole. Due to the Cold War, the plane couldn't fly over China or the Soviet Union, necessitating a detour through the Arctic to reach Europe. An announcement was made, and souvenirs were distributed to passengers. During the meal, they served triangular packaged cheese. Although I had encountered cheese while studying in the United States, I hesitated to eat it due to its smell. The Siberian tundra below during mealtime was a spectacular sight.

As we traveled further, we reached the European grasslands, a refreshing view for me. As the plane approached Copenhagen, Denmark, our first European destination, it flew into dark rainclouds, making passengers nervous. Despite the era of scientific advancements, including lunar exploration, I felt anxious. Upon landing safely, passengers applauded and shouted "Well done!" in relief. I experienced similar situations during later overseas travels. We transferred at Copenhagen Airport to fly to Hamburg Airport in Germany, and then again to Lufthansa, West Germany's national airline, to reach Bonn Airport, our final destination and West Germany's temporary capital. On the Lufthansa flight from Hamburg, we received paper lunch boxes containing two small apples, which I initially thought were welcome gifts. However, after the rough-looking four-winged propeller airliner departed with a loud noise, they announced lunchtime, instructing us to eat from the lunch box, with only coffee or cola served. It was my first time receiving a lunch box on a flight. This was my first impression of Germany, a nation accustomed to a simple and practical lifestyle, saving while creating the "Miracle on the Rhine" in a short time.

♦ Language School in Euskirchen and My Days There

Upon arrival at Bonn Airport, we were warmly welcomed by the Korean Defense Attaché Officer to Germany, Colonel Kim of the artillery. He drove us to the Defense Attaché Office, where he and his wife served us warm Korean food, for which I was very grateful. After the meal, he kindly and meticulously explained our life plans and precautions during our stay. We needed to register for school immediately, so despite the late hour, he drove us a long distance from Bonn to the school. The cadets stayed at the Bachelor Officer Quarters (BOQ), while I was assigned an apartment, one room per person, in the same building as the classrooms, just upstairs.

This was a small city with a population of about 27,000. It was located approximately 35 kilometers (21 miles) from Bonn, and 30 kilometers (18 miles) north of Cologne, a historic and beautiful city known for tourism. The principal of the language school was a lieutenant colonel, while most of the professors were civilians. They primarily taught European languages, including English and Russian, and offered German lessons to foreign officers studying abroad. Classes began at 8:00 a.m., with the fifth period ending at 12:30 p.m. We were given time for self-study until 3:45 p.m., after which we had free time. Each homeroom had about ten students, and the education was largely based on rote learning, with overwhelming amounts of homework. My homeroom consisted of officers from various countries: one from Thailand, one from Morocco, four from Nigeria, one from Turkey, and five from Korea. Three months after enrollment, all officers were moved to a downtown hotel called Concordia, granting us more freedom. However, we still had all three meals at the school cafeteria. Typically, we had simple breakfasts, warm lunches, and took boxed dinners of dried food, milk, and black barley bread back to the hotel.

While observing other German patrons at the Concordia dining room, I noticed many enjoyed drinking 'Spirits' similar to Korean soju from small shot glasses, followed by beer. This spirit, called Korn, has an alcohol content of 32-38% by volume. Due to the poor quality of water in Germany—partly because of frequent rain—Germans often drink beer or wine instead of water, even with meals. They almost always drink wine after dinner and typically pair Korn with beer. Drinking Korn after beer keeps the amount of Korn the same, but drinking beer after Korn increases the effect of the Korn. This method allows people in the countryside to get drunk without spending much money, and they do it habitually.

♦ A Trip to Holland (Netherlands)

Expanding one's horizons is both interesting and essential for personal growth. Therefore, I aimed to broaden my perspective on Europe and compare European civilization to the remarkable American civilization, to assess the present and future of Korea. I seized opportunities during course transitions and school breaks to do so. This was one of my reasons for studying abroad in Germany. Spring break began in late April, so the three of us—officers studying at the German staff college, Lieutenant Colonel Gu of Armor, Lieutenant Colonel Kang of the Marine Corps, and myself—traveled through Western Europe with local residents via local travel agencies. Central Europeans often say, "April is the cruelest month," referring to nature rather than politics, as we do in Korea. Although flowers bloom and sprouts grow in April, the weather remains cold with thick ice, cloudy skies, rain, and wind. Despite this, the weather warmed in late April, and we had some free time. We embarked on a two-night, three-day trip to the Netherlands, meaning "lower countries" in German, to broaden our views. We departed from Cologne, West Germany, and crossed the border. The transportation system was as well-developed as the freeway systems of other countries, with numerous canals and ships on our way to Amsterdam. The Netherlands boasts a highly advanced dairy industry and is a major producer of European cheese. City centers feature flower-lined paths wider than the roads, and downtown areas resemble a paradise for bicycles, with tunnels allowing uninterrupted cycling beneath intersections while cars must stop. Amsterdam, the capital, is a harbor city connected to the North Sea via the North

Sea Canal. Canals play a significant role in downtown transportation, making it convenient and a major draw for tourists. The two-hour canal tour was particularly fascinating. Various buildings, especially offices and homes, were situated on the water, reminiscent of Venice, Italy. Observing people through waterproof windows underwater was a spectacular sight, showcasing the country's advanced science. As a harbor city and tourist destination, Amsterdam is also famous for its alleys where scantily clad prostitutes wave from display windows.

Traveling south along the Atlantic coast, we saw a seaside levee 10 meters (10 yards) wide and over 10 meters (10 yards) high. It made the story of a boy plugging the levee with his fist overnight seem plausible, not just a legend. The vast flower garden complex, primarily of tulips, along the west coast was breathtaking. It generates hundreds of millions of dollars annually through exports and plays a significant role in tourism, making the Netherlands truly a "country of flowers." We stopped at a small village along the way, where quaint and beautiful houses lined both sides of a narrow road, resembling scenes from fairy tales. Each house had large glass windows in their living rooms, displaying the interior like shop windows, inviting passersby to admire them. Flower pots adorned the fronts, and behind cotton curtains lay a flower basket on the table, with a birdcage for parrots hanging from the ceiling. These homes, with their charming decor, seemed like tourist exhibitions, yet they were actual residences. They appeared to be about 66 square meters (78 square yards) in size, smaller and daintier than houses in other European countries, which made them even more endearing. Germans were particularly impressed and reluctant to leave.

A symbolic flower garden in Holland is the enormous 'Keukenhof' park. Spanning 1 square kilometer (247 acres), it features hills, a lake, canals, and trails around a windmill, creating a stunning garden with various flowers, mainly tulips. It's a must-visit for tourists worldwide, and even two hours there felt too brief. Enjoying a Heineken beer, a world-renowned Dutch brand, at a café in the park's center while taking in the view was delightful. The park also offered immediate export counseling for interested tourists. However, Holland wasn't trading plants with Korea at the time, so I couldn't receive counseling, despite seeing flowers I wished to take home.

We continued our journey to The Hague, a seaside city familiar to Koreans due to the story of 'Yi Jun the great patriot.' As King Gojong's secret messenger in 1907, he appealed to peace-loving nations about Japan's forceful occupation of Korea but was denied entry to the palace, leading to deep disappointment. I was deeply moved when we were introduced to the "Peace Palace" in downtown. How long was the journey from Korea to here by land? How much did he endure, navigating immigration processes in unfamiliar countries as someone from a nation that had lost its sovereignty? How sorrowful must he have felt with language barriers and unfamiliar food in Europe, where only Japan's name was known then and now (1969), and the Hague Convention, a convention "for imperialist nations?" Reflecting on all this, I couldn't help but bow my head in humility.

Rotterdam, Holland's largest harbor city facing the Atlantic Ocean, had rows of ships 20,000 tons or larger lined up and anchored. It was so vast that a 70,000-ton ship, the largest possible at the time, was being constructed there. I understood why the Allies landed in Normandy and executed the "big airborne operation" to secure a harbor point for transporting "Red Ball" during the late stages of World War II. Furthermore, this harbor marks the endpoint of the Rhine River, which originates in Switzerland and flows through Germany. Koreans learn about Holland as a country of flowers and a dairy industry producing and selling cheese. Indeed, it was a "park of Europe with blooming flowers" in April and May, but upon closer inspection, it was truly an advanced nation with modern industries and trade.

♦ A Trip to Explore the United Kingdom and Belgium

• Crossing the Strait of Dover to London

Before we parted ways after completing our language courses and heading to separate units for officer practice, we decided to travel to Belgium and the United Kingdom to broaden our perspectives. The three of us joined a local "senior tour" package, a land route trip to Belgium and the United Kingdom designed for older Germans. Considering the time needed to cross the Strait of Dover, we departed from Cologne around twilight, boarding a "Globus" bus, similar to a Greyhound bus in the United States. The bus soon crossed 'Aachen' at the border and immediately reached 'Liege', Belgium. Our tour bus continued, crossing an interchange in 'Antwerpen'. Bright orange streetlights provided a cozy ambiance for travelers at night.

The bus continued its journey and arrived at Ostende Harbor on the Atlantic Ocean coast, at the edge of the European Continent, around 1:00 a.m. the following day. I gazed eastward from the harbor, recalling my time studying abroad in Norfolk, North Carolina, near the U.S. Marine Corps base, about ten years ago. Back then, I imagined Europe from the United States, but now I stood facing west towards the Atlantic Ocean, overwhelmed with emotion.

Travel about 50 kilometers (31 miles) south from here, and you'll reach Dunkerque, a French harbor city. During the early stages of World War II, this was where the Allies, including the UK Armed Forces, retreated to the United Kingdom after Belgium's surrender to the German Armed Forces. Just as President Roosevelt of the United States declared, "Remember Pearl Harbor!" Churchill of the United Kingdom urged, "Do not forget Dunkerque!" and led the troops in this "harbor city of devastatingly painful history." Below Dunkerque lies Calais Harbor, the closest French harbor to the United Kingdom, about 30 kilometers (18 miles) away. It was a crucial strategic point where General Rommel of Germany anticipated the Allies' landing and fortified the 'Atlantic Wall.'

The ferry we boarded was a 5,000-ton vessel, capable of carrying 50 to 60 cars, ten buses, and numerous trucks. The cabins and cafeteria were located on the deck above, reminiscent of the night trains on Korea's Jeolla-do line. Many passengers sprawled or sat on the floor were hippies, men and women with disheveled hair, traveling to the United Kingdom. Currency exchange was available, but the UK's duodecimal system posed a challenge for non-British travelers. The novel "The Moon and Sixpence," translated into Korean, references the sixpence (12 pence equals 1 shilling), a basic currency unit akin to Korea's 500-won coin, used for everyday purchases like a bottle of coke or a phone call.

The ferry journeyed for about four hours at 10 knots across the Strait of Dover, arriving at the Port of Dover, United Kingdom, at dawn. The towering white cliffs, over 100 meters (109 yards) high, and the Union Jack fluttering in the sea breeze left a striking first impression of the United Kingdom. The bus drove on the left-hand side along the Thames River for about two hours, and we enjoyed a morning walk in Canterbury, the legendary and literary capital praised by Joyce, a master of English literature, accompanied by birdsong.

After four more hours of travel, we finally reached London. The sights of London, the hippies at Piccadilly Circus, and the stout at Dirty Dick's were unforgettable. The first things I noticed were the bridges over the Thames River, the Parliament, Big Ben in the distance, police officers in distinctive uniforms, and the massive marble and granite buildings downtown. Everything was impressive, but some memories stand out.

Hyde Park was particularly memorable, a public park about 2 kilometers (1.2 miles) wide and 4 kilometers (2.4 miles) long. In the UK, private parks owned by aristocrats are common, but Hyde Park featured a large river, a marina, a horseback riding arena, a soccer field, and more, serving as a venue for citizens' health and relaxation.

An intriguing nighttime spot was Dirty Dick's, a local pub in front of London's old town central station. The story goes that a man named Dick, who lived about 100 years ago, was so lazy that his wife divorced him. He threw fish and meat bones to the ceiling after meals, and those bones remain there. The walls, covered in 100-year-old stains and dust, are cluttered with tiny customer photos, stamps, business cards, postcards, and scribbles. The century-old log tables and chairs barely supported the patrons and their glasses, yet the place was so crowded that people waited long for refills. Despite—or perhaps because of—its condition, Dirty Dick's, along with the hippies and stout, was a true "delicacy of London."

The next day, we visited Oxford University, about 100 kilometers (62 miles) west of London, still one of the world's top universities. The dining hall walls were adorned with life-size portraits of successful Oxford graduates, serving as "pride" and inspiration for current students. The last page of Oxford's history we learned stated, "The breaks were long, and the semesters were short," and "The ability to grace learning is given to few, but the opportunity to learn the grace is Oxford's gift to all sons and daughters."

Next, we visited Shakespeare's house near Oxford, but it's too famous to need further explanation, so I'll return to discussing London. Downtown London was quiet and empty at night when we returned, but Piccadilly Circus was bustling with drunkards, hippies, and tourists observing the scene. Nearby streets were filled with strip shows, street girls, and old pimps, reminiscent of Myeong-dong in Seoul, Ginza in Tokyo, Pigalle in Paris, and St. Pauli in Hamburg. However, the arcade near Soho, adjacent to Piccadilly, was renowned as the birthplace of the global popularity of gentlemen's suits, much like the tailors' street in Sogong-dong, Korea.

The British say, "Buckingham Palace symbolizes London's protocol, Westminster Abbey is the heart of UK political life, and Piccadilly Circus is London's lighthouse." During World War I and II, soldiers heading to Europe sang "Goodbye Piccadilly" instead of military songs. London's main streets, built from majestic granite centuries ago, seemed capable of enduring for over 1,000 years, steeped in history and tradition. In contrast, in 1969, many hippies roamed the streets, their appearance starkly different from the city's grandeur. About nine out of ten had disheveled hair like The Beatles, seven out of ten girls wore "super miniskirts," and the rest wore bell-bottom pants. Many dressed like Native Americans, and some hippies with uncut, unwashed hair for months wore long capes and went barefoot, accompanied by those in super miniskirts. Our German tourist group exclaimed, "Oh, no!" at the sight.

London's numerous parks offered shaded spots under trees or on benches to relax, watch fountains, and converse with pigeons. The UK's many rotaries feature historic sculptures and monuments. Notably, the Hyde Park entrance rotary boasts the Equestrian Statue of Duke of Wellington, and Trafalgar Square features Nelson's Column. These monuments were particularly memorable to a military serviceperson like me.

London inspires lengthy reflections on a single city. Westminster Abbey, a beautiful Gothic building near the Thames River, is the birthplace of the UK's national church and the monarchy's heart. Established about 900 years ago, when the UK had church-state unity, it still hosts royal coronations. Upon entering, a large bouquet greets visitors, and a memorial monument honors unnamed veterans who died in battle during World War I in Europe. This sight was poignant for us military serviceperson tourists. The brochure we received on entry advised, "I truly wish that you will not forget to look up from time to time to see the glory of this church."

Madame Tussauds' House, a masterpiece I saw in the UK, and Admiral Lord Nelson's words, "Thank God, I have done my duty," were next on our itinerary. We visited the Houses of Parliament, always majestically reflected in the Thames River. Tourists could only see the House of Lords, House of Commons, and Westminster Hall. The hallway walls depicted the British Empire's glory through its history of global colonization and administration, designed to boost British patriotism. I realized that one nation's shining age of glory could be another's age of pain and darkness.

We also visited Madame Tussauds, a place where the British celebrate their national pride. This museum attracts not only foreign tourists but also British visitors in London. The building has two basement levels and three to four floors above ground. The tour begins in the dark and eerie "Chamber of Horrors" on the second basement level. This room displays wax figures of infamous criminals from around the world, along with the torture and execution devices used on them, such as the French guillotine and a large British axe used for executions at the Tower of London, including those of figures like Mary Stuart. There were also shackles and the head of Louis XVI impaled on iron bars. The exhibition featured Oswald, the primary suspect in President Kennedy's assassination, detailing his life in prison and his death. The brochure even warned, "Do not see the exhibition alone," due to its frightening nature. I thought anyone who witnessed these scenes would vow, "I swear I will never commit any crime in my life."

We then moved to the first basement floor and entered "The Battle of Trafalgar Hall," which was the most impressive section for me. Upon entering, we were immersed in a perfect re-enactment of the interior of "Victory," the British flagship commanded by Admiral Nelson. The strong smell of gunpowder and smoke filled the air, accompanied by lights and booming sounds from bombardment, along with the commands of the officers and the chants of the sailors and gunners. It was a complete re-enactment of the final moments of that victorious battle. When the battle concluded, cheers of victory echoed, and Nelson's last words, "Thank God, I have done my duty," were heard. This five-minute re-enactment of "victory in battle and noble death" was more than enough to remind the British of their pride and loyalty to their nation.

We proceeded to the ground floor, with those images still vivid in our minds. There were life-size wax figures of about 30 historical greats, including a scene of Churchill painting at the beach during sunset, smoking a cigar. We ascended once more and entered "The Hall of Heroes of the Era." The wax figures, in various sizes, re-enacted scenes with sound and light effects. One remarkable scene featured Richard Burton and Elizabeth Taylor, a British actress who was incredibly popular worldwide at the time, emerging from a hotel in New York on a rainy day. The scene captured the moment newspaper journalists rushed to them, asking, "Miss Taylor, what did you have for breakfast this morning?" Although these exhibits were created and displayed through the personal vision and investment of Madame Tussauds, a French woman, they contained universal lessons, pride, and joy.

Korea has Bulguksa Temple in Gyeongju and The Independence Hall of Korea in Mok-dong, Chungcheong-do, which all Koreans visit. However, I hope a modernized museum like Madame Tussauds will be established in the heart of Seoul someday. I wish for an even more magnificent version of Madame Tussauds to be built in Korea, including the story of the great Admiral Yi Sun-sin. I heard one has already been built in Tokyo, Japan. When I witnessed the majestic changing of the guards in front of Buckingham Palace at precisely 12:00, I recalled the "military parade in lines" we conducted weekly when I attended KMA in Hwarangdae.

We also visited several other places: the subway with 500 stations and seven lines; the Tower of London, rich in tradition and history but also marked by the Royal Family's tragedies; the Fusilier Museum, a military museum at the Tower of London, housing royal relics, treasures, guns, and cannons; the pure white statue of Queen Victoria in the central rotary; a memorial monument for unnamed veterans in the bustling downtown; Buckingham Palace and Windsor Castle, owned by the Royal Family, and so on. As we left London and concluded our tour of the United Kingdom, we arrived at the Port of Dover at sunset. A cliff facing Europe suddenly stood out. During World War II, a British fighter pilot, shot and wounded, bravely crossed the Strait of Dover and reached the cliffs of Dover in his homeland. He shouted, "I am finally back to my country!" before losing consciousness, crashing onto the cliff, and perishing in flames. I heard a monument commemorating his patriotism is carved into that cliff. As I watched the cliffs of Dover fade into the sunset while we boarded a returning boat, I was reminded once more of the United Kingdom during the era of imperialism, when they proclaimed, "The sun never sets on the Union Jack."

• The Waterloo 1815 Memorial in Belgium

On our way back, we stopped in Brussels, the capital of Belgium and Europe. It's a small city compared to other European capitals, with a population of about 1.1 million, so most tourist attractions are within walking distance. First, we visited the Grand Plaza (Grand-Place of Brussels) and walked to the Mount of the Arts, the old royal palace, the streets of the current royal palace, and the famous Peeing Boy statue. We found shops selling chocolate, potato fries, and waffles everywhere. The Peeing Boy statue, though small, was a must-see attraction, akin to The Little Mermaid statue on a rock at Langelinie Beach in Denmark. This demonstrated that the good nature of humanity is universal, despite differences in ethnicity, history, and traditions.

Next, we visited the Waterloo 1815 Memorial in the Waterloo region. According to the explanation, it was inspired by "The Battle of Waterloo" written by Victor Hugo, a world-renowned French author. They re-enacted the final battle that took place in Waterloo in the form of a panorama. It was another world-famous panorama, alongside the one depicting the final battle of the American Civil War in Atlanta. Outside, a large statue of a lion stood on a gigantic conical hill, made by melting a cannon used by Napoleon's Army of France, which lost the battle. As I gazed at the statue, it felt like I could hear the cheers and shouts from the British Army, commanded by the Duke of Wellington, and the allies who fought in the battle. The military lesson I learned here was: "If you're a military serviceperson, you just have to win in a war (battle).”

• Sightseeing at the River Rhine with our cadets under the guidance of the Korean Defense Attaché Officer to Germany

While attending classes at the West German Armed Forces' language school in Euskirchen, we often visited the Korean Embassy in Germany on holidays because it was close to Bonn. One day, the Defense Attaché Officer (Colonel Kim) invited us (the two cadets and me) to go sightseeing at the River Rhine (Rhein), the lifeblood of Germany (Europe). I don't remember it clearly now, but I think we went to Wiesbaden, about 100 kilometers (62 miles) to the south, and took a cruise there to travel north, up to Bonn along the riverbank. This area is a cruise tour route reminiscent of the Hantangang River in Korea. One side is mostly plains and cliffs, while the other side has relatively less steep hills. They created a scenic route along the riverbank on that side and developed a tourist area with an arcade where visitors can rest or shop. I thought a scenic area near the Hangang River in Korea could be transformed into a tourist destination someday.

As we traveled north for about 30 kilometers (18 miles) from our departure point, we saw a gigantic rock on the right bank of the river near Sankt-Goar, rising about 100 meters (328 feet) high. This was the famous “Loreley,” meaning “the rock of the siren.” According to legend, sailors passing by were bewitched by the beautiful singing voice of the siren from the rock, causing them to stray from their course, get caught in the swirling currents, crash onto rocks, and end up shipwrecked. This legend certainly attracted tourists. If you travel further north from there, you will reach the River Mosel in Koblenz. This river flows from east to west and is quite winding, with many south-facing hills. Its environment is ideal for growing grapes, which is why Mosel wine from this region is more well-received than Rhine wine.

2. Visiting the staff of the Brigade, the 23rd Mountain Brigade (Gebirgs Brigade) affiliated with the 1st Mountain Division

♦ The 23rd Gebirgs Brigade (Mountain Brigade) was stationed in the Alps, nicknamed “Edelweiss Brigade”

We completed our German classes at the West German Armed Forces' language school in July 1969 and individually moved to the 23rd Mountain Brigade to visit the brigade staff (August 1969-September 1969, for two months), which was the next course. This brigade was located in the suburbs of Bad Reichenhall (a hot springs village) in the southeasternmost part of West Germany, right below the Alps, facing Salzburg (a salt village), a famous tourist city across the border.

Nearby was Berchtesgaden, now a famous tourist attraction, known as the "Alpine Fortress," selected as Hitler's final defense fortress. The command center of the 1st Mountain Division was located in Garmisch-Partenkirchen, slightly more inland toward Munich. This troop was established in 1935, fought in World War II, was disbanded afterward, and was restored in November 1956 when West Germany was revived. It had two mountain brigades and one armor brigade affiliated with it. The troop's symbol was the Edelweiss, the flower representing the highlands of the Alps.

The strategic and tactical concepts of the West German Armed Forces at that time were as follows: In the northern plains, operations were conducted using panzer maneuver troops. In the central region, which consisted of mid-sized mountains and forests, integrated maneuver operations were carried out by infantry, artillery, and armor. In the southern Alps, mountain operations were the focus. The West German Armed Forces were a central component of NATO's military forces. Most of their units, with a few exceptions, were transformed into panzer maneuver troops, in line with the general war strategy and the "strategy of flexible response" that gained emphasis in the 1960s. Consequently, even a mountain division included two mountain brigades and one panzer brigade. The mountain brigade comprised one panzer battalion, two mountain battalions, one mountain artillery battalion, and one mechanized logistical support battalion. A mountain battalion included three motorized mountain companies, one armored heavy weapons company (featuring anti-tank guided missiles, anti-aircraft guns, heavy mortars, and anti-tank guns), and one panzer and motorized headquarters company.

For your reference, in West Germany, they referred to it as a panzer division, while in the United States, it was called an armor division. The fundamental strategy for the mountain division was to conduct operations in the highlands (2,000 to 4,500 meters) of the Alps using specialized mountain soldiers and gradually move towards the hills on either side of the Alps, engaging in battles with the panzer maneuver troops. A unique aspect of this unit was its composition and equipment.

To enable independent brigade operations, each brigade's panzer mobilized supply battalion dealt directly with the corps and included a mountain supply company with 80 'Mules' for mountain supply. These 'Mules' originated from Corsica, Napoleon's birthplace, and were bred with high-quality horses to enhance their strength and sturdiness. This allowed them to transport disassembled 105-millimeter mountain guns up the Alps during operations. The infantry's machine guns could fire continuously without headspace adjustments, and skilled soldiers could replace gun barrels in three to four seconds. The firing technique involved straightening the legs while lying in a trench, allowing the gun to stand up with the gunner. This method addressed the inconvenience and delay of firing while bending and standing. The newly developed Leopard tanks, considered the best in the world at the time, were narrow and light, enabling them to travel at speeds of up to 65 km/h. They could also submerge up to 3 meters underwater, earning them the title of "prince on land" in Europe.

Let's conclude this section and discuss professional military topics such as firearms, equipment characteristics, and the training system for officials. In terms of troop operations, the West German Armed Forces prided themselves on pursuing democratized armed forces, but recruitment was challenging. Consequently, they reduced their organized military personnel, with officers often doubling as intelligence officers in a battalion, and the battalion executive officer (a major) also serving as the operations officer. In a company, two officers, the company commander and a platoon leader, worked during regular times. The first sergeant commanded other platoons and was responsible for education, fire direction, and managing vehicles and firearms. This was the framework for education and training within the troops.

In West Germany, unlike Korea where most troops are stationed near the Military Demarcation Line, combat troops were stationed in each province, with border guards handling the front lines. Each battalion had a company designated for new recruits, conducting basic military training for three months, followed by three months of specialist training. Many recruits were then transferred to brigade departments, while the rest-maintained combat readiness as the "company of classmates." After serving for 18 months, company members were discharged, and new recruits were brought in, creating a repetitive cycle. Basic military training, primarily instructed by first sergeants, had a 30% shooting success rate, with general soldiers achieving 50% to 60%. However, first sergeants often boasted of a 90% success rate.

The unit's unique feature was mountain training, with each brigade having a special platoon and each battalion a special squad for this purpose. Members were trained to navigate the Alps, over 4,000 meters high, and all officers and soldiers participated in mountain marching training. They focused on improving proficiency in rope climbing and other skills on less steep terrain. The company commander's motivational speeches often included lessons on Germany's history and geography, occasionally featuring guest speakers. Physical education was mandatory for six hours or more per week, including track and field, swimming, and soccer. Officers were required to run 1,500 meters and swim 300 meters. Despite the rigorous training, everyone enjoyed the opportunity to climb the snow-covered Alps in summer and ski at nearby resorts in winter, enhancing both fitness and leisure activities.

♦ General Situations of the West German Armed Forces on Its 10th Anniversary of Rebuilding: Rebuilt as a NATO Ally from a Defeated Country

When I went to study abroad, the West German Armed Forces had been excused from punishment as a defeated nation due to the need for European power during the Cold War. Rebuilt in 1955, they joined NATO, established in 1949, and had been part of it for 14 years by then. I don't recall the exact location, but the West German Armed Forces participated in NATO's 20th-anniversary celebration and parade, which was a significant event and a protest against the Warsaw Treaty Organization during the Cold War. Observing this event helped me understand the German Armed Forces' structure, which was beneficial during my studies in Germany.

It was a time of conflict for the German people. Having lost the war, disarmed, and punished internationally, Germany was rebuilding its nation but had to rearm due to the Cold War. The German populace, weary of war and the military, held a strong "Ohne mich" (not me) mindset. To counter this, Germany initiated military conscription to enlist soldiers and organize troops as soon as it began rebuilding its armed forces. Consequently, an average of five soldiers per company deserted each month, creating a serious situation. Company commanders were busy filing lawsuits against deserters—a method to civilianize military proceedings by removing military court trials and handling them in civil courts.

Conflict on Promotion Inside the Military:

To democratize the armed forces, commissioned officers were allowed to join political parties, which seemed to cause internal conflict. It was said that political party members of the current administration played a crucial role in promotions to general. Additionally, like many countries, Germany experienced historical, religious, political, and traditional conflicts between north and south, or east and west. At that time, Germany was divided into east and west, but internally it was fundamentally divided into north and south. The north embraced new religions and focused on industry and commerce, while the south adhered to old religions and agriculture, maintaining traditions like the "Barbarian" culture. This division influenced everyone, though it often went unnoticed.

During a federal election in Germany, a competition arose between the Christian Democratic Party's candidate from the north and Brandt, the Social Democratic Party's candidate from the south. Officers engaged in fierce debates in the barracks, but in the southern "Barbarian" region where I was stationed, Brandt was more popular. The brigade commander advised me to listen quietly during discussions with other officers in the BOQ, offering political advice I hadn't encountered while studying in the United States. Political matters varied across countries and armed forces, but in Korean society, despite regional characteristics, there was no sentiment of regional division in the military, which I found reassuring.

• The Officer Education and Training System of the German Armed Forces:

In the past, only aristocrats could become commissioned officers in Germany, similar to many autocratic countries worldwide. However, after the war, the West

German Armed Forces aimed to establish a democratic military. They recruited commissioned officers from soldiers who had completed their mandatory 18-month service, graduated from high school, and held the 'Abitur' certificate (from passing the college entrance exam). During their freshman year at a military academy, these recruits joined an actual unit as staff sergeants, wearing the staff sergeant badge with a white underline, to gain practical experience. The first sergeant of information, responsible for troop education, taught them general education, such as reading and understanding newspaper articles. This approach allowed them to experience life as both soldiers and first sergeants, contributing to the democratization process by eliminating the old aristocratic influences. Unlike in many democratic countries like Korea and the United States, where officers do not experience life as soldiers, in West Germany, a cadet's life was essentially a soldier's life. This system had a minor flaw, as it sometimes led to conflicts with the first sergeant when they became company-grade officers.

♦ Visiting and Observing Field Training for Mechanized Company and Mountain Infantry Battalion

• Accompanying and Observing Field Training for the Mechanized Company (Panzer Infantry Company) at a Distant Training Ground

After becoming a democratic country, West Germany had limited training grounds, so they used the U.S. Army's shooting range in West Germany, with the U.S. Army paying the German government for the land. For heavy firearm drills, the West German Armed Forces had to go to France (mostly for field artillery), the United Kingdom (mostly for tank drills and shooting), and even Crete, an island in the Mediterranean Sea. As NATO allies, these countries supported each other by sharing training grounds. On one occasion, the panzer infantry company formed a convoy of 12 armored vehicles, two ferry motorcycles, and five supply and logistics vehicles. The company commander led them in a jeep with the company flag, traveling over three hours to the training ground. I also drove my own jeep and joined them, witnessing the confidence of the German Armed Forces as the company commander "waved his flag" and independently commanded his company. Upon arrival, as the company set up camp for bivouacking, I drove around the training ground to gauge its size. It took about an hour at 60 km/h (37 mi/h), suggesting a diameter of 7 to 8 kilometers (4.3 to 4.9 miles). The training ground accommodated simultaneous firing of about 20 different firearms, with each unit conducting exclusive live ammunition drills two to three times a year.

I camped with them for a week, observing the drills. A commissioned officer was in charge of the shooting ground, and the drills were conducted under their supervision, but the first sergeant instructed the entire shooting drill. The first

Sergeant of gunnery specifically oversaw the firing of the 120-millimeter mortar, ensuring safety and control, while the platoon leader monitored the results chart. During tactical drills, the platoon leader's and company commander's vehicles were equipped with fixed personal computers (or laptops)—a capability the ROK Armed Forces could only dream of at the time—to receive and relay operation orders without dispatch riders. However, traditional dispatch riders on motorcycles were also used as a backup in case of telecommunication failures. One memorable aspect was the "system of duty responsibility and reward and punishment." For instance, when a company ordnance man accidentally set fire to about ten rifles while working under a gaslight, the German Army did not punish the company commander, and the soldier was only required to compensate for the loss with his own money. This approach was unfamiliar to us Koreans, where such incidents would result in punishment for both the soldier and the company commander. We must be more cautious in punishing service members, especially commanders, not only when we achieve self-reliant national defense but even before that.

• Visiting and Observing Field Training for the Mountain Infantry Battalion in the Alps

The Mountain Infantry Battalion of the 1st Brigade conducted drills on mountain tops or high plains at least once every six months, climbing the surrounding Alps with all their equipment, including mules and heavy firearms. I joined them for their July training to observe the officers' activities in the unit. They loaded heavy firearms for the artillery battalion, disassembling the 105-millimeter mountain gun into 12 parts and having mules carry them. Officers and soldiers then walked to the drill position in the Alps along a valley trail with glacial water flowing down. Despite taking short breaks, the mule troop steadily traversed the narrow, steep uphill mountain path, demonstrating their strength and endurance. The company commander guided me, a newcomer to the path, and pointed out lovely and rare flowers, including Edelweiss, a flower familiar to Koreans and associated with Salzburg. This flower symbolizes the Alps and the mountain troop. We finally reached the snow-covered peak, even in summer. The mule troop rested in the area designated for the rear reserve company of the infantry troop, protected by military horsemen during the drill. The troop's drill resembled the infantry drills in Korea, but I felt they were trained with equipment suitable for a mountain troop, as they used mules to carry equipment, including the 105-millimeter mountain gun, up the mountain. Given Korea's natural and geographical environment, where the front troops should be categorized as mountain infantry, I believed it was essential to study the equipment and drill details of the West German Mountain troop.

♦ Exploring the Beautiful Scenery of the Alps Around the Base

• Exploring Salzburg (The Salt Village) and Salzberg (The Salt Mountain)

Bad Reichenhall, the village where the 1st Mountain Brigade was stationed, was located just below the Alps, offering beautiful scenery and hot springs. It was a popular tourist destination for Germans. Nearby, across a major road (from Munich to Salzburg) to the north, lay the picturesque resort village of Piding. Salzburg, less than 12 kilometers (7.4 miles) away at the 1 o'clock direction across the Germany-Austria border, was renowned as the birthplace and major career hub of Mozart, the master musician. It also gained fame from the musical movie "The Sound of Music," particularly the song "Edelweiss." Salzburg is a beautiful, pure, and kind tourist city, with the snow-covered Alps (Mt. Watzmann) as its backdrop. It is now the top destination for Koreans touring Eastern Europe. Historically, this city was once a sea, which dried up, transforming it into the salt village. About 30 kilometers (18 miles) south of Salzburg lies a real salt mountain (Salzberg), as tall as a large hill. Since the 1200s, people have been mining salt from inside the mountain, which has now become an entertaining and famous tourist attraction.

• Exploring "Berchtesgaden"

The eastern border of the German Confederation resembles a traditional Korean pouch, bordering Austria. This area is filled with the typical beauty of the Alps and boasts numerous famous tourist attractions. Along with Salzburg and Salzberg, there is Mt. Watzmann, a snowy mountain I planned to explore, and Berchtesgaden, known for its views and military connections. This region's geography made it an ideal hiding place for criminals. Consequently, Hitler, the German dictator during World War II, chose it as his last refuge, turning it into a fortress when pursued by the Allies. With Austria as its backdrop, he anticipated assistance from its people, who shared his ethnicity.

Now, it stands as a magnificent tourist attraction, framed by the beautiful Alps at its back and the rolling plains and hills of the Alps at its front, offering visitors a chance to appreciate this beauty from the heights of the mountains. However, in the 1960s and 1970s, it held a deeper significance as a place to visit, observe, and reflect on Hitler's last stronghold. Our car wound its way up the curvy mountain road. Once parked, we loaded both equipment and people—sometimes as many as 50 or more—onto the final path through the Rocky Mountains. We took a gigantic elevator that ascended 150 meters (164 yards) or more, reaching the peak where the combat command center and observatory were located. I was struck by the preparedness (the construction of the fortress), the power of science, and Germany's national defense capabilities at that time.

We climbed Mt. Watzmann and explored Lake Königssee. Traveling about 30 kilometers (18 miles) south from Bad Reichenhall, the snowy Alps unfold before you. Among them stands Mt. Watzmann, a mountain easily accessible to people and serving as a regional landmark. Rising approximately 2,700 meters (2,952 yards) above sea level, the mountain is forested up to the 2,000-meter (2,187-yard) mark, gradually transitioning into highlands with scrub. This area is accessible by car, attracting many visitors. My guide officer and I drove to the 2,000-meter point in the base's exclusive jeep, disembarked, and climbed near the peak in our uniforms, without any equipment or preparation. Beyond the 2,000-meter mark, not even scrub could be found. Despite it being August, we walked on snow piled as high as our ankles, climbing with little struggle and hardly breaking a sweat. We encountered a mountain ranger armed with a shotgun, who was intrigued by my status as a foreign military serviceperson. He kindly explained his duties of guarding the mountain borders. Although I couldn't ascertain if there were stationed soldiers or border police in the Alps, the mountain ranger was both protecting the mountains and guarding the border. I admired the bravery and majesty of these rangers, patrolling and monitoring the snowy Alps alone, albeit armed.

At the base of the mountain lay Lake Königssee, meaning "the king's lake." We returned the next day to explore and sightsee. Nestled deep in the mountains, it was untouched by human presence at that time, enveloped in profound silence. We boarded a tour boat, gliding to the lake's center while listening to explanations. Surrounded by sharp cliffs and snowy mountains like Mt. Watzmann, I marveled at the wonders. When the boat stopped and the engine was turned off, a prehistoric silence enveloped us. A bugler then sounded a bugle, its echo resonating through the surrounding mountains and valleys, lingering for a long time. That echo and atmosphere remain unforgettable. Even during a recent tour in Eastern Europe, when I boarded the same boat on the lake, the echo was no longer performed. I felt a pang of sadness for not hearing it again and realized how much the world has changed.

3. Life at the West Germany Army Command and Staff College (Führungsakademie der Bundeswehr) in Hamburg

♦ Introduction to the School

The literal translation of its German name is "commanding academy," but in the ROK Armed Forces' education system, it's akin to an "Army college," and in the U.S. Armed Forces system, it's a "command and staff college." Therefore, the most comprehensible term for both civilians and military personnel is "command and staff college," abbreviated as CSC. At that time, Germany was still under restrictions as a defeated nation and was attempting to downsize its military. Consequently, organizations and positions were performing dual roles, operating multiple functions in one place. General military functions, such as military court trials during peacetime and school security, were entrusted to civilians or outsourced, as I observed firsthand. The school also offered a course similar to the national security course at Korea National Defense University alongside the CSC. Retired civilians were hired as security guards for the school.

Located in Hamburg during 1969 to 1970 (West Germany), the school was strategically placed in a region where political, diplomatic, economic, social, and international relations were at the forefront. The Academy aimed to equip officer students with an international perspective, fostering continuous improvement and development of the military to an international standard. This was evident when the unified Germany's capital moved back to Berlin, prompting the CSC to return to Berlin as well. This approach was absolutely right. In contrast, Korea's major army academies are now far from Seoul, raising concerns about military officers lacking the necessary international perspective for their era.

Germany welcomed international students from around the world, supporting their studies to align with advanced Western countries and expand their influence overseas. They particularly supported studies in German linguistics, technology education and training, and invited military officers to study in Germany. Many officers who received support for studying abroad hailed from former African colonies—most were captains, yet crucial to their armed forces. Upon completing the course at the military branch school and returning home, they became national leaders. Additionally, officers from allied NATO member nations, such as the United States and the United Kingdom, took regular courses with German officers. Officers from emerging countries like Korea were also present. In 1970, the foreigners' class (a short-term one-year program) comprised 22 students: five German officers, three Koreans, one Swiss, one Nepali, one Moroccan, one Venezuelan, two Brazilians, one Thai, one Iranian, one Spanish, one Indonesian, one Taiwanese, and one Irish.

The school's headquarters consisted of a principal, a brigadier general, and staff officers G-1 through G-5, all colonels. There were no separate active-duty instructors; homeroom instructors and the headquarters staff served as professors. Each homeroom class had a homeroom instructor (Hörsaal Leiter, or lecturing instructors, who were colonels) working with a female secretary and two to three soldiers to prepare and deliver assignments, conduct classes, and handle administrative tasks. These colonels were highly experienced officers who had fought in World War II.

♦ An Introduction to the 'Key (Core) Staff System (Generalstab)' of the German Army

The 'Generalstab' resides in the main command province of the (old) German

Army, traditionally known as the most powerful army in the world. It translates to "general staff (agents)" or "staff of army headquarters." Previously, I used the latter term, but upon reflection, the former seems closer to the actual meaning, so I will use "general staff" more from now on. I will explain how they are trained and operated, why this "general staff" was renowned and formidable after World War II, and their current situation based on my studies and experiences in Germany. I hope this insight will aid the development of the ROK Armed Forces.

Historical Origins

All armed forces worldwide are commanded and directed by a commander with input from the staff. Generally, democratic countries like the United States, United Kingdom, and France have a command structure centered around the commander. In contrast, autocratic countries ruled by dictators, such as Germany and the old Soviet Union, and the Empire of Japan, which emulated them, centered their command structure around the General Staff. The German Army significantly contributed to the unification of Germany in the 1870s under Bismarck, the Iron Chancellor, and Moltke the Elder. Moltke the Elder established the "staff of army headquarters" system to educate and train the "General Staff," composing and operating the "staff of army headquarters" per troop. This system made the German Army the most powerful in Europe, a status it maintains and develops to this day.

They trained a select group of elite officers through specialized education to form the "General Staff (department)," treating them with distinction akin to individuals with doctoral degrees in general society. They wore different epaulettes and pants with red lines and were managed with special care, serving as key members of the Army's organizations. This tradition of command and direction by the German Army's "General Staff" proved invaluable during World War I, following the unification of Germany. As all military personnel know, General Hindenburg, with assistance from General Ludendorff, his exceptional Chief of Staff, and the "General Staff (department)"—particularly through their strategic planning and direction—annihilated four and a half corps of the Russian Army in the Tannenberg region during World War I. This battle is recorded as a significant victory in world military history.

The German Army further strengthened its "General Staff" system, which resulted in its tactics, strategies, and military operations being among the best in the world, instilling fear in the Allies. Despite losing the war due to political figures like Hitler, the Allies and the global community attributed the German Army's "source of power" to war crimes. Consequently, the 'Generalstab' (General Staff), essentially the "staff of army headquarters" of Germany, was put on trial and punished, even though it was not criminal in itself. This made it impossible for the German Army to continue using the system in its original form. When Germany was reestablished as a NATO member after World War II, it eliminated visible symbols of elitism, such as epaulettes and outer covers, and reformed its operational processes. The aim was to ensure that staff members gained experience beyond their specialized roles by mandating that they also serve as commanders, thereby reviving and operating the system.

In terms of training and education, officers for the German Armed Forces were previously selected from the aristocracy. Now, candidates are chosen from soldiers who have completed an 18-month mandatory service and hold an Abitur. They undergo a three-year education course at a military academy, which includes academic education and practical training, before being commissioned. Long-serving commissioned officers go through various certification courses and serve as both platoon leaders and company commanders. To advance to captain, officers must be recommended by their commanders, including the brigade commander, and pass an exam at the Command and Staff College (CSC). Typically, 15% of commissioned officers, including 40 from the Army and 15 from the Navy and Air Force, are selected. They undertake a two-and-a-half-year course at CSC, equivalent to a doctoral course in regular graduate schools, as Germany does not have a master's program. Students immediately begin language classes for six months to obtain an English teaching certificate for middle and high schools—failure results in disqualification. They then return to the main campus for a two-year "core course," living in dormitories and remaining unmarried to focus on spiritual enlightenment. Graduates receive the "im Generalstab" certificate, equivalent to a doctoral degree, and are promoted to major. This rigorous education process is highly regarded, and the title "im Generalstab (i.G)" is as prestigious as a doctoral title, even appearing on business cards. The German public holds these officers in high esteem, contributing to the internal and external strength of the German Armed Forces.

Regarding the operating system and promotion process, after graduating from CSC and being commissioned as Generalstab, officers typically begin as liaison officers for NATO, at a Defense Attaché Office in a German Embassy abroad, or as G3 or G4 staff in a brigade. G3 assumes S2 responsibilities during emergencies. After completing their terms, they are promoted to lieutenant colonels and gain command experience as battalion commanders of combat arms troops. They then serve as staff in high-ranking units (divisions, etc.) before being promoted to colonels and commanding regimental-sized units. This path guarantees their eventual promotion to generals, allowing them to continue serving in high-ranking staff and command positions. The German Army is thus led and strengthened by this elite group.

Meanwhile, some regular long-term officers are promoted to majors, serve as operations officers (S3) at a battalion, complete a one-year short course at CSC, and advance by serving as executive officers or advisors at a regiment or brigade, completing their careers as colonels. Most regular long-term officers (about 85%) serve as captains, rotating through S1, S2, S3, and S4 positions within local battalions and regiments or brigades, and can serve until age 54 if desired. This system contrasts with Korea's, where promotion conflicts are more prevalent. I spoke with a nearly 50-year-old captain, serving as S1 of the mountain brigade where I trained, who shared his perspective on a lifetime career as a captain. He said, “While 'i.G' officers are admired, we are content with our lives. They excel in their units, are recommended by brigade commanders, study diligently even on holidays, and pass competitive CSC exams. They live in dormitories, immersed in study and research for two and a half years, unable to marry or enjoy their youth. After graduating, they constantly relocate, living like nomads with their families, always on edge. In contrast, I've worked in this beautiful unit in a resort town in the Alps, enjoying my role without excessive study or difficulty. I married at the right time, work regular hours, and spend holidays climbing the Alps. I'm satisfied with my life, free from conflicts.” His perspective seemed valid, and I thought it was worth studying for the ROK Armed Forces, which faces promotion conflicts.

♦ I spent days I learning in ‘Allied Forces Course’ at the West Germany Army Command and Staff College

During my time in the “Allied Forces class” at the West Germany Army Command and Staff College, the curriculum and core course classes were structured as a ten-month short course. On the first day, after a simple entrance ceremony, we were introduced to the principal, a brigadier general, and the school's staff, who were colonels. The lecturing instructor (Hősaal Leiter) guided us through the campus facilities and library, where we received about 30 field manuals (FMs) to fill our bags. We were assigned seats and desks in the lecturing rooms, where the FMs were to be kept, indicating that all studies, research, and discussions occurred in the classrooms, with free time outside of that. The key manual among the FMs, “Fűhrung,” is equivalent to the “Operation” manual of Korean FMs and “FM 100-5, Operation” of the U.S. Army's FMs.

The lecturing instructor, a colonel, was responsible for teaching, administrative assistance, field exercises, and staff trips, similar to an elementary school homeroom teacher. His office was adjacent to ours, and he worked with us daily, assisted by one or two administrative agents (including a female secretary). The core courses were divided into three phases: the 1st course (three months) focused on <combat readiness for the unit→emergency→moving the unit to the front>; the 2nd course (five months) on <defense assignment→conducting defense>; and the 3rd course (two months) on <preparation for counterattack and attack>. On the first day, the instructor assigned students to four division headquarters groups (division commander, chief of staff, and major staff of G1, G2, G3, and G4) and regularly reassigned classes to complete the course.

On that first day, I received a “situational task (problem)” for advance study and problem-solving. The initial assignment involved “the situation of discovering signs of enemy invasion→the enemy prepares to attack, and our forces initiate Defcon-2 (establishing defense positions after full armament).” The task: As the division's staff commander (1, 2, 3, and 4), what actions will you take, and what are your plans and conditions? Each assignment typically took two weeks to complete, following the sequence of individual study, group discussion, group presentation, instructor evaluation, and receiving the next assignment. Individual studies involved reading and referencing FMs in the classroom desks, followed by group discussions and presentation preparation based on assigned staff positions. Each group, or division, took turns presenting their solutions. For reference, most West German divisions are stationed in the rear, with border guards (police) operating in border regions.

♦ The curriculum and core course classes were enlightening

The educational approach I encountered was quite unique. There were no preliminary explanations or tips provided before or after the sessions began. Instead, the focus was on individual study, group discussions, and collective conclusions. If a question arose, a relevant member from the school headquarters would address it, offering advice on problem-solving. This method was designed to maximize each individual's motivation for study and research.

Unlike the Korean system, where instructors teach each subject—such as river-crossing, defense, and attack—this system did not assign specific instructors to subjects. There were no separate classes for each topic. Instead, students were encouraged to read field manuals, think critically, study independently, and develop solutions based on their learning. It was an ideal and creative educational system.

From Monday to Friday, groups gathered in classrooms for study sessions, discussing topics to reach group conclusions. For subjects outside the core curriculum, like politics, economics, and history (especially national history), visiting scholars, both German and international, conducted lectures. History, particularly military history, was emphasized as "experience of actual battles in usual times" and was considered crucial.

After two weeks, each group presented their findings. A large clock on the bulletin board added a sense of realism to the presentations. Each group took turns presenting, simulating real-time actions. For instance, the operations officer would receive orders and report them within minutes, demonstrating the process and outcomes as if in a real scenario. Other groups listened, asked questions, and offered opinions.

Once all presentations concluded over two to three days, the lecturing instructor provided evaluations. He summarized each group's presentation, shared his World War II experiences, and concluded, "I respect all groups' presentations and conclusions. Since these situations may occur in real battles, please consider other groups' opinions to develop your own original answers."

At that time, Korean educational institutions still adhered to "the school's original plan," emphasizing it as the sole approach. This could hinder the immediate application of individual creativity in real-world situations.

After conclusions were drawn, the instructor distributed preparation sheets with subsequent scenarios and assignments. Group members were reassigned to foster a fresh learning atmosphere. The following is a summary of the ongoing situations and assignments given to us:

- Receive an order to move the troop and conduct defense in front defense areas; You are the staff of the division/commander. Review the plan to move the troop. It is presumed to be a drill troop similar to an actual troop stationed near Hamburg.
- Start the troop movement; Receive an order to move your troop via highway 000 through 000 city. Review cooperation issues with the city's administrative office and the military road control office during the troop movement.
- Receive an order for river-crossing without a bridge in an emergency; The mechanized troop is in a hasty situation to cross a large stream (e.g., Hangang River) without a bridge. What are your plans and their state?

♦ The staff trip, terrain exercise, and record of personal experiences in West Germany were integral parts of the course.

The German Armed Forces often sent the "general staff" on "staff trips" to confirm and conduct operations according to plan and assess local situations. Our Allied Forces class embarked on a staff trip to compare and confirm our individual plans with actual scenarios. We traveled from Hamburg to the eastern border, exploring local roads, autobahns, and a tributary of the River Elbe. We visited local administrative offices to discuss military support details, such as water supply, traffic restrictions, and supply assistance.

As we progressed, the course involved organizing and conducting defense exercises, terrain exercises, staff trips, and preparation for counterattacks. In the final stage, the regular German Armed Forces class was divided into Blue and Red Forces for a joint exercise involving the Army, Navy, and Air Forces. Our class observed this exercise as we completed our course.

♦ I learned about the West German Army's operation doctrine and management of tactical nuclear weapons

The West German Army's operation doctrine and management of tactical nuclear weapons were also covered. The terms "Fűhrung" in the West German Army, "Operation" in the U.S. Army, and "Instruction on Operation" in the ROK Army were discussed. The U.S. and ROK Armies only have "tactics" and "strategy," while the West German Army included "operation" for regiments and brigades.

In defense, mechanized and panzer units were strategically positioned, with the panzer battalion conducting counterattacks. This model was typical for battles in the European plains. Tactical nuclear weapons, managed by NATO's U.S. Armed Forces, were used in drills by West Germany. However, they were deemed less beneficial than traditional weapons, leading to the cessation of drills in the 1970s and eventual disposal in the 1990s following arms control agreements.

During field exercises and staff trips, I visited various regions and facilities. One notable visit was to Helgoland, a triangular-shaped island used as a Navy ammunition depot. This experience prompted me to consider potential military facilities in Korea's Taebaek Mountains.

We also visited Volkswagen, an automotive company known for producing fuel-efficient, beetle-shaped cars that were highly reliable. These cars were beloved by the German people and were world-famous at the time. On their production line, they managed to produce one car every three minutes. From what I gathered, Volkswagen was just beginning to rise in Germany, producing Opel and Audi with American capital and German technology, while Benz was preparing for production. At that time, Korea was assembling and producing cars called Cortina, and I thought Korea might have started in a similar way.

After that, we visited Krupp, a world-renowned German steel company. Its immense size and grandeur, along with its pride in product quality, were impressive. This company had produced gun barrels for various firearms during World War II. However, it was prohibited from producing military supplies, and a representative from the company lamented that even German Panzer tanks had gun barrels made in the UK, a NATO member nation. He nostalgically boasted about their old gun barrel products.

Every visit and observation allowed me to speculate on Korea's national development, which was rapidly changing under the military government. Germany was accelerating its national revival and building a structure for car production to support heavy industrialization, which piqued my interest. We also visited a communication school on our way and observed the DDD telecommunication system of the West German Army, which was about half a step ahead of the ROK Army. In the evening, we attended a masquerade, enjoying a few hours with local women, likely families of military personnel, who hid their ages and appearances with amusing masks. We disguised ourselves as sailors.

4. Visiting and obserbing the Pnzer Division staff – the 5th Armored Division (Frankfurt am Mine)

In July 1970, after completing my ten-month course at the Command and Staff College in Hamburg, I spent a month visiting and observing staff work in divisions. Germany has two cities named Frankfurt, and one of them is Frankfurt am Main, located on the banks of the River Main in West Germany. Nowadays, most Korean flights to Germany land at this city's airport. I was fortunate to visit the 5th Armored Division and observe the panzer unit, a symbol of the German Army, as the final part of my study in the West German Army. Upon arrival, the division commander and staff warmly welcomed me. I spent most of my time exploring the division's staff departments and attending staff meetings to follow daily routines within the command center. Occasionally, I visited nearby brigades to witness the vigor of the German Armored Division. Unfortunately, they didn't conduct any maneuvering drills or exercises with other units, so I couldn't observe real field exercises. One day, I joined the division staff for a hike up a nearby mountain, where we enjoyed beer at a park on the summit. A German Army comrade offered me fruit wine, saying it was the best drink after hiking and sweating, and I tasted it with him.

As my course was ending, the unit's Chief of Staff asked me about the preferences of the ROK Army's Chief of Staff, who was visiting soon with a Korean assemblyman. As an Army major, I didn't know the Chief of Staff's specific preferences, but I shared general Korean food preferences, appreciating their effort and hospitality. The Chief of Staff seemed indifferent to the assemblyman, perhaps because German assembly members were considered equivalent to a bureau chief among public officials, unlike in Korea.

5. Other stories from studing abroad in West Germany - Travelogues from West Germany, Europe, and Japan in the early 1970

♦ I took historical tour in London, UK, and Paris France

In May 1970, with the dreary winter and homesickness behind me, spring arrived, offering the perfect opportunity to be active. I embarked on a trip to Paris with a German civilian through a travel agency in the city, just before completing my course in Hamburg. I now recall those memories to write a travelogue. We departed from Hamburg, passed through Cologne in northern Germany, traversed Liege and Namur in Belgium, and entered Sedan in the Ardennes Mountains, France. As an officer who graduated from KMA and studied European military history, I was deeply moved by this route. It was the same path the German Armed

Forces took to invade France during World War I, following the Schlieffen Plan, and the German panzer troops used it to bypass the Maginot Line for a blitzkrieg to Paris during World War II. Monuments for unnamed war veterans lined the streets, and in Dinant, national flags of France, Belgium, Germany, the UK, and the U.S. flew year-round to commemorate the fierce battles of the past. Many cemeteries for unnamed war veterans lay beneath a gigantic cross. I heard that representatives from the countries involved in wars gather annually for a significant memorial ceremony.

Before reaching Paris, we stopped in Reims and visited the world-famous REIM Champagne brewery. Underground storage facilities, a few hundred meters long, were connected by numerous passageways around a spot 50 meters below ground. Champagne bottles were stored endlessly, and technicians regularly adjusted them, allowing sunlight exposure. They said ten-year-old Champagne tasted best. The guide randomly selected a bottle, removed the cork, and lightly tapped it with something resembling chopsticks, causing it to foam and rocket without spilling a drop. That was the delicacy of Champagne. They even joked that the German Army got stuck in Reims during its march to Paris because its members wanted to drink this Champagne, leading to endless drinking and drunkenness.

Upon entering Paris, we checked into a tourist hotel at Place de la Concorde, a wide plaza where history, hope, African invasions, and traditions coexisted. After dinner, I ventured outside at sunset, stood in the plaza's center, and admired the night view of the Champs-Elysees toward the distant Triumphal Arch. I witnessed the beautiful night scene depicted in paintings worldwide—the rainy street of Champs-Elysees, rows of cars, and the red hue from their taillights harmonizing with the drizzle. It was already late, so I returned to the hotel and went to the bathroom before bed. In the bathroom, I found something resembling a toilet and used it to wash my hands, feet, and socks, thinking France had peculiar appliances as a country of art. I later learned it was for women, realizing this was the essence of Paris, France. Forty years later, around 2010, it became popular in Korea and is known as a "bidet."

The next day, we explored the plaza, bustling with farmers who had moved to Paris, citizens returning from old overseas colonies, and antique and vegetable sellers in every corner. It exuded a vibrant human atmosphere. We then walked up the Champs-Elysees, a 100-meter-wide street stretching to the Triumphal Arch, with marronier trees and stylish sidewalks on both sides. I was particularly impressed by the marronier trees planted along the street's sides and center. Eight years later, in 1978, when I was a regimental commander, I planted seven marronier trees in front of and beside the headquarters of the 26th Regiment, Nonsan Training Center. If they still stand today, they must be enormous. The trees were evenly spaced, similar in size and shape, and wonderfully designed metal plates were neatly placed below them. They embodied France's public order, caregiving, and beauty.

The street views in large cities of Korea, which have become popular 50 years

After my visit, remind me of the red-colored shops lined up along the sidewalks in Paris, with chairs and tables set out front, creating a peaceful and human atmosphere. When I finally arrived at the Arc de Triomphe, built to commemorate Napoleon's conquests, I was struck by the grandeur of this massive stone structure at the intersection of 12 roads. Constructed over 30 years, it stands as a majestic symbol of Paris and is one of the world's most renowned triumphal arches. I approached it to examine the details on its four sides, which feature group sculptures representing "La Marseillaise" (The March), "La Triomphe" (The Triumph), "La Resistance" (The Resistance), and "La Paix" (The Peace). I wondered when we might build such a triumphal arch in Gwanghwamun, Republic of Korea, and hoped this dream would come true someday.

Our next stop was the first and largest military history museum, showcasing weapons, equipment, military flags, uniforms, and artwork from various battles throughout history. It provided insight into not only the Napoleonic era but also the broader scope of military history. The collection was extensive, taking about two hours to view even for a casual visitor. We then visited a war history building, where I learned about the victories and defeats of the French Armed Forces and world war history. Particularly striking was the brilliant yet solemn marble coffin of Napoleon, elevated in the center of the grand main hall, reflecting the French people's admiration for him. As military personnel, we too hold his achievements in high regard.

The Eiffel Tower, synonymous with Paris, is a 320-meter-tall iron structure standing before a large fountain, crafted by a German technician to commemorate the first World Expo. From the upper observatory, accessible by escalator, you can enjoy a 360-degree view of downtown Paris and its suburbs. A circular direction board marked world-famous cities in 12 directions, yet only Tokyo represented Asia. Disappointed, I submitted a complaint to the tower's management to include Seoul.

Paris is home to many iconic streets, churches, parks, theaters, palaces, and sculptures. Notable sites include the Moulin Rouge, known for the French Can-can dance; Pigalle, a street of nightlife; Montmartre, a hub for street artists; the Palace of Versailles with its historical gardens; the Louvre Museum, a world-renowned art museum; a romantic cruise on the River Seine; and the antique beauty of Notre-Dame Cathedral. However, what impressed me most was the Paris Metro, the largest and widest subway system in the world at that time. With 15 lines stretching over 30 kilometers, it was a vast network that made it seem as though tourists walked above ground while Parisians traveled below. It felt as if downtown Paris floated in the air.

There's a saying that every world traveler should end their journey in Paris, and it's no exaggeration. Many beautiful and traditional European cities aspire to be called "Little Paris" or "the second Paris." Most Parisian buildings are five-story apartments from the Napoleonic urban development era, with shops and offices on the lower floors and residences above. These structures remain unchanged, reflecting European history and traditions distinct from American cities.

As of 2021, Seoul boasts more than 10 metro lines extending over 60 kilometers, connecting the city to regions like Gyeonggi-do, Chungcheong-do, and Gangwon-do. This development was unimaginable in 1970, when France was a symbol of nostalgia and pleasure for Koreans, making my visit all the more impressive. Reflecting on my European travels, I concluded that removing cathedrals from Europe, Napoleon and de Gaulle from France, or Nelson and Churchill from the UK would render European history books irrelevant.

♦ I visited West Berlin by invitation and experienced life in West Germany

From May 19th to May 21st, 1970, we were invited to Berlin as VIPs, along with our instructors, students, and their families, for a government-planned propaganda and graduation trip. At the time, Berlin was surrounded by East Germany, with the Allied Forces controlling over half the city to protect West German citizens. As the former capital of Germany and the future capital of a unified Germany, West Germany sought to redefine itself morally after World War II. Chancellor Willy Brandt's 1970 visit to Warsaw, where he knelt before war victims' tombstones, exemplified this effort.

We were invited to witness evidence of the anti-Hitler movement within Germany, showcasing the military, administrative, and civilian resistance, particularly among elite citizens. We saw the devastation of Berlin post-war and the division by the Berlin Wall, appealing for a change in Germany's war criminal image. Arriving in Berlin by military aircraft, we stayed at the Hotel Palace in the Europe Center complex. The next day, the Mayor of Berlin welcomed us and took us to an old prison, where we learned about the torture and execution of anti-Hitler forces, including German Army officers involved in the July 1944 assassination attempt on Hitler.

The mayor passionately explained how General Rommel, a revered figure feared by the Allies, was accused of plotting an insurgency and executed under the guise of suicide. Many General Staff agents, representing the respected German Army, were also suspected of being anti-Hitler elites, tortured, and executed. Hearing this, I realized the General Staff was indeed the heart of the German Army, punished as a group in the Nuremberg Trials, yet still respected.

We then visited the Brandenburg Gate, a triumphal arch from the Prussian era, symbolizing the Berlin Wall and Cold War tensions. The cement wall divided Berlin into East and West, with barbed wire and sentry posts marking the border between East and West Germany. Standing there, I felt emotional, reminded of Korea's division by the 38th Parallel and the Military Demarcation Line after the Korean War. We took a photo in front of this Cold War symbol, and looking at it in 2021, I reflect on history's flow and feel sorrow for Korea's continued division, perpetuated by North Korea's ruling Kim family.

They built a structure resembling a viewing platform in a sports stadium, slightly adjacent to the triumphal arch, where tourists could stand and look out over East Berlin beyond the wall. The atmosphere was mostly quiet and tense. As we walked further along the wall, we noticed several round bouquets placed on it. These bouquets commemorated the East Berlin citizens and East German guards who were shot and killed or died tragically while attempting to escape, marking the very spots where they fell. It reminded me of North Korean defectors who continue to escape North Korea even today.

Next, we returned to the city center to visit the Kaiser Wilhelm Memorial Church, which had been bombed and destroyed, leaving only its frame. A new octagonal church was built right next to it. This meant I got to see another memorial church constructed when Berlin was rebuilt after the war. Although West Berlin was surrounded by East Germany—essentially within East Germany—and Berlin itself was divided by the wall built by East Germany, the East Germany I saw beyond the wall and the West Berlin I was experiencing were completely different worlds. This visible contrast was a clear way to distinguish between communism and democracy.

On the last day, we had some free time. However, there was a warning: "Be cautious when you take the metro, because you might end up in East Berlin if you take the wrong train." It seemed that East and West Berlin were not completely divided, unlike Korea, and I felt the difference from our situation. As the daytime tour was ending, I met a German officer from my class, and we ventured into an unrecovered three-story building deep in an alley with a "King George V" sign. To my surprise, it was literally a "Ganz Akt Show Striptease," as advertised on the poster. I watched, feeling awkward, and to my astonishment, I turned to see a grandfather and his elementary school-aged grandson watching it together right next to me. The truth is, Germany had "Ero Centrum" across the entire country, and I often saw women selling related items on the streets.

♦ Reflections on Life in West Germany

It is impossible to recount everything I witnessed in West Germany from 1969 to 1970, so I'll highlight a few unforgettable experiences.

• The Quintessential German "Deutsch Punkt!"

I truly felt that the German people are practical, firm, and precise in everything they do. I stayed in a hotel in downtown Bad Reichenhall for two months while working with the Mountain Brigade in the Alps to observe the staff. A German second lieutenant accompanied me when necessary. We arranged to leave the hotel at 9:00 a.m. on holiday. That morning, I finished my preparations and waited in my room. Just as I grabbed the doorknob, not a second late, the accompanying officer knocked. When I opened the door, he saluted and cheerfully said, "Deutsch Punkt!"—a phrase emphasizing that "Germans are great, accurate, and trustworthy." This sentiment was truly reflective of Germany, and all Germans lived with that thought and pride.

One day, I visited a post office to send a letter. Despite the long line, the employee diligently and perfectly assisted each customer. When lunchtime arrived, the hardworking employee left for lunch, regardless of the waiting line. Yet, the people in line remained, seemingly unfazed. I couldn't help but wait in line just as they did. Germans take pride in this, boasting about it, albeit differently from Americans. German-manufactured products, especially weapons—from rifles to heavy firearms I saw in the German Army—appeared somewhat dull and awkward compared to the sleek designs of American weapons, but they were exceptionally sturdy and superior in functionality.

• Weather, Life, Aspirations, and Philosophy in Germany (Central Europe)

During my philosophy classes as a cadet at KMA, our professor often exhibited a peculiar behavior. He would say, "Kierkegaard said..." and then stand there, staring at the ceiling, completely frozen for about three minutes (though it felt like ten). The classroom would fall silent, and the energy of philosophy would make the air solemn. When he discussed Nietzsche, he would say, "Nietzsche said, 'God is dead...'" and again look at the ceiling for what felt like ten minutes. This made me wonder, "Why did that German philosopher say 'God is dead'? What is Germany like to inspire such philosophy?" I found answers to my questions when I visited Germany. Its geopolitical situation and weather influenced such thoughts.

In the mid-late 19th century, Germany was still a federal state composed of about 40 duchies. It was a small power, both in terms of population and nationhood, enduring wars against Napoleon and Russia, conquests, revolutions, and insurgencies. Its history was filled with relentless hardships. It was unified by Bismarck, the Iron Chancellor, and Moltke the Elder, a great general, in the late 19th century, but it remained surrounded and threatened by great powers. As a nation, it faced an era of hardships, turbulence, and an uncertain future. Perhaps this is why Nietzsche thought "God is dead." Furthermore, Germany (Central Europe) experiences cloudy weather year-round, with frequent drizzles, creating a gloomy atmosphere. A sunny day is when the sun shines for just 30 minutes. On such days, women would sunbathe topless. This was their natural environment. They even call April "the cruelest month" because flowers are covered in ice, cold winds still blow, and the weather is disappointing, despite it being technically spring.

When I asked why they work so hard to earn money, everyone, especially civilians, said, "I am making money to go on vacations in summer and winter. I want to visit places with sunny weather and clean water, where people treat me well, like Italy, Spain, Africa, etc., to relax." Perhaps philosophers, civilians, politicians, and all Germans living there think about escaping reality. This might explain why Germany sometimes experiences chaos and struggles, as seen in history.

• Daily Lives of German Civilians

The economy of West Germany was still developing at the time, but it had recovered significantly after the war. The exchange rate between the U.S. dollar and the West German mark was 1:4, and the bank interest rate was 8%. Just a few years later, it reversed to four dollars to one mark. Germany's economy was improving continuously, with its economic indicators rising sharply. The employment rate of non-Germans, especially southern Italians, reached one million, a level Korea reached in the 2000s. Korea was still experiencing inflation at the time, with bank interest rates around 20%, so most companies were compensating for operating losses by securing land rather than profits from business operations.

Germans were still thrifty and well-prepared in their daily lives, maintaining a unified and controlled societal system. In the United States, when invited to an acquaintance's house, they usually host an abundant dinner party. In West Germany, they also invite acquaintances, but usually in the afternoons. Initially, I thought they wanted to talk first and then serve dinner. However, contrary to my expectations, they simply conversed over "a cup of tea," and the gathering ended by dinnertime.

The menus at military base cafeterias or civilian homes were consistent throughout the week. Breakfast typically consisted of simple bread (black barley bread), milk, and sausages. They prepared a hot dish for lunch or dinner. Dinner could also be cold or similar to breakfast, meaning something already cooked. The main ingredients for one hot dish per day were: Beef on Mondays; Lamb on Tuesdays; Leftover soup on Wednesdays; Fish on Thursdays; Other meats on Fridays; Sweets on Saturdays; and often dining out on Sundays. I received a "lunch box" from the base's cafeteria, consisting of barley bread, sausages, and other items, which I enjoyed with beer or milk alone in my room. I only had three eggs per week—at the U.S. Army officer's cafeteria, they prepared two eggs per day as requested (boiled, scrambled, half-cooked, etc.).

Germany cannot produce wheat, so affluent households consumed white bread imported from France. The officer's cafeteria at a German Army base also served one baguette, imported from France, for breakfast only.

The first Thursday lunch I experienced was a simple boiled fish fillet, about the size of a fist, accompanied by a bland dipping sauce. It was too tasteless and fishy for my liking, so I asked if they could grill it for me, as is customary in Korea. They replied, "That's something available only in hotels." The taste was unbearable, and I couldn't finish it. I had heard of a senior who had also come to Germany for studies and couldn't adapt to the German cuisine, ultimately giving up his studies. The dining etiquette was similar to American customs, where it was acceptable to blow your nose loudly without concern for others—a behavior considered disgusting and offensive to Asians. One difference was that Americans tear bread into small pieces with their hands, while Germans slice it with a knife. Additionally, you are expected to move only the parts of your arms above the wrists on the table. Despite this, they almost always enjoy wine or beer at night while watching TV. I was aware that "going Dutch" is common in Europe, but I had an interesting experience in Germany. One day, all the students in my class were invited to the home of a German classmate near the school. While we were eating and chatting in the yard, one of the officer's chairs broke. He explained that it was his neighbor's chair and that he needed to compensate for it. He asked all of us to contribute, as everyone should share the cost. This seemed reasonable in a culture accustomed to going Dutch. However, Koreans were still used to acts of benevolence and were unfamiliar with the concept of splitting costs, making the situation feel strange.

Feeling a deep sense of patriotism, pride, and homesickness, I recalled my first encounter in Europe. A German I met on my first day asked, "Are you Chinese? Or Japanese?" I replied, "I'm Korean." He responded with delight, "Ah, Korea! That's a country with a great national soccer team!" He remembered that the North Korean team had defeated the Italian team and reached the quarterfinals. At that time, many people, especially Europeans, had never heard of Korea or Koreans, but the North Korean soccer team's achievements had brought some recognition.

Traveling abroad often turns people into patriots, and we Koreans became particularly patriotic when overseas. Someone once showed a photo taken in front of Daehanmun Gate of Deoksugung Palace in Seoul and proudly claimed, "This is the gate of my house, and many Koreans live in houses like this." Men would even boast, "Unlike your people, we are the kings at our homes. We never pull chairs for woman."

♦ I pondered what homesickness truly means

However, during my time abroad, I experienced homesickness. Although I felt some homesickness in Vietnam, being busy with important work and facing constant threats kept it from becoming overwhelming. It wasn't too severe during my six months at the German language school or while practicing staff exercises with the mountain troop in the Alps. But for some reason, I became very homesick while living in the VOQ of the CSC in Hamburg. Reflecting on it now, I can identify the reasons, but I was unaware at the time. Firstly, I missed my beloved family in Korea, especially when witnessing the happy moments of my classmates' families from different countries. Secondly, despite being an adult and a serviceperson accustomed to living away from home, the unfamiliar food, bed, and environment caused daily stress and made me long for my life in Korea. Thirdly, I often found myself alone in the quiet dormitory in the forest with little to do after my daily routine, on weekends, or holidays. Seeing families dining together at the school cafeteria on holidays intensified my yearning. To comfort myself, I bought a German-made music recorder and player, repeatedly playing Lee Mi-ja's greatest hits album. I also traveled to other countries on short or long trips to alleviate my homesickness.

To my dear Su-yeon, my beloved wife: A long time ago, a second lieutenant in the Army deeply loved Su-yeon, a charming, beautiful, and graceful college student. From the heights of the front, a building in Seoul, and the United States, he thought of her passionately, night after night. Five beautiful years passed, and we lived happily in Gwangju, even though we rented a small room. The birth of our first son brought us immense joy and a sense of accomplishment, despite the trials we faced due to my hardships. When our second son was born, we settled in House 250 in Hwagok-dong. Yet another trial struck when I was dispatched to Vietnam. My beloved 'Young,' as I affectionately call her, remains the princess waiting for me. Nothing in the world compares to Su-yeon and her love. I promise to bring happiness, accomplishment, and a bright future to Su-yeon, my love. Celebrating our 7th anniversary with love, sincerely yours from West Germany, April 22nd, 1969.

♦ **Hamburg, where the West Germany Army War College located, became familiar Hamburg, where the West Germany Army CSC was located, was the leading city of West Germany, the largest harbor city in all of Germany, and a hub of economic activity and global trends in the 1970s. This is why the CSC, traditionally based in Berlin, was temporarily relocated to Hamburg. Interestingly, this harbor is not on the coast but inland, near the end of the River Elbe, which flows into the North Sea. My Korean classmates and I would sometimes visit Kiel, a true seaside city north of Hamburg, to enjoy the sandy beach. However, I often visited Hamburg's harbor, sitting at a riverside café, observing non-German ships navigating the narrow sea route and interacting with the immigration office. I found the whole scene fascinating and enjoyed the harbor's atmosphere.**

I didn't venture downtown often, but one day, guided by a German classmate, I visited the famous 'Reeperbahn,' a must-see in Hamburg. It was a large area with dance halls, casinos, special restaurants, beer bars, jazz stages, wine tasting areas, circuses, movie theaters, adult clubs, and cabarets. Women, completely or partially naked, sat behind long horizontal display windows, enticing customers. The street was about 200 meters long, and there was a place called "Ero Centrum," surrounded by buildings resembling three-story office apartments. Inside the courtyard, dozens of naked women stood under a veranda roof, winking at passersby, signaling them to choose. Many visitors, especially sailors, came for this purpose, while others were simply tourists. My German classmate warned us before we had free time, advising that if we entered a strip club, we would be obliged to buy a drink, usually high-class German "sekt" or spirits, which were expensive. If a woman joined us and ordered more drinks, we risked being overcharged. Complaining would only lead to humiliation by the bouncers, so he advised us to be accompanied by German classmates if we wanted to visit such places. He also mentioned that, despite being in Germany, these establishments lacked honesty.

♦ I attended the '1970 Osaca EXPO' in Japan and then returned to Korea

The '1970 Osaka EXPO (EXPO 70)' and Japan: Accompanying me at the CSC in West Germany were Major Kang of the Marine Corps and Lieutenant Colonel Gu of the Army's tank branch, whom I've already introduced. Lieutenant Colonel Gu was one of three brothers, with his two elder brothers being successful businesspeople in Osaka, Japan, producing and selling auto parts. They lived confidently, and Lieutenant Colonel Gu honored their family as a Korean military serviceperson. His brothers manufactured "bearings," essential components for car wheels and other rotating parts, under contract, supplying all their products to Mercedes-Benz, the renowned German automotive company. At that time, based on their post-war restoration technology and the combined spirit of Japan, they strived to supply bearings under their own brand to Mercedes-Benz, eventually signing a new contract with initial disadvantages. They were remarkable Korean entrepreneurs in Japan, making Korea proud. Of course, Korea also achieved "the Miracle on the Hangang River" with heavy and chemical industrialization following the May 16th Military Revolution, and the entire nation was filled with pride and determination to "catch up with Japan" within 15 years. Finally, as of 2023, Korea has surpassed Japan and become one of the six great powers of the world.

Proud of their younger brother studying abroad, they invited us to Japan on our way back to Korea, coinciding with the Osaka EXPO (EXPO 70). We joyfully stopped in Japan from August 2nd to August 5th, 1970, on our return journey from Germany. Despite sharing an oceanic climate, Osaka's early August heat was oppressively humid compared to Busan's climate at 35 degrees north latitude. Thankfully, Japan had air conditioning in all buildings, including homes, allowing us to cool off indoors. Despite the heat, Lieutenant Colonel's two elder brothers and their families graciously hosted us, enduring the weather.

One day, we visited the historic cities of Kyoto and Nara, reminiscent of Korea's Gyeongju. At Nara Park, they proudly showcased four deer within fenced areas.

When I revisited in 2015, there were over 2,000 deer roaming freely, much to the tourists' annoyance. The following day, we attended “The Japan World Exposition” or “EXPO 70” in Osaka, which aimed to showcase Japan’s national power and ambition during its recovery. Due to the intense heat, we visited a few indoor exhibitions and stopped by “Dream Land,” a miniature version of Disneyland, in Nara. I vividly remember that all the families and children appeared affluent and sophisticated, prompting me to wonder, “When will Korea reach this level? We need to hurry.”

As the weather cooled at night, people in the neighborhood gathered outside, setting up “flat wooden beds” or low benches in front of their homes. Men, wearing 'fundoshi'—traditional Japanese underwear—sat flapping fans, laughing, and chatting with women. It resembled Korean daily life, but the sight of the “fundoshi,” considered “vulgar” by Koreans, made me think they still held onto barbaric customs.

The next day, Lieutenant Colonel Gu’s elder brothers drove us to Tokyo. We expressed our gratitude for their kindness and hospitality, visiting their auto parts factory along the way. Though not large, the factory was sturdy and gleaming, like a solid rock. They employed many Japanese workers, praised for their trustworthiness, loyalty, and dedication to the company's growth. We arrived in the afternoon, bid farewell to our hosts, and stayed in our hotel rooms during the day to escape the heat. We took the subway to see Tokyo Tower, a 333-meter (364-yard) tall transmitting tower, heavily advertised as being nine meters taller than the Eiffel Tower in France. I noticed that elderly Japanese were shorter than Koreans, allowing me to see over their heads in the subway, but the younger generation seemed to be growing taller than young Koreans. I felt the military government needed to “push things ahead” to expedite our revival and development.

Returning to Korea on August 5th, 1970, I arrived at Gimpo Airport and reunited with my beloved family, who came to greet me. This was my third long overseas trip since getting engaged and married, following my studies in the United States and deployment to Vietnam. Yet, I missed them dearly and was overjoyed to see them again.

6. As an Instructor at Jinhae Korea Army College, living in the official residence

♦ I became qualified as an instructor and lived that life, residing in the official residence with my family and experiencing life in Jinhae

As an instructor at Jinhae Korea Army College, I was tasked with teaching guerrilla warfare, a subject I was assigned due to my studies abroad, combat experience in Vietnam with the Tiger Division, and work at the Army's special warfare office. Despite the rote learning and lecture style, I taught guerrilla warfare for 30 to 45 minutes, followed by a Q&A session. The non-credit system allowed me to teach according to the school's syllabus, totaling about ten hours. I taught two to three courses, balancing teaching with research to develop the subject using Korean and world war history.

The faculty conducted annual lecture tours to front and rear troops to spread new doctrines, pairing instructors for each subject. Officers, including division commanders, attended these lectures with keen interest, respecting the instructors and their content. After lectures, ACK graduates and troop commanders interested in doctrine development hosted us, allowing us to explore various regions of Korea and experience their unique geographies and customs.

Living with my family in the official residence at Jinhae, we enjoyed a stable yet unfamiliar life from September 1970 to April 1972, until I was transferred to a front troop. The Korea Army College, located under Jangboksan Mountain in Yeojwa-dong, offered a stunning view of downtown Jinhae and Jinhae Bay. I recalled taking my final KMA entrance exam there in 1954, feeling nostalgic about living and working there with my family.

The campus was beautifully lined with cherry blossom trees along the central road, leading to the main entrance. Highway 2 (Busan-Mokpo) crossed in front, with a railway crosswalk of the Jinhae Line beyond it, leading to downtown Jinhae. The market was 1.5 kilometers away, and the Republic of Korea Naval Academy was 2.5 kilometers away, near the Naval Station and temporary naval aerodrome. The cherry blossom trail inside the Naval Station was a breathtaking sight in spring, and the Cherry Blossom Festival in late March was renowned nationwide.

• Growing a Vegetable Garden with My Family and Market Shopping

In Korea, during that time, it was common for men to work outside the home to earn money while women managed the household, raised children, and cared for their husbands. This was the norm. Families of instructors moved into official residences, where houses were spaced 5 to 6 meters apart, with roads in front and behind, facing each other with a ten-meter gap. Without fences, all the houses were visible to one another. The residents were of similar ages, fostering an ideal community life. However, the campus lacked welfare facilities, except for a single coffee shop in the faculty area. Consequently, everyone had to visit the market daily for groceries or found joy in planting vegetables in small gardens to alleviate boredom. We grew lettuce, chili peppers, cucumbers, and even zucchinis. A particularly diligent instructor even cultivated a hill behind the residence, creating a 33-square-meter garden to maintain health. Refrigerators were not available then, necessitating daily market trips. Buses ran to the market twice a day, allowing homemakers to travel together, purchase groceries, and explore the outside world.

• Education for Children and Family Hobbies

Most instructors' children were in kindergarten or early elementary school. The school operated a public kindergarten, a rarity in the ROK Armed Forces, offering a privilege to instructors' families. Our second son, Seong-eon, enjoyed his time at the Army College Kindergarten for a year and a half. Our first son, Jeong-eon, attended Daeya Elementary School in Jinhae after previously attending a kindergarten in Hwagok-dong, Seoul. Education for servicepeople's children was a significant issue, affecting family development. Children often moved schools due to their fathers' transfers, leading to frequent relocations and educational disruptions. Our second son finished kindergarten early, read books with friends, or played around the campus. He would wait for his elder brother at the rear entrance, chatting with the guard until his brother arrived. They would then collect snacks and return home together, later meeting me to walk back to our residence. The base lacked officer clubs or restaurants for families, but it did have tennis courts for families to enjoy. A public swimming pool, 25 meters long, was also available, hosting local competitions and providing summer fun for families. Golf was not an option for Army officer instructors until 1979, when it became available by chance, a story I will share later.

Chapter 7

The Establishment of the 102nd Mechanized Infantry Battalion (Oct 24th.1972), and the Capital Mechanized Infantry Division (Mar 22nd.1973)

1. Commander of the 1st Battalion, 98th Regiment, 32nd Division (April 1972)

♦ We assumed armored personnel carriers (APC, M113) and prepared to establish <Rainbow Troop>

• I became a Infantry battalion commander.

In April 1972, I became a battalion commander in a reserve division at the front. Former Army College instructors were prioritized for these roles due to their tactical knowledge. The 32nd Division, a reserve division, was reorganized into a mechanized infantry division. Officers who studied in Germany, known for its expertise in tank and mechanized troops, were ideal candidates for battalion commanders. I was appointed commander of the 1st Battalion, 98th Regiment, 32nd Division.

• The Division Environment and Commander

When the ROK Armed Forces were deployed to Vietnam, Korea and the United States agreed to modernize the Korean Armed Forces. Two divisions were dispatched to Vietnam, and two 'mobilization reserve divisions' were reorganized into combat divisions and moved to the front. The 32nd Division relocated from Chungcheongnam-do to Hyeon-ri, Gyeonggi-do.

• Battalion ATT and Special Assault Commando Platoon

As a reserve division commander, I was required to take an Army Training Test on field combat drills. Our battalion was the last to be tested as an infantry battalion before becoming mechanized. The test included marching, organizing and conducting defense, counterattack, and attack. With prior experience, we achieved excellent results. As a former instructor in guerrilla and commando warfare, I organized a successful 'Special Assault Commando Platoon.' I selected a capable platoon leader and 30 members, assigning them missions. They performed exceptionally, with determination and pride.

The issue of serving food during wartime was problematic. When I was a platoon leader, cooking involved firewood and clay kitchens. By the time I was a battalion commander, anthracite and kitchen sets replaced firewood, but mealtimes remained chaotic, reducing combat power.

2. The 102nd Mechanized Infantry Battalion of the Army (The 1660th Troop of the Army) was Established (October 24th, 1972):

♦ Acquisition of armored vehicles and preparations for the creation of the Rainbow Unit

After completing the infantry battalion test, we moved to the division's command center in Hyeon-ri in early October 1972 to establish the 2nd Mechanized Infantry Battalion. We assumed all APC platoons and members from tank companies across the Army, with platoons traveling dozens or hundreds of kilometers to join our battalion.

At that time, no one in the division or battalion had any real knowledge of APCs, and I was no exception. My experience was limited to disassembling and assembling automobile engines during my weapon engineering class at the Korea Military Academy. Additionally, I had only ridden in a U.S. Army-operated APC for an hour during a combat operation when I was a platoon leader. To address this gap, I assigned a college graduate with prior car driving experience to take charge. I also formed the APC Assumption and Inspection Team with a few ROTC officers, sending them to each division in succession. Their only guiding principle, based on advice from a tank officer, was to select APCs emitting “white smoke from the muffler and an engine that makes a 'whoosh!' sound.” Despite these efforts, inspecting them proved futile.

When the entire troop arrived, I went below the Seopa Checkpoint to welcome them, repeatedly saying, “I'm proud of you, thank you.” The battalion, normally consisting of about 800 members, suddenly swelled to 1,026, and the company grew from 160 A/S members to 260. This overcrowding forced soldiers to sleep in close quarters, leading some to climb onto lockers to sleep, much like passengers on nighttime trains using luggage racks as beds. The battalion remained overcrowded for a while, and everyone had to endure the situation until they were gradually discharged. Our soldiers understood the circumstances and endured them admirably.

♦ Strengthening Combat Power and Reorganizing the Infantry Battalion to a Mechanized Infantry Battalion

Meanwhile, the infantry battalion was quickly equipped with armament and equipment comparable to an infantry regiment. It expanded to include 60 armored vehicles, such as M113 armored personnel carriers, M112 APCs for the battalion commander, and armored ambulances, all managed by a sergeant first class, a vehicle maintenance engineer, and a captain, the chief of vehicle maintenance. Additionally, there were 20 wheeled vehicles of various sizes for administrative, combat, and telecommunication purposes, managed by a sergeant first class and a master sergeant. A mortar company equipped with 4.2-inch mortars, typically used by regiments, replaced the 81-millimeter mortars, with a captain of infantry as the company commander. The signal platoon was upgraded to a company with a signaler and a captain appointed.

The battalion evolved into the second Mechanized Infantry Battalion of the Army, known as the 102nd Mechanized Infantry Battalion, and was soon renamed the 1660th Troop of the Army, an administrative and logistics support unit equivalent to a regiment. This allowed the unit to issue administrative orders and supply logistics directly from the supply depot, bypassing the division's supply point. This expansion was significant, and my responsibilities as battalion commander grew, but I felt deeply proud and honored.

♦ Establishing and developing the 102nd Mechanized Infantry Battalion (The 1660th Troop of the Army), <The Rainbow Troop>

I reviewed everything and set orders, choosing a rainbow as the symbol for the troop, painting it on the front of all armored vehicles. I named it “The Rainbow Troop,” inspired by General MacArthur's “Rainbow Division” from World War I. I reported this quickly and considered making the anniversary of its establishment a holiday for commemoration and rest. We held the establishment ceremony of “The Rainbow Troop,” or “The 1660th Troop of the Army,” on October 24th, UN Day, which was a holiday at the time. The top priority motto after its establishment was

"Operate the equipment 100%." Despite lacking extra parts or military engineers, we had one skilled sergeant first class who taught himself. It was fortunate that he took breaks to fix equipment en route to our troop, but from then on, my troop and I were fully responsible for maintenance and operation.

I transformed a regiment warehouse into a maintenance garage for wheeled and armored vehicles. To train soldiers as they were discharged, especially those driving armored vehicles, I created a training and testing ground in a nearby mountain for obtaining armored vehicle operating licenses. Simultaneously, I built a parking lot and shelter for safe parking and exclusive troop guarding. I embarked on developing an operational doctrine suited to Korea's geography and operation plans, recalling the West German Army's operation drill doctrine I learned. However, this was no easy task.

3. Establishment of the Capital Mechanized Infantry Division (CMID) (March 22nd, 1973)

♦ Transition from the 32nd Infantry Division to <Capital Mechanized Infantry Division>

After October 1972, the 32nd Infantry Division was ordered to reorganize into a mechanized division, preparing by assuming equipment from the withdrawing 7th Division of the U.S. Army. In early 1973, the Tiger Division, or the Capital Division, the heart of the ROK Armed Forces in Vietnam, returned to Korea. It inherited the Tiger Division's long and honorable traditions, history, flags (including those of the division, battalions, and companies), the Tiger Mark, and all written records, establishing the Capital Mechanized Infantry Division (CMID) on March 22nd, 1973. The establishment ceremony took place at the division's command center training ground in Hyeon-ri, attended by the Minister of National Defense. With the naming of the flags and division, the 32nd Division's flag, history, and name returned to Chungcheongnam-do, its original location.

♦ Inheriting the Traditions of the Honorable "1st Battalion of the 1st Regiment of Capital Infantry Division"- "Tiger Division"

Our battalion received the flag of the 1st Battalion of the 1st Regiment of the Capital Infantry Division, the first battalion ever established in the Republic of Korea, a tremendous honor. Holding the flag of the esteemed 1st Battalion was one of the most emotional moments of my life. The flag, adorned with numerous victory ribbons, including one bestowed by the President, proudly signified it as the best battalion in the ROK Armed Forces. The Capital Mechanized Infantry Division comprised the 1st Mechanized Infantry Brigade (formerly the 1st Regiment of the Capital Division), where our battalion was affiliated, the 1st Armored Infantry Brigade, the 26th Mechanized Infantry Brigade, the Artillery Brigade (not yet automated), and a new Logistics and Supply Unit commanded by a colonel. A mechanized infantry brigade included one mechanized infantry battalion, one motorized infantry battalion, one armored vehicle battalion, and one artillery battalion (not yet automated), forming an extremely powerful combat unit.

♦ The Outcome of the Combat Commandment Inspection: 'Happy and Sad'

Six months after the Capital Mechanized Infantry Division was established, the 1st Field Army conducted a "combat commandment inspection on divisions." Our battalion was particularly interested in the newly expanded and organized 4.2-inch mortar and conducted drills, similar to firing cannons, with instruction from an artillery unit. Due to this inspection, I decided to use the "BL (basic load)"—the extra combat-ready bullets for the battalion—and replace them with new models of training ammunition. Using the same Lot Number could ensure optimal conditions for 100% accuracy in live ammunition shooting. From my experience in the "Joint Shooting Competition between ROK Army and the U.S. Army," using new ammunition with the same LOT numbers made it easier to understand the ammunition's characteristics, and accuracy was guaranteed if soldiers were trained with them. Consequently, we achieved 100% accuracy for "firing ten shots in day and night" and received immediate commendation from the division commander. However, due to this accomplishment, everyone in the company was selected for rifle shooting. The shooting results were unexpectedly low, with 40% accuracy during the day and 38% at night. The division commander expressed disappointment, creating an episode of "getting a perfect score in the morning and failing in the afternoon." I decided to view it as a typical result for a newly reorganized troop—it was a normal outcome even for a rifle shooting at a regular company in West Germany. I checked other units during the inspection, and many selected companies supplemented their shooters with experienced regiment members, achieving around 90% accuracy at the test shooting ground. I couldn't do that. I believe a troop commander must train soldiers harder based on effort and strive for improvement. This approach builds actual military power, instilling fear in the enemy and trust in the Army from the people.

4. Serving as Military Logistics Staff (G-4) of the Division, the 1st World Oil Crisis and Its Influence

♦ I managed the unit and overcame hepatitis a while on duty

In October 1973, after successfully completing my tenure as a battalion commander, Division Commander Shin Hyeon-su appointed me as the G-4, or military logistics staff. Initially, I was uncomfortable with this position as it wasn't one I desired, but I resolved to adapt to the situation. The division commander assigned First Lieutenant Shin Hyeon-bae, his younger brother and a junior from the Korean Military Academy, to work alongside me. Through our collaboration, I found Shin to be both trustworthy and kindhearted, which created a satisfactory work environment. He later rose to become the commander of the 9th Division and eventually a corps commander, alongside Captain Kim, another colleague from our team.

During the 1st Oil Crisis of 1973, Division Commander Kim, the new commander, focused on stabilizing the troops and enhancing the training of soldiers to improve the Capital Mechanized Infantry Troop. However, the outbreak of the 4th Middle East War (Yom Kippur War) in October 1973 led OPEC to halt oil exports as retaliation against countries supporting Israel. This resulted in a "sudden cut in oil production" and a "sharp rise in oil prices," which were five times higher than in 1972, severely impacting the global economy, including Korea. The crisis extended into subsequent oil crises, causing prolonged economic hardships worldwide and in Korea. Consequently, the Armed Forces' oil budget was significantly reduced, halved in fact, but we managed to avoid further cuts. We overcame these challenges through frugality and strict control of oil usage within the troops. Despite the budget cuts, oil for education and training was maintained at levels similar to the previous year. We ensured our maneuvering equipment's tanks were full for emergencies, secured oil for engine starts during the winter, and left administrative details for later calculation. The M48 tanks, in particular, consumed a lot of oil, using three gallons (about ten liters) just to start the engine. This made commanders of armored vehicle battalions, who had access to oil, popular again. To conserve oil, the division commander even suspended the carpool for the division's Chief of Staff and staff members, requiring us to walk the 3.5 kilometers (2.1 miles) from our residences to the division's command center training ground.

That winter in Hyeon-ri, from November to February, was extremely cold, with temperatures ranging from negative 20 to 25 degrees Celsius (negative 4 to 13 degrees Fahrenheit). I bundled up in two layers of thick long johns, my military uniform, a thick U.S.-made field jacket, and a wool scarf, and trotted to work, arriving in about 35 minutes. Within ten minutes, I would start sweating, and by the time I reached the training ground around 7:30, my undershirt was almost completely soaked. All officers and soldiers at the command center were required to remove their shirts and perform stretching exercises together. Afterward, I would put my clothes back on and head to my office, where I would sit next to the anthracite stove to dry off and warm up. Although I was in my 40s and could endure the conditions, I couldn't avoid a loss of stamina and a decrease in work efficiency.

During my duty, I contracted hepatitis A. All officers and soldiers in a front division face tough work, but the logistics work for the CMID (Capital Mechanized Infantry Division) was particularly challenging during the Oil Crisis, as it required extreme frugality. As all battalions in the division were motorized, mechanized, or armored, I conducted on-site inspections at least once a week to ensure compliance with the division's logistics guidelines. After a long day of inspections, which included personally checking oil tanks and starting engines, I would have dinner around 10:00 to 11:00 PM. This meal was often brought to me by a soldier from my office, as I couldn't have my family live in the official residence due to my children's education and the absence of a signaler on duty there. After about two months, I caught a severe cold with body aches and was bedridden for ten days. The division commander visited me after a week, offering comfort by my bedside. I remained weak for months afterward, feeling dizzy even on bus rides in Chuncheon. It was only when I became a colonel and underwent a thorough physical examination that I learned I had contracted hepatitis A. Those were indeed challenging times.

♦ Defcon-3 was issued, and all Armed Forces were checked for defense readiness condition

In October 1973, Defcon-3 was issued, and all armed forces were evaluated for defense readiness. Following the "July 4th South-North Joint Statement" in 1972, with Vietnam's fall and the return of ROK Armed Forces from Vietnam, the entire ROK Armed Forces were in a state of complete provision. However, North Korea did not honor the joint statement, ceased talks with South Korea, and engaged in provocations, including infiltrations and attacks, igniting political tensions. Consequently, the Ministry of National Defense reinforced defense readiness and conducted comprehensive inspections across all armed forces, achieving an average readiness rate of 80%. The goal was to reach 100% readiness in all areas, with particular emphasis on the firearms department, which sometimes required immediate action due to limited ammunition supplies.

When the U.S. and ROK Armed Forces withdrew from Vietnam in March 1973, following a flawed armistice agreement, Free Vietnam quickly fell. Despite the activation of the "July 4th South-North Joint Statement," North Korea continued to provoke South Korea, risking a full-scale war. In March 1974, 120 North Korean soldiers violently attacked the United Nations Unit (American soldiers) in the Joint Security Area in Panmunjom, resulting in one officer's death, five injuries, and damage to four sedans. This led to the issuance of Defcon-3, the step before receiving live ammunition (Defcon-2) and initiating battle (Defcon-1). Although the Korean Peninsula's front had maintained a Defcon-3 equivalent due to the armistice, this was a genuine Defcon-3 situation. We followed the Standing Operation Procedure (SOP), ensuring all equipment and combat agents were ready and military personnel returned to their units, without panic. Officers and soldiers on vacation had to return immediately, but I monitored the situation and delayed my decision-making for a day or two. Fortunately, the situation resolved on the third day, relieving me.

Chapter 8

Working as the commander of the rear and staff, a professor, foreign inspection, the Chief of Military Assistance Investigation Commission (March 1975-May 1981)

1. Work in the rear after a long time of frontline activity, G-2 Special Warfare Command (Information Office)

♦ Director of G-2 Special Warfare Command Information Office

• Being promoted to a colonel and recommendation of a new position

Typically, regular KMA graduates were promoted from lieutenant colonel to colonel based on their years of service. I was slightly delayed due to my role as an instructor at Army College, so I was promoted in the second period among my classmates. I owe my promotion to the recommendation of General Yu Byeong-Hyeon, the 5th Corps commander at the time (January 1975), who had been the Korean Tiger Division commander in Vietnam, where I served as his war history officer. After my promotion, I needed to transfer to a colonel's position promptly. Fortunately, Jang Gi-o, my senior and former chief at Dongbok Guerrilla & Ranger School, who was then a G-1 (personnel officer) for Special Warfare Command, recommended me for the G-2 (intelligence officer) position. I am grateful to him for this opportunity.

• Special Warfare Command and G-2 (Information Office)

Thus, I was appointed Director of the Information Office (G-2) of Special Warfare Command, proudly donning a black beret as a special warfare agent of Korea for the first time. This position also allowed me to work in Seoul with a rear unit, enabling me to live with my family after a long period apart.

The Republic of Korea (ROK) Special Warfare Command was originally established as the "Army Special Warfare Command" in August 1969. It was formed to oversee all special warfare units of the Army, evolving from the former 1st Airborne Special Warfare Unit, and initially included the 3rd and 5th Brigades. Over time, the command expanded significantly. In 1974, the 7th and 9th Brigades were added, followed by the 11th and 13th Brigades in 1977, and the 707th Special Missions Group, a counter-terrorism unit, in 1981. The missions of these subordinate units, which I will detail in the chapter about my tenure as Commander of the 7th Airborne Special Warfare Brigade, included preparing for guerrilla warfare in enemy territory, counter-guerrilla operations (securing potential enemy bases), suppressing urban riots, and serving as an opposing force in conventional warfare drills, among other tasks. Notably, it was the only unit with actual military power that could be deployed in the rear areas at that time. All combat troops under the 1st Army, including reserve divisions, were affiliated with the Combined Forces Command and could not be sent to the rear without authorization from the Combined Forces Command. In 1968, the command conducted large-scale counter-espionage operations when North Korean spies infiltrated the Uljin-Samcheok area and Seogwipo, among other locations. It was also deployed in companies to various divisions during the Vietnam War. In 1976, the command was tasked with executing "the operation to cut down the cottonwood tree" in the Joint Security Area (JSA) and destroying four sentry posts of the North Korean Armed Forces. This was in response to the "Korean axe murder incident" in 1976, where North Korea provoked an incident in the Panmunjom security area.

The command's involvement didn't end there. During the Military Revolution of May 16th, it crossed the Hangang River with actual military power, charged into the center of Seoul, led the revolution, and played a significant role in swiftly eliminating so-called political and social gangsters once the city was occupied. From that point on, the special warfare unit became essential for maintaining social order in the rear, in addition to its original military duties. It was deemed important not only for military but also for political reasons, leading to its continued expansion and its role as a major force in maintaining public security, particularly in Seoul. Eventually, it was even deployed as the main military force to suppress the "Gwangju Insurgency," also known as the Democratization Movement, on May 18th.

The primary duty of the G-2 of the Special Warfare Command was to analyze enemy regions (areas in each province north of the Military Demarcation Line) and extract target intelligence to provide to subordinate troops. It also served as the intelligence staff for general troops, frequently supervising the intelligence duties of subordinate staff and visiting them individually or as a group. Particularly, when a subordinate troop marched 400 kilometers (248 miles) in full gear, the G-2 would inspect and supervise their drill state at night by dividing the duties. Starting over with work in the rear took some adjustment, especially getting used to "getting off work on time" at 5:00 p.m., both mentally and physically. I often thought about the officers and soldiers at the front, imagining them still working or engaged in construction work during holidays. When I finally learned to play tennis after work, I felt a sense of guilt, thinking, "The front units must be going through some kind of drill now... I'm sorry..."

♦ I was part of the entourage for the annual 'Asia Special Warfare Commander Meeting, 1975' in the USA

During the annual "Asia Special Warfare Commander's Meeting" in the USA, I attended the 8th meeting in November 1975 as part of the entourage for Commander Jeong Byeong-ju, a major general, serving as the intelligence officer. The meeting was held by the U.S. Army's Special Warfare Center to provide assistance for special warfare in Asia, which was facing indirect invasion by the Chinese Communist Party. The United States had become involved in the Vietnam War in 1963, conducting guerrilla warfare based on the special warfare strategies defined during Kennedy's era. They executed indirect strategy operations to block international communist powers and infiltrated the rear to carry out secret plots to disrupt the enemy and secure bases with armed military power. During the meeting, I revisited the J.F. Kennedy Center in North Carolina, where I had studied counter-insurgency in the spring of 1962, which was an emotional experience. The United States seemed largely unchanged. The first day included a welcoming ceremony and a dinner party. The following day, we observed the nearby 82nd Airborne Division, renowned as the "original airborne troop of the U.S. Army" with its rich history and victories. We also witnessed an operational demonstration by a team from the 7th Special Warfare Unit. I was particularly impressed by their medical officers, who were fully qualified surgeons capable of performing surgeries and running a small field hospital anywhere with the necessary equipment. The intelligence team members spoke a foreign language fluently, which I recall was Polish. At that time, our team's qualifications and skills had not reached that level, and we couldn't even distinguish North Korean regional dialects. I resolved to review and develop our G-2's duties upon returning to Korea. We were also shown new infiltration equipment, with the underwater infiltration gear being particularly impressive.

During my visit to New York before returning to Korea, I unexpectedly met Lee In-gil, a close friend from Dongnae High School, who came to greet me. His older brother, who had lived in Dongnae during the Korean War, studied abroad in the United States, and gifted me a model of the Empire State Building, was the chief executive general of special warfare. It seemed likely that he had been instructed by his brother to guide us. Lee and I were delighted to see each other and took time to catch up on our lives. As I mentioned earlier, he entered the law school at Seoul National University (SNU) and often visited me at the Korea Military Academy (KMA) when I was there. We sometimes met in downtown Seoul when I was on leave. He was one of eight classmates from Dongnae High School who were accepted into SNU's law school. None of them could take the high-rank law official exam due to wartime conditions, and they all became entrepreneurs. After graduating from law school, Lee worked at "Lucky Toothpaste" (later Goldstar, now LG), which was the leading company in Korea at the time, as an employee in charge of foreign trade. He was dispatched to New York for his work in foreign trade, but he eventually resigned to become independent, settling in New Jersey and running an independent trading company in New York. I enjoyed sightseeing in New York under his guidance for one night and two days. Unfortunately, I never saw him again after that, but I wish him well for the rest of his life.

2. I engaged in diplomacy with neutral countries

♦ I served as the Chief of the <Military Assistance Investigation Commission to Morocco>

In April 1976, I worked as the Chief of the Military Assistance Investigation Commission to Morocco, focusing on diplomacy with neutral countries and responding to Morocco's request for military assistance. In 1975, the fall of Free Vietnam and the subsequent communization of three countries by its Domino Effect influenced all of East Asia. Meanwhile, newly inaugurated U.S. President Carter's pledge to withdraw the U.S. Army from the ROK further stimulated Kim Il-sung of North Korea. He traveled to Eastern Europe and African countries seeking war assistance. Upon his return, he intensified indirect infiltration to the rear and direct provocations at the front, disregarding the "July 4th South-North Joint Statement," escalating the war crisis on the Korean Peninsula. The North Korean puppet state engaged in severe provocations, such as announcing "the war is approaching" in July, brutally murdering two American officers with an axe in the Joint Security Area of Panmunjom, triggering a Defcon-3 activation in the ROK, and kidnapping fishing boats and celebrities. Despite this, concerns persisted that the United States might abandon Korea if deemed not in its national interest, driven by U.S. political and civil tendencies and Kissinger's "Detente" diplomacy. This drove President Park and patriotic citizens toward "self-reliant national defense" and "diplomacy for survival." Consequently, the ROK reinforced "diplomacy with neutral countries" to reduce reliance on the United States, expand diplomatic relations with "neutral countries" or third powers, and counter Kim Il-sung's influence in these regions. The ROK focused on pro-Western neutral countries in North Africa's Maghreb, including Morocco, Algeria, Tunisia, and Libya. Following the Military Revolution of May 16th, the Korean Central Intelligence Agency had been building connections with these countries, particularly their royal families, through contributions like training royal bodyguards in taekwondo.

In 1975, Spain withdrew from the Western Sahara in Africa, entering into negotiations with Spain, Morocco, and Mauritania. Seizing the opportunity, Morocco occupied the Western Sahara region and declared its annexation. In response, the local ethnic group formed the Polisario Front, an independence movement, and proclaimed the establishment of the unrecognized state of the "Arab Sahara." They waged a guerrilla war for independence against Morocco in the desert. Consequently, Morocco aimed to establish 20 counter-guerrilla battalions, initially forming two special warfare battalions, and sought military assistance from the Republic of Korea (ROK) Armed Forces, known for their expertise in counter-guerrilla warfare. Algeria, Morocco's neighbor, was hostile towards the pro-Western Morocco and actively supported the Polisario to gain access to the Atlantic Ocean.

During a diplomatic tour of neutral countries, Prime Minister Kim Jong-pil promised assistance, and Minister Shim Heung-seon asked Morocco to support the ROK in the UN. Morocco agreed and reiterated its request for Korean military assistance. Korea had already been aiding Morocco by providing Korean-made combat uniforms and personal equipment.

The April 24th Investigation Commission was formed to maintain confidentiality and commemorate the day of its establishment. The commission consisted of myself as chief, No Yeong-Chan, the chief of the Asia and Middle East Bureau of the Ministry of Foreign Affairs (later Minister of Foreign Affairs), Lieutenant Colonel Jo (who later became a general and Commander of Security), and Colonel Han, a French language professor at KMA, serving as the interpreter. We disguised ourselves as businesspeople from Daewoo Company, with all expenses and schedules arranged by the Ministry of Foreign Affairs, specifically No Yeong-chan.

♦ This involved addressing Morocco's request for military assistance, outlining the missions and structure of the Investigation Commission

The Ministry of Foreign Affairs, led by Minister Park Dong-jin, was concerned about international public opinion worsening due to North Korea's military assistance to countries like Zimbabwe, as reported in "Newsweek." They believed it was challenging to provide the active military assistance Morocco requested. Therefore, our primary goal was to "visit Morocco for investigation" in response to their request for assistance. We were to listen to their request for drill instructors but persuade them to send their instructors to Korea for training. This was reportedly President Park Chung-Hee's opinion.

The Korean Central Intelligence Agency, represented by Hong Neung, emphasized the importance of "non-aligned diplomacy with pro-Western countries" and actively engaging in diplomacy by sending massage therapists and taekwondo instructors to foreign dignitaries and training their bodyguards. Morocco's request for military drill instructors, following their military procurement team's visit to purchase ROK Armed Forces' weapons and equipment, was seen as an opportunity to dispatch a team of drill instructors and complete non-aligned diplomacy.

The Ministry of National Defense, led by General Yu Byeong-Hyeon, Chairman of the Joint Chiefs of Staff, believed the Armed Forces should align with government policy. The chief of the Intelligence Department advised that, after our investigation, we should recommend either dispatching Korean drill instructors to Morocco or bringing Moroccan instructors to Korea for training. General Lee Se-ho, Chief of Staff of the Army Headquarters, emphasized the Army's commitment to dispatching drill instructors for military assistance.

After consulting with relevant bureaus and considering their opinions, I concluded that the ROK Armed Forces were capable of dispatching a team to provide military assistance, such as drill instructors for education and training. We should seize such opportunities to expand our global presence beyond the Vietnam War. Thus, I decided to recommend dispatching ROK Armed Forces drill instructors to Morocco before departing Korea. However, it seemed No Yeong-chan from the Ministry of Foreign Affairs would follow the Ministry's orders.

♦ Conducting local investigations in Morocco

Upon arriving in Morocco, we held our first meeting at the ROK Embassy in Rabat, the capital, with the Ambassador, Diplomatic Minister, and Defense Attaché. They welcomed us warmly and cooperated passionately, considering our task as their own. The Embassy had been using various methods, such as providing taekwondo and massage therapy assistance, to lead neutral countries in the Maghreb region to become pro-Korean. Our government maintained significant influence compared to North Korea's presence in the southern Sahara Desert.

We decided to hold daily meetings at the ROK Embassy, involving the Ambassador, Embassy personnel, and our Investigation Commission members, and send daily reports to the Ministry of Foreign Affairs via Paris. The next day, we visited Morocco's Minister and Vice Minister of National Defense and attended a briefing at the Unified Command, responsible for the military assistance project. The officer guiding us was a classmate from the West German Armed Forces' Command and Staff College, and he provided insights into their opinions.

The Minister of National Defense hosted a luncheon featuring red lobster tails, a local delicacy. It seemed to be a survival habit developed by residents living near the desert. The following evening, the Unified Command agents invited us to a "whole roasted lamb" party, a gesture of hospitality. Despite being full from the whole chicken and eggs, I tasted the tender lamb, which was more delicious than the

Korean dish "Bosintang" (dog meat stew).

My classmate from Germany expressed regret for not inviting us to his home. I learned that women in Arabic countries are slim and beautiful before marriage but gain weight and age quickly afterward. According to customs, women cannot leave home without their husband's permission and remain indoors after marriage.

We visited Morocco's military academy, observing cadets marching, which demonstrated the country's reliance on us. We also toured Casablanca, a world-famous resort city, and Rabat's old town during breaks between meetings. In Casablanca, we encountered Henry Kissinger, a renowned American diplomat, and No Yeong-chan engaged in a friendly conversation with him. This experience taught me that "coincidental chances" exist in both life and diplomacy.

The following day, we visited and observed the commando battalion and the new base under construction in the desert's operational area. Initially, we toured the new training base in Sidi Ifni, a location in southern Morocco prior to the merger, to assess the environment and the status of education and training. The next day, we inspected El Aiun, a newly occupied operations base in Western Sahara, along with the surrounding areas. We spent the night there, literally under the protection of sentinels in enemy territory, and heard gunfire outside during the night. In the morning, I learned that warning shots were fired at a location suspected of guerrilla infiltration. It was evident that tensions between the Moroccan Armed Forces and the Polisario guerrillas were escalating in Western Sahara. On our return to Rabat, we flew over the Sahara Desert within Western Sahara's borders. Although not entirely sandy due to its proximity to the Atlantic Ocean, the landscape remained desolate. I pondered whether territorial battles could indeed occur in such places.

Regarding the Moroccan Armed Forces' determination and the Investigation Commission's final conclusion, as we were concluding our investigation, Morocco sought agreements on the treatment of Korean drill instructors, the training camp's location, and preparations for the trainees. However, we sidestepped these discussions by stating that our primary task was to return to Korea and report our findings. Consequently, the Ambassador, the Diplomatic Minister (representing the Korean CIA), the Defense Attaché, and all members of the Investigation Commission convened at the ROK Embassy to finalize our conclusions. The Diplomatic Minister (of the CIA) and the Defense Attaché Officer advocated for Korean drill instructors to be sent to Morocco. In contrast, the Ambassador, following the Ministry of Foreign Affairs' directive, insisted on sending Moroccan drill instructors to Korea. It appeared unlikely that No Yeong-chan would alter his stance on this order. Morocco's strong desire to bring Korean drill instructors, despite the higher costs, stemmed from concerns that elite Moroccan Armed Forces officers, once sent overseas, might not return, increasing the risk of a coup d'état. Considering these factors, I represented the Investigation Commission at the final meeting with Morocco's Ministry of National Defense. I expressed our gratitude for their hospitality and acknowledged our understanding of Morocco's security environment and their request. We assessed their preparedness, both materially and emotionally, for the potential arrival of Korean drill instructors. I assured them that we would report these findings, particularly Morocco's preference for Korean instructors, upon our return to Korea and inform them of the results promptly. Thus, the Investigation Commission's local investigation concluded, leaving Morocco with anxious anticipation but no definitive conclusion.

♦ Reporting the findings upon returning to Korea

Upon returning to Korea, I drafted the report on the flight back, contemplating it repeatedly. After confirming and recognizing all the facts, I concluded that "the best choice is to send our drill instructors to Morocco." I personally reported this to the Ministry of National Defense and the Army's Chief of Staff upon my return. The Ministry of National Defense acknowledged my report with a "Good job," and the Army's Chief of Staff supported it. However, when I presented it to the Minister of Foreign Affairs, he responded, "Good job. But I will report it to the President myself." The outcome, as anticipated by the Minister and the President, was that "we demonstrated our sincerity to Morocco, ensuring no diplomatic issues with neutral countries and avoiding international criticism due to North Korea's military assistance to Africa. Therefore, we 'welcome the Moroccan drill instructors' invitation to Korea anytime' if Morocco desires." This was the conclusion reached by the April 24th Investigation Commission. I later heard rumors about Moroccan drill instructors visiting Korea by invitation in 1977.

3. Studying at Korea National Defense University Graduate School - Public opinion poll on ROK Armed Forces' nuclear armament, inspecting in the U.S., and my graduation thesis

♦ The process of studying at Korea National Defense University (KNDU) Graduate School

It established and operated by the Ministry of National Defense, KNDU Graduate School is Korea's premier educational institution for national defense. It conducts a ten-month "National Defense Course" annually and has an affiliated organization called "The Korean Journal of Security Affairs (KJSA)." Selected students from the military (colonels/generals), administration (police officers of deputy chief rank, prosecutors, and public officials of bureau director rank), and civilians (newspaper journalists, etc.) participate in this course. Although the system is somewhat cumbersome, the course is mandatory for elite national figures. It is especially crucial for fostering cooperation between governmental organizations for national defense and for individual development and communication. Additionally, it has established and operated a national regular "master's course on military science" since 1980. However, there are some regrettable aspects. Ideally, it should be a mandatory course for military personnel aspiring to become generals and for public officials aiming for class 1 or political executive positions. Unfortunately, it is merely recognized as a short period to pass for public officials or military personnel, which saddens me. Nonetheless, many colonels and generals voluntarily enroll in the course to enhance their resumes and receive education.

• Graduation trip, The U.S. (discussion on human rights issues) and Canada

As I previously mentioned, my cherished childhood dreams were "studying in Seoul" and "studying abroad in the United States." These dreams, aligned with the biblical promise "Ask, and it will be given to you," granted me another fortunate opportunity to visit the United States for observation. This marked my third trip to the U.S. I had studied at the American Special Warfare School as a captain, attended the 8th Annual Asia Special Warfare Commander's Meeting the previous year, and now had this chance. This time, it was a graduation trip for the national defense course. Based on English test scores, one-third of the graduates traveled to the United States, Europe, Asia, or the Middle East, while two-thirds toured military bases and local administrative offices in Korea.

Our team visited research institutes and organizations focused on national defense, as well as the U.S. and Canadian congresses. We first toured the Capitol and the U.S. Department of National Defense. Although I had only seen it from a distance during previous visits to Washington D.C., this time, I explored its interior, guided by an American congressperson. Its size and facilities were incomparable to the United Kingdom's Houses of Parliament, reflecting the extraordinary nature of the United States.

One vivid memory is our visit to research organizations like RAND and Brookings, where they frequently criticized Korea's human rights situation. I found this jarring and, despite others' attempts to stop me, I strongly defended Korea's situation and the government's policies at the time. It was evident that foreigners considered 'Korea's human rights issues' a top priority for discussion. In Canada, we attended dinner parties and receptions hosted by the Department of National Defense. A particularly memorable experience was visiting Vancouver. Enchanted by the beautiful seaside city, I resolved to return someday. This wish was fulfilled when I, my wife, a few classmates, and their wives traveled to Canada after my retirement. Later, during a cruise trip to Alaska with my grandson, daughter-in-law, son, and wife, we stopped in Vancouver once more. As I admired the stunning scenery, I was flooded with old memories and felt deeply moved.

♦ My graduation thesis: "Collective Security in the Pacific Rim, and Planning a Triangular Security among Korea, the U.S., and Japan"

Around 1977, President Park Chung-Hee and the Korean government were grappling with North Korea's increasing threat of invasion to communize South Korea. President Park believed that the United States, prioritizing its national interest, might withdraw its army from Korea by 1980 and potentially abandon Korea if circumstances turned unfavorable. He spearheaded efforts to achieve self-reliant national defense by domestically producing all weapons, including nuclear ones. Amidst this Korean national security climate, we studied national security strategies and wrote graduation theses. I chose the topic "Collective Security in Asia and the Pacific Rim." Chapter 1 provided a detailed analysis of national security in Korea and abroad. Chapter 2 examined Korea's national security system. Chapter 3 discussed problems and solutions, followed by a conclusion.

The conclusion I reached was that we must strengthen the Triangular Security among Korea, the U.S., and Japan until the 1980s, or until it is clearly verified that we have surpassed the North Korean Puppet State. We must also establish mutual or group security systems with neighboring countries to suppress war, achieve peace, overcome current challenges, and aim to defeat communism and unify the two Koreas in the future. Furthermore, we must drive away the northern powers (continental powers) and maritime powers, completing the mission of reviving the Korean nation.

♦ President Park Chung-Hee's determination for 'Nuclear Armament' in 1977

In 1977, President Park Chung-Hee was determined to pursue nuclear armament, a sentiment echoed by the students at KNDU Graduate School. KNDU Graduate School hosted friendly gatherings for high-ranking public officials and special lectures by VIPs, including the President. Located not far from central Seoul, it was one of Korea's premier national defense organizations, inviting many ministers, including the Minister of National Defense, and chiefs of major governmental bureaus to deliver lectures on significant issues. Additionally, VIPs from foreign countries visiting Korea were also invited to lecture. President Park Chung-Hee attended the graduation ceremony every year during his term, but for some reason, the Presidents of leftist governments avoided attendance. This led the students, who were the talented individuals destined to become (or who had become) the nation's leading officials, to say in unison, "I knew it. A leftist government makes national defense seem doubtful." This is an unforgettable memory for me.

President Park worked on "self-reliant national defense" to be fully prepared for an invasion by the North Korean Puppet State and due to a lack of trust in

U.S. security assurances. The final stage of his project was nuclear armament. He became even more resolute when the United States announced its strategy to withdraw U.S. troops from Korea to prioritize its national interests. He posed a question to us students, conducting a survey: "Should we pursue nuclear armament or not? What are its pros and cons?" Although I didn't confirm it, I speculate that all students agreed with this armament.

4. Regiment Commander of Nonsan Training Centor, a Directer of KNDU, Incident of President Park, Chief of Military Assistance Investigation Commission to Saudi Arabia,

♦ I got a new job, the Regiment commander of Nonsan Training Center, so I will be 'the cream of the crop'

Unfortunately, the Army Headquarters assigned talented individuals who graduated from KNDU Graduate School to be regimental commanders of Nonsan Training Center instead of Combat Regiment/Mechanized Brigade. Before starting my assignment, I visited General Yu Byeong-Hyeon (the Chairman of the Joint Chiefs of Staff at that time). He immediately called Lee Se-ho, the Army Chief of Staff, and complained, "I kept telling you that officers from the Capital Mechanized Infantry Division should work in that base. Why are you breaking your promise?" However, it seemed the Army Chief of Staff was only making excuses.

Next, I visited General Park Se-Jik—my senior from Busan Normal School, later the mayor of Seoul, and the chairman of the organization committee for the 1988 Seoul Olympics—and greeted him. He seemed very disappointed and comforted me, saying, "Let's meet again when you finish your duty as a regimental commander." Seeing the disappointment of my superiors, I realized this position was considered to have an unpromising future. But I wasn't discouraged. It reminded me of a story from "Nineteen Stars," a masterpiece on U.S. military leadership, where General Marshall once worked as a vice principal of a school when he was a colonel, a duty considered trivial. I thought, "All units and bases in the ROK Armed Forces have duties to carry out. Units with relatively lower priority have more work to do, and their members will be cooperative. So, I'll do my best to excel."

I was assigned as the commander of the 26th Regiment of Nonsan Training Center. The regiment comprised the regimental commander, the regiment executive officer (a lieutenant colonel), and the regimental staff, including a personnel officer (a major), education and operations officer (a captain), a military logistics officer (a first lieutenant), and a medical officer at the headquarters, along with 12 affiliated companies (with captains as company commanders).

• Training New Recruits and Life in the Unit

Each regiment in the training center trained 2,000 new recruits for the infantry for one month per quarter. The regiment was responsible for the recruits' life in the barracks, discipline, transportation to and from the training ground, and their entrance into and dismissal from the training center. The training center's unit was in charge of training and educating them on various subjects. During training, about 2,000 people in 12 companies, with 180 or more people per company, woke up, used bathrooms, washed their faces, and ate meals simultaneously, leading to overstraining, humorous, and challenging episodes.

• Leading Regiment for Two Consecutive Years

The training center conducted tactical practice competitions between regiments during the hiatus (the period without trainees). The subjects included those the assistant instructors had to teach the trainees in the barracks, such as disassembling and assembling rifles, shooting techniques, close-order drill, and more. The main event was a 10-kilometer (6.2 miles) run with the simplest equipment setup—the front units did it in general armament setup. About 30 assistant instructors from a regiment set off from the training center and returned to the area near Nonsan Station, guided by an officer. Despite the same conditions for every regiment, winners and losers emerged, depending on the regimental commander's interest and encouragement.

Although the regiments at the training center lacked sufficient materials, they did their best with what they had. The regimental commander's interest, or mental encouragement, was crucial. "Hey, we're men, aren't we? Let's do this!" I motivated them, spent time with them during preparation training, checked on them at night to offer comfort and encouragement, and provided everything we could. I gave them twice the fixed amount of hardtacks (dry bread) by saving or acquiring more, along with baked goods from the PX. These weren't even enough to be snacks, but they symbolized the regimental commander's care. I encouraged them during breaks by saying, "You're doing your best," but also trained them strictly to achieve the best score. On competition day, all officers went to the testing ground to cheer and support them directly and indirectly. This resulted in excellent scores in each subject and won the judges' hearts. Consequently, our regiment became the leading regiment with the best scores among eight regiments, earning this honor for two consecutive years.

As the Head Managing Professor at Korea National Defense University Graduate School, Chief of Military Assistance Investigation Commission to Saudi Arabia, and Establishment of Master's Courses at KNDU Graduate School

As the Head Managing Professor of the 2nd Faculty Department (economics and management) of National Defense at KNDU Graduate School, I achieved my goal of excelling and fulfilled my responsibilities in the assigned duty. However, I faced despair once more due to the confusing personnel policies (assigning the right person to the right position and personnel review) of the Army Headquarters. Nonetheless, I decided to remain hopeful and pursue my personal preference, applying for a position as a military officer professor at KNDU Graduate School. I received recommendations from Professor Kwon Mun-sul, my classmate from Dongnae High School with a doctorate from Columbia University, and Professor Lee Han-jong, my junior from the 15th class and a Yale University doctorate holder. I also met Professor Kim Jong-hwi (from a U.S. university), the chief of the Korean National Research Institute of National Security Affairs—later Presidential Special Advisor of Foreign Affairs and National Defense. Consequently, I was appointed as a military officer professor at KNDU Graduate School, automatically becoming the Head Managing Professor of the 2nd Faculty Department (economics and management, later Faculty Department of Management) of National Defense. I maintained a close friendship with them and completed my duties without difficulties, thanks to their cooperation.

Professor Lee Su-han, my senior from the 11th class of KMA, was in the management course faculty. He studied abroad at the renowned Purdue University in Indiana, U.S., and graduated with a master's degree in computer science. Although the United States had just begun working on computer science, Korea was still in the so-called era before "i486" computers. We had just started printing salary payment envelopes with computers, which were previously handwritten, and calculating salaries with computers instead of using an abacus. Still, we were designing the future and planning education for students to use computers to catch up with the United States' level of computer usage.

Jo Mun-hwan, the principal (a lieutenant general) of the Graduate School, was always passionate about everything. He worked tirelessly to establish the "master's courses on national defense and security," by inviting the Minister of Culture and Education, seeking cooperation from the National Assembly, and more. His efforts culminated in the "amendment on the Act on the Establishment of Korea National Defense University Graduate School (Establishment of master's courses)" on December 28th, paving the way for the courses to begin in February 1981.

I became the Chairman of the Master's Course Education Preparation Committee, where I engaged in serious discussions with the existing professors to establish the primary major courses: "International Affairs," "Management of National Defense," and "Military Strategies." Following this, I entered a hopeful phase, reviewing each professor's subjects, class schedules, credit distribution, and other details, negotiating as necessary. This process laid the foundation for the master's courses that KNDU proudly offers. Personally, I drew upon the 'Total Exercise' experience from my final studies in Germany to implement a similar 'Total

Exercise' in our course. This involved a week-long practical exercise called 'Write Total Joint National Security Strategy,' focusing on national defense courses (politics, military, diplomacy, and economics) once students completed their studies. Notably, this was before the publication of the 'National Security Strategy' during President Reagan's administration in the United States and the 'National Strategy of the U.S.A,' which is published twice during a President's term as a report to Congress.

The October 26th Incident and the directly related '12.12 Incident' involved the assassination of President Park Chung-Hee on October 26th. To counter North Korea's aggressive Vietnamese-style provocations with a 'self-reliant national defense policy,' President Park established the Yushin Constitution in 1972, accelerating Korea's heavy and chemical industrialization while suppressing domestic political calls for democratization. However, domestic and international factors, such as the 2nd Oil Crisis in late 1978, led to inflation exceeding 18%, worsening the economy. Additionally, President Carter of the United States mistakenly perceived the growing leftist movement in Korea as a democratization movement—though they were essentially one and the same—and openly pressured Korea by threatening to withdraw U.S. troops. Consequently, Korea faced political and economic crises in 1979. Amidst this turmoil, the "Bu-Ma Protests" erupted in Busan and Gyeongsangnam-do, prompting the activation of emergency martial law and the Garrison Decree, leading to military suppression operations by the Marine Corps and airborne troops, heightening societal tension and danger.

♦ The historical events occurred, <10.26 Incident> and the related <12.12 Incident> ad related <Gwangju Incident>

Kim Jae-Gyu, the Chief of the Korean CIA and President Park's trusted confidant, had been preparing an "ungrateful and treacherous revolt" to address the situation, whether by his own volition or influenced by others (including the United States?). He devised a "plan for the revolution in three steps": 1. Involve Jeong Seung-Hwa, the Army Chief of Staff (and martial law commander), as an accomplice, 2. Assassinate President Park and have Jeong Seung-Hwa activate martial law and take action, 3. Form a revolutionary committee under military leadership to rule Korea. To execute this plan, Kim enlisted the support of key military figures, including the commander of the 3rd armed forces, the nearest corps commander, the nearest division commander, the special warfare commander, and the commander of capital defense. Through meticulous planning, he executed the "Treason Incident of October 26th."

General Chun Doo-Hwan, who had recently been transferred from division commander to Commander of Defense Security, automatically became the Chief of the Joint Investigation Headquarters of the Martial Law Command, overseeing all investigation bureaus in Korea. On October 28th, two days after the incident, he made an initial announcement emphasizing that "Kim Jae-Gyu and his associates, including Kim Gye-Won, the Chief of Staff to the President, were the main culprits. No external powers or organizations, such as the CIA of the United States, were involved." The case of President Park's assassination appeared to be resolved in a straightforward military manner.

The arrest of Chief of Staff Jeong Seung-Hwa on December 12th was part of the ongoing investigation into Kim Jae-Gyu's treason. The investigation revealed that the Army Chief of Staff had received orders from Kim Jae-Gyu, waited for further instructions while hearing gunfire about 50 meters away, and then followed Kim Jae-Gyu's orders, even if briefly. This was sufficient to suspect him as an accomplice, constituting treason against the Commander-in-chief, betrayal of the Armed Forces, and actions advantageous to the enemy—unacceptable behaviors. Despite being the martial law commander, Jeong Seung-Hwa defended Kim Jae-Gyu's actions and used his influence to conduct a hasty reshuffling of military personnel, including promotions for generals, in November to prepare for potential arrest and interrogation. Furthermore, while defending himself, he attempted to remove Chief Chun Doo-Hwan of the Joint Investigation Headquarters, who was investigating him. Consequently, the Joint Investigation Headquarters took decisive action to arrest Jeong Seung-Hwa, despite his powerful position in the Army, as he was clearly implicated in the President's assassination and was attempting to destroy evidence. During his arrest, a pistol shooting occurred between the general's aide and an investigator, known as the "12.12 Incident."

In response to the 2nd Oil Crisis, I was appointed as the Chief of the Military Assistance Investigation Commission to Saudi Arabia. When President Park's assassination occurred on October 26th, the Crisis Management Government, led by the new President Choi Kyu-hah, was established. Meanwhile, politicians with restricted political activities initiated the "Era of the Three Kims." However, society descended into chaos, exacerbated by the 2nd Oil Crisis, which worsened the struggling economy and skyrocketed inflation, creating the worst economic crisis in Korea's history. This presented an opportunity for Kim Il-sung of North Korea, who reinforced his plan to communize South Korea by sending spies and ordering heightened defense readiness on October 27th, anticipating a second "April 19th situation" in South Korea. Violent protests by leftist college students in Seoul and the Gwangju Insurgency (Democratization Movement?) of May 18th followed.

♦ As well as counter measures to the 'Second World Oil Crisis', I was there

In this context, Chief Chun Doo-Hwan and the Joint Investigation Headquarters served President Choi Kyu-Hah in national defense matters while investigating Kim Jae-Gyu. To address the Oil Crisis, as the nation's economy was at immediate risk and the Ministry of Foreign Affairs and Ministry of Trade, Industry and Energy struggled to arrange a meeting with Saudi Arabia's Petroleum Minister Yamani, the "Mugunghwa Plan" was devised. This plan involved the President visiting Saudi Arabia to resolve issues related to military assistance and stable oil supply. As part of this plan, I was appointed as the Chief of the Military Assistance Investigation Commission to Saudi Arabia. Disguised as employees of Arikata Hanil (Hanil Development), we infiltrated Saudi Arabia in March 1980 to "develop measures for military assistance to Saudi Arabia and report on them." Before reporting to Chief Chun Doo-Hwan, I received briefings from the intelligence officer of the Defense Security Command.

TThe key points were as follows: Saudi Arabia had been requesting Korea to provide the following through diplomatic channels: 1. Drill instructors to train pilots and engineers for bombing missions in South Yemen. 2. Nurses for hospitals,

3. A turnkey base hospital and additional nurses, among other things. We had consistently declined these requests. However, given the urgency of the situation, we needed to verify if these requests and conditions were still valid, with the implication that we might now consider fulfilling them. I was also instructed to confirm whether the construction of a turnkey base for special warfare training facilities, ordered by the prince in actual power and an acquaintance of Jo Jung-hun, the president of Hanil Development, was "available for support," and to conduct an investigation to determine if support was necessary.

I reported this to Chief Chun Doo-Hwan of the Joint Investigation Headquarters. He is naturally a kind, optimistic, and passionate man, and he explained the current situation and his intentions in more detail. He was particularly keen on providing military assistance in special warfare education and training to the bodyguard unit of Saudi Arabia's royal family, as he had previously trained Korea's special warfare unit and the President's bodyguards with dedication. He wanted to know: 1. What types of professional instructors were needed to establish special warfare schools for the Saudi royal family and civilians? 2. Information necessary to decide on dispatching instructors, including details of education and assistance. He emphasized considering the current national defense situation, particularly the stable securing of oil, to review and determine if we could provide assistance. 3. If necessary, conduct an investigation into mutual cooperation matters by inviting the person in charge from each nation—the prince in actual power and Minister Yamani were suitable representatives for Saudi Arabia. He also added that I should express our support for the current Saudi regime and our willingness to provide assistance. He stressed that persuading them by demonstrating our capability and willingness to assist in military, security, and defense matters was part of our duty.

Details on the negotiation and maneuvering process were omitted. The conclusion and report suggested that the Investigation Commission returned to Korea and reported to Chief Chun Doo-Hwan in person on March 25th. Despite being tired from excessive workload, he listened attentively for over an hour, comforted and encouraged us, and promised to "apply the details of the report exactly as submitted."

* Summary of the report on "Suggestions for measures of military assistance for Saudi Arabia":
- Provide a medical team (medical officers and nursing officers) to operate military hospitals.
- Provide military equipment for Saudi Arabia to supply to other countries (North Yemen and Afghanistan).
- Assist with education (planning agents, instructors, etc.) for the establishment of a new military intelligence school (to be built soon).
- Suggest converting two airborne battalions into Special Warfare Forces (SWF) and assist with this.
- Assist with education and the expansion of the Special Security School's size and scale.
- Provide pilot instructors and engineers for combat and transport aircraft for Saudi Arabia to supply to other countries.

After completing my report, I spoke to Heo Hwa-Pyeong, my junior and close colleague from our cadet days at the headquarters of the 2nd Company. He had also supported me during my time in Vietnam and was a fellow member of Hanahoe. I told him and the Chief Secretary, "This is already deeply involved with governmental policy. I think it should continue." Heo Hwa-Pyeong replied, "We've drawn our sword already; we cannot put it back without using it." This was a time when military sentiment was deeply intertwined with politics.

• Execution of the conclusion:

Following this, President Choi visited Saudi Arabia in mid-May and secured a deal for a stable oil supply, but it wasn't sufficient. Fortunately, Indonesia developed an LNG gas field and began supplying it to Korea just in time, prompting a shift in Korea's oil policy. This historical fact is one of General Chun Doo-Hwan's lesser-known achievements.

5. I became the Chief of Staff and Head Professor at the Republic of Korea Army College (July 1980 - November 1981) and was promoted to general (January 1st, 1981).

♦ Chief of Staff at ROK Army College:

After forming the 'Special Committee for National Security Measures' on May 31st to address national emergencies and the Gwangju Insurgency of May 18th, General Chun Doo-Hwan's New Military Government and its pro-military political allies dedicated themselves to governmental reform. They made history by boldly eliminating corruption, prohibiting private tutoring, and cracking down on gangsters. During this period, I was appointed Chief of Staff at ROK Army College by Army Headquarters and was promoted to general during my tenure.

♦ I became a general (January 1st, 1981) and aspired to be a battlefield commander and hero:

No one decides or declares, "I will become a general" upon graduating from KMA and being commissioned as a second lieutenant. However, as they work hard for the public good, setting aside personal desires, and as they rise through the ranks, they begin to aspire to become a general. Unfortunately, not all classmates achieve this, despite having the same qualifications, due to the structure. About 30 are promoted to brigadier generals. Thus, one might consider it "50% good luck and 50% skill" during peacetime, not wartime.

The first thought that crossed my mind was to report this to my parents and show them my achievement as a general. Sadly, they had passed away long ago and didn't have proper graves. So, I could only boast about it to them in my heart, thanking them for their love and grace. I especially recalled my mother's words about a rooster with a big cockscomb crowing loudly on our roof in her dream the day before Buddha's Birthday, when she gave birth to me. I have always strived to repay her. Naturally, I credited my wife for this joy and glory, as she has been my life's companion and caretaker of our family. I will remember my parents' dreams, especially my mother's, as I live the rest of my life, and I will do my best for my beloved wife and family.

It was January 1st, 1981, a very snowy day. After reporting, we headed to the National Cemetery. The road was covered in thick snow, slowing our journey. But the world was bright, blessing us and the future of the ROK Armed Forces with the sacred snow of New Year's Day, making me emotional. In the evening, we attended a celebration at the Army Hall hosted by the Armed Forces and the government with my beloved wife, who had endured all the hardships with me, and we reflected on "my hard life devoted to the nation."

It is said that becoming a general comes with about 30 types of better treatment. First, you receive a general's flag and can place a star plate on your car (military vehicle). But more importantly, as a general, you can work in the way you want, whether as staff or a unit commander, applying your thoughts and will. Wars have always existed in history, and stories of commanders leading them to victory have always been told. Figures like Eulji Mun-Deok, Kang Gam-Chan, and Yi Sun-sin in Korean history are revered as "Generals" or "Commanders." I promised myself to strive to become a Commander whose name would be recorded in history during wartime, a hero of victory, with the spirit of devotion to the nation, destroying evil, and upholding righteousness.

♦ Being the Head Professor at ROK Army College, an opportunity to renovate the education system:

• My attempt to reform the education system into a German style:

I was appointed Head Professor at ROK Army College in May, which was exactly what I wanted. I saw it as my chance to work as a general in the way I desired, an opportunity to reform education at the ROK Army College. I immediately formed the Education Development Committee with instructors who had studied abroad at Army Colleges (Command and Staff College) in Germany, the United Kingdom, and France. The committee and I planned to create a new curriculum within six months for the first phase of collecting materials and basic investigation and three months for the second phase, and we began working on it.

* Unfortunately, I couldn't complete it as I was transferred to a front unit. However, General Hong Seong-Tae, my classmate and close friend who studied abroad in German CSC after me, became the Head Professor, and I became the Deputy Chief of Staff of Operations (G-3). Together, we were able to complete it.

• Guiding the exercise on operation plans at the front:

Every year, the Head Professor organizes an event where students enrolled in regular courses are taken to a frontline division to participate in exercises using that division's operational plan. In July 1981, I joined the regular 29th recruits on a ten-day field trip to the 7th Division in Hwacheon, located on the central-eastern front, and the 15th Division in Sachang-ri. Here's how the exercise unfolded: We first arrived at the division's command center, where we received a briefing on the division's current situation and our assignment. We then reconnected the area with a frontline unit smaller than a regiment (GOP-COP-FEBA) in designated groups. Using the field manual, we studied at school, the local geography, and the unit's duties, we developed our own operational plans. The groups were given free time in the frontline region to devise their operations, after which we returned to the command center to complete an integrated draft over two to three days. Finally, we presented our results to the division commander and the commanders and staff of subordinate units, comparing our plans with the division's existing ones. This exercise allowed students to gain practical field experience and provided the unit with a review of its operational plans by Army College students, ultimately enhancing both plans.

During young officer 1958~1971

1959, When I was a platoon leader (first lieutenant) on the Imjingang River of front line.

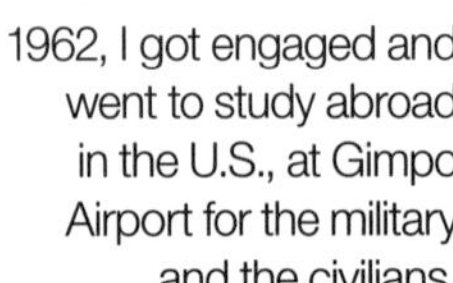

1962, I got engaged and went to study abroad in the U.S., at Gimpo Airport for the military and the civilians.

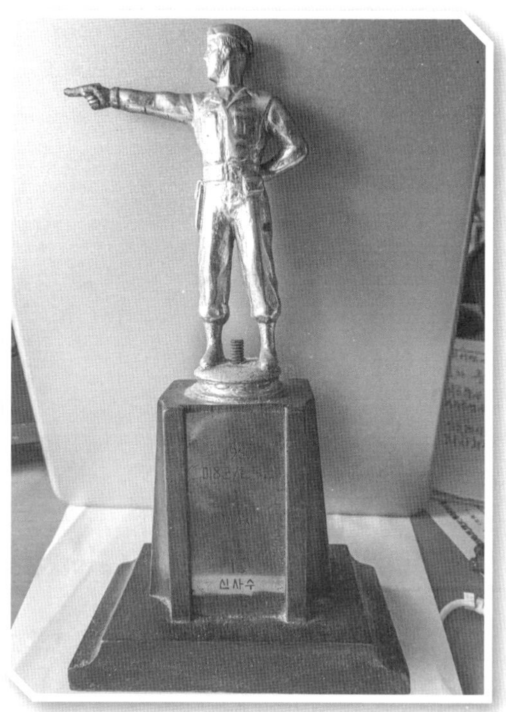

The 1st place trophy for new shooters, rapid fire, in Joint Shooting Competition for the ROK Army and the U.S. Army,

April 1962, The graduation photo from Special Warfare School at Kennedy Center, U.S.A.

April 1962, A road trip in the southern U.S. continent with my classmate from the U.S. Marine Corps.

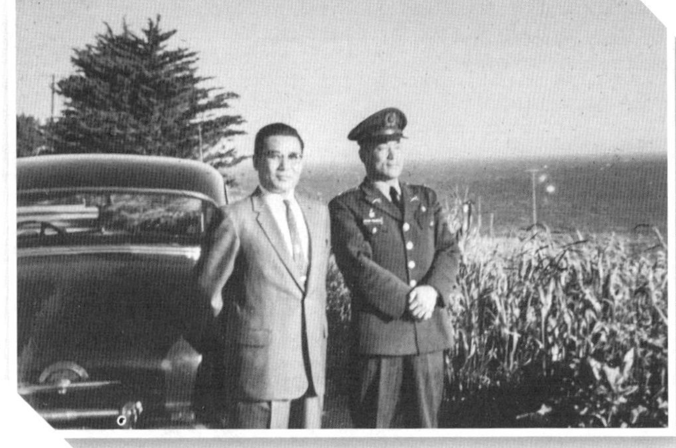

1962, Returning from my studies abroad, in Santa Barbara. Visited General Lee Han-rim, ex-president. of KMA.

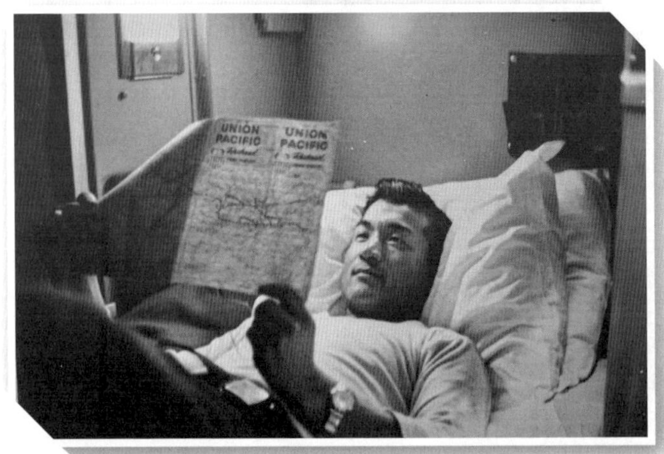

January 1962, in a bed of a Pullman Car of Union Pacific train.

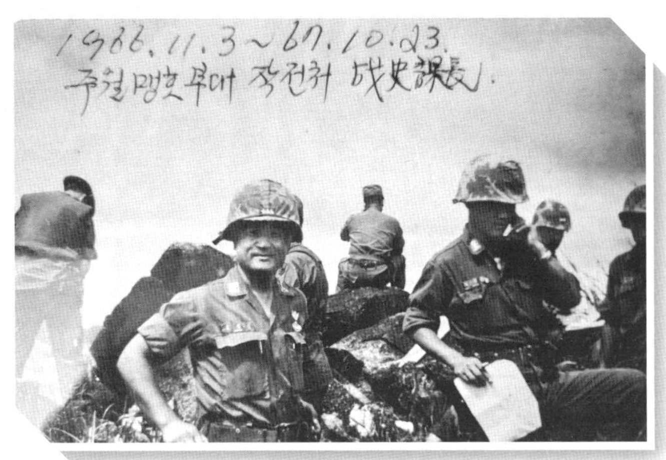

Novenber 1966, At the division's TCP in operation as the military history officer of Tiger Division in Vietnam.

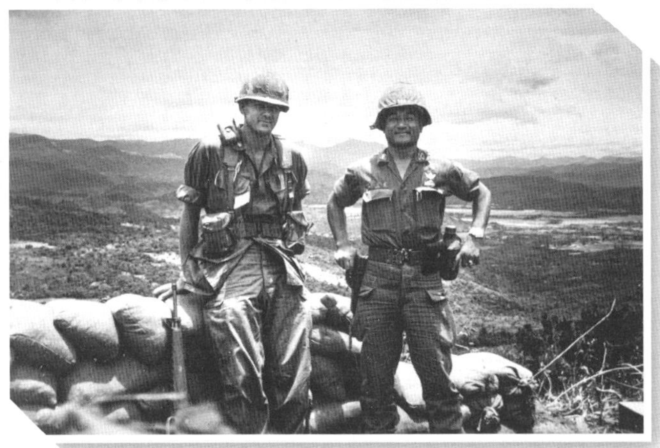

November 1966, At the division's TCP with the U.S. Army's liaison officer for Tiger Division.

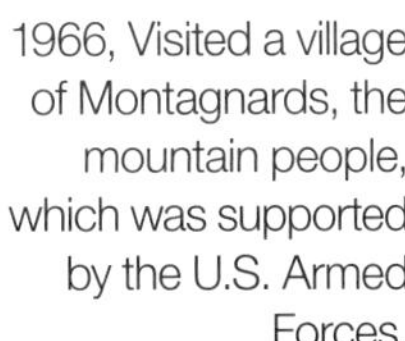

1966, Visited a village of Montagnards, the mountain people, which was supported by the U.S. Armed Forces.

January 1967, The market on Deo Cu Mong for exchange between south and north, just before Operation 8th Tiger.

January 1967, The village of Song Cau retrieved through Operation 8th Tiger.

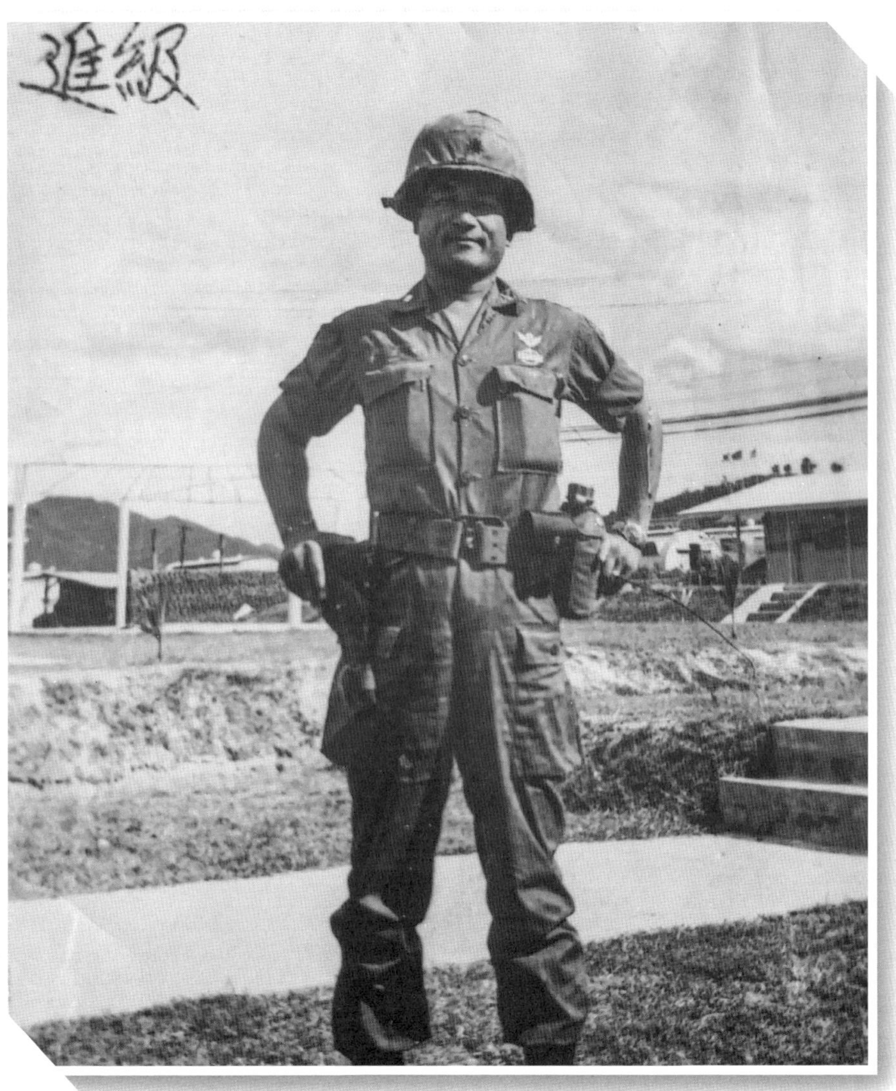

September 1st, 1967, I was promoted to a major in Vietnam.

January 1969, studying abroad at CSC in West Germany, attended language school in Euskirchen, with my classmates from the ROK Armed Forces and Turkish Armed Forces.

may,1969,dinner at Army Langage School in West Germany, with cadet Park Hung-Hwan (Corp commander after), Kim Guan-Jin(Senior Secretary, Blue House after)

July 1969, A visiting staff to a mountain unit in the Alps of West Germany, Bad Reichenhall, with Captain Song, who came for a visit.

1969.8, August 1969, A mule for operation company of the mountain unit in the Alps of West Germany.

August 1969, Climbing the Alps with the staff of West German Army and Captain Song.

September 1969, entered the Allied Forces Class at West Germany CSC, a lecturing instructor introduced officers of ROK Armed Forces.

September 1969, the Allied Forces Class at West Germany CSC, 19 students and a lecturing instructor, a colonel of the West German Armed Forces.

The staff trip of West German Armed Forces, we visited and observed major organizations and facilities, including signal school, and et cetera.

Early winter of 1970, We learned about tactical nuclear weapon warfare and visited a projectile missile unit.

Attended a masquerade at the signal school during the staff trip, and we enjoyed dancing with everyone, men and women, young and old.

Around January 1970, A trip to Spain, in front of Puerta de Alcala, Madrid.

February 1970, Reviewing the unit's placement and strategic plans in actual place after transferring a rear unit to the front.

Around April 1970, A trip to Paris, I stood in front of Triumphal Arch.

1970, Invited to visit Berlin on a graduation trip of West Germany CSC, with the Allied Forces Class in front of Brandenburg Gate, the symbol of Berlin Wall

July 1970, Visited the 5th Panzer Division as the last trip of my studies in West Germany, a conversation with the division commander and a staff of personnel.

Forward and rear Duty, During Field officer 1972~1980

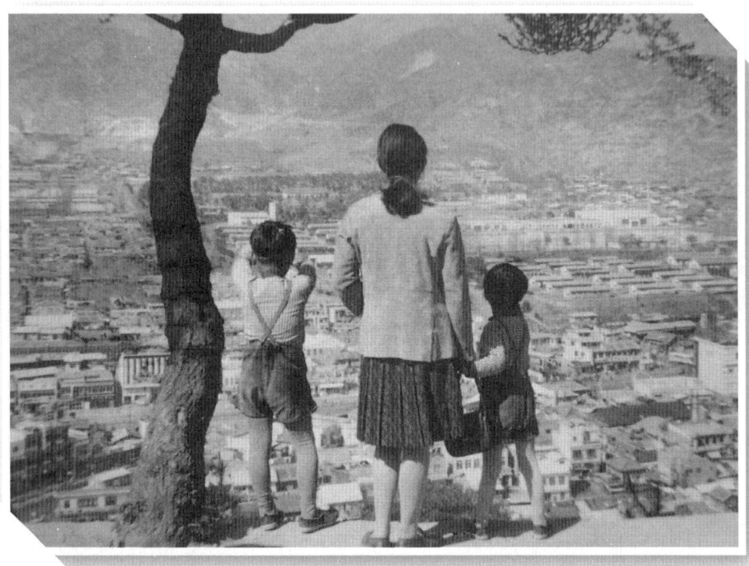

1971, When I was an instructor at Jinhae Army College, my family was looking down at Army College under Jangboksan Mountain from Jehwangsan Park.

1972, The battalion commander's residence with Baegunsan Mountain in the back, my family visited here often.

October 24th, 1972, The 1660th Unit of the Army (the 2nd Mechanized Infantry Battalion) on the UN Day activated.

October 24th, 1972, Holding a commemorative. plate with the staff of the newly established 2nd Mechanized Infantry Battalion on the UN Day.

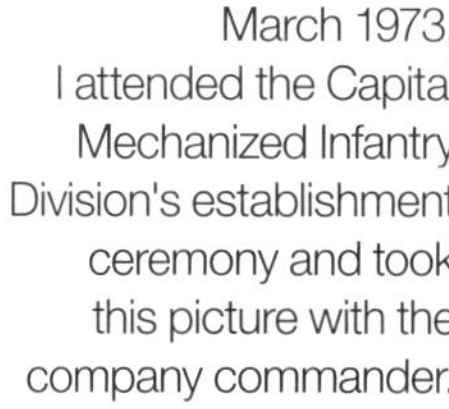

March 1973, I attended the Capital Mechanized Infantry Division's establishment ceremony and took this picture with the company commander.

1973, Singers came to perform when I was commanding for a day as the staff of the division. A picture with Choi Hee-Jun and Jeong Hun-Hee.

1973, A party for establishment of Capital Mechanized Infantry Division, Division Commander Shin Hyeon-Su and his staffs.

1975, As G-2 of Special Warfare Command Information Office, Commander Jeong, Executive Officer Lee, Brigade Commanders Chun Doo-Hwan, Roh Tae-Woo, Jeong Ho-Yong, and the staff.

1975, I accompanied Commander Jeong on his patrol at the 7th Brigade, visited Maisan Mountain, Jeonju, guided by Commander Jeong Ho-Yong.

1975, The celebration for the 9th Brigade, with Brigade Commander Roh Tae-Woo and the staff of information, G-3 and G-6.

1975, I participated with Commander Jeong for the 8th Asia Special Warfare Commander's Meeting, and this is the souvenir for it.

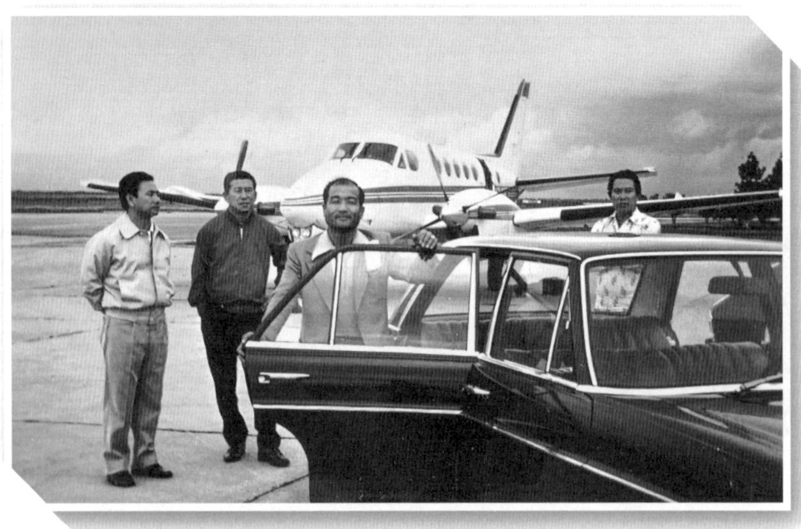

1976, With Military Assistance Investigation Commission in Morocco, just before flying over the Polisario area in the Sahara Desert.

1976, Military Assistance Investigation Commission in Morocco attended a lunch party of Minister of National Defense of Morocco.

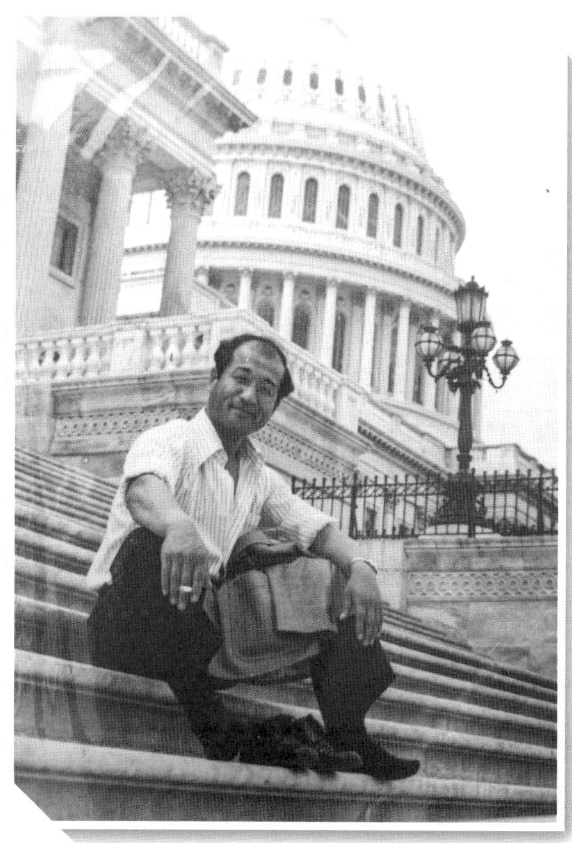

1977, When I studied at KNDU Graduate School, I went to observe the U.S., and took a break after visiting the Capitol.

1977, With KNDU Graduate School's U.S. visiting team (professors and students), including Kim Yeong-su, later a minister, and Kim Jong-hwi, later a senior secretary.

1978, As Regimental Commander of Nonsan Training Center, I worked hard to be the cream of the crop.

Selected as the leading regiment for the training center two years in a row, gave Makgeolli contributed to soldiers as a gift.

1979, KNDU Graduate School's graduation trip to Europe, with UK's House of Parliaments in the back, and with Song Eon-jong, husband of wife's sister, later Minister of Communication.

1979, KNDU Graduate School's graduation trip to Europe, with Choi Chang-Yun, later Minister of CST, a professor, and Song Eon-jong, later Minister of Communication.

1980, With Military Assistance Investigation Commission in Saudi Arabia and President Jo Jung-Sik of Hanil Development's Saudi HQ.

As Chief of Staff of ROK Army College, an at easy between of busy.

1980, I was promoted to a general a bit late, but it was an honor.

January 1st, 1980, I had an honor of being promoted to a general, my wife put the star on me, and we shared this moment of honor and joy.

Part 3

Dreaming of Becoming a ‘Commandant General’, a ‘Hero’

Chapter 9

Commander of Upper Units of the Army,
Deputy Chief of Staff of Operations at the Army Headquarters
(Dangun era 4314-4321, AD 1981-1988)

1. Commander of the 7th Airborne Special Warfare Brigade (November 1981-January 1983)

♦ Missions, Composition, and Capabilities of the Unit

All airborne special warfare brigades under the ROK Airborne Special Warfare Command have identical missions, compositions, and capabilities. The unit comprises four battalions, a headquarters unit, and a parachute maintenance unit, totaling about 2,000 personnel. Each battalion consists of four area units and a headquarters company, led by a lieutenant colonel, with approximately 300 personnel. An area unit includes five companies (teams) and a headquarters unit, commanded by a major, with around 70 personnel. A company (team) includes one captain as the company commander, one first lieutenant as the company executive officer, two medical specialists, two demolition specialists, two telecommunication specialists, two intelligence and operation specialists, and two weapon specialists, totaling 12 members. The specialists are primarily first sergeants with extensive service and middle and high school graduates who volunteered, often recruited during work trips to other regions or selected from new recruit training centers.

The brigade's primary mission is to infiltrate enemy territory (by land, sea, or air) to train anti-government locals, support their needs, and conduct guerrilla warfare, including assassination, abduction, and conspiracy. It may also involve commando warfare, intelligence warfare, and inducing warfare towards us. In preparation for these missions, the brigade performs daily tasks such as counter-guerrilla operations, counter-insurgency operations, and pacification operations during peacetime, including volunteer services for civilians and disaster assistance. Despite its size, the brigade is the only unit with substantial military power in the rear, boasting high combat capability.

♦ Education, Training, and Operations of the Unit

• Counter-Guerrilla Operations and the "Cheonli Haenggun" (400km Long Technical March – Evasion & Escape/Infiltration – in 7 Days Full Setup Along Field & Mountain Road with Full Equipment)

All unit members, both officers and soldiers, are selected from those who have completed air drop (jump) training, obtaining basic wing qualification through three weeks of land training, four daytime jumps, and one nighttime jump, totaling five jumps. They also undergo specialty and basic special warfare training. Once selected, they are transferred to the unit and immediately placed in teams. Members must conduct air drops at least once every three months to maintain their qualifications, receiving air drop payments to replace damaged sleeveless shirts or underwear. In spring and autumn, battalions occupy mountain areas expected to be enemy bases, such as Taebaeksan Mountain, Unjangsan Mountain, and Jirisan Mountain, conducting field battle exercises in underground tunnels for three weeks to deny enemy occupation and practice operations in enemy territory. Upon returning to base, they undertake the infamous "long march in full setup," an escape drill (hit and run) to evade and escape quickly from enemy areas. This challenging drill occurs only at night, avoiding roads, managing scenarios set by supervisors, and returning to base in seven days. Participants must overcome extreme sleep deprivation and endure blisters, using needles and thread to pop them, placing pine needles in shoes, or applying soap or ointment to feet. They march approximately 70 kilometers (43 miles) per day, employing tactics to complete missions and return to base. Only special warfare unit warriors can complete this drill, requiring a mental commitment to national service.

• Special Infiltration Method Drill

In summer, all brigades conduct a month-long summer swimming drill at Byeoksan Beach in Buan Chungcheung-namdo, practicing combat swimming in simple or full armed setups. This demanding drill sometimes results in casualties, despite increasing caution and sophistication each year. In winter, brigades conduct a "special winter drill in snow," or tactical skiing drill, in designated areas or on tours. Previously held in Seoraksan Mountain, our unit used a new ski training ground in Gucheon-dong, Muju. Although tactical skiing has limited practicality in Korea's climate and environment, special warfare units must learn it to prepare for various situations. Maritime infiltration drills into enemy areas in summer are also crucial, conducted in cooperation with the Navy. Naval ships or submarines transport infiltration agents near enemy coasts, about three kilometers (1.8 miles) away, where they use boats and underwater infiltration (swimming) skills to reach enemy beaches. While U.S. Armed Forces' special warfare units use underwater infiltration equipment, we relied on swimming skills at the time, though improvements have likely been made.

• The 'Ulchi-Focus Lens' in Mudeungsan Mountain, and Other Drills

Brigade command centers participate in the annual Ulchi-Focus Lens exercise, conducted by the government, Armed Forces, and Combined Forces Command, as CPX under FTX. Our brigade's command center was located in the northern part of Mudeungsan Mountain's peak. In late summer, we conducted the following: First, we simulated guerrilla warfare in North Korea, checking telecommunication command availability; second, we commanded rear operations to eliminate enemy guerrillas per Presidential Directive 28; third, we operated a field command post for over a week, serving as a drill for opposing force operations in the Armed Forces' 'Foal Eagle' (counter-guerrilla warfare). These experiences were invaluable. The following year, starting from Jirisan Mountain, we conducted a raft operation on Seomjingang River. A battalion commander proposed a sudden river-crossing drill (in full setup) by disembarking mid-river and crossing to the virtual enemy area in Hadong. Unfortunately, the unexpected Seomjingang River water temperature (18°C or 64°F) resulted in three fatalities. I continue to pray for their peace, honoring their national service dedication.

♦ Creative Effort to Improve the Mission-Oriented Unit

• Winning the Special Warfare Tactics and Techniques Competition Between Brigades

The Special Warfare Command hosted a special warfare tactics and techniques competition between brigades that year. Our brigade secured first place, thanks to our members' skills. An episode during the competition illustrates this: When the judge struggled to decide between first and second place, our brigade's competitor confidently stated, "Instructor, I have a government-authorized certificate, while others don't!" The instructor acknowledged this, leading to our victory. The 7th Brigade, based in Jeolla-do's countryside, triumphed over seven brigades, not only due to hard-earned skills but also the confidence and pride expressed in the statement, "I have a certificate, I am a qualified man!"

Everyone, including the officer in charge and the 20 competitors on our team, went on a relaxing vacation at the Gyeryong Spa Hotel in Yuseong Hot Springs, Daejeon, proudly carrying our flag. Even now, I believe it was a worthwhile investment. However, there was an unexpected side effect—something I anticipated but couldn't find amusing. As he earned a government-authorized certificate in technical skills and won the competition, his confidence soared, and he yearned to return to society as soon as possible. I thought this was wonderful. It was a joyful and proud moment for our unit to have someone become a skilled technician, both as an individual and as a member of society. I was willing to grant him permission without hesitation, knowing I would need to train more soldiers to compensate for the unit's capability loss.

• Efforts to Improve Field Meals

Improving field meals was a significant concern throughout my military career. While it was a serious issue in infantry units, it was even more critical in special warfare units. As mentioned earlier, our unit had to conduct outdoor emergency combat operation drills and "long marches in full setup" for over three months each year, alongside opposing force operations and counter-espionage missions. Our unit frequently left the base for independent activities, making field meals a pressing issue. Drawing from my experience, I decided to study this problem and provide portable meals for field exercises and outdoor movements. I supplied pastries and canned food during ambush operations or when we needed to eat on the move. All expenses were handled in cash, up to the battalion level. We received canned food from authorized factories, though they were in poor condition, but they were available in places like Daegu. This process involved trials and errors. I attempted to serve pastries, milk, and sausages for breakfast within the budget, sourcing supplies from a local bakery. However, many soldiers had never eaten pastries before, and they found them unpalatable and unsatisfying. Despite the challenges, I couldn't complete this initiative during my term. Nonetheless, as a general, I was committed to improving welfare for my subordinates and enhancing combat readiness.

2. Commander of the 8th Infantry Division of the Army (January 1983-July 1984)

♦ The Missions of the 8th Division and the Authority of the Division Commander

A division commander bears significant responsibilities, executing all three authorities—commanding, administration, and jurisdiction—necessary for individual command and supervision. While orders typically come from the upper unit (corps), a division commander can conduct independent operations with affiliated combat, artillery, and logistics units. These units can be dispatched overseas if needed, given their appropriate size and power. Thus, a division commander holds the highest authority, sometimes surpassing a corps commander. This is why people say, “A division commander is the highlight of anyone's military career.” I realized this during my time as a corps commander. Consequently, the division commander's responsibilities are greater and heavier than those of any other unit commander.

♦ The Missions of the 8th Division and Its Commander's Motto of Duty

The 8th Division served as a reserve division for the corps alongside the Capital Mechanized Infantry Division. Its primary mission was to besiege and annihilate the enemy in Munhye-ri, Cheorwon, using tactical nuclear weapons, and conduct counterattacks with the main force. During peacetime, the division focused on training, demonstrations for the Army and other armed forces, constructing reserve and rear bases for the corps, counter-espionage operations, and emergency national defense measures. Known for its rigorous training, soldiers often tried to avoid being placed in this division. Upon my appointment as division commander, I established mottos: “Always complete your responsibilities,” “Assault and finish the first battle in three days,” and “Reform old mindsets.” I emphasized these principles throughout my career, believing that individuals and units must fulfill their missions, even at personal risk. At that time, the North Korean Puppet State emphasized “Fight for the first battle of war in three days.” I adhered to the combat guidelines set by President Park Chung-Hee and President Chun Doo-Hwan, which called for immediate counterattacks following successful defenses, even in the worst situations. This approach required a “spirit to assault” and immediate counterattacks, reflecting tactical belief and determination. I also stressed the importance of “reformation of mindset movement,” necessary for reforming the mindset of all Koreans, including officers, soldiers, their families, and local residents, in response to domestic and international political situations, economic rebuilding, and justice.

♦ The Troop’s Field Maneuver Exercise and Demonstration; Participation in the Field Training Exercise for the T/S Combined Forces Command of 1984

• Participation in the 'Team Spirit'-CPX, FTX Drill of 1983 (November 1983)

As an operation officer at the 5th Division’s S-3(1965), I participated in a CPX drill for three nights and four days, even staying up all night. The operations officer, a captain, handled situations by routinely writing, “Yes, it has been taken care of,” without needing the division commander or staff. This was the general perception of CPX, and even as a high-ranking unit commander, I wasn't particularly interested in it.

My focus was on the field maneuver exercise for FTX Team Spirit, although it primarily involved automatic, mechanical movements following a scenario. However, I was keen on adapting to operational and environmental changes in the field, building my experience. The ‘T/S of 1984’ was scheduled for the following spring. In November 1983, the Division command post conducted an outdoor FTX as a unit affiliated with the 7th Corps, as preliminary training. This took place in the “Anseong-Icheon-(river-crossing)-Jipyeong-ri-Hoengseong area,” the only training ground for large-unit field exercises in the ROK Armed Forces, including the U.S. Army. I gained valuable experience operating the division's TAC-CP (tactical command post), which greatly aided future drills.

• The “Winter Operational Plan 5027 Drill” for the Division and the “Drill for Assault and Finish the First Battle in Three Days” (January 1984, for four nights and five days)

Our division was affiliated with the ROK-US Army Corps (in Uijeongbu) under the 3rd ROK Army at that time. Annually, we participated in the “Winter Operational Plan 5027 Drill.” As a reserve unit for the corps, we did not occupy bases even in emergencies, waiting for orders to counterattack or switch with other units. However, operations in the ‘Sincherwon’ area of ‘Munhye-ri’ considered tactical nuclear weapon use, with the FEBA forming a U-shape toward the north limit line of ‘Uncheon’. In emergencies, our unit occupied the lower part of the U-shape, the corps' final protective line. We built a connecting trench on that line, maintaining defense conditions in an underground space similar to a sleeping trench in winter.

The drill was reorganized into two phases this time. Phase 1 was a planned exercise. Following the corps' orders, a regiment was dispatched to the area on the corps' left flank to conduct a drill aimed at halting an enemy attack. Phase 2 was an independent drill devised by the division as an extension of the annual winter exercise, even though it had already concluded. This phase involved drills focused on defending the base at the northern limit line of Uncheon and executing counterattacks. The weather was sunny, but unusually, the temperature rose after “Daehan” (the big cold day), which typically sees a drop, resulting in harsh conditions of around negative 21 degrees Celsius (negative 5.8 degrees Fahrenheit) at night. Despite this, I led the drills day and night, commanding from an open jeep. I also trained the troops to endure extreme cold in the connecting trenches at night. The following day, I conducted a counterattack toward Sincherwon and Jipo-ri, completing the first battle in three days. General Menetrey, the Commander of the ROK-US Combined Field Army in Korea at the time, observed the drill. I recalled my field maneuver exercises in Munsan during the coldest winter days when I was a platoon leader and led my unit through these challenging drills.

♦ In March 1984, I participated in the Field Maneuver Exercise for the Team Spirit (T/S) of 1984, with the presence of the President and the U.S. Army's Chief of Staff.

This followed the T/S CPX-FTX of 1983, which prepared the division. The division's command center and a regiment formed a regimental combat unit for the exercise. Early in the year, I received the order, surveyed the local geography, sought cooperation, and established a drill plan (March 1st-March 9th). The marching unit moved to the location on the 14th, while vehicles and the command center relocated on the 15th. The command center prepared field equipment and tools early, as standardized field equipment was lacking, conducted a final check on weapons, and made close-order preparations for departure from the training ground. The military chaplain prayed for the successful completion of our mission and safe return. To boost morale, the division's military band played the division's song at the intersection of Sampalgyo Bridge (38th parallel north) in front of the command center as all units departed simultaneously. The marching unit walked 30 kilometers (18 miles) to Jeongok, took a train, and headed to Anseong Training Center. The division's command center and motorized unit proceeded directly to the first base in Anseong, the line of defense, and took their positions.

This was in late March, with the warmth of spring beginning to emerge. Our initial stationing area was in Gyeonggi-do, not Gangwon-do, and since spring plowing hadn't started, infantry and motorized units could maneuver over rice paddies. It was an ideal time and location for field maneuvers. The division was affiliated with the newly organized 7th Mechanized Corps of the ROK Army upon arrival. The large-scale field maneuver exercise commenced on March 20th. Initially, we defended the Namhangang River line. Then, according to plan, some units, including the subordinate unit and command center, withdrew toward Anseong and launched a counterattack on the 23rd. We advanced through Yeoju and Icheon, crossed the Namhangang River on a pontoon ferry, and attacked toward Munmak and Namwonju. We besieged the enemy with marching units and helicopter assault operations, annihilating them to reclaim Hoengseong Airfield, the final target, completing the mission on March 26th. The exercise concluded the next day, the 27th, with a review and a victory celebration.

Our division was affiliated with the U.S. Army's 1st Corps, tasked with besieging and attacking Hoengseong Airfield by land and helicopter assault. The commander of the U.S. Army's 1st Corps asked me, “Will the weather be sunny on March

26th?" I confidently replied, "That day is President Rhee Syng-Man's birthday, so I know the weather will be sunny. You can bet on it," based on my past experience. Remarkably, as I predicted, the rain stopped, and the clouds cleared just before the bombardment began and the helicopters took off, allowing us to execute the operation smoothly. President Chun Doo-Hwan visited the 7th Corps and the virtual enemy corps during the exercise on the 22nd, offering encouragement to ROK-US joint officers and soldiers. President Chun visited the exercise annually during his term, always holding events to motivate and support us. The following day, Jeong Ho-yong, the ROK Army Chief of Staff, General Walker, the U.S. Army Chief of Staff, and General Sennewald, the commander of ROK-US Combined Forces Command, visited our division's front tactical command post (TCP). I briefed them on the current geography and situation using a situation chart. They were satisfied and praised our efforts.

- **The U.S. Army's 1st Corps, a reserve corps stationed in Washington State, participated in the exercise.**

This corps is fully organized by recruiting reserve officers and soldiers to fight in the Korean War in an emergency. We interacted with the corps commander and staff (reserves) during the exercise. After the exercise, I made a friendly visit to the corps, thanked them for their participation, effort, and friendship, and presented pears and ceramic plates as gifts.

Regarding differences in techniques and tactics between the ROK Army and the U.S. Army, when our troops prepared to position in the line, three U.S. Army soldiers—two male and one female—were dispatched to the division's CP to assist with satellite telecommunication. I valued them as essential to the operation and offered the female soldier a room in the officers' dormitory. However, she declined, preferring to sleep with the two male soldiers in an A tent (an infantry outdoor tent for three people) at night. I was aware that U.S. servicewomen are not part of a "Women's Corps" and are considered regular troop members, working and staying with male soldiers in bases or the front lines. This experience reinforced that understanding. Additionally, when the division's TCP was organized and positioned, nearby divisions and high-ranking U.S. Army troops requested data for their database. However, the ROK Army had not prepared this data, so we couldn't provide it before the operation began. While the ROK Army completed the mission without significant issues, it seemed the U.S. Army was already using computers to digitize everything, simulate scenarios, and conduct war games, even in military operations. Despite sending agents to assist with advanced technology, we couldn't fully utilize it due to our lack of understanding. This highlighted the level of scientific advancement in Korea at that time.

3. As Deputy Chief of Staff of Operations (G-3) at the Army Headquarters, the Army's Strategy, operations, education, training, organization, and equipment (1984~1986)

♦ I held a position that all Army generals aspire to. It is a role of great importance and honor, and I felt privileged and deeply responsible to have been selected among many qualified generals. Military personnel, whether commanders or staff, are generally granted a degree of authority to fulfill their missions. The Staff of Operations, the Army's key and highest staff, is endowed with general authority, though it can be misused within its scope. The Deputy Chief of Staff of Operations of the ROK Army serves and assists the Army's Chief of Staff. Using the authority granted, the Deputy Chief must design and plan education and training for the Army in both wartime and peacetime, conduct this training, improve equipment and weapons, and manage domestic emergency operations during peacetime. Unfortunately, the authority to command operations in wartime is vested in the ROK-US Combined Forces Command and executed through the "Joint Chief of Staff." I hope for the swift realization of "true self-reliant national defense," strengthening the ROK-US alliance.

♦ In preparing strategies and operations, particularly against North Korea's "Invasion plan to South in 5 to 7 days," which included biological and chemical warfare, the Army had already moved some mobilized divisions slightly north since 1980. After conducting numerous war games to prepare for chemical warfare, it became apparent that transporting weapons from the U.S. mainland in an emergency (taking two to three days) posed a challenge. Therefore, we needed to replace them with binary options and urgently begin research on chemical warfare attack and defense strategies. Additionally, the use of the Hyunmoo Missile in actual combat was considered.

• The Nike-Hercules (SAM-N-25), a surface-to-air missile change to Korean made Hyunmu Missile

It was stationed at a southern base after the Korean War to protect the airspace of the Republic of Korea (ROK). As it was nearing retirement, we expedited work on the binary system and requested the U.S. Army to deploy the 'Lants Battalion,' a missile troop, in Korea. We also sought the deployment of 'Pershing I' missiles. Fortunately, during this period, the ROK Army developed the Hyunmoo missile, which allowed us to address the situation. We searched for strategic locations to station it for actual combat, deciding to use it as a surface-to-surface missile capable of reaching Pyongyang. After considering various factors, we chose a site under Yongmunsan Mountain for its range and secrecy and attempted to purchase the land quickly. However, the landowner, who had military connections, opposed the sale, so we abandoned the plan to maintain confidentiality.

Instead, we selected a valley south of the Namhangang River and established a base there. This enabled us to target Pyongyang in emergencies with a 200-meter (218-yard) diameter HEAT bomb. Meanwhile, scientists continued to improve the Hyunmoo, developing a 240-kilometer (126-mile) cruise missile. We requested the U.S. to lift restrictions promptly but were constrained by longstanding limitations due to concerns over ROK's potential northern advances since President Rhee Syng- man's era. These restrictions were fully lifted in 2021. Taiwan and North Korea had advanced their missile technologies ahead of us, with North Korea posing a particular threat. As of 2024, our defense industry has made significant strides, exporting various missiles, self-propelled guns, F&T-type airplanes, tanks, and more globally.

• Preparation of strategies and operations–3: Attempt to Install Barbed-Wire Fences in the DMZ (Demilitarized Zone)

At that time, the DMZ was marked with 1,292 posts delineating the Military Demarcation Line along its 240-kilometer (155-mile) length, with a vertical width of 4 kilometers (2.4 miles) from the Imjingang River estuary to the East Sea coast. North Korea had already installed electric barbed-wire fences near these posts to prevent enemy invasions and escape attempts to South Korea. Our forces had set up regular fences near the southern limit line to thwart surprise attacks or armed scouts from the north. The Army decided to install robust barbed-wire fences near the Military Demarcation Line as a strategic measure against North Korea's 'Invasion plan to South in 5 to 7 days,' using the fences for primary defense and early warnings against surprise attacks by infantry, armor, and artillery. One front decision temporarily installed these fences, held a demonstration, and ensured they were connected along the front line. This work progressed consecutively, and when I was appointed corps commander, the temporary construction was just beginning for our corps' front. We aimed to prevent surprise attacks by the North Korean Puppet State by adding another layer of defense.

• Preparation of strategies and operations–4: Planning a Counter-Infiltration Operation in the Rear and the Drill

In response to severe provocations from the North Korean Puppet State in the 1980s, the ROK Army reinforced preparations for front-line infiltrations or full-scale war. Concurrently, we declared the 'March 25th Operational Plan' (a counter-infiltration operation plan for the rear) to relevant military, administrative, and civilian bureaus in the rear in 1983, preparing for enemy infiltrations by airborne or sea routes. With the 1986 Asian Games and 1988 Seoul Olympics approaching, we conducted a "drill for dealing with enemy infiltration into the rear" near Honam Expressway in Chungcheongnam-do, attended by President Chun Doo-Hwan. In emergencies, the military and police would respond, but this drill followed a scenario for rear defense. The scenario was as follows: upon reporting enemy infiltration, local residents would initially counter with sickles, pickaxes, etc., and subdue the enemy with military and police support upon arrival. This drill emphasized the need for local residents to be resolute and quick to act against infiltrating North Korean soldiers. Subsequently, rear divisions were required to incorporate this plan into their regular operational plans.

Preparation of strategies and operations–5: Immediate Punishment and Retaliation Against Enemy Challenges

The rule was to immediately punish and retaliate against enemy challenges at the front. However, such situations were rare, leading front troops and commanders to occasionally question the manual. Considering political changes and negotiations with the Combined Forces Command, which was concerned about excessive countermeasures, we issued a revised SOP. From that point, the original plan of "Immediate punishment and retaliation (attack) against the enemy"—involving platoon infiltration into the enemy's main base for attack and annihilation—was deferred, and instead, immediate shooting for punishment and retaliation was increased onefold to twofold.

♦ Development of Education and Training, and Organization of the Army, and Establishment of Central Military School for ROTC Cadets (November 1985)

There were issues with varying levels and standardizations as summer military training for ROTCs nationwide was conducted separately in different regions. To address these issues, we established the Central Military School for ROTC Cadets by presidential order—since the Ministry of National Defense couldn't handle the issue due to budget constraints. Our staff's department of school education conducted extensive research and discussions until the plan was approved by the Army's Chief of Staff (General Jeong Ho-Yong). Consequently, a general from ROTC was appointed as the principal, and facilities were set up within the integrated military administrative and education area under Namhansanseong Fortress. The establishment ceremony took place in November 1985. By having ROTC cadets from across the nation stay at this school for summer military training, we ensured they experienced general barracks life and that commissioned officers from ROTC were equipped with integrated and standardized qualities to become commanders of small units.

♦ Developing the Army's Equipment and Armament

• Developing the Army's Equipment and Armament-1 : K-1, 155-Millimeter Self-Propelled Artillery

Due to President Park Chung-Hee's efforts for self-reliant national defense, the process of domesticating weapons, from rifles to field guns, through reverse engineering or acquiring original blueprints under certain conditions, progressed steadily in the 1980s. Notably, the K-55 self-propelled artillery, the precursor to the current K-9 self-propelled artillery, was manufactured under license from American M109A2 self-propelled artillery at 'Samsung Aircraft Industry' and distributed to all armed forces in the early 1980s. I monitored this process closely. Samsung aimed to manufacture self-produced shell carriers (tracked armored vehicles) alongside the licensed self-propelled artillery. 'Daewoo Heavy Industries,' which was developing various military armored vehicles at the time, attempted to monopolize these shell carriers. I allowed Samsung to manufacture them according to the Army's original ROC.

• Developing the Army's Armament-2: The Failure of MD-500's Maintenance with an Unknown Cause

The MD-500 helicopters, used at the front, is a subminiature model accommodating only one pilot and one passenger. It crashed whenever it returned to its base after regular maintenance in the rear (this occurred twice before my tenure). These incidents caused casualties and equipment damage, making it a priority for my duty. As anticipated, the same accident occurred again. I immediately grounded the entire Army's fleet of the same helicopter model—operational flights were the responsibility of the operations staff—and ordered an investigation into the maintenance depot's technical skills and the accident's cause. An American technician, dispatched to Korean Air for education, was involved in introducing and developing maintenance in Korea. However, after two months, they reported being unable to identify the cause, raising suspicions of concealment. The military logistics division was responsible for equipment maintenance, and while it was operationally disadvantageous to delay flights further, it was impossible to hold them accountable or encourage them directly. They repeatedly requested permission to resume flights, which I reluctantly granted under the condition: "You must find the cause and guarantee safety." This irresponsibility by the technician, the profit-driven company, and those who approved the project resulted in the sacrifice of innocent pilots and the waste of equipment and government funds.

• Developing the Army's Armament–3: A Review on Introducing Future-Type Electronic-Counter-Countermeasure (ECCM) Telecommunication Devices

The Office of Telecommunications was making significant efforts to enhance telecommunication devices for combat arms troops, aiming to develop advanced ECCM (Electronic Counter-Countermeasures) systems in preparation for armored vehicle warfare, particularly electronic warfare. Meanwhile, we decided to introduce a new product from the United States, capable of generating 16 jamming charges, and conducted tests on it for consumers who demanded it while negotiating with the responsible parties. However, Korea's telecommunication technology lagged behind that of advanced countries, although it was beginning to improve. Consequently, we resolved to adopt future-type ECCM systems. Initially, we saw an advertisement for a new telecommunication device developed in the United States, which led us to draft the Required Operational Capability (ROC) and immediately test the necessary functionalities with that device. Unfortunately, we were unfamiliar with the latest telecommunication terminology, so we had to frequently consult the American technician to conduct the tests. Ultimately, the price they demanded was excessively high, and with no alternatives for comparison, the entire plan fell through.

• Developing the Army's Armament–4: Developing and Mass-Producing ROK's First K-1 Tank and 155-Millimeter Gun Carriage

Korea's first domestically produced tank, the K-1 Tank, featured gun turrets newly invented in the U.S.A. and made with composite steel. It was first manufactured in 1985 and was about to be deployed to the troops. However, during the final test, its cast iron body cracked while driving. As a result, we urgently imported tank bodies from overseas to meet the demands and deployment plans on time. Despite our passion and determination, our capabilities were limited, requiring us to rely on foreign equipment for the first year. Nevertheless, after conducting cast iron and other tests, we eventually succeeded in domestic production. We also hastily completed the domestic production of the 155-millimeter towed gun, but as expected, the body continued to crack during tests, and it failed to achieve the target firing speed. Nevertheless, we ultimately succeeded in researching and developing a Korean-made towed gun, eliminating the need for foreign models.

• Decision on the Development of Armament and Equipment: The Best Method is to Introduce Weapons Used by the U.S. Army

The ROK Armed Forces have been striving to domestically produce various equipment and armament, and most of these efforts have come to fruition, allowing us to advance towards self-reliant national defense. However, we must continue to improve or invent new armament and equipment by keeping pace with scientific developments. Consequently, we may introduce and utilize overseas products based on current demands and even develop our own products using these as references. This is why we are still negotiating to introduce equipment and armament from abroad. The best approach for the ROK is to adopt the same armament system as the United States, given our military alliance and the necessity for coordinated operations. For instance, if a radar detects a similar-looking aircraft, it would be problematic if we couldn't identify it as friend or foe. If we purchase aircraft from a foreign country and deploy them simultaneously, but are unable to identify them, it would disrupt operations. Even so, if development conditions or pricing don't align, we sometimes explore products from other countries, although I hope this can be avoided. Based on my extensive military experience, American armament products remain the best globally, and the optimal course of action is to adopt those already chosen and used by the U.S. Army, as their functionality is thoroughly guaranteed.

4. Commander of the 1st Corps of the ROK Army (July 1986-January 1988)

♦ As my term as Chief of Staff of Operations was ending, I was appointed as a corps commander.

I reported to President Chun Doo-Hwan at the Blue House, where I received the honorable 'Samjeongdo' (Sword of Three Pure Spirits) and the ribbon-type flag of a corps commander, which became a treasured family heirloom. President Chun expressed deep trust in me and others during the ceremony and delivered a speech. I vowed to repay his trust and expectations by fulfilling my responsibilities. Chief of Staff Jeong Ho-Yong repeatedly congratulated me on the way back, saying, "I was going to recommend you to be the commander of special warfare, but..." I could always rely on President Chun Doo-Hwan and Chief of Staff Jeong Ho-Yong. However, had I become the commander of special warfare at that time, my future might have been different... Such is the nature of destiny.

♦ The History of the 1st Corps and Its Commander's Immediate Duties Under the Current Situation

• The proudly history of the 1st Corps

The 1st Corps of the ROK Army was the first corps formed immediately after North Korea invaded South Korea on June 25th, marking the outbreak of the Korean War. It left the western front to the main U.S. Army forces and primarily managed the central (Chungcheongbuk-do) region, conducting delaying operations. When the Nakdonggang River line was established, it automatically commanded the main ROK Army forces, defending the central and eastern lines. During the counterattack, the 2nd Corps of the ROK Army (including the 6th and 8th Divisions) managed the central and central eastern lines. The 1st Corps was responsible for the eastern line, from the eastern parts of the Taebaek Mountains to the East Sea coasts, with the 3rd Division and the Capital Division under its command. On October 1st—later designated as 'National Armed Forces Day,' a national holiday—by order of President Rhee Syng-Man, it breached the 38th Parallel and began advancing north. Consequently, it marched to Gilju, North Korea, and Hyesanjin near the North Korea-China border. Unfortunately, they had to withdraw to the South due to China's involvement in the war. Later, it launched another attack and was positioned along the current Military Demarcation Line, advancing to Ganseong-Goseong, the northernmost area. After a brief period stationed in Gapyeong (from 1960 to the early 1970s), it relocated to its current location (Byeokje, Goyang) in 1972, swapping positions with the 1st Corps of the U.S. Army. This is why the 1st Corps is the most distinguished corps of the ROK Army, boasting the longest tradition and war history from the Korean War, and it continues to uphold its honorable reputation as the "top elite 1st Corps."

• Our Corps' Environment for Operations (Geographical and Human-Related) and Its Range

The corps' operational environment was challenging. The operational depth was generally 60 kilometers (37 miles) long, but in this case, it was about 40 kilometers (24 miles) from the Military Demarcation Line to Seoul. This meant the troop's positioning was narrow, limiting the establishment of a sufficient buffer zone in the boundary, which was disadvantageous for defense. However, the Imjingang River served as an operational obstacle between us and the enemy, making attacks challenging but aiding in defense. Meanwhile, the defensive front was generally 30 to 40 kilometers (18 to 24 miles) long (from Jangdan Peninsula to the northeast side of Gorangpo), with an additional 30 kilometers (18 miles) for counter-espionage and counter-infiltration operations in the rear (from 'Unification Observatory' to Haengjusanseong Fortress) during normal times. This added a brigade responsible for defending the inner line of the Hangang River. Furthermore, it lacked the 27-kilometer-long (16-mile-long) civilian control line typical of other corps, complicating the organization of COPs (combat outposts) or GOPs (general outposts) and necessitating extreme caution against enemy surprise attacks. This situation presented numerous challenges. For instance, the barbed-wire fences on the final protective fire line on the main line of resistance (the FEBA line and combat areas at that time) and the integration of crossfire were mixed with civilian properties (rice paddies and gardens), making management difficult and requiring extra caution. Consequently, active cooperation with local residents was essential. The corps was responsible for defending one of the three major avenues of approach (Uijeongbu→Seoul, Chuncheon→Seoul, and Munsan/Gorangpo→Seoul) that North Korea might use to invade South Korea. This avenue was the shortest and had a significant impact on real-time operations. Therefore, in an emergency, as known through the CPX, a large troop of at least 300,000 personnel—including numerous artillery troops, mobilized divisions, and newly affiliated combat divisions and brigades—would assemble in the operational area of this corps and conduct a defense battle under my command as the Corps Commander.

• The Missions of the Corps (and Its Commander) in Wartime, Usual Times, and Immediate Times

Under the strategies and operational environment outlined above, the corps (and its commander) must conduct defense and counterattack battles, typically focusing on counter-espionage operations and front-line guarding according to "Operational Plan 5072" during wartime. Simultaneously, the corps supported the 1986 Asian Games and the 1988 Seoul Olympics as immediate tasks, and I decided to include efforts to "stabilize the political situation" (establishing the values of liberal democracy, promoting anti-communism and unification, educating the public on economic stability, etc.) as part of the basic missions. The corps was also responsible for training reserve forces within the region (Goyang, Munsan, and Paju).

The counter-infiltration operations along the coasts of the East Sea and the Hangang River were deemed crucial in the ROK Army's counter-espionage efforts. Particularly, the operations downstream of the Hangang River, spanning approximately 30 kilometers (18 miles) from the current 'Unification Observatory' to the basin of Haengjusanseong Fortress, were of significant importance. The Capital Corps was responsible for the area south of the river, while our corps managed the area north of the river. Armed spies often used the tactic of navigating the waterways from the downstream of the Imjingang River, following the river's flow to infiltrate the northern part of the Hangang River, and then blending in with the citizens of Seoul. This is why barbed-wire fences for civilian control remain installed along the riverside of the Hangang River, and guards vigilantly monitor for spy infiltration day and night. As is well-known, the "January 21st Incident" (The Kim Shin-jo Incident, January 21st, 1968) occurred because the Blue House was close to the enemy's base. Consequently, operations to prevent such incidents and swiftly eliminate the enemy in emergencies were added to the corps' regular missions.

• The relationship between the Corps (and Its Commander) and the affiliated divisions (and their commanders) was as follows:

Among the four combat divisions, the 1st and 25th Divisions were positioned at the front. The 9th and 30th Divisions were reserve divisions, traditionally dispatched without the corps commander's authorization or even notification for "subjugation of uprising" after the '12.12 Incident.' Therefore, the commanders of these divisions often received orders directly from the Blue House, bypassing the corps commander, but they always reported afterward. However, there were some inconveniences when the President's secret inspection (by a subordinate unit) visited, aside from "subjugation of uprising."

Regarding the relationship with the administration and civilians within the corps, there was little interaction with the mayor of Seoul or the governor of Gyeonggi-do. The governor of Gyeonggi-do visited the corps during the Team Spirit Drill and at the end of the year to offer encouragement, and that was about it. All regions of the corps maintained primary relationships with civilians or contacted them through divisions (and their commanders). The corps (and its commander) attended neighborhood meetings in the corps' command center's region for friendly purposes. However, even though it was a region under the 1st Division's charge, the residents of Gwangtan complained about insufficient drinking water. An engineering unit from the Army's military engineering department, which had completed drilling underground tunnels at the front and was withdrawing at the time, was assigned to stay and successfully drilled three round wells, providing significant assistance. In terms of administration, Munsan and Paju frequently sought help. We met with their mayors at civilian, administrative, and military meetings to discuss governmental issues and emphasize them.

• My Leadership Policy in the Corps and Its Implementation

Upon my appointment as the 32nd commander of the corps, I issued the "Policy on Leadership in the Corps." These policies were: "Always complete responsibilities, no matter what," "Those who believe in victory shall be victorious," and "Support national policy." I believed that the most important and fundamental virtue of a military serviceperson, as a member of a troop, is to "always be responsible for the missions assigned to you as an individual and ensure their completion, no matter what," based on the rules and experiences I gained as a commander and staff member of various troops since my days as a platoon leader. I also believed this was the key to victory. I emphasized that not only the commanders of subordinate troops but also all individual officers and soldiers must fight with "the conviction that we will win this battle, and we must win this battle," and that they can indeed "win" that battle. The Armed Forces' existence was a demonstration of patriotism for the nation and the people, so I emphasized "understanding and practicing national policy" to all officers and soldiers.

• Major Interests in the Area and Extension Situation

Civilians were allowed to enter the front tactical and operational area of the 1st Division, making 'Dorasan Mountain Observatory' and the '3rd Tunnel' subjects of interest as they became tourist attractions for "national defense tourism." An observation post and a combat command center for a general outpost unit were located on the lower floor of the observatory. From there, we could observe an avenue of approach from Kaesong toward the south and even observe military activities within the area up to Songak-san Mountain in Kaesong (about 12 kilometers, or 7.4 miles) with the naked eye during the daytime. The 3rd Tunnel was reported by a defector in 1974, a borehole was installed, and it was discovered in 1978. It is located 73 meters (79 yards) underground, 1,635 meters (1,788 yards) long (1,200 meters (1,312 yards) in North Korea, and 435 meters (475 yards) in South Korea), 2 meters (2.1 yards) tall and wide, and arch-shaped. It was estimated that 30,000 officers and soldiers in full gear could infiltrate and move through it per hour, reaching Seoul in 45 minutes if traveling at high speed. To inspect it, I first walked 300 meters (328 yards) down, met the tunnel, and went north up to the Military Demarcation Line (where a cement wall is installed). The tunnel is slanted 3 degrees toward the north, causing subterranean water to flow northward. Additionally, when President Chun Doo-Hwan was a division commander, he constructed a counter-tank trench in Jangdan, which was over 1 kilometer (0.62 miles) long—20 meters (21 yards) wide and 10 meters (10 yards) deep—considering the enemy's tanks' functionalities and characteristics, using it as an obstacle to prevent surprise attacks by enemy tanks. It was a very good idea. However, civilian residents occupied the southern limit line and even the Imjingang River in this area of the Jangdan Peninsula, which was advantageous for civilian tourism but seemed to present many issues for military operations.

• Counter-Espionage Security Operation on the Hangang Riverbank

After patrolling the frontline (the southern limit line, the main line of resistance, and GP) for a week, I began to understand the current situation of the counter-espionage operational area along the Hangang River, which is the second front. The length from below the eastern part of 'Unification Park' to the booster pump station (sluice)—the line for Seoul and Gyeonggi-do up to Gayangdaegyo Bridge—is about 55 kilometers (34 miles) long, which is twice the length of the corps' defensive front. In other words, the corps' left depth itself is the counter-espionage operational line on the downstream of the Hangang River. Of course, it is another overlapping mission besides counter-espionage infiltration operations on the Imjingang River. As mentioned many times already, in 1959, the 1st Regiment of the Capital Division, which was on the central front, organized the 1st Regimental Combat Team (RCT) and took over this region from the 1st Brigade of the ROK Marine Corps, carrying out defense missions. At that time, I became the platoon leader of the right frontline of "Unification Park," and Second Lieutenant Lee Seung-ju, my classmate, became the platoon leader of the left frontline of "Unification Park." Second Lieutenant Lee's platoon ambushed in the far downstream of Gongneung-cheon Stream, based on intelligence obtained that autumn, and shot and killed three armed spies who infiltrated by floating on the water with volleyball tubes, receiving the Order of Military Merit. Even after that, spies and armed communist guerrillas continued to infiltrate the area from the downstream of the Hangang River to Haengju-sanseong Fortress, the northern part of the Hangang River, and Seoul.

The next day, I moved along the levee on the northern part of the Hangang River—its top just wide enough for one cattle-drawn carriage to pass—toward Haengjusanseong Fortress, receiving reports from company commanders and platoon leaders from important spots and checking the current situation. Especially the gap area near Janghang (the current Ilsandaegyo Bridge and Janghang Intersection) and the area near Sinpyeong Drain Pump Station had a large and lush reed forest and sturdy ground. I even patrolled up to the central area of the Hangang River by tracked armored vehicle. Unlike how it appeared on a map or from the outside, I thought this wide, deep, and lush reed forest would be a route of infiltration into Seoul for North Korean armed communist guerrillas and spies.

Standing on the levee of Sinpyeong Drain Pump Station in Sinpyeong-dong, I could see the Singok Pumping Station across the way toward Gimpo. A truck road, used for transporting agricultural products grown by the riverside, began at Sinpyeong Village, north of the levee, crossed over it, and descended toward the river. As part of the Hangang River Development Project, the construction of the Singok Underwater Levee was underway. I discussed this with the corps commander on the opposite side, Lieutenant General Kim, a junior from the 17th class of KMA, and we proposed the following: 1. Construct an underwater road for vehicles atop the levee, at least 7 meters (7.6 yards) wide; 2. Round the downstream edge of the road to prevent spies from climbing it; 3. Since the Capital Division on the south side is responsible for this area, I suggested building numerous guard outposts on the water at close intervals to prevent spy infiltrations. We agreed to implement these suggestions. Although I never had the opportunity to test the underwater road, which was intended for emergency delay operations, I never heard of any spies infiltrating via that route, as it was completely blocked.

♦ Assistance for the 1986 Asian Games and preparation for the 1988 Seoul Olympics

The first national-level task for our corps after my appointment was preparing for the 1986 Asian Games (September 20th-October 5th, for 15 days). Our objectives were to counter North Korean military provocations during this period, prevent North Korean disruptions through espionage, and ensure complete security for the Games through military, administrative, and civilian cooperation. Our corps was responsible for assisting with security at the Asian Games venues within our area, including Hanyang Country Club for golf (Goyang), cycling routes (entire Tongil- ro), and horseback riding (Wondang Eventing Tracks). I mobilized all agents in the corps to conduct thorough reconnaissance operations, focusing on the Games areas, and maintained this vigilance throughout the preparation and duration of the Games. Officers living outside the barracks worked in plain clothes from preparation to the Games' conclusion. Given that the Games venues were in rural areas, I conducted surveillance to prevent sudden emergencies, such as direct provocations or disruptions like spies or the fifth column throwing sand on the cycling road. I also ensured that animals like chickens or dogs were kept away from the horse tracks. As a result, all events in the region concluded successfully, and I could proudly say that our efforts contributed to the Games' success. I believed this experience would greatly aid our preparation for the 1988 Seoul Olympics, which was two years away.

♦ Tactical discussion for the corps and the guideline for "Charging for three days at the beginning of war and having a decisive battle" (annihilation)

Tactical discussions in front-line troops (divisions or corps) usually involve assembling commanders and relevant staff in the area of concern, with the troop's commander attending. These discussions emphasize the commander's intent or help understand new guideline changes. After completing patrols and assessing the situation, I conducted the first tactical discussion for the corps at the covered outdoor training ground south of the DMZ, overlooking the GP in the DMZ. The discussion focused on whether to defend the GP in place or warn the enemy, attack, and withdraw immediately. The GP in front of us was more of a natural cave than an artificial one, so most commanders and staff favored defending it, even if besieged. After a passionate discussion, I emphasized the tactical guideline as the corps commander: "The GP must warn the enemy upon detection, maintain contact, and quickly withdraw under our forces' supporting fire. This approach conserves manpower early on and boosts troop morale for an early victory."

Next, I participated in the 25th Division's tactical discussion on whether to defend the waterfront with obstacles at Gorangpo, Imjingang River, or lure the enemy inland, besiege, and annihilate them with Gamaksan Mountain as the key point. The latter had been the division's defense strategy. I suggested, "Prioritize the obstacle at Imjingang River and focus on defending the waterfront first. Consider luring and annihilating the enemy as a subsequent step." Ultimately, I determined that the best defense strategy for the corps was to fully utilize the natural obstacle of the Imjingang River from its downstream to Gorangpo, focus on "charging for three days at the beginning of war and having a decisive battle (annihilation)," and annihilate the enemy crossing the Imjingang River through repeated counterattacks.

♦ False report on Kim Il-sung's death

On November 16th and 17th, 1986, our corps observed the North Korean flag in "Gijeong-ri Peace Village" of North Korea's DMZ at half-mast, and Kim Il-Sung's statue in downtown Kaesong was covered in white fabric. Upon reporting this to the Army's superior office, the Armed Forces and government closely monitored the situation, given North Korea's political sensitivity. Meanwhile, we heard North Korean propaganda broadcasts to the south playing a funeral march and reporting "Kim Il-sung shot to death," which was also reported to the superior office. The Eighth U.S. Army's intelligence report, suggesting Kim Il-sung's death, was distributed to the corps. Even the Minister of National Defense believed this information, and Minister Kim addressed Kim Il-sung's death during a government interpellation at the National Assembly. However, Kim Il-sung appeared at Pyongyang Airport on the 18th, shattering the hopes of the South Korean people. The events that transpired remain uncertain, whether they were North Korean Armed Forces' overreaction or an intentional conspiracy against South Korea.

♦ Participation in Field Training (Maneuver) Exercise for the Team Spirit of 1987 with the 1st Corps of the U.S. Army

As a military service member, I had the honor of participating in Team Spirit, the field maneuver exercise for ROK-US Combined Forces. I participated as the commander of the 8th Division in 1984, and this time (March 28th, 1987-April 10th, 1987), I participated as a corps commander alongside the 1st Corps of the U.S. Army, commanded by Lieutenant General Schwartzkopf, who later became a hero for leading the attack on Iraq. The main subordinate troops were the Capital Mechanized Infantry Division, the 8th Division, and the 25th Division of the U.S. Army (mobilized). I will skip explaining Team Spirit's purpose, history, drills, and political and military significance, as they are well-known. Instead, I will share a few unforgettable stories from that time. The 1st Corps of the U.S. Army, which collaborated with the 1st Corps of the ROK Army under my command, practiced delaying operations, defense warfare, and counterattack warfare with our corps. This corps is stationed in Washington State and recruits reserve forces to be sent to Korea's front lines in emergencies, participating in this exercise annually. That year, its commander was General Schwartzkopf, who had an elite background. I met him at the operational meeting at the Combined Forces Command, where he told me, "I'm going to be appointed as the staff of operations at the Army Headquarters (G-3)—In Korea's case, after the General Staff of Army HQ, and then become a corps commander—and I wish to become a commander (general) of a theater anywhere in the world." He was one year older than me, graduated from the U.S. Military Academy, and was commissioned two years before I was. His father was also a general and fought in the Middle East. Schwartzkopf appeared to be a competent, active, and passionate general, both in appearance and past activities. As expected, he became the commander of the U.S. Army troop of the multinational force during 'Operation Desert Shield of the Gulf War.' He then counterattacked Iraq's invading forces in 'Operation Desert Storm,' winning the battle in just around 100 hours, and became the 'hero of the desert.' I truly felt that the saying, "The era creates a hero, and the hero creates an era," was accurate, but it was unfortunate that not everyone gets such an opportunity.

♦ A soldier's claim: The military must not be subordinated usually to politics, but politics must be subordinated to the military depending on the situation for victory in war.

As a cadet, I was deeply engrossed in Clausewitz's "On War." He famously stated, "War is a tool for politics, which is why it has political tendencies, subordinating the military perspective to the political one. Military leaders must be aware of political situations and knowledgeable about the names, personalities, beliefs, and political tendencies of at least a few politicians of their era." I dared to reinterpret his theory on the relationship between politics and the military, as well as military philosophy. Clausewitz developed his theories while teaching a prince in a palace, suggesting that his military philosophy was shaped in a political atmosphere, potentially skewing it towards politics. I concluded that while politicians should understand the military, and military leaders should understand politics, it is incorrect to assume the military must always be subordinate to politics. Sometimes, politics should yield to the military to achieve victory in wars and battles.

An example from recent history is the Korean War. General MacArthur, commander of the UN Command, suggested to President Truman that they bomb certain facilities in Manchuria. Truman, considering political relations with the Chinese Communist Party, refused and dismissed MacArthur. Consequently, the Chinese Communist Party used Manchuria as a base, forcing the Allied Forces to retreat and thwarting the strategy of unification under liberal democracy. In such cases, politics should have been subordinate to the military to win the war, but the politicians' emphasis on "the military as a tool for politics" left a significant resentment in Korean history.

As a corps commander, I witnessed Korea's military ruling politics and society, yet simultaneously being ruled by political military officers. I refused to support these political military officers.

Brigade Commander, Division Commander 1981~1984

May 1981, The inauguration as the commander of the 7th Airborne Special Warfare Brigade, with my wife.

1981, Inaugurated as the commander of the 7th Airborne Special Warfare Brigade, centered on training, recovery from the May 18, and cooperation with administration and civilians.

1982, Reconnaissance on outdoor training ground (the point where the enemy infiltrates) near the East Sea.

1982, Visited Vice President Kim Sam-ryong of Wonkwang University and interacted with him.

1982, I had lunch with special warfare soldiers in the unit's outdoor training ground and comforted them.

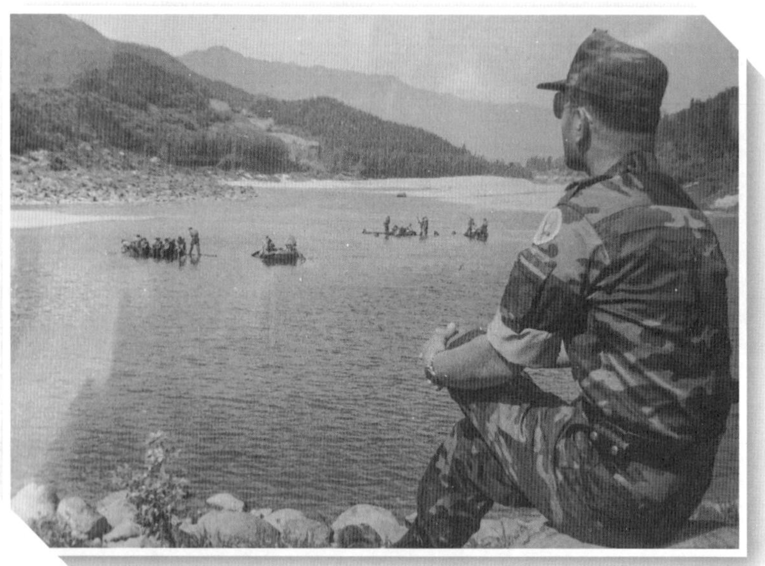

1982, I saw a river-crossing drill on Seomjingang River on rafts, with Jirisan Mountain in the background.

1982, the Commander of Special Warfare visited TCP of the 7th Airborne Special Warfare Brigade on the peak of Mudeungsan Mountain for Foal Eagle.

January 1983, inaugurated as the commander of the 8th Division, and received the flag of the proud Roly-poly Toy Division with history and tradition.

January 1983, Inauguration as the commander of the 8th Division, with my wife.

Summer of 1983, President Park Jeong-Gi of KEPCO, my close friend, and his wife visited the unit, and we played sports to welcome them.

Summer of 1983, I commanded and inspected armaments of the division.

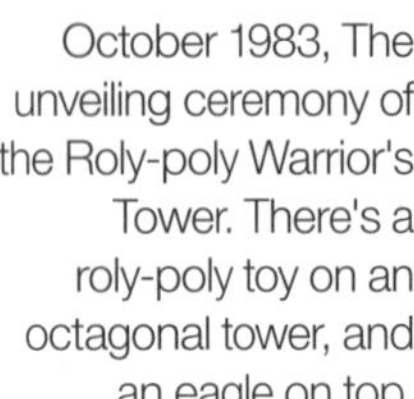

October 1983, The unveiling ceremony of the Roly-poly Warrior's Tower. There's a roly-poly toy on an octagonal tower, and an eagle on top.

September 1983, all officers and soldiers of the division assisted civilians by cutting and harvesting rice.

October 1983, I received the newly made Samjeongdo from Chief of Staff Jeong Ho-Yong, and it became our family's treasure number one.

March 1984, the commanders of the 1st Corps and the 24th Division of the U.S. Army came for a visit before Team Spirit '84.

March 1984, Team Spirit '84, unit inspection, the division's TCP briefing of the training ground, and Lieutenant General Jeong Ho-Geun came for inspection.

March 25th, 1984, Commander of ROK-US Combined Forces visited the TCP of the division, I held a briefing and had friendly conversations with him.

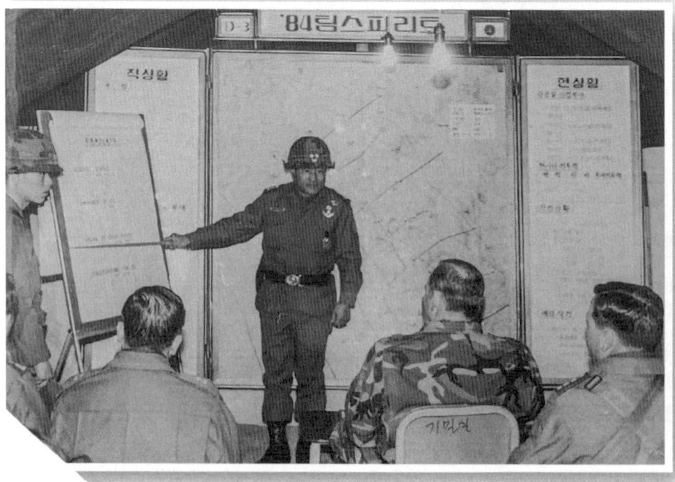

March 26th, 1984,
The final meeting and conversation with the commanders of the 1st Corps and the 24th Division (call-up units stationed in Washington), our allies.

March 26th, 1986, Commander of the U.S. Army visited, I did a briefing and guided him through the operational area.

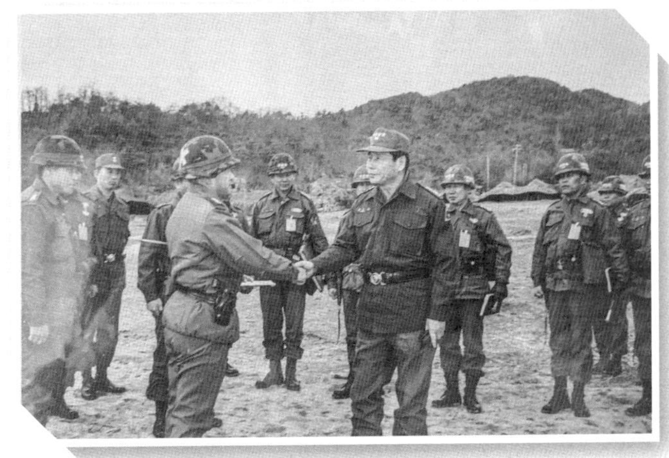

March 26th, 1984, Team Spirit '84, Chief of Staff Jeong Ho-Yong visited TCP of the division to comfort and encourage us. I was thankful.

1984, Team Spirit '84 ended successfully, celebrating the victory with officers and soldiers of the division.

Operations Staff, Corps Commander 1984~1988

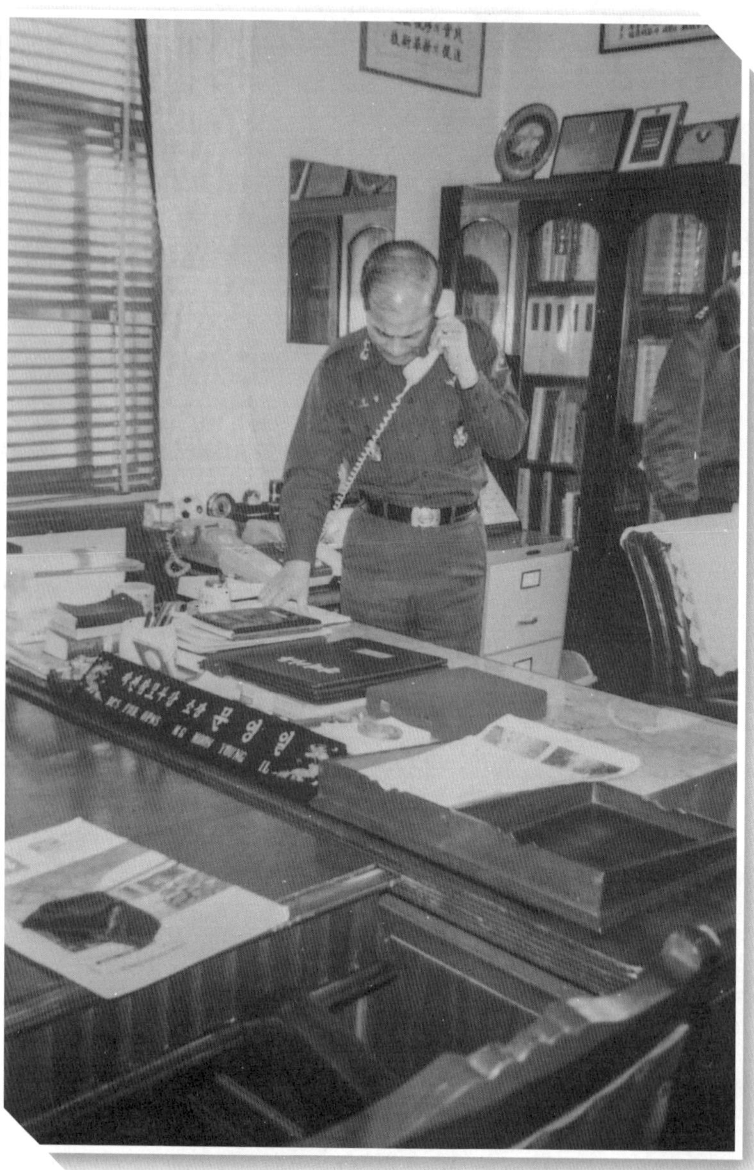

1985, Deputy Chief of Staff of Operations at Army Headquarters, Army Headquarters in Yongsan, It was lucky case to talk with visitors for ten minutes.

I participated often welcome party for overseas VIPs, like UK Army Chief of Staff (visited).

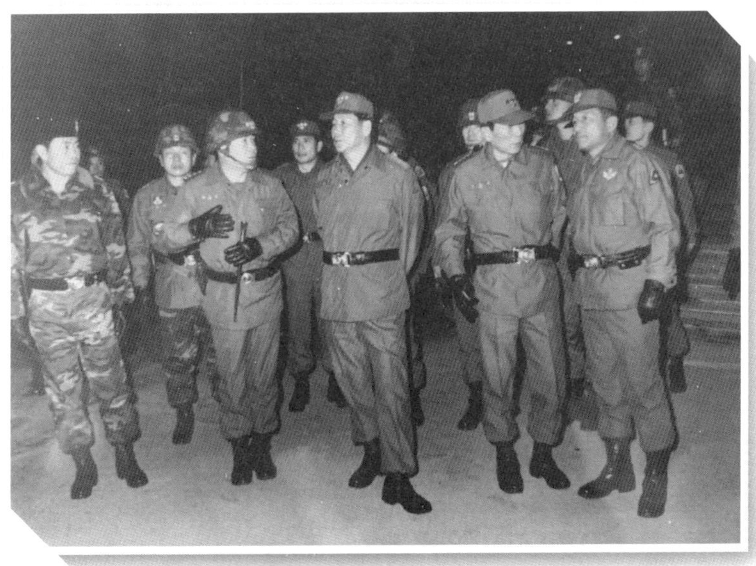

Sometimes I accompanied Chief of Staff when he patrolled major bases at night.

A regular meeting for Staff of Operations of affiliated units.

June 1986, I was inaugurated as the commander of the 1st Corps of the Army, and became highly responsible.

Patrolling the barbed-wire fences of the 101th Brigade, July 1986,

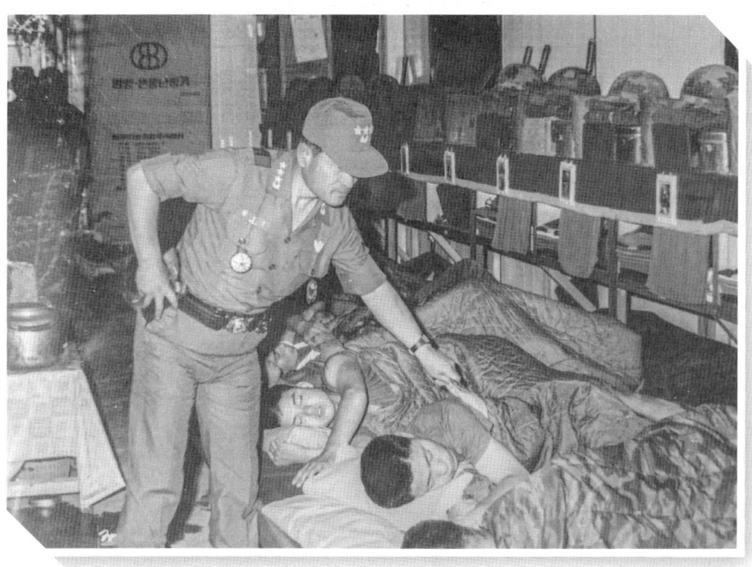

July 1986, Patrolling the life in the barracks of affiliated units at night

January 1987, Focus Clear CPX, evaluation on the corps.

June 1987, Built an octagonal gazebo and a small pool in the park for the corps, named it Baekiljeong after General Kim Baek-il, which was a rare thing.

Patrolling the installation of additional barbed-wire fences adjacent to Military Demarcation Line after the southern limit line wall was built.

팀 스 피 리 트 '87

(1987. 3. 31 ~ 4. 9)

정 예 제 1 군 단 장 중 장 문 영 일

① 제 8 사단장	소장	이 진 백	① 참 모 장	준장	섬 백 관
② 미 25 사단장	소장	CRYSEL.J.W	② 지원참모	대령	임 창 호
③ 제 72 사단장	준장	구 본 중	③ 정보참모	대령	김 정 웅
④ 제 1 포병여단장	준장	이 승 남	④ 작전참모	대령	정 정 택
⑤ 제 1 공병여단장	준장	장 대 준	⑤ 감찰참모	대령	진 병 국
⑥ 제 701 특공연대장	대령	김 명 세	⑥ 본부대장	소령	안 상 질
⑦ 제 101 통신단장	대령	권 정 행	⑦ 비서실장	소령	권 두 환
⑧ 제 101 보안부대장	대령	허 호	⑧ 통역장교	대위	전 인 범
⑨ 항 공 대 장	대령	김 대 선	⑨ 전속부관	중위	신 천 웅
⑩ 헌 병 대 장	중령	오 세 창	⑩ 주임상사	상사	정 홍

March 1987, Participated in Team Spirit 87, the commemorative plaque for the 1st Corps' affiliated unit, of the blue team, the slogan of 'Charge and win.'

熱氣 더하는 87팀·스피리트 韓·美연합훈련

美25·2사단 황·청군에 배속신고

육군오봉산부대 동원예비군 비상소집 작전 돌입

하와이에서 공수된 「열대의 번개」 미보병 제25사단이 지난29일 한국군 황군부대장에게 배속신고 해옴으로써 실질적인 작전훈련 태세에 돌입하게 됐다.

한국군 군악대의 팡파르가 울려퍼지는 가운데 중부전선 ○○기지에서 실시된 이날 배속신고에는 황군부대장인 육군 2127부대장을 비롯, 미25사단장등 많은 한·미장병들이 참석하여 양국의 두터운 결속을 다짐했다.

이날 황군부대장은 미25사단장의 배속신고를 받고 지휘봉을 수여함에 따라 87팀스피리트훈련기간중 미25사단은 황군부대장의 작전통제를 받게됐다.

이자리에서 황군부대장은 환영인사를 통해 「평화를 수호하기 위해 멀리 이곳까지 찾아준 미군장병여러분을 한국군 전장병과 더불어 진심으로 환영한다」고 치하하고 「쌍방간의 긴밀한 협조를 통해 훈련의 성과를 더욱 드높여 줄것」을 당부했다.

또한 「개인적으로 한국에 있는 시간을 보다 즐겁고 유익하게 지낼수있게 되길 바란다」면서 「하와이에 훌라춤이 유명하듯 한국에는 훌륭한 부채춤이 있다」고 문화예술을 소개하기도 했다.

같은날 중동부전선 지역에서도 미보병 제2사단이 한국군 청군부대장에게 배속신고를 함으로써 청군부대와 합류했다.

한편 수도권지역에서 비상소집된 동원예비군 들도 이날 전원의 응소율을 보이며 집결지인 「육군오봉산부대로 속속들이 출동했다.

잠재능력의 극대화로 연합합동작전의 능력을 배양하기 위해 동원된 이날 예비군들은 [illegible] 개인화기를 비롯한 각 총장비를 지급받고 숙영지 편성에 들어갔다.

이날 훈련에 투입된 동원예비군들은 4박5일간에 걸쳐 남침및 도하훈련등 실전적인 작전에 들어간다.

한편 이날 지역주민들은 투입되는 예비군들에게 뜨거운 박수로 환영함으로써 성공적인 팀스피리트 훈련이 되길 기원했다. 【87팀스피리트 특별취재반】

◆87팀스피리트훈련의 황군부대장은 지난29일 미보병 제25사단장의 배속신고를 받고 지휘봉을 수여했다.

TS '87, a division from the U.S. participated, the 25th Division reported the affiliation and I gave the commander's stick.

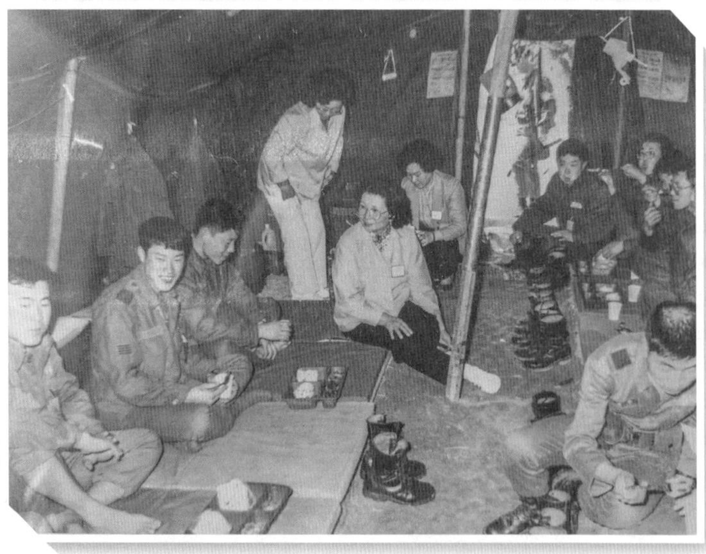

April 1987, the wives of the corps' commanders visited to comfort soldiers (served food, and et cetera) during Team Spirit '87.

April 1987, President Chun Doo-Hwan visited during the Team Spirit '87 exercise, I reported the current status and he encouraged us.

Rehearsing the briefing on the exercise for President Chun Doo-Hwan's visit.

August 1987, The evaluation and commanders' meeting after Ulchi-Focus CPX '87 at ROK-US Combined Forces Command in Uijeongbu.

Autumn of 1987, Went hiking to Obongsan Mountain with families of the corps staff officers.

Part 4

An Old Soldier Serves National Security Until the End

Chapter 10

I Abandoned My Dream of Becoming "The Generalissimo" and Voluntarily Retired as an Old Soldier

1. The 13th Presidential Election and Upholding the Armed Forces' Neutrality and Right to Free Vote

♦ President Chun Doo-Hwan's Call and a Private Meeting at the Blue House

In mid-November, I received a message from the Blue House that President Chun Doo-Hwan wanted to meet me alone. Private meetings with him were rare, so it was considered an honor. I assumed he was calling his subordinates in important positions to commend them as his term ended. I went with an unburdened heart, and he greeted me with a familiar, friendly smile. We sat closely, and he praised me, saying, "You did a great job," before asking about election preparations with an envelope in hand. I was flustered, caught in a sticky situation. "Ah, yes, you see..." I mumbled, unable to lie but finding it difficult to tell the truth. I hadn't "prepared" anything; instead, I had gathered all battalion commanders to educate them on the four rights to free vote guaranteed by the Constitution and shared my history of refusing to vote in electoral fraud as a platoon leader in 1960.

President Chun seemed to know everything about me from some source, as he said, "Ah, I get it. But this election is very important. Please prepare meticulously. This is 'gift money' for you. You can use it personally or for troop operations to prepare for the election." He handed me the envelope, and the election was not mentioned again. I then shared my thoughts, suggesting, "I assume the communists will form a political party and work in the National Assembly in about ten years. Please control these NLs (pro-North Korean National Liberationists) for now." He replied with a noncommittal "Okay, um..." and, after a brief silence, sent me off with a less friendly look.

♦ Upholding the Armed Forces' Neutrality and Individual Rights to Free Vote

On my way back from the Blue House, I regretted not explaining my views on elections, voting, politics, and the military to President Chun. However, I remained steadfast, emphasizing "no interference with votes" to commanders and staff of all ranks, rather than "preparing for the election." The election took place on December 16th, 1987. I went to the corps' main base, lined up with soldiers, and voted in turn, emphasizing to them, "Your votes are guaranteed. Vote according to your own will." The nationwide election result showed Roh Tae-Woo elected President by a very narrow margin, highlighting the importance of every military serviceperson's vote. This is likely why President Chun, meticulous and kind-hearted, urged preparations for military votes, recognizing their importance.

2. I Abandoned My Dream of Becoming "Generalissimo" and Voluntarily Retired as an Old Soldier

♦ Starting New Work as Vice Commander of the 1st Field Army

On December 27th, ten days after the election results were announced, high-ranking military officials were reassigned. I was relieved of my position as commander of the 1st Corps and transferred to vice commander of the 1st Field Army in Wonju, Gangwon-do. Following political controversies, Roh Tae-Woo's administration amended the Election Act, moving military votes to civilian polling stations outside barracks. However, I believe the true issue lies in "the President's decision" during elections, not the privatization of polling stations. I strongly urge the President, as a politician and commander-in-chief, to stop forcing military votes through illegal methods and adhere to the Constitution's spirit, ensuring military neutrality in politics. This is how commanders can maintain authority with honesty and integrity.

♦ "Thank God, I Have Done My Duty"

I have always enjoyed learning history and admired General Nam Yi, one of the nine Chungmu Lords of the Joseon Dynasty. I cherished Bukjeong-ga, a poem he recited as a hero devoted to the nation. I have kept his will in my heart, along with the last words of Admiral Lee Sun-sin, Korea's eternal hero, and Admiral Lord Nelson, the British hero of the Battle of Trafalgar: "Thank God, I have done my duty." I aspired to be a general who won battles, a hero like General Patton, who achieved distinguished victories in World War II. I believed in General MacArthur's philosophy of "political subordination of the military for victory," but ultimately, I concluded my military career with his spirit of "Old soldiers never die, they just fade away."

Now, as an old soldier without the historical fate of "The era creates a hero, and the hero creates an era," I must fade away without regrets. This is the virtue of a true soldier. Realizing I would not achieve my dream of being a 'Generalissimo' or a war hero, I decided to retire. I, an old soldier, let go of my dream of leading as a Generalissimo and being a war hero, and it was time to fade away from the ROK Army. At the farewell ceremony of the corps commander, I simply but clearly stated, "Thank God, I have done my duty." I repeated this in my heart many times as I left the corps, saying nothing more.

- **In December 1987, I was reappointed as the Vice Commander of the 1st Field Army's Command for a brief period, serving until June 1988. General Jeong Ho-geon, the commander, and his wife extended great kindness and hospitality to my wife and me, for which I was deeply grateful. Unaware of my past relationship with the President, General Jeong seemed to believe I had been assigned to this unit as his successor, albeit temporarily, due to various circumstances that had unfolded.**

Upon retiring, I bid farewell to the ROK Armed Forces and the military. After submitting my retirement report, I went directly to the National Cemetery in Dongjak-dong to pay my respects to my fallen comrades who had dedicated their lives to our nation. As an old soldier who did not perish on the battlefield, I quietly stepped away from military life.

Chapter 11

An Old Soldier Serves the Nation,
Focusing on National Security

1. Vice Chairman of the National Security Council and Emergency Planning Committee (October 1988-March 1993)

♦ The nation called upon this old soldier once more.

The day after my retirement, I began frequenting the KMA Library near my home in Jayang-dong, Seongbuk-gu, to study and write about "Korea's Arms Control and Disarmament" as part of my research on national security strategy. At the time, the focus was on the "summit on arms control and disarmament," a significant issue in the waning days of the Cold War between the United States and the Soviet Union. General Min Byeong-don, the principal of KMA and a close friend, was cautious not to cause trouble. He agreed with me on President Roh Tae-Woo's harsh treatment of former President Chun and the unstable political climate. Following this, as is well-known, he expressed his discontent at the cadets' graduation and commissioning ceremony that year, leading to his dismissal and transfer to the reserve forces—a regrettable incident.

In early October, after the successful completion of the 1988 Seoul Olympics, Senior Secretary Kim Jong-hwi of Diplomacy and National Security at the Blue House requested a meeting. He informed me that I was being considered for the position of Vice Chairman of the National Security Council and Emergency Planning Committee. After our meeting, I resolved to accept the role. The National Security Council is the premier governmental body for national security strategies, integrating areas such as the economy and diplomacy based on national security, essentially the military. I saw this as another honorable opportunity to serve the nation, and I accepted the call with joy. Senior Secretary Kim Jong-Hwi, who had recommended me for the position of Head Managing Professor at KNDU Graduate School, was a close friend and aware of my circumstances. I believed his recommendation played a role in my appointment. Although I couldn't ascertain President Roh Tae-Woo's reaction, Kim's suggestion was a memorable act of kindness.

The Committee, despite its lengthy name, was directly affiliated with the Prime Minister rather than a bureau under the Government Organization Act. The chairman held a ministerial rank, and I was equivalent to a vice minister. I wore a vice minister's badge and attended National Assembly meetings and vice ministers' meetings weekly. I engaged in final discussions and reviews of national policies with vice ministers from all government ministries, sometimes substituting for the committee chairman in cabinet meetings. The Committee's history reflects the turbulent evolution of administrative and civilian perspectives on national security. Established in 1963, it was a response to the Kim Shin-jo Incident in 1968, prompting the government to create the Emergency Planning Committee as an affiliate.

The Committee's functions include preparing and hosting National Security meetings, supervising and improving the annual governmental exercise "Ulchi-Focus Lens," maintaining the government's war command situation room, and managing emergency planning officers in private companies. It comprises the chairman, vice chairman, planning and controlling office, mobilization planning office, and investigation and research office, staffed by about 100 employees. The vice chairman, typically a former general, performs duties akin to a governmental vice minister but with the authority of a department head, attending vice ministers' meetings and coordinating affiliated departments.

The Committee's role is similar to the United States' FEMA, but it focuses solely on emergency mobilization, excluding disaster management. Countries like Korea, recognizing the importance of national security, operate a National Security Council (NSC) near the President. Our committee prepared the NSC, which the President convened irregularly for national issues, with the Blue House's Office of Diplomacy and National Security playing a key role.

One of the Committee's primary responsibilities was activating the "Plan Chungmu" for wartime or national emergencies, controlling governmental and key national companies, and conducting national mobilizations. This included the annual "Ulchi-Focus Lens" exercise. Upon Defcon-3 activation, the Committee issued alerts to all governmental organizations, prepared the National War Command Center bunker, and coordinated emergency communications. At Defcon-2, the Committee relocated to the bunker, and organizations prepared to move from Seoul. Defcon-1 saw the President and command center stationed south of the Hangang River, with nationwide mobilization orders executed.

The government, awakened by the Kim Shin-jo Incident, emphasized self-reliant national defense and civil defense mobilization. Since 1969, "Emergency Planning Officers" were appointed in all governmental and major mobilization companies, maintaining wartime preparation plans. Reserve colonels were placed in all governmental organizations and major companies, with lieutenant colonels and majors selected based on organization size.

President Park Chung-Hee's "Strategic Operational Plan to Place Defense in Seoul" remained valid, though updates were needed. Measures ensured Seoul's defense and citizen welfare during isolation, including emergency electricity, water wells, power generators, and stocked emergency supplies. These procedures were strictly followed, especially during the Ulchi-Focus Lens exercise.

♦ I attended vice ministers' meetings and cabinet meetings, fulfilling my duties as Vice Chairman.

I recall that the Vice Ministers' meetings were held every Thursday, while the Ministers' meetings took place every Friday. On meeting days, I would arrive at the Government Complex in Gwacheon earlier than usual, complete my morning tasks, and leave early to avoid being late due to Seoul's traffic. Occasionally, if I had an extra 20 to 30 minutes or deliberately left early, I would stop by Samcheong Park for a walk to clear my mind. Among the vice ministers with military backgrounds were the Vice Minister of National Defense, the Vice Minister of Unification, and myself, the Vice Minister of the Committee. In my role, I rarely collaborated with other vice ministers, so I felt unfamiliar with them initially. However, after working for over four years, I became well-acquainted with them, and we developed close friendships and professional relationships.

The vice ministers' meetings typically included former vice ministers and served as a platform to finalize policy cooperations and adjustments before presenting them at the ministers' meeting. Most discussions focused on general policies, so I seldom had the opportunity to speak. However, about two to three times a month, topics related to national security and emergency planning arose, allowing me to express my opinions and make contributions. When the committee chairman was unavailable due to vacation or personal matters, I attended the cabinet meetings on his behalf. These meetings, led by the Prime Minister, were significant, and I sought to find meaning in simply attending them.

Vice ministers were invited to banquets at the Blue House two to three times a year. I was usually invited to the end-of-year banquet with my wife, but I rarely had opportunities to meet and converse with the President and the First Lady. I recall attending banquets and meetings at the Blue House as an Army general during President Chun Doo-Hwan's term.

2. In May 1994, I became a visiting scholar at the Department of Military Science at Ball State University, Indiana, U.S.A.

♦ I became a visiting scholar at the university's Military Science Department, ROTC.

With the transition from the Roh Tae-Woo administration to the Kim Young-sam administration in 1993, I automatically resigned as vice chairman, ending my governmental service in national security. Reflecting on my career, I spent 37 years in the military, including my time as a KMA cadet and during the Vietnam War, and four and a half years as a public official. In total, I served the nation for over 41 years, with two additional years in public office thereafter. Although I experienced a range of emotions upon completing my military career, I felt a sense of emptiness knowing I could no longer directly serve the nation. However, considering my age, experience, and circumstances, I decided it was too early to retire. I resolved to embark on "my vocation," focusing on establishing military science as a government-authorized academic discipline and studying "national security strategy" independently.

I frequently visited the office supporting generals of reserved forces and the KNDU Graduate School library. I sent applications to ten prestigious universities and graduate schools in the United States. As a leading democratic nation, the U.S. universities responded positively. Professor Paul Kennedy from Yale University welcomed me, offering accommodation. Stanford University suggested preparation for the following year, and Harvard Kennedy School extended an open invitation. While reviewing these options, family matters prompted me to choose a location near my son and daughter-in-law, who were studying in the U.S., ensuring their studies were not disrupted. Fortunately, Dr. Jang Ju-ho, my son's father-in-law, facilitated arrangements, and Professor Park Seong-jae at Ball State University extended a helping hand. Thus, I became a visiting scholar at the university's Military Science Department, ROTC.

In Muncie, Indiana, a small city with a population of about 80,000, I resided in an apartment with two bedrooms and two bathrooms, costing $350 per month. The university welcomed me with a dinner at the president's residence, provided medical insurance costing about $700 per month, and affiliated me with the ROTC. The ROTC staff included a lieutenant colonel, a female captain, a sergeant first class, a female civilian administrative clerk, and a small library. They generously provided me with an office and allowed me to lecture and discuss "issues on North Korea's nuclear weapons" for over ten hours. A female Korean student at the ROTC assisted as an interpreter. Before departing for the U.S., I prepared a lecture and discussion on North Korea's nuclear weapons, coinciding with the 1994 light-water reactor agreement at the six-party summit. I delivered this lecture to approximately 30 cadets, engaging in discussions through the interpreter.

♦ **My focus was on studying "security strategy thought history of the United States," along with American history, and I diligently worked on writing about it.**

Observing the U.S., I noted that President Reagan had "made his final attack on communism and won," publishing "The National Security Strategy of U.S.A. 1987," which garnered significant interest from national defense and security personnel. President Bush (the elder) won the Gulf War and published "The National Security Strategy of U.S.A. 1991," defining a "new world order." As the U.S. became a superpower, President Clinton issued "The National Security Strategy of U.S.A. 1994," advocating Toynbee's "Challenge and Response, and Engagement" in foreign policies. He pursued a "win-win strategy" and the 'Bottom Up Review (BUR) 1993' Policy, focusing on military strategy transition and modernization. Regarding North Korea's nuclear weapons, he aimed for the "US-North Korea Geneva Convention" in 1994, despite opposition. Consequently, the Armed Forces underwent significant reductions and pursued "super modernization," envisioning future warfare involving robots and lasers, moving toward a "Pandora's Box."

In Muncie, the Korean church served as a haven for the Korean community and students. Established as a university city in the early 1800s, Muncie was heavily influenced by Ball State University, which operated a local educational broadcasting station. The university also housed a beautiful Presbyterian church, a cornerstone of local religious life. This church provided space for Korean students to operate a Korean church, which I joyfully visited. It was a wonderful facility, serving as a church, shelter, and meeting place for about 30 Korean students studying abroad. Most students attended Sunday worships led by a student named Kim, and the few Korean immigrant households in Muncie actively supported the church community.

When my wife and I began attending church on Sundays, Koreans from a neighboring county, though somewhat distant, started joining us. Initially, only two or three attended, but eventually, the group grew to about ten. The Korean students would gather voluntarily for lunch on weekends, supporting and comforting each other through various activities at the Korean church. As more students and local Koreans—around 30 to 40 people—began attending weekend services, the church recruited an additional pastor. He was young but knowledgeable and passionate, and the main American church supported him with a modest monthly stipend to cover living and activity expenses as part of their support for Korean church activities. We were drawn to the church's history, the pastor, and the kindness of the congregation, including the students, and it became a significant part of our lives during our stay in the United States. People even traveled from distant neighborhoods, more than an hour away, to attend. Among them were Dr. Kim and his wife, who had immigrated around the time of the Military Revolution of May 16th; a neighbor of theirs who married a U.S. Army soldier from a red-light district in Korea and moved to the U.S., despite the disapproval of American parents; and another woman who had also married a U.S. Army soldier but was already divorced. These individuals deeply missed the Korean community. In the autumn,

we would hold barbecue parties in the vast, tree-filled parks of Bloomington, where Indiana State University is located, enjoying the autumn leaves. At Christmas, we visited Dr. Kim's neighborhood, enchanted by the Christmas trees lining the streets. We also went to Dr. Kim's house for a lavish Korean buffet and conversation. This was how we found happiness in the Korean community in a small American city. I heard that the pastor and his family eventually settled there permanently. I pray that God will bless the Korean community, the students studying abroad, the church, and the pastor in Muncie.

♦ I experienced many new advantages in the U.S.

I had longed to study abroad in the United States since I was young, and I applied for KMA because it offered me the opportunity to do so. As I grew in my military career, I observed and experienced the United States through interactions with the U.S. Army and studying abroad, yet it still felt like an entirely new world, even more than I had anticipated. Experiencing and observing it as a member of an actual community, even for just two years, I clearly saw that this country strives for a utopian ideal for humanity as a democratic nation, rich and powerful with abundant resources. Of course, it has the fundamental flaws inherent in human society, and American capitalism has its own issues, but I found more strengths and lessons to learn from the United States, and I wish to recall some of those insights from the 1990s.

• I was always skeptical of the idea of "national character."

I believed that all countries and their people could share similar traits, with differences arising from whether they are advanced countries—improved and civilized in economy and society—or not. For instance, the German national character is often described as "stopping at a red light at night, even when no one is watching." Another example is "the lost watch you saw yesterday is still there in the United States." People said these were the national characters of the United States and Germany. However, Koreans adopted similar behaviors a few decades later. This demonstrates that it follows the development of a country, and there isn't a separate national character. I saw that the United States was ahead of Korea in this aspect, suggesting that Korea could become like the United States with improvement and development.

- In American apartments—where even one-story townhouses are called "apartments" if they are rented monthly—when a tenant leaves, they either take everything or leave everything behind. The interior is then cleaned, and maintenance work such as repairs and painting is done before the next tenant moves in. The U.S. is full of transients (new immigrants or those relocating for jobs), so this system is convenient and society operates accordingly. New tenants must bring or buy their own furniture. Families from abroad who arrive empty-handed must purchase new supplies based on their needs and circumstances. While American society appears luxurious, it is hard to find a society more thrifty, frugal, diligent, and wholesome. Of course, the U.S. has department stores selling new and luxury goods, specialty stores, and supermarkets for necessities. However, neighborhoods also have markets and stores for those who need these items or for diligent and thrifty people. These include 'Flea markets' (indoor markets always open), 'Free markets' (regular outdoor markets with items displayed on the ground), and 'Charity stores' for community service that accept donations of old and antique goods and sell them at very low prices.

- Curious, I visited one of these markets. Many people were there, displaying old yet usable and clean items such as beds, bedding, new or old clothes, old books, stationery, cassettes, and various other items. Additionally, individual households hold 'Garage Sales' once a week, on different days depending on the region. They display old items they no longer use in their garages and sell them at extremely low prices, almost giving them away but not for free. Consider how Koreans discard items at apartment complexes; this is worth learning. There are also stores between department stores and wholesale markets selling miscellaneous items, both wholesale and retail—for example, T.J.Maxx—known as "general stores with opportunities," popular among residents. They usually sell new products with minor flaws unnoticed by customers or out-of-style items at prices lower than the market rate. Many people visit these stores for window shopping or actual purchases.

Needing more chairs, I heard that Ball State University's warehouse was auctioning or selling used items, so I decided to visit. As expected, the school's warehouse was auctioning slightly worn-out carpets and selling still usable chairs and some crooked ones that seemed fixable. I bought two chairs, and many others also window-shopped and purchased items. A university in a wealthy area was selling old carpets and crooked chairs for money instead of discarding them, which seemed remarkable to me. One day, they even opened a market in front of the female students' dormitory, selling items like used bras. I wondered if anyone would buy them, but they said there was always someone who did. There's a saying in American society: "The early bird catches the worm." This golden advice suggests that diligent birds can find high-quality food. It was true because waking up early and going to garage sales allowed you to find valuable and rare items, and I saw it happen.

- **However, there are stories about social order that are not amusing. Many Koreans immigrated to the United States with the "American dream" in their hearts, bringing their elderly parents. One elderly Korean, following a Korean custom, touched children's heads and commented on their handsomeness, which led to a police officer's intervention. Another Korean parked at a coin meter but didn't add more coins, thinking it would be okay to exceed the time slightly, only to be fined six dollars. Ignoring it, the fine doubled, and when he pleaded, it was not accepted. Postponing it further, the fine increased, causing significant trouble. This experience taught him about American societal order and how America is maintained.**

During my time studying abroad in the United States as a young commissioned officer, I complained with a classmate from Jordan, saying, "The U.S. gets slapped on the face for kissing asses," referring to its emergency relief aid policy, which only provides short-term necessities. However, upon closer examination, the American democracy with its modified capitalism became evident.

- **Helping others and being neighborly is a common social practice among Americans.**

They are particularly kind to social minorities, especially new foreigners. Even if you appear a bit lost on the street, an American, regardless of age or gender, will often approach you and ask, "May I help you?" If you have too many items at the checkout in a market or mall, the cashier will kindly assist you in bagging them. Even if you are unaware of ongoing sales, the cashier will inform you about discounts and may even provide you with discount coupons you didn't know existed, as if they are working for the customers. While these actions are rooted in business ethics aimed at the store's long-term benefits, customers perceive them as kindness and feel good about it. Unlike the "robotic kindness" I experienced in Japan, the kindness in America seemed genuine, especially in rural areas.

- **Socialization in the countryside and golf**

The countryside offers its residents what they need for a happy life, as it is part of a wealthy nation. For instance, residents of all ages become members of a golf club and exercise at a low cost. Being in the countryside, there are just enough golf courses where they don't need caddies. They can carry their own equipment, play alone or with others, and enjoy golf anytime without reservations. The cost ranges from seven to fifteen dollars at the most expensive places. They can enjoy sports, take a quick shower after a game, and have simple meals and tea at the club. These areas also have churches and town halls for official or large gatherings, providing a sense of community even in rural settings. Membership-based golf clubs also exist in the suburbs for the convenience of their members.

3. Visiting Professor at KNDU and Establishment of the Research Center for Security Strategy Thought History of the Republic of Korea

♦ Becoming a Visiting Professor at KNDU (the first recruit) as an Experienced Expert

As my visa's expiration date approached, my wife and I bid farewell to our son and daughter-in-law, who were still studying there, and expressed our gratitude to the local Koreans, especially Professor Park Seong-jae at Ball State University in Muncie and his wife, Dr. Kim and his wife in a neighboring country, the pastor and his wife, and our Korean and American neighbors in the apartment complex. We returned to Korea, our homeland. Upon our return, we decided to live near my mother-in-law, who was residing with my second younger brother-in-law, at the request of Yun-Yeong (Park Jin-Hee), my third younger sister-in-law. The three households chose to live close to each other. We sold our house in Jayang-dong and moved to Madu-dong, Sinilsan, Goyang, Gyeonggi-do in June 1996. Since then, we have been living there post-retirement, up to the present day in 2025, for 29 years with minimal changes.

Upon returning, I frequented the KNDU Graduate School library in Susaek, near my home, to continue my studies and writing on the “security strategy thought history of the United States,” a project I brought back from the U.S. Eventually, the National Science Foundation under the Ministry of Culture, Sports, and Tourism introduced a system of inviting experienced experts as visiting professors at universities. This initiative aimed to utilize high-level human resources and address academic disparities between the capital and other regions. The program offered two to three-year terms in nearby cities and three to five-year terms in hometowns, with the government covering all expenses (2.5 million won per month). I applied and was among the first recruits, which included vice ministers and some ministers. I joined the KNDU Graduate School faculty of national security, teaching subjects related to “national emergency planning” and other topics based on my experiences. Although there were no exams to measure achievements, I believe there were some positive outcomes.

However, it felt slightly mismatched for a retired general, not a professional instructor, to teach regular academic subjects instead of giving special lectures. Over time, I focused more on writing about the “security strategy thought history of the United States,” my hobby and task.

♦ Publishing “A Security Strategy Thought History of the United States of America”

In the past, I would handwrite on manuscript paper or A-4 sheets and submit them for publication in magazines or media. After 1994, I began typing on a 'Gateway' (14-inch) laptop from the U.S. and saved my work. Once completed, I sent it to the publisher, who revised, edited, and printed it. In 1999, I asked President Bang Yong-Nam, who ran “Eulji Books,” to publish 500 high-quality copies of my book titled “A Security Strategy Thought History of the United States of America.” I am grateful to President Bang Yong-nam for his support. Many copies were placed in the KNDU Graduate School library, and it was rewarding to see all copies checked out simultaneously. I would like to quote the foreword to explain the book's purpose, meaning, and outline.

“In the early 1960s, I visited the United States for a short period to study. During my stay, I visited the Washington Monument, Lincoln Memorial, and Arlington Cemetery in Washington D.C. I learned about the 'history of how the United States was created,' its expansion from 13 to 50 states over 300 years, the Emancipation Proclamation, and the concept of civilian control by the people.”

“Later, in late 1990, I visited Washington D.C. again for a 'War History Society' gathering. I toured the Capitol, the White House, and the CIA Headquarters, guided by the host. This was when the United States had just won the Cold War and achieved a significant victory in the Gulf War, leading decision-makers to assert that 'The U.S. must lead the new world order,' convinced that Pax-Americana would shape the 21st Century.”

“Today, the United States stands as the world's sole superpower, and its national security strategy thoughts are becoming global. In this globalized economy, Korea's national interest relies on maintaining and developing economic and military security relationships with the U.S. Therefore, an in-depth study of their security strategy thought history is essential. I wrote this book to contribute to that understanding. I thank everyone who helped me publish this book.”

“I am especially grateful to Professor Park Seong-jae at Ball State University, who facilitated my research in the U.S., Dr. John E. Worthen, Ball State University's president, and related field professors. I also thank Col. Foley, head of the

Department of Military Science, who allowed me to teach American ROTC cadets, and the department's staff. Lastly, if this book aids readers in understanding the U.S. security strategy thought history and contributes to Korea's security strategy thought history, I will be pleased."

♦ Establishment of "The Institute of Korea National Security Strategy Thought History" (Cyber and Private)

As I delved into the United States' national security strategy and authored a book on it, I naturally developed an interest in Korea's national security strategy. As previously mentioned, the document titled "The National Security Strategy of U.S.A. 1987," the first of its kind, was published during President Reagan's administration at the U.S. Congress's behest. It expressed their resolve to "make a final attack on the Soviet Union and communist nations." Until then, the U.S. had focused on "national defense," but this document defined "national security strategy" and introduced the term. Consequently, organizations like the "Research Institute for Strategy" emerged, studying "globalized strategy" within "national defense." This was when General Hong Seong-Tae, a close friend, established the "Korea Research Institute for Strategy" to lead strategy research in Korea.

I considered the issue deeply. To strengthen Korea's national security strategy, which was still vulnerable, I believed the first step was to create a strategy tailored to Korea, rooted in its tradition and history. This required studying the national security strategies of past governments, particularly those of former Presidents and kings, and understanding the historical context of these strategies. I decided that the best approach was to establish "The Institute of Korea National Security Strategy Thought History" and manage it online for a while. I named it IKONSSTORY and set up the website at "www.ikonsstory.com."

I also secured a space on my alumni club's website to contribute to the development of Korea's national security strategy. I compiled various materials into e-books and made them available online. However, due to a lack of funding, my external activities were limited. I did receive invitations to lecture at the ROK Army College a few times. In the 2010s, when the alumni club ceased its activities, my online presence diminished, and I had to abandon part of my ambition. Consequently, ikonsstory.com was shut down, and my external activities naturally ceased. I am now focusing more on my personal research and studies. I plan to publish "Part 3" of "A Security Strategy Thought History of the Republic of Korea" around 2025, and I am diligently working on this study. I intend to have my tombstone read, "The man who created 'A Security Strategy Thought History of the Republic of Korea' lies here." That will be my final word.

Our family

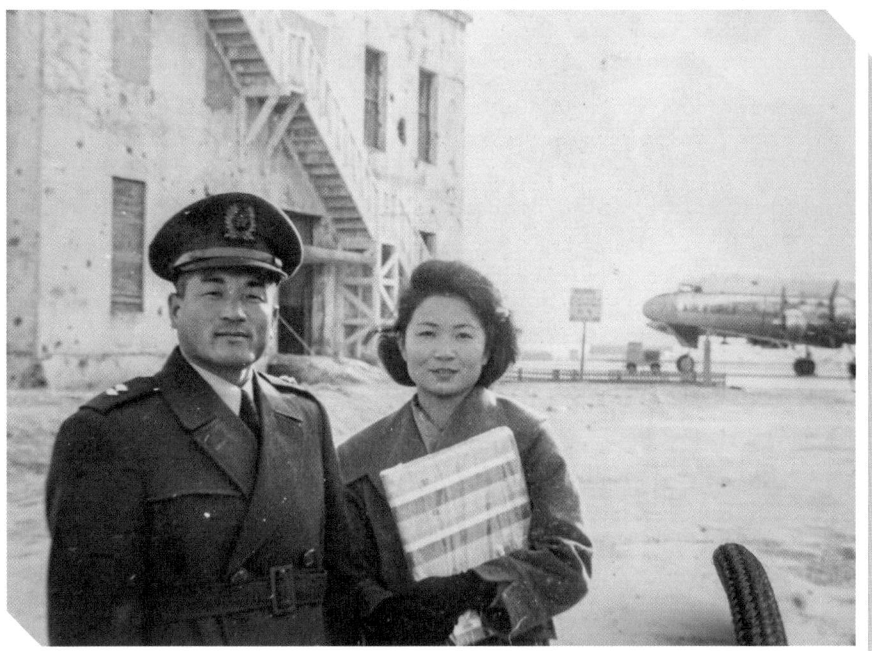

January 1962, I got engaged and went to study abroad at special warfare school in the U.S., and this was at Gimpo Airport for ROK and US at that time.

graduate 61
Ehwa English & literature

graduate Ehwa WU 61. English & literature

April 22nd, 1962, Our wedding at Diplomatic Hall in Sogong-dong with relatives from both families, and my mother attended the wedding.

The friends of my wife and I who came to the wedding, I am especially thankful to Lee Yong-u's older brother and Min Byeong-don for coming.

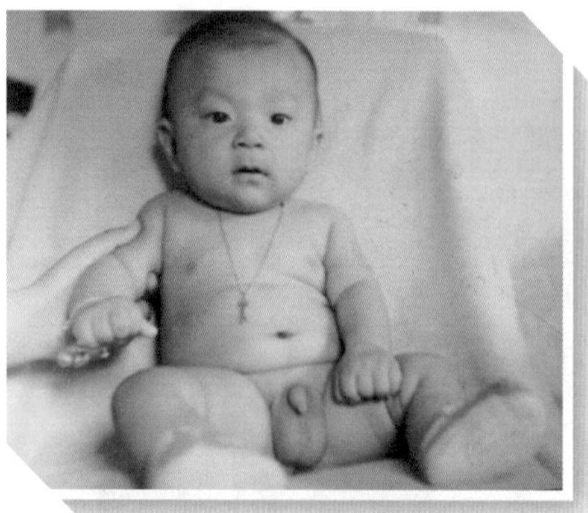

May 1963, Jeong-eon, my elder son, was born.

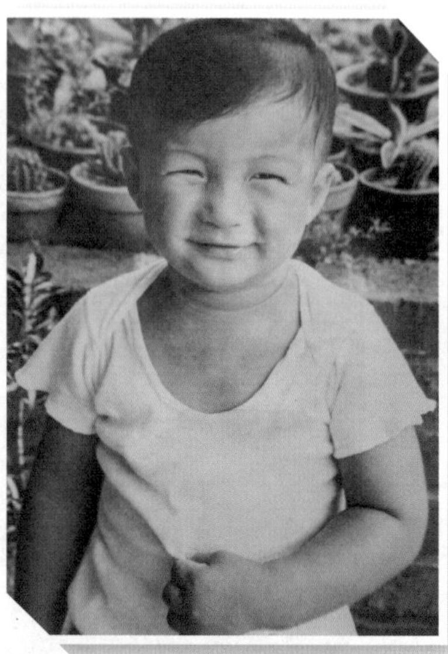

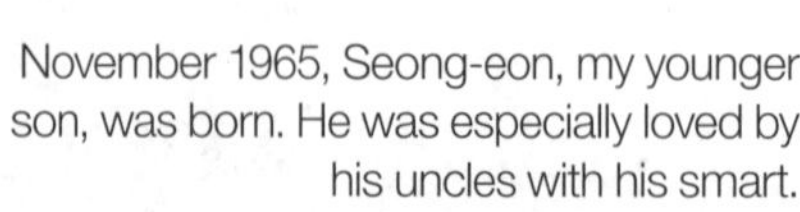

November 1965, Seong-eon, my younger son, was born. He was especially loved by his uncles with his smart.

1966, When I was an ROTC instructor at Yonsei University, the parachute badge and the Night Owl Guerrilla Traning School badge shone with honor.

1965, Our first house, the national housing in Hwagok-dong, she planted grass and made our yard.

Our first house, the national housing in Hwagok-dong, we were the first house to plant grass in the big land of 387 square yards.

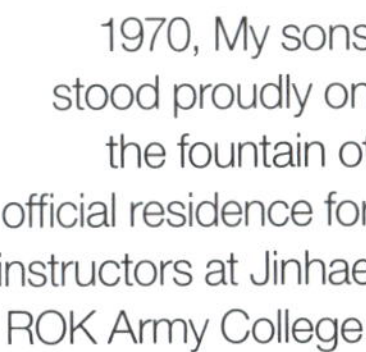

1970, My sons stood proudly on the fountain of official residence for instructors at Jinhae ROK Army College.

1972, My children and wife were happy to visit the residence when I was the commander of the mechanized battalion.

1975, At G-2 Special Warfare Command Information Office, with my family at the parachute training ground in front of the command center (currently Wirye), my sons were Boy Scout

1980, My wife in our house in Banpo on the day I was promoted to a general.

January 1980, at home with my family on the day I was promoted to a general.

1984, When I was a division commander, climbed Hallasan Mountain on Jeju Island on my second official vacation.

1983, A moment at the official residence of the Commander of the 8th Division.

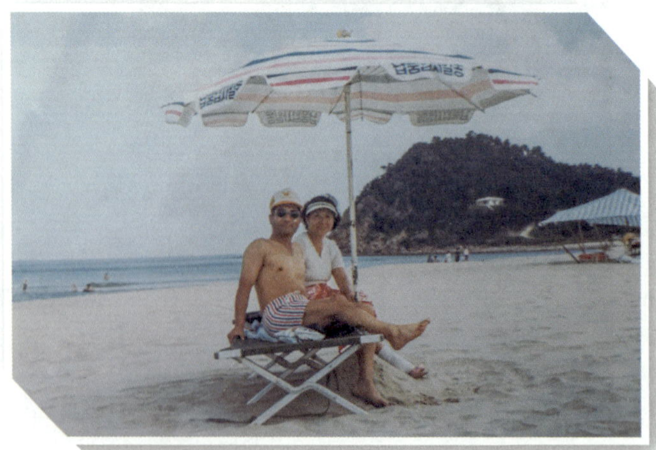

Around 1983, When I was a division commander, my first official vacation after being commissioned, a moment in Hwajinpo Beach.

Around 1987, My elder son was working as the leader of a mortar platoon at a post in the front of Gimpo Peninsula, he was an ROTC.

Around 1987, My elder son was working as the leader of a mortar platoon in a front combat support company of Gimpo Peninsula.

Around 1987, My younger son was commissioned as an ROTC officer, his mother and elder brother attended the commissioning ceremony and congratulated him.

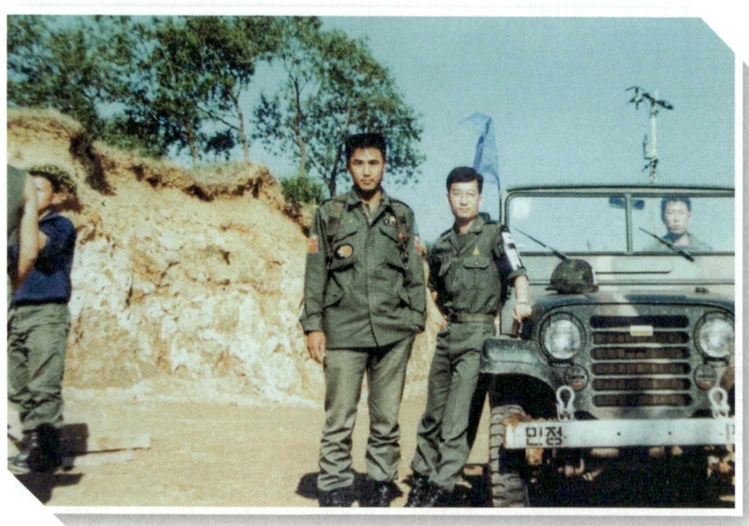

Around 1987, My younger son worked as a platoon leader in a combat support company in the eastern frontline of the 22nd Division near Unification Observatory.

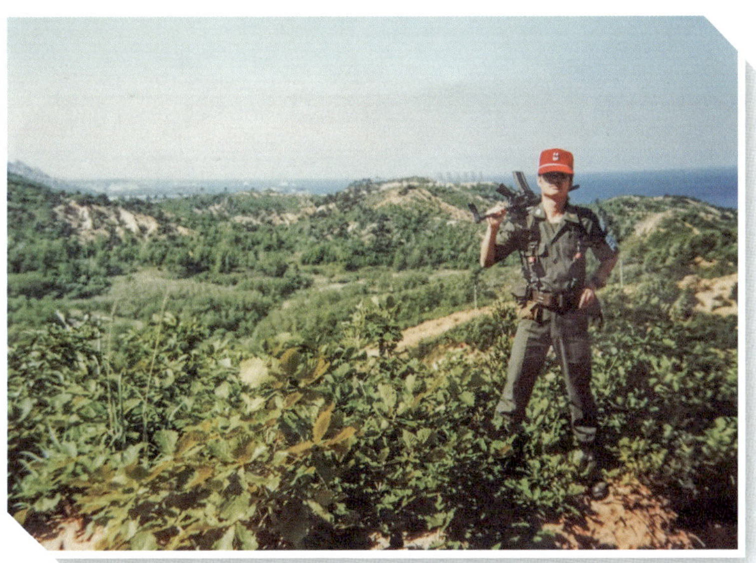

1988, My younger son worked as a platoon leader in a combat support company in the eastern frontline of the 22nd Division near Unification Observatory, Sogeumgang River in the back.

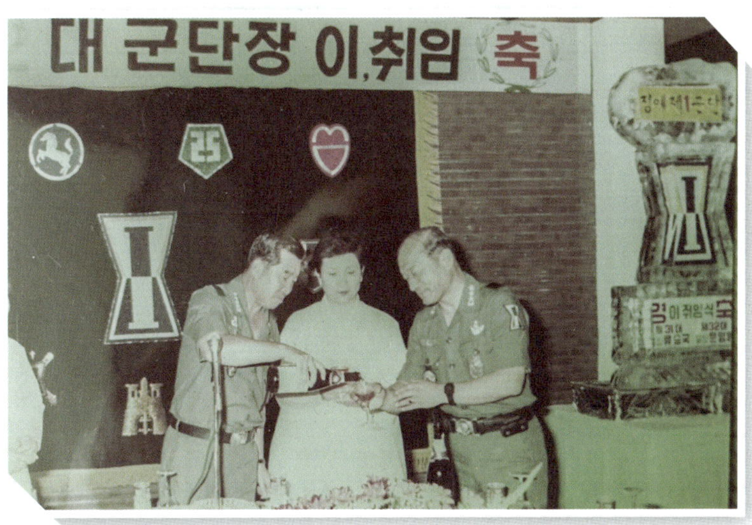

July 1986, Inaugurated as the Commander of the 1st Corps, I was congratulated by the Army Commander with my wife by my side.

Around 1986, A family photo with my sons when they were in college.

My son's wedding took place at Army Hall in Samgakji in 1991. He started a new family. God bless him

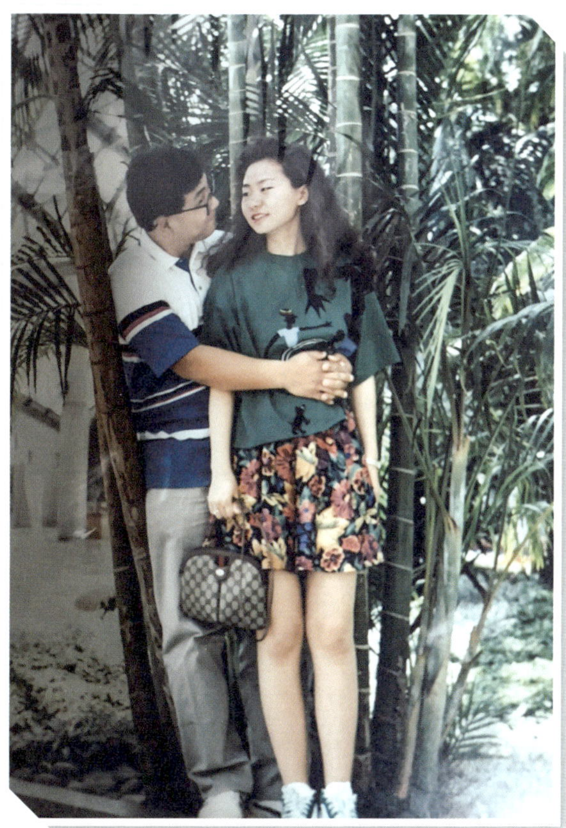

My son and his wife's honeymoon to Jeju Island, may God bless them with happiness.

1991, With Dr. Jang Ju-ho and his wife, our in-laws, after our son and their daughter's wedding.

1995, I lectured on 'Issues on North Korea's nuclear weapons' to ROTC students and civilians as a visiting scholar at Ball State University, U.S.A.

1996, As a visiting scholar for ROTC at Ball State University, U.S.A., I was greeted by Lieutenant Colonel Falley, commander of ROTC, in the university's president's presence.

A moment of my son, my daughter-in-law, me and my wife when we were living together in the U.S. for the university in 1996.

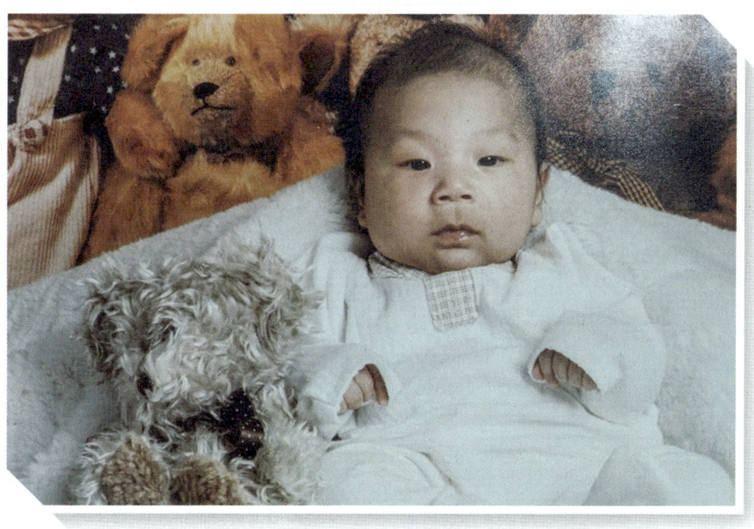

May 27th, 1998, Moon Jun Ho, my grandson, was born in Muncie, U.S.A.

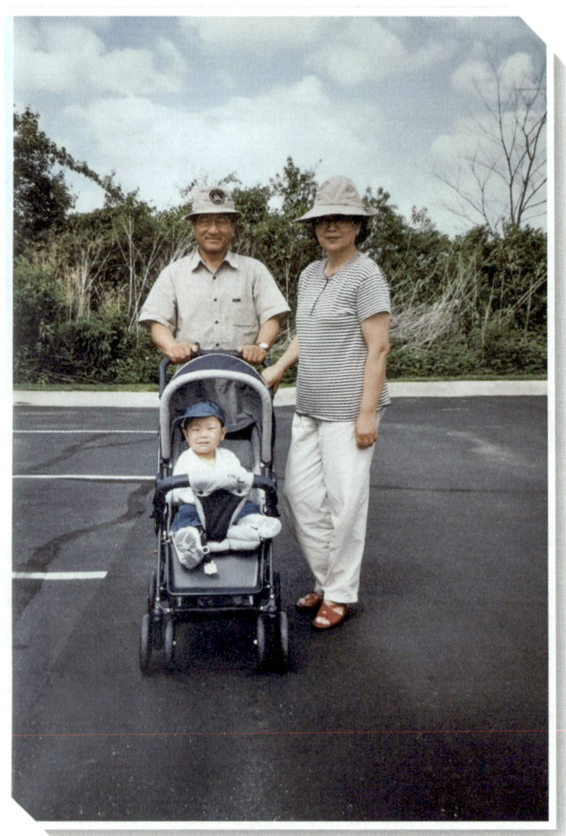

May 1999, We looked after Jun Ho for six months in Mishawaka, Indiana, U.S.A.

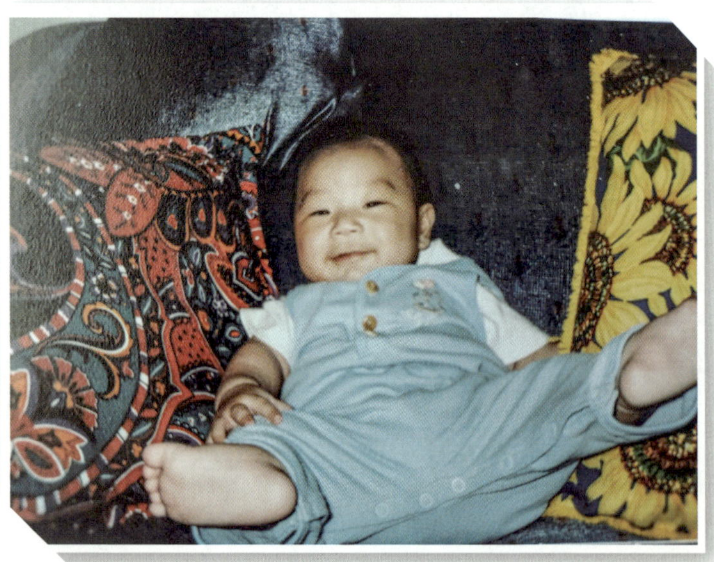

2000, My grandson Jun Ho grew fast into a lovely baby.

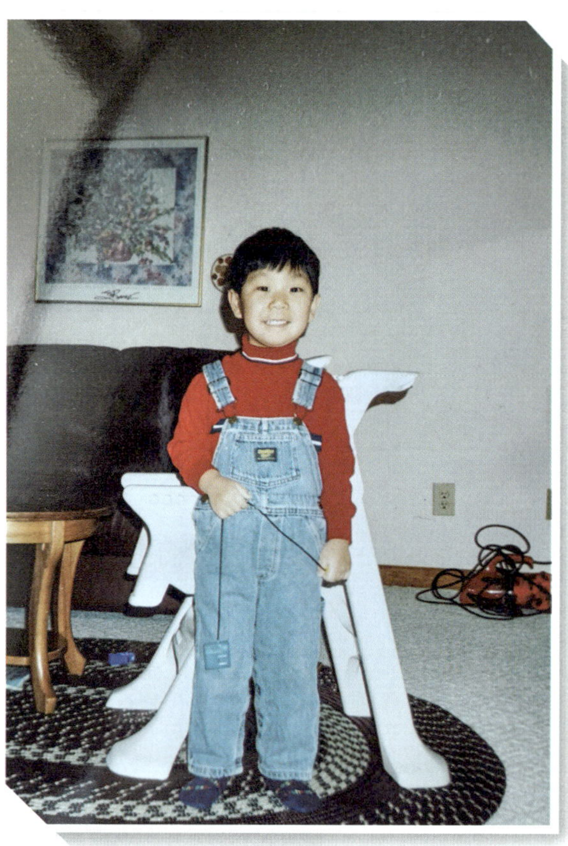

2002, My grandson Jun Ho grew into an adorable and playful boy.

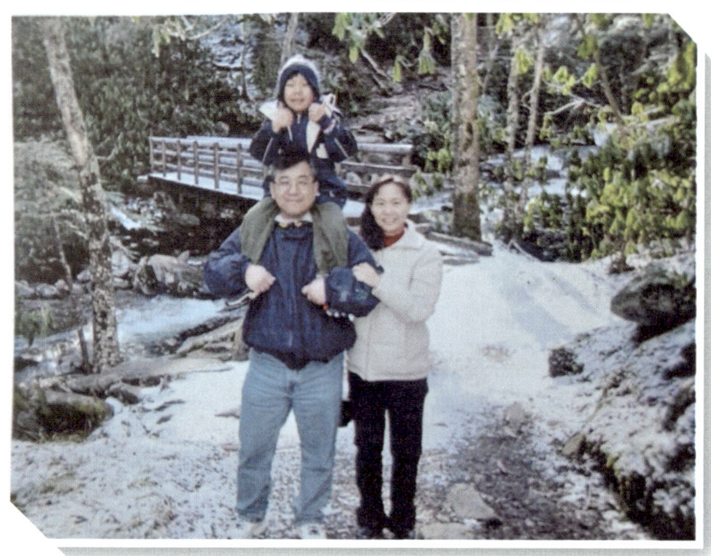

2003, My grandson Jun Ho grew with love from his dad and mom.

After 2000, Dr. Jang Yeong-Mi, my daughter-in-law, was working as a professor at a private university in Ohio, U.S.A.

After 2016, My grandson Jun Ho performing as the leader of the musical team in high school.

May 2019, The three generations of my family traveled to Hakone, Tokyo, me and my wife in front of 'Grandson of the General' statue at a park in Hakone.

May 2020, my grandson Mun Jun Ho graduated from Miami University in Ohio, U.S.A.

December 30th, 2023, my grandson and Kate got married.

December 30th, 2023, My grandson's wedding at a Catholic church in Ohio, U.S.A.

2023.12.30.
Jun-Ho Kate
wedding, bride and
groom, his parents,
her parents, great!

May, 2024 Junho & Kate
Wedding form at Seoul Korean
studio,God bless your wedding.

Afterword:
"To Jun Ho, my grandson, and his descendants"

1. My children's success and their current situations

My wife and I were blessed with two sons. Our elder son, Jeong-eon, graduated from the ROTC at Kyung Hee University, became an officer, and served as a platoon leader near Gimpo. Our younger son, Seong-eon, graduated from the ROTC at Chung-Ang University, became an officer, and served in a frontline division near the Unification Observatory in Goseong-gun. After his military service, Jeong- eon went to the United States and earned a master's degree in physical education from Ball State University in Indiana. He met Jang Yeong-Mi, a fellow student from a respectable family, and they married in Korea before returning to their studies. Yeong-mi also earned a master's degree in childhood education from the same university. They both pursued doctoral degrees at Purdue University, with Jeong-eon focusing on biomechanics and Yeong-mi on childhood education. They graduated together and were employed as professors at Ball State University. They welcomed their son, Jun Ho, after delaying parenthood for their studies. My wife and I, along with Yeong-mi's mother, took turns caring for Jun Ho. Despite challenges, Yeong-mi was dedicated to educating her child. They eventually moved to New Albany, Ohio, for better educational opportunities for Jun Ho, and Yeong-mi became a professor at Ohio Dominican University. Jeong-eon is now a leader in a multimedia group at Ball State University. Jun Ho married an American girl he had known since school, and they both work at J.P. Morgan, leading their family well. Although they live in a weekend marriage, which is common in the U.S., they are happy. I am proud of Yeong-mi for raising Jun Ho while working as a professor, though I sometimes worry for her.

• 'A genius and a fool have a very thin difference between them'

Meanwhile, my second son, Seong-eon, showed signs of being a genius, particularly in music. Although not a prodigy like those in the media, he amazed our family, especially his uncles, who were studying engineering in Seoul (SNU). There's a saying, "A genius and a fool have a very thin difference between them," which refers to their way of thinking. Seong-eon taught himself Hangul and read storybooks aloud before starting school. However, he also displayed a unique way of thinking, often contradicting common sayings with his own interpretations. Despite not wanting to, he completed the ROTC course and served as a respected platoon leader. After his military service, he joined a bank but developed an interest in IT. In the early 1990s, during the era of i486 computers, he struggled to find his path. I, his father, emphasized "diligence, independence, and self-reliance," but he became disillusioned. Eventually, at 26, he left to find his own world. I am at a loss for words and pray that he is happy and at peace in God's kingdom.

2. Jun Ho, my grandson, was born into my son's new family

My son, Moon Jeong-Eon, and my daughter-in-law, Jang Yeong-Mi, earned their doctorates at Purdue University and settled in Muncie, Indiana, where they became professors. I supported their decision to settle in the U.S. as it seemed beneficial for their lives. On May 27, 1998, our long-awaited grandson, Jun Ho, was born in Muncie. He was a strong and healthy boy, weighing 3.3 kilograms. Remarkably, he was born in May, like his father and other family members. I named him Jun Ho, wishing for his bright future and happiness. His name means "an outstanding man with a broad mind and big dreams, like a river flowing deeply and widely, slow and composed, who will do good for everyone."

3. Korea's 5,000-year history and traditions, and its relationship with the United States

I hope my life and military career have given you some insight into the relationship between Korea and the United States during my time. However, I wish to provide a broader overview of Korea's 5,000-year history and traditions, which will deepen your understanding of the relationship between our two nations and convey my central message. This is the Korea that I, your grandfather, have studied and cherished through my love for history.

Korea, often referred to as <Hanguk>, short for 'Daehanminguk' (Republic of Korea), boasts a rich history and traditions spanning 5,000 years. The first form of Korea was established around 5,000 years ago when <Dangun Wanggeom> founded the nation, initiating <the era of Dangun Wanggeom>. Our ancestors lived in regions that are now southern, central, and northern China, along the Yellow Sea, the Korean Peninsula, and the Japanese Archipelago. The geographical formation of these states resembled the Chinese character for "wind (風)" along the Yellow Sea, which was habitable at the time. This is why I assert that "The history of China and Japan is a part of Korean history."

Since then, our enduring state policy has been <The Thought of Extension of Human Welfare>, emphasizing mutual aid and assistance among all people. This aligns with the core beliefs of liberal democracy, led by the United States, which humanity strives for today. Early in history, Koreans defined the three fundamental concepts of humanity as "heaven, humankind, and land." Thus, Korea was founded on principles akin to modern democracy, rooted in nature and humanity. This is why the number "3" holds significance for Koreans, and we have crafted items incorporating "3," such as tripod-shaped supports for religious service plates, since ancient times.

The descendants of 'Dangun Wanggeom' (the Buyeo people) continued to develop the nation, though Dangun Wanggeom's kingdom fragmented into various states around 1000 B.C. Around 200 B.C., the powerful kingdom of Goguryeo emerged in the north, while Silla and Baekje were founded in the south, marking the start of the Three Kingdoms Era in ancient Korea. By around 500 A.D., Silla began a unification war and succeeded in unifying the three kingdoms. However, Tang Dynasty China, initially Silla's ally, unexpectedly attacked, leading to the Silla-Tang War. As a result, Silla lost its territory on the continent, now part of China, and its domain shrank to the Korean Peninsula. Despite this, the Silla Dynasty thrived for 1,000 years, alongside the kingdom of Balhae in the north (Manchuria and beyond), until it was eventually defeated by the Goryeo Dynasty around the 10th century.

During this period, Goryeo historians condensed and altered Korean history to emphasize Goryeo's legitimacy, focusing on the Korean Peninsula. Nevertheless, to remember that current Chinese territories were originally Korean, they renamed regions in the Korean Peninsula after those in the old lands (now China), integrating Korea's geography and history with its ancient territories. For instance, places named "Baekje" and "Honam" exist in both China and Korea.

In the 14th century, General Lee Seong-gye of Goryeo led a successful coup d'état, founding the Joseon Dynasty, which was confined to the Korean Peninsula, with Hanyang (Seoul) as its capital. Joseon maintained a unified Korean Peninsula for about 600 years. Through this history, you can see that the Korean people are the original inhabitants of the East Asian plains, boasting a 5,000-year history. The history of China is part of the Korean people's history—The Central Plain is our ancestral land—and Japanese history is the history of our kin, who migrated to the Archipelago, thus also part of Korean history.

In the late Joseon Dynasty, as European empires sought to dominate Asia and the Empire of Japan acted recklessly, Joseon, under King Gojong, was on the brink of collapse. During this era, the United States engaged in gunboat diplomacy with Joseon due to the 'General Sherman Incident' (1866), but genuine communication between Korea and the United States began with the "Western Disturbance in the Shinmi Year (1871)." Consequently, Korea and the United States signed the "United States-Korea Treaty of 1882," established the "Yeonmu Public Academy," an American-style military academy (1888), and welcomed U.S. Army instructors. However, the school was closed due to pressure from the Empire of Japan.

In 1904, the Empire of Japan initiated the Russo-Japanese War, entered Seoul, coerced Emperor Gojong and officials into signing the "Japan-Korea Treaty of 1905," and stripped Joseon of its sovereignty. In response, Emperor Gojong sent Rhee Syng-Man to the United States to seek assistance from President Roosevelt, but the reply was, "It's already too late." Subsequently, Rhee Syng-Man remained in the United States to study and led the Korean independence movement, thanks to U.S. support. President Wilson of the United States, who was the president of George Washington University and considered Rhee Syng-Man his best student, led the U.S. to victory in World War I and declared "national self-determination" to establish a new post-war order, aiming to dismantle imperialism and colonialism.

This inspired all Koreans, who established a government in exile and conducted independence movements inside and outside Korea, including <the March 1st Independence Movement>. Following these events, Korea was liberated when the Allied Forces, led by the United States, won World War II in 1945, but the nation was left impoverished. The United States provided comprehensive aid to help Korea survive and paved the way for a new beginning. When North Korea invaded – backing Soviet Union and International Communism - South Korea, sparking the Korean War on June 25th, 1950, the United States promptly intervened, subdued international communist forces, signed the "Mutual Defense Treaty between the Republic of Korea and the United States of America," established the ROK-US Combined Forces Command, and continues to contribute to the development of South Korea's military defense and democracy. Therefore, I firmly believe that the United States will always be our ally and closest friend, working alongside us for the democratization of the world and humanity.

4. A message to Jun Ho, my beloved grandson, and his descendants, from me, your grandpa

As you navigate your lives, regardless of your professions or the era, always remember that the relationship between the United States and Korea is one of mutual support. Please play your roles as bridges between the United States, your nation, and Korea, your heritage. Never forget the homeland of your ancestors, me - your grandpa- and your grandma. Always remember how much we love you with all our hearts, as expressed in this autobiography.

Please follow these traditions as much as possible, generation after generation: Learn the Korean language and Hangul to understand it, and don't forget <rice and Kimchi, Hanbok and Norigae, the symbols of Korean culture. Ensure that families gather on 'Seolnal' (the Lunar New Year) and Chuseok (Thanksgiving Day) to honor your ancestors and cherish the joyful and friendly customs of Korea.

This is my wish as your soldier grandpa. If any of you, my descendants, choose a military career, consider joining the U.S. Army in Korea to guard the frontlines alongside the ROK Armed Forces. Meanwhile, explore the beautiful landscapes and mountains of Korea to connect with the sentiments of Korea, me, your grandma, and your ancestors. Moreover, if you are fortunate enough, strive to become a soldier (general) fighting for righteousness and a hero in a victorious war for humanity under the banner of justice, fulfilling my unaccomplished dream. If you succeed, come to me and say, "I made your wish come true, Grandpa." If you do, I will be immensely happy and bless you abundantly.

Your grandma and I will serve God and ensure you all lead blessed lives. My son Jeong-eon, my daughter-in-law Yeong-mi, my grandson Jun Ho, my granddaughter-in-law Kate, and your descendants, in other words, my descendants, will prosper for generations.

On December 30th, 2023, our grandson Jun Ho and Kate celebrated a wonderful, meaningful, and joyous wedding at a magnificent Catholic church in Ohio, U.S.A. My wife, your grandma, and I, your grandpa, send our heartfelt congratulations from Korea. At the same time, I am writing this letter to you, so always keep it in mind. We, your grandpa and grandma, wholeheartedly congratulate our beloved grandson Jun Ho and Kate on their wedding! We wished to attend in person, offer our congratulations, and present you with a gift, but our health prevented us. Nevertheless, we send our heartfelt congratulations from our home in Korea. We especially appreciate that you (as schoolmates) kept your promise to marry on this day. By honoring this promise, your marriage will be a 'hundred-year union' and a happy family for a long time.

With this wedding, I believe a new <MOON's Family (J MOON's)> has been created in the U.S.A. With this honorable and proud occasion, we would like to offer you some advice with deep love. Firstly, build a peaceful home based on love, respect, and trust in each other. Then, we hope that this foundation of peace at home will extend to your work, community, and society. Secondly, we wish for you to have many children, bringing good fortune, laughter, and affection to your family home. May the new Moon Family prosper eternally under God's blessings. Thirdly, prioritize health over wealth. Fulfill your duties but avoid overexertion; "health" comes before "wealth." As you have seen, this grandpa engages in gentle physical exercise every morning. Make it a part of your daily routine, and you will live beyond 90 years.

Fourth, Jun Ho, you are already a 'Creator.' Continue to lead a life that is active, positive, and creative. We believe that you and your partner are 'Givers,' not 'Takers.' Always maintain your kind heart. You empathize with those less fortunate, give coins to beggars, and engage in charitable acts. With a spirit of mutual assistance, you consistently serve your community.

Fifth, throughout your life, do not hold back from engaging with your neighbors and everyone around you. By doing so, you will find peace of mind every day. Especially after retirement, you will enjoy a peaceful and healthy life.

Finally, we pray that God blesses you, Jun Ho and Kate Moon, and that He is with the Junho family, bringing you abundant luck. On the day of your beautiful wedding, December 30, 2023, your grandparents pray that God will bless and protect you both and all your future descendants. "It is Forever!"

your soldier grandpa in Ilsan, Gyeonggi-do, Seoul Korea.

할아버지는 군인이었다

詩와에세이

머리글

1950~60년대 육사생도 때와 청년 장교 시절 많은 기성 장군들이 전역 후 일반 기업에 사장이나 고문으로 취업하였다. 심지어 대장(大將)에서 전역하고도 국회의원이 되는 것을 보고 크게 실망하였다. 나는 끝내 군인의 길을 끝까지 지켜 전역 후 회고록이나 자서전을 쓰면서 여생을 보내리라 다짐하였다. 그러나 그 이후 군대 생활을 오랫동안 하다 보니 그때 그분들의 그런 사정을 여러 면에서 이해하게 되었다.

연이나, 이순신 장군과 같은 전쟁영웅과 한 나라의 대통령과 같이 역사적 인물들은 당대의 업적을 의당히 회고록 등으로 글을 남겨야 한다. 그런데 전쟁이 없었던 시절의 장군, 더구나 스스로 평범한 군인의 길을 걸었다고 생각하는 장군으로서 본인은 자서전을 쓰기가 두려웠다.

그런데 나이 80이 다된 2015년의 어느 날, 서울대학교 '규장각'에서 '김 교수'가 찾아왔다. 서울대학 규장각에서 '한국학중앙연구원'의 '현대한국구술사자료판' 발간 계획 중에서 '한국군 현대 군사사(軍事史)'판을 맡았는데, "어떤 분이 장군님을 추천해 주셨습니다"라고 말하였다는 것이다. 우선 '생도 시절에서 파월 맹호부대까지의 개인 체험 군사사(軍事史)'를 얘기해 달라고 했다. "나는 평범한 군대 생활을 했는데"라고 했더니, 그가 말하기를, '면접 구술을 받게 된 분들 개개인의 구술 자료, 즉 모자이크 조각들을 모아 종합하여 한편의 「구술 한국군 현대군 사사판」을 완성한다'고 했다. 그래서 시작한 이래 예정했던 그 범위의 구술이 끝날 즈음 '김 교수'가 또 찾아왔다. "구술을 녹화하는 동안 장군님의 말씀들이 재미있었습니다. 이 기회에 장군님의 전 생애와 군대 생활 전 과정 구술을 부탁드립니다" 요청하였다.

그 이후 하루 3~4시간, 20여 회 이상 녹화 구술해서 「문영일 장군 구술 녹취문」의 원본과 수정본이 완성되었다. 그 원본과 수정본 그리고 구술 녹화 CVD 등 각 10권을 판권과 함께 증정받을 때 김 교수가 말하기를, "이 자료들에 근거해 자서전을 쓰신다면 후진들에게 참 좋은 읽을거리가 되겠습니다"라고 권하였다. 그 이후 서가에 꽂혀 있는 이 '구술 녹화판'과 그 옆에 그 근거 기록 '카드 철'을 볼 때마다 연이나 '자서전'을 쓰고 싶은 생각이 났다. 그래서 몇 가지 목적을 찾아내고 쓰기로 작심하였다.

이 자서전을 쓰게 되는 주목적은 미국에 정착하게 된 바로 내 유일한 손자와 그 후손들에게 조상의 뿌리를, 후손들이 찾기 이전에 미리 알게 함이다. 특히 나라를 위해 군대에서 '위국헌신하고 파사현정'하려 노력한 이 할아버지와 조상의 나라 한국을 이해하는 데 도움을 주고자 위함이다. 더불어 한국과 그들의 조국 미국과 연관하여 언제든 무엇이든 노력하라고 당부하는 데 있다.

그리고 근래에 와서 국민들은 지나치리만큼 국민의 군대, 자기의 군대를 이해하지 못한다. 일부는 심지어 군대와 군인을 의도적으로 매도하려고도 하고 있다. 이에 나는 비록 평범한 이 나라의 한 사람의 평생 군대(한국군) 생활을 통해서 군인의 일생과 그리고 특히 한국군의 반세기(1950~90년대) 군대 역사를 읽고, 좀 더 우리 한국 군대에 대해서 이해할 수 있기를 간절히 바라는 마음에서도 이 책을 써보기로 하였다.

한편 이 글들은 내 시대 한국군 역사 기록 모자이크의 한 조각으로, 기왕에 한국 군사(사)에 관심을 가진 사람들에게 읽힐 수 있도록 노력하였다. 그리고 앞에 말한 '구술 녹화판'과 함께 이 책이 영원한 기록으로도 남을 수 있기를 바라며 노력하였다. 특히 군인이 되고 싶은 청소년과 사관생도(특히 태릉 육사생도), 그리고 장기 복무 중인 각 병과 각 계급의 현역 장교들에게 위국헌신하고 파사현정의 길을 걸었던 한 군인의 일생을 통해 교훈 또는 반면교사의 지혜를 얻을 수 있기를 바라는 마음으로도 이 글을 쓰게 되었다.

이 글이 완성되는 동안 반갑게도 우리 손자 준호가 중고등학교 때부터 함께 지내며 사귀어 오던 절친 여자 친구 Kate와 미국에서 결혼식을 올렸다. 그리고 한걸음에 바로 우리(할아버지와 할머니)에게 인사 겸 신고하러 한국에 왔다. 정말 평생을 두고 으뜸가는 반갑고 즐거운 일이라 행복한 마음 가득하였다. 우리 손자 준호와 손자며느리 Kate 가정에 하나님의 축복과 가호가 항상 함께하시기를 기원해 마지않는다.

끝으로, 한 군인의 일생을 담은 이 자서전을 세상에 내보이면서 가장 고맙게 생각되는 것은 역시나 나와 평생을 함께한 내 가족 내 아내이다. 한 흙수저 청년으로 이제 막 육사를 나와 중위밖에 안 된 내게 시집와서, 온갖 고난을 다 이겨내며 내조한 아내를 어찌 잊을 수 있으랴. 그 세월이 어언 60주년 '회혼'도 지난 내 사랑에게, 어찌할 말이 없으랴. "나는 다시 태어나도 당신과 함께 살리라" 고맙다는 말을 전한다.

2025년 가을, 경기도 일산 우리 집에서.

차 례

제2장. 화랑대(花郎臺) 육군사관학교 생도 시절(1954~1958)

제2부 장수(將帥), 영웅의 꿈 1

제3부 장수(將帥), 영웅(英雄)의 꿈 II

제9장. 육군 상급부대 지휘관, 육군본부 작전참모부장

마무리 말. "우리 손자 준호와 그 후손들에게"

제1부

위인의 꿈

제1장

할아버지의 어린 시절

1. 할아버지의 고향, 바로 너희들의 본고향

◇ 살기 좋고 전통 깊은 내 고향, '대한민국의 부산—동래'

할아버지는 1935년 5월 9일, 대한민국 부산시 동래군 동래읍 복천동에서 신문명 개척민이었던 '문만준(文晩俊)·박갑아(朴甲阿)'의 6남매 중 둘째 아들로 태어났다. 그 동네 지금 이름은 부산광역시 동래구 복천동으로 개명되었다.

할아버지의 고향이기에 그 자손들인 너희들의 원(옛) 고향이 되는 이곳 동래(東萊)는, 한반도 동남방 끝자락에 위치하여, 한국 역사상 전통적인 경상남도 지역 중심도시가 되어 왔다. 그러기에 부산(釜山/釜山鎮)보다 역사적으로 조기에 동래성(東萊城)—직경 2~4킬로미터, 주로 남의 해적과 북쪽 오랑캐를 상대로 축성—이 축성되고 동래부(東萊府), 오늘날의 광역시 개념으로 발전해 왔다.

특히 동래(주민)와 동래성이 그 역사 가운데 자랑스러운 것은, 1592년 임진왜란 때 현대식 조총으로 무장하여 기습전을 감행해, 부산에 상륙, 북으로 서울을 향해 올라가던 왜군을, 지역 사령관이던 송상현 부사(府使)의 지휘하에 부민(府民)와 함께 군·관이 일치단결하여, 활과 창만으로 대적, 2일간 결사 항전으로 지켜냄으로서 왜군의 북진을 그나마 평양에서 저지시킬 수 있었던 역사적 초기 방어전으로 기록되고 있는 사실이다.

결과적으로 송부사는 지휘소 현장에서 참모 제장들과 함께 전사함으로서 그가 남긴 "싸워 죽기는 쉬워도 길을 비켜주기는 어렵다"는 충언을 지켜 자랑스러운 역사적 교훈이 되어 오늘까지도 송공당(宋公堂)으로 동래 한가운데에 남아 있다.

동래는 지리적으로, 백두대간의 끝자락인 천성산(922)에서 발원하여 서로 금정산(802)맥과 동으로 장산(634, 부산 해운대) 사이로 흘러 내려와 수영만에 이르는 수영강(水營江)의 중하류 지역에 위치하고 있다. 그래서 한때 동래는 물론 오랫동안(낙동강 개발 이전) 부산시의 상수도원(上水道源)이었을 정도로 아름답고 풍족한 친자연 도시였다. 북으로는 '가지산' 도립공원이 있고, 서로는 유명한 '금정산(산성)'을 끼고 있다. 그래서 동래온천과 해운대온천, 해운대 해수욕장이 있고, 한때는 명사십리로 일컬어진 '수영 해수욕장'도 있었다. 지금은 복천동 '확수대'에 자리 잡은, 한반도의 신석기시대 즉 삼한(三韓)시대부터 삼국시대에 이르는 유물박물관이 대표하는 바와 같이, 역사와 전통 깊은 도시임을 알 수 있다.

◇ 개척 정신과 신학문 탐구에 사셨던 할아버지의 아버지

할아버지의 아버지는 '동래읍'으로부터 북동쪽으로 약 2킬로미터 떨어진 '명장동'의 정수장(淨水場) 동네에서, 대대로 농사를 지어오던 농민의 셋째 아들로 1900년에 태어나셨다. 그는 천성적으로 창조적이고 도전적(개척적)이어서 어릴 때부터 농사일보다는, 당시 외세와 함께 밀려들어 오고 있던 신학문에 심취하였다. 그동안 읍내(邑內)에 있는 '명륜동' 서원(書院)에 다니시다가, 거기에 신학문의 전초였던 '명륜학당'이 들어오자 바로 입학하여 수학하셨다.

그러다가 유산을 상속받을 시점이 되었을 때, 그는 두 분 형에게 농토를 양보하고, 지분으로 현금을 받아 읍내로 진출하려 하였다. 그래서 드디어는 결혼하자마자 신부와 장모 함께 농촌과 농사일을 떠나 아예 동내 읍내로, 지금 표현으로는 무작정(?) 진출, 명륜동 바로 옆 복천동 한 모퉁이에 보금자리를 잡으셨다.

그곳은 현재 동래여자중학교와 동래구청 중간쯤으로, 그 선을 따라 실개천이 흐르고 있었는데, 그 실개천 서북지역 즉 명륜동 방면 남향 언덕 지대에는 명륜서당을 끼고 당시 동내 부호들과 양반들의 소위 '아흔아홉 칸' 기와집 저택이 즐비하였다. 그러나 바로 폭 10미터 내외의 실개천과 3미터 내외의 개천길 남동편에 연하여는 농민과 그리고 우리네와 같은 개척민들이 삼 칸보다 더 작은 미니 '초가삼간(三間草家)' 동네를 형성하고 있었다.

우리 집은 당신이 손수 지으신 흙벽돌로 지탱하는 초가집으로, 2평 남짓한 외할머니 방과 여닫이문을 사이로 4평 남짓한 우리 방(할아버지와 할아버지의 아버지와 어머니 그리고 우리 4남매)— 당시까지는 할아버지 외 형과 누님 그리고 손아래 여동생이 있었다.—그리고 작은 가마솥 2개와 부뚜막에 놓인 밥그릇, 그리고 흙바닥에 놓인 나무 부지깽이와 옆으로는 솔잎 불쏘시개와 마른 나뭇가지들이 쌓인, 3평 남짓한 부엌으로 되어 있었다. 그리고 그밖에는 두어 평 남짓한 장독대가 있었는데 어느 달 밝은 밤에는 어머니가 큰 장독에 정화수를 올려놓고 손을 부비며 뭔가를 소원하기도 하셨다.

할아버지의 아버지는 그런 가운데 당시로 보아서는 신학문학원(서당 아닌 신식 학교 즉 '명륜학당(明倫學堂)', 서울의 '배제학당'과 같은 학원)에 다니시며 초등교육을 이수하신 뒤에 상급 신학문 탐구를 위해서, 가정을 할아버지의 어머니와 외할머니에게 맡기고, 무일푼 단신으로, 이 또한 개척자적 도전 정신으로 일본으로 건너가셨다.

낯설은 곳에서 생활 방편인 동시에 과학적 호기심으로 배운 전차(電車) 운전—당시는 지금의 드론 조정수(기사)만큼이나 신기한 직업—을 하시다가 끝내는 그것이 평생 직업이 되었다. 당신은 8·15 광복 전에 귀국하여 부산 동대신동과 동래 온천장 사이 '전차' 노선에서 근무를 시작하여 광복 후 수년간 '감독' 직책에까지 이르러 은퇴하셨다. 은퇴하신 후에는 초망(투망)을, 대나무로 된 망침을 이용하여 손수 짜시고(뜨시고), 납으로 된 봇돌(어망추)

도 납을 녹여 직접 만드셨다.

그래서 당신은 종종 수영강이나 온천천에 나가서 고기를 잡으며 소일하셨다. 하루는 나도 물통(Bucket)에 고기를 담으며, 투망하시는 당신을 따라 온천천을 내려가면서 수영만에 이르기까지 종일 고기잡이를 함께 즐긴 때도 있었다.

◇ 어머니의 평생 가족 헌신(獻身)

할아버지의 어머니의 시집오시기 전 본가는, 아버지가 태어나신 곳의 바로 뒷산 즉 해발 250미터 정도 높이의 옥봉산(玉峯山, 지금은 명장공원)을 넘어 약 1킬로미터 정도 동북쪽으로 떨어진, 500여 미터 강폭에 멀리까지 농토가 전개된 풍경 좋은 수영강(水營江) 변의 근사한 몇십 칸 기와집을 가진 양반댁이었다. 당신은 그곳에서 4자매 중 둘째로 1902년에 태어나셨다. 10여 명의 몸종들로부터 마음씨 부드러운 아씨로 귀함을 받아 가며 자라셨다. 그러나 당신이 시집올 즈음에는 이미 나라와 사회가 개화하여 종과 노비제도가 거의 폐지되어 가세가 기울고 있었다.

그리하여 당신께서는 신문명을 향한 개척자의 동반자가 되어 읍내로 이주해 와서는 이전까지 겪어보지 못했던 고생부터 시작하시게 되었다. 더구나 할아버지의 아버지가 신식학문 공부를 위해서 그리고 이어 일본 유학 떠나신 뒤 우선 당장 식구 생존을 위해서 외할머니가 시장에서 비단(옷배)장수를 시작하였다. 그 후 연로하시게 되자 이를 이어받아 당신이 또한 동래시장 난장에 나가 생업을 계속하셨다.

그런데 그 생업이 알고 보면 참으로 고생스러운 것이었다. 이 할아버지가 옛 기억을 되살릴 수 있는 시점 즉, 대략 5살쯤 즉 1940년경에는, 일주일 중 3일 정도는 동래시장(지붕 덮이고 세금 내는 고정된 자리, 약 3평)에서 나머지 4일은 주변 지역 5일장, 해운대장·구포장·범일동(부산)장을 찾아 비단 봇짐—길이 약 90센치, 폭 약 20센치미터 두께 약 2센치미터 되는 나무판 6~7개 정도에 각각 비단 10마(碼, Yard) 정도를 말아서 꾸린 그 무거운 옷배 보따리—을 머리에 이고, 홀로 또는 보부상들과 함께 기차와 전차 그리고, 특히 '구포장'으로는, 그 험한 산길을 걸어서 '만덕고개'를 넘어 다니셨다.

동래에서 구포장을 오가기 위해서는 반드시 해발 500여 미터의 '만덕고개'를 넘어야 하는데, 그곳은 금정산맥의 중간 안부 지대로 꼬부랑 산길을 이용해도 가파른 곳은 경사도 30도에 이르고 때로는 깊은 계곡 물길도 건너야 했다. 그런데 직선거리 약 6킬로미터에 도보 실거리 약 8킬로미터에 봇짐을 무겁게 인 중년 여자의 거름으로 시간 거리는 왕복 최소 5시간 이상 소요되는 험한 오솔길이고 우거진 삼림 속인데다 호랑이는 안 보였지만 살쾡이는 흔히 볼 수 있는 당시로는 험산 유곡의 길이었다. 할아버지는 어릴 때 손위 누님과 같이 당신을 마중하러 만덕고개 오르막길로 가다가 종종 내려오시는 당신을 만났는데, 그 앞으로 살쾡이가 오고 있는 것을 보기도 하였다.

이러한 고생을 감당하셨던 나의 외할머니와 부모님들은 절약하고 또 절약해서 드디어 1943년에 꿈꾸어 오시던 대망의 집, 30평도 넘는 앞마당과 10평 정도의 대청마루(거실)에

20평 정도의 내실과 사랑방을 가진 본채에, 수돗물이 나오는 데다—당시 근방에는 우물이 있는 집도 드물었고, 수도 있는 집은 더욱 드물어—시멘트로 된 장독대에다 잘 자란 단감나무가 뜰 한가운데에 한 그루 있는 상당히 근사한 집을 사서 '수안동'으로 이사를 하였다. 그리고 그곳에서 해방동이 남동생(화웅(和雄))과 이어서 여동생(말남(末南))을 보게 되어, 온 가족 9명이 되었다.

부모님들은 얼마나 큰 보람을 느끼셨고 행복하셨을까, 그런데 이사하던 날 당신들께서는 다음 목표는 기와집을 갖는 것이라고 하신 말씀을 지금도 기억하고 있다. 그 후 두 분의 그 소망은 형님의 조기 기술 노동과 시집간 누님 노력으로 1960년, 이웃에 있던 아주 좋은 기와집— 신작로 가에 우물과 수돗물이 나오는—으로 이사함으로 소원을 이루었다.

2. 일제 강점기의 고난, 광복의 감격과 혼란(1935~1948)
— 솔깃했던 "사관학교와 사범학교"라는 말

◇ 어머니의 길몽(吉夢)으로 태어난 나, 그리고 어릴 적

어머니께서 나를 낳으시던 그날 밤은 바로 뜻깊은, 음력으로 석가탄신일(4월 8일)을 몇 시간 앞둔 '4월 7일'이었는데, "아주 벼슬이 크고 잘생긴 장닭이 우리 집 지붕 위에 올라 머리를 치켜들고 높이 보며, 크게 부르짖는 꿈"을 꾸셨다고 한다. 그리하여 태어난 내게, —자고로 애를 낳으실 때마다 현재의 고생을 벗고 그 아기의 장래에 기대를 거시는 것이 옛 어른들의 간절한 소망 이였던 때라—영특하고 크게 되라는 뜻으로 내 이름을 영일(英一)로 지으셨다고 한다. 가형의 이름은, 장남이라 부모와 집안일을 받들라는 의미로 '받들 봉'의 봉일(奉一)이었다.

내가 기억할 수 있는 어린 시절은 대략 나이 5살 정도 때부터가 아닌가 한다. 그때는 그저 종일 집 밖으로 나가서 동네 친구들과 어울려 나가 노는 것이 일과였다. 집 앞 사잇길과 개울을 합해 10여 미터 거리를 두고 북서편으로 명륜동(明倫洞)을 중심으로 아흔아홉 칸 고래등 같은 기와집들이 즐비하였는데 당시는 이미 거의 양반집 행세가 끝날 때라 폐가가 된 빈집들이 더러 있었다. 그곳에서 숨바꼭질하며 놀기를 즐겼다.

여름에는 동래에서 부산으로 나가는 길목에, 동래 온천장(금정산)에서 내려오는 제법 큰(폭 100미터도 넘는) '온천천(溫泉川)'에 걸쳐 있는 전차(電車)용 철교가 있었다. 그런데 때때로 그 철교 위에서 놀다가 전차가 오면 7~8미터가량 높이의 강물로 뛰어들기도 하고, 또 때로는 교각 속으로 몸을 숨기고 위로 지나가는 전차 밑을 보며 그 소음을 듣기도 하는 등 개구쟁이 아슬아슬 장난들을 많이 즐기기도 하였다. 여하간에 여름에는 그 온천천이 동래 개구쟁이들의 하루 쉼터요 놀이터인 동시에 자연학습장이 되었다.

그리고 때때로 읍내에서 실거리 10킬로미터 되는 '수영해수욕장'—지금의 광안리해수욕장과 해운대해수욕장 사이, 한때는 간이 비행장이었고 6·25 때는 낙동강 교두보의 유일한 전투기 비행장이기도 하였다, 지금은 유감스럽게도 대형아파트 단지가 되었다—을 걸어서 다니기도 하였다. 한번은 당신들이 애써 벌어 오신 돈, 얼마(당시 돈 5원짜리 동전 한 닢)를 슬쩍하여(평생 딱 한번) 친구들과 함께 기차로 해운대 해수욕장에 가서 잘 놀고 와서는 밤에 당신들께 혼나기도 하였다.

한때는 동네 개구쟁이들을 거느리고 잘도 돌아다니는 것을 친척들이 와서 보고는 칭찬하여(?) 가로되, 마치 '한국 히틀러(즉 골목대장)' 같다고 비행기를 태워 주시기도 했다. 물론 학교에 입학한 뒤에도 다녀오자마자 마루에 책가방을 던져 놓고 그대로 친구들과 함께 잘도 돌아다니며 저녁 늦게까지 놀고 다녔다. 그래도 학교에서는 '전 과목 수(秀)'로 우등상을 받았다.

◇ 국민(초등)학교 시험치고 입학

1942년에 할아버지는 대한민국 부산시 동래구에, 현재도 그대로 있는 동내 내성초등학교—왜정시대 이름은 동래제1공립국민학교—에 입학하였다. 그때는 입학시험도 치렀는데, 그래서 비록 소수이긴 하지만 초등학교도 못 다니는 애들도 있었는데 바로 함께 동네를 휘젓고 다니던 친구 몇 명은 경제 사정도 겸해서 그러하였다.

면접시험 날 어머니께서는 "엄마 직업을 물으면, 집에서 바느질한다고 하여라"고 하셨던 말씀이 지금도 기억난다. 아마도 시장 장사란 것이 당시까지만 해도 농·공·상에 대한 일반적인 관점에서 선생들에게는 좀 어색했던 시절의 반영이기도 하였다.

입학 이후 1945년 광복의 해를 맞이할 때까지 4년 동안은 학교의 모든 생활과 과목을 왜국어(倭國語)를 사용하며, 일제 통제하에 다니게 되었다. 그런데 그때(1940)는 우리 한국이 일제에 의해 강점된 지도 어언 30여 년이 지났고, 일제(日帝)가 제국주의 열강의 번견(番犬) 역할도 모자라 드디어는 세계 3대 군사 파쇼 구축 국가(독일, 이탈리아, 일제)가 되었다. 그래서 미국을 비롯한 연합국을 상대로 태평양전쟁을 도발(1942.12.8)하고, 바야흐로 태평양과 동남아시아 그리고 남태평양에 이르기까지 광범위하게 일제히 침략전쟁을 감행하고 있었다.

드디어는 1941년부터 패전 망국을 앞둔 일제의 최후 발악으로, 국내 독립운동가들을 다시 일제히 감옥에 수감(소위 사상범 예방구금령)하고 초등학교 한국어 학습을 완전히 폐지시켜 왜(倭)말 교육을 강요하였다. 학교에서 우리말을 하면 왜 선생이 즉시 엄벌을 주었다. 또한 왜인(倭人) 선생을 대거 한국 학교에 취업 시키고 교장은 긴 칼을 찬 현역 대위가 자리하였다. 그리하여 매일 아침 운동장에 모여 조회(朝會)를 하였는데, 왜국(倭國) 도쿄에 있는 왕궁을 향해 90도로 절하고 '황국신민(皇國臣民)의 선서'를 제창한 뒤 교장 훈시가 있었다.

◇ 일본 교장 선생의 '육군사관학교와 사범학교' 자랑

그런데 하루는 이 군인 교장 선생이 말하기를 "일본에서는 육군사관학교(시캉각고)와 사범학교(시앙각고)가 제일"이라 하였다. '제일 좋은 학교'라는 말에 솔깃하여 그리고 발음도 비슷하여 그때부터 '사관학교'와 '사범학교'를 막연하게 나마 마음속으로 항상 동경하게 되었다. 물론 그때는 그런 학교가 무슨 학교인지 잘 몰랐지만, 자라면서 마음속에 두었던 이 두 학교와 직접적인 인연을 맺게 되었으니, 지금 생각하면 그가 누구이든 어릴 때 듣는 선생님의 말씀 한마디가 참으로 귀중하게 느껴지고 마침내는 일생 중 어느 때 영향을 미친다는 것을 알게 되었다.

◇ 전쟁 말기 학생생활 ; 방공호에서 본 B29, 고무 공, 맨발

태평양전쟁 말기가 되자 점차 연합군의 공세가 체감되었다. 특히 학교 뒤 언덕은 물론 집집마다 마당에 방공호(防空壕)를 파서 폭격 시 피난처로 지정해 두었다. 공습경보(사이렌이나 난타 종소리 아니면 육성 전달)가 울리면 학교에서는, 평소에 의자 위에 깔고 앉았던 푹신한 깔개를 접어 머리에 덮어쓰고, 나누어 준 건빵 가지고 방공호에 들어가 저 멀리 공중에 제비 새끼 크기만 한 것이 반짝거리며 유유히 지나가는 미군 B-29 장거리 폭격기 편대를 신기하게 그러나 초조하게 바라보곤 하였다.

그런데 결혼 후 아내(즉 너희들 할머니)에게 들은 얘기로는, 할머니의 고향인 전라도 '전주' 교외 '삼례'에서 전주 읍내에 있는 학교로 걸어서 통학하였는데, 하루는 하교 후 집으로 돌아가면서 '만경강' 근처에 다다랐을 때, 갑자기 B-29 미군 장거리 폭격기 1대가 100미터쯤 눈앞에 놓인 철교를 폭격했다고 한다. 그때 실제로 배운 대로 현장에서 양손을 눈과 귀에 대고 가리면서 땅에 바짝 엎드려 피해를 면했는데 평생 '트라우마'로 남아 있다고 했다.

전시였던 당시에는 물자가 귀했던 건 두말할 나위 없어서, 당시 남도지방의 보통 학생들은 심지어 미나리밭에 살얼음이 얼었을 때도 맨발 등교가 여사였다. 그래서 아예 학교 교실 낭하 입구에는 '발 씻는 곳('아시아라이바', 洗足場)'이 설치되어 있었다.

◇ 평생 습관 길들기 ; 밥 잘 씹기, 11자 걸음 바로 걷기, 국민보건체조 하기

그래도 당시 국민(초등)학교는 국민 기본 교육을 한곳임에는 틀림이 없었다. 입학과 동시에 매일 아침 조회 때마다 실시한 국민보건체조는 그때부터 지금까지 근 80년 이상 하루도 빠짐없이 조조에 실시하는 신체 윤활 운동인 동시에 상태 점검 수단이 되어 왔다. 지금이 정도로 건강을 유지하는 비법 중 하나도 이 평생 생활 습관이 된 국민보건체조 덕분임에 틀림없다.

또 한 2학년이 되었을 때부터, 거의 주먹밥에 단무지 수준이긴 하였으나 그래도 점심을 주었다. 학생 당번제로 배식하고 한 반 교실에서 담임 (3학년) 일본 여선생과 함께 식사하였는데, 밥 먹기 전에 항상 선생님은 "밥은 잘 씹어 먹어야 한다, 한 숟가락 입에 넣으면 왼쪽으로 19번, 오른쪽 19번씩 씹은 후 넘겨야 한다"고 강조하였다.

변명일 수도 있지만 그 후 할아버지는 그것이 습관이 되어 평생을 통해 남보다 밥을 늦게 먹게 되었고, 60대에 위암 수술을 받은 이후는 더 늦게 먹게 되었다. 그런데 부대(군대) 생활 중에 외출 나갔을 때 어느 친절하신 친척분은, "문 중위 부대원은 좋겠다, 지휘관이 밥을 저렇게 느긋하게 먹으니 부하들이 서둘러 먹지 않아도 되겠다"고 하였다. 그분은 6·25 전시에 서울에서 피난 내려오면서 종종 행군(도중 휴식) 중인 군부대와 마주쳤는데, 흔히 그 군인들이 "출발"이라는 명령하에 밥도 다 먹지 못한 채 서둘러 일어나 행군해 가는 것을 보고, 지휘관이 밥을 너무 빨리 먹는 사람이라 그럴 것이라 생각했던 것이다. 사실은 지휘관 식성에 따라 부대 행동이 좌우되는 것은 물론 아니지만 때로는 그 친척분의 말씀이 사실일 수도 있기에 웃으며 회고할 뿐이다.

4학년이 되어 광복된 어느 날, 우리 한국 담임 선생님이 체육 시간에, 우리 반 교실 책상을 옆으로 치우고, 바닥에 나 있는 나무 두 결씩에 따라 양발을 11자로 해서 왕복으로 걷기를 반복하였다. 아마도 그래서 이제 90세를 바라보는 할아버지는 지금도 8자 아닌 11자 걸음으로 길을 가고 있다. 아마도 이 모든 초등학교 교육은 내 몸에 배어 평생 습관이 되었다. 어디 이런 습관뿐이겠는가. 윤리, 도덕과 애국심 그리고 미래 꿈 그런 것들도 초등학교에서 터득하여 평생 습관이 되는 것이라 초등학교는 문자 그대로 국민 기본 교육 도장이라 하지 않을 수 없다.

또한 일제는 한국 사람 모두에게 소위 '내선일체(內鮮一體)', '황국신민화(皇國臣民化)' 정책을 강요하였다. 특히 학생들에게는 강제로, 매일 아침 조회 시간에 동쪽을 향해(소위 皇宮을 향해) 90도 각도로 인사하고 이어서 소위 '황국신민의 선서'를 외고, 거의 매주 한 번씩 (온천장) 금정산에 있던 소위 '신사(神社, 왜식 절간)'로 걸어가서 참배도 하였다.

어느 날에는 친구 하나가 교실에서 우리말 하였다고 담임 여선생이 그의 머리를 흑판에 대고 인정사정없이 부딪히는 심한 벌주기를 보고, 여선생과 왜놈(당시는 그렇게 불렀다)들에 대한 민족의식과 함께 적개심이 솟구치기도 하였다. 광복(당시는 해방이라 불렀다)할 때까지 할아버지의 학교 생활은 모범생은 아니었지만 항상 창의적이고 능동적이고 활발하였다. 1, 2학년 때는 2등상을—한 학급에 1, 2등상을 각각 1명씩, 1등상은 공부 잘하고 모범생에게, 2등상은 공부는 잘하나 개구쟁이(?), 3등상은 개근상이었다—받았고, 3학년 때는 3등상을 받고 찢으려다가 왜 담임에게 들켜 과외 남김 벌을 받기도 하였다.

◇ 8·15광복 날, 부엌에서 부지깽이로 어머니께 배운 한글

4학년이 된 그해 8월에 광복되자 일본 담임 선생은 귀국하고, 새로 한국 선생님(成선생)이 오셨는데, 담임을 맡으시고는 곧 할아버지를 급장(級長, 班長과 같다)으로 세웠는데, 아마도 왜색을 단번에 일소하기 위해서였을 것이다. 할아버지의 아버지, 당신께서는 아들이 반장된 것을 기뻐하시고 당시 내게는 공책(노트)이 따로 없어서, 조선 창호지로 공들여 공책을 만들어 주시기도 하였다.

한편 동시에 광복된 바로 그날 저녁(1945년 8월 15일)에 나는, 부엌에서 저녁을 지으시는 어머니 곁에 쪼그리고 앉아, 유식하시던 어머니가 불을 때며 쓰시는 그 부지깽이 끝 검은 숱으로 흙바닥에 쓰시는 한글, '가나나라마바사아자차카타파하' 와, 'ㅏ이ㅑ, ㅓ이ㅕ, ㅗ이ㅛ, ㅜ이 ㅠ, ㅡㅣ·(아), 헨 땡이'— 그 당시는 아래·(아)가 있었다.—를 따라 읽어 배웠고, 그걸로 다음날부터 학교에서 배워나간 '낫 놓고 ㄱ 자도 모른다'로 시작한 한글공부에서 한글 최우등생이 되었다.

그래서 광복 다음 해 졸업식 때는 재학생을 대표한 송사(送辭)를, 그다음 해 할아버지 졸업식 때는 졸업생을 대표하여 답사(答辭)를 읽었다. 그 모두가 그때 부엌에서 당신에게서 배운 '한글 첫걸음' 덕이었다. 나의 어머니 당신께서는 그때, 비록 시장 포목상(때로는 보부상)이었지만 역시나 어릴 적 양반댁 '아씨'였기에, 그때도 물론 유식하고 단아한 귀부인이었다. 그러기에 내 평생을 좌우한 나의 지식과 겸손은 이 모두가 우리 어머니의 가르침 덕이었다.

◇ 광복 직후 동래, 부산 모습

◦ 광복 공간 왜인들의 악행과 우리의 흥분

광복 며칠 후 부산은 어떤 모습으로 변하고 있을까도 궁금하여(초등 4년생, 나이 10살 때) 도보로 도상 직선거리 12킬로미터, 실거리 아마도 15킬로미터는 족히 될 신작로(부산—동래간 간선도로)를 따라 도보로 하루 종일 걸려서 어두울 때쯤에 초량 전차정거장에 도착하였다. 동래를 출발할 때는 무더운 여름 낮 때라, 부산을 향해가는 온천천(溫泉川)상의 유일한 다리 세병교(洗兵橋) 아래에서 옷을 입은 채 통째로 물속에 들어가 강을 건너 나와서 옷이 완전히 젖은 시원한 모습 그대로 부산을 향했다.

서면을 거쳐 부산진 더 밑으로 초량까지, 아마도 그때 점심 굶어가며 8월 땡볕 아래 6시간 정도를 걸어갈 수 있었던 그 고집과 건강이 8년 뒤 육군사관학교를 갈 수 있게 한 원동력이 되었을 것으로 생각된다. 밤이 어두워지자 돌아가야겠다는 생각이 들어, 전차를 타고 동래로 돌아가기 위해 초량역(전차정거장 옆) 대합실에 서 있을 때, 갑자기 몇 분 간격으로 두세 번 천지가 울리는 듯한 굉음과 함께 세상(땅과 건물)이 흔들리면서 유리 창문들이 박살나 내렸다. 동시에 바다 쪽 멀리 지금의 제3부두 방향에 큰 버섯 불기둥이 솟구쳐 오르는 모양이 보였다. 왜놈들(당시의 호칭)이 철퇴하면서 적기(赤畿, 지역 이름)에 설치해서 비장해 두었던 유류를 한국 사람이 못쓰게 하려고 상당 규모 크기의 탱크 수기를 일제히 폭파시켰던 것이다.

한편 광복 다음 날 바로 동래시장 남쪽 입구 광장에는 누구의 짓(쫓겨 가는 일본 관리?)인지는 알 수 없으나 바로 옆 곡식 배급 창고에서 가져다 쌓아 놓은 쌀 산더미에 불까지 질러서 그 아까운 곡식을 불태웠다. 한국 사람들이 했다면 그건 한풀이와 해방감을 맛보려는 순간의 착각 감정에서 온 것이리라. 그러나 그 직후 쌀 배급이 끊기자, 없는 사람들은 와서 그 불탄 쌀을 가져가 씻고 또 씻어도 화근내(불탄 냄새)가 나는 대도 참고 밥해 먹었다.

◇ 급장이 되어 같은 반 어깨(깡패)와 한판 격투

학교에는 동급생으로 '어깨(깡패)'가 2명이 있었는데 한 명은 덩치가 고릴라같이 크고(우리의 2배 정도, 광복과 동시 편입생이 많았다) 우악스러웠으며, 다른 한 명도 덩치는 그만 못했으나 우람하고 뼈대가 굵은 친구였다. 전자는 종종 동급생을 괴롭히기도 했으나 형제나 단짝끼리 뭉쳐서 달려들면 그래도 물러서기도 하였다. 후자는 직접적으로 괴롭히지는 않았으나 위력 시위로 동급생을 제압하였다. 그런데 얼마 후에 전자는 전학을 가고 후자가 남았는데, 동급생들의 공감된 '의로운 저항심'(?)이 한 에피소드를 낳게 되었다.

할아버지는 광복 당시 4학년이었고, 1학년과 2학년 때 받아왔던 2등상(우등상)을, 3학년 때는 일본 여선생이 담임이 되어 3등상(개근상)으로 받았고, 이때는 무난하게 4학년 우등상을 받았다. 그런데, 해방 즉 광복과 동시에 일본 선생들은 가고 한국 남자 선생님(成 선생님)이 부임하셨는데 이 할아버지를 급장으로 뽑아 주셨다.

그런 가운데 하루는 급우들이, 우리 학급에 그대로 남아서 여전히 위협적인 그러나 나와는 친척이기도 해서 친했던 그 '어깨'와 싸움 즉 결투를 벌리도록 선동하였다. 비록 상대가 되지 않아도 좋으니 내가 모두를 대표해서 그에게 달려들고 그리고 한 두방이라도 날려주기를 바라는 것이었다.

그래서 그도 나도 어리석게도 함께 학교 뒷산—즉 지금의 복천동 고분군, 복천박물관이 있는 그 언덕, '학수대'—에 올라가 50여 급우들이 둘러싼 공간에서 둘이 정식 격투를 벌였다. 사실 그 어깨 친구는 힘이 장사여서 내가 이길 수 있는 상대가 아니었기에, 함께 두어 번 치고받고 하다가 그 친구에게 붙들려서 넘어졌다. 처음부터 나를 일방적으로 응원하던 친구들 분위기에 흥분한 그는 내 목을 졸랐다. 금방 숨이 막히고 하늘이 노랗게 되어 가는데도 항복하지 않고 버티었다. 그러나 사태가 위험함을 느낀 급우들 모두가 달려들어 그를 밀어제치고 하마터면 갈뻔했던 나를 구해내 주었다. 급장 하자면 그런 일도 있는 것이거니와 나는 평생에 때때로 그렇게도 정의심에 용감(우직?)하기도 하였다.

3. 부산사범학교 창립과 대한민국 건국(1948~1950), 나의 '위인의 꿈'

◇ 부산사범학교 입학

초등학교 4학년 때 광복이 되었고, 급장이 되었으며, 5학년 말에 담임 '윤의태 선생님'의 권유로 동래중학교로 월반 시험을 치렀으나 준비 부족으로 낙방하였다. '윤의태 선생님'이, 6학년 말이 되자 이번에는 부산사범학교로 추천해 주셨다. 부산사범학교는 광복 후 처음으로 부산 동대신동에서 창립(1946.7)되었는데, 창립과 동시 기존의 국내 유수한 사범학교들(진주·전주·공주·대구·청주사범 등)과 어깨를 나란히 하였다. 양친께서는 아들이 상당한 경쟁을 이기고—각 초등학교에서 우등생 중에서 추천하고, 부산시 학무국에서 다시 선발하고, 사범학교에 가서 2배수 후보 학생들이 시험을 쳐서 최종적으로 합격—유명해지고 있는 부산사범학교에 입학한 것을 자랑하며 기뻐하셨고, 학비도 덜 든다는 사실도 내심 좋아하셨다. 나는 나대로 왜정시대에 들어 귀에 익은 그 '사범학교'에 가게 되어 긍지를 갖게 되었다.

당시 부산사범학교를 창립하고 정진하였던 선생님들은 주로 미국서 교육을 받아왔던 분들로, 학문 실력은 물론이거니와 생각과 생활 그리고 교육관에서 민주주의(Democracy), 선진, 현대화된 분들이었다. 교장 선생님은 후에 연세대학교 총장이 되신 윤인구 박사, 교감 선생님은 광복과 동시 김씨성을 순 한글 성인 금씨로 바꾼 순수 애국자인 동시에 유명한 음악가인 금수현 선생님—그 아들도 잘 알려진 '금난새' 음악예술인—음악 선생은 후에 「한국 환상곡」으로 유명해진(후에 잘못되어 종북 음악인이 되긴 했지만) 윤이상 선생(부인은 국어 담임 이순자 선생), 그리고 우리 담임 선생은 윤인구 교장 선생님의 부인으로 함께 미국 유학하셨던 방덕수 영어 선생님이었다.

방덕수 우리 담임 선생님은 어느 날, 그의 지도로 전국 '학생영어웅변대회'에서 2등 입상하였던 박세직 선배, 당시 부산사범 초급과 2회생 즉 초급과 3학년생—후에 육군 중장, 서울시장, 88서울올림픽 조직위원장—에게 나를 소개해 주셨는데 그 인연으로, 그와는 그 후에 군대 시작에서부터 은퇴할 때까지(사관학교 2기, '하나회' 선배로) 그리고 그 후에도 안면 관계를 유지해 나가기도 하였다.

◇ '5.10 선거'로 '대한민국정부수립'(건국)

'5.10 선거'에 대한 표어는 부산 미국공보원(USIS)—최초 공보원은 지금의 부산 롯데백화점 옆자리—벽보에서 발견하였는데, '대한민국 건국'을 위한 국민총선거(국회위원 선출)였다. 이 투표는 한국 5000년 역사상 최초의 남녀 유권자 전부에 의한 국민투표였다.

당시 우리 담임 선생님은 역사 담임이었는데, 왜 '대한민국 건국'이 아니고 '대한민국 정부수립'이냐고 질문하는 우리에게, "정부의 의미는 3권분립상의 행정부이기도 하지만 국가라는 의미도 된다, 대통령은 행정부 수반이기도 하지만 국가를 대표한다, 그러기에 대한민국정부수립은 곧 대한민국 국가 건국을 의미한다고"고 해석해 주신 것을 지금도 기억한다.

◇ 해방공간, 부산 우마차(牛馬車)시대

왜정시대 말기, 일반민의 교통수단은 기차, 전차, 보기 드물었지만 택시, 인력거 그리고 화물자동차(나무로 불붙여서 운행) 등이었는데, 동래는 주로 우마차였다. 광복이 되자 기차와 전차는 만원이 되어 운행 시간은 따로 없이 출발하는 시간이 그 시간이었다. 미군이 버린, 손가락으로 헤아릴 수 있는 수의 자동차—'스리쿼터'(3/4, 반트럭)와 '지엠시'(GMC) 화물차, '박스차'(Shop, 병기 수리차)를 개조한 버스 등—가 있었으나 물론 대중화되지 못했다. 그런데 미국 서부영화의 마차가 등장하여 대중 교통화하였고, 동래는 여전히 소달구지가 시골과 읍내간의 화물 및 사람의 운반수단이 되어 있었다.

◇ 미국 공보원에서 읽은 미국과 위인들

금수현 교감 선생님은—당시 한국 교육·음악계에서 아주 유명한 분이라 소개를 생략하고—종종, "미국은 사람의 윤리 도덕교육 이미 끝내고 지금은 고양이 교육 중"이라 말씀하면서 우리들의 윤리도덕심과 학구심을 고취하였는데, 그때마다 할아버지는 미국이라는 나라를 동경하였다. 때마침, 부산본역에서 학교까지 약 30여 분간 걸어 다녔던 동선상의 '대청동'길에, 위엄 있고 근사한 건물에 「U.S.I.S」라는 미국공보원이 있었다.

귀가용 통근 기차를 기다리는 시간이 여유가 있었기에 하교 시에는 통상 길가에 있는 책방에 들려 무료 독서도 하고, 그리고 냉난방 좋게 되어 있는 이곳에서 공보원과 도서관 내부를 두리번거리며, 그 질 좋은 미국 학생 교과서를 펴보거나, 각종 잡지—당시 한글로 미국을 소개하는 『희망』이란 잡지도 있었다—를 보거나, 또는 종종 재미있는 미국 소개 영화를 관람하면서 미국의 역사 특히 서부 개척 역사와 3권분립 정치제도, 그리고 풍요한 시민 생활 등을 알게 되었다. 이때부터 풍부한 미국에 관심을 가지면서 장차 미국 유학의 꿈을 키우기도 하였다.

◇ 위인의 꿈을 품다

물론 평소에 나는—우리 위인전은 후에 경제가 좀 발전했을 때 그리고 인문학이 발전된 후이고, 당시는—미국 서적과 일본 서적을 위주로 미국 위인들 특히 미국이 자랑하는 조지 워싱턴, 에이브러햄 링컨, 성공의 화신 룩펠러와 카네기 등의 인물됨과 성공담을 중심으로 탐독하였다. 그리고 틈틈이 '시-저'와 '풀루다크' 영웅전 등도 읽고 감동하였다. 그리고 역사 공부를 좋아하다 보니, 터키 부흥의 영웅 '아타투르크 케말 파샤 장군', 이집트 민족주의자로 식민지를 벗어나 동서냉전에서 위력을 발휘하는 '낫셀 장군' 그리고 당시는 우리보다 훨씬 선진국으로 보였던 필리핀의 국가재건 영웅 '막사이사이' 대통령 등의 혁명정신과 성공담에 마음이 달아오르기도 하였다.

또한 한국의 소년잡지 『소년』과 일본의 소년잡지 『少年(쇼냉)』에서 '소년이여, 대망을 품어라(Boys be Ambitious, Boy Ambition!)' 라는 표어와 격려라던가, "사람은 상(上)을 배워 중(中)에 이르고 중(中)을 배워 하(下)에 이르나니 뜻 있는 자 천하일품(天下逸品)을 지향하라!" 는 금언들을 항시 마음에 색이고 위인의 꿈을 꾸어 왔다.

워싱턴 장군(대통령)의 소년 시절의 정직과 공정함이라던가, 특히 '링컨 대통령'의 정직과 성실— 빌려 온 책 비 맞아 돌려줄 때 빚 갚기 노동을 자처하고, 가난을 오히려 정직으로 극복한다던가, 카네기(학자)의 인생 교훈 그리고 윌슨 대통령의 대학 시절 '10분 늦게 불 끄기'의 가르침 등등으로 이 할아버지는 일찍부터 국가 부흥의 '혁명가', 그리고 사회와 인류의 지도자인 위인이 되기를 마음에 품었다.

◇ 선생님의 수양아들 될 뻔

육사 입교 전까지 가난하여 돼지고기, 소고기는 한 번도 먹어 본 기억이 없고, 중국집은 물론 그 흔한 '짜장면'이란 것이 세상에 있는 줄도 몰랐다. 그러나 비록 처마 끝에 매달아 둔 대나무 소쿠리에 담긴 꽁보리밥을 먹긴 했어도 하루도 세끼 밥을 걸러 본 날은 없었다. 다만 부산으로 사범학교 다닐 때 김치 반찬 국물이 흘러 책에 베여 냄새나고 해서, 도시락을 가지고 다니지 않아 점심때 굶으면서 운동장에 나가 놀고 있었기는 하였다.

그런데 우리 '방덕수' 할머니(인자하시고 섬세하신 바를 나타낸 애칭) 담임 선생님과 '윤인구' 교장 선생님과의 슬하에 자식이 없었다. 방덕수 선생님은, 아마도 우리 집이 몹시 가난해서 점심도 못 먹는 줄 아시고, 한번은 어머니를 학교로 초대해 나를 양자로 입양할 뜻을 논의하였으나 어머니의 겸양된 거절로 무산된 적이 있었다고, 한참 후에야 어머니로부터 들은 적이 있다.

해방 후 설날이 되면, 부모님들이 고향 농촌 이웃들과 일찍이 '고기 계(契)'를 들었다가, 그 설 전날에 소머리 고기를 얼마간 배당받아 와서, 그걸 큰 솥에 끓여 묵을 만들어서 근 한 달간 소고기로 알고 먹었고, 당신은 내장 몇 줄 받아 오셔서 설쇠 위에 신문지 깔고 화롯불에 구어서 소주 몇 잔 하고 잡수셨다. 그러나 식구 누구도 불평 몰랐고, 이 할아버지는 오히려 미국의 위인 '링컨 대통령'의 어릴 때보다 덜 가난한 줄 알았고, 그의 가난한 생활에도 정직을 앞세운 생활관을 본받으려 하였을 뿐이었다.

4. '6·25 남침적란(赤亂)' 시대 부산교두보(1950~1954), 육사가 나를 불렀다

◇ '6·25 남침적란' 발발과 피난민, 천막 가교사(假校舍) 시작

1950년 6월 25일, 그날은 공휴일이었다. 할아버지 옆집에는 학식이 높은 어른들이 살면서 당시 희귀했던 고급 라디오(5球)를 애용해 단파(AM)방송을 자주 들어왔는데, 그날 아침부터 그분들은 아주 긴장한 가운데 무엇인가 되풀이되는 방송을 더 열심히 듣고 있었다. 할아버지도 가까이서 들어보니, 북한괴뢰집단(당시는 그렇게 불렀다)의 선전(Propaganda)방송인데, "남한괴뢰군이 북으로 2km 북침해 왔기에 이를 우리 용감한 인민군이 반격하여 현재 남진 중에 있다"고 허위 선전하고 있었다. 바로 그날 새벽에 문자 그대로 '북한괴뢰집단'은 소련 '스탈린'의 사주로 국제공산주의혁명운동의 선봉이 되어, '한반도 적화통일'을 위해 괴뢰군으로 하여금 38선 전 전선에 걸쳐서 전면 남침을 개시하였던 것이다.

할아버지가 6·25 바로 다음 날 수업(부산사범학교)을 마치고 나오면서 보니, 그사이에 서울서 내려온 피난민이 벌써 길가에 보이기 시작하였고, 그다음 날부터는 대청동, 토성동, 대신동 등 주택가의 온 길가를 메우고 있었다. 우리 학교 또한, 큰길가에 있었고 반듯하였기에 그 열흘쯤 지나자(7월 초순) 미군이 주둔하게 되었고, 우리는 의자와 책상을 들고 이웃 '토성초등학교'로 일단 피난해 갔다. 그리고 그 이후에는 미국군으로부터 대신 받은 24인용 군용 텐트로 아미동 산 언덕에 '천막가교(사)'를 개설하였다. 이후 휴전이 될 때까지 부산은 서울에서 피난 온 각급 학교들은 물론 부산 토박이학교 대부분도 학교 시설을 군부대에 내어주고 '천막 가교사(天幕假校舍) 시대'를 지내게 되었다.

6·25 적란(赤亂) 당시 참전국은 1951년 초까지 총 16개국이었다. 군대 파병은 미국, 캐나다, 콜럼비아, 호주, 뉴질랜드, 필리핀, 태국, 남아공화국, 에티오피아, 영국, 벨기에, 프랑스, 그리스, 룩셈베르그, 네덜란드였다. 이들 참전국들은 유엔이 요구하는 최소 규모인 1개 대대 병력(약 1,200명) 이상을 파견하였다. 1953년까지 한국전에 참여한 연합군은 미국을 포함 총 34만 1천여 명에 이른다.

또한 유엔 결의에 따라 회원국 및 국제기구들이 각종 지원을 하기 시작했는바, 5개국(스웨덴, 인도, 덴마크, 노르웨이, 이탈리아)이 병원 혹은 병원선 등 의료지원을, 그리고 40개 회원국과 1개 비회원국(이탈리아)과 9개 유엔 전문기구가 식량 제공 및 민간 구호 활동에 참여하였다.

◇ 부산본역에서 본 처절한 전사상자 후송

7월 말경부터 부산교두보가 형성되면서 낙동강 전선에서 치열한 전투가 전개되고 있었다. 하루는 할아버지가 학교를 마치고 저녁 통근열차를 기다리면서 부산본역 언덕에 앉아 본역내 군용열차들의 왕래를 보고 있는데, 그때 막 객차 6량가량의 전사 상자 후송열차가 홈에 들어왔다. 열차가 미쳐 정차하기도 전에 일제히, 모든 승강장과 깨어진 창문을 통해서 피투성이의 군인과 전상자들이 담긴 들것들이, 최대로 서두르는 속도로 밀려 나왔다. 그들은 곧 인근에 있는 '영도다리' 근방의 후송 병원과 바다에 정박해 있는 유엔군 병원선으로 이송되어 갔다.

이들은 이곳 본역에서 1시간 거리도 안 되는 '마산'과 낙동강 전장의 치열한 전투에서 지금 막 부상당하거나 전사하여, 지급으로 후송되어 오고 있는 미군 전사 상자들의 일부였다. 그런데 전장 그대로의 처참한 피투성이 후송 광경이 전개되고 있는 홈에는 물론 환영객이 있을리 없었지만, 당시 소문에 들렸던 대로 '대구 금달래'라는 중년의 미친(미친?) 여인이 흰 치마저고리(소복)를 입고, 내복 벗은 아랫도리를 들어내며 덩실덩실 춤을 추며 돌아다녔다. 그녀가 전사자들의 넋을 달래주려는 무당굿을 연출하는 것인지 그것은 알 수 없었으나, 여하간에 처절한 전쟁의 또 한 광경을 그때 목격하게 되었다. 이같이 비참한 전쟁과 전장에서 미국 군인은 한국을 위해 전사하고 전상을 당하기도 하였으니 어찌 한국 사람들이 미국의 은혜를, 또한 참전국 군인들의 희생을 어찌 잊을 수 있으랴.

◇ 임시휴교, 수영비행장 긴급 건설현장에서 본 미군 능력

7월 중순이 되자 여름방학 겸 학교가 일단 휴교 되었는데, 집안이 어려웠던 건 누구나 마찬가지여서 우리들 학생 대분분은 아르바이트에 나섰다. 당시 동래 '수영(水營)' 바닷가에 있는 간이 비행장 겸 수영장(水泳場)을, 대 지급으로 대형 수송기와 제트 전투기까지 이착륙이 가능한 비상 비행장으로 급조하기 시작하였는데, 이 작업장에 할아버지도, 비록 중학 2학년(14세)이었지만, 막일꾼으로 돈벌이 겸 참여하였다. 근 열흘 이상을 밤샘 일과 낮 걸이로, 처음엔 주로 흙과 모래 자갈을 어깨짐으로 나르고 이어서 활주용 철판을 목도(Pole for Shouldering)로, 원하는 지점으로 운반해가는 일이었는데, 특히 밤 2시경에는 졸려서 혼나기도 하였다. 그리하여 불과 10일 여만에 거뜬히 전투비행장이 완성되는 것이었다.

과연 미국의 능력이었다. 그런데 이후 육사 전사학 시간에 배워 알았지만, 이 능력이 태평양전쟁에서 일본의 능력—간이 비행장 하나에 1~3개월—을 압도하여 승리할 수 있었다는 것이다.

그런데 알고 보면 어른들도 중노동에 속하는 일임에도 불구하고, 그러나 그때의 나는 특별히 힘들다는 생각도 없이, 낮일을 마치고 잠간 저녁 식사 겸 휴식하고 바로 밤일로 들어갔었다. 그러나 그때마다 하루살이 노동자로 뽑히기 위해, 힘세고 건강한 어른 모습을 보이기 위해, 얼굴은 밀짚모자로 가리고서도 성년으로 보이게 인상을 만들어 보이면서 어깨를 최대로 펴고 당당해 보이려고 하면서도, 그때마다 일에서 제외되면 어쩌나 하는 초조했던 심정 참 힘들었다. 웃을 얘기로, 그때의 그 고심 때문에 아마도 내 이마에 석줄 주름살이 일찍부터 생겼을지도 모른다.

수영비행장 활주로 공사가 끝나자 공중과 수상—수영비행장 백사장은 당시 전국 최고 해수욕장이어서 멀리 해상의 대형 수송선으로부터 육지로 수륙 양용 수송선 이용—으로 인원과 탄약 수송이 시작되고 이 탄약을 바로 거기에 있는 수영 기차역에서 화차로 이송하여 전방으로 보내고, 계속 들어오는 예비 탄약들은 바로 인접 해운대 기차역으로 가서 다시 하차 시켜 바로 위 지근 거리의 낙동강 전선으로 직송하거나 내륙 임시 탄약창으로 이송하는 작업이 시작되었고, 그를 위한 노동시장이 또 형성되었다.

◇ 미군부대 아르바이트장에서 본 해군 제트 전투기의 처절한 희생

수영비행장 건설공사장에서 해운대역 탄약 적하장으로 아르바이트를 옮겨가는 도중에 건설이 완료되고 전투비행장으로 운용되기 시작한 그 지음(1950년 9월 전후)에 할아버지는 잠시, 비행장을 적의 공중공격으로부터 엄호하는 미군 대공화기부대('애끼애끼부대' ; AA, Ack-Ack, Antiaircraft gun)의 한 반(班)에 심부름꾼(하우스보이)으로 일하기도 했다. 영어 배우기가 주목적이었다. 이 분대의 대공화기는 수영비행장 활주로 맨 북단의 서편 끝에 쌍으로 배치되어 있었는데 활주로 끝으로부터 불과 50미터 거리에 있었다. 그리하여 매일 매시간 활주하여 비상하는 프로펠라 '호주 전투기'와 새로 발명되어 전투에 참가한 항공모함용 해군 '제트 전투기'를 지상에서 엄호하고 동시에 적기 내습시 격추하는 주 임무를 맡고 있었다.

그런데 새로 나타난 짙은 쥐색 제트 전투기는 항상 2기편대로 출동하는데, 아마도 활주로가 짧은 듯 항상 맨 끝 지점(2~3백 미터)에 와서야 아슬아슬하게 급상승하여 하늘로 치솟아 올라갔다. 그런데 하루는 2대 중 한 대가 치솟지 못하고 약 5미터 높이의 북쪽 제방 끝에 몸체를 슬라이딩하면서 박히고, 순식간에 불이 붙으면서 탑재된 탄약(기총소사용)과 함께 폭발하였다. 소방차가 달려왔으나 조종사를 구조할 시간이 없었고, 총탄이 사방으로 나르고 기체가 폭발하기에 근접할 수가 없었다.

그런가 하면 불과 10여 분 눈 깜짝할 사이에 전투기는 잿더미가 되고 조종사는 형적조차 없었다. 함께 출동했던 다른 한 대는 상공을 한 5분 선회비행하다가 전장을 향해 나라갔다. 그때 그 전우 조종사의 심정 어떠했을까. 이곳·이것이 바로 전장이요 전쟁이었는데 내가 그때 불과 50미터 채 안 되는 거리에서 실탄과 폭발을 피해 엎드린 채 그 현장을 목격하였던 것이다. 전쟁과 전장은 이렇게 처참한 것임을 체험하였다.

◇ 해운대역 탄약 운반작업

할아버지는 학교 친구들과 함께 다시 해운대 기차역으로, 동래 시내에서 수영을 거쳐 해운대까지 걸어서 출퇴근하는 아르바이트를 하게 되었다. 주로 화차에서, 각종 구경의 소총 탄약 상자들과 특히 상자에 포장된 105미리 포탄 또는 포장 없는 155포탄(별명, 한되병)을 받아 어깨에 메고 100여 미터 거리에 있는 트럭에 가서 올려 싣는 작업이었다. 포탄의 무게는 155미리가 47여kg 내외, 105미리는 20kg(한 상자 당 2발) 내외였기에 모두 힘에 겨웠지만 특히 155미리 포탄을 받아 메는 순간은 그 자리에 폭삭 주저앉는 기분이 들 정도로 무거움을 느꼈다. 아마도 당시 할아버지 몸무게는 중학생 평균으로 53kg 정도였기에 그랬을 것이다.

그리하여 그렇게도 어려웠던 유엔군의 부산교두보 군수 보급기지 형성이 완성됨으로서 유엔군의 9월 대반격작전(인천상륙작전과 동시 낙동강 전선의 돌파 북진 등)이 성공할 수 있었던 것이다. 그런데 당시 가정 형편은 후방 국민 모두 함께 겪는 가난한 전시 후방 생활이기는 했으나, 그래도 우리 집은 이 할아버지가 직접 생계를 도와야 할 정도는 아니었기에, 여름방학에 휴교가 겹친 짬을 이용해서 아르바이트에 나섰던 것이다.

그런데 마치 그 속을 알기나 하는 듯, 소위 한국 측 고용주(錢主)는 작업 후 바로 현금을 주지 않고 종이로 된 소위 전표(錢票)를 그날 품삯으로 주었다. 그런데 그 전표는 그날부터 최소한 일주일 이상 지나야 전주가 있는 지급 현장에 가서 현금화하는데, 그것조차 30~40% 이상 할인하여 교환해 주었다. 그래서 한 20일 분을 모았다가 교환해서, 모처럼 배밭에 가서 5개 정도 사고 책방에 가서 영어 콘사이스(당시는 일어로 된 사전) 한 권 사고 나니 집에 가져갈 현금이 없을 정도였다. 그런 행위 즉, 공산주의자들이 말하는 소위 '자본가의 노동 착취' 행위가, 지금으로서는 상상하기 매우 어려운 일이나 전시 한국 노동판에는 다반사였다.

◇ 대한민국 '제1회 현충추모식'

'적란'(赤亂) 발발 1주년이 되던 1951년 6월 25일에는 동래고등학교 교정(당시는 '육군간부후보생학교')에서, 이승만 대통령 임석하에 '제1회 현충추모식'이 거행되었다. 지난 1년 동안 전선에서 용전분투하다 전사한 한국군과 유엔군 장병들의 넋을 위로하고 그 가족을 대통령이 직접 위무하였다. 그런데 그때 유가족 일부는 "내 아들 내놓아라!"고 오열을 참지 못하는 경우가 있었는데, 할아버지는 그때(어린 중학생으로) 느끼기를, '전쟁이란 비참한 것이고, 그리고 내 핏줄의 죽음이란, 때로는 애국심도 넘는 것'으로 느껴지기도 하였으나 한편으로는 국가와 민족을 위한 거룩한 희생에 대해서는 선진국의 부모들처럼 좀 더 성숙한 마음가짐이 있어야겠다 고도 생각이 들었다.

◇ 고무신공장에서도 아르바이트 후 사범학교로 복교

1950년 북괴 남침적란 이후 그 여름과 부산교두보가 형성된 그 가을까지 할아버지는, 이미 말한 바 있듯이 중학 2~3학년의 학업을 중단하고 수영비행장과 해운대 기차역에서 전쟁 후방 지원 과업(보수를 받고)에 종사하였고, 그리고 이어서 겨울에는 동네 근처 온천장에 있는 개인이 운영하는 10인 이하 소기업 공장, '고무신 재생공장'에서 일했다.

1951년 봄에 공장 일거리가 일시 중단되자 나는 부산사범학교로 달려가 복교하였다. 당시 풍전등화의 전시 상황에서도 이승만 대통령은 학교 교육을—심지어는 대학생은 병력까지 면제해 주면서—국가 운영상 최우선시 하였다. 그러하였기에, 우리 학교도 토성동 뒷산 언덕 '아미천' 사당(寺堂)—일제가 사용하다 비어 있었던—을 교무실로 그 뜰과 근처 밭을 정리하여 천막 교실—미군은 부자였고 마음씨도 후했다, 부산 전 지역(지역학교와 각급 피란학교)의 각급 모든 학교와 우후죽순으로 생겨나는 기독교 교회당까지 수만 개의 군용 천막(주로 24인용)을 무상으로 제공해 주었다—을 지어서 단절없이 수업 중이었다.

◇ 부산사범에서 동고로 복교 후 주독야경

그리하여 복교 후 고등학교로 진학하기까지 불과 몇 개월이었지 만 방덕수 선생님을 다시 만나 그의 지도하에 즐겁게 부산사범학교 초급과 3학년 말 학기를 보낼 수 있었다. 그런데 전쟁 중 학제 변경으로 졸업 당시 중학 과정은 '사범병설중학'으로 개칭되었는데, 사실상 3학년 거의 전 학기를 결석하고도 '사범병설중학 제1회 생으로 졸업할 수 있었다.

그리하여 새 제도에 의한 고등학교 진학 시험(부산사범학교와 동래고등학교)을 치렀는데, 별 어려움 없이 두 학교에 모두 합격하였다. 그러나 집안 사정—가형의 입대와 기울어진 가세 등—과 교통 사정 등으로 더는 부산사범으로 정시 통학이 어려워, 집에서 300미터 정도로 가까이 있는 동래고등학교를 선택하였다. 그러나 아르바이트는 계속할 수밖에 없는 형편이라, 부산 국제시장 한 부분에 2층 목조 임시 건물(도합 200여 평)에 설치된 국제아동구호소(주로 유럽의료진이 운영), 그때까지도 환도해간 '이화여대 부속병원'의 간판이 여전히 붙어 있었다—에 야간 숙직원(겸 경비원)으로 취직하였다.

그리하여 매일 하교(오후 3시경) 후에는 그 길로 바로 부산으로 내려가서(약 1시간 반 이상 소요), 2층 모퉁이방(1.5평 정도) 숙직실에 책가방을 놓고, 내려가서 병원 열세를 인수받았다. 그때부터는 아무도 없는 병원을 청소(사실은 아주 깨끗하게 사용했던 것으로 기억된다)하고, 내일 사용할 수돗물을 물탱크에 올린 뒤, 건물 내외를 한 번 순시하고, 그때부터는 건물을 지키면서 내 시간을 갖었다. 그때도 여전히 전기 사정이 좋지 않아 밤새 정전이 보통이었다. 나로부터 공부 시간을 많이 앗아 간 이 아르바이트 생활은 고등학교가 거의 끝날 때까지—대학 입학 시험 준비를 위해 부득이 그만 둘 때까지—계속되었다.

◇ 전쟁 중 수복된 서울 관찰 여행

전선이 현 휴전선 전후에서 소강상태를 유지하자, 그동안 부산에 있던 우리 피난 정부가 휴전 성립 이전부터 이승만 대통령의 특단으로 임시수도 부산에서 서울로 환도, 즉 수복해 갔는데, 이 할아버지도 그동안 가보고 싶었던 서울의 모습도 궁금하여 전시하의 서울 여행을 감행하였다. 서울에서는 당시 피난지 부산에서 피난 생활을 마치고 막 서울로 복귀해 간 치과의사 8촌 형님의 '문치과(원효로 2가)'에 며칠간 신세를 지면서, 시간을 아껴가며 서울 시내 즉 태평로(지금 세종로), 종로, 을지로와 용산 등지로 전차를 타고 다니며 구경하였다.

당시 내가 본 서울은 두말할 것 없이 거의 완전히 파괴된 황폐한 모습 그대로였다. 더욱이 수복 직후라 막연한데다 언제 또다시 적의 수중에 떨어질지 모른다는 심리적 압박도 있고 해서인지, 사람들은 우선 살아남은 사람들의 기거 정리로 무너진 벽과 천정 보수 그리고 생필품 상점의 임시수리 등이 한창이었다. 다만 그 가운데서도 하학하여 거리를 지나가는 여학생들의 조잘거림과 웃음만이 그 수복 후 처참한 서울 광경에서 희망을 바라볼 수 있게 하였다.

할아버지는 지금의 세종대로(광화문거리, 세종로, 옛 태평로) 거리 한가운데— 아마도 지금 세종대왕 동상자리 쯤—에 서서, 앞뒤 사방 허허 폐허를 둘러보며, 북악산과 중앙청(지금은 광화문)을 배경으로 남쪽으로 향해 서서 남대문 넘어 멀리 보이는 한강 방향을 바라보며, 마음속으로 "장차 이 나라의 중흥을 위해 일하는 위인"이 되기로 다짐하였다. 그로서 할아버지는 일찍부터 가져왔던 '서울 꿈'을 일차 이루기도 하였다.

◇ 대한민국 육군사관학교에 지원, 합격

1953년 초에, '육사 제3기 추가시험'이 공고되었다. 그 내용 속에 이 할아버지를 끌어당긴 대목은, 육사가 서울로 옮겨간다는 것과 졸업 후 미국 유학의 기회가 있다는 것이었다. 그래서 할아버지는 졸업 학년이 아닌 고교 2학년으로서 시험 삼아 응시해 보았다. 부산에서 학과시험에 합격한 뒤, 대구에 있는 당시 제5보충대(장교보충대)로 소집되 가서 최종적인 신체검사와 면접시험이 있었는데, (짐작하건데) 면접 평가에서, 육사총장이 '육사 지망 이유'를 묻는 질문에, "군의 간부가 되어 군 부패를 개혁하겠습니다"라고 했으니, 지금 나로서도 불합격 판정 내릴 수밖에 없었을 것이다.

그래서 그때는 낙방하고, 가을(10월)이 되어 정상적인 '육사 제4기모집'이 같은 내용으로 공고되었는데, 이번에는 고등학교 3학년의 정식 자격으로 응시하여 별 어려움 없이 합격하였다.

'진해 육사'는, 학교 본부와 교실 외는 모든 건물 특히 생도대는 콘셋(Quonset Hut)—80년대 중후반까지 대부분의 한국군 후방 부대의 막사 그대로—였다. 생도들이 식사한 뒤 이어서 우리 합격생들이 식당을 이용하였는데, 간부사관생도(연대 군수참모생도)가 식사 전에 간단한 소개를 겸하여 말하기를, "여러분이 먹게 될 이 식사는 우리 농민이 힘들여 지은 곡식으로 된 것이기에 농민들에게 감사하며 식사해야 한다"고 하기에 감명받았다. 식사의 질은 '현재 한국 중간 계층의 평균 식사'로 소개되었으나 별루 좋은 형편은 아니었다. 물론 이 할아버지는 그 정도도 먹지 못하고 있었던 형편이라 별생각 없었으나 후에 선배들(1, 2, 3기)로부터 들으니 당시는 배가 고파 혼났다고 했다.

면접이 끝나고 다음 날 합격발표가 있었고 그다음 날은, 즉시 개인 각자에 맞추어 복장(예복, 정복 등) 체천이 있었다. '하! 생전 처음 내 입을 내 옷을 맞추어 보다니!' 기분이 아주 묘하게 훤해졌었지.

그래서 아주 기쁘고 행복한 마음으로 집에 돌아왔다. 그러나 서울대학 시험을 포기할 수는 없었다. 나중에 가고 안고는 그때 가서 볼 일이고, 여하간에 서울대학에 직접 가서 지원서를 제출하려는 동급 반, 아주 친한 친구 이용우에게 부탁하여 서울대 입학원서를 받았다. 그는 일본에서 일찍이 1942년경 한국으로 피난(소개) 나와서 우리 동네에 정착하였는데, 가정은 부유하였고 그 형은 이미 서울대 의대 재학생이였다. 그는 서울대 법대를 졸업, 당시 법대 동기생 대부분이 그러하듯 군 복무와 유관하여 고등고시를 치르지 못하고, 부친의 사업을 이어받아 향리에 주저앉았으나 그 아들들은 2021년 현재 사법부 고위 판사들로 재직 중이다.

이 할아버지는 제1지망과 2지망을 '문리대 정치학과' 그리고 3지망을 '문리대 역사학과'로 기재해서 제출했더니 응시번호가 69번, 이건 부산사범학교 2차 시험번호와 같은 것이어서 행운이라고 믿기도 하였다. 그 학과에 지망한 이유는, 당시 세계에서 구국의 영웅들은 대체로 정치 외교가들로 보였기 때문이었고 또 그 학과가 법대보다 더 인기 있고 전망 있다는 소문에 따른 것으로, 한번 도전의 가치 있다고 생각했었다.

그러나 동기들 모두가 서울로 시험 치러 갈 때 할아버지는 가지 못했다. 할아버지의 어머니는, 아마도 합격하면 당시 형편에 학비와 서울 생활비 감당이 어려울 것이 뻔하기에 말리셨다. 사실은 내가 먼저 그 생각을 했어야 했는데. 물론 할아버지는 서울대학에 도전을 못해 본 것에 대해서만은 좀 아쉬웠으나 모든 사정을 이해할 수 있었다. 그리하여 내게는 육사가 운명일 수도 있을 거라고 생각하고 서울대 입시를 위한 서울행을 포기하였다. 사실 당시 육사 지원자들 대부분의 경제 사정이 그러하였다.

◇ 서울로 육사로 공부하러 간다

드디어 그렇게도 열망했던 서울로 공부하러—군대 입대하러 간다는 생각보다—가게 되었다. 어머니께서 일주일 앞서, 서울대학교에 못 보낸 대신 서울 구경이나 하고 들어가라면서 여비를 좀 주시기에, 입교 일주일여를 앞두고 상경열차(上京列車)에 올랐다. 당시 부산 본역에서 서울 가는 열차는 하루 몇 번 있지도 않았거니와 시간은 연착까지 포함하여 종일 걸리는 것이 보통이었다.

서울 올라가는 그날, 어머니와 누님 그리고 여동생(후에 약사(藥師))이 배웅 나왔는데, 어머니로부터 삶은 계란 몇 개와 감자가 든 봉지를 건네받아 맨 끝 기차칸(당시의 전망열차)의 전망대 섰다. 그래서 기차가 출발하자 손 흔들며 기차가 플랫폼을 빠져나와 어머니와 누님 동생들이 보이지 않을 때까지, 그 자리에 서서, '남아입지출향관(男兒立志出鄕關) 약학불성사불환(若學不成死不還)' —남아가 뜻을 세워 고향을 떠나니, 뜻을 이루기 전에는 죽어도 돌아오지 않으리—을 다짐하였다. 동시에 '나는 돈으로 효도는 못하겠지만, 대신에 '위인이 되어 그 명예를 부모님께 바치리라'고 굳게 마음 먹었다. 부산본역을 떠나오며 본 어머니와 가족, 그때 그 장면과 느꼈던 어머니의 심정과 사랑을 나는 평생 잊을 수 없었으며, 무슨 일이 있을 때마다 나를 앞으로 나가게 해 준 원동력이 되었다.

그리하여 손에 쥐어주신, 당시엔 귀한 계란(집에서는 처음)과 감자를 점심과 간식으로 때우면서, 완전히 붉은 산과 헐벗고 피폐해진 도시와 촌락들 그리고 5천 년 그대로의 초가집과 가난에 찌들린 산하—허기야 그래도 낭만파 시인들은 문전옥답과 때가 되면 피어오르는 초가집 굴뚝의 연기 등을 읊기도 하나—를 보아가며 종일 달려, 저녁 무렵에야 서울역에 도착하였다. 내리자마자 폭격을 면한 서울본역 광장에는 수많은 장사와 호객꾼들(나그네를 상대로 여관방, 밥집, 직업 소개, 노는 곳 알선 등)로 발 디딜 틈도 없어서 이 촌 총각이 정신을 못차릴 정도였다.

그런 가운데 그래도 남 속이지 않게 보이는 한 호객꾼을 따라 할아버지는 역전 바로 건너편에 있는 여인숙(旅人宿)—지금의 거대한 대우빌딩 남쪽 끝, 후암동 길 입구쯤에 자리—에 들고, 여장이라야 손에 든 손가방 하나였으나 그래도 일단 내려놓고, 평생 처음 서울 객지 여인숙, 완전히 파괴된 집들을 우선 추수려 비바람만 겨우 막아 놓은 듯한 여관방에서 내일을 생각하며 잠들려 하였다.

그러나 그날 6월 23일 초저녁에, 바로 여관방 뒤편에서, 당시 서울 복구작업이 한창이던 서울 사람들의 시장이던 남대문시장이 일시에 잿더미가 되어 버린 대화재가 발생하였다. 그날 그 시간에 밖으로 나와 서울역광장에서 남대문시장 쪽을 바라보며 한동안 할아버지 평생 처음 보는 큰불을 구경하면서, 저 큰불이 서울에 온 이 시골 총각을 대환영한다는 의미로 나름대로 좋게 해석해 두었다. 서울의 첫날 밤, 내일부터 서울대 법대에 다니는 친구 이용우와 이인길을 만나 대학 구경도 하고 초토화된 서울을 다시 살펴 본다는 생각을 하면서, 태연하게도 등 뒤로 큰불을 업은 체 곧 잠이 들었다.

다음 날은 전쟁으로 폐허된 서울 중심부(종로 을지로)에서 무너진 벽돌들을 골라내고 그래도 파무쳤던 가제 도구를 파내는 등 작업 중인 시민들의 활동을 통해 재건 중인 서울 시내를 유심히 두리번거리며, 서울역~남대문~태평로~종로5가~동숭동~명륜동을 지나 이용우가 있는 명륜동 하숙집을 찾았다. 당시 서울대 문리대는 현재(2021) '마로니에 공원'에 붉은 벽돌 건물로 있었고 건물 주변으로 프랑스 가로수 '마로니에 나무'가 무성하였던 생각이 난다.

이용우 하숙집은, 이 문리대 맞은편 대학 본부(당시) 북편에 자리한 전형적인 명륜동 하숙촌의 한집으로 단칸 3평가량 공간에 2명, 한 사람은 역시 동고 동급생인 김규식—역시 법대생, 후에 '롯데삼강하드' 사장, 본부장—이 함께 생활하고 있었다. 이후 2~3일간, 함께 하숙집 점심 얻어먹어(물론 하숙집 인심은 공짜가 없어, 찾아온 친구에게 제공된 한두 그릇도 월말에 이용우가 값을 치르게 되어 있었다) 가며 바로 대학로 건너 문리대 법대 강의실(1층으로 생각난다)로 들어가, 무단 청강도 해 보았다. 그런데 강의 내용은 지금 기억이 없으나 강의실과 강의 모습 학습 모습은 고등학교의 그것들과 별 차이를 느끼지 못했다.

남은 날들은 종로와 을지로(전차가 다니는 길) 그리고 남산에 올라 완전히 파괴되어 잿더미가 된 서울을 돌아보았는데, 그 속에서 무너지고 타버린 자기 집 벽과 담을 세워 단층집이라도 일단 복구 중에 있는 서울 사람들 표정에는 굳게 다문 가운데 희망을 가지고 열심히, 벽돌 한 장이라도 찾고 골라 집을 이르켜 세우는 굳건한 모습이 역력하였다. 나머지 날들은 일 년 전에 잠시 올라와 보았던 원효로 2가 문치과(198촌 형님)에서도 재개업을 위해 식구 모두가 집안 곳곳 부서져 내린 잔해를 치우고 벽과 천정에 신문지와 교과서 종이로 도배를 하는 과정을 도우기도 하였다.

6월 30일이 되어 친구 이용우와 이인길과 작별하고, 드디어 대망의 '나의 군인의 길'의 제1 관문인 태능 육사, '화랑대(花郞臺)'즉 '대한민국 육군사관학교'로, 서울에서 전차 버스 기차를 바꾸어 타가며 벅찬 마음을 억제해가며 태릉으로 향했다.

◇ 그때까지, 위인의 꿈을 향한 마음가짐

- 한때는 잡지가 좋아 '잡지 왕'이 되려 했다.
- '남아입지출향관 약학불성사불환'(男兒立志出鄕關 若學不成死不還)을 마음속으로 외우며 고향을 떠나 서울로 향했다.
- 남이장군의 시조 '백두산석마도진 두만강수음마무 남아이십미평국 후세수칭대장부'(白頭山石磨刀盡 豆滿江水飮馬無 男兒二十未平國 後世誰稱大丈夫)를 항시 마음에 두었다.
- '사람은, 상을 향하면 중에 이르고 중을 향하면 하에 이르나니 뜻 있는자 천하일품(天下逸品)을 지향할지니라'를 항상 외우며, '소년이여 대망을 품어라'(Boys be Ambitious)를 항상 마음속에서 외쳤다.
- 선과 정의 그리고 동정(同情)을 위한 '희생정신'(양보, 배려, 봉사, 희생, Give)을 미덕으로 삼았다. 그리하여 겸손과 친절로 살아가려고 노력하였다.
- '사람 위에 사람 없고 사람 밑에 사람 없다'를 인생관으로 하여 직계가족, 아주 친한 친구 외는 존댓말을 사용하였으며, 이후에도 손아래 처남, 동서들에게도 존대말을 사용했다. 물론 장단점은 있었다.
- '남아일언중천금'(男兒一言重千金)을 천금으로 여기고, '말로서 말 많으니 말 많을까 하노라'를 속으로 다짐하면서 가능한 한 말을 참으려 하였다.
- 미국 대통령 '에이브러햄 링컨'의 '가난과 정직과 성실과 신용'을 귀감삼아 살아왔다.
- 미국 초대 대통령 '조지 워싱턴'의 '정의와 정직 그리고 공평무사'를 일생 교훈 삼아 살아왔다. 특히 친구에게도 공사를 지킨 사실을 평생 길잡이로 하였다.
- 어머니의 거룩한 '내 생일담'과 연세대 양주동 박사의 "어머니의 용꿈으로 난 나는 '남에게 함부로 고개를 숙이지 않는다'"를 마음에 색여넣고, 하나님과 부모 말고는, 대통령에게라도 실천하려 하고 있다.
- 고등학교 2학년 한때 '고등고시'도 생각이 나서 상당 시간 '유진오의 『헌법해석』과 『법제대의』' 그리고 '행정법'에 관한 책(이름 잊음)과 『고시(考試)』라는 월간지를 구입해 보는 등 한때 공부하기도 하였다.
- 로마역사 중 푸르다크 영웅전과 시저 등 탐독
- 터키의 국가 영웅 '아타투르크 케말파샤' 전기 탐독하며 혁명과 개혁의 의미 터득
- 제법 많고 다양한 독서를 했는데, 마음에 담은 책은, 앙드레 지드의 『좁은 문』, 앙드레 모로아의 『영국사』와 '프랑스 패망하였다', 모파상의 「진주 목거리」, 귀스타브 플로베르의 『보바리 부인』 등.
- 누구나 다 읽으려고 펴본다는 괴테의 『파우스트』와 단테의 『신곡』 등을 열어 몇 페이지 보다가 놓았다.
- 잡지는 아주 좋아했다, 그래서 한때는 장차 잡지왕이 되려했다. 일본의 『문예춘추』, 『중앙공론』, 『세계』, 『소년(文藝春秋, 中央公論, 世界, 少年』) 그리고 한국의 『소년』, 『희망』, 『아리랑』, 『경향』, 『리더스 다이제스트』, 그리고 미국의 희망(미 공보원).

'Reader's Digest'는, 초기에는 일본 '리더스 다이제스트'와 한글판이 나왔을때부터는 대조해가며 몇가지 테마를 읽었다. TIME, NEWSWEEK은 독해 강의를 받은 이후 앞 몇 면 시사뉴스만 반쯤 이해하며 읽었고, LIFE, Geography 는 속 사진에 매료되어 계속 독자가 되었고, 육사 입교 후는 내 여동생이 수집해 주었다.

- 장교 신체검사 불합격일 수 있는 좌심장 판막증 보유자
- 백낙준 박사의 '가장 실망적인 현재 한국 환경이 곧 한국 청년의 희망과 기회이기도 하다'라는 말씀도 마음에 두다.
- 스스로의 긍지와 고집 그리고 '개척자 정신'에 충일하다.
- 교과서 실력은 6·25 충격과 조기 근로로 반감됨. 특히 수학을 비롯한 이과.
- 겸손과 겸양은, '산에 가면 호랑이가 제일이고, 학교 가면 선생님이 제일이고……그런데 아직 과공은 금물임을 미쳐 깨닫지 못하고 있었다.
- 선심과 동정 그리고 적선(積善)을 알고 배풀어야 했으나 가진 것이 별로 없어서, 필요한 남을 위해 그저 친절과 희생봉사 정신으로 처신하다.

제2장

태릉 화랑대(花郎臺) 육군사관학교 생도 시절 (1954~1958)

1. 입교, 기초군사훈련(1954.6.30~8.31)

◇ 대한민국 육군사관학교와 교훈 '지(智)·인(仁)·용(勇)'

1951년, 전쟁 중이었음에도 불구하고 전체 한국군 간부들에 대한 교육의 강화와 정예 장교 육성의 필요성에 따라, 이승만 대통령과 당시 유엔군 사령관이던 미군 '벤프리트 대장'(Gen. J.A Van Fleet)의 '위대한 용단'으로, 10월에 4년제 정규 육군사관학교가 경상남도 '진해'에서 개교되었다.

학교 교훈은 지(智)·인(仁)·용(勇)인바, 지(智)는 사리를 판단하고 분별하는 능력으로 군인의 사명을 인식하고 무력의 관리라는 부여된 기능을 올바르게 이해하는 덕목이고, 인(仁)은 어진 감성과 신의를 바탕으로 서로 사랑하고 이해함으로써 부대의 단결력과 전투력을 고양시키는 덕목이며, 용(勇)은 굳센 행동으로 어떠한 위험에서도 옳은 일을 실천함으로써 책임을 다하는 덕목이다, 라고 정의되어 있다.

커리큐럼은 미국 육사(West Point Academy)를 모델로 민주주의(Democracy)의 신념 아래 이과(理科) 위주 교육과정에 미 육사식 교육 성과제도(Thayer System)를 도입하여 일일시험(Daily System), 장말시험, 기말시험을 실시하는 등, 전쟁 중인 현실에서 당시 국내 교육기관 중에서는 가장 엄격한 학사제도가 이행되었다.

1952년 1월에 정규 육사 1기생도 입교, 국가 교육 학제 변동에 따라 동년 8월에 2기생 입교, 휴전 직전인 1953년 7월에 제3기생이 입교하였다. 1954년 드디어 수도 서울의 환도와 함께 육사는 진해에서 올라와 '태릉,' 즉 현재의 '화랑대'에 다시 자리 잡았다. 그리하여 1954년 7월 1일에 정규 육사 4기생, 즉 우리 기가 입교 선서를 함으로서 4년제 육사 교육 체계와 생도대 4개학년 체제도 완편되고, 학제 또한 국가 인정으로 이학사 학위로 졸업함과 동시 육군 소위로 임관되게 되었다. 정규 육사 1기생의 졸업 및 임관식은 1955년 10월 4일이었다. 이후 대한민국 육군사관학교는 대한민국 군대의 역사는 물론 대한민국 국군의

역사와 함께 도도히 흘러 내려오고 있다.('Long Long Gray Line !')

◇ '정규 육사 4기', 입교와 입교식(1954년 7월 1일)

단기 4287년(1954. 6월 30일) 오전, 당시는 오늘과 같은 근사한 육사 정문은 물론 없었음으로, 학교 북서쪽 모서리에 자리 잡은 '육사 제2연병장'의 야외 등록소에서 입학 등록을 하였다. 그때 써낸 '입교 서약서' 본문을 보면.

1. 대한민국에 충성을 다할 것
2. 상관 명령에 대하여 절대복종하여 교칙을 엄수할 것
3. 가사에 대하여 후려됨이 없을 것
4. 상기 사항 위반시는 여하한 처분이라도 이의 없이 받을 것, 이었다.

등록을 마치고 '제2연병장(B 연병장)' 바로 위 언덕에 있는 A교사로 가서, 사관생도로 탈바꿈하고 생활하기 위한, 이름도 생소한 관물(官物)들을 가득하게 지급받았다. 그때는 일상에서 생소했던 품목들 예를 들면, '화이바 속 머리지지대, 화이바 턱 끈, 탄띠, 수통, 수통카바, 타올, 단화, 워커군화, 구두약, 치분, 칫솔' 등을 받으면서 무조건 고함으로 복창하였는데, 물건 하나씩, 물론 군대답게 던져주고 떨어뜨리지 않고 받기를 거듭하면서 신기하고 당황스럽기도 하였다. 물론 이 모든 관물은, 심지어 팬티, 런닝, 양말까지 그 모두가 미제(made in U.S.A)였다.

내 것이 된 그 신기한 군용 '따블빽(더플백, Duffelbag, 야전낭, 야전낭(野戰囊)'에 가득 찬 보급품을 짊어지고 교실 언덕 반대편 평지에 자리 잡은 생도대 내무반(內務班, Soldier's Quarters—주거생활) 지역으로 안내되어 내려갔다. 생도 내무반 지역은 길이 약 40미터, 폭 약 30미터의 '콘세트' 막사(반달형 양철지붕막사, Quonset House, 미군 이동용 간이막사)로 형성되어 있었는데, 횡으로 5개(1개 중대), 그것이 종으로 8구간(198개 중대)으로 구성되어 자리하고 있었다. 신입생 부대는 2개 중대, 8개 구대로 편성되었고, 1개 콘세트에 2개 분대(1개분대 9명 내외)가 수용되었다.

배정된 콘세트 안으로 들어가 보니, 물론 냉난방시설은 없고, 한가운데 통로(폭 약 1미터)를 따라 좌우에 철침대가 죽 놓여 있고 가운데쯤에 관물함(옷장겸용)으로 양개 분대를 분리해 놓은 것을 볼 수 있었다. 그런데, 내 자리는 하고 두리번거리자 내 눈에 내 이름과 교번이 적힌 명찰들이 들어 왔다. 나는 평생 처음으로 내 이름이 또렷하게 적혀 있는 침대와 그 옆에 놓인 관물장 즉 옷장을 찾아가, 보고 또 보며, 순간 '문영일'이라는 내 존재를 육사가 국가가 그리고 생도대가 알고 있고 또 나타내 주었다는데 대해 감개무량했고, 이러한 대우에 만족하며 내 존재에 긍지를 느끼며 마음속으로 이들(국가와 군 당국)에게 대단히 감사했다.

내 교번은 '704번'으로 1기생 1번으로 시작하여 704명째 입교자인 동시에, 4기 동기에서

는 651번으로 시작하여 성적순으로 259명 중 54번째로 입교했다는 것이다. 이 교번은 생도 생활 4년 동안 나를 대표하였고 동시에 정규 육사 4년제 생도 순번에서 육사가 소멸되지 않는 한, 정해진 영원한 순서 교번이었다. 그래서 생도 때는 언제나 "예! 704번 문.영.일!"이었다.

더구나 내 이름이 똑똑하게 적혀 있는 관물장(官物欌)을 열어보니, 진해에 갔을 때 재었던 여름 생도 정장과 예복 세트가 걸려 있고, 그 오른쪽 칸에는 정모와 여름 간편복과 체육복 그리고 미제 국방색 '롱 타올' 등이 두부모처럼 기계로 만들어 낸 듯이 각지게 잘 정리되어 있었다. 실은 오늘 저녁부터 당장 그렇게 정리정돈하기를 강요받을 줄은 아직 미처 모르고 그저 또 한 번 감동하였다.

드디어 이날, 4287년(1954년) 7월 1일, 오전 10시에 제2연병장에서 하계 육사생도 정복을 입고 259명이, 우리 동기로서는 물론 정규 육사 창설 이래 처음으로, 태릉 육사 연병장에서 '군인선서식'을 겸하여 '역사적인 입교식'을 거행하였다.

◇ 절벽에서 떨어트려진 새끼 사자의 생존 단련

이제 '태릉 육사'에서 처음으로 4년제 정규 육군사관생도 생활을 시작한 우리 4기 생도들은, 우선 2개월간의 하계(夏季) '기초군사훈련'을 받기 시작하였다. 육군사관학교 교육훈련이란, 크게 일반학기 학술교육과 하계 2개월간 군사훈련으로 대별한다. 거기에 신입생에게는 입학식에 이어 바로 1학년 하계 군사훈련을 받는데, 이를 '기초군사훈련'이라 한다. 군대 기초군사 교육훈련인 신입생 하계 기초군사훈련은 주로 군인 기초 심신단련과 기초전술 교육훈련이기에, 실제로 간단명료한 원리를 반복 실습하여 완전히 몸과 마음과 정신에 주입하여, 습관화되도록 하는 것이다. 2개월간에 2개 과정으로 나누어, 첫 1개월은 주로 교내(내무반, 교실, 연병장)에서, 다음 1개월은 교외훈련 즉 태능 숲속에서부터 남한산성에 이르기까지 서울과 경기 동남부지역 일대에서 실시되었다.

첫 단계 교내훈련은, 전적으로 조교 생도(3학년 모범생도) 지도하에 모든 훈련이 실시되고, 후기는 자치 생활이라 하여, 조교 생도의 지명에 의해 임명된 신입생 자치 분대장 생도가 남은 1개월 동안 분대를 대표하고 자치 내무 생활을 해 나간다. 물론 여전히 조교 생도는 있었으나, 다만 4학년 생도로 된 구대장(區隊長)이 자치 분대장 생도들을 감독 지휘하였다.

할아버지도 그 후기 자치 분대장 생도로 선발되어 1개월간 일반훈련에다 추가하여 거의 봉사하는 근무 기간을 보내 보았다. 그 기간은 어려웠으나 그래도 선발된 긍지와 동시에, 특히 같이 선발 자치 분대장 생도로 근무하게 된 이웃 분대 동기 박정기 생도—그때부터 평생 친구가 되었다—를 알게 된 것이 가장 큰 보람이었다.

신입생의 기초군사훈련을 책임진 상급생 조교 생도는 훈련을 시작하기 전에 이렇게 선언한다. "사자는 새끼를 낳아 천길 낭떨어지에 떨어뜨려 살아남는 놈만을 자기 새끼로 키운다. 제군들에게 가해지는 이 기초군사훈련은 절벽에서 떨어진 새끼 사자와도 같이 쓰라린 시련을 겪게 하는 것이니 여기에서 낙오한 자는 우리의 이 보람찬 대열에서 서지 못할 것이며, 역경을 극복한 자에게는 영광의 문이 열리는 것이다."라고 하면서 우리를 선무하고 동시에 우리의 의기(意氣 Spirit)를 한껏 북돋우었다.

특히 군인으로서 국가에 충성하는 결의를 나타내는 경례법, 완벽한 전투 준비 생활화를 상징하는 똑바른 군복 착용법, 허위와 위선을 배격하고 파사현정의 길을 걷는 직각 보행과, 평상시는 물론 위기에서도 장교와 장차 장수로서의 의연함을 보여주는 식사 행위와 '세계적 신사'—Gentleman, International Standard—수양을 위한 직각 식사법이 있다.

그리고 항재전장(恒在戰場) 의식과 함께 치밀하고도 완벽한 전투 준비 태세를 습관화하는 관물 정리정돈법, 그러기에 이는 내무 점수 삭감의 주범이 되고 학교 성적 기록에 영향을 미치는 것이기에, 모두가 심지어는 침을 발라가며 두부모 각을 내어야 했고, 그래도 일석 점호시에는 지적 감이요, 흔히 고의적 기압감이 되기도 했다. 기타 관물 및 군장품 관리법 특히 구두와 예복용 장식인 벅클 등은 '슈샤인보이' 못지않게 지급된 미제구두약과 '브랏소'를 이용하여 광을 내었다. 이 모두는 개인(사고와 행동)을 통제하여, 구성(군대, 내무생활 단위 공동체)원 즉 단체 상호협력과 전우애를 확립하고 밖으로는 명실공히 '국제 젠틀맨 스탄다드'를 지향하였다.

개인 위생(개인 청결)은 어디까지나 '개인 책임'임을 강조하면서 특히 주말 점호 때 심지어 팬티까지 벗고 검사하기도 하였다. 그리고 단체 위생과 관련하여 내무반 청소는 반듯이 매일과 주말 점검을 실시하였다. 생도 회장실은, 당시는 변소(便所)라 불렀는데, 생도대 변소는 재래식으로 내무반 지역 남편 언덕에 있었고, 비바람을 막을 수 있을 정도의 목재 건물 속에 있었으며, 매일 나무 바닥과 주변 청소를 했다.

◇ 3보 이상 구보의 하루하루

기초군사훈련 중 내무 생활에는 쉰다는 개념은 없다. 내무반 내외에서 한 동작 끝나면 다음 과정을 대기하거나 다음 동작으로 이전하는 것이지 휴식 시간이란 따로 없다. 물론 내무반 안에서도 책 보고 앉아 있는 한가한 시간은 없고, 문밖에 한 발이라도 나오면, 식당에서 숟가락 '직각 식사'에 버금가는 '직각 보행'에다 '3보 이상 구보'를 해야한다. 그러니 조금 먼 곳에 있는 변소나 저 밑에 있는 세면장에 드나들 때는 더 말할 것도 없이 직진 속보 아니면 구보다. 그러나 10시 소등 이후에는 금방 쥐 죽은 듯 고요해지며 즉시 누운 자리에서 자유의 천국행이다. 그리고 주말 토요일 오후부터 일요일 일석 점호 때까지는 숨 돌려가며 쉬어가며 편지 써가며 빨래 해가며 시간 가는 줄 모르다가, 특히나 휴일 일석 점호를 조교 생도가 선심으로 '취침점호'라 하면 그 순간에는 지극히 행복해지기도 한다. 그러나 그것조차 초기엔 몇 차례, 조교 생도에 따라 다르게 빼앗아 가기도 했다.

◇ 땡볕 속 연병장훈련

연병장은 태릉 숲속이 아닌, 그 옆의 풀 한 포기 볼 수 없는 맨땅바닥, 문자 그대로 '연병장(練兵場)'에서 7, 8월의 땅바닥 온도 평균 35도 섭씨 이상에서 펄펄 끓고 있는 그런 곳이었다.

사실, 기초군사훈련 동안에는 학교가 태릉 근처 어디쯤 있는지조차도 모를 만큼, 학교 교훈인 '지·인·용'의 깊은 뜻을 삭일 지능의 작동도 멈추어 둔 체, 그저 매일 매시간 분초를 헤아리며 '차렷', '경례', '직각 보행', '직각 식사', '제식훈련', '16개 동작 우로어께 총', '36개 방향 앞으로 가', 교가 또는 군가를 부르며 분열 행진을 하는 등, 칼날 같은 시간 50분 교육훈련, 10분 휴식, 그리고 땀과 땀 속에 물(얼음을 넣은 워터백 물 꼭지로)을 마시고 소금 먹고, 또 물 마시고, 당시는 연병장 주위에 그늘나무를 찾을 수 없어 울타리를 겸한, 무릎 높이도 안되는, 20센티도 되지 않을 폭의 관목, 그것도 그늘이라고 마치 타조가 급하면 얼굴만 땅속에 묻는다는 식으로 우리도 다투어 얼굴만 그 속으로 밀어 넣어 휴식 시간 10분을 그래도 쉬는 채 해보았다.

그리고 특히나 총검술 훈련 시간은 완전히 기압(氣壓)받는 시간이었다. 총검술(銃劍術, Bayonet exercises)이란 주로 전투 마지막 순간 피아간에 적과 1대1로 마주쳤을 때, 문자 그대로 내가 가진 총과 칼을 사용하여 적을 1격에 공격, 적을 물리치고 나는 살아나는 기술(전술)이다. 때문에 내 총과 칼을 평소에 막대기 다루듯 능수능란할 수 있도록 숙달시키는 것이 이 훈련의 요체이다.

그러기에 무게 5kg여에 달하는 M1소총에 총칼(단검)까지 꽂으면 7kg여인데, 이를 양손으로 움켜쥔 채 쭉 뻗어서 몸 아래위 옆으로 돌리다가 몸도 함께 앞뒤 옆으로 따라 돌리면서, 적이 내게로 뻗어오는 총칼을 즉시 피하면서 그 주인을 향해 내 총칼을 찔러 넣어야 하는 하나의 무술인 것이다.

때문에 그 기본 동작에 속도까지 더하여 휘두르고 무찌르기를 몇 번 반복하다 보면 이 훈련이야말로 교관과 생도 사이에 갈등이 섞이지 않은 대기압이 되는 것이다. 그만큼 힘이 들었는데, 알고 보면 이 총검술 훈련이야말로 군인 정신 배양에 큰 한몫을 차지하는 훈련 종목이었다. 그러기에 한편 얄궂게도 상급 생도가 후배 생도 기압 줄 때 가장 흔히 사용하는 수단이 되기도 하였다.

기초군사훈련 제2단계로 구분되는 8월이 되면, 물론 본격적인 군사학교육이나 연구단계는 아니고, 약간의 실내교육과 함께 태능에 임시로 조성한 사격장에서, 임관후 부대원들을 지도할 수 있는 능력배양을 위한 사격훈련, 각종 구기훈련과 규칙 연구를 한다. 그리고 마무리 체력 단련으로 야외 단계별 구보훈련, 태릉 숲속에서 이전에 실습했던 각개전투훈련을 종합하여 마무리하는 분대 각개전투훈련이 실시된다. 그리고는 이어서 단계별 행군훈련을 시작한다.

◇ 종합행군훈련 겸 남한산성 병자호란 전사 탐방

기초군사훈련의 대미를 장식하는 마지막 종합훈련은 바로 남한산성(南漢山城) 1박 2일, 실거리 약 60km, 역사 탐방을 겸한 완전 무장 행군이었다. 학교 정문을 나와 남방을 향해 역시나 한독약품(화이자) 앞을 지나—당시 시야에 들어 온 사방은 행군 때면 항상 지나가는 한독약품, 좀 멀리 동으로 망우 기차역, 서로는 좀 멀리 청량리 위생병원, 남북으로 따라 흐르는 중랑천과 그 위에 동서로 걸쳐진 중랑교, 그리고는 훤하게 논과 밭이 모두였다—남으로 죽 내려가다가, 아차산을 끼고 동남으로 방향을 바꾸어, 당시 한강에 놓인 2번째 인도교(1936년 현대식 건설, 첫 인도교는 한강대교 1917년)인 광진교를 이용하여 한강을 건넜다.

그리하여 잠실과 송파를 지나 남한산성으로 등산하여 남문을 통해서 입성하였다. 남한산성(南漢山城)은 조선조 수도 서울인 한양 방어를 위해 조성된 주변 전략적 요충 거점 3곳 중 하나였다. 전통적인 핵심 거점은 해협을 방패 삼은 강화도다. 그 둘은 지대내 생존 여건과 성곽 방어 능력이 유력하다고 판단되는 남한산성이고 그다음이 깊은 골짜기를 다수 확보하고 공자에게 불리한 지형지물을 제공해 주는 북한산성이 있었다. 남한산성의 북동편은 상당한 개활지로 농작이 가능하여 산성 농성에 유리한 조건을 제공하였다. 그래서 그때 할아버지는 남한산성을 둘러보고 특히나 북쪽에 한강을 바라보면서 이 지역이야말로 역사적으로나 지형적으로나 대한민국 육사 교육의 요람지가 되기를 즉, 현 태릉에서 이곳으로 육사를 이전하는 것이 좋겠다는 생각을 해 보았다.

병자호란(丙子胡亂, 1636) 때는 청나라 태종이, 명나라를 정벌하기 이전에 후방 안전을 확보하기 위해, 12만 명의 정예군을 지휘하여 조선으로 공격해 들어왔다. 그리하여 왕자와 왕실 주력 일부가 피난 중인 강화도를 비롯하여 조선조 전 지역을 석권하였다. 그리하여 마지막으로 그 주력이 현재 송파 거리 즉 남한산성 턱밑인 탄천을 연하여 주둔하면서 남한산성 전체를 포위하고 인조의 항복을 겁박하고 있었다. 청군은 조선조 외부 지원군의 접근과 성 내외 연결작전을 차단하면서, 주력군은 연일 산 위를 향해 공성의 기세를 놓지 않는 가운데 장기전(絶糧作戰)을 시도하였다. 수차에 걸쳐 전국에서 산성 사방으로 구원군이 성 내외 연결 작전 또는 성내군 증원 작전을 시도하였으나 모두 무력하고 비 작전 계획적이어서 청군에게 차단 또는 격퇴당하고 말았다.

그리하여 완전히 고립된 성내 1만 3000여 명의 조선군은 격렬한 방어전을 전개하며 43일간을 버티다가, 강화도에 간 왕자가 항복하여 인질이 되고 조선군에 의한 구원은 희망이 없고 저장된 군량미는 거의 소진되었기에 부득이 국치와 개인적 능욕을 무릅쓰고 항복할 수밖에 없었다. 그리하여 남한산성 밑 삼전도(三田渡)—1954년 당시는 현 가락시장 근처 논밭으로 기억—에 내려가 조선조 국왕 인조는, 청 태종 앞에 엎드려, 소위 삼궤구고두(三跪九顧頭), 즉 세 번 큰절하면서 9번 이마 조아리기로 항복의 예를 행하였다. 우리는 남한산성에서 이 같은 역사를 연구하고 현장을 답사한 뒤에 그 길을 따라 하산한 뒤 삼전도비석 앞에 가서 국치 역사의 현장을 확인하고 새삼 조국을 그 어느 나라도 침노하지 못하는 국방에 충성을 다할 것을 다짐하였다.

그날 오후에는 비바람 속에 송파 언덕에서 야영을 하고, 다음 날 오던 길 그대로 하계 기초군사훈련의 대미를 장식하는 귀교 행군을 실시하였다. 드디어 우리 행군 대열이 학교 정문에 도착하자, 학교 군악대의 "만세 만만세 우리 장사들 돌아오누나…" 힘찬 연주 소리가 태능 하늘에 울려 퍼졌고, 그와 함께 학교 전 간부들의 환영 박수를 받으면서 우리는 기초

군사훈련의 대장정을 마무리하며 학교로 돌아왔다. 특히 그 군악대의 「승리의 노래」는 지금도 귀에 쟁쟁하다.

고난도의 훈련 고비마다 그 순간마다 '이것이 국가에 대한 충성이다'고 속으로 외치면서 극복해 내었던 지난 2개월이 주마등같이 회상되었다. 이렇게 대미를 장식함으로서 평생 잊지 못하는 육사생도 기초군사훈련과정을 마치게 되었다. 이리하여 2달 전까지의 청년 시민모습은 이제 간데없고 씩씩한 육사생도로 완전히 탈바꿈하게 되었던 것이다.

2. 1학년 생도의 일반 학기 내무·학과 생활(1954.9~1955.6)

◇ '3금지대(三禁地帶)' 생활, 군사학과 문·리(文·理)학 병행 수업

8월 말이 되자 2, 3, 4학년 상급생들이 모두 일제히 도착하였다, 그들은 지금까지의 진해(鎭海) 생활을 뒤로 하고 대망의 서울 태릉 화랑대로 올라온 것이다. 아마도 신입생인 우리보다 그들이 더 기대가 컷을 것으로 생각된다. 이제는 4개 학년이 완전하게 구성된 본격적인 대한민국 육군사관학교가 되었다는 사실에 흥분도 되었을 것이었다. 더구나 그 참담)했다던 진해, 춥고 배고팠던 생활을 뒤로하고 새로운 기대도 컷을 것이다.

육군사관학교는 역시나 학문의 전당이기 이전에 군대이기에 모든 편성은 군대 그대로이다. 육사는 크게 학교 본부, 교수부, 생도대 그리고 이를 지원하는 근무지원대로 편성되었다. 생도 생활의 본거인 생도대(生徒隊)는 훈육부서로 생도대장(육군 준장), 부대장(중령), 생도 8개 중대 훈육관(소령 각 1명), 체육과(과장 소령, 특기 담당교관 약간 명)로 편성되었다. 이들은 사관생도 자치 조직인 생도연대를 훈육하고 지원한다.

생도연대는 2개 대대 8개 중대로 구성된 생도 자치연대로서, 이를 지휘(만)하기 위한 생도 연대본부에 연대장 생도와 부관 생도 그리고 4개 참모 생도가 있고, 그 아래에 2개 대대장 생도 와 그 아래에 8개 중대장 생도가 임명되어 1년간 근무한다. 1개 중대는 2개구대로, 1개구대는 2개 내무반 4개 분대로 편성되었다. 1개 분대는 대략 8~9명으로, 분대장 3학년생도 1~2명, 아래 2학년생도 3명, 1학년생도 3~4명으로 되었다. 4학년 생도들은 독립된 별도 자치내무반을 구성하였다.

모든 일과와 생활은 각 생도 독립생활이나 2개 분대가 상하의 계급을 가지고 한 지붕 아래 생활하기 위해서는 단체 생활의 임무와 의무가 있게 마련이다. 실내 청소는 물론 1학년, 야간 실외 보초 물론 1학년, 기타 공용 용무(보급품 수령 분배 등)도 주로 1학년 임무요 의무다.

육사생도대 생활에는 '명예제도(Honer System)'와 지도자(지휘관) 수양을 위해 생활 통제의 한 규칙인 소위 '육사 3금제도' 등은 아주 철저하고도 엄격하였다. 잘 알려져 있는 바와같이 명예제도(名譽制度)란 곧, 거짓 행위(예, 컨닝 등)와 거짓말을 하지 않는 것으로, 이를 보고도 묵인하는 것까지 처벌(퇴교) 대상이다. 그리고 '3금(禁)제도'란, '금여(혼), 금주, 금연'으로 여자와의 부적절한 관계나 결혼을 금지하고, 물론 교내외에서 금주와 동시에 어느 곳에서도 금연하는 제도이다. 이를 어기면 '명예위원회(생도들로 구성된 자치체)'에 회부되고, 인정되면 가차 없이 퇴교 처분된다.

이 제도야말로 육사생도 수양을 위해서뿐 만 아니라 앞으로 국가와 사회에서 모범 생활을 할 청년들에게는 필수적인 규정이고 덕목인 것이다. 실제로 육사생도 생활 중에 이 규정으로 조치된 자에 대한 소문을 별로 들어 본 적이 없거니와 특히 우리 동기생은 전혀 없었다고 기억된다. 다시 말하면 수양의 도장인 육사에는 이런 규정이 반듯이 지켜져야 하고 그것은 실제로 가능하여 졸업후 각계각층의 지휘관의 덕목으로 작용하였다.

◇ 학교 대표 '럭비부' 선수 생활과 일반학 중첩 생활

그날은, 어찌된 영문인지는 모르나 내무반 지역에서, 한눈으로 보아도 당당한 스포츠맨으로 보이는 한 3학년 상급생이 다가오더니 나를 불러 세우고는 무턱대고 물었다. "어이 귀관, 탁구 잘하지?", "아 아닙니다, 못합니다"—실제로 그때까지 그런 것 만져보지를 못했다—. 그랬더니 "아 그럼 그렇지, 내일 럭비부로 와!" 나는 고향에서 그동안 조금은 어머니를 도와 시장 옷 가게 봇짐을 아침저녁으로 어깨에 메고 집과 시장터를 몇 왕복함으로서 아마도 체격이 운동선수 모양이긴 하였다.

그래서 생도대 내무반 길거리에서, 불과 3분 정도의 면접으로 본의 아니게도 육사 럭비 대표선수로 선발이 되었다.—이후에도 육사 대표 운동선수들은 입교 후 신입생 중에 무작위 현장 면접으로 선발되어 혹독하리만큼 훈련을 거쳐 년중 1~3번 정도 있는 외부 시합에 출전한다.

그리하여 나도 신편된 생도(연)대 제6중대의 4내무반 즉 '학교 대표 럭비선수 내무반'에 편성되었다. 문자 그대로 졸지에 1954년도 육사 대표 럭비선수가 되어 학과 생활과 동시에 내무 생활,—우리 선수들은 3학년 이하 모두 한 내무반에 기거— 그리고 병행해서 학교 대표 선수 생활, 당시는 대한민국에 성인팀은 거의 없었기에 오로지 앞으로 개최될 3군사관학교 대항 시합 준비만을 위한 훈련을 시작하게 되었다.

그런데, 1학년 일반 학기의 내무 생활 얘기 또한 일상의 생도 생활 얘기이기에 아주 단순하게 보이기도 하나 사실은 '깊고도 많은 애환과 애증의 얘기'를 포함하고 있다. 특히 1954~55년도의 1학년 생활이 그러하였다. 그러기에 실감이 나기 위해서는 오히려 몇 가지 일화를 소개하는 것이 좋을 것 같다.

1학년 생도는 내무반 편성에서 보는 바와 같이 한 내무반 한 분대 내에서 층층시하에 노이게 되어 거동이 지극히 조심스럽고 할 일은 어렵고도 많다. 내무반 안팎으로 매사에 'Old boy first'이고 다만, 궂은일은 'Junior first'로 도맡아 한다. 그러나 반면에 바로 옆 침대에서 함께 생활하니 상급생의 간섭을 받게 되는 건 물론이지만 동시에 형제지간의 지도와 편달도 받고, 정도 들고, 인연도 되어 군대 생활 내내 유익한 점이 더 많기도 하다. 사실상 어려운 일이란 것도 실내외 청소이고 보급품 수령 및 분배 그리고는 상급자에 대한 예의 정도이다.

◇ 사관생도 일과 시간

일반학과 기간에는 전 생도가 똑같이 하루 일과를 시행한다. 시작은 언제나 같이 새벽 6시, 실내 스피커에서 나오는 기상 나팔 소리—'억지로~ 억지로~'로 들린다?—에, 마치 전기를 탄 듯 벌떡 일어나 이불 개고, 메트레스 반 접고, 바닥 청소를 위해 철침대 빈칸에 밑에 놓아둔 군화와 운동화, 세면기 그리고 휴가용 '보스톤 백' 등을 올려놓고, 마치 100미터 시합하듯 500여 미터 멀리 있는 연병장(각 대대별)으로 가서 일조 점호를 실시한다.

인원 파악 보고, 애국가 4절까지 봉창, 사관생도의 맹세 제창, 각자 고향을 향해 돌아서서 부모 형제에 대한 묵념 인사. 일조 점호가 끝나면 빠른 걸음으로 돌아와 세면장행, 어서 돌아와 침구 정리—두 부모보다 똑 바르게, 그리고 바닥 청소 후 신발 정돈하고 조식 집합, 돌아와 학과 출장 준비, 그리고 7시 40분, 전 연대 생도가 동시에 학과 출장 집합한다. 교가와 군가 등을 합창하면서 학년 별로 집단으로 자기 교실 앞까지 행진해 가서 각 교실로 해산해 들어간다.

그래서 8시 정각에 학과 개시, 학과 시간 단위는 60분이고 50분 수업에 10분간 휴식 겸 교실 이동, 11시 50분에 일단 내무반으로 돌아와, 다시 식사 집합하여 전체가 동시에 12시 점심, 다시 내무반으로 내려왔다가, 다시 교실로 가서 1시에 오후 학과 개시, 15시 학과 끝, 이후 전생도 일제히 석식(18시)까지 자습 및 자유시간, 다만 학교 대표 운동선수 특히 매년 3군사관학교 체육대회 메뉴인 럭비와 축구 부원은 3시부터 5시까지 의무적으로 운동장에서 운동 연습 실시, 19시~21시 야간 학습 출장, 21시 30분에 일석 점호, 22.00시 소등. 하루 일과 끝.

학교 수업, 즉 학과는 당시는 미국식으로 9월에 시작하여 12월 하순에 1학기 종료하고 방학, 즉 겨울 휴가를 가며, 2학기는 1월에 시작하여 6월 중순까지이고, 약 10일간의 여름휴가를 가진 뒤 7, 8월 2개월 간은 하계 군사훈련 기간이었다. 1학년은 태능 육사에서 기초군사훈련을, 2학년은 육군의 주요 전투병과(보병·포병·전차·통신·공병, 5개 병과)를 순회 교육훈련 받으며, 3학년은 육군·해군·해병대·공군을 각 사관학교 방문과 함께 현장 순회 교육 받고, 4학년이 되면 하계 훈련 기간 중 최일선 전방부대 소대장 근무실습을 실시한다.

◇ 장군 교반, 'daily 시스템, Honour 시스템'

교과 수준은, 미국 West Point 육사 교과를 거의 그대로 옮겨왔기에 선진국 수준이었고, 더구나 6·25 전시 직후라 서울대 등 시내 유수 대학의 유명 교수들이 대위 계급으로 시작하는 예우로 초빙되어, 한국 최초일 수 있는 4년제 사관학교 생도들을 위해서 아주 성의껏 가르쳐주고 때로는 생도대 훈육관들보다 더 애국심과 군대식 규율을 강조하기도 하였다.

경제 분야에 '케인즈'와 사무엘슨의 경제학과 국부론에 거시, 미시 경제학 등, 정치학에 비교 정부론 등, 인문 학습은 물론, 측량학도 실습을 겸하여 학습하였다. 특히 건축학에서는, 당시 무너져 내려앉아 있던 제1한강교(인도교, 지금의 한강대교)의 손상된 교각을 설계하고 제작하는 현장을 방문하여 'I—beam'을 계산해 보는 등 실습도 하였고, 병기학에서 일반 병기는 물론, 군용 자동차 엔진을 분해결합 해 보기도 하였다. 후에 우리 동기생 공학교수 한 사람은 국산 자동차 엔진 제작 선구자가 되어 한때 그 학계 수장이 되기도 하였다.

또 미국 육사식으로, 특이한 'Daily System'을 적용하였다. 그래서 50분 수업에 40분 강의 및 토의 후 10분간 시험—'명예제도(Honor System)'라고 하며 거짓말은 절대로 용서가 없다, 그 일환으로 시험 칠 때도 교수가 시험지를 나누어 주고 출제한 뒤 가고, 생도들은 10분간 시험하고 반장이 '시험 끝 퇴장' 선언하면 그 즉시 연필 놓고 퇴장하며, 시험지는 반장이 거두어서 교수에게 제출한다. 이 점은 완전해서 이를 위반해서 퇴교한 동기생은 4년 내 들어 본 적이 없다.

교반 편성을 보면, 한 학년을 20명 내로 하여 12개교 반으로, 이를 A, B조 각 6개 교반(教班)을 편성한다. 매월 성적 결과에 따라 성적순으로 제1교반에서 제6교반으로 소속하게된다. 1학년 1학기는 시작 때는 입교 성적 순으로 편성되었는데 할아버지는 많은 과목에서 1교반에 편서되었었다. 그래서 1교반은 '우등생(한 학년 2명 내외)' 후보 교반이나, 6교반은 흔히, 아니 전설적으로 '장군 교반'으로 위로와 격려를 겸하여 불려졌다. 그런데 실제로 몇십 년 세월이 흐른 뒤 실제로 6교반 출신에서 장군들이 많이 배출되었다. 이 할아버지도 전사(戰史) 과목에 시간을 많이 할애하다 보니 이과 과목에서 '장군 교반'에 몇 번 편성되기도 하였다.

매 월말이 되면 교수부 게시판에 그동안 시험 친 각 과목별 성적과, 그 결과 신 교반 편성이 공시되고, 한 학년말 성적은 심지어 고향 집의 학부형에게 우송 전달도 되었다. 그런데 이 게시판 앞에서도 1학년은 직각 보행으로 행동해야 하며, 게시판을 볼 때도 자세가 불량하면 2학년 상급생에 의한 특성 훈련감이 된다. 할아버지는 '김복동 4학년 선배(夏訓구대장)'가 말한바 "남자가 소심하게 성적표를 들여다 보아야 하느냐"는 말을 좋게 생각하고 게시판을 멀리하였다.

한편 1학년 학기말에 종합 기말고시 결과 60여 명이 낙제 점수에 해당되어 남과 같은 때 휴가도 못 가고 학교에 남아서 3일간 자습한 뒤 소위 추가시험을 치르고, 그 결과 50여 명이 성적 미달로 그 즉시 퇴교 되기도 하였다. 그 후 2학년이 되어서도 성적 미달 생도를 도태시켰는데, 우리 동기생은 애당초 259명 입교하여 졸업 즉 임관할 때는 179명— 약 35% 탈락—이 되었다. 대부분이 1학년 기말시험 결과 도태자였다. 참으로 육사 교육은 여러모로 원칙과 정직 그리고 엄정 그대로였다.

◇ 학교 대표 럭비 선수 생활—과외훈련과 학습 부담 갈등

할아버지는 비교적 양호한 성적으로 육사에 합격하여 초기에는 모든 학과가 1교반 등 상급반으로 편성되었다. 그래서 학과 초기에는 대부분의 과목이 고등학교 과목의 연장선상 수준이라 방심하였고, 또 '데일리 시스템'이 시간 내 외우기 위주의 시험이요 그 결과라 멋없다 생각하여 소홀하였다. 특히나 모두가 공부에 열중하는 과외 자유시간에는, 전적으로 내게는 과격한 럭비 운동 훈련을 매일 함으로서, 공부 시간을 제한받는 것은 물론, 신체적 피곤이 누적되어 날이 가면서 학업 성적이 저감됨을 면치 못했다.

이미 말한 바와 같이 나는 럭비 대표 선수 상급생에 의해 급행으로 선발되어, 전혀 생각할 겨를없이, 선수 내무반으로 편성되 가서 선수 생활을 하게 되었던 것이다. 그렇다고 해서 억지로 생활하게 된 것은 아니다. 사실인즉 그것은 행운이요 영광된 사건이었다. 그래서 연습 시간마다 자유 학습 시간을 희생하고 대신 힘을 다해 연습하고 단련하였다. 내 연습 포지션은 스크람조 포와드 왼편 날개 즉 번호 1번이었다.

오후 3시에 연병장에 나가면 먼저 가벼운 구보와 준비 운동부터 시작하여, 댓쉬(Dash), 패스, 그리고 볼을 가진 상대를 향해 정면 또는 후면 돌격 태클 연습, 그리고 형세 불리할 때는 볼을 가슴에 안고 절대 빼앗기거나 놓지지 않기 위해 등을 상대편으로 드러누워 밟히고 채이는 연습, 그리고 H 크로스바(골문) 넘기기 킥 연습, 그리고 볼을 받아 뎃시해서 골라인 선상 또는 H 바 후방에 텃치(TOUCH) 하거나 공을 안고 몸 전체로 튜라이(TRY)/센터 츄라이 등등의 연습 훈련.

다음에는 포지션에 따른 훈련, 나는 스크람 포워드 1번이기에 상대 스크람 조와 동시에 격돌하여 제압하고, 앞으로 밀고 나가기 또는 밀리지 않으려고 결사적으로 스파이크를 전면 땅에 붙이고 버티기, 그리고 볼을 발밑에 끼고 옆으로 스크람 전체 돌기 등, 그런데 물론 그때는 사명감과 일체감 그리고 훈련 코치의 풋시로 하루하루 훈련을 넘기고 있었다. 아마도 그 때문에, 야간 자습 출장으로 교실에 가면 몸이 고단하여 그만 2시간 내내 잠 오는 것을 참아낼 수가 없었다, 그러니 하루 일과 중 오후 자습 시간과 야간 자습 시간 최소 4시간은 일반 동기생보다 희생될 수밖에 없었다. 거기에다 문리(文理)에 더 관심을 가진데다 정치·사회 관련 독서와 역사 탐구에 치중하다 보니 1학년 기말시험과 2학년 1학기말시험에 물리와 수학 과목 추가 시험을 치르기도 하였다. 그래서 아쉽기 짝이 없었으나 2학년으로 오르면서 '학교 대표 럭비선수' 생활을 자퇴하였다.

* 참고로 물론 그때도 내가 좌심방판막증이 있다는 사실을 전혀 모르고 있었다. 심장판막증이란, 심장내 4개의 심방 출입을 지키는 4개의 판막이 협착이나 폐쇄부전 등의 고장으로 피의 흐름이 일정하지 않거나 혈액이 역류되는 상태를 의미한다. 선천적 또는 후천적 원인은 알 수 없으나 아마도 사관학교 이전 오래전부터 있어 온 현상으로 짐작되며, 당시 군입대용 약식 신체 검사시는 감지가 곤란하였을 것이다. 평상시는 불감이나 증상은 1. 심장에 무리가 가면 숨차고, 진행되면 호흡곤란, 2. 피 순환장애로 쉽게 피로하고 어지러움, 3. 기침 가래와 함께 흉통 증상도 발생할 수도 있다는 고질병이다.

◇ 1학년의 첫 휴가(1954.12.23~1955.1.2)

생애를 두고 이렇게 즐겁고 기뻤던 날로 추억되는 것 중에 이 '첫 휴가' 만한 것은 더 없었다. 그것은 6월 하순에 집 떠나 12월 하순까지 타향 그것도 군대하고도 특별하고 엄격한, 외출 휴가 단 하루도 없었던 육군사관학교 1학년 1학기 생도 생활을 마치고 드디어, 그 기다리고 기다리던 부모 형제를 만날 수 있는—집 나가봐야 알 수 있는, 부모에게 효도하고 싶은 마음, 형제자매들에게 잘해 주고 싶은 마음을 드리기 위한—내 집으로의 휴가이기 때문이었으리라.

또 한 그것은 단 며칠간이라도 규칙과 시간 생활의 내무반과 공동체 생활에서 벗어나 자유와 인정이 넘치게 될 10일간 휴가, 크리스마스와 새해를 부모 가족 친구와 함께, 인정미 흐르는 고향 동네에서 보낼 수 있는, 특히나 부모님에 대한 효도의 마음이 절절하여, 정말 이렇게도 기다려지고 희망과 즐거움에 한껏 부풀러 올랐던 휴가(겸) 귀향 여행이기 때문이었다.

그래서 나라에서 마련해 준 '사관생도'만을 위한 특별 열차—당시만 해도 일반 열차는 가운데 통로는 물론 만원이라, 심지어는 짐을 올려놓는 선반에도 사람이 누워 밤새워(부산-서울)—가는 기차 형편에, 우리 전 생도들은 고향 가는 방향에 따라 자리 잡았는데, 특히 순 1학년 생도들만의 특별 전용칸이 배려되었다. 기차는 화랑대역을 떠나 서울역에서 각각의 노선에 따라 일반 열차 뒤에 연결되었으며, 고향을 향해서는 해 질 무렵에 서울역을 출발하여 밤새워 가서, 부산본역에는 다음 날 아침에야 도착하였다.

그런데 화랑대역 출발에서부터 우리는, 군가와 유행가 무엇이던 부르기 시작하여, 정말로 끊임없이 밤새워 부르고 또 불러서, 각 역에 동기들 하차해 갈 때도 노래하며 전송하고, 그리고 또 계속 노래하여, 부산 출신들의 하차역인 부산본역에 도착할 때까지 잠 한숨 안 자고 계속 불렀다. 아마도 그것으로도 다 풀리지 않았던 기분이라, 그 휴가 기다림이 그러하였다.

그런데 막상 집에 도착하여 부모님을 뵙고 인사를 드린 뒤 부터는—부모와 함께 지내며 '부모에게 효도해야 한다'는 초심은 어디가고—친구와 어울려 하루 이틀 사흘 가면서 부모님과의 지냄을 미루어 가다가, 그만 시간을 다 보내버렸다. 그래서 귀대(복교)하기 위해 집을 나설 때는 특히 부모님께 죄송한 마음으로, 다음에는 꼭 효도해야지 하고 속으로 변명 겸 다짐하면서 그리고 내려올 때와는 달리 서운하고 섭섭한 마음을 가지고 학교로 돌아갔다.

◇ 잊을 수 없는 '1955 남산 부활절 예배'

1학년 학업 중에도 주요 사적지 견학이 여러 곳 있었다. 바로 옆에 있는 '태릉'을 위시하여 남한산성, 동구릉, 그리고 강화도의 전적지와 '전등사'의 하룻밤 등 배움과 동시에 뜻깊은 경우도 많았다. 그런데 그중에서도 지금까지도 잊지 못하고 남아 있는 참 인상 깊었던 경우는, 바로 1955년 봄, 남산공원에서 거행된 한미 합동 민간인 '부활절 예배'였다. 다른 건 잊어버렸으나, 새벽 남산중앙공원의 그 신선함과 고요함과 지원 나온 미 8군 군악대 소속의 '트럼펫' 병이 단독으로 연주(부른)하는 찬송가 소리가 공중에 울려 퍼지면서, 메아리까지 치면서, 정말 신비하기 그지없었다. 그 소리는 마음과 뼛속에까지 스며들어 지금까지도 그때를 생각하면 그 신비에 여전히 사로잡히기도 한다.

3. 상급 생도 생활(1955~1957)

◇ 이승만 대통령, 정규 육사 재건하고 사랑하다

대한민국의 국부로 평가되는 이승만 대통령은 1952년, 비록 전선이 소강상태였으나 그래도 여전히 치열한 전투가 전개되고 있던 그 시점에, 한국군의 실질적인 전력 증강을 위해 미국에 요청하여, 국군 간부들을 미국 본토 군사학교에 교육훈련 차 유학 보내기로 하는 한편, 국내에서도 중단되었던 정규 군사 교육기관을 재개하거나 육군대학과 같은 고급 군사 교육기관을 설치하여 정예 국군 간부 배양에 심혈을 기울였다. 그리하여 1951년 10월, 진해 임시 교사에서 4년제 정규 육군사관학교로 재개하였고, 1954년 7월에 현 태릉 화랑대로 이전해 와 오늘에 이르고 있다.

이승만 대통령은 본인이 학구열에 불타 미국에서도 굴지의 대학에서 당시 미국 사회에서도 드문 학사, 석사, 박사학위를 취득함으로써, 학문이 국가 부흥 그리고 선진국으로의 대들보라는 교육사상을 포지하고 있었다. 그러기에 그는 전시에도 대학생은 군대를 일단 면제해 주었으며 외국 유학, 특히 미국 유학은 불법도 묵인할 정도였다.

그러한 이승만 대통령은 독립운동 시절에 그렇게도 가지고 싶었던 국군과 그 국군을 지휘 통솔할 군 핵심 간부를 양성하는 육군사관학교를, 당시 유엔군 사령관이던 미 육군 대장 벤프리트와 함께 대단한 관심을 가지고 지원하였으며, 대통령 임기 중 소망대로 일취월장하는 육사를 수시로 방문도 하고, 외국 귀빈이 오면 안내해 생도 퍼레이드를 소개하며 자랑하기도 하였다. 특히나 그의 독립운동의 한 기지였던 하와이 교포들을 초대하여 육군사관학교를 견학시키고 자랑하며 그들의 꿈에도 그리던 대한민국 국군의 참모습과 미래 모습을 보여주어 평생 소원을 풀어 주기도 하였다.

이승만 대통령은 육사를 찾아 생도들과 대면만 하면 언제나, "여~러분, 훌륭한 국군 지도자 되시고 위대한 이 나라 지도자 되세요, 대성공하세요~" 하면서 대한민국 국군의 미래를 크게 기대하면서 우리 생도들을 격려하였다.

◇ 이승만 대통령 생신 축하 서울 시가 행진, 3월 26일의 기억

특히 1955년 3월 26일 이승만 대통령 생신일부터는 서울 시내에서 육해공군사관학교 생도들을 앞세운 국군 시가 행진이 전개되었다. 그 행진 연습을 위해 행진 참가 부대들은 여의도 비행장—현재 여의도가 당시까지는 경항공기(연락기)용 비행장이었다—에서 2개월여 합숙 훈련을 하였는데, 사관생도들은 2월에 매주 1회씩 동참하여 연습하였다.

그런데 그때마다 육사생도대는 비포장 추럭을 이용하여 태릉에서 한남동을 거쳐 여의도로 왕복하였는데, 2월의 그 차가운 겨울철에 귀마개 없는 철모를 쓰고 트럭 위에 4열로, 한 손은 트럭 적재함 상단을 잡고 다른 한 손은 M1소총을 잡고 정열하여, 눈비 속에도 흔들리지 않는 생도 기개를 보이려고 직립 자세를 유지한 채 스쳐 가는 그 2~3월의 차가운 눈 비바람을 피할 수 없어, 닦지도 못한 채 장시간 인내하다 보니, 모두가 귀와 손발 동상에 걸려 평생 고질병이 되기도 하였다. 물론 그렇다고 해서 이승만 대통령을 원망해 본 적은 없거니와, 오히려 시가 행진 참여가 자랑스럽기만 하였다.

3월 26일 시가 행진 그날이 되면, 9시 이전에 전 부대는 현 시청 앞 서울 플라자호텔 입구—육사가 선두이기에—에서 서울역까지 정렬하여 10.00시 출발을 기다렸다. 그런데 그 시간까지 날씨는 잔뜩 흐리고 때로는 진눈깨비도 내려서, 힘 드려 정성으로 연습한 결과가 손상될까 걱정을 태산같이 하였는데, 아주 희한하게도 10.00시가 되어가면서 날씨는 쾌청으로 변해갔다. 정말 이승만 대통령이 하늘이 주신 통수권자로 회자될 수 있게 하였다.

그런데 이 기상 현상이 그 후 해마다 거의 같이 반복되었기에 나는 군대 생활 내내 이 현상을 잊지 않고 활용하였다. 특히 1987년 3월에 있었던 '한미연합 팀 스프리트(Team Spirit)' 기동 연습(演習)에 군단장으로 참여하였는데, 마지막 단계 공세 작전 계획에, 3월 26일 '헤리콥터 강습 작전'이 포함되었다. 그런데 역시나 그 전날부터 눈비 온다는 예보를 들은 연합군 지휘관이 상당히 염려하면서 내게 취소 여부 의견을 물어왔다. 나는 눈 딱 감고 단호하게 그러나 '3·26 이승만 생일날'을 확신하면서 'Go 사인'을 보내고 그 이유를 설명해 주었다. 그들은 웃으면서 내 말을 믿었다. 아니나 다르랴, 11.00 공격 개시 그 시간이 되자 그때까지 흐려서 시야를 가리고 있던 하늘이 맑아지면서 공격 준비 포병사격과 헬기 공중 기동작전이 계획대로 개시되고, 계속되어서 성공적으로 적을 포위하여 승리할 수 있었고, 그리하여 그해 '팀 스프리트 연습' 대미에 유종의 미를 거둘 수 있었다.

◇ 상무대(尙武臺, 전남 광주) 전투병과학교 교육훈련

하계 휴가 복귀와 동시 광주 상무대로 열차 이동하여 육군 5개 전투병과학교에서 교육훈련을 받게 되었다. 당시 광주에는 상무대(尙武臺)에 '육군전투병과 교육훈련사령부' 전교사(戰教司)가 있었고, 지대 내에는 김해에 있는 공병학교를 제외하고, 보병 주 전투병과인 보병학교를 비롯하여 포병학교, 기갑학교, 통신학교 그리고 부수 지원부대들이 있었다. 생도들은 전용 열차로 호남선 열차 여행을 하는 동안, 말로만 들어왔던 호남평야를 보면서 감개무량하였다. 그 드넓고, 까마득히 지평선이 보이는 호남평야 특히 만경평야는 자연스럽게 가슴을 펴게 하고 그 들판 가득한 녹색 볏잎의 흔들거림은 절로 마음을 배부르게 하였다.

2개월의 과정 중 제1단계로는 보병학교 과정을 이수하게 된다. 보병의 개인 무기인 M1 소총으로부터 시작하여, 중대 화기인 60미리 박격포, 3.5인치 대전차 로켓포, 대대화기인 81미리 박격포, 56미리 대전차 총 등, 장교로서 알아야 할 이론과 사격법은 물론 전술 적 용법과 동시 소부대(소대 중대 대대) 지휘관 지휘 요령을 강의듣고 실습한다. 또 대대급 참모학과 전술을 배우고 연습한다.

이어서 기갑학교에서는 전차의 구조와 기술 그리고 전술 지식을 배우고 익힌다. 포병학교에 가서는 포병 소개는 물론 포탄 유도 즉 착탄 관측 요령과 실사격 계산법 및 실사 요령 등을 익히고 통신학교에서는 보병부대 지휘 통신 장비와 사용 요령 그리고 전투 단위부대의 통신 체계를 배우고 익힌다. 그리하여 마지막 단계 교육훈련은 '비학'이라는 광대한 평지 실습장에서 '보전포 합동 시범'훈련을 견학한다.

◇ 생도들의 Proletariat 지식 성향

1959년 11월, 미국 상원 분과위원회에 '미국의 대아시아정책'이라는 이름의 '콜론 보고서(Colon Report)'가 '대한(對韓) 정책 권고서'용으로 제출되었다. 그 보고서의 핵심 내용은, 한국군의 '쿠데타 가능성은 희박하나 그러나 필연적'이라는 것이었다. 그러면서 그 가능성을 지적하여 가로되, 한국에서는 가난한 집안의 유능한 재원들이 학자금 때문에 대학교육이 국비인 사관학교에 들어가, '지식 프롤레타리아트 성향'으로 발전할 수 있는 청년장교가 되고 있다. 그런데 이들은 특권적 관리와 정치가에 분노를 가지고 있으며 폭발할 우려도 있다고 평가 및 전망도 하였다.

실제로 우리 정규 육사 4기생(1954년 입교)부터는 그전 선배들과 달리 90% 이상이 그해 고등학교 졸업생이었고, 이들은 최소 25대 1 이상의 경쟁률을 뚫고 사관생도가 되었으며, 그중에는 서울법대·의과대와 고려대 법대 등의 재학생들도 있었다. 더욱이 6기생(1956년 입교생)은 당시 한국 최우수 고등학교였던 경기고와 서울고에서 각 30여 명씩 집단으로 입교도 하였다. 듣건대 이들은 당시 경기와 서울고 교장을 지낸 유명한 김인규 교장이 육사로 와 직접 견문하고 체험해 본 후 자기 학교(두 고등학교 연임)에 가서, '대한민국 제1의 유망 대학교가 육사'라고 장려하였다고 한다.

그런데 당시 육사생도들은, 특히 재학 중 한때—임관 후 군대 생활을 통해서는 대한민국에 대한 위국헌신의 화신으로 정형된다—프롤레타리아트 적 사고와 행위를 나타내기도 한다. 그때는 그것이 아마도 국가에 대한 충성과 파사현정의 길로 인식되었기 때문이었다.

4. 이학사로 졸업과 동시 육군 소위로 임관

◇ 대한민국 육군 소위 임관의 영광을 부모님께 드립니다

1954년 7월 1일, 벼랑에 떨어트려졌던 '새끼 사자' 우리 4기생이, 그동안 '지·인·용'의 수신(修身)으로, 그리고 무어라 형언하기 어려운 물질적 정신적 고난도의 교육훈련을 이수하고, 이제 1958년 6월 16일에, 이학사 학위와 함께 당당한 대한민국 육군 소위로 영광스러운 임관을 하게 되었다. 더구나 내가 '부(富)보다는 영광을 돌려 드리겠다'고 마음으로 언약한 대로, 어머님만이라도—안타깝게도 아버님은 몸이 불편하셔서—졸업식장에 모시게 되어 한없는 행복을 느끼게 되었다. 이제 부모님께 이 아들이, 이 대한미국 육군 소위 임관의 영광을 드립니다.

◇ 육사(졸업)반지, 조국과 영원한 결혼반지

단기 4288년(1955) 정규 육사 1기 졸업식 그날부터 전통화되어 온, 깊은 의미를 담고 있는 '육사반지'를, 우리도 후배들의 정성으로 이런 금반지를 졸업 기념으로 증정받았다. 졸업식 그날 증정식도 겸하는데, 대형 모조 금반지 안으로 한 사람씩 지나 나오면 기다리던 바로 아래 15기 후배로부터 왼손 4번째 손가락에 직접 끼워 받았다. 우리에게 이 반지는 결혼반지 바로 그것으로 영원한 애인 우리 조국과의 결혼을 의미하였다. 이 반지는 실제 황금으로 항상 빛나기에, 언제 어디서나 굳은 지조를 견지하고, 반지 중앙에서 빛나는 주홍빛 루비와 같은 충성과 정열을 다 하라(한다)는 의미의 상징이 되었다. 그래서 이 반지는 평생 소지하며 '육사인'이라는 자부심의 상징이 되기도 한다.

반지에 얽힌 얘기야 수없이 많으나 한 가지만 한다면, 1995년에 미국대학 군사학과 방문교수(R.O.T.C의 Visiting Scholar) 시절, 〈미국전쟁역사학회〉 회원이 되어 그해 행사로 미국 워싱턴(D.C.) 행사—소련 스파이의 접선 방법 및 현장 답사와 실내 토의 등—에 참여하였다. 그런데 일행이 그날 일정으로 미국 CIA 본부 견학을 갔을 때, 우연히 내가 끼고 있는 반지(미국 육사반지와 닮았다)를 본 한 미국 신사가 말을 걸어왔다. "혹시 그 반지가 한국 육사 것이냐, 누구냐?" 자기는 미국 육사 1953년 졸업생으로 그해 임관과 동시 한국전쟁에 참전하였고 철의 삼각지 지금 '백골부대' 지역에서 전투하고 휴전을 맞이했고, 자기 육사반지는 '남강' 지역 전투 중에 분실했다고 했다. 그래서 나는 5년 선배로서 예우하고 그의 한국전 참전에 감사하였다. 그러자 그는 육사 출신 상호 관심사 얘기로, "우리 반지는 장교 집회 등에서 육사 출신끼리 상호 교신할 때 반지로 책상 밑을 두들겨서 신호를 보낸다"고 하면서 금방 한미 육사 출신끼리 동질감·친숙감을 나타내면서 친해졌던 일이 있었다.

◇ 육사에서 배우고 익힌 것, 나의 특성

∘ 전사 연구(Military History)

나는 소시적 학교에서 역사 공부에 능하였다. 초중고를 통해서 95점 아래로 내려간 적이 없다. 그래서 일찍부터 웰스의 『세계문화사』와 토인비의 『역사 연구』를 탐닉했고, 육사에서는 클라우제비쯔의 『전쟁론』, 토인비의 『문명사관』, 암파문고(岩波文庫)의 『왜 사회주의를 선택하는가』, 『사회사상』 등 역사와 사상개념 등도 사고를 넓히는 의미에서 통독하였으며, 특히 '미국 육사' 『전사교본』과 『전사부도』—임관 후 하퍼의 『전사 백과사전』—를, 학과 시간에는 물론 하루 종일 시간이 날 때마다 옆에 끼고 생활했다. 심지어 '추가시험'을 몇 번 치르면서도 특히 이과 계통 학과는 도외시하고, 교양지 독서와 군사학 특히 좀 더 광범위한 전사(戰史), 즉 전쟁 역사 연구에 골몰하였다. 그 덕분에 군사 실무에서 전략전술의 기본 지식으로서도 물론, 후일 국가 안보 전략 사상 연구에도 크나큰 도움이 되었다.

∘ 원리 원칙, 공평무사(公平無私), 공사 구분(公私區分), 신상필벌

말로는 쉬우나 행하기는 쉽지 않다. 자칫 인정사정과 의리와 법리까지 얽히고설켜 있기 때문이다. 나는 내 양심에 따라 내 의지에 따라 내가 믿는 인간적 도리에 따라 이를 이행하며 생활해 나갈 것을 신조로 하였다. 비록 대단한 모범은 아니지만 '옳다'고 믿는 것 즉 '원리 원칙'에 충실하였다. 또한 그렇지 않을 수 있는 것이 통상인데도, 흔히 남도 나와 같으려니 하며 동기생은 물론 특히 생도 때는 하급생을 믿었고, 부대에서는 부대원들은 물론 특히 예하 지휘관(자)들을, 감독 간섭없이 내가 했던 것처럼 그렇게 해 줄 것으로 믿었다.

우리는 우리 가족을 남보다 더 사랑하고 소중히 여긴다. 이는 하늘의 섭리다. 그러나 공인(公人)으로서 특히 군대 지휘관이 되어서는 공평무사하고, 공사구분이 확실해야 하고 지키려고 노력해야 한다. 누구 하나를 특별히 미워할 수도 없거니와 동시에 하나를 특별히 사랑할 수도 없다. 왜냐면 전장과 전투 앞에서 누구는 뒤로 돌리고 누구는 앞으로 밀어 넣을 수 없는 것이다. 모두 함께 일심동체가 되어 총체적 전력을 발휘해야 하기 때문이다. 그러기에 그 모든 관계는 공평무사해야 한다고 생각한다.

그러기에 상과 벌 또한 공평해야 하고, 군기를 확립하기 위해선 벌 또한 공평무사하게 반듯이 그리고 엄격히 처리되어야 한다고 믿는다. 그러나 예하 지휘관에 대한 무한책임은 특히 고려해야 한다.

∘ Civilan Control의 진정한 의미

한국에는 정치인들이 군대를 경원시하면서도 지배하고자 하는 의도가 엿보이는 경우가 많다. 정치와 군사 관계에서 '클라우제빗즈'는 말하기를, '군사는 정치에 종속되어야 한다'고 했으나 나는 이렇게 생각한다, '정치와 군사는 서로 종속 관계이고 때로는 최후의 전쟁 승리를 위해 군사 전략에 정치가 종속될 수도 있어야 한다'고.

그간 내가 배워 알기를, 처칠은 1차 세계대전 시 해군장관 때 해군 제독들이 건의한 건함 계획에 두배 이상을 승인하며 이것이 'Civilian Control'이라 하였다. 사복이 군복을 지배하는 것이 곧 '민의 군 지배'라고 하는 것은 오해이다. 미국 군 통수권자인 대통령이 선전포고를, 또는 군 증편이나 해외 파견을 할 때는 반듯이 의회의 승인을 받아야 한다. 즉 국민에 의해 선출된 의회가 군대를 지원하고, 운용하는 원칙을 결정하는 이것을 두고 'Civilian Control'이라고 하는 것이다.

◦ 겸손과 상호 존중, 존대(尊待)

나는 잘 모르는 사람으로부터 더욱이 내보다 나이가 많다고 해서 반말을 들으면 기분이 상한다. 나는 천성으로 '사해 평등'(四海平等)을 믿고 '남녀노소 인간 평등'을 믿는 사람이라 아예 남에게는 존대한다. 내 아들·손자와 친조카 외는, 아래 동서들과 처남 처제들에게도 존대하고, 처음 대하는 사람은 남녀노소간에 일단 존대한다. 흔히 과공이기도 하다. 이것이 특히 서열이 엄격해야 하는 군대에서 과공이 되기도 하겠지만, 물론 '지휘 명령'엔 존대가 없지만, 내가 남이 그러기를 바라는—비록 바로 위 상관(중대장)이라도 소대장인 내게—이상 내가 남에게 그렇게 해야 한다고 믿는다. 그러기에 남에게서 잘 볼 수 없는 일이기에 이 또한 '내 평생 고집'이 될 수밖에 없다.

◦ 자주·자립·독립 정신

나는 이미 말한 바와 같이, 사범학교 담임 선생이시던 방덕수 선생님의 가르침도 있고 하여, 육사 입교 전에 이미 '남에 의지하지 않는 경제적 자립으로부터 울어 나는 자주적인 삶, 그리고 타의 간섭을 배제한 독립 인생 정신'이 강하였다. 이제 그에 더하여 육사생도 생활을 통해서 그리고 이제부터 군대 생활을 하게 됨으로써, 생활적으로나 경제적으로나 부모 슬하를 완전히 떠나야 하는 성인으로서도 당연하지만, 한 사람의 군 지휘관(자)으로서 부대를 지휘함에 있어 스스로의 생각과 능력으로 감당해 나가야 하며, 타인의 간섭이나 눈치 또는 조언을 기다려가며 책임을 완수할 수 없는 것이기에 더욱더 이에 충실할 것이다. 따라서 참모의 의견은 하나의 참고로 하는 '지휘관 책임 정신'을 앞세울 것이다.

그래서 내 결심으로 내 인생을 개척해 나감에 있어 물론 어른이나 선배 또는 어떤 선도자의 조언이나 충고를 고맙게 생각할 수도 있겠으나 스스로 찾아가 청탁하지는 않을 것이다. 또한 의식적으로 상급자 밑으로 줄 서지 않을 것이며, 동시에 후배 또는 부하들을 내게 줄 세우지도 않을 것이다. 특히 나는 시중의 세력가들에게 고개 숙이지 않을 것이다.

그리고 경제면서도, 이제부터 나는 국록에만 의지하여 푼수대로 생활해 나갈 것이며 남에게 손을 내밀거나 빚지는 일은 하지 않을 것이다. 그러나 나는 남을 도울 수 있다면—특히 부하를 위해서—할 수 있는 범위 내에서 흔쾌히 그렇게 할 것이다.

◦ 의리(義理)와 일편단심

의리의 참뜻은 '사람으로서 지켜야할 도리'를 말하는 것이지 '어떤 조직체나 지배자에 대한 절대복종 또는 비리에도 뜻을 같이해야 한다'는 것을 의미하지 않는다고 생각한다. 나는 내 부모 형제와 같이 우리 군대와 국민은 물론 진리와 이치와 원리 원칙을 존중하여 필생의 업으로 생각하고, 일편단심으로 의리를 지켜나갈 것이다. 물론 군대 생활과 일반 사회생활에서는 뜻을 같이하여 올바르게 나가기에 존경하는 상급자와 선배 그리고 후배와 동료(동기)들에게 의리를 지켜나갈 것이다.

그러나 불의와 도리와 원리원칙 특히 헌법과 양심에 어긋나 가면서 상하 간 또는 동료 간 관계를 지키려 하지는 않을 것이다. 그것은 내 본연의 생각과도 다르거니와 천성적으로 그러지를 못할 것이다.

◦ 술, 노래 못해 사교 불비(社交 不備)

인정하건데, 내게는 앞으로 군대 생활에서 핸디캡으로 작용할지도 모르는 요소가 몇 가지 있다. 이미 말한바 '좌심방 판막증'이라는 신체적 문제는 물론이고 그 외로, 하나가 선천적(체질적)으로 술을 잘못한다. 소주 한 잔에도 벌겋게 취하고 석 잔이면 머리가 흔들리고 배가 아파 누워야 한다. 술로 사교를 하는 세상에, 참으며 버틸 수 없는 경우에는 그 자리를 실례할 수밖에 없을 것이다.

그리고 아마도 이 또한 천성적으로, 엄연히 사범학교에서 '코류분겐'을 배웠음에도, 예능에 소질이 없어서—개발이 안 되어서?—노래도 잘 못한다. 대단히 부끄러우나 애국가도 혼자서는 잘 부르지 못하기에 대중가요 어느 것 하나 외우고 있는 것이 없다. 군가는 강요된 것이긴 하지만 우렁차게 부르기만 하면 되는 것이기에 별문제로 생각지 않는다만. 그러기에 자연적으로 춤(댄스)이라는 것도 할 줄 모른다. 그러나 이 춤은 담배와 같이 개인 기호품으로 필요할 때 배우면 되는 것이기에 별문제 없을 것으로 생각되어 미쳐 배워 두지를 못했다.

- 천성적인데다 후천적 노력 또한 그 방향으로 경도되어, 사물에 대한 분석적 능력보다 종합적인 판단 능력이 앞선다고 생각된다. 전장에 임해서 유리하게 작용하리라고 믿는다.
- 이미 말한 바와 같이 이 할아버지의 아버지의 천성에 따라 나 또한 '개척자 정신' 즉 '무(無)에서 유(有)를 창조하는 정신'에 충일해 있다고 믿는다. 따라서 임지에서나 인생살이 전반에서 주어진 여건이나 부여된 임무에만 연연하지 않고 가능한한 무에서 유를 창조한다는 창조적 정신으로 '절대 책임을 완수'하고도 그 의미를 다하기 위해 최선을 더하여 다할 것이다.

끝으로, 재 교중 매일 매시 부르고 또 불렀던 육사 교가와 맥아더 장군의 기도를 마음에 색이며, 정규 육사 4기생으로 졸업과 임관의 영광을 누리고자 한다.

◦ 당시 부르고 또 불렀던 우리 〈육사 교가〉 (1951년)

— 공중인(孔仲仁) 작사, 김순애(金順愛) 작곡

1절

동해수 구비 감아 금수 내 조국
유구 푸른 그 슬기 빛발을 돋혀
풍진노도 헤쳐 나갈 배움의 전당
무쇠같이 뭉치어진 육사 불꽃은
모진 역사 역역히 은보래 치리

2절
아사달 기리 누려 여기 반만년
변함없는 그 기상 하늘을 내쳐
천추만리 바람결에 이야기 하리
백사 고쳐 쓰러져도 육사혼이야
가고 오지 않으리 오질 않으리

후렴
아 — 영용영용 이 제도 앞에도 한결 같아라
온 누리 소리 모아 부르네
그 이름 그 이름 우리 육사

◦ 맥아더 장군의 기도를 마음에 새이다

A Father Prayer by General Douglas MacArthur (May 1952)

Build me a son, O Lord,
who will be strong enough to know when he is weak;
and brave enough to face himself when he is afraid;
one who will be proud and unbending in honest defeat,
and humble and gentle in victory.
Build me a son
whose wishes will not take the place of deeds;
a son who will know Thee ?
and that to know himself is the foundation stone of knowledge.
Lead him, I pray, not in the path of ease and comfort,
but under the stress and spur of difficulties and challenge.
Here let him learn to stand up in the storm;
here let him learn compassion for those who fail.
Build me a son
whose heart will be clear, whose goal will be high,

a son who will master himself before he seeks to master other men,
one who will reach into the future,
yet never forget the past.
And after all these things are his, add, I pray,
enough of a sense of humor,
so that he may always be serious,
yet never take himself too seriously.
Give him humility,
so that he may always remember the simplicity of true greatness,
the open mind of true wisdom,
and the meekness of true strength.
Then I, his father, will dare to whisper,
"I have not lived in vain!"

제2부

장수(將帥), 영웅(英雄)의 꿈 I

제3장

임관 초기, 중·서부 최전선 소대장·중대장 근무 (1958~1961)

1. 상무대 보병학교 초등군사반(OBC)

육사 출신 장교는 임관과 동시에 일단 전투병과로만 분류된다.—3사관학교와 ROTC 출신 장교들은 처음부터 전 병과 지원이 가능한데 예를 들면, 병참, 헌병 병과 등—전투병과란 보병, 포병, 기갑, 공병, 통신병과를 포함하는 5개 병과를 말한다. 문자 그대로 최전방 최일선 최고도 근무에 생명 위험까지 무릅쓰는 근무병과이기에 일단 모든 준비가 된 육사 출신 위주로 배치하고 있다. 그 중에서도 보병은 가장 힘든 병과이나, 그래도 미래 야망을 가진 장교는 이 병과를 택한다. 나도 대장부 결심으로 보병을 택했다.

육사 출신 장교는 졸업과 동시 일단, 각자가 택한 병과학교의 초등군사반 즉 OBC 과정(16주)을 거친다. 그래서 우리 보병 동기 일동은 졸업 휴가를 마치고 광주 상무대—전투병과교육사령부가 있고, 그 예하에 보병·포병·기갑·통신학교기 있으며 부대 앞에는 '신촌'이라는 군인 상대 마을이 있었다—에 설치된 보병학교 초등군사반(OBC, Officers Basic Course)과정에 입교하였다.

교육훈련 내용은, 중·소대장 지휘 실습을 비롯하여 무기 장비의 운용 요령, 대대 전술, 참모 편성 및 운용 등에 관하여, 실내와 야외 교육훈련이다. 그런데 물론 이론 교육이라 해도 육사 교육과는 현저한 정도의 차이가 있고, 또한 주로 실습 위주 야외 교육훈련이라, 모두가 주말은 서울과 자기네 집으로 다녔고, 평일에도 가벼운 기분으로 교육훈련받고, 일과 후에는 신촌이나 광주시내로 시간 외출을 다녀올 수도 있었다.

2. 명예에 찬 수도(首都)사단 제1연대 소대장 되다(1958.10)

◇ '1' 자가 선명한 전통과 명예의 제1연대 보병 장교 배지

휴전된 지 얼마 되지 않았기에 국민들에게는 '수도사단(Capital Division)', 그리고 제1연대의 혁혁한 전공과 창군 서열 등으로 한국군에서는 가장 자랑스러운 명예와 전통에 빛나는 부대로 알려져 있었다. 그러기에 나는 수도사단 제1연대 제1대대 제1중대 제1소대장이 되기를 소망하였다.

당시 육사 출신 보병 초임 장교 부대 배치는 부대 서열순에 따라 군번 순으로 전방 사단당 7~8명으로 배당하였는데, 나에게는 비록 최고 소망이요 최대 영광이기에는 좀 미흡하였으나, 그래도 바라던 소망에 가장 근접하여, 바로 수도사단하고도 제1연대로 배치된 것이다. 이로써 나의 부대 근무 시작이 정말 영광스러웠고, 자신과 긍지에 찬 것이었다. 우리 연대에는 이승주 동기와 함께 2명이 왔는데, 정규 육사 출신 선배는 아무도 없었다. 그런데 실제로 부대 부임해 보니 장교용 보병 배지 자체도, 보병 마크 한가운데에 1자 표시가 뚜렷하여, 실제로 전장교가 1연대를 그렇게 자랑스러워하고 있었다.

◇ 중부 전선에 선 '마이티(Mighty) 소대장'

드디어 그날이 되어, 원주 제1야전군사령부 보충대를 거쳐 '철의 삼각지대'를 담당하고 있는 제5군단의 예비사단(당시)인 수도사단의 제1연대 제3대대 제11중대 제3소대장으로 부임(1958.10)하였다. 우리 부대는 포천군 이동면에 우뚝 솟은 국망봉 아래에 주둔해 있었고, 근처 마을은 심재리이고 지척에 '이동'과 '일동'이 있었는데, 우리 제1연대는 이동에서 일동에 이르는 도로 연변에 위치하여 평강에서부터 서울로 향하는 주접 근로 후방을 장악하고 있었다.

당시는 휴전된 지 5년이 아직도 다 가지 않은 여전한 전시 체제라, 전방 군단 소속 사단 단위 전후방 교대를 2년 단위로 실시하고, 최전선(전방부대 중 휴전선 담당부대) 사단은 2개 GOP 연대를 운용하는데, 통상 6개월마다 부대 교대하였다. 때마침 수도사단은 최전선에서 나와 5군단 예비사단으로, 군단 사령부지역 일대 후방에 주둔하고 있었다.

당시 1개 사단이 전후방으로 교대 이동할 때는, 실제로는 1개 군단이 이동한다고 농담을 겸한 얘기를 하였다. 실제 사단과 그 식솔들 집단 그리고 그들과 공존하는 상인 집단이 모두 동시에 사단 따라 이동하였기에, 가히 군단 이동이라고도 농담을 겸했을 것이다.

당시 우리 수도사 단장은, 6·25전쟁 당시 제1연대장으로 용명을 떨치고 지금은 전군에서 가장 청렴결백한 '한신' 장군이었고, 연대장은 군사 지식이 해박하고 실전에 달통하여 존경받는 '김영환' 대령(옛 5기생)이었다.

나의 부임을 계기로 우리 소대는 연대 전입 신병에 대한 현지 적응 및 강병훈련소대로 편성되었고 1개월간 전입 신병 교관이 되었다. 당시 전방 부대는 전투 경험을 가진 강한 군대였기에, 후방의 특히 논산 훈련소 신병교육으로는 수준이 안 맞아, 부대 전입 후 각 부대별, 사단 또는 연대 단위로, 임무형 보충훈련을 실시후 실무부대로 배치하고 있었다.

나는 1개월간 '전지전능(Mighty)한 지휘자'가 되어 '커리큘럼' 즉, 훈련 과정, 내용 그리고 그 수준까지도 내가 정하고, 전 과정을 혼자 책임으로 완수하였다. 어디까지나 내 부대원으로 내 식구로 실시하는 것이기에 엄정에 친절 그리고 관용이 따랐다. 그러자 이 신병 친구들, 휴식 시간이 되면 겁 없이 교관에게 다가와 얘기를 하다가, '휴식 시간 끝 집합!'하면 어느새 군대 예절(거수경례)은 잊고, 자기 형님에게나 하는 것처럼 모자를 벗고 꿉벅 고개 숙여 절하고 뛰어갔다. 앗불싸!

연대장과 연대 간부 입회하에 훈련 수료식을 마치고 그들이 연대 내 각부대로 배치되어 갈 때, 허허, 마치 '내 제자 객지로 방출하는 기분'을 처음으로 느껴보았다. 이후 부대 내외 또는 연대본부로 갈 때마다 이들이 반가워해서 마치 제자들을 만나는 듯했다.

◇ 우리(소대장) 환경과 일상생활, 부하와 동고동락

우리 부대는 군단 예비사단의 한 대대로 한 울타리 안에 집결되어 있었다. 우리 중대는 중대장(대위)과 선임 소대장(화기소대장 고참 중위) 그리고 나와 일반 장교 출신으로 '최소위'가 있었다. 우리 소대는 1개월간 전입 신병 강병 및 적응 교육을 마치고 새로 소대 편상이 되었는데, 선임하사는 KLO 출신—당시 38선 이북도(주로 황해도)출신으로 반공사상이 투철하여 서해 연안에서 첩보 작전으로 미군 작전을 지원한 '한국 연락처 요원'으로, 휴전 후 해산하기 전 일단 군번을 부여하고(부여하기 위해) 군 복무시킨 요원—으로 나이가 지긋한(30넘어) '김 하사'였고, 분대장들은 인접 중대서 차출되온 병장들이었는데도 아주 유능하고 충실하였다.

우리 소대에는 기능공이 많았다. 지금은 고등학교 이상 졸업자만이 군에 입대할 수 있으나 당시는 대한민국 남성 전원이 입대(징병) 대상이었는데, 고등학교 졸업만 해도 고학력의 시대여서 다른 부대와 같이 우리 소대에도 초등학교 출신 각종 기능공이 많았던데다 문맹자도 있었고, 심지어는 드물었지만 저능자도 소대당 한 사람 정도는 있었다. 충청도 '담배 닢 말리는 전문 화공'도 있었고, 우리 소대 '마(馬) 씨 성 아무개'는 서울 명동 핸드메이드 여자 핸드백 기능자였고, 곰같이 생긴 마음씨 좋은 '김 아무개'는 이발사였다. 후에 천호동 어느 골목 이발소를 지나다가 "소대장님!"하고 뛰어나온 그를 만나기도 했다.

그런가 하면 글 잘 쓰는 고등학교 출신이 있어 소대 내 문맹자 편지 대독과 대필을 담당하였고, 문맹자로 약간 모자라 언제나 우리 소대 잔류 경계병 즉 '고문관'—말이 잘 안 통하는 미군 고문관에 빗대어 회자—도 있었다. 그래도 이 고문관은 자기 집에 편지 대필해 보낼 때는 아주 의젓하여, "으흠, 동생 받아 보아라"로부터 시작하였다.

그런 수준이라 흔히 부대 야외훈련에서 현장 시찰 나온 상급자가 무얼 지적하면 그가 누구든지 무조건 "예! 시정하겠습니다"라고 대답만 하도록 대대장(중대장)으로부터 교육되기도 하였다. 그러나 반면에 잔소리 군소리 없는 무조건 복종하는 순진한 부하들이라 지휘하기에는 편하였는데, 멀지 않아 곧 학력을 높여 입대시킨다고 하여 당시 지휘관들은 그 병사들이 복종심이 부족할까 걱정하기도 하였다.

막사는 비록 흙벽돌 벽에 볏짚 지붕이었지만 내부에는 빼치카가 설비되어 있어 실내에서만은 철원 지대 강추위를 피할 수 있었다. 마침 우리 중대에는 앞에서 말한, 충북 출신으로 그 지역 담배 건조 화공(火工)이 있어서 2개의 중대 내무반 무연탄 사용 빼치카를 전담해서, 교육훈련 경계 등 모든 임무를 배제해 주어, 겨울내내 중대 난방을 잘 지켜주었다.

그런데, 명색이 대대 BOQ가 있었는데, 그건 문자 그대로 오두막이었고 발로 차면 근방 무너질 수 있는 형편이었다. 흙벽에 초가지붕으로, 5개 개인 방이 있었으나 고개 숙여 들어가는 건 물론 각방은 회초리나무에 신문지 바른 벽으로, 옆방 친구 숨 쉬는 소리도 다 들렸다. 허, 그정도만 되어도? 그러나 바닥은 드럼통 뚜껑을 뜯어 얹어 그 위에 흙을 바른 바닥이라 부실하기 짝이 없어, 나무로 불을 넣기만 하면 오소리 잡는 연기로 가득 차고 화재 위험도 있었다. 그래도 일과 후 고단해서 곯아떨어지면 모포가 타는지 온 방에 끄름이 끼는지도 몰랐고, 그래서 자고 나면 코 속이 까맣게 되어 있었으니 실제로 가슴속은 어땠을까, 지금 생각하면 아찔하다. 그러기에 여기에 잠자는 장교는 육사 출신 이승주 동기와 나 둘 뿐이었다.

육군 전방 부대는 통상 일과 후 지휘관(자)을 대리하는 주번사관 제도를 운용하였다. 그래서 1주일을 양분하여 3일 또는 4일간씩 연일 야간근무를 하게 되어있다. 예를 들면 중대에서는, 통상 고참 선임 부중대장—당시 대부분은 결혼하여 현지에서 살림하고 있었다— 은 열외(列外)함으로, 남은 장교 소대장 2명(통상 예비사단의 중대, 그중 1개 소대는 선임하사관이 소대장을 대리함)이 맞교대한다. 그러다가 한 소대장이 휴가 가면 아예 남은 소대장이 그동안 새벽 기상 때부터 낮은 물론 내리 밤샘 근무해야 함으로, 정상적인 부대의 소대장은 외출 외박이 사실상 어려워, 특히 육사 출신 신임 장교들은, 1년 365일을 거의 소대원과 같이 몸과 마음을 부비며 동고동락하게 되어있다. 그래서 소대원은 소대장을 'Mighty Leader'로 알고 중대장과의 알력 때는 두말없이 소대장 편에 선다. 듣기로는, 전시에, 한 중대장이 소대원 앞에서 소대장을 꾸짖으며 총부리를 겨누자, 소대원이 즉시 자기 소대장에게 총을 내밀어 중대장과 대치하게 하였다는 얘기가 있었다.

◇ 국망봉(國望峯) 밑 소부대와 소대장 근무

전방부대 장병들은 겨울이 되면 예상외로 할 일이 많아진다. 특히 눈이 오면, 첫째로 연병장을 매일 매시간 눈이 내리는 즉시 치워야 하고, 둘째는 부대와 부대 간의 연락로를 항시(매일 매시간) 사용 가능하도록 유지하기 위해, 특히 담당 지역 내 전술도로 즉 보급로를 그때그때 마다 제설해야 했다. 생각해 보시라, 전방 겨울에 눈은 얼마나 많이 그리고 자주 오는지. 그것이 전방 군대의 일과요 훈련이요 군대 생활이기도 한 것이다.

위에서 말한 바와 같이 전방 소대장은 일 년 365일의 대부분을 중대 주번사관 임무를 수행한다. 나는 한겨울에 폭설이 내려도 야간 순찰을 쉬지 않았다. 대대 내 전 중대 막사와 탄약고 그리고 정문 후문 보초까지 한 바퀴 순찰에 대략 2시간 정도 소요되었다. 중대 내무반 초병은 내무반 안에서 근무하며 첫째 임무는 외부로부터 침략자를 방어하는 것이고, 둘째는 각종 비상사태에 대비하고 연락을 유지하며, 그리고 틈나는 대로 동료들의 건강 상태를 돌보아주는 것이다. 따라서 여하한 방문자, 비록 중대장이나 주번사관이라 할지라도 반듯이 문을 열기 전에 일단 오늘의 암구어를 확인하여야 한다.

그러기에 주번사관은 일일이 이를 확인하고 교육하면서 순찰하는 것이다. 문밖은 한밤의 폭설이 쌓이면서 보행이 어려우나 외부 초소 특히 좀 멀리 있는 탄약고까지 모두 순찰하고야 중대로 복귀하고, 중대 본부에 돌아와서는 가면 상태 근무를 계속한다. 그런데 전투복은 물론 젖어 있지만 특히 다 젖은 군화, 아직도 국산 군화가 보급되지 않아 시장에서 개인적으로 구입한 미제 '워커 군화' 를 말리기 위해 빼치카 철판 위에 올려 놓았다가, 시간을 놓쳐 그만 오징어구이 구두가 되어 낭패 보는 일도 가끔 있었다.

3. 제1연대 전투단(RCT-Regiment Combat Team), 문산 임진강 전선으로 가다

◇ 문 소위, 서부 전선 임진강 최전선에 서다

1959년 6월경에 우리 수도사단 제1연대는 연대전투단을 구성(1개 포병대대+보급부대 등 증강)하여 미 제1군단 예하 제1기병사단(Cavalry Div)에 배속된 한국 해병여단—문산·파주·임진강 전선 담당—과 교대하기 위해 준비하였다. 그 때문에 나는 최전선 담당 중대의 소대장으로 전보되었다. 그런데 지금 소대원들은 '가시면 안됩니다'며 연판장을 돌린다 했다. 군대에서는 그런 행위가 허용되지 않음으로, 겨우겨우 말려서 진정시키고 난생처음으로, 참으로 아쉽고 섭섭한 마음으로 내 소대원들과 헤어졌다.

군대서 '골육지정(骨肉之情)'이란 소대장의 경우에 가능한 것이리라. 지금까지도 그때 그 '집 보기 고문관', 키타 제작 전문가, 핸드 메이드 핸드백 전문가, 보석깎이 전문가 그리고 털보 이발사 등등이 생각난다. 그 후 아마도 10년은 지나 하루는 친척 볼일로 천호동 탄산수 마을 근처 이발소 앞을 지나가는데 이발소에서 한 털보 청년이 뛰어나오더니, "아이고 우리 소대장님, 다시 만나 뵈어 반갑습니다"라고 하기에 보니 허, 그 우리 소대 털보 이발사가 아닌가. 정말 반가웠다.

드디어 우리 연대전투단은 강원도 포천에서 행군으로 출발하여 경기도 금촌에 도착하고, 우리 중대는 '탄현' 방향으로 야간 행군하였다. 중대는 '대동리'에, 우리 소대는 '성동리'의 현 '헤일리 문예촌'을 지나 현 '프로방스' 동네 앞동산에 밤 12시에 도착하고, 소총 3개 분대는 다시 전방으로 나아가 최전선 임진강 가에 병행 배치되었다.

나는 피교대 부대인 해병대 소대장 '문 소위'로부터 부대 상황을 인계받고 즉시 임무를 개시하였다. 해병 문 소위는 종씨라고 반가워하며 상세하게 그리고 친절하게 현항을 소개해 주었는데, 마지막으로 철수해 갈 때는, 대한민국 해병대답게 아랫마을(지금의 프로방스 마을)을 향해, "야 영자야! 육군 문 소위 왔다, 잘해 보아라!"고 고함치고 웃으며 집결지로 내려갔다. 나는 그동안 이곳 전선을 지켜준 해병대 문소위와 그 소대에 행운을 빌었다.

◇ 6·25 말기 구축된 원목 전투진지

다음 날 즉시 소대 진지를 돌아보았다. 우선 소대 본부(소대장+전령+선임하사+향도+기재계(記載係),+화기분대) 진지(陣地)는 길이 20여 미터 둘레 50여 센티미터가 되는 4각 원목을 10개로 나란히 엮어 지붕으로 하되 적을 향해 지붕 끝을 땅에 묻고, 비가 흘러내릴 만큼 약간 위로 올려서 원목으로 받치고, 앞부분 전체가 비록 엎드려서 일제히 들어갈 수 있고 나올 수 있도록 하였고, 사람이 드나들 수 있도록 간격을 두고 자연 흙벽으로 앞을 막았다. 웬만한 적의 포격(155미리 직격탄 정도까지도)은 충분히 대피할 수 있는 정도였다. 6·25 전쟁의 여운이 그대로 남아 있었다. 전방 3개분대진지도 유사하였다. 생각해 보시라, 이런 유개참호가 1개 중대에 20여 개, 1개 대대면 60여 개 이상……, 서부 전선 1개 군단만 해도 그량이 어떠했을까. 그리고 그것들이 전방 참호 구축시까지, 그 자재 보급 능력과 그 수단들은 또 어떠했을까. 이것이 미국의 실력이요, 미군의 전쟁 능력 즉 이승만 대통령이 북진할 수 있다고 판단했던 그 6·25 마지막 단계 전투력이었다.

전방 3개 분대는 임진강 물결치는 바로 위 언덕(10미터 이상)에 자리 잡았는데, 야간 정밀 경계를 위한 수제선 강변 진지(가변형 매복 진지)를 운용하였다. 그 수제선에서는 약 10미터 차이의 간조 시점에, 그동안 무서울 것 없이 뛰놀던 큰 물고기들이 가끔 마음 놓고 물을 박차고 뛰어 올라와 소대원의 밥상을 풍족하게(?) 해 주기도 하였다.

소대장은 거의 매일같이 어깨높이로 구축되어 있는 전투(참호)교통호를 따라 임진강변을 순찰하였는데, 몇 곳에서는 바닥에 똬리를 튼 그놈들이 입을 벌리고 길을 막아 부득이 피해 가기도 하였다. 소대 참호의 총길이는 대략 1.5킬로미터로 토질이 좋아 교과서와 같이 모범적으로 잘 구축되어 있었다.

◇ 피난 복귀 중인 최전선 마을 성동리

소대 본부 막사가 위치한 반대편 바로 아래로 단차선 군 보급로가 있었는데 이 도로선을 기준으로 전방은 민간인 출입 금지 구역이었다. 후방 즉, 그 남쪽으로는 대략 2만여 평방미터에 '성동리'의 30호가량의, 우리 소대가 책임지는 한 마을이 자리하고 있었는데, 전방 민간 마을 지역 복귀가 허가되어 이제 막 한두 집씩 피난지에서 돌아오고 있었다. 마을 남쪽 어귀에 간이 검문소를 설치하고 출입 민간인을 체크하면서 보호하였다. 이 마을 사람들은 말하자면 우리와 생사를 함께해야 하는 그야말로 최전방 민간인들이었다.

당시 이들의 생활은 이제 막 빈손으로 복귀한지라, 물론 후방 국민들과 대동소이하게 어려웠으나 특히 겨울 땔감이 어렵게 보였다. 물론 근방은 전장터라 지금은 아주 드물게 고사목이 몇 뿌리 보이는 황량한 동산이었다. 그래도 필요하기에 평소엔 고사목이나 크다 마른 나무를 캐다가 이용하고 겨울에는 그날 그날따라 눈이 오는 날에도 나와서 나무뿌리를 캐어갔다.

우연이던가, 우리 소대 선임하사는 가끔 소대 본부 앞 언덕에 올라 임진강 건너를 바라보면서 그리워 한숨을 쉬기만 하였는데, 전쟁 중에는 친척들끼리 임진강을 건너 서로 왕래하던 그곳 즉 북의 개풍군 임한면에 있는 자기 고향, 자기 동네가 저기에 보이기 때문이었다. 참으로 안타까운 북한 괴뢰집단이 일으킨 민족 비극의 한 장면이었다.

◇ 임진강 하류 지역 강변 방어진지 보강 구상

임진강 북쪽 북괴군은 전국에서 징집한 '인민 보국대'가 맞은편 강변을 연하여 전투참호를 구축하고 동시에 오늘날에도 볼 수 있는 5~6층짜리 유사 아파트촌 '전시마을'—현재 오두산 '통일 전망대' 올라 바로 앞에 보이는 '선전마을'—을 조성하였다. 그 집단의 작업 모습은 쌍안경 없이도 바로 보이기에 그들의 노예와 같은 일거수 일동작을 잘 관찰할 수 있었다.

아침 6시에 종소리 울리면 일어나 점호하고 작업하기 시작하여 점심 종소리에 멈추었다가 저녁 6시 종소리에 작업을 끝낸다. 그동안 종종 배구 시합 같은 구기 종목 놀이로 사기를 올리는 듯하였다. 그때면 그들의 고함 소리 즉 응원 소리가 그대로 생생하게 다 들렸다. 밤에 잠자리에서는 북에서 밤새 삽과 곡괭이로 작업하는 소리가 들리는데, 한때는 아주 크게 들려서 행여나 땅굴을 파는 게 아닌가 의심이 들었으나, 낮에 보이는 그 규모와 모습으로 임진강 밑으로 감히 어려울 것으로 생각되었다.—1980년 이후 현재까지 그를 의심하여 그 강변을 연하여 거리 4~5미터 간격으로 심정을 수 100개 굴착하면서 엄중 감시 에 있다.

나는 전방 진지 순찰 도중에 때로는 강변 언덕에 앉아 임진강과 적 지역을 동시에 바라보면서, 임진강 방어 문제를 생각해 보았다. 탄현면 전방 임진강은 만조시 최장 강폭 약 3킬로미터, 만일에 시속 10킬로미터 모터보트로 일제히 도강해 온다면 불과 2~30분 만에 기습당할 수 있다. 그리고 간조시는 강 한가운데 대략 100미터 미만 강폭으로 줄어들고 갯벌이 들어나, 걸어서는 어려우나 엷은 판자 또는 양철판을 깔면서는 얼마든지 건너 올 수 있다. 자 그러면 우리의 준비는 일차 수제선에서 2차 상륙지점에서인데, 이는 사전 경고되었을 경우이다. 그렇다 하더라도 방어 보장을 위해서는 우리 측 강변에 장애물 즉 각종 종합 장벽이나 수중 장애물 등의 설치가 반듯이 필요하다고 생각했다. 마치 노르망디 해안 방어진지처럼. 그러나 건의의 기회를 놓치고 구상으로만 끝났다.

◇ '춥고 배고프다'를 실감하는 비상훈련(Defcon-2)

임진강변 전투전초(COP)의 소초(소대)장 생활도 6개월여가 되자 전쟁 당시 관습대로 그해 12월경 임무를 교대하고, 우리 대대는 연대전투단의 예비대대로 전환되어 월룡산 밑 예비대대 집결지로 이동하였다. 그런데 여기에서 진짜 전투 소대장의 경험을 다양하게 충분히 쌓게 되었는데 그것은 군대 생활 전체를 두고도 행운이었다. 그 시작이 바로 매월 1회 불시 비상진지투입훈련(Defcon-2 훈련)이었다. 우리 제1연대전투단은 당시 휴전 전후로 최서부 전선을 담당하고 있던 미제1군단 예하 제1기병사단(Cavalry Div)에 배속되어 있었다.

그래서 매월 1회 정도의 '군단 불시 비상전투진지투입훈련'을 실시하고 있었다. 그해 12월 임진강변은 섭씨 영하 20도를 훨씬 하회하는 강추위가 몰아치고 있었다. 그달 어느 날도 체감온도는 영하 30도를 넘는 시점인 새벽 3시경에 비상이 걸렸다. 대대는 완전 군장을 하고 즉각 출동하여 월룡산 근방 방어진지(소대는 교통호)를 점령하였다. 점령 배치 완료 후 한 30분이 지나면서부터 추워 오기 시작하였다. 보급된 내복은 다 입고 나간 것 같은데도 그 자리에서 벗어나지 못하고, 눈과 얼음 위라 물론 앉을 수도 없고, 보온 방법은 내 체온밖에 없었다.

대대장 이하 전 전투원이 꼼짝없이 체감온도 영하 30여 도의 체감 냉동 고속에서, 급히 올라오느라 흘린 땀은 속에서 얼어가는 듯한 상태에서, 새벽 3시부터 아침 9시까지 참고 견디는데, 6시쯤 되니까 그 추위 속에서 이제는 배가 고프기 시작하였다. 새삼 6·25전쟁 당시 철수하면서 겪은 아군의 극한지 '장진호전투상황'을 이제사 진정하게 이해할 수 있었다. 이러한 상황은 평생에 몇 번이고 겪게 되어있는 것이 우리 군인이기는 하나 그때 그 '춥고 배고프던 생각'은 군대 생활 내내 결코 잊을 수 없었다.

또 다른 훈련 얘기도 하겠지만 당시 미군—특히 제1군단, 예하 제1기병사단—은 정말 똑바른 전투훈련을 하는 걸로 보아 미 기병사단의 긍지가 과장이 아님을 재확인할 수 있었다.

◇ 동계(혹한기) 부대 야외 현지 기동훈련(FTX, ICE CAP)

1960년 1월, 당시 미 1군단은 휴전 상황의 돌변을 대비하여 각종 전투 준비 태세를 실전과 같이 유지하고 있었다. 수시 비상 진지 점령훈련을 포함하여 또 하나가 군단 야외 현지 기동훈련이었다. 물론 최전방 COP '문산 서부지대'나 GOP '문산 동부지대' 부대는 현지에서, 각급 예비부대(대대급 이상)는 현 작전 계획에 의거하여 후방 1차 예비 전선으로 후퇴 이동 후 즉각 반격 작전에 돌입하는 상황으로 전개되었다.

연중 최하 기온—그때는 아마도 영하 20도보다 훨씬 아래—인 소한에 우리 대대는 월룡산 아래 주둔지를 떠나 가상 반격 개시선 바로 아래 즉, 일산(현 정발산 서북지역)에 도착하여 하룻밤 소대 숙영용 극한지 야외 빼치카형 참호를 준비하였다. 출발 전에 교육받기를, 혹한기 야외 숙영 시설은, 땅을 최소 1미터 이상 파고 한편에 빼치카용 굴뚝을 내고, 아래는 판쵸 우의를 깔아 습기와 냉기를 방지하고, 위로는 나무를 걸쳐 A형 텐트로 덮어서 비·바람을 피하고 온기를 보존하기로 하였다. 첫날 집결지에서는 비전투 상황이고 그래도 시간 여유가 있어 야전삽으로 10~20센티미터 이상 언 땅을 파내고 밑으로 30센티미터 가량 더 깊이 파내어—그러나 더 이상 작업은 현지 극한상황으로 불가능하였다—소대 야간 취침용 호를 구축하듯, 흉내 내듯이 준비하였다. 물론 전투 복장 그대로 첫날밤을 지냈다. 결코 편하거나 따뜻하거나 간단하지 않았다. 그 차가운 겨울밤에, 땀나고 힘들고 시간 가는 작업이었고 뜻대로(교육대로) 되지 않는 또 하나의 실전 상황 그대로였다.

다음 날 아침, 트럭으로 식사(밥과 국)가 왔는데, 분배하는 도중에 강추위로 다 식고 얼어버린 밥과 국을 반합에 받아먹고, 우리 소대는 인접 소대와 함께 공격(반격)개시선에 전개하였다. 그날은 약 10킬로미터를 10여 시간에 고지 공격 점령과 야지 전투형 전진을 계속하다가 캄캄한 밤이 되어 어느 평지에 도달하였다. 아마도 현 교하읍의 파주 운정신도시 한 가운데쯤 되리라 짐작된다. 칠흑같이 어두운 밤—당시 근처에 전혀 불빛이 없었다—이라 손으로 더듬어가며 소대 참호 구축 가능한 평지를 확보하여 자리 잡고, 소대 극한지 야영 작업을 시작하였는데 야전삽으로 무릎까지도 파내기 어려웠다. 모두가 지치고 기온은 영하 20도 이하 체감온도 30도가 넘는 때라 일 분이라도 빨리 드러누우려 했다. 그래서 그 정도에서 밑은 근처 논에서 얻은 볏짚을 깔고 위는 그냥 판초우의와 A텐트 조각들을 덮어쓰고 소대원 모두가 한곳에서 나란히 누워 골아떨어졌다. 물론 보초 세우기도 어려웠지만 그러나 그것은 전투 기본이었다.

다음 날 새벽 6시 출발을 위해 일찍부터 서둘렀으나 식사 보급이 늦은데다 완전히 언 주먹밥을 깨물어 가며, 차디찬 국을 선체로 먹는 둥 마는 둥 먹어치우고, 명령에 따라 비포장도—당시는 국도를 비롯 모든 지방도로는 비포장—로 나갔다. 날이 밝아 뒤 돌아 보니 어젯밤 숙영지는 공동묘지의 한구석 빈자리였다.

도로에 도착해, 미군 APC 5대에 1개 분대씩 탑승하였는데 속에는 미군이 있고 그 차운 날 APC 밖 발판 위에 서서 각종 돌출물을 붙들고 체감온도 영하 30도 겨울바람을 정면으로 맞아 코와 귀가 어는 듯한 추위를 견디며—비록 시속 5킬로 서행이었지만—적을 추격해 갔다.

약 5킬로미터 전진 후, 공릉천의 장애물을 통과하기 위해—아마도 교량 파괴 상황—하차하여 도강 준비를 위해 전개하였다. 정찰 결과 도보부대는 물론 차량부대도 빙판 위로 그대로 통과 가능하리만큼 두껍게 얼었음을 확인하고 공병의 연막탄(통) 차단을 방패 삼아 우리 중대는 일제히 빙판 위로 공격도하(강)하였다.—당시 공릉천은 별도의 뚝이 없이 남북 1킬로 모래밭과 뻘, 중간 강폭 약 100미터였다.

도강 즉시 우리 소대는 월룡고지(산), 255고지 우리 대대 주둔지 뒷산, 공격을 명령받고 남쪽 와지선(산의 밑바닥 가장자리)에서 공격대형으로 전개하였다. 현 위치에서 고지 중간 지대까지는 대략 4~50도 경사였고, 그 이상에서 정상까지는 7~80도 경사였다.

공격 개시 이후, 마음은 구보였으나 가파른 고지를 네발로 기다시피 오르는 현상이라 바위와 잔솔가지, 밟으면 굴러 내리는 자갈흙 등등 실제 거름은 등산 행보였다. 5부 능선쯤에서, 중대장 지시로 소대원을 선임하사 지휘로 우측 방향으로 돌려서 오르게 하고, 나는 포판(布板) 병을 대동하고 온갖 힘을 다하여 계속 등진(登進)하였다. 그리하여 드디어 고지 정상을 점령하고 방어를 위한 재편성을 시작하였다.

이후는 예비대대의 일부가 되어 전진부대를 후속하게 되었다. 그러나 내복 속은 아직도 젖어있는데 해가 지면서 추위가 엄습해 왔다. 차라리 공격부대가 되어 전진 또 전진하는 것이 낫지, 예비대로 서서 소한 강추위를 감당한다는 것은 참으로 어려웠다. 야간이 되어 1킬로 전방의 신 집결지로 이동하였는데 사방을 더듬어 소대가 들어갈 수 있는 인조 동굴을 발견하고 천행으로 그 밤은 서리를 맞지 않고 지새울 수 있었다.

다음 날은 임진강으로 도주해 가는 적을 추격하여 마지막 일격을 가하는, 그래서 이번 'FTX, ICE CAP'의 대미를 장식하는 임무를 영광스럽게도 우리 소대가 부여받았다. 그리하여 새벽같이 출동하여 대기 중인 탱크 3대에 전 소대가 분승, 드디어 파주 '오금리' 근방 임진강변을 향해 최후의 일격을 가하기 위해 돌진해 나갔다. 아, 그 선봉대 선봉장의 기분! 그것은 바로 군인의 특권이요 지휘관의 영광이리라. "나를 따르라!" 그것은 진짜였다.

다만, 영하 20도에 얼대로 얼어 있는 무쇠덩이 위에 올라타, 손이 닿는 곳마다 쫙쫙 얼어서 달라붙는 상태에서, 체감온도 30도 되는 임진강변 찬바람 속을 돌격해 나가는, 탱크의 속도 따라 얼굴과 온몸에 와 닿는 그 한겨울 임진강변 어름 바람을 맞받으며 돌격해 나가는 그때 그 어름장 같은 냉기 또한 지금도 잊지 못한다.

◇ 보병대대 실전(실탄) 훈련시험(ATT)

전쟁 당시부터 서부 전선을 당당하였던 미 제1군단의 휴전 이후 전투 준비 태세는 변함없이 계속되는 실전훈련이었다. 여단 예비대대로 훈련 중, '대대TEST'를 위해서 아직도 추위가 다 가시지 않았던 3월 초순경에 트럭을 타고, 지금의 산정호수 지역 '여우고개'에 위치한, 미군(주로) 종합훈련장 중의 하나인 'Nightmare훈련장' 집결지로 이동하였다.

먼저 야영을 위해 교범대로라면, 소대원은 A텐트를 설치해야 하나, 이미 말한 바와 같이 한국군은 아직도 가난하여 1개 소대당 3동분—3인당 1동이 근본—뿐이라 부득이 소대 전체가 합숙하는 임시 텐트 즉, 부근 나무를 꺾어와 아치형 골조를 만들고 그 위에 A텐트 조각들과 판초우의로 덮었다. 다음날, 보전포(步戰砲)와 공지(空地) 합동 또는 한미 연합 작전 훈련 시범장으로 주로 사용하는 훈련장으로 이동하여 방어훈련 시험부터 시작하였다.

집결지에서 중대장으로부터 방어 명령을 수령하고 소대 대기지점으로—그동안 소대 선임하사가 지휘하여 집결지에 소대는 이미 도착—가서 소대 방어 명령을 하달하고 즉시 방어진지로 투입하였다. 이후 시나리오대로 공격 대항군이 공격해 오고, 적절한 시점에 소대는 후퇴하여 신 방어진지를 점령하였다가 방어 테스트 상황이 종료 되면 다시 숙영지로 돌아갔다. 당시 중소대간 통신은 유선(대대 통신병이 가설)이었다. 그리고 다음 날, 다시 공격 명령—대대 우일선 소대로서 전방에 보이는 제1 목표 고지를 점령하고 이어서 좌로 90도 회전하여 전방의 대대 최종 목표를 공격한다—을 수령하고, 소대는 공격개시선을 점령, 전개하였다. 실전과 같은 실사격 훈련이라, 전방으로 가상 공대지 사격(가상)이 있고 바로 이어 포병에 의한 사격(가상)이 실행되었다.

드디어 공격 개시 시간에 발포되는 유색 신호탄을 신호로 일제히 진지를 박차고 뛰어나가면서, 소대는 M1에 실탄을 장진하고 자물쇠를 푼 채 구간 기동으로 우선 제1목표 고지를 향해 용감하게 전진해 나갔다. 그동안 몇십 발의 대대 중화기중대 81미리 박격포 포탄이 최종 목표 고지에 작열하였다. 소대장인 나는, 왼손에 칼빈소총을 쥐고 오른손으로는 칼빈소총 무게의 소대장용 무전기를 들고, 그 긴 안테나는 흔들리면서 지휘봉 역할까지 하였다.

그런데 막상 거의 엎드렸다 뛰거나, 포복 자세에서 보이는 지형은 명령 수령시 그리고 공격개시선에서 보던 지형과 판단이 어려워 제1목표 고지(오판) 와지선에서 소대는 돌격형으로 전개하여 일차 일제히 돌격 준비 사격을 가했다. 그러자 중대장으로부터 그건 중간목표 고지이고 제1목표는 그다음 고지라 무전으로 지적해 왔다. 나는 즉각 사격을 멈추게 명령하였으나 소대 일제 사격하의 목소리는 불통이었다. 부득이 총탄을 피하면서 전방으로 나가 뒤로 돌아서서 목소리와 함께 손짓으로 겨우 사격을 저지시키고 그 고지를 지나 다시 구간 전진을 시작하였다. 그리하여 제1목표 즉 중대 공격 목표를 탈취하는데 성공하였다.

그리고 쉴 사이 없이 작전계획대로 90도 좌회전하여, 대대 최종 목표 공격을 위한 핵심 전력 우일선(右一線) 소대로서 다시 전개하였다. 일단 화기분대 바주카포 반(班)을 불러 실거리 300미터도 넘는 고지를 향해 공격 준비 사격 2발을 발사하였다. 그런데 이 바주카포는 물론 6·25 때 미 24사단장 '딘 소장'이 대전에서 북한 괴뢰 탱크를 향해 직접 사격했던 포와 같은 것으로, 이미 폐기직전의 구형 로켓포였다. 때문에 사격할 때마다 반동이 심한 건 물론이고 발사 순간 품어져 나오는 가스 때문에 사수가 얼굴에 손상을 입을 정도였다. 그래서 당시 사수는 손상을 각오하고, 손수건 마스크로 얼굴을 감싸고 대담하게 사격하였다. 다행히도 우리 로켓반 사수는 이 소대장을 믿고 용감하게 임무를 완수해 주었다. 그리하여 소대는 로켓포탄의 목표지점 작열을 신호로 중대 2차 공격 대기 지점을 뒤로하고 전면 계곡지대 적 지역을 일제히 전진해 내려갔다. 그리하여 와지선에 도착과 동시 분대 구간 전진으로 계곡을 신속히 횡단하여 대대 최종 목표 고지의 와지선에 전개하였다.

물론 도착과 동시 지체없이 40~50도 경사진 고지를 오르기 시작하였다. 물론 구간 전진하려 했으나 그건 마음이지 경사진 고지를 오르기에 전력을 다하기에도 어려웠다. 물론 상급부대 지원사격이 우리의 전진을 보장해 주는 상황이라 상정하고 대략 6~7부 능선에서 사격 연신 요청 신호를 보내고, 소대는 소총 일제 사격을 실시하였다. 그리고 정말 젖 먹던 힘까지 다하여 일어선 자세로 정상을 향해 돌격해 올라갔다. 헐덕거리는 숨이 헐덕거리는지도 모르고 포판병을 앞세우고—바로 직전에 실시했던 혹한시 FTX 당시 월룡산 고지 공격하던 때와도 같이—네발을 다 사용하며 오르고 또 올랐다. 그리하여 드디어 숨을 헐떡이며 고지 정상을 점령하고, 소대는 만세 부를 사이도 없이 적 반격에 대비한 방어 편성을 실시하였다.

다음 날, 그동안 실시한 대대 전술시험을 우수한 성적으로 평가받고 철수를 위해 숙영지 정리를 하는 도중, 웬 여자들 여러 명이 달려들어 텐트 밑에 깔았던 가마니때기—그들의 영업용 밑천—를 서로 가져가려고 밀고 당기며 싸우는 것이었다. 그곳은 여우고개 정상이라 당시는 화전민 몇십 세대와 양공주—부대 시험받기 위해 계속 들어오는 미군을 상대하여 위안해 주며 돈벌이하는—몇십 명이 살고 있었는데, 그토록 가난하였던 것이다. 나는 난생 처음으로 '처량한 인생, 인생 허망'을 마주 보았고, 지금도 그 광경과 그걸 보던 심정을 잊지 못한다.

◇ 국군 최초 시멘트벽돌 막사 신축

1960년 봄, 문산 지역 제1연대전투단의 월룡산 밑 우리 예비대대는 미군이 지원해 준 시멘트로 휴전 이후 한국군 최초로 시멘트벽돌과 양철지붕 막사를 짓게 되었다. 당시 전방 군부대 막사들은 휴전 이후 여전히 가막사 상태로 부대 생활을 영위하고 있었다.

예를 들면, 미군 담당 서부 지역은 최전선이 원목 벙커, 연대 후방지역은 대체로 나무 벽 가막사와 양철 '콘센트' 등이었고, 한국군 담당지역 전 후방부대 대부분은 손으로 만든 흙벽돌 벽에 초가지붕의 가막사였다. 거기에다가 매년 사단급 부대 교대를 실시하였고, 전방 사단 연대급은 매 6개월마다 부대 이동을 하면서 막사 내부 시설은 서로가 뜯어 가는 등, 참으로 불편한 거주 형편이었다.

이제 대대 내 각 중대에서 1개소대씩 차출하여 자기중대 건축분과 여타용 시멘트벽돌을 제조하게 되었다. 우리 중대에서는 이번에도 우리 소대가 만능소대 본보기—대체로 육사 출신 소대장들은 만능 지휘자가 되어, 전술훈련 때는 우 1선, 전방투입 때는 COP 최전선, 각종 시범 주연 등, 어렵지만 자긍심으로 책임을 다한다—가 되어 시멘트 제작 작업에 투입되었다.

부대 주둔지에서 약 5킬로미터 지점에 임진강으로 흘러 들어가는 문산천이 있는데, 그 뚝방 아래 강변에 소대 숙영지를 설치하고, 수제 벽돌 제조기를 보급받아 지체없이 작업을 시작하였다. 작업을 분담하였는데, 대체로 1조는 숙영지 관리와 식사 담당, 2조는 모래 체취와 채로 고르기, 3조는 벽돌 제조와 시멘트 관리, 4조는 제작된 시멘트벽돌 관리—벽돌을 물에 옮겨 일주일가량 담그고 다시 볕에서 건조 그리고 보관 등—를 담당하였다.

처음 상당량 시행착오 후 제조 기술을 완전히 터득하여 대량생산에 들어갔다. 시멘트는 미국 제품(made in U.S.A)이라 한 포대로 20장이 정량인데, 때로는 23장을 찍어내라는 요구도 있었으나, 이 또한 보급 투쟁 개념으로, 기어이 20장을 고집하기도 하였다. 지금부터 65년여 전 일이라 숫자 개념은 명확하지 않으나, 대략 하루에 100여 장씩 약 20일간 2,000여 장을 생산하였다. 다만 도중에 위생 상태 부주의로 나를 비롯한 상당수 소대원이 수인성 질환(적리)으로 어려움도 있었으나 경험으로 생각하고 오로지 젊음의 힘으로 그리고 소대원의 완전한 단결력으로 극복하고 소대 임무를 완수할 수 있었다. 부대 복귀하여서는, 각 중대용—전대대가 일제히—장방형 단일막사를 신축하였다.

◇ 3·15 부정선거에 저항하다

1960년 3월 15일은 대한민국 역사상 또 하나의 수치를 기록한 소위 '3·15 부정선거의 날'이었다. 우리 부대 투표 장소는 금촌에 있는 연대전투단본부에 설치되어 있었다. 당시 인접 중대 소대장으로 와 있던 바로 아래 후배(5기) '임승해 소위'와 투표장 옆 사무실 난로 앞에서 만나 최종 결심을 하였다. 후배는 투표통지서를 난로불에 태우고 나는 현장 확인을 위해 투표장으로 갔다.

이미 1개월여 앞서부터 연대 파견 기관에서 소대장들에게도 (부정)투표 준비에 대한 비밀 교육이 있었다. 소대원을 A·B·C·D·E로 분류하고 분류별로 철저하게 교육하고 감독하여 100% 찬성 투표하게 하란 내용이었다. 부대 생활에서 내 소대는 나와 동일체(골육지정으로 뭉친)로 생사고락을 함께 하고 있는 내게, 우리 헌법상 선거 4대 원칙인 보통, 평등, 직접, 비밀을 미리부터 부정하고, 내 소대원을 분류하여 일심동체 아닌 감시와 감독의 대상으로 하였다가, 자유당 도당들의 부정선거에 무조건 동참하라는 것이었다. 나는 결코 우리 소대원을 그렇게 할 순 없었다. 그래서 일체 내색하지 않은 채 오히려 헌법상 선거와 투표의 4대 원칙을 특히 '비밀'의 원칙을 강조하였다.

당시 전 육사 출신(당시는 소대장 중대장 등 초급 간부)은, 이미 우리끼리는 모두 이심전심이었기에, 자의 또는 고의로 휴가를 갔거나 자의로 기권(난로불에 투표권을 태움 등)하였다.—물론 후에 대통령이 된 '박정희' 장군도 불태웠다고 했다.

나는 무엇인가. 거짓의 죄책감에 눌린 듯한 삼엄한 투표현장에서 용지를 받아들고 기표소로 갔는데, 허, 바로 우리 중대장이 상사 계급장의 전투모를 쓰고 그 안에서 들어오는 대로 중대원 전원의 표를 받아서 대신 찍어주고 있었다. 그리고 그걸 가지고 투표함에 오면 민간인 두 사람이 앉아서 표를 받아 펴서 확인하고 그들 손으로 투표함에 넣고 있었다.

이와 같은 모든 부정선거와 투표과정이 내게 각인되어 "앞으로 군대 내 부정선거는 무슨 일이 있어도 두 번 다시 있어서는 안 되겠다"고 결심하고 또 다짐하였다. 이후 대대장 시절에 '유신헌법 투표'가 있었고, 군단장 때 '제6공화국 대통령 선거'가 있었다. 나는 무슨 후환은 생각할 것 없이 여하간에 내 신념, 양심, 헌법을 기어이 지켜내었다. 그 시점에 가서 다시 한번 상세하게 말하기로 한다.

◇ 대대대항 연대 전술전기(실습)대회

당시의 군대는 쉴 사이 없이 각종 훈련과 전후방 이동 그리고 부대대항대회(전술, 체육, 사격 대회 등)를 실시하였다. 이 시절에 제1연대전투단에서도 '대대대항연대 전술대회'가 개최되었다. 이때도 여하간에 육사 출신 보병 소대장은 '전지전능'하기에 이번에는 중대 화기소대 무기인 60미리 박격포를 책임졌다. 그래서 즉시 M2 60미리 박격포자체(라고 해 보았자 포신, 포판, 포다리, 가늠대, 조준구, 사거리 2킬로미터 내외)를 추가로 공부하고 그 전술(차려포, 가늠대와 조준경 가늠줄 일치 요령)을 익혔다.

그런 뒤 박격포 요원들(화기소대원)과 함께 시험 요령에 대한 숙달을 위한 연습훈련을 거듭하였다. 당시의 60미리 M2 박격포는 2차대전과 한국전에서 사용된 구형이었으나 성능은 여전하였고, 포 1문당 포수, 부포수, 1번 2번 탄약수로 구성되었다. 시합 과제와 순서는, 포반 계산병(FDC)으로부터 하달된 사격명령에 따라, 1. 시합대기선에서 포반 전체가 뛰어나가 포를 설치함과 동시에 2번 탄약수가 전방으로 나가 가늠대를 설치하면, 동시에 2. 포수가 조준구를 꼽고 숫자를 조정한 뒤, 3. 조준경으로 가늠대와 조준경내 조준선 왼편으로 정밀 정확하게 일치시키고, 4. "사격준비 끝"을 외친다.

그 결과 심판관은, 먼저 조준선 일치를 확인하고 "합격!"을 주고, 전 요원 협동 및 숙달성과 총소요 시간 점수 등을 합산하여 등수를 결정하였다. 우리 선수 팀은 우승하여 연대 내 최고팀으로 선정됨으로써 대대 최고 성과에 크게 기여하였다. 내가 얻은 교훈은, 전술시험 또는 기타 대회에 승리하려면, 1) 팀원과 울고 웃고 즐기고 긴장하며 동고동락하라, 2) 선수 사기를 앙양시켜라, 건빵이라도 좋고 라면이라도 좋으니 형편대로 수시로 제공하고 위로하라, 3) 감독 또는 훈련관은 현재 기록에 앞서는 목표치로 훈련시키고, 시험 현장에서는 승부욕에 불타 적극적이고 열정적으로 참여하고 독려하며 편들어 주면, 그 결과 승리가 가능하다는 교훈을 군대 생활 내내 절감하고 실천하였다.

4. 전투전초(COP) 중대장, 60년도 육군 권총 사격 최우수선수

◇ 중부 전선으로 복귀, 4·19혁명 지나다

60년 4월 초순경, 우리 제1연대는 다시 수도사단으로 복귀하고 군단사령부 인근 포천군 노곡리, 연대 신 주둔지로 교대 이동하였다. 얼마 있지 않아 '4·19혁명'이 일어났다. 지금 한 창 밑으로부터 부정부패 척결에 나서고 있던 우리 4년제 정규 육사 출신들로서는 정말 기대하는 바가 컸다. 그러나 시간이 흘러가도 국가적 사회적 변화는 별로 보이지 않았다. 다만 우리 주둔지 인근의 인적 분위기 변화는 잠깐으로 끝나기도 하였다.

이곳은 바로 뒷산 여우고개 정상 지점에, 주로 미군이 사용하는 '사격장 겸 중·대대급 기동훈련장, 'Nightmare'이 있었다. 이 훈련장으로 연중 계속되는 미군의 이동 편의를 위해, 남쪽 영평천변 도로에서 바로 여우고개 정상으로 이동할 수 있도록 군사도로를 내고 이를 당시의 대통령 이승만의 아호를 따서 '우남(雩南)도로'라 명명하였는데, 이 길에는 항상 시험(ATT)장으로 가는 미군 차량, 장갑, 탱크부대가 밀려서 줄지어 서 있게 마련이었다. 그래서 생겨난 것이 양공주 영업이었다. 4·19 이후 이 동네 변화는 이들이 집단으로 퇴출되었다가 대략 1개월 후부터 개별로 다시 돌아온 정도였다, 더구나 군대 내부로는 전혀 변화나 영향을 미치지 못하였다. 그러기에 우리는 크게 실망하고 다시 변화를 추구하였다.

◇ 사단대항 육군사격대회, 한국 육군 최고 권총 사격 선수 되다

한국 육군은 당시 휴전 상황하 전투 준비 태세를 유지하기 위해 부대대항 운동시합, 전술시합, 사격시합 등을 연중 계속 실시하고 있었다. 당시 수도사단 장교들은 육군 최고 엘리트—당시 일반 장교는 임관 성적순, 사단 서열순으로 배치했음으로 서열 최고인 수도사단 장교단은 엘리트 집단이라 해도 과언 아님—들이었는데 그중에서도 제1연대 간부 구성원들은 육군 제1의 긍지를 가지고 있었다.

그래서 연대대항 사단 대회에서는 그것이 무슨 시합이던, 거의 항상 타 2개 연대 성적 합보다 높은 성적으로 리드하고 있었다. 그러다 보니 사단대항 군단 또는 육군 시합에서도 수도사단은 항상 월등한 성적으로 전군 제1위를 유지하고 있었다. 특히 사격대회는 가히 타 사단이 따를 수 없는 대회 전승 전통을 유지하고 있었다. 여기에서 '사단의 전통' 즉, 사기(士氣) 그리고 그것이 불러오는 부대 단결이라는 것이 전장에서도 승리를 좌우할 수 있는 큰 전투력이라는 것을 알 수 있었다.

1960년 봄, 제5군단 주최 사단대항 전군 사격대회가 '일동'에 있는 군단사격장에서 개최되었다. 이럴 때면 각 사단은 대체로 1개월 이상 전부터 사단 대표 사격선수단을 구성하고 별도로 실탄사격 연습을 실시한다. 대구경 총포는 주로 전투 검열 때 별도로 시행함으로 시합에서는 제외한다. 따라서 시합 때는 주로 기관총 이하 권총 포함 소구경화기가 해당되었다.

특히 우리 사단 승리의 일등공신 하사관들은 매년 합숙 연습 때마다 팀원들을 혹독하게 훈련시킨다. "야 너희들 잘 들어, 작년엔 00초를 끊어서 겨우 이겼는데, 지금 이 기록으로는 안된다. 3초 더 단축해야 한다. 자, 반복 연습이다 알았나!" 하며 목표 달성 때까지 그리고 그것이 문제없이 유지될 때까지 쉼 없이 피나는 노력을 다한다. 그러다 보면 연습용으로 실탄은, 전투 요원의 1년치 교탄 중 1/2, 예를 들면 개인당 30발의 교탄(교육용 실탄) 중 15발을 사격선수들이 연습용으로 소모하기도 한다.

이 때문에 과연 이런 시합이 전체 전투원/부대의 실제 전투력을 향상시킬 수 있는 건지 의문을 갖기도 한다. 그래서 그로부터 10여 년 뒤 시합이 폐지되었다. 그러나 장점도 많이 있었다. 실제 전장에서 그리고 전투에서도 다수의 엘리트 장병들에 의해 전투가 리드될 수도 있다는 대는 이의의 여지가 없을 것이기 때문이다. 그때도 우리 수도사단은 전 종목에서 우승하였거니와 장교 권총 사격에도 우승하였다. 그 권총 사격대회에서 나는 92점(%)을 받아 그해 육군 최우수 권총 사격선수가 되었고 사단 우승에 크게 기여도 하였다.

그런데, 에피소드가 한두 가지가 생겼다. 하나는 바로 권총 사격 시합 현장에서이다. 우리 대표선수는 5명이었는데 나를 포함 중위가 두 명, 대위 두 명, 선수 겸 대표선수로 소령 1명이었다. 그런데 이들 모두가 상당 회수 출전한 경험 선수들이었다. 그래서 평소 연습 때는 평균 92% 적중률을 보이는 우승 후보들이었는데, 막상 시합 전날이 되자 안정심을 얻기 위해 신경안정제를 복용하는 것 같았다. 올림픽에서 흔히 회자되는 소위 '약물 도핑' 이었다. 그리하여 시합 당일 사선에 올라가서는 그만 정신이 오락가락하여 오히려 평상시 기록을 못 내고 마는 것이었다. 반면에 그런 사실을 모르는 나는 평상시보다 좋은 기록으로 우승하였다.

또 하나는 행사의 대미를 장식하는 의미에서 마지막에 사단장 이상 지휘관들에 의한 (친선) 권총 시합이 있었다. 우리 사단이 소속한 5군단장은 오늘의 결과에 의기양양하여 앞서 시합장으로 나오면서, 오늘 권총 사격 최우수선수의 권총 즉 내 권총을 빌려 갔다. 내 권총은 내게 맞게, 특히 격발 장치를 연하게 해 두었기에 사전주의가 없으면 실수하기 좋게 되어 있었다. 아니나 다를까, 사격 결과 우리 군단장은 최하위를 면치 못하고, "역시나 총보다 사람이 말하는구나"라고 했다 한다. 나는 우리 동료 선수들과 함께 미안한 웃음으로 총을 돌려받았다.

◇ 철원 전방 백마고지 인접 '남방한계선 전투전초'(COP) 중대장

나는 사단 사격단에서 부대 복귀와 동시 소대장을 면하고 제2대대 작전 장교로 보임되었는데, 대대장은 생도 10기 '이상익 중령'—5·16군사혁명 당시 '한신' 내무장관 비서실장, 후에 국회의원, 충청도 양반—으로 높은 학식은 물론 인덕이 누구나 존경할 수 있는 분이었다. 부대대장은 일반 장교 출신 '최상화 소령'으로 외모가 장수같이 거구였고 인간성 또한 훌륭하여 대대본부는 항상 인정이 훈훈한, 마치 대대 단결력의 상징 같았다. 그러기에 나는 이 시기가 상급자로부터 가장 큰(완전한) 신임을 받으며 마음의 부담 없이 충성을 다한 행운의 한 시기였다.

당시에 대대 S—3(작전 장교) 직책을 수행하고 있었는데, 연대장으로부터 '화학전 방어 연대시범'을 지시받았다. 그런데 어느 중대도 주저하기에 또 '육사 출신 전지 전능 정신'을 발휘하여, 내가 직접 계획하고 지휘하여 준비한 뒤, 연대 전 장병을 상대로, '화생방 상황하의 야전 행동과 방독면과 키트 내용물 사용법'을 시범 행동으로 실시하였다. 그 결과 연대장(김영환 대령 #5기)의 공개 칭찬과 대대장의 격려 말씀을 듣고 전방 생활의 한 기쁨을 만끽하였다.

이제 최전선 이동이 임박한 시점에, 나는 이찬우 선배(3기생)가 전방 가족생활을 벗어나 육사 교관으로 전보되면서 나를 그 후임으로 추천하여, 나는 제1연대 제2대대 제5중대장이 되었다.

당시 특히나 우리 수도사단에는, 대위급을 비롯한 고참 장교들이 많았는데도 내게 기회를 준 것은 아마도 요긴한 이유가 있었을 것이다. 우리 대대는 휴전선 GOP연대(General Out Post, 수도사단 제1연대)의 전방 전투전초(COP, Combat Out Post) 대대 임무를 맡아 강원도 철원 동송리 전방 독서당 지역—당시는 대광리 위 '신탄리(역)'에서 민통선 시작이라 그 이북엔 민간인 거주프랑스가 지역—으로 이동하고, 우리 중대는 전방으로 더 나가 '삼자매(三姉妹)고지'에 중대본부를 두고, 그 전방으로 휴전선 남방 2킬로미터 즉 비무장지대 남방한계선을 연하여 3개 전투전초소대를 배치하였다. 중대 경계 작전 담당 구역은 '백마고지' 하단 '역곡천'에서부터 우로 '월정리역'까지 대략 5킬로미터였다.

작전 환경은, 폭 4킬로미터 비무장지대 넘어 북으로 멀리 500고지 능선 지대가 북진을 저지하는 장벽으로 가로막혀 있고, 비무장지대 내 북측에는 북괴가 휴전 조약을 무시하고, 일찍부터 대대 본부를 비롯한 예하 단위 부대를 중화기와 함께 전진 배치해 놓았고, 전투참호 구축과 동시 전기 철조망을 가설 중이었다.

당시 휴전선 이남 아군 비무장지대에는 휴전선 표지 말뚝 외 철책선도 방벽선도 없었다. 다만 아군은 휴전 조약에 따라 지대 내 순찰과 적동향을 감시하는 '비무장지대 순찰 겸 감시조'(MP)만을 운용하였다. 그 부대 단위는 한 지점에 증강된 1개소총 소대 규모로—상대인 북괴는 대대급 부대와 그 중장비들로 무장—순찰(Patrol) 중 휴식 및 숙소와 감시초소를 겸하는 GP(Guard Post)만 존재하였다. 이들은 좌우순찰조들과 수시로 교신하며 만나고 또 직후방 우리 중대와도 협조하였다. 우리 중대 앞 GP는 '왕관고지'에 있었는데 마침 우리 육사 5기생 후배가 있어서 협조에 문제가 없었다.

우리 전투전초 중대의 전시 임무는, 최전방 파견초로부터 시작한다. 이들은 전시에는 분초에서 매복 또는 보초로 전방 감시 요지에 파견되었다가 적 공격이 시작되면 즉시 이를 분초로 보고하면서 철수하고, 분초는 이를 확인하고 즉시 소초로 보고하면서 철수해 합류한다. 소초부터는 상급부대 화력 지원하에 적과 접촉을 유지하면서, 명에 의하여 사격과 후퇴 이동으로 중대에 복귀한다. 전투전초 중대는 미리 준비해 둔 전투배비 위치에 전개하여 일단 적을 저지하면서 감시하다가 대대명에 의해, 또는 대대 전투SOP에 의해 전투 행위를 수행한다.

평소에는 남방한계선에 배치된 소초가 중대장 명에 의거 비무장지대 내 야간 매복작전을 위해, 지점을 매일 변경해 가며 매복작전을 수행하고 일출전 철수한다.

전투전초 중대장은 지역이 광범위하기에 순찰용으로 지프가 배차돼 있었다. 나는 그 기회를 이용하여 지역 내를 부지런히 순찰하고 적을 감시하며 전투전초부대 임무를 충실히 수행하면서 휴전 직전 20회 이상 주고받은 고지 쟁탈전으로 유명해진 백마고지를 견학하고, 때로는 역곡천의 전술적 활용도 검토하고, 그리고 지역 내에 들어와 있는 해골만 남은 북괴 '철원노동당사'를 보며 북괴의 잔인성을 상기하기도 하고, 월정리역을 지날 때는 6·25의 참상을, 바로 눈앞에 전개되어 있는 북괴군 모습과 함께 연상하기도 하였다.

거의 매일 소대를 순찰하는데, 어느 소대는 불과 몇 달 사이에 야채밭을 가꾸어 자랑도 하였는데, 그 소대장은 일반 장교 출신 '옥 모 소위'로 부지런하였는데, 아니나 다르랴, 후에 육군병참감이 된 성실한 장교였다.

◇ 한미8군합동권총사격대회 속사 1등

한국 중부전선 철원지역에서 전투전초 임무를 개시하여 3개월여가 지나는 동안 이상익 대대장과 부대대장(최상화)의 친절하고도 적절한 지도를 받아가며 지형 익숙과 평시 임무 그리고 전시 작전 임무 등에 숙달이 되어 가고 있었다. 그런데 뜻밖에도 '한·미합동사격대회' 출전을 명받았다. 육군 권총 대표선수 자격을 가졌으니 본인인 나도 어쩔 수 없었거니와 대단히 섭섭한 표정이 역력한 대대장도 어쩔 수 없이 "여긴 걱정 말고 좋은 성적 거두고 오라"고 격려하며 허락하였다. 중요한 임무를 수행해야 하는 내 중대와 중대원들을 두고, 비록 1개월여이지만, 어딘가 간다는 것은 참으로 무책임하고도 안타까운 마음이었으나 명령인 것을 어쩌랴.

서울에 모여보니 '60년 한미8군합동권총사격대회'가 준비 중에 있었고, 참가자들은 태릉에 이미 자리잡고 있는 '한국국가대표사격선수단' 요원 5명(단장은 소령)과 그리고 우리 육군 대표 신참 3명(대위 1, 중위 2)이었다. 우리 한국 권총 사격 대표팀은 사전 연습과 행사 기간을 합쳐 대략 1개월간, 장충단 공원 동쪽 산마루턱 당시는 공터, 지금의 '반얀트리 서울호텔', 전엔 '서울타워호텔' 자리에 천막을 치고 야영하였다.

사격 시합장은 미군 권총 사격장으로, 현 남산 2호와 3호 터널 위 능선상에 있었는데, 남쪽으로 미8군사령부가 내려다보였다. 사격 시합 종류는 권총 50m 완사, 25m 완사와 시간사, 10m 속사였고 선수 자격 구분은 master(수상 경험자), expert(2번 이상 출전자), new shooter(처음 출전자)였고, 그해 나는 뉴 스타에 속했다.

대회 사격통제관은 놀랍게도—우리네 생각으로는 이 정도 대회면 최소한 영관급 통제관 범위 같은데—하사관(중사)이었는데, 듣기로는 소령으로 전역했다가 재복무자라 했는데, 그 말 대로 능숙하고 당당하였다. 한국군 대표선수와 한국 주둔 미군 즉 미 제8군 대표선수와의 시합인데도 아무런 잡음이나 차질없이 통제해 나갔다. 미군과 미국민의 자치, 자존의 힘이 얼마나 강한가를 새삼 알 수 있었다.

그런데 당시 기준으로 미국과 한국의 실상(격차)을 실감하는 몇 가지 사실을 잊을 수가 없다. 그 하나는, 권총 그 자체에 관한 것으로, 이 총은 한미 양군이 같은 형식 즉, 흔히 '포리 파이브'(구경45)라고 하는 미국 콜트(Colt) 회사 제품을 사용하고 있었다. 그러나 '사격 시합'이라는 상황을 놓고 말하자면 한미 양군의 총의 질(성능)에는 현격한 차이를 보였다.

미국 선수들은 각자 개인 소유 권총 전용 보관함(가방)—사격에는 가늠쇠와 가늠자 역할이 중요함으로, 최상의 조준 상태를 유지하기 위해서라도 필요한 것이다—을 가지고 다니는데, 그 속에는 순 사격시합용 자기 권총(상아 손잡이에 자기 이름이나 이니시얼을 넣은)을 2~3정이 들어 있고, 그것들은 모두 최신 생산품으로, 가늠자는 앞뒤로 움직이고 가늠쇠도 좌우로 조정할 수 있는 그야말로 시합용 권총이었다. 그래서 연습 때나 시합 때도 이것저것 바꾸어 써 가면서, 동시에 정밀하게 설계된 가늠자 가늠쇠를 조정해가면서 그야말로 시합 도구도 최상의 컨디션으로 사격에 임한다.

하, 그런가 하면 당시 우리의 현실은 그들과 비교해서 정말 기막힌 것이었다. 그나마 사격 국가 대표선수는 본 것이 있어서 각자가 나름대로의 솜씨로 나무로 만든 가방 속에 제2차 세계대전 때부터 쓰던 권총—모델은 미군과 같은 '포리파이브'(구경45)—을 넣어 다니기는 하였으나, 우리 선수 모두는 2차대전과 한국전쟁을 거친 고물(?)로 현직 지휘관용(사용하고 있는) 권총으로, 전투용이기에 가늠자와 가늠쇠는 물론 고정되어 있었다.

그나마 태릉 선수촌 선수들은, 그래서 종종 가늠쇠와 가늠자가 오래 써서 닳지 않은 상태의 '슬라이드'만은 병기창에 특별히 주문하여 가능한 최신 제품으로 보급받아 와서는 시합 직전에, 부지런하게도 원시시대로 돌아가, 대장간에 가서 가늠쇠에 쇠를 더 붙여와서 '줄'로 일일이 갈아 좀 큰 모양 가늠쇠를 만들면서 수없이 시험 사격과 갈기를 반복하여 자기에게 맞는 가늠쇠 모양을 만들어 내는 수고를 조금도 마다하지 않았다. 이들은 시합 전 며칠간은 거의 반나절을 대장간에 갔다가 방에서 줄로 갈았다가 시험 사격해 보았다가 하는 것이 연습장 일과였다.

육군 대표선수로 나온 우리 중에도 그렇게 하는 동료가 있었으나 나는 그러지 않고, 있는 그대로를 내 눈과 체력에 맞게 적응해 나갔다. 내가 가지고 온 권총은 현직 전방 대대장 이상 지휘관용으로, 물론 2차대전에서 한국전 그리고 지금에 이르기까지 어느 지휘관 옆구리에 차는 가죽 케이스에 들어 있던 권총 그대로여서 가늠쇠는 닳아서 모서리가 없을 정도이고 햇빛에 번쩍였다. 시합 때는 야전교범대로 라이터 불 검정으로 그을려서 반사를 막으며 사용하였다.

그런데 실탄은 그해 시합용 실탄—실탄 탄피 하단에 1960년도의 60.match가 선명한 번쩍이는 신탄—으로 한정판으로 생산해 나와 시합장에 보급되는데 미군은 그것을 연습용으로도 사용하기 때문에 여러 가지 조건에서 한국 선수들보다 훨씬 유리한 입장에서 시합 선에 나가게 된다. 우리는 시합 전까지 한국전쟁 때 생산하여 사용하던 것, 지금은 여분의 교탄(교육훈련용)이나 잘하면 비축된 BL(전투비축용)탄 등 이것저것 얻어지는 대로 사용하여 연습하였기에 미군에 비해서는 불리하기가 뚜렷하였다. 그런 미군과 감히 시합하다니!, 그러나 결과는 다를 수도 있었다.

시합 종류와 시상 종류는 역시나 풍족하고도 원칙적인 미군답게 다양하여 사격 선수라는 기분을 그리고 자기 기량을 충분히 발휘할 수 있도록 제도화되어 있었다. 사격 선수 구분은 우선 선수 자격 급수 구분으로, 3개 파트로 구분하였는데, New Shooter로 신참 선수, 다음은 Expert로 신참을 면한 선수, 그 위가 Master로 여러 번 우승하거나 우수한 기록 보유자로 규정하였다. 그리고, 시합 종류 또한 다양하여 50m 완사, 25m 시간사와 완사, 그리고 10m 거리의 속사 등이 있었고, 선수들은 모두가 여기에 참가할 수 있었다. 시상은 자격 급수 구분대로, 사선과 종류대로 우승자는 트로피, 2, 3등은 은메달 및 동메달 그리고 각종 류별사 선별 통합 성적에 따른 우승 트로피와 등급별 메달, 그리고 참가 기념 문양품 등등, 여하간에 선수들은 자기 기량을 그리고 사격의 재미를 마음껏 발휘하고 느낄 수 있었다. 대단히 미안하나, 한국군 권총 사격대회는 선수 구분도 사격 종류도 없이 25m 사선에서 완사 10발 한 번으로, 우승자 상장 하나로 행사 끝이였다.

시합이 시작되면 선수끼리 물론 조용하면서도 눈에 들어오는 응원도 한다. 아마도 시합 결과는 개인은 물론 단체 성적이나 기록도 되는 것 같았다. 그 중에는 자기 부대기(아마도 대대 단위급)를 가져와 꽂아 놓고, 그 꼭지에 피 묻은 여자 붉은 팬티를 걸어놓고는 진지하게 사격 과정을 지켜보며 외치기도 한다. 미군이 저런 것도 할 만큼 신기한 광경이 흔히 있었다. 시합 판정에서도 '판별 확대경'을 통해서 점수선에 물린 탄흔은 가능한 한 선수에게 유리하게 판정하는 것을 당연한 원칙으로 하고 있었다.

미군은 간식 시간은 물론이고 종일 이동 PX차가 와서 선수들의 식욕을 달래 주고—주로 도넛과 커피 아이스크림 등—심신의 피로를 위로해 주고 동시에 즐거운 휴식을 도와주었다. 이미 이런 풍습을 알고 있는 우리 국가대표 선수 중에서는 미리 몇 달러 준비해 와서 활용하는 사람도 있었다. 그런데 나는 처음 보는 물자 풍족한 미군 생활의 한 광경을 보면서, 아 우리 군대는 언제쯤 저 정도로 윤택해질 수 있을까, 한시바삐 될 수 있도록 우리가 노력해야지, 하고 다짐도 하였다.

시합 결과 나는 10m 12초 속사에서 한미군 통합해서 신사수로 우승하여 우승 트로피 — 물론 지금도 내 서가에 진열되어 있다—하나를 확보하고, 25미터 시간사에서 실버메달, 완사에서 브론즈메달, 전체 합산하여 신사수로서 종합 5위의 성적으로, 내가 처음으로 출전한 '1960년도 한미8군합동권총사격대회'를 마감하였다.

그런데, 국가 대표선수들은 Master급으로, 위에서 본 그대로 모든 것이 불리함에도 불구하고, 전 국민 무장이 허용되고 사격 연습이 일상화되어 있는 미군을 상대하여 실로 악전고투 끝에 체면을 세울 수 있는 성적을 기록하였는데, 참으로 대견하였고, 올림픽 후보 선수들로서 기대될 수 있었다. 나는 그들로부터 올림픽 국가 대표단에 합류할 것을 제의받았으나, 제의한 그들도 나도 육사 신으로 그 방향은 무리한 것으로 결론짓고 대신 차순위의 일반 장교 출신이 참여하기로 하였다.

그리하여 다시 전방 나의 COP중대로 복귀하였는데, 훌륭한 군사 실력자요 인격자로 친절하였던 분들, 대대장 이상익 중령은 사당 참모부로, 연대장 김영환 대령은 야전사 전투검열단장으로 영전하고, 부대대장도 후방으로 동시에 보직변동이 되어 있었다. 그때 느꼈던 정말 인간적 허탈 기분과 섭섭한 기분은 지금도 잊을 수가 없다.

그러나 다행하게도 중대는 비록 대대 예비 중대로 후방에 나와 있긴 하였으나 5기생 후배(임승해 중위)가 중대를 지휘하고 있어서 큰 공백은 느끼지 않았고, 비록 예비 중대 임무는 생소하였으나 다시 최전방 생활에 적응을 시작하였다.

◇ 아주 마음에 드는 아가씨를 좋아하다

사관학교 생도 때부터 외출·외박 때는 유일한 서울 근거지, 문치과 형님댁(용산 원효로)으로 신세를 지는 일이 다반사였다. 4학년이 되어 외출했을 때는, 문치과 형수님의 언니의 딸 즉, 조카뻘 되는, 이화여대 영문과에 갓 입학한 청초한 여학생이 하숙생으로 와 있었다. 그래서 외출·외박 때 집안에서 마주치기도 하였는데 그때마다 어쩐지 아주 좋은 아가씨로 보였다. 그녀의 이름은 '박진영(鎭榮)', 애칭은 '수연(秀淵)'이었다.

임관 후 박정기 동기가 그동안 사귀던 이화여대 영문과 졸업생과 결혼 약속을 하고, 주변 동기들 다수가 이대 여학생들과 잘 사귀고 있는 소식들을 들으면서 귀도 마음도 솔깃하였다. 그러던 중에 이미 말한 바, 전방 같은 부대 '이 선배' 결혼식에 다녀온 뒤부터, 서울에 외출 나간 기회에 문치과 형수님 조카 여대생을 새삼 다시 보게 되었다. 여러 가지가 다 마음에 들었으나 특히 그의 사람 대하는 모습, 친절하고 차분하면서도 성실(진심)한 자세가 마음을 끌었다.

지난번 문산 근무 시절 몇 번 외출에서 보아왔고, 이번 한미사격대회에 나와서도 만나보니, 보면 볼수록 더욱 마음에 들었다. 그래서 형수님께 내 마음을 말해 두었다. 61년 2월, 바로 중대로 복귀하여 예비 중대의 중대장 임무를 수행하게 되는 때, 그녀는 학업을 마치게 되었고 나는 형수님의 초청으로 그 졸업식에 참석하여 졸업을 축하도 해주고 자연스럽게 그 부모도 보게 되었다. 모두 좋은 분들로 보였다.

◇ FEBA 개념 거점대대의 작전 장교, 근무와 사랑의 데이트

◦ FEBA 개념의 전방 대대 거점

1961년 2월 말경에 한국군은 미군과 함께 '전방 전술핵 방어작전·전략'의 도입에 따라 휴전선에 연한 전군 재편성과 동시에 최전선 진지 재형성과 재구축을 시작하였다. 즉 지금까지는 '주저항선(MLR, Main Line of Resist)' 개념으로 최전선이 대체로 횡으로 일찍선으로 형성되고, 진지가 구축되었으며 부대가 지면 편성되었다. 그러나 이제부터는 전술핵을 사용하여 방어하기 위한 전략개념에 따라 전장지대 내 '최후방어(거점, Strong Point)'을 형성 구축하고, 이들 방어지역 전단을 연결하는 최전선 개념 즉, 피바(FEBA, Foward Edge of Battle Area)를 방어해 나가는 개념이었다.

그리하여 최전선 GOP부대와 그 지대 외의 종심 주저항선은 지대 내 주변 거점을 대체로 대대 단위로 형성하고 고수하면서 적을 지대 내로 깊숙이, 예를 들어 문혜리 전선이라면, 운천 지역까지 최종 방어거 점 포켓안으로 유인한 뒤—즉 자연적으로 적이 아군 거점을 피해 전진하여 아군 포위망에 들어오면—전술핵(통상 5kt)을 투하하여 적 1개대대 규모를 섬멸하고, 즉시 반격한다는 전략전술 개념이었다.

그래서 나는 다시 제1대대 작전 장교가 되어 부대 이동을 계획하고 그해 3월경 밝은 달밤을 이용하여 백마고지 지대에서 '동막리' '을지 거점'으로 평행 이동하였다. 우리 연대는 종으로 지포리 깊숙이까지 3개대대 거점으로 된 연대 FEBA 전선을 형성하였다. 그리고 몇 개월에 걸쳐 대대관측 및 지휘소를 겸하는 대대OP와 전투참호 등을 구축하는 진지 편성을 실시하였다.

◦ 전방 근무와 사랑 데이트

그러는 동안, 서울로 외출 외박하는 기회에 문치과에 들려 그 여학생을 만나 정말 마음가는 데이트를 하였다. 그런가 하면 전방으로 데이트를 대신하는 '연서'가 오면, 연대 정보주임 '이 소령'—한때 군대 탈모비누 사건의 피해자 본인, 한때 우리 권총 사격 선수 인솔 책임자—이 즉시 전화로 "왔어, 왔어!"하며 가능한 즉시 가장 빠른 연락병 편으로 보내주었다.

그런데 이분이 사람이 참 인정스럽고 내게 친절하였다. 그때쯤에 서울에 있는 '영 아가씨'가 내가 근무하는 전방으로 한 번 면회를 왔는데, 당시는 연대 정문이 곧 면회소였고 정보참모 소관이었다. 그런데 그 양반이 알고는, 누구 반가운 자기 친척이나 온 듯이 안내하고, 급히 전화로 나를 찾아, "뭐 하느냐, 빨리 안 나오고" 독촉하며 자기 지프를 보내주기까지 하였다.

그런가 하면 같은 대대에 근무하며 친한 중대장(대위)들은 나에게 진담 겸 농담조로 "장가들면 기선을 잡아 여자를 지배해야 한다. 그래야 평생 조용한 가정이 된다"고도 하였는데, 마치 그 나이에 인생 다 살아본 것처럼 조언도 하는데, 역시나 인정을 다하여 진지한 것은 틀림없었다. 부대 근무하다 보면 이런 친절하고 인정스럽고 믿어주는 상급자들이 있어서 나는 부대 생활에 크게 낯설거나 외롭지 않았다. 지금 그 모든 분들께 거듭 고마웠다고 인사드린다.

정보참모의 인정과 친절한 독촉에 따라 전방 근무지에서 나와 문혜리에서, 비록 보잘것 없는 100여 호 초가마을, 그러나 그래도 전방에서는 사람이 살고 군인 가족들(하사관부터 연대장에 이르기까지)이 살고 있는 이 전방 마을까지 와 주다니 더 이상 정들 수가 또 있으랴. 비록 데이트라는 것이 '영계백숙집'에서 한 그릇 같이 먹으며 앉아서 얘기하는 것, 당시는 커피점 뭐 그런거 전혀 없었고, 그 밥집에서 그저 숭늉 한 그릇으로 입가심이 다였다. 그때 그녀의 그 낯설고 먼길 찾아온 성의와 인정 정말 고마웠고, 아마도 서울에서 하는 일 년 치 데이트 보다 진한 것이었기에 지금도 결코 잊을 수 없는 행복한 추억이 되어 있다.

당시 서울에서 이곳 문혜리로 올려면, 우선 청량리나 미아리고개에 있는 시외버스터미널로 가야 한다. 거기서 하루 서너 번밖에 없는 운천행 시외버스를 기다리다 타야 한다. 당시는 4시간 내지 5시간 소요되었다. 낯설은 시골 군대 도시 운천에서는 또 문혜리로 가는 지선 버스(이건 더 드믈었다)를 기다렸다가 타고 문혜리에 도착하면 연대본부 면회실로 묻고 또 물어서 걷고 또 걸어서 찾고 찾아가야 했다. 그렇게 어려운 길을! 그래서 그 어찌 정들지 아니하였으랴.

◇ 고대하던 '5·16 군사혁명과 콜론 보고서'

◦ '콜론 보고서'

이승만 정권 말기, 자유당과 그 도당들에 의해 정치적으로는 대한민국의 헌법에 없는 영구 집권을 노리고, 경제적으로는 미국 원조가 급감하면서 도당적 부패가 극에 달하여 문자 그대로 한국 사회가 도탄에 빠지고 있을 무렵인 1959년 11월에 미국 상원분과위원회에 '미국의 대아시아정책'이라는 이름을 가진 '콜론보고서'가 '대한정책권고서'용으로 제출되었다.

이 보고서에는, 한국의 실정을 "미국 원조 없이는 한국 경제는 곧 붕괴할 것이고, 한국에 민주주의가 껍질만 남은 것도 기적이고, 부의 양극화, 수단 방법을 가리지 않는 출세 제일주의의 만연 등"으로 규정하고, '쿠데타 가능성이 희박하나 필연적'이라는 다소 모호하나 암시적인 군사혁명의 긴박성을 공공연히 강조하였다.

군사혁명의 가능성을 분석하여 가로되, "한국에서는 가난한 집안의 유능한 재원들이 학자금 때문에 대학 교육이 국비인 사관학교에 들어가 지식 프롤레타리아트 성향으로 발전할 수 있는 청년 장교가 되고 있다. 그런데 이들은 특권적 관리와 정치가에 분노를 가지고 있으며 폭발할 우려도 있다. 현재 한국에서는 군사 지배가 정당을 대체하는 그런 사태가 있을 수 있다"는 사실을 강조함으로서 미국 일부 정계의 한국 군사쿠데타에 대한 기대를 반영하는 것이기도 하였다. 나는 생도 때부터 청년 지식인용 교양잡지 『사상계(思想界)』

를 탐독해 왔는데, 60년 1월부터 소개된 이 '콜론보고서'를 읽고 아주 고무되었고, 스스로 국가와 국군 개혁에 대한 어떤 역할을 자각하게 하는 자극제가 되었다.

◦ 5·16 군사혁명

드디어 1961년 5월 16일, 박정희 장군을 비롯한 쿠데타 주동자 24명이 지휘하는 3,600명의 봉기군이 별다른 저항—단, 한강 입구에서 10여 명의 경계헌병 사상—을 받지 않고 시내로 진입하여 목표 지점을 장악하였다. 그리하여 봉기군 지휘부(박정희-김종필)는 KBS방송국을 통해 계엄령선포를 공고하였고, 혁명군 지휘부와 육해공군 및 해병대 참모총장들은, 숨어버린 장면 총리 대신 대통령을 면담, 윤보선 대통령은 "(드디어) 올 것이 왔구나" 하면서 그들과 상면하고 '무혈 해결'을 강조하였다. 즉 혁명을 인정한 것이었다.

혁명 주체 세력은 거사와 동시에, 당시 국민들이 믿고 있던 육사생도들의 지지가 곧 거사 성공의 보장이 될 것으로 인식하고, 일찍부터 육사생도 지지 동원의 방법을 모색하고 있었다. 그래서 전두환 대위—정규 육사 1기생으로, 미군 보병학교 RANGER(특공부대) 교육을 이수하고 귀국, 당시 서울대학 학군단 근무, 5·16 직후부터 하나회도 조직하고 육사총동창회를 지도하였다.—가 주동이 되어 동기생 이동남(동창회장)과 이상훈 대위(서울 근무)와 함께, 물론 육사교장과 학교본부가 반대하는 가운데 우여곡절 끝에, 적극적으로 육사생도들을 동원하는데 성공하였다.

그리하여 5월 18일 오전에 역사적인 육군사관생도들의 무장 예복 시가 행진이 서울시내 중심가(동대문에서 시청 앞까지 시가 행진 후 시청 앞에서 혁명지지를 선포)에서 전개되었다. 이로서 결과적으로 우리 모두 잘 알다시피 육군사관학교와 사관생도들을 깊이 신뢰하고 있었던 국민들은 이 혁명을 비로소 완전하게 지지하게 되었고, 민심은 문자 그대로 하루아침에 안정을 되찾았던 것이다.

◦ 육사생도들이 정규 육사 선배들 주도로 혁명시위에 나선 뿌리 깊은 이유

이미 말한 바와 같이 정규 4년제 육사생도(1~4기)들은 기성 장교 세대들의 부정부패와 부조리에 대해 파사현정의 개혁 정신으로 저항해 왔다. 제1기가 임관 이후에도 현지 보급투쟁을 통해 전방에서 후방 등 전군에 개혁 바람을 불러 이르킴과 동시에, 제2기 졸업 시에는 거의 전 동기가 육사로 와서 졸업식장에서 공식 행사 후 별도로 선배(1기) 장교와 졸업생 그리고 재학생도들이 한데 뭉쳐, 교가와 응원가 그리고 응원 구호를 외치며 '부정부패 척결, 파사현정'의 기치를 내걸고 단결하고 또 단결하였다.

이 행사는 매해 졸업식 때마다 계속되어, 군에서는 이제 거슬릴 수 없는 개혁 기풍이 일어났고, 육사 출신 초급 장교들은 가는 곳마다 개혁의 기세를 더하였다. 이러는 중에 바로 '5·16군사혁명이 일어났던 것이다. 그러기에 최고 선배인 육사 1기생, 총동창회 간부들이거나 서울 지역 근무 정규 육사 출신 장교들이 즉각 혁명에 호응하고 그들에 의해서 즉시 육사생도들을 설득하게 되였던 것이다. 당시 정규 육사 출신들의 위국헌신, 파사현정을 핵심으로 하는 일심동체 단결력은, 그 정도도 사실은 훨씬 넘고 있었던 것이다.

◦ 5월 16일 새벽 4시 30분에 KBS 방송망을 통해 발표된 「혁명공약」

1. 반공을 국시의 제일의(第一義)로 삼아 반공체제를 재정비 강화
2. 유엔헌장 준수, 국제협약 충실 이행, 미국과 자유우방 유대공고, 증진
3. 부패와 구악 일소, 퇴폐 국민 도의와 민족 정기 쇄신 위한 기풍 진작
4. 기아 선상의 민생고 시급 해결하고, 자주 경제 재건에 전력 집중
5. 국토 통일을 위해 공산주의와 대결 실력 배양에 전력 집중
6. 위의 과업 성취되면 정권 이양 후 본연 임무 복귀

"조국은 새롭고 힘찬 역사가 창조돼 가고 있다. 조국은 단결과 인내와 용기와 전진을 요구하고 있다. 대한만국 만세!, 궐기군 만세! "

혁명 구호 ; "간접침략을 분쇄하고 혁명과업을 완수하자 !"

궐기군의 혁명 목적은 일부 불만 소장파 장교들이 정군을 내걸고 군대 내부적인 진급 문제나 처우 개선 문제들에 대한 해결을 위해서만 쿠데타를 감행한 것이 아니었다. 30대의 이 청년 장교들은 당시 한국 내 어느 집단보다 선진적으로 민주주의 문물을 민주주의 본령에서 배우고 체험한 바 있어서, 문자 그대로 죽도록 가난하여 공산주의로 막 넘어가려는 나라와 민족을 구하려는 구국의 결심으로 가진 수단(무력과 조직의 힘)과 방법을 다하여 결단하고 감행하여 성공하였던 것이다.

그들이 표방했던 궐기공약 즉 선언문을 통해서 그들이 국민들과 전 세계에 전달하고자 했던 초기 혁명 전략 사상 즉 국가 안보 전략 사상은 박정희의 구국 사상과 정군 개혁 장교들의 우국충정 그리고 정규 육사 출신 장교단과 육사생도들의 파사현정(破邪顯正) 사상에서 발로된 것이 틀림없었다.

◇ '한국 사단대항 전군사격대회'와 '한미합동사격대회' 출전

그해 7월이 되자 제2군단에서, 해마다 실시되는 61년도 사단대항 전군사격대회가 개최되었는데, 이 해에도 사단 대표 권총 사격 선수로 선발되어 출전하는 영광을 갖게 되었다. 사단 사격 선수단은 일찍부터 구성하여 사단 사격장에서 이미 집체 연습훈련을 하였고, 우리 권총반은 반장 겸 선수 소령 1명에 선수 장교 4명으로, 이번에는 임박한 10일 전쯤에 구성하여 제2군단으로 이동, 사격장 근처 '아래샘밭' 근방 적당한 장소에 선수 야영장을 설치하였다.

사격 연습은 그 위에 있는 동네, 그때만 해도 비록 춘천에서 멀지 않은 곳이었음에도 불구하고 첩첩하고도 산골 동네인 '윗샘밭'으로 가서 사격 연습을 하는데, 동네 노인네들과 아이들이 모여서 구경도 하였다. 식사 때가 되어 반합에 담아간 밥과 된장국을 준비하려면 나무를 좀 구해야 하는데, 동네 사람들이 와서 그 밥쌀(보리30 대 쌀 70)을 좀 주면 그

곳 주산물인 감자를 많이 주겠다고 했다.

그래서 바꾸어 먹기도 했는데, 왜 그렇게 그 정도의 밥쌀도 욕심을 내는가 했더니, 옛날에 듣던 '강원도 특유의 사연'이 아직도 거기에 그대로 남아 있었다. 즉, 그때도 이 동네 사람들은 평생 쌀 한 말 먹고 죽으면 행복한 사람에 속한다고 했고, 처녀 시집갈 때는 신랑집에서 최소 쌀 한 가마, 과부가 재혼할 때는 보리쌀 한 가마로 때워야 하는 것이 이 동네 전통 풍습이라 했다. 사실 알고 보면 5·16 군사혁명 당시 우리나라는 전국 전 민족적으로 이렇게도 가난하였던 것이다.

이 해 육군사격대회에서도 우리 수도사단은 여유 있게 여타 모든 사단을 따 돌리고 수위의 성적을 거두고 사단장을 비롯한 전 부대원 환영 속에 귀대하였다. 그런데 귀대와 동시에 이번에는 '한미합동사격대회' 참가 선수 소집 명령을 받고 다시 해를 연이어 국제대회에 출전하는 영광을 가졌다. 이번 대회(61년 9월, 문산 미군 종합사격장)는 규모를 좀 크게하여 소총(M1과 Carbine)과 권총 분야를 동시에 시합하게 되었다. 따라서 군에서는 각 사단 기록 우수 선수를 선발하여 국군 선수단을 만들고, 시합 후 우수 선수는 국군 국가대표선수로 선발하려 하였다. 당시 대한민국에는 민간 사격 선수는 있을 수가 없었다.

권총 분야 시합 모습은 작년과 다를 바 없었고, 특히 우리 국군사격선수단팀은 그 어려운 환경을 이겨내고 50미터 완사에서 개인적으로 90% 이상 기록도 내며 기염을 토하기도 했으나, 역시나 정밀한 무기 소유자들에게 밀릴 수밖에 없었다. 나는 금년에는 작년 입상 기록도 있어서 숙련 선수(Expert)로 참가하였다.

나와 친한 후배 민병돈 중위와 동기생 강 중위와 나 이렇게 육사 출신 세 사람은 고군분투했으나, 원천적으로 2차 세계대전과 한국전쟁 때부터 미군과 한국군 현역 대대장과 연대장들이 휴대해 다니며 사용했고 지금도 사용하고 있는, 휴대용 가죽 케이스에 넣어다니는, 사격 시합용으로는 무디고 무딘 권총을 사용하였다. 그러나 미군은 선수 혼자 자기 애용 권총 3자루를 007가방에 넣어 다니며, 수시로 닦고 또 조이고, 가늠자 가늠쇠를 움직여서 조정해 가며 사용하는 그들이었다.

그래도 어떻게 하던 권총 가늠자 가늠쇠를 미군 것처럼 잘 보이게 하려고, 용접하고, 쓸고 쏘아보고 또 쓸어서 가늠쇠를 만들어보는 그 지성들이는 국가대표선수들과도 애당초 시합이란 말이 어폐가 있었다. 그리하여 대체로 동메달과 종합 5위 정도가 최상 기록들이었다.

이번 대회는 규모가 커서 지원 부대로 미군 1개 중대가 동원되었다. 그동안 미군을 많이 보아왔지만 미군 부대나 부대 행동을 보게된 것은 처음이었다. 그들은 중대장 지휘하에 일사불란하게 행동하는 것이 웬만한 한국군 중대보다 훌륭하게 보였다. 가만히 본즉, 중대원 모두가 하나같이 수염을 기르고 있었다. 아니 특히 당시 미국 남자들과 미군은 매일 면도하는 것이 신사도라며 특징으로 알려져 있었는데 의외였다. 그래서 병사 하나를 붙들고 물어보니, 중대장의 명령이란다. 중대장의 명령?, 미국과 미군이야말로 자유 국민이요 군대일텐데, 중대장의 명령이 그렇게 먹혀들고 있었다. 정말 의외의 미군을 새삼 발견하였던 것이다.

제4장

미국 유학, 결혼, '동복 올빼미' 교관, 연세 ROTC교관 (1961~1966)

1. 미국 유학, 'J.F, Kennedy Center', Ft.Bragg, N.C로 가다

◇ 유학 길이 열리다

6·25 전쟁 중에는 국군의 질적 능력을 향상시킨다는 의미에서 거의 전 장교가 단기 과정으로 미국 본토의 미군 각종 병과학교의 OBC와 OAC 또는 육군대학에 다녀왔다. 그러나 전후에는 주로 고위직 전속 부관들 정도로 극히 소수 인원이 다녀왔다.

그러다가 60년 전후해서 포병에 '미사일', 보병에 Special Warfare(특수전)—Psychological W(심리전), Unconventional W(비정규전), Counter Insurgency W(폭동 진압 작전)—와 Ranger(특공부대) 과정이 추가되었다. 그러자 61년 봄에 이미 결혼해 있던 내 절친 박정기 동기가 포병 미사일 과정을 다녀오고 김진규 동기도 다녀와서 광주 포병학교 교관으로 자리 잡았다. 그들이 전하는 미국 얘기도 흥미진진했지만 유학 과정이 더 관심사였다.

그리하여 그해 늦은 가을 '비정규전 과정' 유학 모집에 지원하고 휴가를 내어 서울로 와서 문치과에 유숙하며 한 열흘 동안 명륜동의 서울문리대 도서관에 가서 오랜만에 영어 책을 좀 들여다보았다. 그래서 군사학(지휘/참모)과 영어 시험—지금의 '토플 시험', 당시는 '부관(副官) 시험'이라 하였는데, 부관참모부에서 주관하였기 때문이리라—을 치르고 마지막으로 미군 관계관에게 면접 시험(Interview-Oral Ex)을 치렀다.

재미있었던 것은, 최종 면접 시험에서, 미군 주 시험관 소령이 내 나이, 임관 출신, 가족관계, 현 직책 등을 질문해서 확인하고는 최전방에 근무한다 하니, "요즈음 북한군 대남방송에서 뭐라고 하느냐?"고 묻길래, 나는 웃으며 친한 사람들끼리의 솔직한 마음으로 "American Go Home!" 한다고 주저 없이 말했더니, 그들은 폭소하면서 "그래서 당신은 어떻게 생각하느냐?"고 하길래, 내 생각 그대로 "You are Our Friend!"라고 강조했더니, 그들은 또 한 번 기분 좋게 웃었고, 주시험관 소령은 흔쾌히 "Good, I Recommend

You!" 하였다. 그래서 또 한 번, 너도 나도 모두 웃는 가운데 나는—뒤에 들으니 일반 통역 장교 경쟁자들보다 좋은 면담 성적으로—합격하고 나왔다.

그리하여 전방 생활(소대장, 작전 장교, 중대장) 3년 3개월을 아주 의미 있게 보람 있게 마치고, 중학생 때부터 희망하고 육사에도 유학 조건이 있어서 지망하여 그날을 고대하였던 미국 유학을, 비록 짧은 기간이지만 다녀오게 되어 기쁘기 한량없었다. "구하라 그러면 주실 것이다"를 믿고 열심히 노력한 결과임에 틀림 없었다.

◇ 약혼(언약)하고 유학가다

◦ 형수 씨 주선으로 약혼(언약)하다

그동안 서울에는 다른 연고 없이 그저 8촌 형벌 되는 문치과 형님 댁에, 서울 나올 때마다 내 집같이 드나들었는데, 그 형수님은 나를 믿고 좋아하셨다. 그런데 그분은 '영 아가씨'의 이모가 되는데, 그동안 나와 아가씨와의 관계 진행을 눈여겨보아 오다가 드디어, 이 유학 시점을 기해서 내 마음을 물어보며 권하기를, '자기 언니의 딸 즉 자기 조카와 결혼하란다'. 나는 즉시 고맙고 반가운 마음으로 동의했다. 그러나 결혼(식)은, 지금은 무일푼이라 좀 어렵고, 미국 다녀와서 한 일 년 월급을 모아서 전세값이라도 장만되면 하겠다고 말했다.

그랬더니 '아 그거야 자신이 맡아줄 테니 여하간에 빠른 시일 내 결혼하기로 하자' 해서, 부산 집으로 내려가 부모님께 자초지종 말씀을 드렸다. '전주 과수원집의 큰딸로 전주사범학교를 나오고—여기에 부모님은 일차 기분 좋아하시고—, 서울에서 당대 최고 학부인 이화여대 영문과를 이제 막 졸업한 정말로 내 마음에 드는, 그리고 부모님께도 잘하리라 생각되는 규수를 서울 문치과 형수님으로부터 소개받고 청혼받았다'고 말씀드렸다. 그랬더니 처음에는 "전라도 사람인데…"—당시 경상도 사람들은 무조건 '전라도 사람?'이었다—하다가, 그러지 않아도 서울 문서방(문치과 8촌 형님)한테서 얘기 들었다면서 바로 승낙하셨다. 그러자 옆에서, 당시 한창 열심히 일해서 돈 잘 벌고 있던 누님이, 내 신접살림 전세값—아마도 당시 10만 원, 지금 1,000만 원 정도—과 예물은 맡아서 해결해 주겠다고 약속해 주었다.

그래서 서울로 올라와 말씀드렸더니, 그럼 바쁘기도 하고 형편상 그러하니 약혼(언약)한 것으로 하고, 결혼 예물용으로는 마음에 드는 시계 한 쌍을 사 오는 것으로 대신하자고 했다. 이렇게 해서 말로 약혼하고 희망차고 벅찬 마음으로 미국 유학을 떠나게 되었던 것이다.

◦ 소망했던 미국 유학을 가다

1962년 1월 14일, 드디어 나는 그렇게도 소망하던 미국 유학을 가게 되었다. 이제는 아주 약혼까지 하게 된, 미래 나의 신부 '영 아가씨'가 홀로 김포공항까지 귀중한 선물을 들고 나와 나의 미국행 장도를 축하해 주었다. 정말 따뜻하고 정스럽고 고마웠다.

나와 함께 가게 된 선배(육사 3기) 한오경 대위'는 생도 시절 안면이 있었거니와 친절하고 좋은 대인 관계를 가진 선배로 그때부터 귀국할 때까지 항시 전우조(戰友組)와도 같이 고락을 함께하는 행운을 가져 참으로 다행이었다. 그 시작으로, 미군 지원으로 미국 가는 길이라 우리는 미군 사무실(퀀셋 건물)—당시 김포공항은 한국 민간항공과 미군용 비행장으로 공용하였다.—에 가서 여권과 함께 15장의 동일 복사 서류를 받아쥐고, 바로 옆에 대기중인 미군 쌍발 군용기(C-46 코만도)에, 일본으로 휴가 가는 듯한 미군들과 함께 올랐다.

'제투 비행기'와 같이 하늘로 치솟아 올라가는 스릴은 없었으나 그래도 창을 통해 송영대—그 옛날에는 3층 김포공항 옥상에 송영대(送迎臺)라는, 가고 오는 여객에게 손 흔들어 주는 곳—에서 손을 흔들어 주는 고마운 '영 아가씨'를 보아가며 이륙할 때는 정말 감회가 깊었다.

전쟁 복구 중이지만 서울의 모습을 공중에서 보니 아직도 처참한 상황이 여전하였고, 그런가 하면 좀 멀리 떠 오르자 바로 아래로 내려다보이는 김포 지역의 무질서하여 꾸불꾸불한 논밭과, 'ㄱ,ㄷ,ㅁ' 글자 모양으로 지어진 5000년 내려온 초가집들의 모습은, 5·1 6군사혁명의 구호처럼 "민족중흥"이 간절한 상황을 말해 주고 있었다.

우리가 탄 미군 수송기는 약 4시간가량 비행하여 현해탄을 건너가자, 아래로 일본 영토가 서해안부터 보이기 시작하였다. 첫인상은 푸르른 산 그리고 숲과 들, 잘 정돈된 논과 밭, 잘 꾸며진 기와집 마을과 마을들의 풍경들이 주마등같이 전개되어, 방금 떠나온 우리의 헐벗어 시뻘건 강산과 대조를 이루며 무언가 나라를 위해 해야 할 일들이 생각나고 또 생각났다.

◇ 미국 가며 전후 '일본 동경'에서 본 것들

드디어 일본 수도 동경의 '다찌가와(立川) 미군 비행장'에 착륙하였다. 우리는 비행장 근처 미군 숙소인 '방문 장교 숙소(VOQ)'에 안내되어 단 며칠이지만 그곳에 여장을 풀었다.— 동경 도심에서 1시간 거리, 지금은 일본 자위대 기지와 유명해진 '소화(昭和)공원' 으로 변해 있다고 한다.—우선 샤워장에 가서 참으로 오랜만에 따뜻한 물로 몸을 씻으니 그동안의 피로가 가시고 새 힘이 솟구치는 것 같았다. 솔직히 말해서 우리나라에서 맛보지 못한 편안함과 따뜻함이, 마치 최전선을 갓 벗어난 바로 그 후방의 분위기 느낌이었다.

다음 날, 일찍 민간복으로 갈아입고 서둘러서 밖으로 나가 일본 슈샤인보이—당시 일본에는 구두닦이도 기생(妓生)도 흔했다, 전후 사정은 어느 나라 없이 가난하게 마련이니까— 한테 구두를 번쩍이게 닦고는 물어 물어서 일단 버스를 타고 동경 시내로 향했다.

당시 일본도 우리와 같이 버스 여차장이 있었는데, 참 상냥하고 부지런하였다. 왼팔에 버스 차장 완장을 차고 한 손에 빨간 깃발을 들고 정차하는 곳마다 재빨리 내려서 교통정리를 하고 올라타면서 "오라잇"하는데 우리 차장 아가씨와 꼭 닮았다. 그리하여, 아마도 지금의 '긴자거리' 중앙통 6가쯤 되는 곳에서 내려 약속 지점을 찾아가, 사전에 김진규 동기로부터(한 선배) 소개받아 온 일본 여자 대학생과 만났다.

만나서부터 이틀간 여학생이 안내해 주는 대로 동경 시내 갈만한 곳 몇 군데와 극장 등을 중심으로 관광하였다. 1961년 1월 당시의 일본은 지가 저지른 전쟁 탓으로, 미군의 계획적 폭격에 의해 특히나 파괴가 심했던 동경 시내는 15년이 지난 그제사 임시 복구로 겨우 안정을 되찾아가고 있었다. 그런 가운데 여학생이 안내한 곳 중에 지금도 생생히 생각나는 곳은, 도쿄 중심거리에 있는, 우리의 옛 명동거리처럼 보이는 '유라구초(有樂町)'에 있는 극장 '에라이샹'(夜來香)이었다.

이 극장은 3층이었고, 앞 중앙 무대가 3층으로 오르내리면서 가수가 계속 등장하면서 노래로 서비스하는 양식이었다. 당시 일본에서 이 정도면 상당히 유명하고도 훌륭한 극장에 속했다. 그런데 더 유명했던 것은 바로 당시 일본에서 애달픈 곡절을 간직하여 대 인기곡 중의 하나였던 〈에라이샹(夜來香)〉이라는 노래를 직접 그 주인공인 '이향란(李香蘭)'이라는 여가수가 무대에 나와 불렀고 그래서 그 유행곡 이름을 따 극장 이름조차 '에라이샹'이었다. 뭐 감상할 줄 모르긴 하나 3층으로 무대가 오르내리며 그 가수가 부르는 애절한 노래는 역시 들어 줄만 했고 지금까지도 기억할 만했다.

당시 일본에는 '8·15 무조건 항복' 이후 '미조라 히바리'라는 어린 여가수가 전후 일본 현상을 노래로 위무하여 인기 절정에 있었는데, 6·25 적란 중에 미국 다녀온 우리 청년 장교들이 일본에 들러 '미조라 히바리'의 '도넛 판'—LP시절에 발명된, 지금 CD 크기—을 많이 사 들고 들어와 우리나라에도 많이 알려져 있었다. 특히 미군을 향해 '무엇이든 드릴테니 우리 집으로 오세요(come on my house come on!)'는 노래는 당시 일본 실정을 그대로 대표하는 유명한 유행곡이었다.

다음 순서로 뒤따라온 한 동기생 얘기로는, 어쩌다 일본 기생의 서비스를 받았는데, 당시 우리에게는 좀 큰돈인 30달러도 서슴없이 쥐어 줄만큼 서비스가 좋았다고 한다. 그런데 그 기생 아이들 얘기로는, 이 미국 달러는 곧 국민 저금이 되어 일본 부흥에 도움이 된다고 말하더라면서 일본 기생들의 애국심에 감탄했다고도 했다.

전철에서 본 당시 남녀 성인 일본 사람들의 키가 우리 턱 아래로 전철에 서서 보면 몇 칸 앞뒤로 다 보였다. 내가 나서 처음 본 외국, 처음으로 만나 본 일본 사람과 수도 동경, 벌써 질서 잡히고 부흥하는 일본, 자기 일 희생해 가며 성의를 다해 안내해 주는 아가씨와 일본 사람들—길가다가 보이는 여자에게 급하다 말했더니 자기 집안 화장실(고전풍)도 쓰게 해주는—의 친절에 고마웠다.

우리는 비록 며칠간이지만 여대생의 친절하고 정다운 안내로 일본의 수도 동경을 관광도 하고 겸해서 상황도 관찰한 뒤에 다음 돌아올 때를 다시 기약하고 평생 처음 일본 동경 방문을 끝내고 드디어 미국으로 향발하게 되었다.

◇ '하와이'를 지나 '샌프란시스코'에 오다

동경에서 하와이 비행은 장거리라 군용 4발 프로펠러 수송기인 C—130(허큘리스 전술 수송기)로 이동하였다. 야간에 '다찌가와 미군기지'를 이륙하였는데, 태평양으로 나올 때까지 한 30여 분간 동경 상공을 비행하였는데, 복구 중이라 여전히 밤이 어두운 한국 서울보다는 길고 넓고 밝았다.

듣기로는 6·25 당시 미국으로 유학갔던 선배 씨들은 군 수송선으로 태평양을 건너갈 때는 15~6일이 걸렸다고 했는데, 세월이 지난 지금은 비록 4발 프로펠러 수송기 일지라도 아마도 15시간 정도에서 하와이에 접근하였으니—3개월 뒤 돌아올 때는 민간 제트 전세기로 더 빨리— 그동안 얼마나 문명이 발전하고 있었는지 실감이 났다.

하와이로 접근한다는 방송을 듣고 내려다보니 안전에, 지금까지 보아왔고 생각해 왔던 바와는 전혀 새로운 풍경, 섬이지만 비행기가 낮게 나르니, 넓고 아주 반듯하게 잘 정리된 경작지의 아름답고 풍요한 모습이 한 참 전개되다가 드디어 호놀룰루 국제공항이 가까워지자 더욱 아름다운 풍경, 짙푸른 바다에 높직한 야자수의 가로수들, 물론 말로만 듣다가 지금 바로 눈앞에 전개되고 있는 세계 제일의 남국 자연풍경, 거기에다 정말 확 다른 양옥집들과 잘 정비된 신작로 등 이국 풍경을 보면서, '아 좋구나, 그런데 우리는 언제?' 로 생각하며 정말 미국의 첫인상이 감명 깊었다. 그러나 하와이공항에서 상당 시간 지체하였음에도 밖으로 나가보지 못해 유감스러웠다. 다음 어느 땐가는 관광 오리라고 다짐하며 호기심을 달래었다.

하와이에서 미국 본토로 향발하여 10시간여, 역시나 광대무변한 듯한 태평양 상공을 지나 드디어 미국 본토의 태평양 측 제1관문이며 세계에 잘 알려져 있는 '샌프란시스코(San Francisco)' 공항에 안착하였는데, 대기하고 있던 미군기지 당직 장교의 라이드 안내로 'Ft. Mason'에 도착하였다. 드디어 그렇게도 소망하던 미국에 그것도 유학(비록 단기간이지만)을 또 그것도 공짜로 온 것이다. 실로 감개무량하지 않을 수 없었다.

이곳 '포트 메이슨'은 전통 깊은 육군 해외 보충대 기지로 특히 한국 유학 장교들은 과거는 수송선으로 지금은 군용 수송기로 와서, 이곳을 거쳐서 출입국하였다. 기지 내 출입국 사무실로 가서 가져온 15장의 복사 서류를 내밀자 혼자 근무하는 중년 여사무원이 기다렸다는 듯 반갑게 "Welcom!"이라 인사하고 서류를 확인한 뒤, 금방 안내해 주었다. 우선 오늘은 시내 호텔 몇 곳 중 하나 골라서 쉬고, 내일부터는 원한다면 'Mrs Ko' 집으로 가서 다음 여행 명령 나올 때까지 쉴 수 있다고 했다. 그래서 우리는 우선 아는 이름 'YMCA 호텔'—나중에 알고 보니 미 육군과 할인 서비스 계약된 중류급 호텔—로 가서 뜻깊은 미국의 첫날밤을 위한 여장을 풀었다.

그런데 그 시간부터 이제 미국이라는 나라와 사회 시스템에 적응하기 위한 에피소드가 수많이 전개되었다. 우선 방을 배정받고 가르쳐준 엘리베이터를 탔는데, 어떻게 운전할 줄 몰라—당시 서울에는 현 롯데호텔 자리에 과거 일본 백화점으로 쓰이던 6층 건물이 있었으나, 상관없던 우리야 타 본 경험이 없어, 솔직히 우리는 생전 에리베이터가 처음이라—한참 연구하다가 수십 층 숫자와 문자가 있는 걸 발견하고 무엇이던 눌렀는데, 에리베이터가 한참 올라가는데 우리가 내려야 할 층에 서지를 않고 계속 올라갔다가 다시 내려가 올라탔던 그 자리에 문이 열리고 저기 프런트가 보여 미안한 얼굴이 되었다. 이제는 하고 눌렀으나 그 또한 잘못된 것이었다. 한 두어 번 오르락내리락 하는 걸 보고 프런트 아저씨가 오더니 우리 층 번호를 눌러주어 그제야 우리 층에 내릴 수 있었다. 그래서 보고 실습하고 연구해서 이제는 엘리베이터는 운전할 수 있을 것 같았다.

그러자 날이 이미 어두워서 각자 방에 들어가 여장을 풀고는 일단 샤워— 아마도 당시는 개인 방에 샤워가 없었던 같다.—를 하기 위해 수건을 들고 문밖으로 나오는데 문이 자동으로 닫혔다. 열쇠를 가져 나오지 않은 것 같아 돌아서서 문을 열려는데 열리지 않는다. 할 수 없이 고민 끝에 프런트로 내려가 직원과 함께 와서 문을 열고서야 들어갈 수 있었다. 오늘날 우리 어린이에게도 얘기 못할 에피소드가 미국 도착 첫날부터 이렇게 전개되었다. 이럴 줄 알았으면 도미 경험자에게 상세히 물어서 알아둘 것을, 사실은 경험해야 미국 맛을 안다고 하길래 이 에피소드를 택하였으니 누굴 원망하랴.

다음 날, 일찍이 한국계 미국 여인 '미세스 고(高)'가 와서 우리를 자기 집으로 안내해 갔다. 당시 미국 유학 장교들은 대부분 이 집과 이 중년 여자의 집에 며칠간 합숙, 하숙 신세를 진 경험을 가지고 있었고, 그래서 다음 도미 동료들에게 어렵지 않게 소개해 주고 있었다. 단순한 이유로는, 우선 아직도 말이 제대로 트지 못한 초행들이 며칠이라도 말에 대한 큰 불편함 없이 지낼 수 있고, '미세스 고' 자신은 한국 이화여대를 나온 인텔리 여성으로, 미 해군 장교와 결혼하고 미국으로 이주, 이곳 해군기지 근방에 자리 잡았고, 남편은 지금 해군 중령으로 독일에서 파견 근무 중이고, 그녀 또한 미국이 처음인 한국 군인 만날 겸 서비스도 제공하는 아르바이트하는 것으로 알려 있었기에, 물론 경제적이기도 하고 우리 음식 먹을 수 있기도 했지만, 무엇보다 우리 장교들이 그녀와 동족적 동정심을 가진데다 신뢰감을 가질 수 있었고, 그래서 미국에 대한 기초 정보들을 쉽게 얻어들을 수 있다는 장점들이 있었다.

그녀의 집은 전형적인 샌프란시스코 시내 언덕으로 올라가며 길 양면으로 계단식으로 지어진 집이었고, 호출 버튼을 누르면 제법 듣기 좋은 음악이 들렸고, 방은 많지 않은 것 같아, 앞 팀에게 양보하고 우리는 아예 방도 아닌 거실에 5~6명이 기거하면서 불편한 줄도 모르고 미국 본토의 첫 만남의 날들을 보냈다.

이곳 샌프란시스코는 전 세계적으로 미항(美港)으로 이름나 있는 도시라, 당시 기준으로 거의 완전한 미개발 국가였던 한국, 거기다가 최전방 심심산골에서 근무하다 온 호기심 많은 총각 장교들이라 보는 것마다 놀랍고 신기하고 탐스러웠다. 그 수많은 샌프란시스코의 첫 인상 즉 미국의 첫인상 중에서도 지금까지 잊지 못하고 있는 몇 가지만 얘기하여야겠다.

관광의 첫인상은 바로 '금문교(Golden Gate Bridge)'로부터 시작되었다. 이 다리는 길이 약 2.7킬로미터, 수면 높이 67미터—왼만한 크루즈 배도 통행 가능한 —의 상판, 이를 받혀주는 교각은 2개로 하나는 육지에 붙어 있고 하나는 반대편 육지에서 좀 떨어진 곳, 마치 이 교각 하나로 전체 교량이 버티고 있는 것처럼 보이는 위치, 그리고 물론 교각으로 방해받지 않는 아치형 다리라 선박들의 넓은 시야가 확보된 설계였다. 그 길이와 위치를 굳이 우리 한국 지형으로 연관시켜보면, 군산과 장항항구 사이 약 3킬로미터에 크루즈 배가 그 밑으로 다닐 수 있도록 높이 그리고 가운데 거슬리는 교각 없이 단 2개의 양옆 교각으로 길게 걸려 있는 구조물로 생각할 수 있겠다.

다리 위를 걸어가며 구경도 하고 관찰도 하기 위해 남쪽 끝 공원에서 올라와 인도 입구에서 자동 출입 게이트—오늘 우리의 전철역 게이트, 그것도 생전 처음 보는 것으로 신기했다.—를 한 사람씩 통과해서 인도로 올라섰다. 첫 눈에 들어온 것이 바로 거대한 쇠밧줄

(Main Span Cable)이 저 앞 좌우 양편 교각 꼭지에서 여기까지 쭉 느려져 있는데, 가까이 가보니 직경 1미터도 넘는 거대한 상상하기 어려울 정도 굵기였다. 좀 더 들어가면 이 편 교각에 도달하는데, 쇠 아이빔 덩어리로 뭉쳐져 바다에서 솟아올라 저 위로 버티고 서 있는데, 둘레는 아마도 장정 여덟 사람이 팔을 벌려 둘러도 맞닿지 않을 것 같은 거대한 철골 구조물이었다.

이런 거대한 쇠 구조물이 이 미국 사람들의 꾀와 힘으로 그것도 1930년대에 가능했다는 사실에 감탄을 금할 수 없었으며, 동시에 역시 미국이 선진국이고 거대하고도 위대한 국가임을 새삼 체감 실감할 수 있었다. 그런데 돌아 나오다가 아래로 내려다보니 바로 밑 'I-Beam 난간'에 사람이 편하게 앉은 자세로 메달려 무언가 작업을 하고 있었다. 나와서 물어보니, 페인트공으로 1년 만에 이쪽 끝에서 저쪽 끝으로—왕복은 2년 소요—저렇게 페인트(사람 눈에 잘 보이는 해난 구조용 '인터내쇼날 오랜지 색')칠을 하고 있다는 말을 듣고, '아 위대한 사물의 그늘 또는 배경에는 저러한 사람도 있구나' 하는 인간 사회생활에 대한 새로운 발견도 할 수 있었다.

사실 '샌프란시스코 만'에는 2개의 큰 교량이 있는데 하나는 'Bay Bridge'이고 또 하나는 'Golden Gate Bridge'이다. '베이 브릿지'는 금문교와 같은 현수교이고 상하 복층 왕복 6차로로 무려 14킬로미터의 위대한 작품이었으나 금문교가 건설되자 그 인기를 금문교로 넘겼다고 한다. 그동안 한강철교와 인도교(한강대교)를 위대한 작품으로 알고 지내던 나에게, 이 명물들은 나에게 미국이라는 나라의 거대하고 위대함을 실감하게 하는 큰 충격을 안겨 주었다.

또 'Marina District(요트 계류장)'를 관광 겸 산책하였는데 수많은 호화 요트와 모터보트들이 그 넓은 계류장에 정박해 있는가 하면, 그 앞으로 해변가에는 수많은 서양 미인들)이 '비키니' 차림으로 풀장용 침대나 그냥 수건이나 또는 잔디밭에 그냥들 줄지어 누워서 햇빛 쬐기를 하고 있었다. 당시 우리네 여자들은 감히 그런 옷을 입지도 못하고 그저 아래위로 붙은 수영복을 입고도 부끄러워했고, 또 감히 밖에 나가 사람들 산책 다니는 곳에 드러누워 있을 수도 없던 때였다.

그런데 여기 이 값비싼 요트들을 타고 즐기며 이 아름답고 평화스러운 해변가에서 한가하고 풍요하고 즐겁게 일광욕을 하고 있는 사람들 모습을 보니 새삼 '인생이 무엇이냐?'가 생각났다. 우리네는 지금 '먹기 위해 살고 있는데, 여기는 살기(즐기기) 위해 먹고 있지 않는가', '아 우리는 언제 이것이 가능할까?'. 불현듯 사범학교 시절 금수현 교감으로부터 들은 얘기, "미국은 이제 사람 문제는 끝나고 고양이 교육시키고 있다" 는 것이 새삼 마음에 와 닿았다.

거기에다 대형 선착장에서 많은 외국 국적 표시 선박들이 줄지어 정박되어 있는 곳에서 어쩌다 비록 몇천 톤급 정도의 화물선이라 할지라도 태극기가 달린 걸 보고 그 어찌나 반가운지. 사람들이 흔히들 외국 나가면 모두가 애국자가 된다고 하였는데 이 감정이 바로 그것이구나고 느끼게 되었다.

시내 즉 다운타운에 가 보았는데, 아마도 메인 스트리트였는가, 왕복 10차선 정도의 넓은 거리에 인도도 넓어서 광광객으로 보이는 사람들도 함께 그러나 비교적 한가하게 사람들이 오가고 있었다. 그런데 거리를 두리번거리며 걸어가고 있는 우리 곁으로 아주 기분 좋고 경쾌한 걸음으로 젊은 한 쌍이 지나가는데 한 10미터쯤 앞서갈 때까지 그 모습이 하도 좋게 보여 눈으로 뒤쫓고 있었는데, 그중 예쁜 애인 아가씨가 뒤돌아보며 쫑긋 윙크를 하는 게 아닌가. 어 기분이 좋아 나도 그렇게 따라 해 보았지, 어리석게도 설마 나를 좋아해서(?), 물론 그건 아니고.

당시만 해도 바쁜 사람들이 오가는 그 '스트리트'에서도 사람들은 눈이 마주치면 "하이 굿 모닝!"은 누구나 서로 주고받았고, 어떤 이들은 '윙크'해 주기도 하였다. 우리도 그저 분위기 따라서 "하이 굿 모닝" 정도는 할 수 있었다. 참 좋은 나라요 낭만이 흐르는 샌프란시스코 시민으로 보였다.

길거리를 돌아다니다 보니 큼직한 아이스크림 그림이 그려져 있는 상점이 있어서 안으로 들어가서 주문해 보았다. "헬로, 아이스크림 플리즈" 했더니, "웟 카인?" 그런다, 어 분명히 무슨 종류? 그러는데, 아니 아이스크림이나 아이스케이크에 종류?—웃지 마세요, 당시 한국은 '아이스케이크'만 있었고, 그것도 그냥 한 가지 종류 뿐이였고, 아이스크림은 더더구나 웬만한 사람들은 잘 듣지도 보지도 못했다.— 두리번거리자 이 친구 눈치채고 앞에 진열된 그림을 가리킨다, 아 그제야 "응 저거" 했는데, 또 주지는 않고 질문한다, "가져갈래 여기서 먹고 갈래?" 하는데도 무슨 말인지 못알아 들었으나 그저 눈치로 알아듣고, 손짓으로 가져 나가겠다고 했다. 그제야 이 친구 몇 사람 분인가 또 물어보고는 잘 포장해 주었다. 한국 '프로레탈리앗' 청년 장교들인 우리는 이런 것들이 참으로 생소했다.

또, '다운타운'과 '엎타운'의 개념과 실제도 보고 경험하였다. 즉 '다운타운'(Down Town)은 주 중 대낮에 공동체 일상 활동 구역으로, 그곳에 출근하여 일하고 생활하다가 밤엔 전부 철시한다. 그래서 사람 사는 지역, 주로 비교적 높은 지대에 자리 잡은 주택지구, 그래서 '업타운'(Up Town)이라는 주거지역으로 가서 쉬며 자고, 다음 날 다시 다운타운으로 내려와 낮 직장생활을 한다.

허 이거 별천지고 신천지네, 건물들을 보라 벽돌집에 화강암 집들, 잘도 설계된 도시, 물론 그 편리하고 질서정연하고 아름답게 보이는 동네, 어딜 가나 숲이 있는 널찍한 공원들, 거기에 사람들은 앉아 쉬고, 젊은이들은 뛰놀고, 어떤 사람들은 산책하고 책보고 누워 있고, 남녀들은 짝짝이 함께 산책하는 모습들은 정말 보기 좋아 탐스러웠다.

◇ 미대륙(북부) 횡단 기차 관광여행의 행운

며칠 뒤 우리는 목적지를 향한 기차여행 명령서(티켓 함께)를 받고 상당히 긴—현재까지 생애 최초요 마지막, 단 한 번뿐이었던—북부 미국 대륙 횡단 기차여행을, 아주 운 좋게도, 하게 되었다. 이름답고 인간미 풍부한 샌프란시스코의 항구 관광은 예정되어 있기에 돌아올 때 다시 하기로 하고, 우리(한 선배와 나)는 'Union Pacific train'의 'Pullman(ship) car(쾌적한 설비가 된 침대차)'의 2인용 칸—아래위 침대차로 3면 거울이 달린 화장실에 큼직한 관관용 창문, 일반 호텔과 같이 매일 시트 교환해주고 청소해 주고, 문 열고 복도에 나가면 반대편 창문으로도 기대여 광광할 수 있고—에 몸을 실었다.

이 열차는 넓은 창이 지붕이 되어 있는 전망차와 식당차 그리고 침대차 수량으로 구성되어 있었고 밤낮 쉬지 않고 5일간 계속 달려서 종착역인 '시카고'로 가는 장거리 고급 관광열차였다. 거듭 말하지만 개척자 정신을 가진 나는 관광여행을 물론 좋아하였는데, 특히 미국의 모든 것이 보고 싶은 내게, 이렇게 호화 관광열차를 타고, 최고급 예우를 받으면서, 이 젊은 때 미 대륙을 횡단하는 기회를 가지게 된 것은 참으로 큰 행운으로 생각되었다.

기차는 샌프란시스코역을 출발, Sierra Nevada 산맥을 지나자 문자 그대로 광활하고 끝이 전혀 보이지 않는, '가도 가도 끝이 없는' '네바다' 사막을 지나가는데, 이야말로 그동안 그림에서 그리고 서부영화에서만 보아 오던, 그래서 생전 처음 보게 된 대 사막지대를 지나갔다. 그런가 하면 그대로 이어서 '유타주'로 들어가 사막 한가운데 있는 '그레이트 솔트 호수(Great Salt Lake)' 가운데를 가로질러 지나가는데, 좀 낮은 속도로 아마도 2시간여를 지나가는데, 그야말로 문자 그대로 거대한 '소금호수'라는 이름이 실감 났다.

기차는 하루에 한 번 정도 서든가? 여하간에 밤낮없이 달리고 또 달리는 동안 나는 이렇게 광활한 사막, 이렇게 거대한 풍경 속에서, 자고 일어나면 하루 몇 시긴씩 밖을 보며 감탄하고 또 감탄하고, 식당에 가서는 레스토랑형 메뉴로 제법 매일 바꾸어 선택해 서비스를 받았다. 그런데 청소나 식당 서비스 등은 주로 흑인이 도맡고 있었다. 그런데 이를 며칠간 반복하였으나 그래도 워낙 생소한 것들이라 그때마다 메뉴 읽기를 배우고 익히려 하였으나 끝내 익숙하지를 못하였다. 그런데 식당에서 아주 자주 나오는 치즈에 친하지 못해 우리는 자주, 함께 마주 앉아 식사해 주는 친절한 신사에게 다른 반찬과 바꾸어 먹기도 하였다.

2일쯤 지나면서 정차한 역의 이름을 보니 와이오밍주의 '라라미(Laramie, 레러미)'였다. 사막 한가운데서 친구를 만난 것처럼 반가웠다. 그 이유는 한국에서 당시 서부영화 시리즈가 대인기였는데 그중 하나가 「'라라미'에서 온 사나이」였다. 아주 재미있게 본 영화 기갑 장교인 동생의 억울한 죽음을 복수하고자 '라라미' 출신으로 역시 기갑장교 대위인 형이 범죄자를 추적하여 기어이 복수하는 서부영화, 서부 개척 시대의 용감하고 정의롭고 불패의 총잡이 사나이들과 사필귀정의 얘기—라 그 이름이 아주 반가웠던 것이다. 그래서 내려서 두리번거리기도 하고 뭔가 살펴보기도 하다가 역내에 '30분 세탁'—당시는 각자 여행용 다리미를 휴대하여 여행하던 시대라—이 있기에 맡겨서 와이셔츠를 바꾸어 입기도 하였다. 이어서 며칠간 '네브레스카' 주의 'Omaha' 지나고, '아이오와'주를 지나 '일리노이'주에 들어와서 드디어 중간 정착지인 '시카고' 서편 역에 도착하였다.

◇ '시카고'를 지나 수도 '워싱턴'에 오다

바야흐로 한겨울이라 눈에 푹 파묻혀 있다시피 한 'Chicago' 시내를 택시로 지나 '동부 기차역'으로 바쁘게 이동하느라 그 유명한 시카고를 둘러보지도 못하고 그저 다음을 기약하고 갈 길을 서둘렀다. 그래서 다시 워싱턴행 기차로 바꾸어타고 시카고에 연접한, 마치 우리 남한 크기와 비슷한 '미시간호'와 '이리호'에 인접하여 지나가면서 밤새워 동으로 동으로 달려, 미국 지형 구분과 역사 구분상 유명한 '애팔래치아' 산맥을 통과하여 다음 날 오전에 미국연방의 수도 '워싱턴(Washington D.C) 기치역에 도착하였다.

약 3시간 정도 환승 여유시간이 있어서 우리는 택시 투어를 하게 되었다. 역전에 대기 중인 관광용 택시를 타고 시내 관광에 나섰는데, 제일 먼저 안내된 곳이 '워싱턴 모뉴먼트'였다. 그냥 보기에는 뾰족한 첨탑으로만 보이나 가까이 가면 역시나 거대한 구조물이었다. 높이 약 170미터에 내부는 올라가는 엘리베이터와 내려오는 와선형 계단이 설치되었고 꼭지 부분에는 사방으로 워싱턴 시내를 볼 수 있는 창문을 비롯하여 도보로 내려오면서도 밖을 볼 수 있는 창문들이 있었다.

이 탑은 미국 초대 대통령 '조지 워싱턴 장군'을 기념하여 1886년에 완성되었는데 바로 몇 년 뒤 프랑스 파리의 '에펠탑'이 건조될 때까지 세계 최고 높이였다고 한다. 그런데 듣기로는, 이 재료들은 아프리카 이집트에서 유럽을 거쳐온 것이라 하였다. 그런데 그 근방에 노신사 몇 명이 점잖게 서서 동전 동냥을 하고 있었는데, 야 이 부자나라 미국에도 동냥꾼이 있나(?) 하여 대단히 신기하였다.

다음은 그 건너편에 마주 보고 있는 '링컨 모뉴먼트'에 갔다. 이것은 우리에게도 잘 알려져 있긴 하나 그래도 막상 거대한 석상 앞에 서보니 감회가 무량하였다. 나는 특히 어린 시절 즐겨 읽던 위인전기 중에서도 '링컨 대통령'의 어린 시절 가난에도 불구하고 정직하게 열심히 살았고, 그리하여 노예해방에 이르게 된 그를 위인으로 존경하며 나의 인생 지표로 삶아 살아왔기에 이제 그의 거대하면서도 새하얀 거상 앞에 서니 더욱 보람을 느끼지 않을 수 없었다.

이 외도 웅대한 국회의사당을 설명을 들으며 지나가고, 거대한 국립항공우주박물관인 'Smithsonian'에 들려서는 물론 항공기와 우주개발 역사와 실물 등을, 그리고 '쥐라기' 시대 북아메리카의 공룡 전시물을 보고 압도되기도 하고, 또 이외도 근방 여러 곳에 역대 미국 대통령을 기리는 모뉴먼트가 많이 있다기에 들리고는 싶었으나 다음을 기약하고, 미국 대통령 관저인 '화이트 하우스'—우리나라도 이를 본떠 대통령 관저를 '청와대'라 한다.—로 갔는데, 참으로 청아하고 우아하면서도 아름답게 보였다. 그런데 대통령이 산다는 이 집이 이렇게 길거리에 있어서 국민들에게는 물론 심지어 이런 관광객들에게도 볼 수 있게 되어 있으니 과감한 도시 배치라는 생각과 함께 과연 미국식 민주주의 상징이라는 생각이 들었다.

다음은 우리가 군인이라는 걸 알고 교외에 있는 '알링턴 국립묘지'에 안내되었다. 당시만 해도 우리나라에 동작동 국군묘지가 있었으나 이렇게 거대하고도 위엄 있는 그리고 아름다움을 더하여 외국인까지 관광할 수 있을 정도의 모습일 줄은 미쳐 몰랐다.

그곳에는 6·25 남침적란(南侵赤亂) 시 한국에 참전하였다 전사한 대부분의 미군이 잠든 '한국전 참전용사묘지구역'이 있었는데, 그 구역에는 전체 묘역을 지키는 초소 그리고 기념행사를 할 수 있는 단이 조성되어 있었다. 그래서 그곳에는 2명의 의장 대원이 약 50미터를 사이에 두고 교차 의장 행진을 하고 돌아서서 다시 적당한 시간 간격으로 교차 행진을 실시하는 등, 전지역 순찰(돌봄)과 경비를 대신하는 간단 명료하고 의미 깊고 보기 좋은 소구간 교차 보행 의장 행사를 계속하고 있었는데, 여기에서 기념일마다 또는 주요 인물 방문시 헌화 행사가 이루어지기도 한다는 설명을 들었다.

이제 다시 환승할 시간이 되어 기차역으로 갔는데 보아하니 거의 시내 한복판에 기차역이 있어서 워싱턴 시내 관광에는 안성맞춤으로 보였다. 과연 이 '워싱턴시'는 자연 조성이 아닌 완전한 계획 도시로, 아름답고 웅대하게 그리고 미국 역사를 써나가며 보여주는 도시, 그리하여 미국 정치의 중심인 동시에 오늘날 세계 정치의 중심이 되어 있는 도시로 전혀 손색이 없을 듯하였다. 이 또한 내게는 경탄할 수밖에 없는 완전한 신천지의 상징 도시로 보였다.

◇ 드디어 'J.F, Kennedy Center'에 오다

이제는 객석이 침대차 아닌 걸터앉는 의자로 된 '코—치 카(Coach Car)'로 환승하여 직선거리 약 500킬로미터 남쪽에 위치한, '노스캐롤라이나(North Carolina)' 주의 옛 수도 '페이예떼빌(Fayetteville)'에 도착하였다. 도중에 길고도 길면서 아름답게 전개되는 초원지대와 우거진 원시림 지대 그리고 현대식 도시지대를 지났는데, 그런대로 미국 역사와 전사를 연구하면서 귀에 익은 '리치몬드'나 '포츠머스' 등을 지날 때는 유심히 관찰하며 지나갔다.

저녁이 다 되었을 때 드디어 목적지인 '페이예떼빌'에 도착하고, 학교 당직 장교에 의해서 안내된 곳은, Ft.Bragg, N.C의 John F. Kennedy Center 내에 있는 Special Wafare School 의 V.O.Q였다. 이 숙소는 단순한 방문자 숙소라기 보다 피 교육생을 위한 기숙사였다. 가운데 화장실을 사이에 두고 양편으로 화장실 출입문을 두었고, 그 한 편을 보면 물론 개인용으로, 옷장이 달린 침대방과 엷은 벽을 칸막이로 공부방(책상과 책장 그리고 거실을 겸하는)을 가진 한 건물 2인용 숙소였고, 물론 침대 책상 의자 등 모든 것이 전통 미국 거실 가재도구 그대로였다. 아 드디어 미국에 유학 왔구나 하는 기분이 실감났다.

이곳 군사 유학 생활을 얘기하기 전에 먼저 여기 'J.F Kennedy Center'와 'Fort Bragg N.C'부터 소개하겠다. 제2차 세계대전 후 최고조에 달하고 있던 동서냉전 시기에, 소련 수상 '흐루시초프'가 겉으로는 소위 '평화공존론'에다 '데탕트(Detente)'를 내세우면서 그 이면으로는, 스스로 핵무장을 강화하면서도 세계적으로는 얼치기 공산주의자들을 통해 소위 '반전, 반핵, 평화'운동(데모 시위 등)을 선동하여 위장 평화를 가장하였다. 그와 동시에 실제로는, 제3세계 특히 남미와 아프리카 그리고 동남아시아 국가에 침투하여 '분란(Insurgency)'을 일으켜 적화(赤化)하려는 전략—핵전쟁을 피하되 제3세계 민족해방전쟁을 적극 지원하는 세계 간접 적화침략 전략—을 적극 전개하였고, 드디어는 미국의 코 앞인 '큐바'에 핵미사일 기지까지 건설하여 미국을 직접 위협까지 하였다.

이에 '미국 중흥의 기치(New Frontier Spirits)'를 내걸고 나타난 '케네디' 대통령은 1961년의 '베를린 사태'—동부 베를린과 동독을 봉쇄하는 장벽 설치 소동—를 현지 공수작전과 지상 돌파작전으로 극복하고, 62년에는 쿠바에서 소련과 대결하여 단연코 소련 침략(도전) 의지를 분쇄하였다. 그리하여 케네디 대통령은, 소위 'Missile Gap'을 보완하고

'상호확실파괴전략(MAD)'을 확립하고 '3탄도체제(TRIAD)'를 수립 시행하였다.

동시에 소련의 '제3세계 해방전략전술'에 대응하기 위해, '테일러 장군'—101공수사단장으로 노르망디 상륙작전 지휘·미육사교장·한국전 참전 8군사령관·육참총장·합참의장·주월남대사, 'Uncertain Trumpet' 저술, 비정규전 이론가—의 건의에 따라 '정치/군사 통합전략'인 '유연대응전략(Flexible Response Strategy)'을 확립하고, '폭동진압작전(Counter Insurgency OP)' 개념을 정립하여, '특수전사령부(Special Warfare Center)'를 이곳 '노스 캐로라이나 주'의 'Ft.Bragg'에 설치하고, '특전부대(Special Warfare Forces—별칭 Green Beret)'를 창설하였다. 그리하여 미국은 특히 이에 유관된 국가에게 이 전략·전술 교리를 전파함과 동시에 미국 주도하에 공동전선을 형성하려 노력하고 있다.

이곳 Ft. Bragg은, 서울시보다 조금 큰 크기로, 남북전쟁 당시부터 'Camp Bragg'으로 시작하여 1, 2차 세계대전을 거치면서 확장을 거듭하였다. 오늘날에는 신전략 개념의 중심지가 되어 종래의 전통을 자랑하는 '82공수사단'을 비롯하여 특수전 센터와 '그린베레 부대' 등 명실공히 "Special Operations Forces의 본거지(Home)"가 되어 있다. 그래서 이 모든 군사 요원들과 가족과 가정을 위한 제반 민간 생활 터전은 물론 4개의 코뮤니티를 포괄하는 큰 도시가 형성되어 있었다. 그래서 군사기지 한가운데로 대형 고속도로가 관통하고도 있었다.

◇ Kennedy Center의 철학과 특수전(Special Warfare)의 개념

이곳 'Special Warfare School'에서는 초청된 동맹 또는 연합국가 군인들에게, '특수전'에 대한 철학과 이론 그리고 3가지로 분류된 주과목 즉, 심리전·비정규전·폭동 진압전, 에 대해서 주로 실내 토론과 질의응답을 통한 사례연구(Case Study)를 통해서 이론을 배우고, 동시에 야외에서 간단한 시범과 실제 부대, 82공수사단과 제7특수전 부대를 방문하고 거기서 시범을 통해서 익히도록 하였다.

특수전(Special Warfare)이란, 흔히 비정규전(Irregular), 비재래식 전쟁으로 이해하기도 하나 바르게 말하면, 정규전(Regular Warfare, 또는 Conventional Warfare)이 아닌 문자 그대로 '특수한 방법에 의한 전쟁'을 의미한다. 교육을 위한 특수전 분류는, 심리전(Psychological Warfare), 비정규전(Unconventional Warfare), 폭동 진압전(Counter Insurgency OP)의 3과목이 주류다.

심리전이란 사실은 특수전에서 아주 중요시하고 있는 전략 전술 분야이다. 그래서 이 유학 과정 명칭도 엄연히 '심리전 과정'이다. 이미 잘 알려져 있어 더는 설명이 불필요하리라고 생각한다.

비정규전이란, 정규전에 대한 비정규전 또는 비재래전(예, 핵전쟁)을 의미한다기보다 완전히 새로운 의미의 특수전, 정치와 무력을 배합한, 그리고 전쟁법규 범위를 벗어나는 수단과 방법을 가리지 않는 전쟁 양상(Black/Dirty 불사)을 의미한다. 그 진짜 의미는 미특수전부대에 가서 한 팀의 시범을 보면 이해할 수 있다.

작전팀은 통상 12명으로, 팀장과 부팀장, 복수의 정작(정보·작전) 전문가, 복수의 피아 화기 전문가, 복수의 피아 통신 전문가, 복수의 폭파 전문가, 그리고 복수의 외과 수술 가능 군의관으로 구성되어 있다. 이들 전원은 파견(침투)국가 언어를 구사할 수 있어야 한다. 당시 특전 부대에 가서 본 시범 요점은, 1개 팀이 적 후방 반정부 지역에 침투(육해공)하여 토착민 게릴라 부대를 조직, 지휘/지원하고, 때로는 직접 정치공작 암살 납치 등의 작전을 담당한다고 했다. 부차적으로 극한 상황에서 생존을 위한 단련훈련을 실시한다고 했다.

특수전 3대 요소 중 또 하나는, '대 분란전' 또는 '분란 진압전' 또는 '폭동 진압전'이라는 이름을 가진 'Counter Insurgency Warfare(또는 OP)'이다. 이 과목의 요점은, 제3세계 사태를 중심으로 착안한 것으로, 사태 발생 이전 조치와 사태 발생시 조치 그리고 사후 안정조치 들이다. 사태 발생 이전 조치는 곧 사태 발생 요인(Rising Expectation), 예하면 물론 정치 사회적인 문제를 비롯하여 특히 식량·물·의료 불만 등의 환경 개선 문제 등이고, 사태 발생시는 '폭동(반란) 진압 작전으로 들어가되 단호하고 위엄 있는 그리고 집중적인 병력 투입, 가능한 비살상 제압 등의 과제이고, 그 후는 지속적인 안정 작전을 시행하는 문제 등의 과제였다. 물론 말하기는 쉬우나 각국과 각 지역 환경과 조건 그리고 상황에 따라 그대로 실천되기는 어려운 과제들이었다.—그래서 미국이 사전에 이렇게 교육하고 지원하면서 성과를 기대하였으나 그후 월남전쟁이나 남미 아프리카 지역 등지의 대 게릴라전에서 바람직한 성과를 거두지는 못했다.

◇ 미 특수전학교의 수업 및 생활 이모저모

◦ 나는 민족주의자

그동안의 생활 에피소드 몇 가지를 소개한다. 나는 상대를 처음 대할 때마다 물론 영어로 "나는 문영일 중위이고(I come from KoRea)"라고, 좀 Rea 부분을 악센트를 더주어 말했더니, 교관이 공부 시간에 '비정규전 성공 요건 중 하나로 굳센 민족관'을 강조하면서, 나를 두고 '민족관이 강하다'고 소개하고 좋은 현상이라 하였다. 심지어는 그다음 반으로 다녀온 친구들로부터도 그 말을 듣기도 하였다.

◦ 친하게 된 요르단 장교와 미해병 장교

우리 반(1962.1~3)은 11개국(한국, 요르단, 이란, 중국(대만), 이탈리아, 베트남, 니카라과, 노르웨이, 캐나다, 버마, 서독)에 미 육해공 해병대를 포함하여 80명이 한 교실에서 동시에 수업하고, 대령에서부터 중위에 이르기까지 전 계급을 망라하였는데, 최고참 최고령 미군 대령이 반장이었다. 단 3개월 단기 과정이라 많은 국가 장교들과 사귀지 못하는 것이 단점이었을 뿐 전체 교육 내용이나 학생 관리 대우 식사 예우 그 모든 것이 만족스러웠다.

나와 비교적 친하게 지낸 외국 장교는 요르단군의 '소령, A. Rafie'였는데, 그는 당시 왕세자의 비서실에 근무하고 있다고 했다.—60년대 말경에 요르단 왕세자의 방한을 수행하여 서울에 와서 문치과 주소를 통해 나를 찾았으나 서로 시간이 맞지 않아 만나지를 못해 아쉬웠다.—우리는 손짓발짓 다하여 "미국은 'X 주고 뺨 맞는다', 즉 원조 잘해 주고도 그 나라로부터 원성 듣는다"면서, 의사 소통하고는 그다음부터 만나면 그저 즐거운 말동무가 되었다. 또 한 친구는, 학업을 수료하고 귀국시에 같은 반 출신 '미해병 대위 J.E, Hennegan'과 함께 그의 자동차로 남부 미대륙을 횡단하며 사귀게 되었다.

그런데 교실에서는 좀 의외의 장면을 보기도 했는데, 미 해병대 장교들의 수업 자세가 상당히 무례하게 보였다. 겪어보니 미국 사람들(서양 사람들)이 남녀노소 간에 별 격의 없이 소파 등에 편하게 발 올리고 스스럼없이 지내는 걸 서양 문화라 생각은 하고 있었지만 이건 좀 과하게 보였다. 그들 몇 명(주로 대위급)은 끼리 이웃하여 자리 잡고, 마치 그들의 기질을 과시라도 하는 양, 가끔 서로 좀 큰소리로 대화하고, 주변 기타 병과 미군을 무시하듯 보이기도 하였다.

그런데, 수업시간 내내 그들 중 몇 명은 몸을 완전히 의자에 기대어 뒤로 누운 듯, 양 구둣발을 책상 위에 얹어서 바로 앞 장교 뒷머리에 닿을 만큼 쭉 뻗은 체 교관을 향하고 수업하였다. 물론 수업에 방해가 되는 건 아니었기에 미국 교관도 이에 개의치 않았다. 그러나 아무리 서양이 또 미국이 자유스럽다 하더라도, 과연 그런 수업 자세가 미국 해병대 장교다운 태도로 좋게 평가될 수 있을 것인지 나는 이해하기 어려웠다.

◦ 폭동 무력 진압 전술

야외 시범 실습 시간에는 각종 장비 소개와 '폭동 진압전 시범'을 보았는데, 요지는, 처음 계는 통행 금지와 함께 요지 요부 경계 그리고 각종 제압 장비 활용으로 격상하고, 이어서 지체없이 꽂아 칼 돌격 자세로 일보 일보 또 일보씩 밀고 나가다가 폭도가 밀리기 시작하면 그때는 기세를 올려 뛰면서 돌격해서 분열시켜 격파하고 해산시킨다는 작전 요령이었다.

◦ 기타 생각나는 것들

그런데, 물론 견학 및 실습 복장은 자국의 전투 복장이었는데, 보아하니 미군 전투복을 입은 나라는 우리나라와 베트남뿐이었다. 야외 실습 시간마다 느끼는 것은 우리도 하루빨리 발전하여 자기 나라 복장에 자기 나라 생산 무기로 무장할 수 있는 '자주국방'을 이루어야겠다고 다짐하고 또 다짐하였다.

우리들 모두는 종종 주말에 미군 장교 클럽에서 초청 모임이나 단체 '빙고 게임'을 즐기기도 하였는데, 젊은 미군들 특히 해병 장교들은 그 지역 병원 간호 장교들과 어울려서 댄스파티를 즐기는 것 같았다.

◦ 풍족한 미군 영내 장교 식당

우리는 한국 출발과 동시 거의 모든 것이 처음이라 눈치로 생활—특히 식사 때—을 시작하였는데, 첫날 장교 식당(Officer's Mess Hall)에 안내되었을 때는 새삼 옛날(1950년 전후)에 들었던 '벙어리 코스(한국군 집단 통역장교 대동 과정) 에피소드'가 생각났다. 식당에 들어서자 낯설은 식판을 들고 계란 조리대 앞에 줄을 섰는데 차례가 되자 요리병이 뭐라고 물어보았다. 처음 듣는 단어라 머뭇거리자, 이 요리병이 웃으며 모양을 그려가며 보여주어 가며 설명한다. 미국 사람들(군인은 물론 대부분)은 하루아침에 계란 2개씩 먹기에, 여자 젖 가슴처럼 흉내 내보이며 "브레즈"라고 하다가 다시 "선 라이즈"라 하고, 다음엔 막 섞는 모양을 하면서 "스크램블"이라 하였다. 그제야 얼른 눈에 익은 '후라이 2개'를 주문했더니, 즉석에서, 스탠 철판 위에서, 요리해 건네준다. 그래서 다음 날부터 스크램블도 시켜 먹는 등 그 단어들에 익숙해졌다. 솔직히 나도 그때까지 계란을 그런 식으로 즉석 요리로 먹어보지를 못했었다.

그래서 계란 담긴 식판을 들고 다음 빵으로 갔더니 또 선택해야할 고민을 안겨주는 여러 가지 종류가 있었다. 식빵, 바겟빵, 여러 가지 생과자, 프랜치 토스트 등등, 식빵 옆에는 토스터가 있고, 그 옆으로는 각종 모양의 소세이지와 햄 등, 그리고 옆으로는 싱싱한 야채 샐러드, 그리고 음료수로는 오랜지 주스를 비롯한 각종 주스, 우유, 그리고 코카콜라와 팹시콜라, 연한 커피 진한 커피 등이 나오는 기계와 그릇들, 홍차 등등이 풍족하게 보기 좋게 진열되어 있었다. 그리고 후식 과일로는 이스라엘 산 오랜지가 있었는데 배 부른대다 보기도 좋고 그냥 먹어치우기엔 아까워서 종종 방으로 가져와서 놓고 보기도 맛보며 먹기도 하였다.

지금이야 이름들을 다 알고 사용하거나 먹을 줄도 알지만 그때는 모든 것들이 생소하였다. 이것이 소위 '지중해식'과 비교되며 값으로도 차이를 내는 이른바 '아메리칸 블랙퍼스트'였던 것이다. 우리의 속담에 '지 멋대로', '지 마음대로' 그리고 '지 맛대로'가 있는데 이제야 그 뜻을 알게 되었다. 여하간에 미국은 질 좋고 풍족하다.

그런데 점심식사는 더욱 풍족하여 스테이크 포함해서 레스토랑의 세트 요리와 비교해 손색이 없었다. 미국에서 군인과 특히 장교에 대한 대우는 각별함을 알 수 있었다. 밥값은 아침 3달러, 점심 7달러 저녁 5달러였다. 호화 식사였기에 전혀 비싸다고 느끼지 않았으나 매주 받는 포듐이 월간 약 600달러(?)였기에 빠듯하였다. 그래서 어떤 한국 장교들은 입맛도 다스리고 돈도 아낄 겸 영내 가족 상대 'commercially(PX품 외 식료품 등 생활 필수품 판매장)'에 가서 한국 음식 재료를 구입, BOQ에서 밥(국)해 먹기도 하였는데, 그 냄새가 풍겨서 외국장교로부터 신고가 되어 주의를 듣는 경우도 보았다.

미군 PX도 우리에게 개방되어 있어서 면도용품 등—예, Skin Bracer, Dial 비누 등은 그 이후 내 평생 동반물이 되었다.—일용품과 특히 담배 등 기호품을 애용하였다. 미군 PX 및 commercially 제도는 우리 한국군도 반드시 본 받아야 할 제도 중 하나였다. 그것들은 근무 지역 위험 강도별로 3지역으로 구분 운용되는데, 제1지대가 전장터나 최전방지대 즉 한국과 같은 지역으로, 거의 원자재 값 정도, 제2지대는 그 후방지대 즉, 일본 같은 지역 주둔 지대로 아마도 면세액의 절반 정도, 그리고 본국의 주둔지에서도 면세로 운영되었다. 미군 급여 자체도 그리 나쁘지 않은데도 국가에서 그렇게 대우해 준다는 의미가 포함되어 있다.

◦ 그때는 생소했던 '서양 풍속'

비록 소경 코끼리 만지듯 보고 들은 것이긴 하나 당시는 참으로 신기한 서양 문화요 풍습으로 보였는데, 지금(2025년 한국)은 우리네가 거의 그러하다. 당시 내게도 미군 고참 대령 한 분이 스폰서였는데, 부인과 어린 손자와 함께 생활하고 있었는데, 종종 나를 자기 에 초대해 주었고, 한때는 바닷가 해군·해병대 사령부가 있는 해군기지 도시 'Norfolk'에 가서 바다 구경도 하고 해산물 식사도 하였다.

그런데 그들이 집안 밖에서 여자가 의자에 앉으려면 반듯이 남자가 와서 의자를 빼주고 바쳐준다. 정말 들었던 데로 옛날 서부 개척 시대에 여자가 귀해서 그때부터의 '여존남비'의 풍습이란다. 그런가 하면 집안에서는 여자가 출, 퇴근하는 남편에게 반듯이 옷을 입혀주고 살펴주고, 벗겨주고 가져다 걸어 주고 한다.

대체로 주말이 되면 '장교 파티 홀'에서 모임을 갖는다. 그때 남자는 여자의 돌봄으로 집 현관을 나와 차고에서 자동차를 몰고 현관에 세우고 조수석 앞에 서서 앞문을 열면 기다리던 부인이 타면 문을 닫아주고 운전대로 와서 운전해 간다.

파티장에 도착하면, 현관에서 남자가 부인석으로 와 얼른 문을 열어주고 여자가 내린다. 남자는 차를 주차장에 세우고 돌아와, 기다리고 있던 부인의 코트를 벗겨주며 모자를 받아 카운터에 맡긴다. 그리고 함께 안으로 들어가, 여자의 의자를 빼주고 앉힌 뒤 자신의 자리로 가 앉는다. 모임이 끝나면 남자는 부인의 코트와 모자를 찾아와 건네주고, 곧바로 주차장으로 가 차를 몰고 와 기다리던 부인의 문을 열어주고 닫은 뒤 운전석으로 돌아와 함께 집으로 향한다.

집에 도착하면 남자가 차문을 열어 부인을 내리게 하고, 차를 주차시킨 뒤 현관으로 온다. 그때부터는 여자의 차례다. 현관문 앞에서 남편을 기다리다가 문을 열어주고, 그의 외투를 벗겨 들고 모자와 함께 장롱에 걸어둔다. 생각해보면, 참으로 지극히 합리적인 일 아닌가. 그런데 왜 그 당시에는 그런 모습이 우리 눈에는 그렇게도 '여존남비'로 보였을까. 그래서 낮에 동료 미군을 만나면 "야, 우리는 집이건 밖이건 남자가 왕이다."라며 자랑 아닌 자랑을 하곤 했다. 세상이 지금처럼 달라질 줄, 그때 누가 알았겠는가.

◦ 하와이 출신 일본계 미군 장교가 준 병김치와 김치 맛내기

우리 반에는 하와이 출신 일본계 미군 장교(대위)가 있었는데, 아주 정스러웠다. 그는 종종 우리에게 주먹 크기의 유리병 김치(6달러)를 가져다 주어서 고맙게 잘 먹었는데, 그때 김치를 공장 생산할 수 있고 저렇게 상품화할 수 있구나 하는 것을 알게 되었다. 실은 우리가 김치 생각이 나서 야채에 '핫소스'를 좀 뿌려 먹으면 맵고 새콤한 것이 김치 8촌의 맛은 볼 수 있었으나 물론 본 맛은 아니었다.

◦ 효도도 하는 미군 초급 장교 생활

관심을 가지고 보았던 미국 장교(위관급)들의 생활은 의외로 부지런하고 절약형이며 우리 못지않게 효도하고 있었다. 우리와 한 반이었던 미군 장교들은 주로 대위였는데, 나를 자기 집으로 초청해준 친구도 대위였다. 그 대위의 미 국내 생활 월급(주급으로 지급)은 당시 3,000여 달러(우리 돈 500여만 원)였는데, 30년 월부 주택기금으로 월 700여 달러, 각종 보험료 500여 달러, 생활비 및 공공요금 1,000여 달러 공제하고, 그리고 부모님께 월

300여 달러씩 송금—아 미국에도 이런 효자가 있었다, 모두가 그럴 수도—한다고 하니, 실제로는 경제 생활이 우리네 생각보다는 풍족하지는 않게 보였다.

그는 저녁에 통상 일과 정리하고 파티 다니고 클럽 생활 등 하다 보면 늦게 잠자리에 들게 되고, 기상과 동시 바삐 출근 준비하다 보니 면도하며 빵 하나 입에 넣고 우유 한잔하고는 부인이 운전하는 자가용으로 출근한다. 그래서 10시~10시 30분쯤 되면 'Coffee Break'으로 도너츠 또는 토스트 등으로 커피와 함께 아침을 보충한다. 그리고 퇴근 시간이 되면 부인이 운전해 온 자가용으로 일단 집으로 퇴근한다. 그리고 저녁 시간을 가족과 함께 지낸다.— 댄스파티, 클럽활동, 공식 리셉션 참석 등등. 당시 우리는 언제 저런 자동차를 가지고 가족과 함께하는 생활을 할 수 있을까를 생각하며 그때마다 국가 개혁, 국가 발전을 다짐하지 않을 수 없었다.

◦ 솔방울도 강냉이도 이렇게 클까

그런데 이곳에서 놀라웠던 또 하나는 소나무가 많아서 반가웠는데, 아주 굵고 잘 자란 나무들이고 그 솔방울 들은 우리 솔방울의 10배 정도 크게 보였고, 옥수수도 많았는데 반가웠는데 그 옥수수 아마 우리 것의 5~6배는 되지 않을까, 과연 모든 게 크고 굵고 풍족하게 보였다. 심지어는 날씨도 사 계절이 따로 있지 않고 하루에도 사계절이 다 있는 것이 느낄 정도였다.

◇ 철저한 흑인 차별

이곳 '노스캐로라이나' 주는 역시 미국 남부에 속해 있어서 당시까지만 해도 여전히 흑인에 대한 차별이 심했다. 특히 여기 가까운 '페이예트빌(Fayetteville)' 도시는 100년 전의 남북전쟁 이전, 공식 대형 노예시장이 있었던 곳이기도 하였다. 극장 정문은 백인이, 저 구석 옆문으로 흑인이. 좌석이야 물론 구별되었고, 버스도 앞에서 8/10은 백인이, 흑인은 저 뒤 구석 좌석 몇 개 정도, 기차 정거장은 완전히 한 지붕 밑 두 방으로 나누져 있었다. 물론 인구 비율이 그 정도였을지도 모르나 내가 보기에도 아주 극심하였다. 그래서 학교 당국의 주의 사항은 외국인 특히 동양인은 외출할 때 반듯이 군복을 입고 나가야만 봉변을 당하지 않고 동시에 "yes sir" 대접을 받는다고 하였는데 실제로 그러하였다.

◦ 미국인의 대단한 국기 사랑 곧 나라 사랑

미국인 남녀노소 군관민 할 것 없이 애국심 특히 국기에 대한 사랑은 유별나게 보였다. 길거리에는 관공서가 아닌데도 명절이 아닌 평일에도 많은 집이나 다운 타운의 사무실과 상점들이 성조기를 내걸고 생활하고 있었다. 그런데 하루는, 교실에서 공부 좀 하고 귀가(BOQ) 길에, 막 영내를 가로지르는 고속도로를 건너가려는 데 때마침 5시 예포 한 발과 함께 하기식 나팔소리가 나서 멈추고, 건너편 연병장에 게양된 성조기를 향해 거수 경례를 하였다. 그러자 고속으로 지나던 자동차들이 모두 멈추고 대부분은 밖으로 나와 곧바로 서서 내가 보고 있는 곳을 향해 경례를 하지 않는가. 미국은 유치원에서부터 성조기에 서약하고, 국가 행사 때는 물론 민간 행사(각종대회) 때도 애국가를 연주하고 합창하며 성조기를 올리기도 한다. 이것이 미국이고 대국의 힘임을 여행 가는 곳마다 절감하였다.

◇ 뉴욕 및 웨스트포인트(미 육사) 견학 여행

학기 중간쯤(2월)에 학교 당국 안내로 뉴욕과 웨스트포인트(West Point, 미국 육군사관학교) 견학 여행을 가게 되었다. 뉴욕공항으로 이동하여 버스로, 우선 웨스트포인트(뉴욕주 뉴욕시 북부 허드슨 강변에 위치)로 가서 유서 깊고 우리 육사 출신 장교에게는 관계도 깊은 미국육군사관학교를 견학하였다.

우선 허드슨강 요충지에 위치한 이곳은 북미대륙 패권을 두고, 옛 영불전쟁과 독립전쟁 등에서 군사 주둔지로 중요한 역할을 한 이 유서 깊은 자리에, 미국군을 대표하는 미 육사는 1802년, 당시 주로 미국 국토 건설을 위한 인재 즉 공병 장교를 양성하기 위해 개교하였고, 그 후 남북전쟁 등을 거치면서 발전을 거듭하여 현재 모습이 되었다. 학교 대부분은 석조 건물로 미육사 설립 당시 강조되었던 미군 공병기술의 대표작—주로 미군 요새 모양으로 현재 미군 공병 배지가 상징하듯—으로 오랜 세월 전통을 자랑하며 건재하였다. 웅대하고 든든함이 보기에도 미국 육사에 대한 또 미 육군에 대한 신뢰감을 느낄 수 있게 하였다.

미 육사의 교훈은 의무(Duty), 명예(Honor), 조국(Country)이다. 우리 육사의 표어는 유교 국가 인재 양성소답게 또 수양의 도장답게 '지(智), 인(仁), 용(勇)'이다. 그런데 임관 이후 막상 미 육사 교훈을 대하니, 이것이 군대를 통솔하는 지휘관 특히 초급 장교에게는 오히려 현실적이고 격에 맞는 교훈이라고 생각도 되었다.

학교 교수부를 지나며 보니, 이제 막 수업을 마치고 생도대로 가기 직전, 아마도 월말고사 결과를 보느라고, 넓은 게시판 곳곳에서 절도 있고 정연하게 움직이는 생도들을 만날 수 있었는데, 특히 성적 게시판 앞에서 좌우로 차려 자세로 한 발자국씩 움직이며 지기 성적과 교반 편성표를 바라보는 모습에서 우리의 화랑대 생도 시절 생활 모습이 떠올라 정겨움이 앞섰다.

학교 도서관 겸 기념관에는 미국에서 흔히 볼 수 있는 '자유 아니면 죽음을 달라' 고 하는 선언문과 '나라가 당신을 요구하고 있다'는 전형적인 미국식 애국 포스터를 보면서 미국에 대한 인상이 더 깊어졌다. 그런데 좀 보다 보니 옆에 젊은 서양 여자가 있길래 통성명을 했더니, 자기는 여기보다 더 시골 "코네티컷"주에 있는 국민학교 여선생인데 학생들 데리고 견학왔다고 했다. 그래서 우리는 한국에서 왔는데 했더니, 놀래면서 어떻게 그렇게 먼 곳에서 여기까지 왔느냐고 했다. 당시만 해도 세계 여행이란 미국 사람들에게도조차 '소수 사람들에게 주어진 행운'으로 생각되고 있었다.

우리는 생도 식당 한편에서 생도들과 식사를 함께하였는데, 나는 특별히 옛 육사 생활을 떠 올리며 그들의 일거수일투족을 관심을 가지고 살펴보았다. 전 생도가 오전 일과를 마치고 일제히 식당으로 들어와 거대한 v자형으로 자리를 잡고 정좌한다. 그러자 식당 도움이 군인들이 동시에 각 분대 식탁으로 가 음식 이 담긴 접시 한가지씩 테이블에 올려주면, 맨 끝자리 하급생 오늘의 당번 생도가 접시를 들고 왜친다. "여기 맛있는 스프가 왔습니다"고 하면서 안쪽으로 밀어주면 저 끝 상급생에게까지 패스된다. 그러기를 여러번—아마도 5번 정도, 그날 메뉴에 다르겠지만—하고 나면, 전생도 분위기를 내려보고 있던 2층 높이의 베란다에 자리하고 있던 연대장 생도가 "차렷! 식사 개시" 한다. 그러면 일제히 식사를 한다.

그리고 모두가 열심히 일제히 식사를 끝내는 듯하면 연대장 생도가 이후 일정 등 간단히 훈시 형식으로 말하고 "식사 끝 퇴장"을 명한다 그러면 일제히 일어나 퇴장해 나갔다. 이들을 닮아서 했던 우리네 회랑대 생도 식당 생활 모습이 생각나 감개가 무량하였다.

미 육사를 소개한 영화에 「Long Long Gray Line」이 있다. 평생을 육사에서 근무하며 생도들을 뒤바라지 해온 상사가 전역하는 날 생도들이 그에게 사열과 분열로 그를 환송하는 영화이면서 동시에 정의와 의무와 국가 충성의 생도 대열이 금년도 내년도 또 그다음 해도 끝없이 대열지어 국가와 국민에게로 전선으로 나가고 또 이어져 나가는 그 대열, 즉 그레이 예복 입은 육사생도들의 끊임이 없는 나아가는 퍼레이드 행렬, 그 진수를 여기 웨스트포인트에 와서 진짜로 보았다.

이어서 우리 버스는 눈이 많이 와 미끄러운 시골길을 조심해서 달려 드디어 세계 제일의 상업 도시 '뉴욕'에 도착하였다. 우선 시내 '타임스퀘어'에 내려 중심가를 걸으며 주변을 관광하는데, 말로만 듣고 사진으로만 보아 오던 미국 뉴욕이라는 곳에 와 그 중심가에 서서 두리번거리며 사방을 눈여겨보았다.

아마도 6~70층 이상 되는 듯한, 문자 그대로 높고 크고 우람한 빌딩의 숲속을 걷는 그 기분, 마치 시골 촌사람과도 같이, 특히나 한곳에 서서 몸을 뒤로 재치고 고개를 들어 위를 처다 보며 몇 층이나 될까, 한두 번 시도하다 어림도 없어 포기하고 그저 감탄과 감탄으로 지나가는데, 또 시내를 지나다니는 뉴욕의 명물 그 'Yellow Cap(택시)'는 질서 정연하고 보기도 좋았다.

다음에는 맨해튼 5번가로 가서 그 유명한, 미국 가면 반듯이 보고 싶었던 'Empire State Building(엠파이어 스테이트 빌딩)'을 오르게 되었다. 1962년 당시에도 여전히 세계에서 가장 높았고 유명했던 이 빌딩은, 세계 대공황기에 불과 몇 년 만인 1931년에 완성되었다는데, 전체 102층에 높이 381미터의 문자 그대로 마천루(摩天樓)였다. 콘크리트로 되어 있는 86층까지는 한 엘리베이터로 단숨에 올라가고, 그 위로 16층짜리 전망대와 방송안테나로 올라가기 위해서는 다시 엘리베이터를 환승하여 올라가 전망대에 이르게 된다. 그렇지 않아도 저 아래 거리를 지나면서 놀라기도 했거니와, 이제 여기에 올라와서는 사방으로 저 멀리 끝없는 지평선까지 바라볼 수 있는 것은 물론, 그 수 없고 거대한 빌딩 숲을 한 눈 아래로 전부 내려다볼 수 있으니 실로 가관이라, 더욱 놀라고 김탄스러울 뿐이었다. 그리하여 다시 한번 국가 건설과 민족 발전에 헌신할 것을 각오하였다.

가히 1950년대 선배 장교들이 집단으로 이곳을 방문하고, "인생관이 바뀌려 했다"는 실토가 결코 빈 소리가 아니었음을 저절로 확인할 수 있었다. 생각해 보시라. 1950년 전에도 부산에서는 6층짜리 일본 백화점 하나, 서울에서도 6층짜리 일본 백화점 하나 한국인 5층짜리 백화점 하나가 있었는데 그것조차 '6·25 적란'으로 파괴되었던 시절이라, 충분히 이해할 수 있었다.

2020년대에도 미국 대통령 '트럼프'는 북한 지배자에게 "'비핵화'하면 '엠파이아스테이트 빌딩'과 같은 발전을 도와 줄거라"고 약속하는 것을 보아도 능히, 당시의 우리 방문 장교단의 심정을 짐작할 수 있으리라고 생각한다. 나는 그 이후 일생 동안 3번 더 뉴욕을 방문하였는데, 그때마다 옛날 감격을 되살리며 이 빌딩의 그 전망대에 오르고 또 올랐다.

◇ 첫 미국 유학의 마무리, 남부 미대륙(과 멕시코) 횡단 여행

◦ 다시 와본 미국 수도 워싱턴

불과 3개월 기간이었지만 내게, 다방면의 미국 견문을 통해 신천지 미국에 대한 지식은 물론, 더불어 세계적 안목을 넓힘과 동시에 폭넓은 지식을 습득할 수 있는 기회가 주어졌던 사실에 대해 미국에 감사하고 하나님께 감사드린다.

이제 짧은 기간이나마 학업을 마치고 귀국길에 오르게 되었는데, 때마침 미군 해병대 대위 'Hennegan'이 자기 자동차로 '캘리포니아의 샌디에이고'에 있는 미 해병대기지로 귀대한다기에, 우리(한 선배와 나)는 함께 미대륙 남부를 자동차로 횡단 여행할 수 있는 행운을 갖게 되었다.

그리하여 먼저 위로 올라가 워싱턴을 2일간 방문하게 되었다. 이 워싱턴 2차 방문에서는 주미대사관 무관부 '박보희 소령'을 만나 워싱턴에 거주하는 한국인들에 대한 소개와, 특히 5·16 군사혁명 때문에 망명한 고위 장군들에 대해 소식도 들었는데, 그중 몇 분이 우릴 만나자고 하기에 만나보기도 하였다.

사실은 6·25 적란과 함께 한국 전선에서 맺은 미국 전우들의 도움과 한국과의 미래를 생각하는 미국 국가 정책으로, 어쩌다 '반혁명 분자'가 되버린—이후 많은 장군들이 귀국하여 군사 정부에 협조하였다.—이분들이 미국으로 망명 온 지도 1년 여가 되었다. 그래서 그동안 군대와 사회 정치 분위기와 소식 등이 궁금하였던 지라 우리같이 초급 장교에게도 만나자고 한 것이다. 솔직히 우리는 그들의 기대를 물론 만족시키지 못했는데, 우린 기관원도 아니었고 단순히 유학 온 초급 장교에 불과하였던 것이다.

친절하고 사교적인데다 영어를 아주 유창하게 구사하는 '박보희' 소령은, 나중에 아주 유명하게 되는 인물이기에 간단히 소개해 두려고 한다. 내가 육사생도 2학년 시절 하기 군사훈련을 위해 광주 상무대 보병학교에 갔을 때 그는 대위로 M1소총 교관이었다. 물론 간단하고 보병의 기본 병기이지만 아주 흥미 있게 아주 기억하기 좋게 설명해 줌으로써 우리는 그를 최우수 교관으로 점찍고 있었다.

앞에서 잠깐 언급했지만, 그는 '육사생도 2기' 출신 장교로 한국전쟁 때 한국군 제3군단이 '상진부리'에서 후퇴할 때 군위문연예단을 무사히 인솔하였다. 아마도 그 인연으로, 주미 무관부 근무 후, '통일교 문선명' 씨 후원으로 한국 고아들로 된 '리틀 엔젤스(Little

Angels)'를 창단하여 세계 참전국 16개국 순회 공연을 하면서 좋은 반응은 물론 인기를 얻게 되었다. 그래서 드디어 한국 대표 '어린이합창단'이 되어 한때 유명해지고 한국의 대외 문화 인상도 드높인 바 있었다. 그 이후 본격적으로 문선명을 도와 통일교가 세계화하는데 크게 기여한 인물이다.

우리는 그가 소개해 준 예쁜 한 여대생—주미한국대사관 아르바이트생—의 안내로 지난번에 못 가본 워싱턴의 여러 구석을 돌다가 하루는 버지니아 12번가—워싱턴 근교의 가난한 흑인 주거지역—를 둘러보면서 미국 워싱턴에도 그리고 자본주의에도 저런 어두운 구석이 있구나를 느끼기도 하였다.

◦ 미국 고속도로와 남북전쟁 결전장 '애틀랜타'의 '사이클로라마'

두 번째 워싱턴 방문을 마치고 우리는 다시 '해니건' 미 해병 대위와 만나 이제 본격적으로 개인 자동차를 이용한 제2의 대륙 횡단 여행을 시작하였다. 워싱턴에서 남으로 내려가 다시 '노스캐롤라이나'주를 지나고 더 남쪽으로 '사우스캐롤라이나'주의 '컬럼비아'에서 방향을 서로 돌려 '조지아' 주의 '애틀랜타'에 도착하였는데 대략 1,500킬로미터를 약 15시간 정도 걸렸다. 고속도로가 부산에서 북한 신의주를 거쳐 만주 심양까지 있다면, 하루에 그 거리만큼 이동한 샘이 된다.

특히 워싱턴에서 출발한 그때부터 당분간 고속도로는 한 방향 8차선 왕복 16차선이었고, 군데군데 4입 클로버 형 인터체인지가 다이나막하게 건설되어 있었고 무인 톨게이트에는 노란색 소쿠리가 있어서 동전을 거기다 던져넣고 지나갔다. 내가 미국 가서 찍어 온 사진 중에 많은 부분이 바로 이 아주 웅대한 고속도로들이다. 2025년 현재 한국에서 이 사진들은 아무 의미가 없고 오히려 싱겁게도 보이나, 1962년 당시에는 참으로 신기하고도 위대한 볼거리요 뉴스 거리였으며 일거리(국토 혁신/개혁)였다. 그후 10여 년이 지나서야 겨우 힘겹게(타국에서 돈을 빌려와) 대한민국 최초 고속도로 '경부고속도로'가 개설되었기 때문이다. 미국 유학 와서 이런 고속도로 보고도 한국 고속도로 건설을 꿈꾸지 않는 장교가 있었다면 그는 분명 한국군 장교가 아니었을 것이다.

애틀랜타 근교 군사기지 VOQ—미국군 군사기지마다 VOQ가 있어서 출장/여행 중인 현역 및 예비역에게 침식의 편의가 제공된다— 에서 잠자리를 해결하고 다음 날 일찍부터 미국 남북전쟁의 결전장으로 알려진 애틀랜타의 남북전쟁 박물관 '애틀랜타 Cyclorama(원형파노라마)'로 향했다. 과연 생전 처음 보는, 축구장 크기만 한 거대한 실내 전장 파노라마(바닥과 벽화)가 있었다.

파노라마의 내용은, 미국 남북전쟁 당시 결전을 위해 '셔만' 장군이 지휘하는 북 '돌격군'이 적진을 돌파하여 남군 후방으로 깊숙이 돌격해 들어가 후방의 핵심 요지 애틀랜타에서 승리의 결전을 벌리는 장면(1864년)이다. 한때 미국군이 애용했던 '셔만전차'가 말해 주듯이 미군 전쟁 역사에서 '셔만 장군'은 '적진 돌파, 무자비, 초토화, 적후방 강타'하는 전략 전술의 상징으로 추앙되고 있다. 그 내용도 유명하지만 이 거대한 전장 '사이클로라마'가, 이후 독일 유학에서 '워터루 결전장'의 전쟁 박물관에서도 이런 모습을 볼 때까지, 특히 전쟁 역사 공부를 열심히 해온 내게 더 감격과 감명을 안겨주었다.

다음에는 멀지 않은 곳에 솟아 있는—실은 애틀랜타 일대는 분지형 대평원으로 멀리 까지 잘 보이는—'Stone Mountain'으로 갔다. '스톤 마운틴 공원'으로 잘 가꾸어져 있었는데 한가운데에 거대한 돌산 하나가 웅장하게 자리하고 그 한쪽 벽에 3명의 남군 영웅(당시 남부연맹 대통령 데이비스, 리 장군 그리고 잭슨 장군) 기마상이 크게 부조(浮彫)되어 있다. 3명의 석공(작가)이 60여 년간 교대로 조각하였다고 한다. 이 규모는 사우스 다코타에 있는 4명의 위인상에 버금간다고 한다. 돌산 위에서 저 멀리 애틀랜타 시내를 포함한 전경을 내려다보고 내려와서는 옛 전장터—지금도 당시 사용했던 지휘소(관측소) 등이 남아 있는—를 순방한 뒤 그 유명했던 영화 「바람과 함께 살아지다」와 같이, 그때 그곳을 다시 생각하며 '자동차와 함께 살아지면서' 다시 남부 횡단 고속도로 위로 다음 행선지를 향해 달려갔다.

◦ 텍사스로 가다가 속도 위반 벌금 물다

미국 서부 개척을 향한 최초의 장벽이었던 '애팔래치아 산맥'을 통과하고 '앨라배마'주를 지나 초원 지대의 '미시시피'주에서는, 서부 개척 시대 많은 일화를 남기고 있는 북미대륙 중앙을 남북으로 종단하며 흐르는 거대한 '미시시피강'을 건너 잠시 직선거리 약 300킬로미터 '루이지애나'주를 횡단하여, 드디어 광활한 초원 지대로 카우보이와 보난자로 유명한 '텍사스'주에 도착하였다.

그리하여 불과 몇 년 뒤 '케네디 암살사건'으로 세계에 알려지는 '댈러스'를 별생각 없이 지나 '포트, 워스' 근방의 '카즈웰' 미 공군기지 VOQ에서 1박 하였다. 오는 도중 어느 도로 구간에 '여기는 레이더 체크 구간'이라 표시가 있었는데 미국 친구 얘기로는 '실제로 속도 위반하면 경찰이 즉시 뒤따라 온다'고 했다. 물론 시험조는 아니었지만 당시 미국 고속도로는 통상 60마일 시간인데, 어쩌다 방심하여 70마일을 달리게 되자 진짜로 "왱~!" 사이렌 소리 울리며 경찰이 뒤따라와 거울 속에서 손짓으로 옆으로 정차하라 한다.

길옆으로 붙여 세웠더니 경찰이 와서, 우리가 군복을 입은 장교라 정중히 인사하고, 보아 줄줄 알았더니, 천만의 말씀, 면허증 보여달라 하고 두말없이 딱지 떼고는, 친절하게 '조금 더 가면 마을이 나오는데, 거기 은행에 가서 벌금 내고 가시라'고 하고, 또 정중히 "먼 거리 조심해서 안녕히 가십시오"라고 인사까지 껌벅하고 살라졌다. 딱지를 보니 마일당 7달러 합계가 70달러였다. 먼 길 가는 우리 나그네에게는 상당한 액수라 좀 억울하였으나 세 사람이 '더치페이'로 납부하고 또 가던 길을 재촉했다. 실제 미국은 범법에 대해서는 가차 없이 집행하는데 특히 교통 법칙 준수는 대단하였다.

◦ 텍사스 카우보이와 기름 도시 엘패소 그리고 인접한 멕시코 도시

당시에도 '텍사스 카우보이'는 유명했다. 이후 미국 역사를 연구하면서 알게 되었지만, 1980년대 서부 개척 첫 단계에서 더 더 서부로 가보느라 지나쳐버린 이 초원 지역에 실제로 4000만 마리 이상의 야생들소(Buffalo)가 '인디언' 원주민을 살려가며 생존해 있었다. 그래서 2차 서부 개척 당시에는 이를 발견하고, 미국 역사상 '제2 횡재'(Windfall)로, 또 한차례의 야생들소 떼, 보난자(Bonanza, 뜻밖의 행운)로 기록되기도 하였다. 그래서 이

들소 떼를 몰고 소비 지역 북쪽(시카고 지방)으로 올라가기를 반복했던 전문 카우보이들이 이 텍사스의 상징이기도 했다. 역사책에 보면, 이 들소 떼가 오늘날 비교적 체구가 큰 유럽 인류의 골격을 형성하는데 큰 공을 세웠다고도 할 정도로 대단한 행운이었다고 한다.

이런 역사를 품고 있는 대초원 지대 텍사스를 서쪽 방향으로 지나고 또 지나 드디어 멕시코 접경도시, 그리고 당시로는 미국 유수의 갑부들의 도시 '엘패소(El Paso)'에 도착하였다. 한 선배와 나는 '포트 블리스'(Fort Bliss) 육군 기지에 숙박하고 미국 친구는 아는 여자 집— 미 해군 중령 부인으로 딸 한 명과 거주, 상당한 석유 유산 보유로 부유 생활—에 투숙하여 3박 4일간 지역 관광에 재미를 가졌다.

엘패소는 당시 텍사스 석유 생산 단지에서도 질과 양적으로 최고 수준의 생산 지역으로, 그로서 시민들은 경제적으로 풍요를 누리고 있었다. 예하면, 초대해 준 중령 부인은 날씨만 좋으면 수시로, 14살 먹은 딸과 함께 비행장에 가서 개인 격납고에서 '세스나' 경비행기를 둘이서 밀고 나와 탐승하고 그대로 날아올라서 하늘 위 드라이브를 즐긴다고 한다. 다음 날 우리도 함께 가서 타 보았는데, 5명이 세스나에 올라 14살 딸애가— 한국 나이로는 15살 이긴 하나 훨씬 조숙해 보였다—조종하고 뉴멕시코 상공 등 주변을 근 1시간여 비행도 해 보았다. 사실은 그동안 긴장하고 마음이 졸였다. 그런데 통상 한 집에 자동차 2~3대는 물론 세스나 등 경항공기 1~2대씩은 누누나 소유하고 있다고 한다.

그래서 공중 드라이브는 엘패소 전 시민들 일과의 한 부분일 뿐이라 하니 당시 우리 계산으로는 그 부유함을 가늠하기 어려웠다. 그리고 밤에는, 보기에는 매일같이 동네 '파티홀'에서 남녀가 서로 어울리는 댄스파티가 열리고 있었다. 석유 부자들의 호화스런 생활, 과하게 말하면 동양식 '주지육림' 모습을 언제나 목격할 수 있었다. 우리도 그 부인과 함께 매일 밤 동행해 가보았는데, 나는 춤을 못 추긴 하였으나 그들과 한 자리에서 자주 시간을 보내다 보니—그 이웃들이 우리 한국 장교를 신기하게 보고—특히 중년들과 친하게 되었다.

그래서 귀국 후에도 때가 되면 카드도 보내왔는데, 어떤 카드 그림엔, 늙었으나 더욱 풍만해져 힘이 더 센 듯한 큰 암탉이, 야위고 힘 빠진듯한 늙은 장닭을 불쌍하게 보고 있는 재밌는 것도 있었는데, 그때 젊을 때는 몰랐으나, 지금 생각하니 즐거운 인생 후기의 한 모습이기도 한, 그 동네 삶의 한 단면이기도 하였다.

원래 이 도시는 '리오그란데강'을 끼고 남북으로—마치 서울이 한강을 끼고 강남 강북으로 있듯이—형성된 한 도시였으나, 1888년에 '텍사스공화국'이 성립되면서 다른 나라로 분리되었고, 북쪽은 미군 국경 수비대를 비롯한 석유 개척민들이 점차 증가하여 오늘날의 풍요한 '엘패소'가 되었다. 그런데, 어떻게 된 것인지 강을 하나 사이에 두고 남쪽은 멕시코 전통 도시 '시우다드 후아레스'로 불리며, '북 천당, 남 지옥(가난)'이 되어 있었다.

하루는 국경 검문소—미국인과 관광객은 통과, 멕시코인은 엄중 조사—를 지나 강남 멕시코 동네로 가보았다. 신호등에 차가 멈추면 금방 애들이 달려들어, 한 손은 유리창 닦는 시늉을 하면서 다른 한 손은 벌려서 돈 달라고 하였다. 식당에 앉으면 여지없이 멕시코풍의 고깔모자 쓰고, 통기타를 어깨에 멘 노래꾼이 다가와 키타 치며 노래하면서 팁 줄 때까지 열창한다. 관광객(주로 미국인들)들은 이들과 함께 노래도 하고 팁 주고 앙콜해서 즐긴다.

동시에 그림 그리는 친구가 와서 초상화 그리라고 조른다. 우리에게도 재밌으니 그림 그리도록 맡겨 보라고도 했다. 거리 주변에는 합법 비합법으로 성매매가 이루어지고 있었다.

미국인들은 이런 풍습을 이제는 즐기기 위해 찾아온다고 한다. 사실 미국 내에서는 성매매가 법적으로 금지 되어 있어 국경 근처 미국인은 이렇게 멕시코로 관광을 즐기고 있다는 것이다. 미국은 한동안 금주를 단행하여 술꾼들은 군대에 자원하여 복무하면서 술을 마실 수 있었는데, 그렇지 못한 사회에서는 밀주(Moon Shine)로 생업을 유지하는 소위 깽 단(Gangster)'이 횡횡했다고 한다. 지금도 미국 사람들은 절주하는 편이다.

그런데 멕시코에서 본 것 중 지금도 기억나는 건, 빈부의 격차가 하늘과 땅 사이로 느껴졌다. 시내를 한 바퀴 돌아보는데 어느 한 곳에서 황금색으로 번쩍이는 아주 고급 저택이 있는가 하면 그 바로 얼마 떨어지지 않은 언덕에는 곳곳에 땅굴을 파고 들어가 살고 있는 모습도 보였다. 과연 이 나라는 자본주의의 최악 사회상태에 있고, 때문에 남미의 좌경화가 이유 있음을 알게 되었다.

◇ '애리조나 카우보이'를 노래하며 미 해병 기지 '샌디에이고'로

◦ 모뉴먼트 밸리, Ghost town, 광야를 달려가는 '애리조나 카우보이' 기분

풍요하면서도 질서정연하고, 참으로 즐거웠고 친절한 인간미가 흐르는 석유 부자 도시 '엘패소'를 뒤로하고 중간 도착지, 미 해병대 기지 '샌디에이고'를 향해 뉴멕시코 사막 길로 출발하였다. 뉴멕시코에서 직선거리 300여 킬로미터를 달리자 '애리조나'주에 들어왔는데, 저 머리 아득히 '로키산맥'을 바라보며 2~3시간을 달려도 직선 그대로인 사막 한가운데 고속도로를 달릴 때는, 저절로 당시 유행하던 노래 그대로 '황야를 달려가는 역마차, 광야를 달려가는 카우보이' 기분이 절로 나기에 우리는 '아리조나 카우보이' 노래를 부르며 사막 여행 기분을 만끽하였다.

가다가 도중에 '나바호 인디언 보호 구역' 을 지나게 되었는데, 길가에는 인디언이 운영하고 관리하는 관광안내소와 기념물 판매소가 있었고, 좀 더 가면서 가까이로 정말 이국풍의, 붉은 황야에 우뚝우뚝 서 있는 '모뉴먼트 밸리'가 보여서 멈추고 한동안 신기한 풍경을 혼자 보기엔 아깝다는 생각으로 감상하였다. 그 주변에는 군데군데 'Ghost Town'이 산재해 있었는데 물론 인적도 없고 특별한 흔적도 없었으나 설명으로 듣고 보면 알 수 있었다. 조금 더 가다 보면 이 풍경을 배경으로 서부영화 촬영소들이 몇 곳 있었는데, 가짜 배우들이 흉내를 내며 관광객을 상대로 돈벌이 중이었다.

나바호 보호구역은 미국 서부 개척 시대 이후 잔존 '나바호족 인디언'을 보호하고 감시하기 위해서 일정 구역을 그들의 생존 지역으로 정해 주었는데, 그들은 이 황량한—우리가 보기에도—뿌리 터전을 되찾아 들어왔다고 한다. '나바호 보호구역만 하더라도 현재 남한 크기라고 하는데, 미국 국토에 이런 인디언 종족별 보호구역이 수 십 군데 있다 하니, 그렇게도 많이 희생되고도 이만한 생존력을 보존하고 있다니 과연 백인 침탈 이전에는 그 세력이 어떠했을까 짐작할 만하였다.

◦ '투손' 공원의 신기한 명물 '기둥 선인장'과 만발한 꽃

가다가 투손(Tucson, 서부영화 주무대) 국립공원 지역에 들어가자 동부 '사구아로(Saguaro ; 기둥선인장 등)' 국립공원이 전개되었는데, 때마침 꽃피는 4월이라— 한국에서 선인장 큰 것이 주먹만 하고, 30여 센티면 귀물이고, 꽃은 100년에 한 번 핀다고 알고 있었다.—거대한 기둥 선인장(사람 키 몇 배짜리도 있고)과 군데군데 손바닥 선인장도 섞여 있어서 정말 귀물 동네에 와 있는 신비감조차 들었다. 조금 더 북쪽으로 가면 진짜 거대한 '그랜드캐니언'이 있다는데 그건 다음으로 미루기로 하였다.

'샌디에이고'를 약 250여 키로미터 앞두고 애리조나의 마지막 도시 '유마(Yuma)'에 도착하였는데, 우리 생각 외로 유마 교외에 있는 감옥 구경을 하게 되었다. 그 당시는 이 동행 미국 친구가 미국에는 이런 곳(감옥)도 있다는 의미의 안내였나 했는데 알고 보니 이 또한 애리조나 즉 미국 서부 개척 시대 역사를 상징하는 유명한 관광지였다. 그런데 기억으로는, 그때는 여전히 감옥도 운영 중이었고 교도소 안으로 들어가 실제로 죄수가 간수에게 말로 무언가 불평하고 호소하는 모습을 보기도 하였다는 생각이 지금도 들고 있다. 지금(2020년)은 순수 광광 명소로 알려지고 있는 듯하다.

◦ 드디어 도착한 '샌디에이고' 해병대 기지, '롱비치'에서 헤어지다

이제 마지막 자동차 드라이브의 기분을 다하여 달려서, '캘리포니아'주(최 남단 지대) 아름다운 초목 지대를 지나고 드디어 우리 자동차 드라이브와 미국 남부 자동차 횡단 여행의 최종 목적지, 미 해병 '해네건' 대위의 집이 있고 직장(해병대 기지)이 있는 '샌디에이고'에 도착하였다.

기지를 둘러보다가 어느 길엔가 영내 24마일 속도 제한이 붙어 있는 옆에 'Korea Street' 라는 자동차 도로 길 명칭이 붙어 있는 것을 발견하고 반가웠다. 그만큼 미 해병대와 한국이 인연이 깊다는 상징이 거기에 있었다. 그 거리를 지나 역시 영내에 있는 '해네건'의 집으로 가서 그 부인도 만나고 차 한 잔 대접받으며 그동안의 얘기와 한국 얘기 주고받았다. 참 좋게 보이는 부인이었다. 서로 얼마나 반가우랴.

우리의 다음 최종 행선지는 샌프란시스코의 '포트 메이슨'인데 도중에 'L.A'와 '산타 바바라'에 들려서 지나가기로 했다. 그래서 그 미군 친구가 자기 차로 우리를 'L.A'의 '롱 비치'까지 전송해 주었고 거기서 정말로 아름다운 석양을 바라보며 여행의 대미를 장식하고, 정말로 아쉬운 작별을 하였다. '롱비치' 해변은 말 그대로 길기도 하였지만 아름다웠고 태평양 쪽에 있어서 더욱 감회가 깊었다.

◇ 미국 유학 소망 결실, 평생 길잡이 된 그때 그 견문과 각오

◦ 다시 와본 아름답고 웅장한 '샌프란시스코'에서

우리는 미국 대륙 횡단과 종단 여행의 대미를 장식하기 위해, 당시 타 보고 싶었던 유명한 '그레이하운드, 장거리 버스'를 타고 미대륙 여행의 최종 목적지 '샌프란시스코'로 향했다. 이 버스는 미 대륙 횡단, 종단의 기차 또는 비행기보다 편리하고 싸기에 많은 미국 사람들은 물론 특히 미국 여행을 즐기는 외국 사람들에게는 대인기였다.

직선거리로 500킬로미터가 넘는 고속도로를 흔들림도 없이 오히려 비행기보다 편하고 즐겁게 여행하게 된 이 장거리 버스는 실내에 회장실도 있고 밤새 달리며 취침할 수 있도록 자리가 곧 침대가 될 수 있게 되어있다. 주요 도시 곳곳마다 들리면서 내려서 볼일 다 보고 또는 관광 다 하고, 다음 차를 이용할 수도 있게 되어 관관 버스로도 아주 편리하다. 그리고 쉬지 않고 밤낮 24시간을 달리는데, 8시간마다 운전수만 교대하고 달리며, 도중에 차량 정비를 계속 점검해가면서 그대로 그 차로 달린다. 그래서 미대륙 종단은 물론 횡단도 보통 10일 정도로 해결해 준다. 선진국 미국의 또 하나 상징이었다.

달리는 버스에서 왼쪽으로는 태평양 오른쪽으로는 로키산맥의 지류들인 '시에라네바다 산맥'과 그 서쪽 아래에 전개되는 코스트산맥을 번갈아 보아가며 그동안 미국에 대한 견문을 반추해 보았다. 미국의 첫인상은 하와이 상공에서 본 광활하고도 잘도 정비된 미국 농토를 내려다보면서 속 시원하면서도 엄정하고 아름다운 선진국이라는 인상을 받았고, 샌프란시스코에서는 질서 정연하고 아름다우며 풍요하고도 자유스러운 사람들이 잘사는 선진국 도시를 보고, 당시 여전히 '밥 먹기 위해 살고 있는 우리'는 언제 어떻게 하면 저렇게 '살기 위해 밥 먹는 삶'을 살 수 있을까를 생각나게 인상 깊었다.

◦ 미국은 신천지 ; 크고 풍족하며 서로 믿는 사람들 세상

기차로 1주일을 주야로 달려가야 다른 한쪽에 닿을 수 있는 거대한, 광활한 미국을 보았고, '골든게이트 브릿지'와 '엠파이어 스테이트 빌딩' 같은 거대하고도 위대한 건축물과 웅장하고도 탄탄하며 질서정연하게 건설된 선진 도시들, 그리고 그 도시들을 출입하거나 도시 간을 이어주는 고속도로, 이 모든 것들이 당장은 추종 불가능한 신천지로 느껴져, 역시나 그것들로 '내 인생관이 변하려고 한다'는 것이 총체적 인상들이었다. 그러했기에 내 마음로는 '우리도 한번 잘살아 보자'는 결심이 절로 솟구쳤다.— 그 후 유럽에 가서야, 아 우리도 일단은 유럽 발전 단계를 거치면 미국 같은 선진국이 될 수 있을 것이라고 확신할 수 있었다.

이제 실상, 견문과 체험을 통해 각인된 미국과 미국 사람들에 대한 생각은 한마디로 '미국과 미국 사람은 믿을 수 있다'는 것이다. 행선지 'J.F, Kennedy Center'를 가기 위해 이용했던 '유니언 태평양철도'의 'Pullman ship Car'에서 우리(한국군 장교)는 미국 일등 시민의 대우를 받았고, 목적지에 도착하여 '여행 중 비용명세서'를 적어내면, 물론 그대로 믿고— 예, 그동안 집으로 한 전화 비용도, 식사 외 특별히 부담한 비용 등—두말없이 보상해 주었다. 당시 특히 그 지역에서는 유색 인종에 대한 차별이 여전했음에도 불구하고, 숙소는 미군 장교와 1대 1로 배정했고, 'PX와 Commercially'도 미군과 구분 없이 이용하게 하였다. 당시 미국은 우리 한국 장교에게 여행부터 시작해서 먹고 자고 공부하고 용돈까지 완전히 부담해 주었다.

그러하기에 행정의 편의성도, 잔소리 군소리 없이 그저 현장에 도착만 하면 기다리고 있었다며, '어서오세요'하며 일사천리로, 우리에게 편리하게 물어가며 조치해 주었다. 샌프란시스코에 도착하여 한국으로 쓴 편지 답장이 케네디 센터에서 기다리고 있었고, 케네디 센터에서 여행 출발하며 한국으로 쓴 편지 답장이 샌프란시스코 '포트 메이슨'에서 기다리고 있었다. 기간 중 그 모든 면에서 그들이 그들 장교 서로를 존중하고 믿듯이 우리 외국 장교 특히 한국군에게도 믿고 존중해 주었다.

◦ 내 나라로 돌아오면서 생각과 각오

샌프란시스코에 도착하여 그동안의 휴가비를 지급 받고 결산하였으며, 다시 '미스 고' 집에 며칠간 하숙하다가, 드디어 미국을 떠나 귀국길에 올랐다. 그동안 과학이 발전하여 이제는 미군도 제트 여객기를 이용해 해외로 드나들 수 있게 되었다. 그래서 우리도 올 때는 미군 수송기로 왔으나 갈 때는 민간 제트 여객기 'Tiger 전세기'에 탑승하여 '웨이크 섬 미군기지, Wake Is'를 거쳐서—시간 관계로 시내(비행장 근처에 단층 건물들로 조성된 시가지)를 돌아볼 수 없었으나 태평양 원주민 색이 농후하였다.—서태평양을 횡단하여 김포 공항에 도착하였다.

내 조국 대한민국 서울에 가까이 올수록 누구보다 나를 기다리고 있을 '영 아가씨', 아니 약혼녀를 다시 만나게 될 생각을 하니 마음 설레였다. 그리하여 밑을 내다보고 또 내다보는데, 우리의 '삼천리 강산'과 '폐허된 서울' 그리고 더 가까이에는 꾸불꾸불 논밭과 거의 전부가 초가집으로 된 김포 평야 지대였다. 그때도 나는 이제 '5·16 군사혁명'의 '국가 재건'과 '역사 부흥'의 바람이 더 거세게 불어 조속히 한국 천지개벽이 성취되어야 한다고 굳게 굳게 결심하였다. 다른 한순간에는, 기회가 된다면 미국을 다시 한번 가보고 싶은 생각이 스쳐갔다.

2. 결혼과 광주 신혼생활, '동복 올빼미 유격교육대' 창설

◇ 결혼하고 광주에서 신혼생활 시작하다

미국 유학 후 보직은 규정대로 광주에 있는 육군보병학교 교관이었는데, 이는 내가 바라던 직무였다. 한편, 광주 보병학교로 부임한 지 얼마 안 되어 결혼 날짜가 정해졌다. 그래서 그날에 앞서 우선 가형이 '전주'로 가서 사주단자(納采)를 직접 전하고, 장차 장인어른 되실 분은 직접 '동래' 우리 집으로 보답(擇日) 방문하는 등의 절차를 밟았다. 그리하여 결혼식이 임박하자 남자 측에서 보내는 예물을 신붓집(전주 처가)으로 직접 가져가는 행사를 하게 되었다.

당시 경상도는 남자가 여자 집에 예물을 가져가는 풍습이었다. 그래서 내 바로 주변 동기생들이 기꺼이 나섰다. 나보다 앞서 결혼하고, 미국 포병학교 미사일 유학 과정을 마치고 여기 상무대 포병학교 교관으로 와 있는 절친 박정기 동기와 기갑학교 교관으로 와 있는 사람 좋은 김종태 동기, 기혼자들로 함께 근무 중인 신우식, 장기하 이승주(총각) 동기들이 총출동하여 전주에 있는 신붓집에 예물 전달 퍼포먼스를 가서 행하게 되었다.

그때는 광주에서 기차를 타고 이리로 가서 여관방에 하루를 지나고, 다음날 기차로 전주로 갔다. 그래서 태평로에 있는 처갓집 근처에서, 기갑 김 중위가 예물 보따리—귀국시 가져온 샘소나이트 케리어 하드백 속에, 비단 장사하시며 며느리 주려고 아껴 놓았던 옷감과 내가 미국서 사 온 하이힐과 예식용 팔 장갑 등—를 짊어지고 벙어리 행세를 하고 박정기 중위가 흥정꾼이 되고 다른 친구들은 들러리 꾼이 되고 나는 모르는 척 뒤따라 가며 눈치 통신하는 모양새로 태세를 갖추었다.

전주 태평로 한국은행 골목길을 들어서면서 큰소리로, "물건 사려! 물건 사려!" 하며 여기 신붓집이 어디냐? 이 동네 맞느냐? 등 떠들고 온 동네가 알만큼 선전하다가, 신부네 식구가 나와 사정사정해서 집으로 모셔가는데, 드디어 대문 앞에 와서는 한바탕 들어가느니 마느니 실랑이를 하면 돈다발이 나오고, 못 이긴 척 마당에 서서는 짐을 내려 놓지 않고 떠들기만 하면 또 돈이 나오고, 그래서 한참 실랑이 끝에 동네 사람들에게 구경 다 시킨 뒤에는 또 돈 받고 아주 못 이긴 척 짐 내려주고서 '퍼포먼스 임무 끝' 하였다.

1박 2일의 힘들었던 일정이었지만 재밌는 우리네 풍습이라 친구들이, 모두 새삼 재미있어하며 성의를 다해 주었다. 그러자 장차 장인어른 되실 분이 배포가 크시고 기분파시라 아주 기분이 좋아지셔서 우리 일행에게 전주에서 알아주는 큰 한 상을 차려서 우리 친구 수고에 보상해 주셨다. 뿐만 아니라 전주에서 광주 상무대까지—당시는 기차를 환승하면서 1박 2일로 다니는 먼 길인데도—택시를 제공해 주고 또 귀가 후 만찬 파티 비용도 보태 주었다. 지금도 즐겁게 생각나는 결혼 전 퍼포먼스로 수고 많았던 동기생들이 정말 고마웠다.

그 얼마 뒤 서울 문치과 형수님 덕분에, 문치과 옆 소공동 골목길에 있는 '외교회관'에서 결혼식을 올렸다. 막상 가친께서는 거동이 불편하여 오지 못하고 어머님과 형님 그리고 친척들이 올라와 참석하시고, 정말 고맙게도 평생 친구 이용우의 형님(서울의대 졸업 서울에서 개업 중)이 오고, 사관학교 교수 동기생 10여 명—친했던 박돈서 동기와 차호순 동기 포함—과 역시나 절친 박정기 동기 그리고 후배 민병돈 중위들이 와서 축하해 주었다. 이 기회에 모두께 거듭 감사드립니다.

신혼여행은 당시 일반 사람들이 흔히 선택하는 '온양 온천장'을 다녀왔는데, 때마침 꽃들이 만발한 화창한 봄날이라 정말 기분 좋았고, 이로 미루어 우리의 앞날에 축복이 가득하리라는 믿음으로 마음이 따뜻해졌다.

그런데 신혼여행에서 돌아오자마자 문자 그대로 신부는 시집으로 직행하지 않으면 안되었다. 앞으로 우리는 객지에서 살아갈 수밖에 없는 형편이니, 시집 형편과 가족 관계를 숙지하기 위해서는 몇 개월간의 시집살이가 필요하다는 집안 여론이 일리 있기에 신접살림을 잠시 뒤로 미루고, 신부 혼자 시집에 남아 독수공방하며 시집살이를 해야 했다. 그동안 내 본가는 누님의 노력으로 기와집에 수돗물과 우물이 집안에 있는, 전주 처갓집 환경과 비슷했으나, 그래도 시할머니와 시부모 그리고 세 명의 시동생들이 있었고, 어머니가 시장에서 포목장사를 하였기에 여러 가지로 어려운 환경에다가, 전주와 다른 전혀 생소한 지방과 풍습 등에 신부는 심신 양면으로 고생이 많았을 것이다.

한 3개월 뒤 시집에서 해방되어, 드디어 우리는 광주에 신혼살림을 꾸리게 되었다. 때마침 마음씨 좋으시고 폭넓은 교제를 가진 처고모부가 광주 한전지사에 근무하고 있어서, 그분의 마음속으로부터의 친절한 도움으로, 처음 전세로 입주한 동네가 광주 양림동의 대나무밭 아래 양옥집으로 아주 깨끗하고 단정한 단층집인데, 그 집 한 칸을 빌려 전세 살림을 시작하게 되었다.

살림 도구(광주 생활 3년간)는 사관학교 졸업 때 나누어 준 알루미늄 가방(현재 32인치 TV 크기에 깊이 40센티 정도) 한 개와 군용 더플백(Duffle Bag) 그리고 이부자리—신부가 정성드려 수놓아 만들어 가져온 이부자리에 내가 지금까지도 애용하는, 한때 월남까지 가져갔다 온 베개까지—와, 거기에 현지에서 구입한 다리 접이식 2인용 아크릴 밥상과, 결혼 때 준비한 은수저, 그리고 선물 받은 '토스터', 그리고 신문지를 발은 사과 상자 2개가 2층 옷장을 겸하였다.

그래도 우리 신혼살림은 이렇게 후방에서 온정(溫情) 가운데 좋게 시작은 하였으나 진작 신랑인 본인은 광주 시내에서 최소 3시간 거리—당시 교통 사정—에 위치한 '동복 유격교육대'에서 주로 생활하지 않으면 안되었다. 그리고 1기당 교육 주기가 4주였기 때문에 내가 집으로 가는 날은 한 달에 2~3일이어서 그때는 신혼신부가 전방 생활처럼 독수공방 생활을 여의치 않게 감당할 수밖에 없었으니 이 또한 미안한 마음 지금도 가득하다.

◇ 동복(올빼미) 유격교육대 창설, 교관 생활

◦ '동복 올빼미 유격교육대'를 창설, 교육 준비하다

전라도 광주의 육군보병학교에서는 나와 같은 '미 특수전 교육 과정'을 이수하고 바로 이어서 미국 보병 특공부대의 'Ranger 과정'까지도 이수하고 돌아와 보병학교 유격학부 교관으로 막 보임된 2기 선배 '장기오' 대위(곧 소령)가 나를 기다리고 있었다. 그래서 즉시 미군 '레인저 과정'과 미군 '비정규전 과정'을 혼합한 새로운 과정을 입안하고, 과정 즉 학교(Scool)를 설립하기 위해, '장기오 선배'(유격학부장)가 예정해 두었던 장소와 정립된 커리큐럼에 맞는 확장된 전체 교육장을 물색하기 위해 전남 전체를 두고 정찰을 실시하였다.

요건은, 영 내외 체력 단련장을 구비할 수 있고, 근처에 'Rope Climbing'이 가능한 큰 바위 산악훈련장, 급속도하훈련이 가능한 하천훈련장, 그리고 대외로, 광범위한 정찰 활동이 가능한 산야 활동장, 역사적으로는 북괴 무장 간첩 주 침투로 산 등을 고려하였다. 그리하여 정찰결과 학교(과정) 본부는 '화순군 동복면 독상리 동복'에서 동복천변에 위치하고, 근처 넓고 풍족한 저수지와 하천 그리고 산악훈련에 적절한 '제비바위', 그리고 무장 공비의 해상 침투지역 광양만에서 무등산에 이르는 접근로 일대, 공비들의 주 활동지역이었던 지리산(노고단 지대) 일대를 지정하였다.

그리하여 24인용 천막과 불도저 한 대를 끌고, 유격학부장 겸 유격교육대장인 장기오 대위와 우리 동기 교관 5명은 과감하게 상무대 보병학교를 출발하여 광주 시내를 지나고 화순 너릿재를 넘어 동복 강가에 도착하여, 그곳에 일단 자리 잡고 유격교육대본부를 설치함과 동시에 교과 과정을 기획하면서, 동시에 '장기오 부장(소령) 지도하에 교육 준비를 완료하였다.

◦ '유격교육'의 정의, 과정 내용, 올빼미 흉장, 교육 개시

동복유격교육대는 1962년 여름부터 야외 천막 생활장에서 교육을 시작하였는데, 당시는 지원 제도로서 장기 근무를 원하는 장교에게 의무적으로 부과되었다. 그래서 양질의 중위 대위급으로 1개기 50여 명으로 편성되고 4주간의 엄격한 훈련 과정이었음으로 낙오하는 장교도 흔히 발생하였다. 그래서 그때부터 군에서는 보병학교 '죽음의 올빼미 교육과정, 유격훈련'이라 크게 알려졌고, 지금도 '올빼미'라는 단어는 군필자들이 사랑하는 단어가 되었다.

올빼미라는 새는, 주로 야밤을 친구로 삼고, 날카롭게 야생(새 등 짐승 상대)해야 하며 동시에 그 울음소리로도 적을 공포로 몰아가는 새임으로, 우리 교육대 피교육생에 대한 교육훈련 목적과 일치하였다. 그래서 우리는 이 '올빼미'를 피교육생의 상징으로 정하고 이를 구호로 외침으로서, 피교육생으로 하여금 엄정한 훈련을 용기 있게 극복하게 함과 동시에 한국 특공 즉 유격대의 정신을 함양하려 하였다. 이후 미군에 Ranger 과정 있으면 한국군에는 '올빼미' 과정이 있다면서, 지금도 군대에서는 또는 군대 다녀온 사람들은 '올빼미' 말만 들어도 일단은 고개를 저을 만큼의 육군 상징이 되고 있었다.

그래서 일단 입소하면 그날 그 시간부터 '올빼미'라는 구호는 수료하는 그 시간까지 입에 달고 다니게 하였다. 다만 한 가지 단점은 구보를 할 때 박자 맞추기가 어려웠는데, 그저 고난도의 훈련 때마다 무조건 외치게 하다 보니 그 자체가 더 무게 있게 되었다.

◦ 한겨울 눈 오는 날의 정찰, 땀과 어름의 이중고

나는 본 과정의 주요 과목인 정찰 과정을 담임하였는데, 겨울에도 '올빼미'들과 정찰과정을 함께 가다 보면 여름보다 더 어려운 신체적 고난을 겪게 된다. 내 형편에 따라 걷고 쉬어가고 돌아가는 것이 아니고 피교육생들의 계획과 실력과 능력에 따라 함께 행동하다 보니 몸에 무리도 감수할 수밖에 없었다. 전라남도도 겨울에 영하 10도 내외 날씨는 흔히 경험하였는데, 어느 한겨울 한밤, 당시 시골(길)은 밤이 되면 칠흙같이 어두웠고, 다만 맑은 날 별빛에 산과 들을 분간할 수 있을 정도였는데, 춥고 눈이 제법 오는 밤에, 목표 고지를 향해 수직 방향으로 올라가다 보니 밭도 지나고 숲속도 지나고 또 제법 발목까지도 빠지는 눈 속으로도 지나면서 강행군이 계속되었다.

그러자 추위를 이기기 위해 두껍게 입었던 윗몸에서는 땀이 차고 머리와 목은 방한모에 두꺼운 목도리라 땀을 닦아야 형편인데도 장갑 벗고 닦기가 어렵고 귀찮아 그대로 갈 수밖에 없었다. 한편 신발은 두꺼운 모 양말을 신고 고지를 오르고 내리면서 안으로는 땀이, 그 더위로 눈에 계속 젔고 가죽에서는 땀이 밸 정도로, 즉 속과 밖이 얼고 더워 병 나기 아주 좋은 상태로 임무를 완수해 나가는 때도 여러 번 경험하였다. 여하간에 참으로 '실전과 같은 훈련'은 결코 쉬운 것이 아니고 인간 의지의 시험도 쉬운 것이 아니어서 오로지 '젊음의 힘' 그것으로 버티어 내었다.

◇ 공수(낙하산)교육 자청, 15기생되다

1963년 초, 교육대의 겨울 정비 기간을 이용하여 우리 동기 교관들(신우식, 장기하 그리고 나)은, 당시 고난도 교육훈련으로 평가되 오던 제1공수특전여단의 낙하산 위탁 교육을 자원하여 허락받고 2월에 제15기로 입소하였다. 우리 생각은, 이 어렵다는 교육조차 극복한 우리 교관이 교육훈련시키는 '동복유격교유대'의 '올빼미 교육훈련'은 한국군 최고 난이도 훈련이 되고, 그럼으로 그 과정을 마친자는 영광스럽고, 그들을 지도한 우리 또한 자랑스러울 것이라고 믿었다.

당시(지금도), 제1공수특전여단은 김포공항에 가까운 서울 김포 '오쇠리'에 위치하여 한국 최초 공수특전부대 위용을 자랑하고 있었으며 특히나 4주간에 걸친 공수교육은 악명을 날리고 있었다. 4주간의 훈련 중 1~2주는 주로 반복되는 공수부대 요원용 P.T(체력 단련)기간, 제3주는 낙하기술지상훈련, 그리고 드디어 4주째는 수송기에 탑승하여 한강 상공에서 낙하하는데 주간 4회 야간 1회 계 5회를 마스터하면 낙하산 휘장과 함께 자격증이 부여되고 과정을 모두 수려하게 된다.

우리 일행은 교육대에 입소하여 일과시간에는 철저히(50분 훈련, 10분 휴식) 훈련하고 일과 후는 자유시간을 갖는데, 피곤하여 외출할 엄두를 내지 못했다. 첫 주는 주로 지상 PT체조와 함께 1단계 3킬로미터 급속구보훈련, 2주째는 모의 낙하장에서 지상 낙하 동작과 함께 2단계 6킬로미터 강속도 구보훈련, 3주째는 10미터 상공의 '막타워'에서 공중낙하훈련과 낙하중 낙하산 조종훈련 그리고 낙하후 현장이탈훈련을 겸한 3단계 12킬로미터 장거리 구보훈련 등이였다.

각오하였던 훈련이라 곤란을 느낀 경우는 없었으나 단, 장거리 김포가도 구보에서 나는 예의 그 지병(좌심방판막증)으로 어려움을 겪었다. 부대에서 출발하여 일단 김포가도로 나와, 김포비행장으로 그런대로 경사진 도로를 뛰어가는데 역시나 가슴이 답답해져서 도리없이 열외하여 내 심장 뛰는 대로 뒤따라 뛰었다. 대열은 김포비행장 북동쪽 모서리에서 반전하여, 울타리를 오른쪽으로 끼고 부평 방향으로 가다가 '오쇠리' 부대 앞길로 들어서는데 여기에는 '그식이 여인네' 들이 우르르 나와 휘파람과 기성 그리고 진짜 응원과 격려의 박수를 받게 되는데, 이상하게도 마지막 힘이 나기도 하였다. 나는 대열로부터 100미터 이상 낙오하지 않았다 하여 12킬로미터 마지막 체력시험에 통과되었다.

평일 일과 후 장교 피교육생은 자유시간이었으나 피곤하여 전혀 외출 생각도 나지 않았거니와 가족 또한 모두 광주에 있기에 필요도 없었다. 그런데 김포 지역—당시는 개활지 벌판—의 2월 날씨는 고약하여 낮에 땀 흘리기를 반복하며 야외에 있어서인지 거의 모두가 감기에 걸린 상태면서도 그저 '젊음의 힘'으로 이겨나갔다. 그런데 유일한 휴식과 위로는 주말에 김포 시내에 있는 목욕탕이었다. 우리는 매 주말 함께 나가, 과하게도 목욕탕 속에 들어가 30분 동안 몸을 녹이는 그 행복감, 탕에서 나와서는 바닥에 누워 2시간 이상 잠자고 났을 때 그 가볍고 상쾌해진 몸과 마음의 기분, 참으로 경험하기 드문 단련이요 행복이었다.

그 지루하고도 지겹던 체력 단련과 낙하 기술 과정을 통과하여, 드디어 기다리고 기다리던 4주째 실지 실제 낙하 실습 과정이 되었다. 처음 1회는 단독 군장으로 낙하하는데, 김포비행장에서 C-40 한국 공군 수송기에 탑승하여 서에서 동으로 한강 인도교(제1한강대교)로 향발하는데, 비행기 가운데 문을 열어 놓은 채 시퍼런 한강 물 위를 그대로 비행하여 오다가—이륙과 동시에 그리고 한강 물을 내려다보면서 뛰어 내릴 때까지 '피가 마르는 긴장감'을 회를 거듭해도 '그때마다' 맛본다—한강대교 근접하면서 'Jump Master'의 명에 따라 일어서고, 고리 걸고, 앞사람에 바짝 붙어서서 상호간 군장 검사 끝나면, 앞사람부터 차례로 그 억센 바람부는 공중에서 열린 문턱에 선다. 점프마스터의 "뛰어!" 명에 따라 속으로는 '나는 죽었다'하며 뛰어내리면서 "일만!, 이만!, 삼만! 사만!" 무의식중에 외친다. 그러면 신통(?)하게도 "이만!" 정도에서 몸이 공중으로 솟구치는 기분을 느끼면서 '살았다'는 외마디가 절로 나오면서, 머리 위로 활짝 펴진 낙하산을 확인하게 되고, 그때부터 불과 60초 내외에, 그 살아서 공중에 떠 있는 최고의 '다행한 기분'에 스릴을 느끼며 땅에 근접한다. 그러면서 죽어라 하고 남산 방향으로 낙하산을 조종하여 그 시퍼런 한강 물을 피한다. 쉴 틈 없이 허리띠에 메어둔 소총을 분리해서 끈 달린 채 내려트리고, 이어 땅이 내게로 솟구쳐 오르면 배우고 익힌 대로 땅에 발이 닿는 순간 옆으로 딩구르는 낙법을 실시하여 몸을 일으킴과 동시에 땅에 막 닿고 있는 낙하산 방향으로 신속히 뛰어가 그 뒷면에서 낙하산 바람을 죽이고, 이를 재빨리 회수한 뒤 둘러메고, 전술 상황으로 재빨리 뛰어서 현장으로부터 신속하게 이탈해 갔다.

그런데 당시 한강 백사장 지금의 제1한강대교와 반포대교 사이—경의선 기차선로 이남지대 백사장, 지금의 한강공원과 유명 아파트단지들 터—가 주 낙하장으로 사용되었는데, 드물었지만 때로는 한강대교에 낙산이 걸리는 피교육생도 있었고, 어떤 사람은 지상에 닿으면서 약간의 시간 지체로 그대로 바람에 끌려가 기차가 오고 있는 경의선 '서빙고역'까지 가다가 멈춘 적도 있었다. 또는 경우에 따라 백사장 모래를 퍼내고 웅덩이가 생긴 곳에 떨어지기도 하는데 모두 미리 경계병들이 대기하고 있다가 도와준다. 그래서 교육 기간에 피교육생 낙하사고는 거의 없다고 하였다.

그렇게 해서 4번의 주간 낙하훈련 시험을 실시하는데 2번은 단독 군장, 2회는 완전 군장 낙하시험인데 요령은 단독 군장 때와 같다. 이렇게 모두 무사히 마치면, 이어서 마지막으로 1회의 야간 낙하 시험이 실시된다. 더구나 당시 한강 위 야간비행은 비행기 문 열어놓고 세찬 바람 직접 맞으며 위로는 별 아래는 시커먼 한강 물줄기, 그 현장에서 생명을 줄 고리에 걸고 하늘을 향해 무조건 뛰어내리는 것이다.

물론 비행기에 오를 때까지는 절차 지키느라 잠깐 잊었다가 막상 비행기가 공중에 올라 컴컴한(당시 서울은 야간통금까지 있었으니까) 한강 상공에 이르기까지 '피마르는 긴장'감 속에서, 단체 행동이기에 반 무의식으로 앞사람 따라 뛰어내리고, 그리고는 '아 살았다, 내 세상이야' 하다가 금방, 한강 물 반대 방향으로 낙하산을 조종하고, 모래밭이 솟구쳐 오르면서 발에 닿으면 '낙지법'에 따라 딩굴어서 일어나고, 이 모두 60초 동안의 일. 그런데 이번에는 일어서보니 바로 웅덩이 곁이 아닌가.

곧 미끌어져 웅더이로 내려갈 지경에 온 힘을 다해 뛰어서 낙하산을 접고 막 집결지를 향해 뛰려는데, 미군 특전병— 한국 특전부대에 1개 팀이 파견되어 있었다—한 명이 뛰어와 잠깐 나를 멈추어 세우고, 내게 '죠니워커' 뚜껑을 열고 거기에 한 모금의 술을 따라 건네주며 말했다. "Well Done, Well Done! Congratulation!"이라고. 그는 오늘의 무사 착지와 성공적인 교육 종료 및 '낙하산 요원'자격 획득을 축하해 주었다.

아 이번에도 죽었다 살아온 듯한, 더구나 야간 첫 점프에서 성공하였다고 희열을 느끼는 그 순간에, 이 한 모금의 술이, 그 한마디의 축하가 그 어찌 고맙지 아니하였으랴, 지금도 물론 잊지 않고 그 미군 특전요원을 고마워하고 있다. 살다 보면 미군과 미국은 이런 고마운 때가 많았다.

그렇게 해서 우리는 자부심과 긍지를 가슴 가득 안고 우리의 올빼미 본고장에 돌아와서는, 어디 해병대교육이 센가, 우리 올빼미 교육훈련이 센가 다투어보기로 마음먹기도 하였다. 이후 실제로 해병교육대 요원이 한두어 번 입교하여 훈련받고는 나름대로 인정하고 가기도 하였다.

◇ 참모총장 참관 시범으로 올빼미 교육 과정이 장교 임관 필수 과정되다

1963년 봄, 아마도 이세호 교장의 초청으로 김종오 육군참모총장과 당시 미군사고문단장(소장)이 내교하여 '동복유격교육대' 현장에서 우리 올빼미 교육 과정을 설명 듣고 거대한 '제비바위' 앞 'Repell' 교육 현장에서 시범을 참관하였다. 물론 다 시범할 수는 없었지만, 첫 번째는, 환경이 뛰어난 하천 도하 현장에서 도르래를 이용한 하천 도하훈련을, 장기하 동기가 '육사 체육부장' 솜씨를 다하여 능숙하게 시범하여 박수와 칭찬을 받았으며, 둘째 시범으로는, '제비바위'—1단계 약 50미터 이상 직하—교육 현장에서, 장기오 교육대장과 신우식 동기가 아주 능숙하고도 자신만만하게 그 위험하면서도 거대하고 우람하게 생긴 거대 바위에서 로프를 이용해 오르내리면서 1. '로프 클라이밍', 2. '로프 레펠링', 3. '레스큐 레펠링'(Rescue Repelling)—'들 것'을 이용한 부상자 구조 하강—을 성공적으로 시범하였다. 시범 도중에 마치 쇼를 볼 때처럼 수시로 휘파람 불고(미 고문관), 큰 박수를 연거푸 쳐주고 고성으로 위로해 주는 등 시범 보이는 우리를 정말로 격찬해 주었다.

아 그런데, 격찬을 받은 것까지는 기쁘고 보람 있는 일이나, 문제는 그다음이었다. 육군참모총장의 특명으로, "당장 지금부터 모든 육군 전투병과 장교후보생은 의무적으로 4주간의 '올빼미교육훈련'을 이수하고 임관하라"는 것이었다. 일반인이 들으면 바람직한 조치라 할 수 있으나, 한국군 최강 교육훈련을 자랑하려는 우리 교관들에게는 고민이 생기고 말았다.

그렇게 되어 우선 간부후보생 제180기부터 마지막 4주 동복유격교육을 받게 되었는데, 결과 기준에 따라 미달자를 몇 명 지적했더니, 학교장 말씀이, "야, 1년여 후보생 교육 다 잘 마치고 마지막 4주 교육 과정에서 힘 좀 모자라 낙제하면 억울하지 않겠느냐, 그러니 좀 봐 주자"고 하였다. 참으로 인지상정이라 그럴 수밖에 없었다. 그렇게 되어 올빼미교육훈련은 애당초 우리 혈기왕성했던 동기 교관들의 뜻을 조금은 접고 교육의 질은 유지하려고 노력하였다.

◦ 각개전투, 침투훈련 우수교관

그렇게 해서 한국군 '보병학교 유격교육대'의 시스템과 교육 과정을 안정궤도에 올려놓은 뒤, 축차적으로 육사 후배— 미국 레인저 과정이나 특수전 과정 이수자—들에게 교관 업무를 인계하고, 우리 동기 교관들은 본교에 복귀하여 전술학 교관이 되었다. 그런데 이제는 늦깎기 교관이 되어 다른 이들이 기피하는 각개전투훈련과 침투훈련과목 등을 맡았다.

나는, 옛날 생도 때 멋진 교관들의 멋진 교수법과 언행을 상기하며, 더구나 지금 어려운 고비를 넘기고 있는 후보생들을 위로하면서도 요점(요령) 위주로 각개전투훈련을 실시했고. 침투 훈련장에는 휴식시간을 엄정히 지켜주면서 스피커를 틀어 휴식 시간에 노래로 조금이나마 심신을 위로해 주며 훈련 시켰다. 보병학교 간부후보생 183기부터 187기까지 담당하였다. 그래서 우수교관으로 지명되기도 하였다.

◇ 첫아들 '정언'이 소식, 훈련 중 산속에서 듣다

그날도 '화순군 남면'지역 산속에서 '올빼미'들의 정찰 과정을 따라 함께 헤매고 있는데, 화순경찰서 순경 한 사람이 찾아 올라와 "유격대에서 연락이 왔는데, '문 중위는 득남했으니 빨리 집으로 가보라'는 내용"이라 하였다. 경찰서에서 한 참 먼 산속인데 그리고 이동 중인데도 이렇게 기어이 찾아서 알려 주니 정말 고마웠다. 옛날엔 이런 인심도 있었다. 그래서, '여하간에 어서 가 보아야지'하는 마음으로, 그 길로 바로 하산하여 지나가는 화물차와 버스 등등을 환승하며 집을 향해 뛰다시피 서둘렀으나 저녁때가 되어서야 도착하였다.

'서석동' 조선대학 철로길 밑 '사글세' 집에 들어서니 기다리고 있던 주인 할머니(중앙초등학교 선생님의 어머니)가 얼른 반가워하며 자초지종을 얘기해 주었는데 곁으로 들으면서 얼른 방문을 열었다. 아, 거기에 건강한 애기와 기진맥진이면서도 그래도 아주 반가워하는 아기엄마인 내 아내가 함께 있었다. 정말로 일생에 더 이상 사람답고 정겨운 장면이 또 있으랴. 한편 정말 혼자서 이렇게 미비한 환경에서 그 얼마나 고통스러웠고 외로웠을까 하는 마음으로 미안하고, 그리고 안쓰럽고 고맙기 이를 데 없는 마음으로 아내에게 "욕 봤다"고 맘속을 다하여 말하며 위로하고, 내 자식을 보며 실로 감개무량하였다.

◇ 광주에서 신혼생활 이모저모와 잘 만난 인연 등

◦ 전세에서 철롯길 밑 사글셋방으로

광주에서 신접살림— 정말 미안하게도 3~4일 집에 와서 겨우 남편 노릇 하다가는, 한 달 이상 독수공방시키기를 거듭한 신혼생활—을 차린 지 1년이 훨씬 지나서야 동복유격대 격리지대 생활에서 해방되어 상무대 보병학교 전술학부교관으로 복귀하였다. 그동안, 그런대로 아담하고 편안했던 양림동 첫 살림집은 남에게 팔려서, 부득이 서석동 조선대학 앞 철로길 밑 중앙초등학교 선생님 집 안쪽 동남 향방 딴채 사글셋방—전세 1년 지나니 전세값이 올라 가진 돈으로는 부득이 사글셋방 신세—으로 나와서 '첫아들 정언이'를 낳게 된 것이다.

그런데, 그 방은 진짜 소문대로, 기차가 수시로 지나다니며 조선대학 들어가는 건널목 경보를 핑계로 철길 밑 살림집들 아주머니들을 향해 기적 울리며 농담하며 지나가기를 그냥 보통 일로 알고 있는 그런 방이었고, 여름에는 폭풍우가 바로 창호지 문을 강타하고 방안으로 들어와 방을 다 적시기 때문에 아이는 아예 그네 매달아 잠재웠다. 그제서야 주인은 방문밖에 비바람막이 챙을 달아주었으나 폭풍우에 견디지 못했다.

그 집에서는 더 이상 애기를 키울 수 있는 환경이 못되기에 아쉬웠지만 부득이 서석동 그 근처 집 사글셋방을 찾아 다시 이사하였다. 가재도구는 여전히 육사 졸업 당시 지급품인 휴대용 알미늄 가방 하나와 발 폈다 접는 2인용 호마이카(?) 식탁 하나, 신문종이를 바른 사과상자 2개, 이불과 요 그리고 그 외 2인용 부엌살림이 전부였다.

그래도 지금 생각하면 신혼살림은 행복하였다. 서석동 같은 동네에 절친 박정기네(도미 미사일 과정 유학)와 김진규네(마찬가지), 그리고 이제 막 고등고시 합격하여 전남도청에 발령받아 내려온 손아래 동서 송(언종) 서방네—후에 통정부장관 됨—와 함께 문자 그대로 그 시대 외지 출신 신혼부부들의 애환을 함께하며, 매일 상부상조하며 즐겁게 3년여 광주 생활을, 지나고 보니, 참 좋은 추억이 많이 남은 것 같다.

◦ 어려웠던 경제 살림살이

당시 얘기로 빠질 수 없는 것은 경제생활이다. 모두들 자립 독립하는 초급 장교 생활이라 당장 가진 것은 무일푼 마찬가지나 그래도 배경은 그런대로 좋아서—박동기는 대구역장 아들이고, 김동기는 삼촌 등이 상류 사회 분들이고, 우리는 물론 독립심으로 일관하지만 배경은 전주 과수원하는 처가가 있었다—아주 조금씩은 본가 도움을 받아, 사글세 내고 삼시 세끼 굶지 않고 지내면서 수시로 모여 함께 먹고 얘기하며 희망과 포부를 가지고 지냈다.

그런데 당시는 5·16 직후 국가 재정 사정이 여의치 않아 장교들의 월급 대부분을 '알랑미'—미국 원조 물자, 원래는 '월남 쌀'이나 그때는 아마도 미국 캘리포니아 산?—현물로, 그리고 약간을 현금으로 지급해 주었다. 그런데 그 사정을 듣고 전주 처가에서 한때 직접 농사지은 맛쌀을 보내주어서 그걸로 밥하고 '알랑미'는 기타 반찬감으로 바꾸어 먹기도 하였다.

◇ 절친 박정기 동기생의 추천, '하나회' 가입

하루는 절친 '박정기 동기'(포병학교 교관)가 찾아와 평소와 좀 달리 은밀히 신중하게 말했다. "하나회가 있는데…, 우리 육사 출신으로 뜻맞는 동지끼리 힘을 합쳐서 군대 발전을 기하고, 상부상조하며, 선배는 후배를 이끌어주고 후배는 선배를 뒷받침하며 군대 생활을 동고동락하는 하나의 잘 뭉쳐진, 동기생 중에서는 선발된 인재들로 구성되는 친목 그룹이다. 위로는 1기생 중 전두환 선배가 대표 지도자이고, 지금은 우선 4기까지 조직 중이고, 각 기별 한 10명 정도로 예상하고, 우선 4기생 우리가 먼저 구성 중이다. 동기생으로는 자기와 아무개, 아 무개기 이미 가입했고, 이번에 여기 상무대에 있는 나와 아무개를 추천하고자 하는데, 우리 함께 하자"는 것이었다.

그러면서 5기 '민병돈 후배'가 "문 선배도 함께 하겠다면 자기도 가입하겠다"고 했단다. 정말 그 얘길 듣고 민 후배에 대하여 더 깊은 의리를 느꼈다. 그런데 물론이다, 박정기 말이라면 무엇이던 좋다는 생각에다 물론 동기생 몇 사람은 마음에 들지 않았으나 그런대로 괜찮은 동기, 선후배들 모임이니 주저할 것은 없었다. 그리하여 군대 생활 일생에 영향을 주고받은 '하나회'에 가입하였다.

그러나 이후 끝까지 특별한 단체 활동은 없었고 다만, 주로 전두환 리더가 구해준 용돈으로 주기적으로 동기회별로 회식하면서, 다음엔 각자 집으로 돌아가며 전두환 선배 대표를 모시고 동기회 모임을 하며 우의와 동지애를 다졌다. 그 이후 '12·12사태'가 날 때까지—이 사태 자체도 '하나회' 조직과는 직접적인 관계가 아니었다.—전혀 정치 활동은 없었고, 다만 친목과 진급과 보직에 상호 도움을 주고 받았다. 그러나 결코 진급이나 보직의 독식이나 배타는 물론 없었다. 그동안 우리 내외는 전과 같이 박정기 동기생 내외하고는 친애하였으며, 평생 우의가 유지되었다.

3. ROTC 제2기생 교육 중대장, 육군병원 신세, 연세107학훈단교관

◇ 학군단 제2기생 초군반(OBC) 교육 중대장

◦ 대학 문화 속의 ROTC 초군반 장교

1963년 봄에 보병 ROTC 과정 제2기생의 초등군사반교육훈련을 위해서 중대장 직책으로 우리 동기생들이 다수 선발되었다. 여기에는, 이 또한 군대 생활 동안 인연이 되는 '이종구' 대위도 나와 같은 중대장이 되었다. 나는 13중대 중대장으로 내무반은 바로 상무대 간이비행장 곁에 있었다. 구대장(소대장 격)으로는 후배 8기생들 4명이고 부중대장(행정담당)으로 일반장교 중위 1명이 있었다.

이 과정은 주로 중, 소대급 전술과 참모, 지휘기법을 수련하는 코스였다. 그런데 ROTC의 OBC 과정은 2가지 의미(목적)가 부여되어 있었다. 그 하나는 원래의 '장교초등군사반' 교육이고 다른 하나는, 특히 그 당시는 아직 '학생중앙군사학교'가 설치 되어 있지 않았음으로 내무 생활 경험 부족과 4년간 교육 과정의 종합 즉 장교 기본교육을 보충하려는 의미도 가지고 있었다. 그래서 비록 장교로 임관은 되었지만 새삼 중대 편성을 하고 당분간은 내무 생활을 하면서 간부 후보생 출신이나 장교 기본을 갖추도록 '마감교육'을 실시하는 과정을 두었던 것이고, 그래서 중대장과 구대장은 주로 육사 출신으로 구성되었던 것이다.

우리 중대는 때마침 간이비행장 바로 옆이라 언제든지 넓은 공간을 사용해서 무슨 과목(얼차려도 포함)이던 가능했음으로 특히 우리 중대 출신들은 좀 호되게 과정을 보냈다고 그들은 추억할 것이다. 내게는 그들에 대한 이런 추억이 있다. 훈련 과정의 마지막 과정은 '송정리' 기차역까지 왕복 12킬로미터 구보였는데 내가 직접 지휘하여— 생도 3학년 때 6기생 여름 기초군사훈련 구보 중 순직 사실을 생각하며— 속도 조절하며 군가도 박수도 쳐가며 뛰었는데, 한 명 낙오 없이 성공적으로 의기양양하게 훈련 전 과정의 대미를 장식하였다.

그런데 그날 밤 회식을 희망해서 허락했더니,—4주간 외출 외박 없고 회식도 없는 강행군 과정이었기에—비록 한정된 양의 음주 가무였지만 막판에 전원이 일어서서 줄지어 노래하며 짱가리(식기류) 치며 이 내무반 저 내무반 들락날락하며 문자 그대로 한판 굿을 벌였다. 육사 문화에 그런 일이 있을 리 없었고, 내가 살아온 생애에서도 그런 음주 문화는 처음이었다. 과연 한국 대학생들의 음주 문화는 자칫 사람을 잡을 수도 있을 만큼 대단히 요란한 것이었다.

그런가 하면 이제 수료식을 2일 앞두고 부대 정비 시간이 되었는데, 외출 외박을 신청하기에, 절대 '미귀 없기로 약속'하고 허락하였다. 아 그런데 수료식 시간이 다가오는데 한 사람씩 한 사람씩 도착해 식장으로 급히 입장시켰는데 끝내 식장에 들어가지 못하고 밖에서 수려한 장교도 한둘 있었던 걸로 생각난다. 서울과 광주 그리고 송정리 기차역 간의 교통이 당시는 의외로 특히 초행인들에게는 그렇게 어려웠기도 했지만, 근본적으로 지나치게 자유 분방한 한국 대학 사회 문화는 하루 이틀의 군사교육으로 변화될 수 없었다.

◇ '큰 시련의 고비'를 넘고 넘다

∘ 시련의 한고비, 불효

그러니까 1964년 5월 하순, 아들 정언이 첫돌을 기해서 누님이 어머님을 모시고 광주 우리 셋방으로 오셨다. 이는 어머님의 두 번째 광주 방문으로 처음에는 양림동 양옥집이었으나 이번은 사글셋방 집이었고, 더구나 정언이 돌날에 맞추어 오신 것이다. 그런데 편히 지내시기는 고사하고, 돌잔치—정언이에게 첫돌 기념으로 행운의 열쇠가 달린 금목걸이를 주시고 축하해 주시고는 줄곧 이웃에 사는 육사 선후배 한 다섯 그룹 차례차례로 상 차리시고 치워주시면서—감당해 주시느라고, 거기에 비좁은 방에 편히 눕지도 못하신 가운데 수고만 하시다 가시게 되었다.

누님이 사전에 귀가하실 때는 비행기 편을 얘기해 주셨으나 그때만 해도 내겐 엄두가 나지 않은 일이라 그저 평상대로 기차 편으로 보내드렸다. 그러나 그것이 불효였다. 당시 교통은 참 불편해서, 간선이라 하더라도 하루 몇 편 없었고 언제나 만원이었고, 심지어 야간 완행열차는 짐을 얹는 칸에까지 사람이 올라가는 것이 보통 일인데, 더구나 호남선은 더했다. 광주에서 송정리를 거쳐 대전에 가서 경부선 열차로 환승하여 부산까지 12시간도 — 운이 좋아야 앉을 수 있었고—더 걸리는 기차여행이었다.

집에 도착하셔서 그동안 고단하셨던 심신을 푸시기 위해 방을 평소보다 좀 더 따뜻하게 하고 두 분이 함께 주무시다가 그만 가스 중독 사고로 함께 저세상으로 가셨다. 생각할수록 불효했던 일, 지금은 오로지 하늘나라에서 하나님의 보살핌으로 평강하실 것으로 믿으며, 내 인생에 그런 불효가 있었음을 여기에 말해 남기고자 한다.

◦ 시련의 또 한고비

중대는 규정된 정비 기간을 지나고 새롭게 특별간부후보생(법무관, 경리관 군목 군종 등) 교육 과정을 위해 준비를 끝내고 절차에 따라 이들 후보생들을 인수하기 위해 '논산훈련소'로 가게 되었다. 가는 도중에 전주를 들리게 됨으로 가족들도 만날 겸—그때는 가족이 전주 처가로 가 있었다.—유명하게 큼직한 무등산 수박도 2개 준비했다. 다음 날 아침 일찍이 하숙집 우물가에서 세수를 하려고 한 손에 칫솔을 들고 두 쪽짜리 우물 뚜껑을 여는데 부주의로 그만 한쪽이 우물 속으로 떨어져 버렸다. 이런 경우 일반적으로는 '아차 오늘'해야 하건만 바쁜 것만 생각하고 그냥 무심결에 지나치고 말았다.

학교에서 제공된 '지프'(Jeep)로 출발하였다. 그런데, 우리 차가 정읍 가까이에 이르러 S형으로 굽으며 오르막길이 되는 곳에서 갑자기 그 S자형의 중앙 위쯤에서 광주를 방향으로 질주해 오는 버스를 피하려다가 비포장 자갈길에 미끄러져 바로 1미터쯤 아래 논으로 차와 함께 굴러떨어져, 나는 중상을 입었다.

아, 그 순간 하늘이 샛노래지고 나는 반의식을 잃으면서 내 가족, 내 사랑하는 아내와 정언이가 전면에 나타났다. 내 평생 전무후무한 환상이었다. 그 후 1시간여 지난 뒤 마침 지나가던 군인—광주 상무대로 가던 장교들—들에 의해 수습되어 보병학교 77 야전병원에 응급 후송되었다. 그때 정말 하나님과 그들의 천운으로 운전병과 수행 부중대장 두 사람이 별 이상 없이 복귀할 수 있게 되었던 것을 나는 지금도 하나님께 감사드린다. 동시에 때마침 그 시간에 사고 현장을 지나다가 발견 후 수습해준 그들 헌병요원에게 감사드린다.

그리하여 광주 전투병과사령부소속 육군 제77병원에 이송되어 응급치료를 받게 되었으나 중상이라 대몰핀을 맞아가며 사경을 헤매었다. 전주에서 놀란 아내가 장인어른과 함께 뛰어왔는데, 나는 아내에게 정말 미안해하지 않을 수 없었다. 이제 막 인생 일막으로 가정 가족생활 시작하는가 했더니 어처구니없이 중환자로 침대에 누워 있는 모습을 보여주다니. 아내는 열악한 입원실에서 죽어가는 듯한— 제3자 평가—나를 한시도 곁을 떠나지 않고 지성껏 돌보았다. 당시 광주육군야전병원에서는 더 이상 감당하기 어려워 서울(수도육군병원)로 후송하게 되었다.

◦ 하늘의 도움으로 중환자실에서 걸어 나오다

그리하여 일단은 치명적 고통을 면하고 안정적 중환자 생활을 시작하게 되었으나 중상당한 지 10여 일이 지난 이제야 엉덩이 우측 엉덩뼈가 단순 골절된 것을 발견하였는데, 이미 치료 골든 타임을 놓치고 약 6주 이상 지난 뒤 결과는 왼편 요골이 응축되어 발이 2.5센티미터 짧아지게 되었다.

그런 가운데도 내게 대한 최대 관심은 언제쯤 '찢어진 5미리미터 굵기의 요관'—쉽게 말해 굵은 성냥개비 만 한 파이프—이 자연 원복될 것인가, 그러지 못하면 한쪽 신장의 제거

수술을 할 수밖에 없고, 그렇게 되면 군대 장교 생활은 마감해야 한다는 예측이었다. 그 시점에서 나는 또 한 번 운명의 갈림길에 놓이게 되었다. 즉 치료보다 운수가 절대 가치를 갖게 된—당시 의료 환경—또 한 번의 터닝 포인트를 맞이했던 것이다.

입원 후 약 한 달이 지나도 '시험용 잉크'가 여전히 요관에서 새어 나오자 의사들이 점차 수술할 날을 잡기 시작하였고, 드디어 그 어느 날 수술날을 결정하고 내게 통보한 뒤 준비를 서둘렀다. 그런데 바로 그 수술 예정일 전날 밤에 마지막으로 점검하러 왔던 의사가 무릎을 치며 진지하고도 반가운 표정으로 혼자 탄성을 질렀다. "드디어 붙었다"는 것이었다. 그러자 또 다른 의사가 와서 확인하고 "기적이다, 당신은 이제 수술 안 해도 되고 군대 생활 계속할 수 있다"고 말해 주었다.

내 운명은 이렇게 해서 또 한고비를 넘기게 되었다. 기적이란 무엇이고 운명이란 무엇일까, 무엇보다 먼저 하나님의 뜻일 것이고, 그리고 돌아가신 내 부모님의 보호와 사랑하는 내 가족의 지성(사랑)에서 유래되는 것이라 지금도 믿고 싶다.

◇ 연세대학교 제107학군단(ROTC) 교관

◦ ROTC의 존재 의의, 군사 교육훈련과 학생시위 간접 억지 역할도

내가 입원해 있는 동안 내 뒷바라지를 위해서 아내는 정언이를 데리고 서울로 올라왔다. 때마침 처남들—모두가 수재를 넘는 인재들로, 첫째 박은오 학생은 전주에서 월반하여 서울 경기중학에 들어왔고, 둘째 박도현과 셋째 박진섭 학생들도 전주에서 경복중학으로 유학와 있었다. 그래서 이들을 돌볼 사람, 쉽게 말해 하숙집이 필요하였기에 겸사겸사 동교동에 집을 하나 전세하여 우리 가족과 함께 있기로 하였다. 말하자면 아내는 하숙집 주인과 스폰서를 겸하긴 하였으나, 그리고 도움이도 두긴 하였으나, 참으로 고생스런 가정 주부 생활의 연속이었다. 특히 내가 입원해 있었을 때 가정 형편을 생각하면 내가 더욱 미안할 수밖에 없었다.

일생 초기 시련을 극복하고, 나는 연세대학 학군단(제107 ROTC)에 교관으로 전입하였다. 연세대학 학군단은 단장 대령과 교관으로 대위급 3명 그리고 2명의 행정병으로 구성되었다. 연세대학교 학군단 위치는 '언더우드 동상 서편에 있는 '신학대학' 건물 1층(행정실, 강의실 등)과 지하(장비 격납고용)실을 이용하였다. 인원 구성과 시설 그리고 대학과의 관계 등은 별다른 문제 없었다. 다만 몇 가지 에피소드를 겸하여 회상해 본다.

그 하나는, 당시 학생과 학군단과 학교 당국과 시국과의 관계가 얽혀 돌아가던 때 얘기다. 내가 전입하기 1년 전에 소위 '6·3사태'가 학원을 휩쓸고 간 뒤였다. 즉, 63년에 '한일관계 정상화' 반대 학생시위 사태로 교내 진입했던 군인들을 학생들이 포위하여 한 병사의 총을 학생들이 탈취했다가 나중에 반환했던 사건이 있었다. 따라서 뭔가 침침한 학생 분위기가 감지되었으나 나는 그와 무관하게, 강의 시작과 동시에 원칙을 강조하고 방공을 강조하고 국가 안보 질서를 강조하였다.

연세대학생 중 특히 공산주의에 물들여진 이들은 듣기 어색했을 것이리라. 그러나 육사에서 익힌 파사현정관에 입각하여 그리고 국가안보와 반공 정의관에 입각하여 나는 거침없었다. 그러자 하루는 좀 친해진 학생이 걱정해 주는 마음으로 찾아와 말해주기를, "현재 특히 상과대학생에 공산주의자들이 더러 있다. 그들이 웅성거리기도 한다. 그러니 교실에서 '반공'에 대해 조금 조심하시는 것이 좋을 것 같다"고 귀띔해 주었다. 그러나 나는 교실에서 그 말조차 공개하면서 공개적으로 반공을 설득하였다. 그렇다고 해서 결코 그들 중 누구를, 물론 알지도 못하였기에, 지목해서 언급하지는 않았다.

당시 서울대학교를 비롯해서 유명 대학의 총학생 회장과 각 단과대학 학생 회장들이 대거 ROTC 과정을 밟고 있었다. 그래서 당시는 이 ROTC 교육 과정과 훈련단의 존재에 대해 정부는 물론 각 학교 당국에서도 상당한 비중으로 긍정적으로 생각하고 있었다. 그 이유 중의 하나는 바로 반정부 시위의 주동자들을 ROTC 교육 과정과 훈련단 요원 그리고 그 시스템이 상당히 억제해 주고 있기 때문이었다. 예를 들어 인정사정없는 군대식 출석 강조와 국가안보 강의와 그에 대한 강조 등으로, 특히나 학생 회장들은 일단 학훈단의 피교육자 신분의 약점을 가지고 있었기 때문이었다.

◦ 학생 시위와 단식투쟁의 뒷모습

연세대학 정문에서 '언더우드 동상'까지는 그런대로 깊숙하였다. 중앙로 서편으로는 야구장 축구장 그리고 잔디광장이 길게 펼쳐져 있어서 실외 군사교육장 즉 연병장으로 불편함이 없었다. 처음엔 그 친구들, 연병장훈련이 생전 처음이라 낯설어했고 특히 여학생—당시 막 부산에서 여학생반(가정과)이 올라와 연세대 여학생회가 자리 잡아가고 있었다.—들이 훈련하며 기합(특성훈련, 얼차려 훈련)받는 모습을 보고 뭐라 할까 봐, 처음엔 약간 계면쩍어 하였으나 금방 재밌는 얘깃거리로 되면서 개의치 않게 잘도 숙달되었다. 특히 내가 연병장(운동장)에서 교육하는 기본제식교련과 36방향행진 그리고 총검술들은 더욱 재미있어 했고 나중엔 여학생 총회에서도 찾아와 인터뷰도 하는 등 관심을 보이기도 하였다.

6·3사태—64년 6월 3일에 '한일회담반대운동' 진압 위해 계엄령 선포—를 계기로 정부는 소요 대학교에 군을 투입하는 등 군경 등 공권력을 동원하여 대학생들의 농성, 가두 시위 등을 적극적으로 진압하였다. 그러나 학생들은 계속 저항하였고 당국은 진압과 회유를 거듭하였다. 그 과정에서 연세대학생들은 시위가 어려우면 주력들을 대표하는 몇 학생들은 '언더우드 동상' 주변에서 소위 공개 단식투쟁이라는 행사를 하였다.

내가 근무하던 학군단은 언더우드 동상이 직선거리 약 100미터도 안되는 거리에서 잘 보이는 바로 옆 언덕 위 신학대학 건물에 있었음으로, 근무 시간은 물론 과외 당직 시간에도 그들 학생들의 동정을 잘 볼 수 있었다. 한때 도하 각 신문에 크게 발표되고 있었던 '연세대학생 단식투쟁'의 쇼 현장을 목격도 하였다.

아마도 대표자 10여 명씩 교대로 언더우드 동상을 둘러싸고 낮에는 앉았다 일어섰다 누웠다를 반복하며, 물 아닌 우유를 마셔가며 뭔가를 논의하다가, 요청한 신문사 기자들이 10여 명 들어오면, 미리 준비한 팸플릿을 나누어주며 그대로 낭독하고 팔을 흔들며 주장하다가, 기자들이 가고 나면, 아마도 그 기자들도 선배들이거나 그 수하들이었을 것으로 짐작하는데, 그 자리에 앉거나 누워 쉬다가 하였다.

그러다가 저녁이 되면—보는 외부 사람은 나밖에 없었다.—여학생들이 가져다주는 식사)를 하고는 아마도 다음 조와 교대하였을 것으로 생각된다. 이렇게 학생답게 낭만스럽게 소위 '연세대학생 교내에서 단식투쟁'을 신문에 계속 광고하는 한편으로는 교내 시위 또한 주동하였다. 그러다가 기회가 되면 시내로 나가기 위해 신촌 로터리 방향으로 진출하다가 종종 경찰에 의해 막히곤 하였다.

◦ 연세대학생들의 '낭만(?) 시위' 현장에 가다

그런데 하루는 그런 시위대가, 신촌 로터리 경찰 저지선을 돌파에 성공하여 이화여대 앞을 지나 아현고개를 넘어 삼거리(서대문-신촌-마포)까지 진출하였다. 그래서 곧바로 서대문 방향으로 들어서려는데, 경찰이 아현삼거리 3방향에서 계획적으로 급습 포위하여 선두 주력을 와해시키고 주동자 체포에 나섰다. 나는 학교에서부터 이들을 따라 나와 우리 학군단 학생들을 살펴보고 있었다. 학훈단장 지프를 타고 뒤따라와서 아현동 삼거리 마포 방향 길가에 세우고 관찰하고 있었는데, 아니나 다를까 우선 충정로 방향 선두로부터 경찰 포위 공격에 쫓기는 학생들의 모습을 보게 되었다. 그때 학군단 우리 학생들 수명이 나와 지프를 알아보고 도망해 오기에 순간 숨기고, 형편 보아가며, 즉시 뒷골목길로 그들(아마도 10명쯤)을 도망가게 해 주었다.

그 이후 시위 학생들은 밀려서 신촌 로터리 방향으로 후퇴해 갔는데, 가다가는 자기 학교도 아닌 이화여대 안으로 거의 다 들어갔고 이대 운동장에서 이대학생들 보라는 듯 한바탕 시위하다 더 이상 호응이 없자 뿔뿔이 헤어졌다. 그러니 이들 대부분 학생들은 시위가 전문이 아니고 그저 나도 '한번 해보았다' 이고 참가했다는 것에 의의가 있었고, 또 이대—당시 이대생들은 이웃 연세대학생들을 좀 만만하게 보는 경향이 있었다. —학생들 앞에서 위세도 부려보는데도 의미가 있었다.

◦ 지 엄마는 아들 찾아 신촌 장마당까지 갔다

이 할아버지는 전통 한국 남자를 벗어나지 못해 가정에 무심하였으나 아이들에게는 엄하게 대하였다. 거기다 한국에서 본격적으로 직업 군인 생활하는 군인들은 직장과 집이 원격되어 있고 일과 자체가 보통 민간 생활과 달랐다. 그러다 보니, 집을 돌볼 겨를이나 겉으로라도 가정에 대한 깊은 관심조차 내색할 수 있는 생활(생각) 여유가 없어서 특히 아이들에게 소홀할 수밖에 없었다. 그러다 보니 아이들과의 정다움이 일반인들에 비해 모자랐던 터에 내 생활 신조로도, 아이가 길에서 넘어져도 스스로 일어나 옷 털고 다시 걸어가도록 두었고, 혼자서 나가 골목 어린이들과 어울려 놀도록 놔두었다. 그래서 자립 정신과 개척 정신을 갖도록 하였으나 그로서 아이들과의 인정 관계는 깊어질 수가 없었다.

토들러를 면치 못했던 어린 시절의 큰아들 정언이는, 밖에 나가 놀기를 좋아했는데, 골목에 나가면 다들 좋아했다. 물론 동래 또래들이 제일 좋아 하지만 길가 가겟집 아주머니도 '특별고객'—공짜로 집어가 먹으면 나중에 그 엄마가 후불하니까.—이라 좋아하고, 특히 이웃에 있는 큼직하고 널찍한 어느 기업가 저택의 집지기 할아버지가 특히 좋아하였다. 그런가 하면 그는 나를 닮아 모험도 좋아하였다. 한 뼘 남짓한 폭을 가진 시멘트 담장 위를,

이제 막 토들러를 면한 아이가 기어 올라가 한발 한발 걸어가는 걸 보노라면 아슬아슬하면서도 담대함을 느껴 흐뭇하기도 하였다.

우리 집은 동교동 삼거리에서 100미터 정도 못간 신촌로 북쪽 바로 뒷골목에 있었는데, 때때로 엄마에게 업혀서 그 골목길 따라 창천 삼거리 뒷골목 언덕길을 넘어 실거리 약 1킬로미터에 있는 신촌시장을 함께 다니기도 하였다. 하루는, 지 엄마가 잠깐 집을 비운 사이 이 토들러가 그 길을 따라 겁 없이 홀로 '엄마 찾아 십 리 길'(실제는 1킬로미터) 탐험을 하였다. 아이가 보이지 않자 엄마와 동네 사람들이 놀라서 애태우는 동안 그는 신촌시장에 도착하여 땀에 젖은 모습으로 두리번거리며 엄마를 찾고 있었다. 이를 본 노점 단골 아주머니가 의아하게 생각하며 주시하다가 혼자 헤매고 있음을 확인하고, 고맙게도 자기 노점을 남에게 맡기고, 애를 앞세워 우리 집으로 오고 있었는데, 도중에 그 방향으로 찾으러 나선 애 엄마와 만나게 되었다. 참으로 고마운 노점상 아주머니였다. 그때는 신촌과 동교동의 뒷골목 인심들이 그러하였다.

◇ 큰 경사, 둘째 성언이의 탄생, 화곡동에 자리 잡다

그 무렵(1965년) 우리에게는 두 번째 경사가 났다. 둘째 아들 '성언'이가 태어난 것이다. 이번에는 첫아이 때와는 달리 미리부터 벼루였다가 당시 이름 있던 서울 시내 '고려병원'으로 가서 출산하였다. 그런데, 좀 무리하게 활동(새집 보기 위해)했던 탓으로 조산이 되었으나 다행히도 '인큐베이터' 신세는 면하였다. 그는 신생아 때부터 아주 귀염둥이로 특히 함께 살고 있었던 외삼촌들로부터 크게 귀여움을 받았고, 자랄수록 똑똑하여 외삼촌들의 '시험감'이 되기도 하였다. 이 두 녀석들을 데리고 길에 나서거나 버스를 타면 특히 동네(화곡동) 어른들이 많이 귀여워해 주었다.

1965년에 우리가 원하던 모양의 집과 동네 즉, '화곡동 10만 단지 국민주택'이 건설되기 시작하였다. 즉시 응모하여 행운으로 97평 대지에 15평 국민주택, 80여 평의 정 네모꼴 마당을 가진, 소원하던 바로 그 집을 갖게 되었다. 처음부터 그 현장 건설 과정을 거의 매 주말마다 버스를 타고 가서 걸어 다니며 구경 겸 시찰하였다. 특히 언덕 위의 '시범주택'들이 철근 콘크리트로 기초를 다져가며 잘 시공되고 있는 것을 보고 믿음이 갔고, 입주하는 날을 고대하게 되었다.

드디어 66년 봄에 서울의 강서 지역 최초의 10만 평 국민주택단지가 완성되고, 우리는 그곳에 진짜로 아담하고 아름다운 전원주택을 갖게 되었던 것이다. 물론 오늘날 것과 비교하기는 그저 우스울 뿐인 것이었다. 당시 잘 나가던 부산 누님이 집값(약 12만 원, 당시 돈 값)을 원조해 주었는데, 이를 시작으로 그 이후 전세나 사글세를 면했는데, 우리 동기생 중에 당시 비록 단칸방이라도 자기 집 가진 경우가 아마도 열 손가락 이내였을 것이다. 그만큼 군 간부 생활이 열악하였다.

화곡동 10만 단지 내로 진입하는 주도로가 8미터 폭밖에 되지 않는 도로라 지금 기준으로는 보면 어림없는 도시 계획이었지만, 당시로는 그 얼마나 넓고 훤해 보였는지 모른다.

내가 전방과 베트남 그리고 독일 유학에 가 있는 동안, 아내는 견문과 지혜를 발휘하여 멋있게 블록 울타리를 치고 쇠 대문을 달고 '시다 나무' 2그루를 입주 기념을 겸하여 식목하였다. 이 나무는 그 후 40년 뒤인 2000년대 들어와 화곡동이 새롭게 변화할 때 화곡동 생성 기념수로 지정되었다는 얘기를 전해 들었다.

특히 80여 평의 넓은 마당에 잔디를 심어 10만 단지 내 가장 아름다운 집으로 가꾸어서 지나다니는 사람들과 집 구경하러 다니는 사람들에게 좋은 눈요기가 되었다. 당시 잔디는 상품으로 아직 나오지 않았기에 동네 집 청소 도움이 아저씨에게 부탁하여 근처 들에서 조금씩 뜯어오면 그걸 거의 해체 하다시피 하여 드문드문 줄잔디로 심고, 쉴 사이 없이 관리하여 조성하였는데 그 정성이 잔디 깔린 양옥집의 꿈을 이루게 하였던 것이다.

4. 다시 전방 사단 대간첩작전 장교·중대장으로, 중대원 전원 파월 지원

◇ 제5사단 대간첩작전 과장

그동안 나는 광주 보병학교 고등군사반 과정을 우수한 성적으로 이수하고, 다시 연세대 107학군단으로 보직되었다가 이듬해(1966) 봄에 경력을 쌓기 위해 전방으로 가게 되었다. 사단 사령부로 가서 사단장께 신고하고 작전참모부 근무를 소원하여 사단 작전참모부에 소속되었는데, 거기에 이미 고참 작전 과장이 있어서 나는 사단 '대간첩 작전 과장'의 임무를 맡게 되었다. 당시 북한은 대남적화공작을 위해 수많은 간첩과 무장 정찰대를 전후방을 가리지 않고 침투시켜 활동하였음으로 대간첩작전의 중요성은 전후방을 막론하고 매우 강조되고 있었다.

◇ 군단 예비사단의 대간첩작전 현장

당시 제5사단은, 중부 전선을 담당한 제5군단의 예비사단으로 군단 후방 지역 대간첩작전도 책임지고 있었다. 특히 지대 내 주요 산악 침투로인 광덕산-백운산-도마치봉-도마치고개-국망봉-강씨봉-오뚜기고개-서울, 또는 도마치재(도마치고개)에서 124번 도로(현재 75본도로)-적목리—가평, 그 중간에 적목리에서 가평천을 따라 올라 오뚜기고개길, 또는 그 반대 방향 등의 루트를 중심으로 병력을 배치하고 작전을 수행하였다.

그러나 일단 적 침투 징후가 보고되면 전 지역에 '바둑판식 병력 배치'로 기간이나 동원 상태 한정 없이, 소탕될 때까지 작전을 계속하였다. 평소에는 요소요소(접근로 목 지점)에 분대급 대간첩작전 병력을 상주시켜서 주간에는 지역을 수색 정찰하고 야간에는 요소에 매복 작전을 실시하고, 일단 유사시에는 즉각 조치(사살 또는 생포)하고 보고하기로 규정 즉 SOP화 하고 있었다.

나는 사단 대간첩작전 담당관으로 수시로 지대 내를 지프를 이용해 점검 및 순찰하면서 작전을 파악, 판단 건의하고 실행하였다. 순찰로는 주로 '이동'에서 '도마치고개'와 '광덕고개' 즉 '카라멜고개(김일성고개)'에서 현 372번도로, 이어서 현 75번도로(구124번), 그리고 '적목리'(실제로 거대한 붉은 소나무림 지역)에서 가평천을 따라 '오뚜기고개길'로, 또는 '도마치고개길'로 해서 '일동'—'이동'으로 돌아오는, 또는 그 반대 방향으로 기동하면서 순찰하였다. 실제로 이 지역에서 1964년 부터 1966년까지 무장 간첩을 사살도 하고 생포도 하였다.

그 기간 중 웃지 못할 에피소드도 있었다. 지금은 우스게 삼아 또는 교훈 삼아 하는 끼리끼리 얘기로, "소대장님! 쏠까요 말까요?"가 있다. 봉쇄 지역을 바둑판 모양으로 개인별로 배치하여 야간 근무 중에 돌현이 바로 눈앞에 나타난 간첩을 보고, 순간 병사가 사살 여부를 판단 못해,—즉 교육이나 훈련이 미숙하거나 명령 자체가 애매해—소대장에게 다급하게 물어보는 것이다, 허, 그 순간 간첩은 살아짐으로써 작전은 실패하고 만다는 것이고 이런 사례가 작전 현장에서는 흔하게 있을 수 있다는 교훈이 되었던 것이다.

◇ 중대장과 함께 전 중대원 파월 지원

5·16 군사혁명 직후 당시만 해도 제3국가군을 제외하고 우리보다 못사는 나라가 별로 없었기에 외국으로 나가보는 것이 선망되고 있었던 때에, 마침 군사혁명으로 해외 진출 붐이 막 일어나던 시점을 계기로, 개인적으로는 해외 유학, 해외 돈벌이, 해외 경험 등의 욕구가 치솟던 시절이었다. 그래서 그렇게도 우리에게 선망의 대상으로 알려진 독일의 탄광 인부 모집에도 대학생들이 대거 지원하였고, 여자 간호사들은 해외 대학 유학을 가고 싶었던 여학생들이 대거 지원하였다. 그들은 선진국 독일에 가서 일해서(탄광이라도, 간호사라도 좋으니) 돈 벌어 유학을 또는 선진국 진출을 해 보고 싶었던 것이다.

그동안 나는 사단 인사 환경 변화로 사단참모직에서 새삼 부대 지휘관으로 전보되었다. 중대장으로 부임(1966.9)한 지 1개월쯤 지나자 월남 2차 파병 요원, 즉 1965년에 제1차로 파병된 요원들의 복무 기간이 1년이라 이들에 대한 교대 요원 장사병 지원자 모집을 지시받았다. 그때는 이미 상당수 동기생들이 1차 파병 중대장 요원으로 지원해 가서 복무 중이었다. 그러기에 정규 육사 출신 장교로 특히나 전투병과 장교들은 전투 경험이나 참전 경력이 필수적이라는 생각이 들고 있었기에 나 스스로를 포함해서 우리 중대원들에게 월남 파병 지원을 권유하기로 했다.

그리하여 전 중대원을 한자리에 집합시키고 명령 아닌 권유를 시작하였다. '남자로 시대에 맞게 해외 진출과 견문욕을 충족할 수 있고, 국가에 충성은 물론 개인 경제적으로도 병사도 적게는 황소 한 마리로 가사에 큰 도움이 될 수도 있다. 그리고 1년 피해 통계는 국내 행정 손실과 별 차이 없다'고 역설하고 나도 지원한다고 했다. 그랬더니 중대장과 함께라면 우리도 흔쾌히 함께 가겠다면서 전원이 지원하였다. 이건 그냥 하는 얘기가 아니고 진정이었다. '중대장과 함께라면'이라는 단서가 달렸었다.

그러나 유감스럽게도 '제1차 교대' 자원은 부분 교대이기에 부대별 교대가 아닌 보충 병식 교대로 실행됨으로써 부득이 자원자 개별로 파월하게 되어, 나는 내 중대를 거느리지 못하고 개별적으로 파월될 수밖에 없었다. 그래서 우선 내가 먼저 떠나기로 하고, 월남 전장에서 만나 각자 분투하기로 약속하고 양해를 구한 뒤 그들과 석별하였다. 먼저 떠나면서, 그들의 안전과 건투를 그리고 무사히 귀국하기를 기원해 마지않았다.

때마침 파월 맹호부대 전사 장교 홍성태 대위—육사 동기생으로 전사(戰史) 1교반에 상당 기간 함께 연구했던 전사(戰史) 연구가—로부터 연락이 왔다. '자기는 보병전투 중대장으로 나가고 싶은데 후임으로 와 달라'는 것이었다. 마침 잘 되었다고 생각했다.

제5장

파월맹호(派越猛虎)부대 전사(戰史) 장교로 월남전 참전

1. 파월맹호부대, 월남 '퀴논'에 진을 치다

◇ 패망한 월남전쟁의 역사적 배경

본격적인 월남전쟁 얘기에 앞서 한국과는 다르게 월남이 패망하게 된 연유와 한국군이 파병하게 된 국제 정세적 환경을 먼저 간단히 알아보기로 한다.

'월남(越南, Viet Nam)'은 '안남(安南)'으로도 불렸는데, 3모작을 한다는 '안남미(安南米)'는 독특한 쌀로 알려졌다. 월남은 동남아시아 한편에 나 있는 거대한 반도 동쪽 해안을 따라 남북으로 뻗어 있고, 북은 중국과 서쪽은 라오스 및 캄보디아와 국경을 이루고 있다.

국민은 단일 민족인 우리 한국과 달리 다종족으로 구성되어 있는데 주로 평지족인 비엣족(Viet)이 90%, 나머지 10%는 주로 산악 부족(53개)이다. 현 산악 부족은 원래 원주민이었으나 현 평지족의 침략에 쫓겨 국토 80%가 험산 산악 지역으로 이주하여 지금도 거의 원시생활을 하면서 평지족을 원망하며 문화와 문명과는 거리가 먼 산악 생활을 하고 있다. 그리하여 현재 '베트남'에 관한 얘기는 모두 평지족에 관한 것이다. 종교는 전래로 불교 60%, 가톨릭 20%, 기타 20% 정도이다.

우리나라 삼국 시대가 전개될 지음인 BC 690년경 월남 최초의 왕국이 성립되었으나 곧이어 중국 침략 세력의 지배를 받아오다가 938년경에 독립 왕국을 재건하고 이후 수차에 걸친 중국과 몽골군의 침략을 물리쳤다. 그러나 1400년 경에는 17도선—한국의 청천강선 비슷한 역사적 분할선—을 중심으로 남북 왕조로 분활되었다가 1700년대에 남북 통일 왕조가 성립, 그러나 19세기 초부터의 서세 동점 시대에 프랑스 침략을 받고(1858), 드디어 1885년에 (바오다이) 왕조는 괴뢰 정권화하고 실질적인 프랑스 식민지가 되었다.

1940년에는 일제의 침략을 받았는데, 당시 프랑스(괴뢰 비시 정권)의 약세로 프랑스와 일제의 2중적 식민지가 되었다가 제2차 세계대전이 종결되자 프랑스와 일제의 식민지는 면했으나, 우리 한국과는 달리 일제 청산이나 토지 개혁 등이 이루어지지 않은 채 식민지 괴뢰 정권이 복귀한 가운데, 다시 강대해진 프랑스 세력이 개입하였다. 그런데 일제 강점기 우리의 '임정'과 같은 독립운동 기구가, 국제 공산주의 영향을 받는 '호찌민(Ho Chi Minh, 胡志明)'의 유일적 지도하에 중국 영향 지역인 북부에서 '베트민(Viet Minh, 越盟)'을 결성하고(1941.5), 반불/반일전선을 형성하고, 전 지역에 '해방구'를 설치, 전 베트남에 조직적 인민 봉기를 준비하였다. 이때부터 호찌민은, 마치 우리의 이승만 김구처럼, 민족 독립의 우상이 되었다.

이들은 일본의 항복(1945.8.15)과 동시에 하노이에 진출하여 중국과 한때 미국의 지원을 받아 '베트남민주공화국'을 수립하고 전국적인 독립운동/독립무력전쟁(프랑스 정규군 상대)—전후 복귀한 프랑스 식민 세력과 바오다이 괴뢰 정권으로부터—을 전개하였다. 그리하여 프랑스 군의 난공불락의 거점 요새 '디엔비엔푸'전투— 에서 승리(1954)하여 일단 17도선 이북을 확보하고 이어서 2년 뒤 남북통일의 길을 개척하였다.

그러나 1955년에 미국이 지지하는 '고 딘 디엠' 이 남부에 '베트남공화국'을 성립시키고 소위 '족벌 독재 정치'를 행하며, 토지 개혁을 하지 못한 채 부정부패하여 민심이 이반되어 갔다. 이에 (남부)공산주의자들은 지역별 자위대 즉 '베트콩(Viet Cong, 越 共)', 약칭 VC을 조직하고, 나아가 이들을 통합하는 '남베트남민족해방전선'을 결성(1960)하여 남부 자유 민주 정부 전복 무력 투쟁을 전개하였다. 동시에 북으로부터는 월맹 정규군 3개 연대 규모가 남으로 침투하여 베트콩과 지하로 연결되어 있었고, 중부 지역에서는 이미 월맹 정규군 지휘자가 소부대별로 베트콩을 지휘하고도 있었다.

한편 미국은 아시아지역 공산화 도미노 현상을 우려하여 월남 전선에서 방어벽 고착화를 기도하였다. 그래서 이 할아버지가 미특수전학교로 유학갔던 그 시점 1961년에, 케네디 대통령은 미국에 특수전사령부를 설치하고, 월남에 '미국군사원조사령부(U.S, MAC.V)'를 설치, 월남 정권을 정치, 군사 경제적으로 지원하기 시작하였다. 이어서 자유우방 25개국에 '월남지원'을 요청(1964.5)했다.

◇ 한국, 월남에 파병 군사 지원

당시 한국 정부는 일찍(1962)부터 미국 대통령 '케네디'의 확고한 '반공 전략'과 국제 정세 그리고 한반도 정세를 분석하여 미국을 지원하기 위한 한국군의 파월 불가피성을 판단하고, 물밑으로 미국과 월남 정부를 접촉해가며 파월 군사 지원 전략 정책을 준비하였다. 그러던 중 미국 존슨 대통령으로부터 공식 '베트남 지원 요청'을 받았다.

이에 한국 정부는 다음과 같이 명분과 국가 이익을 정하고 파월 군사 원조를 단행하였다. 명분으로, 1. 한국 안보에도 간접적 영향을 주는 자유 우방 월남공화국 지원 필요, 2. '6·25 적란'시 자유 우방으로부터 받은 은혜, 공산 위협 공동대처 도의적 의무, 3. 동맹국 미국의 요청, 4. 월남 정부의 요청, 5. '헌법 제4조의 국제 평화 유지와 침략 전쟁 부인' 정신으로 '월남 지원 필요' 등이었다. 물론 궁극적으로는, 월남 전후 부흥 수요에 참여하는 경제 발전 전략과 실 병력 대거 파월시 창출될 수 있는 달러(전투 수당) 수입 전략과 동시에 한국군 2개 사단 정도의 군사력 증강 전략 등도 고려되었을 것이다.

그리하여 제1차로 제1이동 외과병원(붕타우)과 태권도 교관단(육해군 사관학교와 보병학교)을 파견(1964.9)하였다. 2차로 '한국군 군사 원조단'(비둘기부대)—각군 혼성 여단 규모(2,000여 명), 공병대대, 수송 자동차 중대, 해병공병 중대, 해군수송 분대(LST), 그리고 기 파견된 제1이동 외과병원과 태권도 교관단, 그리고 이들을 경비해줄 경비대대로 구성—을 파견(1965.3)하였다.

3차는 본격적인 전투부대 지원으로, 맹호부대(수도사단)와 해병 제2여단(창설, 청룡부대)을 선발하여 각각 중부 빈딩성의 '퀴논' 일대 전투지역에, 남부 '깜란만' 지역으로 파견하였다. 그 이후 해를 넘겨 다시 제4차 파병으로 육군 제9사단(백마부대)이 파월되어 맹호부대 아래 '닌호아' 지역에 배치되었다.

◇ 맹호부대, 월남 중부 '퀴논'에 진을 치다.

맹호부대(猛虎部隊, 즉 首都師團)는 1965년 10월에 월남 중부 '빈딘성 퀴논' 일대에 전개하여 작전 책임 지역(TAOR, 일단 1,200평방km)을 미군과 월남군으로부터 인수하고, 전투 중대별로 거점 지점을 점령하여 원형방어진(중대 전술 기지)을 구축하였다. 사단사령부도 작전 책임 지역 내 대체적인 중앙 지점을 점령하여 독립된 방어진지를 구축하였다. 그와 동시에 전 부대는 전술 책임 지대 내 베트콩과 주민을 상대로 평정 작전—베트콩 소탕전/민사 심리전—을 전개하였다.

맹호부대가 진을 치면서 시작된 전투 작전은 내가 부임할 때(1965.10~1966.11)만 해도, 물론 중대 단위 작전은 매일 매시간이었고, 대대 단위 작전 30회, 연대 단위 작전 12회, 사단 단위 직전 3회를 기록하고 있었다.

2. 파월 한국군 전사 기록, 역대 모범 전사 기록으로 남기다

◇ 홍성태 육사 교수, 한국군 최초 전사과(戰史課) 편성

태능 육사 개교 이후 전사교육은 주로 미국 육사 교재를 번역한 것으로, 내용은 유럽 전사와 미국 전사였고, 심지어 '6·25 한국 전사' 또한 미국 교재 전사 기록을 이용하였다. 그러니 모든 전쟁 원칙과 교훈 등은 외국군 용이나 마찬가지였다. 우리 고대 전사나 특히 6·25 전사 조차 불비하였고 전투 상보는 거의 존재하지 않거나 정리되어 있지 않아 교재로 사용할 수 없었다. 그래서 절실히 느꼈던 것이, 앞으로 우리 군의 최소한 사단급부대에는 '전사과'가 전시는 물론이고 평시에도 편성되고 운영되어야 한다는 것이었다. 그래서 파월부대 편성시 때마침 육사 전사교관이던 동기생 홍성태 대위는 군에 건의하여 파월 사단 작전처에 '전사과'를 편성하는데 성공하고, 그가 그 맹호부대 전사과를 맡아 파월까지 하였던 것이다.

◇ 맹호는 간다, 가족을 두고 월남 전장터로 가다

나는 홍성태 대위의 요청(즉 현지 수요)에 따라 서둘러서 제1차 교대 제2진(1966.11)으로 편성되었는데, 춘천 외곽 '오음리' 파월훈련소 입소를 생략하고 춘천 기차역에서 막 출발하려는 제2진 주력에 합류하였다. 춘천역에서는 주로 남녀 학생들이 총출동하여 환송해 주었다. 청량리역에서는 서울 시민 대표들과 함께 우리 가족, 사랑하는 아내와 두 아들, 이 환송 인파 속에서 나를, 우리를 환송해 주었다. 물론 그동안 아내에게 상당 시간 설명하고 설득해서 이 시간에 전장 마당으로 가게 되었지만, 앞으로 내가 무사히 돌아올 때까지 내 아내와 가족의 마음을 생각하면 내 스스로도 죄책감이 있으나 이 또한 직업 군인의 의무요 임무요 운명인 것을 어찌하랴.

아내는 청량리역 승차장, 즉 환송장에서 잠시 내려선 나에게 부적 삼아 악어 가죽 지갑을 내 손에 꼭 쥐어주었는데, 그때 그 기분/감정, 내 책임의 가족을 두고 전장으로 가는 사나이의 어떤 마음이 울컥 솟아올랐다.—이후 그 지갑은 오랫동안, 모서리가 다 닳아 못 쓸 때까지 내 포켓을 떠나 다른 곳에 놓아둔 적이 없었다.—기차가 출발할 때 나는 다시 한번 '한 1년, 그동안 내 염려 말고 애들과 함께 잘 지내주길 바란다'고 속으로 빌고 또 빌었다.

드디어 부산본역에 하차하여 제3 부두에서 미국 여객선(2만여 톤급)으로 환승한 후 이곳에서도 부산 시민들의 열렬한 환송을 받으며, 특히 부산에서 사업하시는 가형이 나와 '형제 믿음'의 마음으로 환송해 주었다. 역시나 전장터로 가는 전사들에게 친지들과 국민들의 환송(식)은 반듯이 필요하다고 느껴졌다.

문자 그대로 뱃고동을 울리며 제3 부두를 떠나 전장터로 가는 수송선 데크에서 부두의 환송객과 형님이 흔드는 태극기 물결이 점점 멀어져갈 때, 또 한 번 어떤 감회가 스쳐갔다. 그리하여 항해한 지 1주일 만에 예정지인 월남 중부 '빈딩성 퀴논'에 도착(1965.11)하여 맹호부대에 부임 신고를 하였다.

「맹호는 간다」, 그때 춘천역에서, 청량리역에서, 부산 부두에서 들었던 환송가

1.
자유통일 위해서 조국을 지키시다
조국의 이름으로 님들은 뽑혔으니
그 이름 맹호부대 맹호부대 용사들아
가시는 곳 월남 땅 하늘은 멀더라도
한결같은 겨레마음 님의 뒤를 따르리다
한결같은 겨레마음 님의 뒤를 따르리다

2.
자유통일 위해서 길러온 힘이기에
조국의 이름으로 어딘들 못 가리까
그 이름 맹호부대 맹호부대 용사들아
남북으로 갈린 땅 월남의 하늘 아래
화랑도의 높은 기상 우리들이 보여주자
화랑도의 높은 기상 우리들이 보여주자

3.
보내는 가슴에도 떠나는 가슴에도
대한의 한마음이 뭉치고 뭉쳤으니
그 이름 맹호부대 맹호부대 용사들아
태극깃발 가는 곳 적이야 다를 소냐
무찌르고 싸워 이겨 그 이름을 떨치리라
무찌르고 싸워 이겨 그 이름을 떨치리라

◇ 전장 감찰로 전훈(戰訓) 전파

전장 감찰이라는 말은 공식적 표현은 아니나 그런 의미는 실재하였다. 사단 전사 과장의 임무 중 또 하나가, 과에 보직된 1~2명의 전사 장교와 함께 전사 기록이나 현장 관찰 또는 보고와 전언 등에서 도출되는 전투(전쟁)교훈을 기록하고 전파하는 것이었다. 특히 수시로 발생(전개)하는 '우연한 충돌'(우발 사건)에 대해서는, 가능한 한 직후 현장에 출동하여 사태를 파악하고 평가하여 교훈화하였다. 그래서 가능하면 어느 때던 어느 장소건 불문하고 현장에 입회하여 보고 듣고 판단하려고 노력하였다.

그러다 보니 어느 때, 바로 앞서 베트콩으로부터 기습당한 그 자리에 홀로 가서 사태 현장 분석을 하다 보면 완전히 단기로 노출되어 위험한 지경도 몇 번이나 있었다. 그런가 하면, 연대 작전 회의나 작전 지휘소에 참석하여 열심히 살피다 보면 그 부대 지휘관이, 사단에서 왜 왔는지 오해를 하는 경우도 있었다.

나의 일상생활은, 사단 상황실에서 매일 아침 사단장 임석하에 실시되는 일일 상황 보고에 참석하여 오늘의 작전 상황을 파악하고, 전투식량 미군 C-Ration 한 박스를 싣고, 무장한 운전병과 함께 단둘이서 전용 지프로 작전 연대 지휘소 또는 주요 지점으로 사방을 살펴 가며, 그러나 전운(戰運)에 맞기고 겁 없이 전장으로 이동한다. 때로는 퀴논 시내를 지나기도 하나 통상은 마을을 지나고 인적이 없거나 드문 산지와 야지를 지나는데 때로는 몇 10킬로미터, 몇 시간 이동하여 목적지에 도달하기도 하고, 또 때로는 하루에 여러 지점에 가보기도 하였다. 물론 저녁에는 사단으로 복귀하나 때로는 부대 야전(작전) 지휘소에서 밤샘을 하기도 하였다.

사단 작전 경우에는 기간 중 전방전술지휘소(TCP)에 며칠이라도 머물면서 작전 회의와 상황실을 드나들고, 밖으로 나가서는 전방 전투 현장으로가 전장관찰을 실시하였다. 그리고 상황이 끝나면, 또 다른 작전 현장에 전사 장교를 파견하고 나는 전사 기록을 위해 전사과 사무실(퀀셋)에 앉아 초고를 쓰고 그것이 일단 완성되면, 이어서 선임하사는 복사지를 한글 타이프라이터로 쳐서 등사 준비를 하였다. 그런데, 언제나 그걸로 시간과의 싸움에 이길 수 없기에, 때로는 고장도 나기에, 나는 아예 쇠받침 위에 초가 묻은 푸른 복사지를 올려놓고 골필로 한자 한자 글을 써 나갔다. 물론 그때는 시간 가는 줄 모르거니와 밤을 지세우는 작업도 여러날이었다.

3. 작전 현장 체험, '맹호8호· 홍길동· 오작교작전'

◇ 맹호8호작전

주월 한국군은 애초부터 월남전 즉 '대게리라작전' 개념을 점과 선을 넘어 점에서 면으로 확장전략작전을 계획하고 실행하였다. 최초 인수 받은, 즉 할당된 '작전 책임 지역'(TAOR)을 면의 작전으로 완전 평정하기 위해 일단, 지대 내 요점에 중대 단위 거점 진지를 편성하고 이어서 중대 주변 지역을 매일 위협 사격과 위력 정찰 또는 은밀 정찰을 통해 평정(중대작전)하고, 이어서 중대 기지와 중대 기지 사이 지역의 적을 소탕—평정작전(대대작전)을 실시하고, 이어서 대대와 대대간의 적을 소탕—평정작전(연대작전)을 실시하고. 또 이어서 지대 내 적 주요 활동 거점 완전 소탕을 위해서 그리고 그 작전 이후 면의 확장작전 즉 '작전 책임 지역' 확장직전을 끊임없이 계속적으로 실시하였다.

그래서 내가 부임한 그 시점까지 우리 맹호부대는 사단급 작전인 '맹호 5호작전'과 '맹호 6호작전'을 실시하여 'TAOR'를 북으로 이미 상당한 면적으로 확장하였다.(1,400평방km). 그래서 이제는 남쪽 방향으로, 추후 '투이호아'를 중심 책임 지역으로 활동하며 북으로 확장작전 중인 우리 '백마사단'(9사단)과의 연결작전까지도 염두에 두고, 우리 맹호부대는 남진 확장작전을 계속 실시하게 되었다. 이름하여 '맹호 8호작전'이었다. 그런데 본 작전 전사 기록상 아군 측 요지 요부의 한곳은 바로 '꾸멍고개(deo Cu Mong)'였다.

이 고갯마루는 퀴논에서 1번 국도를 따라 남으로 해안 촌락 도시, 송카우(Song—Cau)로 가는 도중에 위치하며, '퀴논'에서 직선 거리 약 40킬로미터 실거리 60여 킬로미터(고개길)에 있어서, 베트남 역사상에서도 일찍부터 유명하였다. 15세기 베트남은 남북왕조로 분립하였는데 그 중앙 대척점에, 마치 우리의 '판문점'과 같은 역할을 담당하는 꾸멍고개가 있었는데, 바로 1965년 이후 '맹호8호작전' 이전까지, 또한 그 역할을 담당하고 있었다. 즉 맹호부대가 작전 지역—베트남 행정 즉 주권이 미치는 지배 지역이나 '낮이면 베트남, 밤이면 베트콩 세상'—을 인수 후 베트콩이 장악하고 있는 즉 베트콩 해방구인 남측('송카우' 지역)과의 경계 선상 유일한 통로상의 '만남 지점'에 이 꾸멍고개가 위치하게 되었던 것이다.

그래서 맹호부대는 일찍부터 이 고갯마루에 분단된 한반도의 역사 경험에 따라 남북교역의 시장을 열고, 남북 물물 교류를 허락하고 있었는데, 이는 분단 현실 속에 가능한 최소한의 이웃 간 소통 사정을 풀어주면서, 동시에 남쪽 적 지역에 대한 정보도 입수할 수 있었다. 그래서 나는 부임 후 그 사정을 알고 종종 이 고갯마루에 올라와 남북 시장 교류를 눈여겨 보아왔다.

◇ 작전이 시작되다

작전 지역은 '꾸멍고개'이남 '송카우'시 지역으로, 작전 개시선(LD)는 따로 없고,—각 부대별 헬기 탑승장—공격 개시 시간은 바로 각 부대별 제1번기의 이륙 시간이었다. 다만 최초 작전 통제선은 각 부대의 강습 착륙지점(LZ, Landing Zone)을 이은 선이다. 즉, 부대는 목표 지역을 포위하는 개념으로 부근 고지지점에 있는 LZ들에, 미군이 지원해주는 헬리콥터(UH-1H ; 무장병 9명)로 분대별로 이동하여 착륙(랜딩)하고,— 탑승/착륙 지점은 일단 '고엽제'로 사전 작업, 여의치 못하면 로프하강으로 강습 착륙 시도— 일단 전개하였다가, 명에 의거 '송카우' 시내(해 보았자 밀림 속의 촌락)로 밀림을 헤치며 지역 내 베트콩 소굴을 소탕해가며 내려가 포위망을 좁혀서(즉 '토끼몰이 전술'로 평지 시내에 몰리게 된 적(베트콩)을 소탕하고 지역을 점령한 후, 이어서 평정(안정)작전으로 새 행정조직과 민심 안정작전을 실시하고, 형편대로 가능한 조기에 월남 정부에 주권(특히 행정권)을 이양하는 것이었다.

D-Day H-Hour는 1967년 1월 3일 10시 30분이었다. 나는 새벽 일찍부터 꾸멍고개 — 작전지역으로 차량 이동할 수 있는 유일한 길은 1번 국도이고 그 고갯마루에 있는 유일한 집결지인 동시에 전방작전 지휘소가 위치하는 요점—로 달려가 전투 개시를 관찰하였다. 꾸멍고개 시장은 평일과 다름없이 아침부터 송카우 상인들이 걸어서—이미 수처에 베트콩 적이 1번 도로 길을 차단해 놓았다.—올라와 전을 벌려놓고 퀴논에서 온 상인들과 거래를 시작하고 있었다.

어제 밤새 폭풍우가 몰아쳤고 오늘도 35 knot의 폭풍우 속에, 10시 30분이 되자, 그 시간에 바로 150여 명의 남북 상인 모두는 강제로 억류되고, 동시에 송카우 시내로 수십 발의 포탄이 작렬하고 왼쪽 편 해안 고지대를 따라 전투부대(사단 수색중대)가 소총 사격을 계속하며 남으로 내려가고 동시에 하늘에는 수많은 헬리콥터가 날라들어 왔다. 이 무시무시한 광경을 본 송카우 상인들은 울음, 신음과 함께 공포에 질린 모습으로 어쩔 줄 몰라했다. 이 지역과 이 주민들이 평화에서 전쟁으로 변하는 순간이었다.

유병현 사단장은 꾸멍고개에 설치된 26연대 TCP에 사단 이동식 TCP를 설치하고(거느리고), 주로 26연대장의 작전 지휘를 전적으로 지원하였다. 때때로 헬기(지휘용 따로 없이)를 이용하여 전장 상공을 선회하며 관찰하고 돌아와 작전을 지휘하였다.

나는 2일째 되던 날, 수색 중대 요원과 함께 남으로 1번 국도를 연하여 2킬로미터 정도를 전진하다가 돌아왔으며, 다음 날은 26연대장과 함께 도보로 2중대 호위병과 함께 아군이 탈취한 '싼록(Chanh Loc)마을'—'송카우'의 한 마을—에 들어갔다. 1번 국도는 군데군데 50여미터 길이로 짤려 있었으며, 피란민들은 남부여대하여 마치 수재민 같은 모습으로 마을 속을 헤매고 있었다.

5일째는 사단장과 함께 그동안 보수한 1번 국도를 따라 장갑차에 동승하여 일단 무력저항을 진압한 상태의 송카우 중심부 들어가서 주민의 환영도 받고 그 자리에서 주민에 둘러 쌓인 채 주민 대표들과 추후 시정 논의를 하였다. 사단장은 가능한 빨리 새 행정 수장(아마도 군수 격)을 선출하여 주민 자치체를 확립할 수 있도록 격려하였다. 전투가 진행중인 현재는 물론 우리 지휘관의 명령으로 질서가 유지되어야 하나 한국군은 당분간이라도 군정을 실시할 의사가 없음으로 전투 종식과 동시 자치 행정으로 복귀시켜줄 것이라고 약속하였던 것이다. 그리하여 그들도 뜻밖의 한국군 조치에 감사하며 새 수장 선출을 서둘렀으나 나서는 자마다(두 사람) 숨어 있는 잔류 베트콩의 저격으로 한동안 어려움을 겪기도 했다.

송카우 군 중앙에는 야자수 밀림으로 덮힌 광장이 있었는데, 한쪽은 피난민 수용소 겸 '함렛' 구역이고 또 한쪽은 4~500명의 포로수용소인데 여자 포로들이 많았다. 사실은 전투 현장에서 피체된 실제 베트콩은 물론 근처에 서성거린 준 베트콩까지, 당장 구별은 불가하여 일단 수용소에 수용 후 심문하여 전투 정보 입수 후 진짜 가짜를 구분하고 진짜 포로는 일단 정부군에 인계하였다. 그런데 진작은 피란민 수용소에서 진짜 포로가 더 많이 배출되었는데, 그만큼 베트콩의 처신은 교묘하였다. 일반민들은 순진하여 총을 가져오면 돈 준다 했더니 개인당 2~3정씩 순식간에 몇 백정이 수집되기도 하였다.

2월 1일부로 '맹호8호'의 실질적인 작전은 끝나고 지역 안정작전을 시작하면서 '함렛'(주민 격리 수용소)에 수용되었던 주민 전원을 귀가시키고, 480여 명의 색출된 포로만 월남군 당국으로 후송하였다. 아 저 꾸멍고개! 전설의, 비극의, 슬픔의 그러면서도 희망의 꾸멍고개, 이제 다시 맹호부대 얘기와 함께 또 한때의 전설로 역사 한 페이지에 추가되겠지. 작전이 끝나자 남은 것은 열대 지역에 설치된 퀸셑막사 속 책상에 붙어 앉아 내가 몰두해야 할 본격적인 전사 기록 업무였다. 이후 4월 중순까지 1개월 반여 만에 탈고하였는데 10센치 볼펜이 2개 닳았고, 골필이 더 이상 쓰기 어려울 정도로 무디어졌다.

◇ '오작교작전(烏鵲橋作戰)' ; 1967. 3~5월

맹호8호작전에 이어서 같은 해 3월에서 5월까지, 주월한국군사령부계획으로 '오작교작전'이 실시되었다. 여기에는 맹호부대(수도사단)와 백마부대(9사단)가 각각 남북으로 작전 책임 지역을 넓히면서 연결 작전을 실시하는, 한국군 대게릴라작전의 특징인 면의 확대작전을 야심차게 전개하려는 의도가 내포되었고 이를 달성하였다.

작전 지대가 맹호 지역 '송커우'에서 백마 지역 '투이호아'를 통하는 국도 1번의 해안길 지대였기에 평소와 같이 미군 헬기부대는 물론 해군과 공군의 지원도 받는 군단급 작전으로 실시되었다. 작전결과, 한국군 양개 사단의 지역 연결로 1번 국도 400킬로미터가 회복

되어 안정이 확보되고, 한국군 전술작전 책임 지역—월남 정부 행정 및 군관구 지배하—을 6,800평방킬로미터(제주도의 약 3배)로 확장하고 안정 확보하게 되었다.

나는 맹호8호작전 기록에 열중하기 위해 이번 작전 기록은 육사 후배 16기 노영한에게 전적으로 위임하였다. 우리 전사과에는 내 밑으로 대위 1명, 중위 1명, 하사관 1명으로 구성되어 있었다.

◇ 홍길동작전(1967. 7~8월), 사단 TCP 피습

주월한국군지원사령부는 월남 정부의 대통령 선거에 대비할 겸 '오작교작전'으로 확장된 지역 내 적군(월맹 정규1개 연대 포함)의 잔적을 소탕하여 안정작전을 실시하려는 의도로 맹호 사단과 백마사단이 동시에, 역시 미군 포병, 미군 헬기부대, 미공군 전략폭격(ARC Light) 등의 지원을 받아 앞선 오작교작전 지역에서 잔적 소탕작전 즉 '홍길동 작전'을 전개하였다. 여기에 참가한 우리 맹호부대는 확장된 지역에서 26연대의 확장 배치와 안정 확보의 목적도 가지고 있었다.

금번 작전은 월맹 정규군과의 충돌이 예상되기 때문에 전쟁 준비를 강화하였다. 따라서 사단사령부 또한 '전술전방지휘소'(TAC.CP)를 남쪽에 위치한 제26연대본부 지역에 전진하여 설치하였다. 그리고 작전 개시 이전에 적 지역 내에 미공군 B—52 전략폭격기에 의한 'Arc Light(渡洋)' 폭격도 선행되었다.

*통상 '1소티'당 B—52전략폭격기 3기 편대— 대당 108발 적재—가 태평양 기지(주로 괌)에서 출격하여 태평양을 가로질러 베트남의 적 밀집 밀림 지역 한 목표에 100톤의 폭탄 투하로 1.6평방킬로미터를 일시에 초토화하였다. 전쟁 중 1,200소티로, 1967년까지만 해도 이미 한국전시 사용 폭탄의 2배 100만톤 이상이 사용되었다. 그리하여 어떤 지점(내가 가서 목격한)은 마치 우리 이리역 폭파 지점과도 같이 깊이 10여미터 길이 10여미터 되는 거대한 웅덩이가 수십 개 앞으로 줄지어 파여지기도 하였다. 그러나 장거리 도양 도중 소련 함대가 그 길목에 위치하여 이 폭격기들에 대한 정보를 월맹에 타전하고 월맹은 베트콩에 제공하여 실제로 직접적인 인명 피해는 거의 없었다. 다만 전후 베트콩 지휘자의 고백에 의하면, 고막을 파괴하는 그 폭음과 거대한 웅덩이의 형성 과정 그리고 내습의 공포에 의한 심리적 압박으로 베트콩의 사기에 상당한 영향을 미쳤다고 했다.

나는 공격 개시 시간—07시 15분, 공격부대가 작전 현지에 헬기 등으로 landing 하는 그 시간—이전에 새벽 일찍이 단기(單騎)로 'Toy An'에 지정된, 거의 모두가 정글을 고엽제로 말려 베어내고 조성한 헬기 '픽업' 존으로 가서 관전하였다. 헬기 도착을 기다리며 장병들은 분대별로 모여 '한발 뛰뛰기 내기'를 하며 스스로 긴장을 달래며 사기를 올리고 있었다.

작전 개시 후 약 1주일이 지나면서도 적 주력이 포착되지 않고 있던—포위망 밖으로 도주 또는 땅 밑 토굴로 피난—15일 초저녁, 일반 공개 이전에 전장 전방에 있는 군인 사기를 배려해 먼저 공개하는 미국 영화를 보기 위해 기밀실 앞 공간에, 상황실 당직자들을 제외한 TCP 요원들이 모여 있는 가운데, 영화를 막 시작했을 때, "짜 짱!"하는 소리와 함께 돌아보니, 약 150미터 거리에 포탄이 작렬하였다. 낙탄 거리가 좀 있다고 생각하는 순간 또 1발, 그러자 전원 해산하면서 함께 있던 참모장과 함께 대부분은 바로 옆 언덕 교통호(참호)로 뛰어들었다. 사단장은 지휘용 삽차에 그대로 있었다.

숨을 돌릴 사이 없이 머리 바로 위로 "쌩~,쓩~"하며 포탄이 지나가는가 했더니 불과 얼마 안 되는 뒤에서 "짜 짱!" 했다. 적은 장교 숙소와 지휘부를 노렸던 것으로 판단된다. 헤어 보니 모두 12발! 적의 82미리 박격포탄은 장교 숙소 지역에, 57미리 무반 동포는 영화보는 관중을 노렸으나, 운 좋게, 간발의 차이로 비켜나 머리 바로 위 10미터로 지나갔던 것이다. 다행히 큰 손실을 입지는 않았으나 동기생 1명이 때마침 장교 숙소 샤워실에서 샤워하다가 파편 경상을 입고 후송되었다.

그런데, 즉시 연대장은, 예비대 일부로 남아 있던 즉 연대 본부 중대로 하여금 맞은편 언덕 발포 지점을 수색 소탕하고, 그 지점에 경계조 잔류를 명하였다. 물론 적은 이미 도주한 뒤라 출동 주병력은 수색 정찰 후 철수하고 1개 분대가 '크레모아(지향성 대인지뢰)'로 무장하여 잔류하였다. 23.00시경 폭발음과 동시에 사고가 발생하였다. 잔류 경계 중이던 연대본부 중대요원—거의 현장 교전 경험을 갖지 못한—이 크레모아 설치 중 방향 오인(앞뒤 구분이 약간 어려움)과 사격 방법 부주의로 오발되어, 아군 방향으로 분탄되어 6명이 전사하고 3명이 부상당하는 1개 분대 자멸의 사고였다. 즉시 '다스탑(Dust Off, 구호 헬기)'이 날라 이들을 후송시켰는데 당시 그 '다스탑' 헬기(UH-1H)의 날개 소리, "타타타타"는 그 후 내 평생 당시 상황과 함께 '트라우마'로 남게 되었다.

◇ 베트콩 지역 수색작전 참가

7월 18일, 이날은 26연대 수색중대와 함께 'Ba산' 밑 계곡수색작전에 사단 정보참모와 함께 참가하였다. 하늘이 보이지 않는 정글 속의 계곡을 따라 바위와 나무 사이로 길 아닌 험한 길을 따라 전진하면서 여기가 과연 베트콩(VC)의 근거지였고, 격전지였음을 확인할 수 있었다. 두개골이 넘어져 있는 옆에 아직도 썩지 않은 월남인의 삿갓 모자가 뒹굴고, 곳곳에 저격용 개인 호가 산재해 있고 각종 불발 부비 추렙이 널려 있었다.

정글을 헤매며 땀을 닦아가며 눈을 360도로 쉴새 없이 돌려보며 신경은 온통 주위와 발밑을 살피기에 집중하며 3시간여, 드디어 정상쯤에 다다르니 한 움막집과 개간지가 나왔다. 근접전에 사격으로 탐색하였으나 저항이 없음을 확인하고, 그 집을 샅샅이 수색한 뒤 소각하고, 앞으로 더 나갔다. 도중에 '파인애플'밭에서 참외만 한 것을 따 칼로 껍질을 벗기고 생생한 속을 먹은 맛, 잊을 수 없었다. 18시 30분경, 어둠이 깔릴 때 중대원과 헤어져 헬기로 복귀하였다.

21일에는 역시 사단 정보참모와 함께 기갑연대 3대대 12중대를 동반하여 월맹 정규군 포로 2명을 앞세우고 그들 대대본부를 찾아 정글수색전에 참전하였다. 전 신경을 곤두세워 정글을 헤쳐나가기 3시간여, 드디어 그곳에 도착해 보니 3일 전에 있었다던 대대의 인적은 간곳없고 흔적만 남아 있었다. 소규모 훈련장, 의무 시설 장소, 대대장 숙소, 통신 시설, 큰 우물도 있었다. 아마도 홍길동의 무지개 칼날 빛이 번쩍일 때 이미 삼십육계 한 모양. 돌아오다가 길을 잃고 O-1기를 불렀으나 오히려 포로의 길 안내로 무사히 귀환할 수 있었다.

4. 1960년대 월남전쟁의 실상 ; 한국군과 미군의 이모저모

◇ 케네디 대통령의 적극 개입과 맥나마라 국방장관의 참전 후회

이미 미국 유학편에서 자세히 소개한 것처럼 미국 '케네디 대통령'은 소련 '후루시쵸프'의 '평화공존론'의 속임수를 간파하고, 60년대 초에 정치 모략전을 포함하는 '특수전(Special Warfare)' 개념을 확립하고, 베트남전쟁에 깊이 개입하였다. 특히 'Green Beret, 미특수전부대' 도시에서도 운용하였다고 소설에 나와 있으나, 확인 못하였고, 다만 '호치민 통로' 지역인 국경 산악 지역 요소요소(월맹군의 남하 통로상, 캄보디아와의 국경 감시 지점)에 평지 월남인을 싫어하는 산악 부족(Mountaineer, 몽타냐)—역사적으로 월남 원주민이었으나 침략자를 피해 산악 지역으로 피난 후 정착한 원주족—을 고용하여 'CIDG, Civilian Irregular Defense Group' 기지(基地)를 편성, 직접 운용하였다.

미국 케네디와 존슨 대통령 당시 미국방장관이던 '맥나마라'는, 당시 국제 정치학계와 함께 '전쟁의 과학화 즉 계량화'—특히 '비용대 효과(PPBS, Planning, Programming, Budgeting System)' 이론이 한때를 풍미하였음—를 주장하면서 '워게임'을 실시(1968년경)한 결과, 월남전쟁은 1966년에 이미 미국 승리로 끝났다고 나왔다. 그럼에도 실상은 오히려 더 불리해 지기만 했다고, 자신의 이론에 대한 회의를 나타내었고, 결국 1995년에 발간된 회고록을 통해, 그는 '베트남전쟁을 후회한다(Rrgret Vietnam War)'는 말로 '월남인의 전쟁 의지에 대한 오판을 후회한다'고 했다.

◇ 부자나라 미국의 월남 물량전(物量戰)

말한 바와 같이 'Arc Light폭격(또는 융단폭격, Carpet Bombardment)' 양상에서 본 바와 같이 전쟁과 전투에 우리네의 상상을 초월하는 거대 물량을 투입할 수 있는 나라는 전 세계에서 오로지 미국뿐일 것이다. 초기 파월 한국군은 한국에서 하던 대로 미군 '대포(보급창, DEPOT)'에 가서 요구서(예, 435개)를 내밀면 창고 담당 미군은 웃어가며 자기 펜으로 동그라미 2~3개를 더 붙여서, '박스떼기'로 차에 실어 주었다. 이를 처음 경험한 한국군은 미군의 풍족한 전쟁 지원에 처음엔 감탄하다가 나중엔 습성이 되어 이후부터 그렇게 알고 신청하고 그렇게 알고 수령해 왔다.

예를 들어 한 번의 전투에서 전투 손실된 수통, 삽, 탄피 등을 신청하고 수령하고는 소모품으로까지 생각하고 소홀히 하면서 전투 후에 또 신청하고 수령하였다. 특히 전투식량인 'C-Ration'도 무한정으로 보급받아 사용하였다. 그러다가 1970년대 들어서면서 미군 물자 정산 과정에서 한국군은 'C-Ration'을 3년간에 7년 분을 소모하였다는 기록이 나오기도 했다고 한다.

한 전투가 끝나면 '위문품 세트'라 하여 고등학생 개인 책상보다 큰 박스 하나를 1개 소대마다 선물해 온다. 내용은 주로 기호품으로 담배, 커피 과자, 각종 식품 캔 그리고 '덩어리 초콜릿' 등으로 구성되어 있다. 그런가 하면 한국군에게는 기본적으로 미군 전투식량에다가 한국 쌀을 포함해 보급하여 식량은 먹고도 남았다. 사단사령부에서는 한국 쌀 등을 주변 월남 시장에서 채소로 바꾸어서 먹기도 하였는데, 병사들은 원망하기를, "우리에게는 고기만 주고 장교들은 채소를 먹는다"고 하는 말이 유행하였다.

1966년 12월 25일 크리스마스 때는 각 부대에 여러 선물 박스와 함께 종이로 된 크리스마스 추리들이 보급되었으며, 그날은 한국군 부대 위로 연락기를 띄워 '화이트 크리스마스 노래'를 종일 방송하면서 이 열대지방의 전투 현장에 크리스마스 분위기를 고조시켜주기도 하였다.

한국군 참전 장병 모두에게 계급별로 다르게 전투 수당이 지급되었다. 대위에게는 월 150달러였는데, 30달러 정도 현지에서 쓰고 나머지 120달러 정도를 한국 집으로 보내면, 집에서는 한국 월급으로 생활하면서 보내준 돈을 1년간 적금하면 30여만 원이 조성되는데, 이는 당시 서울 변두리의 15평 국민주택 구입이 가능할 정도였다. 농촌 병사들은 그렇게 해서 황소를 구입할 수 있었다.

그런가 하면 전투부대는 중대까지 주둔지역 안정작전용으로 월남 돈(월 100달러 정도)으로 지급되어 중대장이 지역민과의 소통용으로 활용하였다. 어디 그뿐인가, 전후 고엽제로 인한 신체장애자에게 전상자 수당으로 적게는 70만 원에서 많게는 150여만 원까지 평생은 물론 다음 세대까지 혜택을 주고 있다. 본인도 전장 고엽제 영향으로 발병한 '허혈성 심장병'으로 그 수혜자 중 한 사람이다. 이렇게 할 수 있는 나라가 앞으로도 미국 외 있을 수 없을 것이다.

나는 단기(單騎)로 전장을 누벼야 하기에 종종 도로 가까이에 있는 미군 부대 주유소에 들려 휘발유를 보충하였는데, 언제나 무한정 그리고 반갑게 주유해 주었다. 또한 전장으로 갈 때는 미군 'C-Raion'을 6개 들이 큰 박스 그대로 차에 실어서 출발하였고, 어디에서나 머물러 운전병과 함께 풍족하게 식사하며 다녔다. 사단사령부에는 한국군에서 못 보던 아늑하고 아담한 '장교 클럽'이 신설되어서 틈나는 대로 이용했고, 양주는 물론 커피와 사이다 등 청량음료수 등은 무료로 서비스되었다. 이 모두 미군의 지원으로 되었다.

미군부대 각 지역별로 'PX(편의점)'가 운영되고 있는데, 말이 편의점이지 생필품에 사치품까지 다 있었는데, 전장인 월남 지역에서는 한국 지역과도 같이 완전 면세였다. 미군이 주문해서 후방 자기 가정에 배달시키기도 하고 후방으로 전속 가면서 주문해 갈 수도 있었는데, 일제 냉장고 등 가전 제품에서 프랑스 화장품(샤넬5 등)에 이르기까지 부족함이 없었다.—특히 당시는 미국이 전후 일본을 민주화시키기 위해 경제를 부흥시키면서 관세 특혜를 주어가며 일제를 수입 사용하였는데, 그래서 군대 'PX'에도 일제 물품이 상당하였다.
그 덕에 한국군(사단급 이상)에도 그런 'PX'가 설치 운용되었는데, 다만 일부 물품은 제한(가전제품 등)되었으나, 예를 들어 프랑스 화장품 '샤넬 5' 등은 얼마든지 구입할 수 있었다.

◇ 미군은 전술적 승리 단, 전략적 패배

미국 군대와 장병은 우수하고 용감하며 낙천적이고, 형식보다 실제로 절대 책임 완수하였고, 'Arc Light 폭격'을 비롯하여 전장정찰 사진 및 위성 사진 정보, 헬기는 물론 개인 M16소총 등, 월맹 정규군이나 베트콩보다 월등하였다. 특공대(Kommando)는 헬기 양편 발판에 서서 기동하며 정글 속의 적 지역 상공을 저공으로 날으며 적을 수색 및 소탕하였고, 헬기 조종사는 심지어 정글 속에서 올라온 적탄에 맞아가면서도 저공 비행하며 임무를 수행하고, 웬만한 폭풍우라 할지라도 한 번 나왔으면 기어이 임무를 수행하였다.

한국군 사단사령부에 파견된 '화력협조관(통상 소령급)'은 평소 철모도 벗고, 장교 클럽에서 한잔하기도 하나 때가 되면 1분도 틀림없이 제자리에 나타나 책임을 완수하였다. 미군 장병의 책임성과 그 능력은 모범 직업군인 그대로 였다. 월남에서 패배한 것은 미국(군)의 정치 안보전략과 군사안보전략 이지 미군 전술이나 미군 개인이 아니었다.

일제가 중국을 침략하여 패배한 것은 '점과 선의 전략'— 그럴 수밖에 없었지만—의 취약성 때문이었다. 물량전에 익숙하고 기동전에 전통화된 미국(군)의 전략은 더하여 지상에서는 점과 점(요지요부)만을 확보하고, 정보에 의해 공중에서 적 주력을 찾아 타격하여 섬멸하고, 곧 기지(점)로 철수해 다음 큰 먹이를 기다리는 것이었다. 말하자면 선이나 면의 확보 없이, 다만 적 핵심 전력들을 골라 섬멸하면 전쟁에 승리할 것으로 믿는 것이었다. 지금도 미국은 물량을 동원한 전략 폭격이나 적 핵심 지역(지점) 타격을 중요시하고 있다. 역사가 증명하듯이 특히 게릴라전에서는 백전백패의 전략 전술인 것이다.

* 2021년 8월 31일의 '아프칸' 철수에서 다시 한번 미국(군)의 전략에 문제가 있음을 증명하고 있다 .

월남전에서 좀 구체적으로 말하면, 충분한 공중기 동력과 화력으로 무장한 미군 부대는 일정 지역에 대부대로 기지화하여 주둔하면서 여러 가지 정보 수단을 이용하여 획득한 정보를 통해서 또는 실제 소규모 부대 수색작전을 통해 적을 확인하고 이를 물고 있으면, 그 즉시 헬기로 타격 부대가 신속히 출격하여 이를 소탕한다는 개념이고, 동시에 공중으로도 마치 매가 먹이를 찾아 날듯 수시로 헬기를 이용해 정글 위를 날아다니며 'Search & Destroy" 전을 전개하는 개념이었다. 객관적으로 보기에는 그때마다 주력이 섬멸되면 전력이 상실됨으로써 전투에 승리할 것으로 믿었다. 그러나 더구나 정글 속의 대 게릴라전은 그것이 아니었다.

또한 미군의 각 수단에 의한 정보 특히 항공정보와 위성 정보 등은 정확하나, 수집—분석—에하전투부대 전달되고도, 작전 계획 수립, 작전 개시 등 최소 3일 정도의 시간 소요로, 실시간 정보가 되지 못한 반면, 적은 그 2~3일 사이에 보다 한발 빠르게 도피 및 도망하였다.

◇ 한국군의 월남전 전략과 작전

한국군은 기동전을 위한 물리적 수단이 불비하였던 영향도 받았지만, 보다 근본적으로 전략 사상을 달리하고 있었다. '전투에서 승리는 마지막으로 보병이 그 땅을 밟고 서 있어야 하는 것'이었다. 그래서 비록 월남 정부의 주권이 미치는 전장터라 할지라도 한국군은 면의 작전인 '전술 책임 지역'(TAOR)을 원했고, 무력으로 지역을 평정 후에는 주민 안정작전(Counter Insuergency)을 실시하여 게릴라 물고기가 놀 수 없게 물을 마르게 하면서 축차적으로 지배 지역을 확장해 나갔던 것이다. 허기야 월남전에서 완승을 위해 이런 전략을 구사하려면 당시 투입된 병력의 수배에다가 특히 월남군의 전투 역량 회복이 필수적이었는데, 그렇게까지는 다하지 못하였다.

파월 한국군은 전략적으로나 전술적으로 '깔아뭉게기작전(重複反轉作戰)'과 '토끼몰이작전(망치모루작전, Hammerhead-Anvil OP)'을 활용하였다. 특히 사단규모작전일 경우 대규모 병력이 헬기로 일시에 정글 속 적을 포위하여 랜딩하고 망치가 되고, 동시에 모루가 되는 병력을 육로 또는 육지기동으로 투입하여 쇄기를 박았다. 그리하여 포위 병력은 토끼몰이식으로 포위망을 좁혀오면서 모루 방향으로 내려쳐 갔다. 또한 일단 지나갔던 곳도 전술적으로나 전략적으로 다시 되돌아와 땅굴이나 논, 밭의 굴속에 잠적했다가 되돌아(온)오는 적을 수색 소탕하였다. 다시 말하면 문자 그대로 지역소탕작전을 끈질기게 실시하여 청소하였던 것이다.

다만 사단장(유병현 장군)의 명령으로 모든 착륙부대는 현지점에서 일단 주변작전을 전개시키고 포위 토끼몰이작전은 며칠간 지연 통제하기도 하였다. 예하 연대장들이 포위망 속의 적을 다 놓칠 것 같다는 건의에도 그러했다. 당시 사단장의 지휘 의도는, 치열하지 않은 전투에서 가능한 아군의 손실도 고려—이점은 전투 원칙에 어긋나지만, 추측건대 박정희 대통령의 은근한 당부였을 지도 모른다.—하고, 적과의 접촉을 유지하면서 포위망을 조급히 압축해 나가는 것보다 적이 미리 알고 스스로 도피/도망하여 포위망 속에 들어가게 하려는 의도로 볼 수 있었다. 그리하여 당분간 현장을 유지하다가, 며칠 후 일제히 내려가면서 평지 시내로 소탕 겸 적 몰이를 해 나갔다.

◇ 전장에서 1승 1패는 병가지상사(兵家之常事)

전쟁(작전)에는 공격도 있고 방어도 있으며, 성공도 있고 실패도 있으며, 성과도 있는가 하면 손실도 있게 마련이다. 그래서 일찍부터 '일승일패는 병가지상사'라는 말이 있다. 내가 현장에서 체험하고 목격한 아쉬운 손실 사항 몇 가지를 보자. 하루는 기갑연대 대대장(육사 11기 선배)이 단기(單騎, 운전병 1명과)로 Anke Pass—'플레이크'로 가는 19번 도로 길목—지역의 예하 중대기지 순찰 방문길에 베트콩의 기습을 받고 분전하였으나 전사하였다.

같은 연대 모 중대는 중대 인접 바나나밭으로 접근한 여자 3명을 베트콩으로 오인, 경계 과잉으로 모두 사살하였는데, 알고 보니 그 동네 처녀들이었다. 며칠 뒤 베트콩이, 동네 앞을 가로지르는 보급로 안전 확보차 출동한 1개 분대 정찰조를 매복 기습하여 전원을 무참히 살상하고 무전기를 포함 장비 일체를 피탈당하는, 파월맹호부대 전사상 전무후무한 사고가 발생하였다. 그래서 나는 급히 현장에 출동하여 상황 파악과 교훈을 도출하여 전파하였다. 사단에서는 군법회의를 개최하고 중대장을 엄벌한 뒤 고국으로 즉각 후송하였다.

또한, 내일 작전출 동을 앞둔 모연대 2중대가 경계 소홀로 메트콩의 중대기지 기습(식량 조달용)을 받아 순식간에 전사 11 부상 22명, 상당수의 총기 장비는 물론 출동 준비용 '전투식량' 모두를 피탈당하는 맹호부대 치욕의 날도 있었다. 또한 바로 다음 날, 천하 제1을 자랑하는 연대가 수색 정찰 활동 중 베트콩의 유인 매복에 걸려 1개소대 1/18명이 전멸(3명 부상)하는 또 한 건의 불상사가 발생하기도 하였다.

또한 '홍길동작전' 중에 주력 연대 전투 요원들이 약간 명 전사와 부상이 있었는데, 그 중에서도 5중대가 점심 식사 시간에 적의 기습을 받아 5명 전사, 6명 부상하였다. 그런데 안타깝게도 소대장은 파월 3일 만에 전사하여 전우들의 마음을 울렸다.

또 전투 중에 잠간 휴식 중이던 아군 1개 분대를 아군 4.2인치 포대가 계산척 오산(10도각)으로 오폭, 분대 전원이 전사한 사건도 있었다. 사단사령부 김 소령은 귀국 며칠 앞서 '플레이크' 미군기지로 귀국 선물 보러 갔다가 헬기 사고를 당하는 경우도 있었다.

◇ 전장 심리 ; '뽕짝', '아리랑 잡지', '담배'만이 낙일 수도

전쟁 철학자 '클라우제빗츠'는 말하기를, "전쟁은 참혹한 것"이라고. 한국전쟁에 참전했던 한 용사는, "전투 현장 상황은 언급 불가하니 묻지도 마시라"고 하였다. 사실이다. 전장/전투 현장의 묘사는 물론 당시의 심리 현상도 말로는 설명하기 어려운 현상이 전개되기 때문이다.

(일기장) ; 어젯밤 야간 매복에서 베트콩의 빈딩성 재무 담당을 비롯한 간부 5명이 동시에 사살되었다는 보고를 받고 혹시 중요한 정보를 건질 수 있을까 하고 사단 정보참모와 함께 다음날 헬기로 현장에 가보았다. 내리는 순간 그 야릇한 시체 썩는 냄새가 주변에 진동하기에 여기가 바로 그 전쟁터라고 보기도 전에 알려주었다.

예상되는 적 보복 공격 등 긴장된 분위기에서 현장에 도착해 보니 우리 전투 요원들이 경계하고 있는 가운데 5구의 베트콩 시체가 나란히 있었는데 특히 여자 시체가 바로 최고 간부라했다. 성공적으로 작전을 지휘했던 중대장의 안내와 설명으로 '사전에 입수된 정보'에 의한 전투 상황을 파악할 수 있었고, 더불어 탈취한 문서 등을 넘겨받아 차후작전에 도움되도록 분석하기로 하였다. 돌아서니 병사들이 시체 처리를 하면서 여자 속을 헤집어

보기도 하는 모양이 보였다.

미군의 사기 앙양 방법에는 여러 가지가 있으나 특히 미국 국민들의 관심의 표현으로, 최고 인기 배우들의 전투부대 방문 장병 위로 행사와, 개봉전 인기 영화의 전장 현지 개봉 등도 있다. 우리나라는 아직 그런 수준의 전장 장병위로 전통이 수립되지는 못하였지만 그래도 군부대 '위문 공연'의 전통은 있어 왔다. 일 년 기간 중에 한국 유명 가수들의 방문이 한두 차례는 있었던 것으로 기억된다.

하루는 당시 한국의 유명 가수 '패티 김'과 '길옥윤' 팀이 단독으로 왔었다. 1차로 사단 사령부와 근처 부대—제1군수지원단 과 제1야전병원—장병들이 사령부 연병장에 모여앉은 가운데 공연이 시작되었다. 그런데 자기 자랑으로부터 시작하여 영어 노래말 해설까지 하면서 영어로 된 노래 즉 미군들이 선호하는 미군 부대용 노래를 가창하기 시작하였는데, 장병들은 기대한 것이 아닌 듯 흥겨워하지 않았다. 그런데도 도중에 청중 태도에 대한 설교도 해가며 영어 노래를 계속하였다. 그러자 박수는커녕 야유가 나오기 시작했다. 좀 가서는 여기저기서 나중에는 합창으로 "치워라, 그만하고 돌아가라"며 모두가 일어서려는 것을 지휘관들이 겨우 말려가며 끝내었다. 주월 한국군 전부대가 그랬는데, 미군부대에 가서는 환영을 받았다고 한다.

그런가 하면 하루는 한국 당대의 유명 '뽕짝'—당시만 해도 한국에는 유행가 즉 트롯 전성시대였다—가수들 이미자, 현미, 김세레나 등이 방문하여 위문 공연을 가졌는데, 정말 그 인기는 물론 완전히 가수들과 정서가 맞아 때창과 춤으로 한바탕 난리가 나섰다. 본국에서 같은 멤버들에 의한 위문 공연 때보다 비교할 수 없으리만큼 열광의 도가니였다. 말할 것도 없이 '패티 킴' 공연과는 완전히 다른 현상이었다. 이 현상은 첫째로 집 떠나 그리운 내 나라 향수에다가 '전장 심리'가 작용하고 있었던 것이다. 전장에서는 좀 심하게 말하면, '아리랑 잡지'와 '우리 유행가' 그리고 담배만이 낙일 때가 많았다.

◇ 월남과 미국은 왜 패망하였는가—'Saigon Dep Lam'

1967년 여름, 내 퀸셀 사무실을 찾아온 어떤 미국 기자가 월남전쟁의 전망을 물었다. 나는 주저하지 않고 말했다, "미군이 철수하면 그 5분 뒤에 월남은 패망한다"고. 1975년 4월 30일 조조, 마지막 헬기로 미국이 완전히 철수해 가자 그 바로 2시간 뒤(10시)에 월남 정부는 무조건 항복하였다. 이는 곧 미국 역사상 드문 전쟁 패배이기도 하였다.

미국의 패배 원인을 간단히 말하면, 미국 정치가들의 '잘못 판단된 국가 이익과 그에 따른 잘못 선택된 전략'에 있었다. 당시 미국 국가안보(전략) 키워드들은, 키신저의 '리얼 폴리티크(Real Politik), 데땅떼(Detente)', 닉슨의 '발란스 오프 파워(Balance of Power)', '차이나 카드(China Card)' 등으로 점령되어 있었다. 그 때문에 미국은 한국전 이후 또다시 정치가 군사를 지배하여, 잘못된 국가 전략 즉 공산 월맹과 휴전 협정을 '평화 협정'이라는 명분으로 감행함으로서, 그나마 전술적으로는 '선제를 장악하고 있던 미군'에게 패배를 감수하게 하였던 것이다.

물론 미국만의 탓이 아니다. 오히려 직접적인 패배 원인은, 월남 자신에게 있었다. 첫째는 월남 역사가 말해준다. 프랑스 제국주의자가 서세동점시기 일찍부터 침략하여, '바오다이' 봉건 왕조를 그대로 괴뢰 정권으로 하여 식민지 지배를 받아오는 동안, 민족주의자들은 끈질긴 저항 즉 독립운동을 전개하였는데, 우리나라 임정(임시정부)과는 달리 월남은, 후반에 가서 국제공산주의 특히 중공의 지원을 받은 '호지명'파가 주도권을 행사하였다.

2차 세계대전 후에도 프랑스 제국주의와 바오다이왕이 식민지 체제 그대로 지배하려 하자, 직접적으로는 중공의 지원— 실은 국제공산주의 운동—으로 17도선 이북을 지배하게 된 호지명 집단과 남쪽 월남 내 민족독립운동자(베트콩)들이 합세하여 무력으로 이들을 타도하고 독립을 쟁취함으로써 월남전쟁이 발발하게 되었던 것이다. 그러기에 월남 내 (국민) 분위기는 일차적으로 '호지명'을 옹위하여 민족독립 운동이 계속해서 불타고 있었던 것이다.

나는 파월 1년 근무 종료를 앞두고 월남의 전통적 수도인 동시에 당시 월남공화국의 수도인 '사이곤'(Saigon)—1965년부터 유행된 '사이공 데프람(Saigon Dep Lam, 아름다운 사이공)'이라는 노래도 있는 그곳—을 3박 4일로 위로 여행을 가보았다. 밤에는 경비가 철저한 연합군 숙소용 호텔에서 자고 낮에는 주로 온 도시 구경했지만, 당시 주월한국군사령부도 있었기에, 혼자서 낯설지도 않은 그런 곳, 중국인 화교 거리인 '쵸론(Cho-Lon, Big Market)'에서 먹으며 시간을 보냈다.

1967년 전시에 잠깐 가본 사이공에서 아주 깊은 사회 불평등과 그로 인한 갈등 요소 그래서 '민란의 원인' 즉 불과 몇 년 전 미국 '케네디 센터'에서 배운 'Rising Expectation'이 생각나지 않을 수 없었다. 당장 대부분의 시민들은 그저 걸어서 활동하고 소수는 겨우 낡은 오토바이 등으로 이동 수단을 삼고 있는 터에, 뚜렷이 표나는 상류사회 지배 계급은 프랑스제 자가용으로 그것도 여자가 운전하며—한국도 당시에는 꿈도 꾸지 못한—시내를 누비는 호화사치가 있는가 하면 내 숙소인 호텔, 현재 한국의 4스타급, 에는 밤낮으로 몸 팔려는 아가씨들로 길이 막힐 지경이고, 밤에는 아예 호텔 내 복도 여기저기에 누워 자는 등, 극도의 계급 차 즉 사회 불평등을 보여주었다.

그런가 하면, 당시 90% 가까운 농촌에서는 여전히 소작농 시대를 벗어나지 못하고 대부분은 지방 부호들의 봉건 시대 가렴주구 대상이 되고 있었다. 예를 들면 소작농 아이들이 토호(호농, 지주)들의 소를 먹이며 생존하는데, 만일에 한 마리라도 잘못되면 그 아이는 벌로, 밤에 들판에서 지세우며 모기에게 뜯기게 하는데, 월남 모기는 군용 담요 한 장쯤은 쉽게 뚫을 수 있기에 이는 보통 인권 유린이 아닌 것이다. 그렇지 않아도 공산주의자들의 선동선전에다 실제 사회 현상이 이러한데다 새로 생겼다는 '월남공화국'마저 '구 식민지 그대로 체제'에 부정부패가 더 극심해지다 보니 월남 패망은 나 같은 일개 외국 군인 대위에게도 확실하게 보였던 것이다.

광복 당시, 이와 아주 유사하였던 우리 대한민국은 제국주의 시대가 종식되고 잠깐의 군정 시대가 지나자 말자 바로 민주주의 국가로 건국되어, 이승만 대통령에 의해 토지 개혁으로 소작농 시대 마감은 물론 '일제 식민지 청산'하고 수정자본주의 국가 체제로 출발함으로써 심지어 '6·25 적화남침'에도 민란이 없이 안전이 보장될 수 있었던 것이다.

◇ 월남전쟁이여 안녕, 드디어 귀국(1967.10.13~23)

인명재천이라, 나를 포함한 전우들(대부분 소령 이하 장병들)은 1년간의 파월 전투 지원 임무를 마치고 한국에서 온 보충 전투 요원과 교대하고, 군목기도와 함께 거행된 귀국 신고식을 마치고, 무사히 드디어 귀국선—미군 고용선 'Barret'호 18,000톤—에 올랐다. 이 귀국선은 맹호부대의 전쟁터 '승리와 비극'의 퀴논을 뒤로 해안을 따라 서서히 북상하여 다음 날 '나트랑'에 기항하고, 귀국 해병대 요원 등을 승선시킨 뒤, 그다음 날(15일) 긴장의 연속이었던 월남전쟁터를 뒤로하고 만감이 교차하는 가운데 그리운 내 조국을 향해 일로 북상하기 시작하였다. '비극의 월남이여 안녕 !'

그러나 출항과 동시에 태풍 'Color'호가 태평양상에서 우리를 환영해 주었다. 수송선이 태풍의 뒤를 따라 '핏칭' 20피트(파고 6미터)와 동시에 비슷한 '요잉'을 반복해 가며 대략 7.5노트 서행으로 항행하여 24시간 정도 지나자, 병사 2/3와 장교 1/2가 K.O로 들어누웠다. 그렇게도 풍족하고 구미 좋았던 식당도 텅텅 빈 날이 며칠간 계속되었다.

다행히도 나는 괜찮아 로비에 앉아 그러나 처음 당해보는 태풍 속 항해에 불안한 마음으로, 좌우 앞뒤로 바다만 보였다가 하늘만 보였다가 반복하는 사태를 관광할 수밖에 없었고 때때로 선원들의 행동을 눈치해 보기도 하였다. 일엽편주란 말이 있는데, 실제로 그 태풍의 바닷속에 3~4백여미터 근방에 몇백 톤급 선박 하나가 정말 아슬아슬하게 마음대로 흔들리면서 파도 위에서 보였다 살아졌다를 반복하는 문자 그대로 일엽편주의 모습이 정말 안타까워 보기가 어려웠다.

한 4일 뒤부터(22일) 마지막 일찍사령을 명받고 총원 상태를 파악하면서 선장과도 월남전쟁을 논하고 얘기하며 수송선 마지막 밤을 보낸 뒤 23일 08시 정각에 1년 전에 떠났던 그 부산 부두에 되돌아와 시민들의 환영과 가족 친지들의 환영을 받으며 무사히 귀국하였다. 전장에서 살아 돌아온 나는, 비록 무공훈장은 없었으나, 우리 가족 특히 아내를 당당하게 온몸으로 안으며 잠깐이나마 그 간의 심신의 고생을 위로해 주려 하였다. 실로 감개무량하다는 말은 이때 실감하였다.

제6장

서독 지휘참모대학(Fűhrungs Academie der Bundeswehr) 유학(1969~1971)

1. 서독 지휘참모대학으로 유학가다

◇ 서독 군사학교 유학 목적과 준비

월남전쟁에 참전하였다가 귀국 후 잠시 육군본부 특전감실에서 근무하였다. 그런데 이 시대 '라인강의 기적'을 이룬 서독은 국가와 사회 전반적으로 우리 한국에 아주 큰 부흥의 모범으로 인식되어 있었다. 더구나 서독에 광부와 간호원들이 파견되어 가고 박정희 대통령이 가서 그들을 위로 격려하면서 다시금 서독이 우리 민족 부흥의 마스코트로 상징되기도 하였다. 그런가 하면 우리 직업 군인 하고도 전략가에게는 배움의 대상이었다. '보불(普佛)전쟁'과 '보오(普奧)전쟁'의 군사 정치적 승리 전략을 비롯하여, 제1, 2차 세계대전에서 군사적 승리와 정치적 패배, 위대한 '크라우제빗츠'의 전쟁 철학, '롬멜과 구데리안'의 전격전(電擊戰)과 기갑 전술, 그리고 전쟁 중에는 연합국 전략가들을 놀라게 하고 끝내는 전범재판에 넘겨진 독일군의 'General Stab(본인 주 ; 핵심참모제도)', '슐리펜의 함마헤드 전략 계획' 등과 이러한 역사를 남긴 독일군 자체에 대해 견문 또한 소원이었다.

이러한 생도 시절 이후 본인의 희망을 위해서는 물론, 당시 한국 안보전략의 화두였던 '자주 국방론'과 동맹국 미국이 구상 중이던 '환태평양 안보기구'와의 관계 연구를 위해서도 서유럽의 NATO와 서독군과의 관계 등을 현지에서 관찰하며 연구해 보려는 목적도 있었다. 또한 감히 접근하기 어려운 신천지 미국 문화에 비해 근대 문명의 선도자로 볼 수 있는 유럽의 문화 문명을 현지에서 체험하며 관찰하여 우리 한국의 미래 발전에 기여할 수 있는 연구 과제를 찾아보려는 목적도 가지고 있었다.

그런데 당시 한국군에서 외국 육군대학(급)에 유학은 미국이 주류—전적으로 미국 원조 부담—를 이루어 오다가 3년 전부터 케나다 독일까지 확대되었다. 5·16 혁명 후 계속해서 국가GDP가 증가됨에 따라 외국 유학 비용도 생활비는 한국, 교육비는 해당 국가 부담으로 발전하였다. 그래도 여전히 기혼자 동반 유학까지는 경제적 사정이 허락되지 못했다.

한편 당시까지만 해도 독일 군사 유학은 사실상 잘 알려지지도 않았거니와 특별한 '메리트'도 없는 것 같이 보여 지원자가 거의 없었다. 이번(1970년)으로 3회차인데 금년에는 영관급 참모대학 과정에는, 기갑병과 장교 1명, 보병병과 장교 1명 그리고 해병대 장교 1명을 선발하였는데, 보병병과 후보자는 나 혼자뿐이었다. 참모대학 과정외 독일 병과학교 과정(대위급) 2명, 사관학교 과정 2명도 동시에 모집하였다.

그런데 당시에는 그와 같은 여건으로 아직도 독일 유학 준비는 생소하였는데, 고등학교 때 잠시 독일어 공부를 해 보았으나 새삼스러웠다. 최종적으로 주한 독일대사관에서 무경쟁으로 필기시험과 간단한 면접을 본 뒤 바로 출발 준비를 통보받았다. 사실은 이미 독일 국가 어학 기관에 유학 다녀온 민병돈 육사 교수, 바로 절친 후배로부터 전 과정에 걸쳐 전적인 도움을 받았었다. 지금도 그에게 감사할 뿐이다.

그런데 막상 생각해 보니 월남전쟁에서 귀국한 지 1년여 만에 다시 가족을 두고 앞으로 1년 8개월여를 떠나 있어야 할 것을 생각하니 참 안타까운 생각이 들었다. 나야 100% 배움의 희망을 가지고 유학 가지만 남아 있어 아이들과 오랫동안 살림을 해나가야 할 아내를 생각하니 미안하기가 말이 아니었다. 내가 다짐하였다, 앞으로 성공하고 또 발전해 가는 그것으로 당신의 고생을 보상해 주리라고.

◇ 북극으로 돌아 유럽, 서독 여정

그런데 서독 어학 학교 개강일을 맞추어 출발해야 하나 국회에서 신년도 예산이 통과되지 못해 그해 전용 예산으로 겨우 69년 1월 3일에야 출발할 수 있었다. 내 책임(주독 한국대사관 무관실까지)으로 함께 가는 두 사관생도가 있었는데, 둘 다 육사 2학년 진급생으로 한 생도는 서울고교 출신의 김관진(후에 국방장관, 안보실장), 또 한 생도는 경기고교 출신의 박흥환(후에 군단장)이었다.

우리는 육군본부 신고에서 "몸 건강히 소기의 성과를 달성하고 돌아오라"는 참모총장의 훈시를 되새기면서 대한항공 'DC—9'으로 김포공항을 이륙하였다. 김포공항에는 가족과 친한 동기생들이 환송 나와 주었는데 특히 우리 가족과 함께 민병돈 교수 내외도 나와주어서 고마웠다. 특히 비행기 타랍에 올라서서 환송대에 있는, 앞으로 또 1년 반 동안 떨어져 있어야 할 내 가족에게 인사 전할 때는 책임감과 함께 감개가 벅차기도 했다.

불과 2시간여 뒤에 일본 동경(東京) Haneda 국제공항에 도착, 하룻밤 하루 낮 일정으로 체류하였다. 다음날 6시간 반 5달러짜리 패키지로 시내 관광 하였다. 기억에 남은 것은, 'Tokyo Tower'로 다음 해 '세계 EXPO'를 위해 만들었는데 프랑스 에펠타워 모형으로 덩치는 작았으나 높이는 '2피트'가 높다며 자랑하였다.

다음은 우리 한국인에게는 일제(日帝) 시대 상징물로 각인되어 있는 소위 '메이지 신궁(神宮)'에 안내되었는데, 마침 정초라 많은 일본인들 특히 여성들이 우리 한복과 같은 유형의 '기모노'라는 원피스를 입고 정면에 서서 소원을 말하고, 바로 앞에 깊이와 폭 약 1미터에 길이 30미터도 넘는 쇠바구니 안에 동전을 던져넣는데, 벌써 쌓이고 쌓여서 눈대중으로 보아도 20가마니는 넘을 것 같았다. 그럼에도 폭 20미터 길이 1키로미터는 족히 되보이는 신전으로 가는 길은 정초 소원 기도를 위한 남녀노소 시민들로 가득하였다. 물론 각 나라마다 나름대로 국민 단결의 방법이 있지만 일본은 이렇게 독특한 정서적 전통 관습으로 국민의 정신을 통합시키고 있었다.

다음은 일본인의 '천연 진주 양생법'을 보여주며 기술 자랑도 하였는데 당시는 관광객 모두가 신기하고 흥미롭게 볼 수 있었다. 어두워질 무렵 마지막에는 바로 '밤거리'로 안내하였는데, 인간의 말초신경을 자극하는 강한 색조에 밤거리 여자의 향기, 술과 춤과 도박 그리고는 바가지! 일본은 그런 동네와 기생들을 예나 지금이나 사회적으로 공공연하게 묵인하며 돈벌이와 관광객을 유치하는 수단으로 삼고 있었다. 특히 전쟁 직후에는 주둔 미군을 상대로 '달러 박스'로도 번성하였는데, 소위 '기생 외교'로도 한몫한 곳이기도 하였다. 일본에는 지금도 '특히 사람의 아랫도리에 관해서는 말을 삼가라'는 사회적, 특히 언론적 묵계가 있다고 한다.

그럼에도 약 8년 전 미국 유학을 위해 김포비행장을 출발할 때의 지상 풍경이나 그 감회도, 또 그리고 일본 나리타공항(당시는 미군용)에 도착하여 시내를 돌아보던 그 흥미로웠던 감회는 없었다. 그동안 '5·16 군사혁명 정부'와 박정희의 제3공화국이 이룩한 우리 강산 천지 개벽의 민족 중흥으로 일본 동경의 풍경도 그렇게 낯설지 않았고, 김포의 양철지붕 풍경을—불과 8여 년 전에는 초가지붕 일색이었는데—내려다본 감회 또한 별다르지 않았다.

다음날 새벽(지연)에 SAS(스웨덴 항공)편으로 동경을 이륙하여 미국 '알라스카'의 수도 '앵커라지'로 향하였는데 한때는 집중 폭우와 천둥 번개 속을 비행하기에 긴장도 되었다. 일단 '앵커라지'에 기착 후 바로 이륙하였는데, 새벽의 동경에서 불과 3~4시간 사이에 해가 지고 밤이 되었다. 비행기는 북극 방향으로 비행하는데 좌전방으로 '진한 오로라'와 유사한 현상이 한참 계속되었다. 새벽이 되자 북극점을 통과하였는데—당시는 동서냉전 중이라 중공이나 소련 상공을 통과하지 못해 북극으로 우회하여 유럽으로 비행하고 있었다.—기내 안내 방송으로 설명하고 기념품을 나누어주기도 하였다. 여기 북극점까지 오는 동안 식사 시간에는 삼각형 포장 치즈가 나왔는데, 옛날 미국 유학 때 경험이 있었으나 여전히 그 냄새 때문에 금방 입에 넣지를 못했다.

식사 전후해서 밑으로 보이는 눈 덮인 시베리아 툰드라 지대는 보기에 정말 가관이었다. 조금 더 지나자 유럽의 초원 지대가 나왔는데 이 풍경 또한 처음이라 마음을 아주 시원하게 해주었다. 그러다가 일차 목적지 유럽 덴마크의 '코펜하겐'으로 접근해 가자 점차 캄캄한 비구름 속으로 비행하였는데, 하강하는데도 주변이 보이지 않은 비구름 속이라 승객 모두가 긴장된 모습이었다. 나 또한 속으로 이제는 '달에도 착륙하는 과학 세상'인데 하면서도 긴장되었다. 그런 가운데 비행기 바퀴가 땅에 닿으면서 안전 착륙을 알리는 방송이 나오자 승객 모두는 그제야 요란하게 박수 치며 "웰던, Well Done"을 외치며 안도하였다. 그 이후에도 외국 여행을 하는 동안 이런 경우를 여러 번 당하기도 하였다.

코펜하겐 공항에서 환승하여 독일 함부르크 공항으로 와서 다시 독일 국적기 '루프트한자(Lufthansa)'로 환승하여, 입국 최종 목적지 서독 임시 수도 '본' 공항으로 오게 되었다.

그런데 함부르크에서 '루프트한자'에 오를 때 조그만한 사과 2개 정도 들어갈 손잡이가 달린 종이상자(도시락)를 주었는데, 환영하는 선물이려니 생각했었다.

그런데 그 시금털털하게 보이는 4발 프로펠러 여객기가 소리도 요란하게 이륙, 잠시 후 식사 시간을 알리면서 '그 도시락'으로 식사하고 커피나 콜라만 제공하겠다고 하였다. 그동안 비행기 여행에서 도시락밥으로 대접 받아 본 적이 없었는데, 과연 듣고 알아 온대로 짧은 기간 내 '라인강의 기적'을 이루는 동안 근검절약과 실질적인 생활이 체질화된 독일의 첫인상으로 각인되었다.

◇ Euskirchen(오이스키르헨) 어학학교, 생활

'본' 공항에 도착하자 우리 일행을 마중 나와 기다리고 있던 주독 무관(포병 김 대령)이 반갑게 환영해 주었고, 바로 무관공관으로 직접 운전해 가서 부인과 함께 따뜻한 한국 음식으로 대접해 주어서 아주 고마웠으며, 식후에는 우리들의 체재 중 생활 계획과 주의 사항 등을 친절하고도 세밀하게 지도해 주었다. 그리고는 입학이 임박하였기에 늦은 밤인데도 본에서 상당히 먼 거리를 손수 운전하여 우리를 학교까지 안내해 주었다. 학교 숙소는 생도들에게는 'BOQ', 나(즉 우리)에게는 교실과 같은 건물 위층의 1인 1실 아파트를 배당해 주었다.

이곳은 인구 약2만 7,000여 명의 시골 도시로 '본'으로부터 남동쪽으로 약 35킬로미터 거리에 있고 그 북쪽으로 30여 킬러미터에 고풍 찬연하고도 관광도시인 '쾔른'(일명 코롱, Colon)이 위치하고 있다. 어학학교 교장은 중령이고 교수들은 대부분이 민간인으로, 어학 종류는 주로 유럽 국가 언어에 영어와 러시아어 등이고, 특히 유학 오는 외국인(장교)에게 독일어를 교육하고 있었다. 기간 중 일과는 8시에 시작하고 5교시는 12시30분까지이고, 오후 3시 45분까지는 자습이며 이후는 자유시간이었다.

교반은 10명 내외로 편성되고 주입식이며 숙제는 상당히 부담되는 정도였다. 우리 반은 전원 장교들로, 태국 1, 모로코 1, 나이지리아 4. 튀르기예 1, 한국 5명으로 구성되었다. 입교 후 약 3개월쯤에는 장교는 모두 시내 호텔 'Concord(ia)'로 숙소를 옮겨 주어서 더욱 자유스러웠다. 그러나 식사는 물론 호텔 식사가 아니고 학교 식당에서 3식을 해결하였는데, 다음에 또 설명할 기회가 있겠지만, 아침은 식당에서 간단한 보통 식사, 점심은 따뜻한 요리, 저녁은 우유와 검은 보리빵이 포함된 도시락(마른 음식)을 호텔로 가져가서 먹었다.

콩코드 식당에서 도시락을 먹으며 다른 독일 손님들을 보면, 상당수가 우리의 소주잔에다 소주 같은 술을 한입으로 마시고는 그 위에 맥주를 마시며 기분 좋아하고 있었다. 그 술은 바로 우리의 소주 같은 콘(Korn)이라는 32~38도나 되는 술이었다. 독일은 물이 좋지 않아서—땅도 그렇지만 비가 자주 와서 수질이 좋지 않아—밥을 먹으면서도 물 대신 주로 맥주를 마시거나(그래서 독일에는 300개가 넘는 맥주회사가 있다) 포도주를 마시며, 특히 저녁 식후에는 상식(常食) 수준에서 포도주를 즐겨 마신다. 보통 '콘'은 맥주하고 궁합이 맞아 같이 마시는데, 맥주 위에 콘을 마시면 마신 콘 그대로이나 콘 위에 맥주를 마시면 맥주

만큼 모두 콘이 된다. 경제적으로 술에 취할 수 있는 방법으로 특히 시골에서는 흔히 그렇게 습관으로 마시고 있다고 하였다.

◇ 화란(홀랜드 Holland, 네덜란드 Netherlands) 여행

세상을 살아가며 견문을 넓힌다는 것은 흥미로우면서도 자기 발전에 중요한 의미를 가진다. 때문에 나는 독일 유학을 계기로 과정 간 이동 공간이나 방학을 이용해서 기회만 있으면 유럽에 대해 견문을 넓힘과 동시에, 위대한 신천지 미국 문명과 유럽 문명을 비교해 우리 한국의 현재와 미래를 가늠해 보려했다. 이는 서독 유학의 한 목적이기도 했다. 4월 하순이 되자 봄방학이 생겨서 우리 세 사람—독일지휘참모대학 유학생, 기갑병과 구 중령과 해병대 강 중령 그리고 나—은 지방 여행사를 통해 지방민과 함께 서유럽 여행을 다녔다.

유럽 특히 중부 유럽 사람들이 '잔인한 4월'이라고들 흔히 말하는데, 그것은 우리나라 같이 정치 관련 얘기가 아니고, 진짜 자연을 경험한 얘기인바, 4월은 분명 꽃도 피고 새싹도 올라오건만 바깥 날씨는 춥고 살얼음에다 비바람 부는 우중충한 날이 계속됨으로 모두들 봄은 봄이로되 '잔인한 4월이라 말하고 있었다. 그래도 4월 말쯤 되어서는 봄기운이 돌고 시간 여유가 생겨서, 2박 3일 예정으로 바로 이웃 나라 네덜란드(독일말 뜻으로 '저지대 나라')로 견문 여행을 떠났다.

서독의 '쾰른(Koln, Cologne)'에서 출발하여 국경을 넘어서면 현재 수도 '암스테르담'에 이르기까지, 수많은 운하와 선박들로 다른 나라의 고속도로 못지않게 교통 시스템을 갖추고 있었다. 이 나라는 유럽 치즈의 주산지로 낙농이 발전되어 있고, 도시마다 시가지는 도로 폭 이상의 꽃길이 도로 중앙선으로 전개되고, 동시에 자전거길은 고속도로를 따라서도 나 있고, 시내는 십자로에서 차는 멈추어도 자전거는 밑 터널을 이용해 멈춤 없이 지나갈 수 있는 '자전거 천국으로 보였다.

수도 '암스테르담'은 항구도시로 '북해 운하'를 통해 북해와 연결되어 있고, 시내 교통은 운하가 주축이 되어 있어 편리함과 동시에 '관광 입국'에 큰 몫을 하고 있었다. 특히 2시간여의 운하 관광은 흥미로운데, 마치 이탈리아 '베니스'처럼 물밑에 자리 잡은 각종 건물과 특히 사무실이나 가정집까지도 수중에 있고 방수 유리창 속에서 사람이 활동하고 있는 모습을 물밑으로 보는 것은 가히 별경(別景)일 뿐 아니라 발전된 이 나라의 과학 수준도 실감할 수 있었다. 역시나 항구도시요 관광도시라 반나의 콜걸들이 쇼윈도 속에서 손짓하는 골목 거리도 세계에서 몇 번째로 유명하다 하였다.

대서양 연안을 따라 남으로 내려가면서 바다 쪽으로 보이는 것은 수면 위 폭 10미터 높이 10미터 이상의 해안 뚝으로서, 이 뚝을 맨주먹으로 밤새 막고 있었다는 소년의 미담은 전설이 아니라 실감이 되었다. 그렇게 해서 조성된 서해안 일대 거대한 꽃밭 단지(주로 튤립)는 가관이었는데, 년간 수억 달러의 수출 실적에다 관광 사업에도 큰 역할을 하고 있으니 이 나라는 가히 '꽃의 나라'라고 할만도 하였다.

지나다가 어느 조그만한 시골 동네에 들렸는데, 가운데 폭 좁은 길을 사이에 두고 양편으로 그렇게도 아담하고 아름다운 문자 그대로 동화의 살림집들이 죽 자리 잡고 있는데다 마치 집집마다 '내 집 보아주소'라도 하는 듯 거실은 통판 유리로 '쇼윈도처럼' 내부가 훤히 보이도록 되 있고, 창문짝에는 각가지 꽃 화분들이 놓여 있고, 면사 커튼 안쪽으로는 탁상 위 꽃바구니에 천정에는 앵무새 집이 매달려 있는 등 인테리어 만점으로, 마치 관광용 전시물처럼 보였으나, 실제로 사람이 살고 있는 가정집 동네였다. 더욱 귀여웠던 것은 집 크기가 20평 내외로 보이면서 다른 유럽 가정집에 비해 낮고 작고 아담하게 보인 것 또한 특색이었다. 독일 사람들이 보고 감탄하며 떠날 줄을 몰랐다.

홀랜드의 꽃밭 중에 상징적인 곳은 '코이켄호—프'라는 대형 꽃 공원으로, 대략 1킬로미터 평방 내에 언덕과 호수 그리고 풍차를 낀 운하와 길을 조성해 놓고, 거기에 주로 튤립을 중심으로 다양한 품종의 꽃밭을 가꾸어 아름답게 정비해 두어, 세계 관광객이라면 반듯이 들려볼 만한 곳이라 2시간도 길지 않았다. 또한 중간 카페에 앉아 공원 전체를 보며 마신, 이 나라가 세계에 자랑하는 맥주 '하이네켄'의 맛이 또한 일픔이었다. 그러기에 흥미를 갖게된 관광객에게 즉석 수출 상담도 하였는데, 당시 우리나라와는 식물 교역 대상이 아니어서 탐나는 꽃씨를 보았어도 상담이 불가하였다.

조금 더 내려가자 우리에게 '이준 열사'의 역사와 함께 잘 알려진 해안 도시 '헤이그(Hague)'가 나왔는데, 특히 도심에서 '평화의 전당'이 소개되었을 때는 감개가 무량하였다. 도대체 우리나라에서 여기까지 육로로 얼마나 될 것인가, 여기까지 오는 도중 수 없는 낯선 나라들을, 나라조차 빼앗긴 존재도 희미했던 국민으로, 입국 수속을 밟아가며 얼마나 고초를 당하며 여기까지 왔을까. 거기에 언어가 불통하고 음식도 어려우면서, 예나 지금(1969)이나 일본밖에 알려져 있지 않은 이 유럽 환경에서 '제국주의자들끼리'의 소위 '만국평화회의'에서 얼마나 서러움을 겪었을까 생각하면 절로 머리가 숙여졌다.

그 아래 대서양 방면 최대 항구도시 '로테르담(Rotterdam)'에는, 2만여 톤 이상의 선박들이 줄지어 정박해 있고, 7만 톤급(당시로 최대급) 선박을 건조하고 있을 만큼 거대하였다. 2차 대전 말기 연합군이 '놀만디'에 상륙하고 뒤이어 'Red Ball' 수송작전을 위한 항구 거점을 확보하기 위해 '대공수작전'을 감행한 이유를 알만했다. 또한 이 항구는 저 멀리 내륙의 '스위스'에서 발상하여 독일을 관통해 내려온 '라인강'의 최하류 지점이기도 하다. 우리가 배우기엔 화란을 꽃과 치즈만 만들어 파는 낙농 농업국이라 하였는데, 물론 4~5월의 이 나라는 '꽃피는 유럽의 공원'이었으나, 다시 보면, 현대 선진 산업과 무역의 선진국임이 확실하였다.

◇ 영국·벨기에 탐구 여행

◦ 도버해협을 건너 런던으로

이곳 어학학교 과정을 마치고 각자 참모실습부대로 헤어지기 전에 가까운 벨기에와 영국으로 견문을 넓히기로 하였다. 그래서 이번에도 우리 세 사람은 이 지방 '효도관광' 패키지(독일 노인네들 육로 벨기에와 영국 여행)에 합류하였다. 도버해협 도섭 시간을 고려해

'쾰른'에서 출발은 황혼 무렵이었고 'Globus(미국의 Grayhound 버스 격)'로 이동하였다.

잠시 후 버스는 국경 선상에 있는 '아악헨(Aachen)'을 지나고, 국경을 지나자 바로 '벨기에'의 '리에-게(Liege)'를 만났다. 우리가 탄 관광 버스는 계속 달려 '안트베르페(Antwerpen)' 들려볼 만한 지나는데, 오렌지색의 휘황한 가로등이 여행객들의 밤 마음을 아늑하게 해주었다.

버스는 계속 달려 다음 날 새벽 1시경에 유럽 대륙의 동쪽 끝인 대서양 해안의 '오스탕드(Ostende, 오스트엔데)' 항구에 도착하였다. 10여 년 전 도미 유학시에 미국 해병대 기지인 '노스캐로라이나'주의 '노퍽' 항구에서 대서양을 동쪽으로 바라보며 유럽을 그려보았는데, 지금은 대서양을 서쪽으로 바라보면서 서 있게 되었으니 감개무량하였다.

그런데 여기서 남으로 50킬로미터쯤 내려가면 프랑스 항구도시 '덩커끄(Dunkerque)' 즉, 2차 세계대전 초기 '벨기에'가 항복하자 영국군을 포함한 연합군이 독일군에 패하여 영국으로 철수해 간 항구도시가 나오는데, 미국 루즈벨트 대통령이 "진주만을 상기하자!"고 한 바와 같이, 영국의 처칠도 "잊지 말자 덩커끄!"라고 부르짖으며 전쟁을 지도한 '단장의 역사적 항구도시'이다. 바로 그 아래에 '깔레(Calais)' 항구가 있는데, 영국에서 가장 가까운 프랑스 항구(약 30킬로미터)로 2차대전 말기 독일의 '롬멜'장군이 차후 연합군 상류 지점으로 판단하고 '대서양 방벽'을 설치한 전략적 요충이기도 하다.

우리가 승선한 연락선(Ferry)은 5000톤의 크기로 아래층에 자가용 5~60대, 버스 10대와 화물차 수대가 적재되어 있고, 그 위층에는 객실과 식당이 있었는데, 과거 호남선 야간열차 분위기와 비슷하였다. 바닥에 눕거나 앉은 사람들 중에는 영국으로 원정 가는 더벅머리 남녀 '히피족(Hippy-ie)'으로 가득하였다. 거기서 환전도 하였는데, 유독 영국만은 여전히 12진법을 사용함으로 외국인들은 셈하는데 고통을 겪기도 하였다. 우리나라에도 번역된 『달과 사랑과 6펜스』라는 소설이 있었는데, 그 6펜스(12펜스가 1씰링)는 우리 돈 500원 동전과 같이 경제 생활의 가장 기본— 한 병의 코크, 아이스크림 하나, 한병의 냉밀크, 한통의 전화 걸기 등—되는 화폐 단위였다.

배는 시속 10노트로 밤의 도버해협을 4시간 동안 항해해서 드디어 새벽녘에 영국 땅 '도버' 항구에 닿았는데, 특히 듣던 바와 같이 10미터도 더 높이 솟아 오른 병풍 절벽과 거기에 새벽 바닷바람에 나부끼는 '유니온잭'기는 영국의 강한 첫인상이었다. 버스는 좌측 통행으로 '템스강'을 따라 2시간여를 달려서, 영문학의 거장 '초이스'가 예찬한 전설과 문학의 고도 '켄터베리'에서 새소리를 들으며 아침 산보를 즐기다가 다시 4시간가량 더 달려서 드디어 '런던'에 도착하였다.

◦ 런던의 풍경, '피카딜리 샌터'의 히피족과 '더티 딕'의 흑맥주

우선 내 시야에 들어온 것들은, '템스강에 걸린 여러 교량과 '파를리먼트' 즉 국회의사당, 저 높이 보이는 '빅—벤', 특이한 복장의 경찰, 그리고 굵직 굵직한 대리석과 화강암의 육중한 시내 건물들이었다. 옛날에 본 것들 모두 인상적이었으나 그중 가장 인상 깊었던 몇 가지만 회상해 보면, 우선 '하이더 파크 공원'인데, 폭 약 2킬로 길이 약 4킬로미터의 공공공원—영국에서는 주로 귀족 개인소유 공원(Private Park)도 도처에 흔하다.—인데 큰

강과 보트 마리너, 승마장과 축구장 등등이 있어서 명실공히 시민들의 건강과 휴식의 장이었다.

밤거리에 흥미로웠던 것은 구 런던시 중앙역 앞에 자리 잡은 'Dirty Dick'이라는 간이 술집(로컬)이었는데, 얘기로는, 100년 전쯤에 'Dick'이 청소도 안 하는 게으름뱅이라 이혼당하고, 혼자 살면서도 생선 먹고 난 온갖 동물 뼈다귀를 천정으로 집어 던져 지금도 붙어 있고, 시커먼 먼지는 곧 술잔에 떨어질 것만 같고, 온 사방 벽은 100년 묵은 검정 떼 그리고 먼지들로 가득한데, 그동안 손님들의 코딱지만 한 사진들과 우표, 명함, 그림 엽서, 그리고 헛갈린 낙서들이 잡동산이 되어 있고, 100년 묵었다는 통나무 탁자와 의자들은 사람과 술잔을 겨우 받쳐주는 데도 한잔 술 하고 다음 잔까지는 한참을 기다려야 하는 정도로 붐볐다. 그럼에도 아니 그러기에 이곳, 이 광경은 '히피족'과 '흑맥주'와 함께 가히 '런던의 별미'였다.

다음날은 런던에서 100여킬로미터 서쪽 방향으로 떨어져 있는, 여전히 전 세계 최상위 랭킹에 있는 '옥스포드대학'을 방문하였는데, 특히 인상적이었던 것은 대식당 벽면에는 실물 크기 정도의 인물 벽화가 온 벽을 장식하고 있었는데 그들 모두는 이 학교를 빛낸 성공한 인물들이라 하였는데, 재학생들은 그들 선배들을 '프라이드'는 물론 귀감 삼아 열심히 대학 생활을 영위하고 있었다. 소개된 옥스퍼드 역사의 끝장에는, "방학은 길었고, 학기는 짧았다"고 하였고, 또한, 'The ability to grace learning given to few, but the opportunity to learn the grace is Oxford's gift to all sons and daughters'.라고 쓰여 있었다.

다음에는 근처에 위치한 '세익스피어 본가'를 관광하였는데, 워낙 많이 알려 있기에 일단 런던 얘기를 이어 가고자 한다. 다시 돌아온 밤의 런던 시내는 조용하고 한산하였으나 도시 중심에 자리 잡고 있는 'Picadilly Circus'만은 취객과 히피족 그리고 이를 구경하는 관광객들로 붐비며, 주변 거리는 서울의 '명동', 동경의 '긴자', 파리의 '피가레', 함부르크의 '쌍 파울'과 같이 스트립 쇼, 스트리트 걸, 그리고 늙은 펨푸가 우글거렸다 그런가 하면 바로 옆 'Soho' 근처 상가는 우리의 소공동 양복 거리와 같이 세계 신사 양복 유행의 근원지로 유명하였다.

영국 사람들은 말하기를, "'버킹엄 궁전'이 런던(영국)의 의전을 대표한다면 '웨스트민스타 사원(寺院)'은 영국 정치 생활의 중심이고, '피카딜리 서커스'는 런던의 등"라고 하는 바와 같이, 유럽으로 원정가던 제1, 2차 세계대전 당시의 병사들은 '굿바이 피카딜리'라는 노래를 군가 대신 불렀다고 한다.

런던 중심가는 장엄한 화강암의 도시로 대부분이 몇 세기 전에 건조되어서 앞으로도 1000년 이상 유지될 수 있는 역사와 전통의 도시로 보였다. 한편 이와 대조적으로 당시(1969년)의 거리와 건물 밑에는 수많은 히피족들이 거리를 방황하고 있었는데, 어림잡아 10명 중 9명은 비틀즈 더벅머리였고, 소녀 10명 중 7명은 '초미니'요, 3명은 나팔바지였는데, 아예 인디언 차림도 많았다. 뿐만 아니라 몇 달을 깎지도 씻지도 않은 머리에 발끝이 보이지 않는 망토에 맨발인 히피와 초미니 히피가 함께 다니는 모습들에 독일에서 온 우리 관광객들은 '오, 노!' 연발이었다.

또한 시내 곳곳에는 수많은 공원이 있어서 길 가다가 잠간 나무 그늘 및 벤치에 앉아 분수를 바라보며 비둘기와 얘기하며 쉬어갈 수 있었고, 수많은 영국 특징의 로터리에는 역사적 기념 조각들이 많았는데, 그중에서도 '하이더파크' 입구 로터리에는 '웰링턴 장군'기념물과 '트라파르갈 스퀘어'이 있는 '넬슨 제독'의 기념물은 내 같은 군인에게는 여러 가지 의미에서 기억될만 하였다.

한 개 도시의 견문록 치고는 좀 길어질 수밖에 없는 곳이 런던이였다. '템스강' 가까이에 아름다운 '꼬띡'형 건물로 '웨스트 민스타 사원'이 있는데, 여기가 바로 영국 국교 교회의 본산지요 왕정의 중심으로, 과거 영국은 완전히 정교 일체 국가였던 시절 근 900년 전에 건립되었으며, 그로부터 지금까지 왕의 대관식을 거행하는 곳이다. 입구에 들어서면 바로 정면에 커다란 꽃다발이 놓여 있는데, 제1차 세계대전 때 유럽 대륙에 출전하여 전사한 무명용사 안치 기념비가 있어서 우리 군인 광광객에게는 인상 깊은 모습이었다. 들어가면서 받은 안내장에, '바라건데 이 교회의 영광을 보기 원한다면 종종 위를 올려다보는 것을 잊지 마시길'이라고 안내되어 있다.

◦ 내가 본 영국의 걸작, 'Madame Tussaud's House' 넬슨 제독의 "나는 나의 임무를 다하였다"

다음은 바로 '템스강'에 항시 근엄한 영상을 비추며 자리 잡고 있는 국회의사당(Houses of Parliament)을 가 보았는데, 관광객이 볼 수 있는 곳은 상, 하 양원과 '웨스트 민스타 홀'이었으나 지나가는 통로 벽면에는 영국 제국주의 시대의 영광이, 세계 식민지 점령 역사와 경영 역사로 표현되어 자국민에게는 정말 큰 자부심을 기질수 있게 되어 있었다. 어떤 나라의 영광과 그 빛나는 시대는 어떤 나라의 고통과 암흑의 시대였음을 나는 새삼 느끼기도 하였다.

또 하나 영국인들의 애국심 고취의 도장인 '마담 투소도스 하우스(Madame Tussaud's House)'에 가 보았다.

외국 관광객은 물론 런던을 찾은 영국인들도 반듯이 들리는 유명한 '마담 투소도'라는 전시관이 있는데, 지하2층 지상 3~4층으로 되어 있고, 관람은 지하 2층 컴컴하고 으슥한 방 '공포의 방'에서 시작한다. 거기에는 세계 각국의 유명 범죄인들과 그들에게 사용된 고문과 참형 도구들, 특히 프랑스 '기로틴'(guillotine)과 영국의 처형용 큰 손도끼(Axel)—런던 타워에서 있었던 처형, '마리아 스투아르다' 등—, 쇠고랑, 쇠창살에 꽂혀 있는 피 흐르는 루이 16세의 베어진 머리 등등. 그리고 그 옆에는 당시에 세계적 미스터리 사건이었던 '케네디 암살사건'의 1차 용의자 '오스왈드'의 감옥살이 모습과 자살에 관한 것들이 전시되어 있었는데, '혼자서 보지 마세요'라고 안내서에 있을 만큼 끔찍한 광경들이라 아마도 이 광경들을 본 그 누구도 '절대로 죄짓지 말아야지'를 다짐하게 될 것이라 생각되었다.

이어서 지하 1층으로 올라오면 특히 내게는 가장 인상적인 '트라팔갈 전투 홀'이었다. 들어서자 말자 실내—넬슨 제독이 승선하고 있었던 당시 영국기함 '빅토리아 호'의 일부—를 그대로 옮겨다 놓은 듯, 화약 내음과 연기가 가득히 풍기면서 각종 포화가 작열하는 빛과 포성, 그리고 지휘자의 명령과 수병 및 포수들의 복창 등등, 당시 승리의 전투 최후 장면이 그대로 실연되었다. 이윽고 전투가 끝나자 승리의 환호성이 들리는 가운데 '넬슨'의 최후의 말, "나는 나의 임무를 다하였다"는 소리가 들렸다. '전승과 위대한 영웅의 최후'에 대한 5분여간의 이 실연 장면은 특히 이를 관람하는 영국 국민에게 분명 그들의 조국에 대한 긍지와 충성심을 일깨워 주고도 남는 것이리라.

그 잔상을 가지고 지상층으로 올라오면, 30여 명 가량의 세계 중요 역사적 인물들의 실물 대형 밀랍 인형이 있는데 특히 처칠이 여송연을 물고 석양 노을의 바닷가에서 화폭에 그림을 그리고 있는 장면이었다. 다시 위층에 올라가면 '시대 영웅관'으로, 텔레비와 영화 그리고 실물 크기의 조각들이 음향 효과와 조명을 받으면서 입체적 실연을 해 보이는데, 그 중에 한 장면이 가관이었다. 당시 유명했던 '버튼'과 '엘리자베스 테일러'—당시 세기적인 인기를 누리던 영국 여배우—가 어느 비 오는 날 아침, 미국 뉴욕의 한 호텔에서 막 우산을 받쳐 들고나오는데, 기습적으로 달려든 신문 기자들이 "테일러 양, 오늘 아침 식사로 무엇을 먹었는지요?"라고 물어보는 소리와 장면이 연출되고 있었다.

비록 프랑스 여인(마담) '투소도'의 개인적 아이디어와 투자로 제작되고 전시되는 것이지만, 범인류적인 교훈과 자랑과 즐거움이 거기에 있었다. 우리나라에도 온 국민이 가보는 경주 불국사와 충청도 목동의 '독립기념관'도 있다. 그런데 이같이 현대화된 또 다른 철학적 개념의 전시관이 서울 한복판에 언젠가는 훌륭한 '이순신' 장군의 얘기를 포함해서 더욱 멋진 '마담 투소도스 하우스'가 세워지기를 바란다. 이웃 일본 도쿄에는 이미 세워져 있다고 들었다.

또한 버킹엄궁전(영국왕 집무처)에서 12시 정각에 시작되는 그 근엄하고도 장려한 근무교대식을 보노라면, 옛적 화랑대 육군사관학교 시절의 매주 거행한 '사열과 열병식'이 생각나 감개무량하였다. 이 이외도 방문 관광한 곳은 500여 곳의 역과 7개 노선을 가진 지하철, 전통과 역사 깊은 그러나 알고 보면 특히 왕실의 비극을 담고 있는 '런던 타워', 거기에 있는 왕실 유물 보관소(특히 보물들)와 주로 총포가 전시된 군사박물관, 중심가 로터리에 있는 순백색의 '빅토리아여왕'의 기념상, 복잡한 시가지 한가운데 무명용사 기념비, 영국왕실 소유의 '벅킹엄궁전'과 '윈저성' 등이었다.

이제 런던을 떠나 영국 관광을 마치면서 석양 무렵에 다시 '도버'항구에 도착하였는데, 새삼 돋보인 것은 유럽 쪽을 향해 버티고 있는 절벽이었다. 제2차 대전 당시 유럽으로 출격했던 한 영국 전투기의 조종사가 적탄에 맞아 부상하였음에도, 용감한 조종사는 끝까지 도버해협을 건너 조국 땅 도버 절벽에 도착하자, "드디어 나의 조국에 왔다"고 부르짖으며 의식을 잃고 절벽에 부딪쳐서 산화하였는데, 그 애국 충혼비가 저 절벽에 새겨져 있다고 들었다. 다시 돌아오는 나룻배에 올라 석양 노을에 멀어져가는 도버 절벽을 보면서 '대영재국은 해질 날이 없다'한 제국주의 시대 영국을 새삼 재인식하게 되었다.

∘ '벨기에'의 '워털루 전쟁기념관'

돌아오는 길에 벨기에의 수도(王都)인 동시에 유럽의 수도이기도 한 브뤼셀(Brussel)에 들렸는데, 110만여 인구의 소도시—여타 세계 각국 수도 규모에 비하면—로 관광 명물들은 대개 걸어서 다녀볼 수 있었다. 우선 들른 곳은 '큰 광장(그랑플라스

grandeplacebrussels)', 그리고 그 근처로 걸어서 '예술가의 언덕', 옛 왕궁, 현 왕궁 거리, 그리고 유명한 '오줌싸게 동상', 그리고 가는 곳마다 즐비한 초콜릿과 감자튀김 그리고 와플 가게들을 얼마든지 만날 수 있었다. 특히 '오줌싸게 동상'은 덴마크 '랑겔리니' 해안 바위 위에 올라앉아 있는 '작은 인어상'과 같이 작으면서도 온 세계 관광객들의 필수 방문명소인 것을 보면, 민족과 역사 전통은 달라도 인류의 선한 본성은 닮았음을 보여주는 것이리라.

다음은 '워털루'(지방)로 가서 '워털루전쟁(전투)기념관'을 방문하였는데 설명하는 바에 의하면, 프랑스의 세계적 문호 '빅토르 위고'의 '워털루 전투'에서 본을 따 제작된 것이라 하였다. 실내에는 당시 워터루 그 장소 지방에서 실시된 최후 전투 모습을 그대로 파노라마 형태로 재현시켜 놓았는데, 미국 '애트란타'에 있는 '남북전쟁 마지막 전투 장면'의 파나라마 작품과 함께 세계에 자랑하는 전시물이 되고 있었다. 밖에 나오면 거대한 원뿔형 언덕 위에, 당시 패전 프랑스 나폴레옹군의 대포를 녹여 만든 거대한 사자상이 우뚝 세워져 있었는데, 처다보고 있노라면, 과연 웰링턴 장군 휘하 영국군과 참여 연합군의 승리의 환호성이 들리는 듯하였다. 여기서 얻은 전쟁 교훈은 "군인은 전쟁(전투)에서 여하간(무조건)에 승리하고 볼일"이라는 것이였다.

◇ 주독 무관 안내로 생도들과 '라인강' 유람

'오이스키르헨' 서독군 어학학교에서 수업하는 동안, 주독한국대사관이 있는 '본'까지는 가까웠기 때문에 휴일을 기회로 자주 들리기도 하였는데, 하루는 무관(김 대령)이 우리(두 생도와 나)를 초대하여 독일(유럽)의 젖 줄기라 할 수 있는 '라인(Rhein)강' 유람을 하게 되었다. 지금은 잘 기억이 나지 않으나 아마도 본에서 100킬로미터 가량 남쪽에 있는 '비스바덴(Wiesbaden)'으로 이동하였고, 거기서 유람선을 타고 북으로 올라와 강가에 있는 '본'에 이르기까지 유람하였던 것으로 기억된다.

선상 관광코스인 이 지대는 우리나라의 한탄강과 닮은 모습으로 대부분이 한쪽은 평지 절벽으로 되어 있고 다른 한편은 상대적으로 덜 가파른 언덕과 같은 모양이라, 그쪽에는 강변을 따라 관광도로를 내고 그 도로를 연하여 강을 바라보며 휴식도 쇼핑도 할 수 있는 상점가를 포함한 관광대를 이루어 놓았다. 우리 한강의 어느 경관 좋은 한 지대도 그와 같이 관광 구역을 만들 수 있을 것으로 생각되었다.

사방을 두리 번 거리며 출발지점에서 약 30킬로미터쯤 북상하다 보면, '장크트고아(Sankt-Goar)' 근방의 강 우편 기슭에, 배에서 한 100미터 위로 솟아나 있는 큰 바위가 있는데 그곳이 바로 '로렐라이(Loreley)'—요정의 바위라는 뜻—인바 전설에 의하면, 지나다니는 많은 배들이 그 바위에서 들리는 요정의 아름다운 노랫소리에 선원들이 도취되어 넋을 잃고 뱃길을 놓쳐 굽어지는 물살에 휩쓸려 암초에 부딪혀 난파한다는 전설로 관광객을 끌고 있었다.

거기서 조금 더 북상하면 '코브렌즈'에서 '모젤강(Mosel)'을 만나게 되는데, 이 강은 동에서 서로 꾸불꾸불 흘러들어오기 때문에 남쪽을 향한 언덕이 많고 주변 환경이 포도 생산에 적합하여 이곳에서 생산된 '모젤와인'은 '라인와인'보다 좀 더 알아준다고 했다.

2. 여단참모 견학, 산악사단의 제23산악여단(Gebirgs Brigade)

◇ 알프스 주둔 제23산악여단, 별칭 '에델바이스' 여단

1969년 7월까지 서독군 어학학교 독일어 수업을 마치고 다음 과정인 여단단위부대 부대참모 실습 및 견학(1969.8~9, 2개월)을 위해 제23산악여단으로 개별적으로 이동하였다. 여단은 서독의 최동남단 알프스의 산 바로 밑, 오스트리아의 그 유명한 관광도시 '잘츠브루크(Salzburg, 소금마을)'와 바로 국경을 마주 보고 있는 마을 '바드 라이헨할(Bad Reichenhall, 온천마을)' 교외에 있었으며, 바로 근처에는 '히틀러'의 최후 방어기지로 예정되었던 '알프스 요새', '베레흐테스가덴(Berchtesgaden)'—역시 현재는 유명해진 광광지 —이 있었다. 당시 제1산악사단 사령부는 '뮌헨' 방향으로 조금 내륙 쪽인 '가르미슈파르텐키르헨'에 위치해 있었다. 이 부대는 1935년 창설되어 2차 세계대전에 참전했다가 해체된뒤 서독군 재검과 함께 1956. 11월에 재건되었는데, 예하에 2개 산악여단과 1개 기갑여단으로 구성되어 있었으며, 부대 마크는 알프스 고산지대 대표 꽃 '에델바이스'였다.

당시 서독군의 전략·작전 개념은, 북부의 평야 지대에서 장갑기동부대 작전을, 중부의 중형 산악 및 산림지대에서는 보, 포, 기의 종합기동작전을 그리고 남부의 알프스 산악 지대에서는 산악지 작전을 적용하고 있었다. 동시에 당시의 나토군의 중부 구성군이었던 서독군은 핵전쟁을 예상하는 전면 전쟁 개념에다 60년대에 강조된 '유연대응전략'개념에 따라 일부 부대외는 장갑기동화 되어 있었다. 그러기에 심지어 산악사단이라 할지라도 2개여단은 산악부대이고 1개여단은 장갑여단으로 편성되어 있고, 산악여단 또한 1개 장갑대대, 2개 산악대대, 1개 산악포병대대, 1개 기계화(장갑 기동화) 보급대대로 구성되어 있다. 산악대대 또한 3개 차량화 산악병중대와 1개 장갑화 중화기중대(대전차 유도탄, 대공화기, 중박격포, 대전차총포), 1개 장갑 및 차량화 본부중대로 되어 있다.—서독에서는 장갑사단, 미국에서는 기갑사단으로 불리고 있다.

산악사단의 기본 전략·작전 개념도 1차적으로 알프스 고산지대(2000~4500미터)에서 산악병(산악특화병)에 의한 산악전투에서 개시하여 점차 알프스의 산 이편 또는 저편의 구능(평야) 지대로 전이되어, 장갑기동부대(전술)로 결전을 한다는 것이었다. 그런데 이 부대 편성 및 장비상의 독특한 사항은, 여단 단위의 독립작전을 수행하기 위해 각 여단의 장갑기동화 보급대대가 군단과 직접 거래하는 한편, 산악보급을 위해 80필의 '노새(Mule)'로 편성된 1개 산악보급중대가 있다. 이 노새의 원조 산지는 나폴레옹의 고향인 'Corsica' 섬이며, 이들(수놈)과 양질의 말(암놈)과 수차례 교배시켜가며 생산해 냄으로 말보다 든든하며 힘이 세다. 그래서 산악작전 시 포병대대의 산포 105미리를 12개 부분으로 분해하여 12필의 노새로 알프스를 운반해 올라간다.

보병부대 기관총은 두격 조정 없이 연속사격이 가능하며, 총열 교환은 훈련된 병사일 경우 3~4초만에 가능하다. 사격 시는 다리를 세워서 사격하고 즉시 참호 속으로 엎드리되 총 다리 발톱은 그 자리에 있고 다리가 굽었다가, 사수가 다시 일어서면 총도 그 자리에서 따라 일어섬으로 총을 들고 몸을 꾸부렸다가 다시 일어설 때 들고 일어서서 거치하여 사격하는 불편과 시간 문제를 해결하고 있었다.

당시 막 새로 개발되어 세계 제1을 자랑하던 '레오파드(Leopard, 표범)' 전차는 폭이 좁고 가벼워 재래식 전차의 약 2배속도(65km/h) 주행 가능하고, 수중 3미터 잠행 가능함으로서 유럽 전역에서는 가히 지상의 왕자를 자칭하고 있었다. 기타 화기나 장비의 특성 그리고 간부 양성 제도 등 전문적인 군사 얘기는 다음 기회로 미루고 여기서는 이만 줄이기로 한다.

부대 운용면에서, 당시 서독군은 민주화 군대를 지향함을 과시해야 하고 실제도 징병 또한 어려웠음으로 'TO, 편제' 병력을 최대한 절약(AS, 허용)하였다. 특히 하급부대에 그러하였는데 예를 들면, 대대는 인사 장교가 정보 장교를 겸하고, 부대대장(소령)이 대대작전 장교를 겸한다. 중대는 평시에 중대장과 소대장 1명으로 2명의 장교가 근무하고 여타 소대는 하사관이 지휘하며, 이 하사관들이 차량 및 화기에 관한 일체를 책임하에 교육, 사격 지휘, 감독하며 유지하였다.

부대 교육훈련을 보면, 지방 주둔부대—우리나라는 휴전선에 연하여 대부분의 부대가 전방에 배치되어 있으나, 서독은 전방은 일단 국경 경비대에 일임하고 전투부대는 각 지방별로 주둔해 있다.—가 직접 신병을 받아 대대당 1개중대가 신병중대가 되어 3개월간 기초 군사훈련, 이후 3개월간 특기병훈련을 필하고 여단 내 소요 부서에 편입되고 남은 주류는 '동기생 중대'로 전투력을 유지하다가 18개월 만기가 되면 그 중대원은 동시에 제대하고 또 새 동기생 신병중대가 되는 등 반복해 운용하고 있다. 주로 하사관들이 주도하는 사병들의 기초 군사훈련 중 사격 성적은 30%, 일반병은 50~60%였는데, 그러나 하사관은 90% 이상이라고 자랑하고 있었다.

이 부대 특징인 산악 교육훈련은, 여단에 1개소대, 대대에 1개분대 규모의 특수 전위부대가 있어서 해발 4000미터를 넘는 알프스의 산을 오르내리는 훈련을 실시하고, 그 외 전 장병은 주로 산악지 행군 위주 훈련으로 로프 등반훈련 등은 완만한 지형에서 숙달 중점으로 한다. 중대장의 정신 훈화 시간에는 자국 역사와 지리에 많은 시간을 할애하였고, 때로는 중대 단위로도 외부 인사를 초빙하여 강의도 하였다.

체육 시간은 장사병 불문 주당 6시간 이상이며, 주로 육상과 수영 그리고 축구 등인데, 장교에게는 1500미터 야지 구보와 300미터 수영은 의무적이었다. 그런데 이 부대에서는 여름에는 시원한 눈덮인 알프스의 산 등정, 겨울에는 수시로 바로 인접 스키장에서 즐길 수가 있어서 장사병 공히 이 부대 입대/근무하는 동기를 체력 향상과 취미 배양으로 생각하고 있었다.

◇ 재건 10주년 당시 서독군대 일반 실정

◦ 패전국 상황에서 나토동맹국으로 재건 중

내가 실습 간 당시 서독군은 동서 냉전에서 서방의 필요성에 의하여 패전국 징벌에서 벗어나 재건(1955)되었고, 그 즉시 나토(1949년 창설)에 가입하여 당시는 14년이 되었었다. 정확한 장소는 기억나지 않으나 나토 창설 20주년 기념식과 식후 퍼레이드에 서독군도 참가하였는데 아주 볼만하였고 특히 냉전 당시의 '동방군사조직(WTO)'에게는 깊은 관찰을 요하는 시위용 퍼레이드였다. 이 행사 참관을 계기로 독일군의 개요를 파악할 수 있어서 유학 기간 중 큰 도움이 되었다.

이때가 독일 국민에게는 갈등의 시기였다. 패전하고 무장해제 당하고 국제적 징벌을 당하면서 국력이 총동원되어 재건을 위해 노력 중이던 차에, 동서냉전을 이유로 재무장을 하게 되었던 것이다. 당시 국민들은 전쟁과 군대에 질려서 '나만 빼고(Ohner mich)' 정서가 이심전심이었기에 이를 극복하기 위해서라도 군대 재건 시작부터 징병제도를 단행하여 모병하고 조직하며 편성하였다.

따라서 도망이나 탈영병이 1개중대 월 5명 평균 정도로 상당하여, 중대장은 이들 탈영병에 대한 고소장 작성—전후 군대 냄세 없애기(군 약화)의 하나로 군대 조직상의 군법회의를 없애고 1회 재판에서부터 민간 재판에 의뢰하기 위한 소장—하는 등의 행정 업무 보기에도 바쁘다고 했다.

◦ 군대 내부 진급 갈등 현상은 현존

또한 군대를 민주화한답시고 장교들의 정당 가입이 허용되어 있어서 뭔가 내부적으로 갈등이 있어 보였는데, 특히 장군 진급 시에는 현 정권의 정당원 여부가 거의 결정적인 역할을 한다고도 했다. 또한 웬만한 국가들은 남북이나 동서 간에 역사, 종교, 정치, 전통에 따라 갈등을 앓으며 역사를 이어가는데, 이 나라 독일도 당장은 물론 동서독으로 분할되어 고통을 앓고 있지만 근본적으로 역사적으로 종교적으로 남북간 갈등—북은 신교 위주 남은 구교 위주, 북은 공상업 위주 남은 농업 위주, 북은 산업 문명화 남은 '바바리언(야만)' 등등의 전통 정서적—으로 내부적인 구분을 하여 알게 모르게 영향을 받고 있었다.

당시 때마침 서독 대선(총리선거)이 있었는데, 북은 신교 주류의 '기독교민주당' 후보, 남은 가톨릭 주류의 '사회민주당' 후보 '브란트'의 경쟁이었다. 그래서 영내에서 장교들 간에도 격렬한 토의가 있었으나, 본인 참관부대 지역이 남부(바바리안)라 '브란트' 지지가 우세하였다.

여단장이 슬쩍 귓속말로, "BOQ에서 간부들과 대화 시 가능한 듣고만 있는 것이 좋겠다"고 얘기해 주었다. 미국 유학 때는 들어보지 못한 정치 유관 충고였다. 그토록 정치 문제는 나라마다 다르기도 하고 군대마다 다르기도 하였다. 그런데 우리나라 일반 사회에서는, 물론 여전히 지방색이 남아 있으나, 그래도 신통하게도 우리 군대 내에는 전혀 지방색 구분이나 느낌이나 정서가 존재하지 않는다. 참으로 다행이라 하겠다.

◦ 독일군대 장교 육성 제도

옛날에는 전 세계 웬만한 전제 국가들과 같이 사회 귀족 계급들만이 장교가 되었다. 그러나 특히 전후의 민주주의 군대화를 지향하는 서독 군대의 장교는 18개월의 의무 복무를 마친 병사들 가운데서 고등학교를 이수하고 '아비투어(수능시험 합격)' 자격증을 가진 자 가운데서 지원자로 모집하며, 사관학교 1학년 때는 하사 계급—실제 하사 계급장에 밑줄 하나는 흰색으로 표시—으로 실무부대에 와서 부대 실습을 하며, 이들 교육 과정 중 일반학 교육(예 신문기사 해석 등)은 부대 공보하사관(전문 지식 하사관)이 맡아서 교육하고 있었다.

아마도 옛 귀족풍을 없애고 철저히 민주화를 한답시고 병 생활은 물론 부대 하사관 생활도 상당 기간 경험시키고 있었다. 그러나 우리와 미국 등 상당수의 민주주의 국가 군대에서는 장교 육성 과정에서 굳이 병 생활 경험을 직접 거치지 않으나 사관생도 생활 그 자체가 바로 병 생활임으로 알고 보면, 그들과 별로 다를 바 없으나 다만 우리네는, 초급 장교 시절 하사관과 약간의 갈등 관계를 겪을 수 있는 단점이 있기도 하다.

◇ 기계화중대와 산악보병대대 야외훈련 참관

◦ 기계화중대(장갑보병중대) 원거리 훈련장 훈련 동행 참관

서독 군대도 민주 국가가 된 이후 역시나 훈련장이 귀하여 서독 내 미군 사격 훈련장에 가서 훈련하고 있었다. 이곳은 미군이 독일 정부에 사용료를 지불하는 곳이었는데, 특히 중화기 사격훈련을 위해서는 서독군도 프랑스(주로 야포)로 영국(주로 전차훈련 및 사격)으로 또 때로는 지중해 'Crete 섬'까지 가서 훈련을 한다는데, 모두가 나토군 예하니까 상호 훈련장 교환씩으로 편의를 도모하고 있었다.

그래서 한번은, 장갑보병중대가 훈련차 12대 장갑차와 2대의 연락 오토바이 그리고 5대의 보급 및 기재 차량 등이 한 제대(梯隊)를 이루고 중대장 깃발을 단 지프로 중대장이 지휘하며 훈련장으로 대략 3시간 이상 거리에 있는 훈련장으로 이동해갔다. 나도 단독 지프를 타고 함께 가면서 보니, 우리나라에서 흔히 말하는 '깃발 날린다'는 말이 실감나게 중대장이 깃발을 날리며 자기 중대를 독립적으로 지휘해 가는 당당한 독일군의 모습을 볼 수 있었다.

훈련장에 도착하여 중대가 숙영지를 편성하는 동안 훈련장 규모를 알아보기 위해 주변을 지프로 한 바퀴 돌아보았다. 주변 시속 60킬로미터로 1시간여 걸렸으니 직경은 대략 7~8킬로미터 되게 보였다. 훈련장 내부에서는 20여 개소의 각종 화기 동시 사격이 가능한데 부대별로 년 2~3회 집중적으로 실탄 사격을 실시하고 있었다. 일주일간 함께 야영하면서 보았는데, 사격장 총책임은 장교에게 있고 항시 장교 감독하에 사격을 실시하나 일체 현장 사격 지휘는 하사관에 의하여 집행되었다. 특히 120미리 박격포 사격은 포술하사관에 의해 실시되었고 선임하사는 안전 및 통제를 맡고 있었고 소대장은 집계되는 성적표를 보고 있었다.

전술 훈련 간에 소대장과 중대장(본부) 지휘 차에는 고정(또는 노트북) PC 컴퓨터가 장착되어 있어서—당시 한국군은 꿈도 꾸지 못하던 때—작전명령을 전령 따로 없이 수령하고 복창하고 있었다. 그러나 전자망 불통 시를 고려하여 전통적인 오토바이 전령 운용도 시험하고 있었다.

한 가지 더 기억나는 것은 '임무 책임제 상벌 제도'였다. 예를 들면, 훈련 기간 중 중대 병기계가 단독 3각텐트 속에 여분의 소총을 비치하고 있었는데, 밤늦게까지 개스 등 아래 작업하다가 깜빡하는 사이 불이나 소총 10여 정을 태웠다. 당시 한국군에서는 아직도 자체 생산이 아니어서 모든 화기들이 귀하여 총의 구성품 하나도 잊어버리면 찾을 때까지 밤 세워 전원이 연병장을 샅샅이 찾아다녔다. 그러기에 물론 이 정도면 계원은 물론 중대장도 책임지고 처벌되었을 것이다. 그런데 중대장 책임 추궁은 물론 없었거니와 병조차도 개인 변상—이건 좀 우리로서는 생소하나—으로 끝내었다. 이제 우리도 자주 국방 수준이 되면 물론이고 그 이전에도 처벌 특히 지휘관 처벌에 더욱 신중해야 할 것이다.

◦ 산악보병대대 알프스 산악훈련 동행 참관

제1여단의 산악보병대대는 전 장비(노새와 중화기 등)를 동원하여 최소 반기 1회 이상 지정된 주변 알프스의 산을 오르내리고 산 정상 평지 등에서 전개 훈련을 실시하고 있었다. 부대참모 활동 참관 중이던 나도 7월 훈련에 함께 동행하며 산악훈련을 참관하였다.

우선 포병대대 중화기—이미 언급한 바와 같이 105미리 산포를 12부위로 분해하여 12필의 '노새'에, 기본 탄약도 포함하여— 를 노새 등에 적재하여 빙하수가 흘러내리는 계곡길을 따라 대대 전 장병은 걸어서 알프스의 산 전개 진지지역으로 올라갔다. 도중에 몇 번 쉬기는 했으나 꾸불꾸불하고 가파롭고 한 사람씩 지나갈 정도의 좁은 오르막 산길 통로를 노새부대는 성큼 성큼 잘 올라가 주었다. 그만큼 노새의 힘이 강하였다.

초행길인 나를 안내 겸하던 중대장이 산마루 가까이 오르자 나지막한 고산 지대 관목들에 보기 드믈게 잘 피어나 있는 꽃들을 가르키며, '잘츠부르크'와 함께 우리 귀에 익어 있는 '에델바이스' 꽃에 대해 설명해 주었다. 이 꽃은 알프스의 상징이고 동시에 이 산악부대의 '부대 마크'가 되어 있었다. 드디어 한여름에도 눈 덮인 산 정상 부분에 도달하자 함께 따라 올라오던 노새부대는 보병부대 후방 예비 중대 지역에 전개하였고, 훈련이 계속되는 동안 노새들은 마부 병사들에 의해 보호되며 쉬고 있었다.

이 부대 훈련 내용은 바로 우리의 보병부대 훈련과 유사하였으나, 다만 산을 오를 때 105미리 포 등 장비를 노새가 운반하는 등 본격적인 산악부대다운 장비로 훈련을 하고 있다고 생각되었다. 사실 우리나라 전방부대들이야 말로 문자 그대로 산악보병부대로 평가되어야할 자연과 지형 환경에 놓여 있어 이 서독 산악부대의 장비와 훈련내용을 잘 검토해 보아야할 것이라고 생각되었다.

◇부대 주변 알프스 절경 탐방

ㅇ '잘츠부르크(Saltzburg, 소금마을)', '잘츠베르그(Saltzberg, 소금산)' 탐방

제1산악여단 주둔지 '바드라이헨할' 마을 자체가 알프스의 산 바로 아랫마을이라 아름다운데다 온천장으로까지 기능하고 있어 독일 내국인들의 관광지로 유명하다. 그런데 바로 위(북) 큰길(뮌헨-잘츠부르크로 가는 길) 하나 건너면 아주 아름다운 휴양마을 'Piding'이 이웃에 있고, 1시 방향으로 독일—오스트리아 국경선 맞은편 12킬로미터도 안 되는 거리에는 '잘츠부루크' 마을이 있는데, 물론 악성 '모짜르트'의 고향이고 활동 무대라 전통적으로 유명하지만, 세계에 잘 알려진 「Sound of Music」이라는 음악영화—그 속에 「에델바이스」 노래는 유명하다.—로 더욱 유명하다. 오늘날 한국인의 동유럽 관광 제1번지로 되어 있을 만큼, 특히 연중 눈 덮인 근처 알프스의 산(Mt. Watzman) 등을 배경으로 아름답고 순하고 친절한 관광 도시다.

그런데 이 도시는 그 이름 그대로 고대에 바다였다가 바다가 사라지고 건조되면서 소금마을이 되었고, 남으로 30여킬로미터 내려가면 상당한 언덕 높이의 진짜 소금산(Salzberg)이 있는데, 1200년대부터 산 위로부터 아래로 파 내려가면서 소금을 캐내었다. 그런데 지금은 재밌고 유명한 관광지가 되어 있다.

ㅇ '베레히테스가덴(Berchtesgaden)' 탐방

독일연방 동부 국경선의 맨 아래 끝부분은 우리나라의 삼지주머니 같이 생겼으며 오스트리아와 접경하고 있다. 그곳에는 전형적인 알프스의 아름다움이 가득하여 유명한 관광지가 옹기종기 모여 있는데, '잘츠부르크'와 '잘츠베르그'를 비롯하여 곧 탐방하게 되는 '밧즈만(Watzmann)' 설산과 특히나 풍경과 함께 군사적으로도 유명한 '베레히테스가덴'이 있다.

그러기에 이 지역은 지형 특성상, 행여나 잘못을 저지른 자가 숨기가 좋을 듯하다고 생각할 수 있는 모양세라, 그래서인지 제2차 대전 당시 독일 독재자 '히틀러'가 연합군에 쫓기면서 숨을 곳으로 준비한 곳 즉, 같은 민족으로 유사시 지원을 기대할 수 있는 오스트리아가 배경이 되어 있는 그곳을 최후 거점으로 택해 요새화하였던 곳이다.

지금은 다만 관광 명소로 뒤로는 아름다운 알프스의 산을, 앞으로는 알프스 평지 구릉지대의 아름다움을 산 위에서 만끽할 수 있는 정도로 알려져 있으나 60~70년대에는 '히틀러' 최후 거점을 방문하고 견학하며 감상한다는 의미가 더 깊었다. 평지에서 꼬불꼬불 산길을 따라 차량이 올라가서 주차하고는, 마지막 코스에 특히 그 바위 산속을 뚫어 50명이상 또는 그 중량의 장비나 인원을 동시에 탑재하여 150미터 이상을 상승하는 거대 엘리베이터를 이용하여 정상에 오르면 바로 전투 지휘소 겸 관측소가 위치해 있었다. 실로 그 준비성(요새 건축술)과 과학의 힘 그리고 당시 독일의 국방력에 대해 새삼 감탄하지 않을 수 없었다.

◦ **'밧즈만(Watzmann)' 등산, '퀘닉(Konigssee)'호수 탐방**

'바드라이헨할'에서 약 30여킬로 남으로 내려가면 Alps 산맥의 눈산(雪山)들이 전개되는데 그중 흔하게 사람 접근이 가능한 산 Watzmann이 우뚝 솟아 있다. 이 산은 이 지방의 지표로도 활용된다. 산 높이는 해발 2,700여 미터인데 2,000여 미터까지는 삼림지대로부터 시작해서 점차 고산 관목지대로 변화해 가는데 여기까지는 차량으로 접근 가능함으로 많은 사람들이 찾아오고 있다. 우리도(나와 안내 장교) 2,000미터까지 부대 지프(전용)로 가서 다음은 하차하여 별다른 장비나 준비 없이 정복 입은 그대로 걸어서 정상 근처까지 등정하였다. 2,000미터 하차 지점부터는 관목조차 없는 그러나 8월 여름인데도 발목 깊이의 눈을 밟으며, 그런대로 땀을 흘리지 않아도, 별다른 힘을 들이지 않고 올라갈 수 있었다.

도중에 만난 사람은 엽총으로 무장한 산악 감시인이었는데 외국 군인이라 신기해하며 친절하게도 산악 국경 경비 임무에 대해 설명해 주기도 하였다. 알프스 국경 지대 산악에 주둔병이나 국경 경찰의 존재는 알 수 없었으나 산악 감시인이 산악 보호와 국경 경비를 동시에 수행하면서 이 알프스 설산을, 비록 무장은 하였으나 혼자서 정찰, 순시하는 모습에 이 산악 감시인들의 용감성은 물론 존엄조차 느낄 수 있었다.

그런데 그 바로 오른쪽 밑바닥에는 '왕의 호수'라는 이름의 'Konigssee'가 있었다. 그래서 다음 날 다시 그 호수로 가서 호수 관광을 겸하여 탐방하였다. 당시는 문자 그대로 첩첩산중 무인지경이라 문자 그대로 쥐 죽은 듯이 조용하였다. 그래서 관광선을 타고 설명을 들으며 호수 가운데로 문자 그대로 미끌어지듯 나아가면서 사방 단애들과 그 위의 설산 즉 '밧즈만'과 같은 눈 덮인 산봉우리들을 올려다보며 신비함을 감상해 가다가, 배를 잠시 멈추고 엔진도 끄고 보니 이건 완전한 태고의 정적 상태가 되었다.

그러자 나팔수가 한 가락 나팔을 불었더니 산과 계곡 사방에서 메아리가 돌아오는데 연속으로 길게 이어졌다. 그 메아리와 그때 그 분위기는 지금도 잊을 수 없다. 더구나 그때 들었던 그 이후 지금까지의 평생에 두 번 다시 산 메아리 소리를 들어본 적이 없다. 심지어 최근에 동유럽 관광을 가서 그곳 그 호수에 그 배를 탓건만 그 메아리 연출조차도 이제는 없어 그 옛적 메아리 소리를 듣지 못해 아쉬웠고, 세상 변화 또한 실감하였다.

3. 서독 지휘참모대학(Fűrungs Academy der Bundeswehr)과 '함부르그' 생활

◇ 학교 소개

독일어 그대로 번역하면 '통솔학원'이지만 한국군 교육 체계로 말하면 '육군대학'이고, 미군 체계로 말하면 '지휘참모대학'이다. 때문에 일반인이나 군인 모두에게 이해하기 쉽게 표시한다면 역시 '지휘참모대학'이 적절한 표현이기에 앞으로 그렇게 사용하도록 하며 때때로 줄여서 '지참대'라고도 쓰기로 한다.

당시 독일은 패전국에 대한 제재를 벗어나지 못한 상태고 동시에 군사 축소 지향 상황이어서 조직이나 직위 등이 하나가 둘의 역할을 하고 한곳에 둘 이상의 기관을 통합 운용하고 있었다. 통상 군대 기능 중 평화 시의 군사 재판이라던가 특히 학교 경비 등—눈으로 관찰한 범위 내에서 보건데—은 민간인에게 위임하거나 직접 고용하여 운용하고 있었다. 그래서 이 학교에는 '지참대'와 한 울타리 안에 우리의 국방대학원 안보 과정 같은 과정이 함께 있었고 경비 요원은 은퇴 민간인으로 편성 운용되고 있었다.

학교는 당시(서독, 1969~1970) '함부르크'에 있었는데, 설명으로는, 정치 외교 경제 사회 및 기타 국제 관계가 첨단으로 작동하는 지역에 학교가 있어야—외국 대통령 등 주요 외빈강의를 청강하는 등, 통일 독일 수도가 베를린으로 복귀하자마자 이 '지참대' 또한 동시에 베를린으로 복귀하였다.—바로 최고학부 간부 피교육생이 국제적 현실 감각을 그대로 받아드려 군대를 항상 국제 수준으로 발전시켜 나갈 수 있다는 것이었다. 아주 맞는 말이다. 오늘날 한국의 주요 군사학교가 서울 아닌 곳 멀리에 있어서 군 간부들이 시대적 국제 감각이 뒤떨어질 수 있다는 우려를 낳고 있기도 하다.

독일도 타 서구 선진국들과 같이 뒤질세라 추후 외세 확장을 위해서 다방면의 외국 유학생을 받아드려 독일 연구에 지원을 다하고 있다. 특히 독일어학 연구 분야를 비롯하여 기술 분야 교육훈련 그리고 군사 간부 유학 지원을 하고 있었다. 군 간부 유학 지원은 특히 과거 아프리카 인연 식민지군대 간부—이들은 주로 대위급이지만 주요한 군 간부들로 (병과학교) 이수 후 귀국하면, 국가 지도자가 되고 있었다.—들이 상당수였고, 다음은 미국 영국 등 동맹 나토 국가 군 간부(이들은 독일 간부와 함께 정규 과정) 그리고 우리같이 앞으로 여지가 있게 보이는 국가 간부들이 있었다. 우리 1970년 외국인 반(1년 단기)에는 22명 중 독일 장교 5명과 한국군 3, 스위스군 1, 네팔 1, 모로코 3, 베네수엘라 1, 브라질 2, 태국 1, 이란 1, 스페인 1, 인도네시아 1, 대만 1, 아이랜드 1, 으로 구성되었다.

학교본부는 학교장 준장, 참모 G—1, 2, 3, 4, 5로 대령들이었고, 현역교관은 따로 없었으며—각반 담임과 학교본부참모가 교수 업무 수행함—각반에는 담임교관(Hősaal Leiter, 강좌장(講座長))(대령)이 있어서 여비서 한 명과 계원 2~3을 거느리고 소속 반원에 대한 교육 과제 해결, 교육 진행은 물론 행정 업무까지도 수행하였다. 당시에는 이들 대령들은 2차 세계대전 참전 고참장교들이었다.

◇ 독일군 'General Stab, 핵심참모' 제도 소개

전통적으로 세계 최강의 군대로 자타가 공인하는 옛 독일 군대의 지휘 통솔 본령(本領)에는 바로 '게너럴 스탑(General Stab)'이 자리하고 있는데, 우리말로는 '핵심참모'(요원) 또는 '참모본부 참모'로 번역할 수 있는데 본인은 그동안 후자 용어를 사용해 왔으나 거듭 생각해 보니 전자의 용어가 더 가까운 의미로 생각되어 앞으로는 '핵심참모'를 주로 사용하려고 한다. 이제 그 양성 과정과 운용 과정 그리고 제2차 대전 종전 후 현재 현상을 통해서 이 '핵심참모'가 무엇이었기에 유명하며 두려운 존재였고, 그리고 지금 형편은 어떠한지를 당시의 직접 현지 연구와 견문을 통해 밝혀보려 하니 한국군 발전에 도움되기를 바란다.

◦ 역사적 유래

세계 모든 군대는 참모(부)의 건의에 따라 지휘(통솔)관에 의해 지휘 통솔되고 작전을 실시하고 있다. 그런데 대체로 미국과 영국 그리고 프랑스를 비롯한 민주주의 군대는 지휘관 중심 구조이고, 반면에 독재 국가들이었던 독일과 구 소련 그리고 이들을 복사한 일제 군대가 참모 중심이었다.

독일 군대는 일찍이 1870년대 철혈재상 '비스마르크'와 '대 모르트케 장군'에 의해서 통일 독일을 완성하는데 결정적으로 기여하였다. 그때 '대 모르트케 징군'은 일찍부터 이 '참모본부' 제도를 창안하여 '핵심참모'를 육성하고 이들로 '참모본부'를 단위 부대별로 구성하여 운용함으로써 유럽 최강의 군대가 되었고 현재까지도 유지 발전되고 있는 것이다.

그리하여 일찍부터 소수의 엘리트 장교 집단을 특화 교육하여 '핵심참모(부)' 집단을 형성하고, 그들을 각별한 대우—일반 사회 박사학위자와 같은 예우, 그래서 견장도 달리하고 바지에는 붉은 줄을 넣어 입게 하는 등—와 관리로 군대 조직의 핵심으로 운용하였다. 그리하여 이 '핵심참모' 중심의 독일군 지휘 통솔의 전통은 통일 독일전쟁 달성에 이어 제1차 세계대전에서 더욱 그 가치를 발휘하였다. 직업 군인이라면 다 아는 바와 같이, 세계 제1차 대전 중 세계 전쟁사에 대승으로 기록된 '탄넨베르그(Tannenberg)' 전역에서, 독일군의 노 지휘관 '힌덴부르그' 장군이 그의 명 참모장 '루덴돌프' 장군과 '핵심참모'(부)—특히 작전참모 호프만 중령의 지혜와 활동(계획 및 현지 참모감독)—의 지원을 받아 러시아의 4+1/2군단을 전멸시켰던 것이다.

그리하여 그 이후 독일군은 '핵심참모 제도'를 더욱 강화하여, 제2차 세계대전에서도 독일군대의 전술 전략과 군사 운용술은 가히 세계 최강을 자랑하였고 연합군의 두려움의 대상이었다. 다만 히틀러 등 정치 야심가들에 의해 전쟁에서 패배하였으나 연합군과 세계는 독일군의 '강대했던 원인'도 전쟁 범죄로 몰아 '뉴른베르그 전쟁 재판'에서 범죄자 아닌 'General Stab, 핵심참모 제도' 즉, 독일군 '참모본부 시스템'을 재판에 회부하여, 단죄하고, 앞으로 독일군은 이 제도를 그대로는 사용할 수 없도록 하였다.

그리하여 2차 대전 이후 NATO의 한 멤버국으로 재건될 때는, 견장과 외부 표지 등 두드러진 엘리트 의식의 상징적 외관은 접고, 운용 과정도 전적으로 참모 근무만 경험하여 참모 특성으로, 참모 집단으로만 운용하지 않고 새롭게, 제대별 '참모 독단 행위'등을 제거하고, 지휘관 근무도 의무적으로 부과하도록 절충하여 부활, 운용하게 되었다.

◦ 양성 제도와 교육 과정

독일군 장교는, 물론 과거에는 귀족 가문에서 선발되었으나, 지금은 18개월 의무병 근무를 끝낸 병사들 중, '아비투어(Abitur)'를 가진 자를 선발하여 사관학교 3년 교육—학교 학술교육과 부대 실무교육을 통해—을 이수시켜 임관한다. 그래서 장기 복무 장교는 각종 자격 과정을 거치면서 소대장과 중대장을 역임한다.

대위가 되어 중대장 근무를 필하고 나이 30세가 되었을 때 여단장 등 부대장 추천으로

1차 선발되고, '지참교'에 가서 2차 시험에 합격하여야 최종 선발된다. 대체로 전투병과 장교로서 육군 40여 명, 해공군 15여 명으로 장교 중 15% 정도가 해마다 선발되는 것이다.

이들은 '지참교'에 입학하여 2년 6개월간 명실공히 일반 대학교의 박사과정—독일은 석사과정이 별도로 없고, 대학 졸업 후 바로 3년여에 걸친 박사과정을 갖는다, 단 2000년대 이후 E.U기준으로 변화했다.—과 같은 수준의 학업을 2년 6개월에 걸쳐 이수한다. 입교 후 바로 외국어 어학학교에서 6개월간 수업하고 중고등학교 영어교사 자격증을 획득한 뒤,—미달자는 낙오—본교로 돌아와 2년간 본교 '정규 과정(Core Course)'으로 들어가며, 2년간 결혼도 못 하고 기숙사 생활하면서 도(?)를 닦는다.

졸업 시에는 성적 서열 없이 소정의 과정을 이수한 자격으로 'im General Stab'의 증서—일반 사회 박사학위와 동등한 학위와 자격증서—를 수여 받고 소령으로 승진하면서 졸업을 하게 된다. 그 얼마나 확실하고도 보장된 교육 과정인가! 이 'im General Stab, (i.G)' 칭호는 사회 'Doctor' 칭호와 같이 불리며 명함에도 새겨져 사용된다. 독일 국민들은 이 사람들을 크게 존경한다. 그래서 독일 군대는 내외로 또다시 강한 군대로 군림해 가고 있다.

◦ 운용제도(진급 과정 포함)

'지참교'를 졸업 즉 'General Stab'으로 임명됨과 동시에 최초 보직은 NATO 연락 장교와 주외국 대사관 무관 또는 여단의 G-3, G-4—여단참모는 S1, S2, G3, G4로 구성된다.—로 근무하게 된다. 근무 중 유사시는 G3가 S2를 장악한다. 근무 시한이 경과하면 다음은 중령 진급과 동시에 전투병과부대 대대장으로 지휘관 경험을 하게 된다. 이후 상급부대(사단 등) G1, G2, G3 G4 등 참모 근무를 하고 이어 대령으로 진급하면서 연대 단위 부대 지휘관을 경험하고 다음은 장군이 보장된다. 이어서 상급부대 참모와 지휘관을 거치면서 군무를 계속한다. 이와 같이 독일군은 일단의 엘리트 집단에 의해 지휘 통솔되고 이들에 의해 성장하고 강화된다.

한편 일반 장기 복무 장교 중 일부는 부대에서 소령으로 진급한 후 부대대장 겸 대대 작전 장교(S—3)를 거쳐 '지참교' 단기 과정(1년)을 이수하고 연대나 여단급의 부지휘관 또는 보좌관 생활을 통해 진급하고 최종 계급은 대령으로 마감한다. 한편 장기 근무 장교 중 대부분(약 85%)은 대위 계급으로 자기가 원하는 그 지방의 토박이 부대의 대대 S1, 2, 3, 4를 거쳐 연대/여단의 S1, S2, 그리고 G3, 4 밑의 S3, 4로 근무하면서 원한다면 54세까지 근무할 수 있다.

한국 실정과 정서로는 좀 이해하기 어려운 현상이기에 내가 실습한 산악여단의 S1으로 근무하는 50세가 다된 인사 장교(대위)에게 물어 보았다. 그는 주저 없이 자기 입장 즉 종신 대위의 군대 생활관을 말해주었다. 물론 'i.G' 장교를 선망도 하고 존경도 한다, 그러나 우리 같은 생활에도 만족하고 있다. 저 사람들은 우수하게 부대 근무한 자들로 여단장의 추천을 받아, 휴일도 쉬지 못하고 열심히 공부하여 '지참교'에 가서 경쟁시험 쳐서 입교한다. 거기서 장가도 못 들고 청춘 재미도 못 보면서 2년 6개월간 꼬박 기숙사 생활하면서 오로지 공부와 연구에 몰두한다. 그리고 졸업하면 한 지역에 있지도 못하고 다른 나라로 갔다가 저 부대로 갔다가 또 다른 부대로 가는 등 평생을 긴장된 가운데 떠돌이 가정생활을 한다.

그런데 우리는, 특히 나는 여기 아름다운 휴양지 알프스 산밑 좋은 부대에서 한 번 익힌 인사 행정 근무 경험을 가지고 평생 별다른 공부 노력 없이, 별 하자 없이, 어려움 없이 지내면서 적절한 시기에 결혼하고 정시에 출퇴근하며 휴일이면 알프스의 산 등산해가며 만족한 생활을 하고 있다. 물론 생활 갈등도 없다, 고 했다. 그 말도 맞을 것 같았다. 앞으로 특히 진급 문제에 갈등이 많은 한국군에서는 연구해 볼만한 가치가 있다고 생각했다.

◇ 서독 '지참대' '연합군 반' 학습 생활

◦ 학교 안내 및 수업 준비

우리 반은 〈연합군 반〉으로 10개월 단기 과정으로 책정되어 있었다. 입학 첫날, 간단한 입학식 후 학교장 준장, 학교 참모부 대령들 소개 후 '강좌장(Hősal Leiter, 앞으로 '강좌장'으로 사용함)'이 인솔하여 학교 내부 시설물과 이용 방법 등 소개 후 도서관으로 가서 가방 가득 30여 권의 『M(군사야전교범)』을 수령하여, 숙소가 아닌 강좌실(강좌 교실, 토의 겸 모임방)로 가서 자기 자리와 책상을 배정받고, 책상에 책을 넣어 두었다. 이 교범들은 정위치가 숙소 아닌 교실의 내 책상 속이었다. 다시 말하면 모든 공부와 연구와 토의는 이 교실에서 이루어지며 여타 교내 시간은 자유 시간이라는 것을 의미하였다.

* 야전교범 30여 권 중 『Fűhrung』이 핵심 교범인데, 한국 교범의 『작전』, 미군의 『FM 100-5, Operaion』과 같은 내용의 교범이다.

지금부터 졸업 때까지 학업 지도와 행정지원 야외실습 참모 여행(후에 설명)등 피교육자들의 모든 것을 담당—옛날 초등학교 담임 선생 역할+행정명령 및 집행—하는 강좌장은 대령으로서, 바로 옆방에 위치하고, 행정 요원(여비서 겸) 1~2명과 함께 상주하면서 우리 피교육자와 일과를 함께 하였다.

학교 본 수업(Core Course)은, 1기(3개월)로 '부대 전투 준비 태세→비상→전방으로 부대 이동', 2기(5개월)로 '방어 편성→방어 실시', 3기(2개월)로 '반격 및 공격 준비'로 책정되어 있었다. 그래서 수업 첫 시간에 강좌장에 의해서 반원을 4개 사단본부조(사단장, 참모장과 주참모 즉 G1, 2, 3, 4)로 편성하고, 각 기마다 반을 재편성하며 진행하기로 하였다.

◇ 커리큘럼과 Core Course 수업

그래서 그날(첫날) 바로 예습 문제와 해결을 위한 '상황 과제(문제)'가 제시된 페이퍼를 수령하였다. 첫 과제(요약)가 "적 침략 징후 발견→적군 공격 태세, 아군 Defcon—2(완전 무장 후 방어진지 배치)" 상황에서 귀 부대 전방으로 작전 이동 명령을 수령하였다.

과제 ; 귀하는 사단참모(1,2,3,4), 지휘관이다. 현재시간 00시 00분, 귀하의 행동 및 계획 여하?

대체로 한 과제(문제) 당 2주간을 할당하여, 개별 연구, 조별 토의, 조별 발표, 강좌장 평가 그리고 다음 과제 제시 순으로 진행하였다. 개별 연구는 교 실내 자기 책상에 넣어둔 야전교범을 참고하여 준비하고 조별로 각자 맡은 참모직책에 따라 토론하고 발표 준비하며, 발표일에는 각 조 즉 사단별로 나가서 직책별로 의견을 발표한다.

* 참고로 현재 대부분의 서독사단은 후방에 주둔해 있고 국경 지대는 국경 경비대(경찰)가 근무 증이다.

시작 전후에 별도의 상황 설명이나 요령 제시는 없다. 오로지 개인 연구와 조별 토론과 조별 결론이 중요시되는데, 다만 질문이 있으면, 학교본부 참모 중에 질문에 해당되는 부서 참모가 와서 질문에 대한 대답만을 해주고 문제 해결을 조언해 줄 뿐이다. 그래서 개인의 연구심을 극도로 고양시킬 수가 있는 것이다. 한국과 같이 각 과목(도하, 방어, 공격 등)별 교관(교수)이 있어서 자기 과목을 강의하고 설명하고 진행하는 것이 아니다. 과목 담당 교관은 없기에 과목 강의는 물론 별도로 없고, 각 개인이 스스로 야전교범을 참고하여 생각하고 연구하여 해결책을 창출해 내게하는 참으로 이상적이고 창의적인 교육제도이다.

월요일부터 금요일까지 교실에 조별로 모여 연구하고 토론하면서 수시로 조별 결론을 창출해 낸다. 그런데 '코어코스' 아닌 기타 과목 즉, 정치. 경제, 역사(특히 국사)는 초빙강사가 강의 또는 강연(자국 또는 외국 귀빈)하는데, 특히 역사는 일반 부대에서도 중요시 하던데, 여기 학교 코어코스에서도 아주 중요시하며, 그중에서도 전사(戰史, War History)는 '실전(實戰)의 평시 경험'으로 생각하고 중요시한다.

이제 2주 지나 각 조별 발표 시간이 되자, 게시판에는 큰 벽시계를 걸고, 단상에 한 조(각 사단별)씩 번갈아 점령하여 자기 직책별로 문제 해결책을 발표한다. 시계는 실시간적 행동을 실감나게 한다. 예를 들면, 작전참모가 군단에 가서 명령을 수령해(또는 전령을 통해) 오고, 그 몇 분 뒤에 어디 가서 누구에게 보고하고…… 그래서 몇 시간 뒤에 어떤 결과가 되었는지 등, 실상황이나 실제 행동과 같이 실감나게 문제를 해결해 나간다. 물론 도중도중에 경청하는 다른 조들은 질문하고 다른 의견을 토의하기도 한다.

2~3일간에 걸쳐 각 조별 발표가 끝나면 '강좌장'에 의한 강평이 있는데, 각 조의 발표 내용을 요약해 주고, 자기가 참전했던 2차 대전 시 유사한 경험을 얘기하고는, "각 조별 발표 내용 및 결론(의견)을 모두 존중한다, 실전에서도 그런 상황들이 전개될 수도 있을 것임으로, 오늘 나온 타의 의견도 참고하여 자기 것을 창안해 내기를 바란다"로 결론 내린다.

당시 한국 교육 기관에서는 여전히 '학교측 원안'—그래서 시험 치고 학교 측 원안대로 성적을 부과한다.—을 내 걸고 강조하고 있었다. 사실은 학교 안 자체도 한가지 안일 뿐인데, 굳이 유일한 원안으로 강조함으로써, 실제 현장(작전 환경)에 적시 적응할 수 있는 개별적인 창안력 발휘를 어렵게 할 수도 있었다.

강좌장은 결론 후 곧바로 진전되는 상황과 해결과제(문제)가 제시된 예습지(숙제?)를 배부해 주면서, 일부 조편성을 바꾸어 학업 분위기를 바꾸어 주기도 한다. 계속되는 상황과 부여되는 과제를 요약해 보면

• 부대 이동 및 전방 방어지역 전개 명령 수령 ; 귀하는 사단 참모/지휘관이다, 부대 이동

계획을 검토하라.—함부르크 인접 실 주둔 부대를 시범부대로 상정.

- 부대 이동 개시 ; 귀 부대는 00도시 0번 고속도로 이용 명령 수령 ; 부대 도로 이동 중 해당 도시 행정청과 군 도로통제소와 협조문제를 검토하라.
- 유사시 무교량 하천 도하명령 수령 ; 귀 부대(기계화부대)는 대하천(大河川, 예, 한강), 무 교량, 급속 도하 상황이다. 방책(계획) 여하 등.

◇ 참모 여행 겸 현장 실습, (서독) 지방 견문록

◦ 부대 전방 전개를 위한 이동 과정 현장 실습 겸 참모 여행

독일군은 전통적으로 사령부, 군, 군단급 '핵심참모'가 작전 중 작전 계획대로 수행되는지 그리고 현지 정세 파악을 위해 그리고 현지 지도 겸 확인을 위해 예하 부대로 '참모 여행'을 거듭하여 실시한다. 이제 우리 연합군 반도 실내에서 2개월여 작전을 연구하여 계획하고 토의하면서, 일단 완성한 '자기의 안(독자 안)'을 가지고 실제 현장에서 대조하며 확인해보는 현지 실습 겸 참모 여행을 가지게 되었다.

함부르크를 출발하여 동부 국경선(당시는 동서독 접경선)까지 지방도로와 Autobahn(고속도로) 그리고 '엘베강' 지류 등지를 현지 답사해 가면서 실습을 하며 전진해 나갔다. 그리고 가는 곳마다, 지방 관청에 들려 '대군(對軍) 지원 사항'을 브리핑받고 질문 및 토의 등을 통해 점검하고 확인하였다. 주 착안 사항은 이동하는 군대에 대한 각종 민간 지원 사항 특히 '물 보급',—유럽이나 미국 도시를 지나는 길에 흔히 둥그렇게 공중에 떠 있는 듯한 거대한 물탱크를 보게 되는데 바로 군사/재난 목적의 시설이다.—교통 통제 문제, 보급지원 문제 등이었다.

이와 같이 과정을 밟으면서 다음 단계 방어 편성과 방어 실시, 현지 실습 겸 참모 여행, 그리고 이어서 반격 준비와 실시 단계로 이어지고 역시 현장 실습과 참모 여행으로 학과가 진행되었다. 독일군 정규반은 과정 말기에 청군과 홍군으로 편성하여, 육해공 합동 연습을 실시(예, 아프리카 내란 국가에 긴급 원조물자 수송 과제)하였는데 우리 반 또한 과정 마감을 겸하여 그 과정을 견학하였다.

◇ 서독군의 '작전교리'와 전술핵 운용

- 서독군의 'Fűhrung', 미군은 'Operation', 한군군은 '작전요무령'
- 작전 운용 단위와 용어 ; 전술(Tactics)는 대대 단위까지, 작전(Operaion)는 연대, 여단 단위, 전략(Strategic)는 여단 이상 통상은 사단 단위, 미군과 한국군은, '전술'과 '전략'으로만 구분되어 있다.

∘ 전차 및 기계화부대 운용(+차량화 보병)

방어시 ; 2개 기계화보병대대(중대)(APC)를 전방 고지(구능)에 좌우로 배치, 전차(Panzer-Leopard)대대는 후방에 배치, 적 공격 시 좌일선 또는 우일선 중 한 대대(중대)는 진지 고수, 한 대대(중대)는 기동 방어, 기회 도래 시 전차대대가 역습하여 방어진 지회복 후, 기회 포착하여 전차대대 선봉으로 공격태세로 전환.—이는 유럽 평원전투의 일반적 모형임.

◇ 전술핵무기의 운용과 전망

전략 핵무기는 물론 전술핵무기도 지역 NATO의 미군이 평시에 보관하고, 훈련지도하다가 유사시 사용 시는 감독한다. 따라서 훈련만은 서독군 단독으로 행하고 있다.

- 사용 화기는 8인치, 175미리, 155미리, 로켓포 등으로 투발 가능하다.—한국군도 이와 같이 가용 화기를 가지고 있었고 훈련도 받았다. 그러나 1990년 이후 미군이 각 화기의 핵무기 투발용 특수장치를 회수해 갔다.

∘ 운용

전술핵무기 표준은 5kt로 5평방킬로미터 유효 범위이고, 통상은 방어 전개된 기계화 1개 대대 범위이다.

방어시는 적 기계화/기갑부대의 아 전선 돌파를 저지하고 섬멸시키기 위해서, 공격 시는 적 방어진 지상의 기계화/기갑부대를 섬멸시켜 돌파해 나가기 위해서 운용한다.

- 60년대부터 계속 발전시키면서 훈련을 실시해 보았으나 핵무기 투발 이후 후유증에 대한 연구와 실증 자료가 재래식 무기보다 실리가 많지 않은대 비해 인류에 대한 도덕적 피해가 크게 부담됨을 알고 1970년대—NATO와 서독군은 72년—부터 운용훈련을 중단하고 폐기 준비를 하다가 90년대에 들어와 미소간 핵무기 군비 통제 협상 성공을 계기로 피차 폐기하였다.

∘ 견문록

현지 실습 및 참모 여행 중에 여러 지방과 군관민 시설을 순방하고 여러 가지 견학도 하였다. 해군기지 방문에 이어 해안에서 46킬로미터로 가까운 거리에 있는 '헬고렌데(Helgo länder)'라는 유인도—세모꼴 모양의 약 1킬로미터 평방, 해발 61미터—를 방문하였는데 2면은 완전히 절벽이고 한 면의 일부가 바다로 이어지는 경사 평면으로 사람이 거주하였는데, 독일에서는 이나마 아주 귀한 바다 휴양/관광지로 유명하였는데, 알고 보면 그 절벽 면과 지하에는 독일 해군 탄약 기지로 이용되고 평지 일부는 해군 보급기지로 이용되고 있었다. 그와 같이 독일 알프스 산속에도 수 없는 군사용 동굴 탄약고와 요새가 존재해 있다. 그런 설명을 들으면서 문득, 우리의 태백산맥에는 어떤 군사시설들이 가용할까, 생각되었다.

'폭스바겐' 지동차 회사도 방문하였는데, 고장 없는 유류 절약형 딱정벌레 모양의 승용차—당시 독일의 국민차로 애용되고 세계적으로도 유명했던—를 생상라인에서 3분에 1대씩 생산해 내고 있었다. 거기서 듣기로는, 당시 독일에서는 이제 막 부흥 중이라 미국 자본(독일 기술)으로 'Opel'과 'Audi'가 생산 중이고 '벤츠'는 생산 준비 중이라 하였다. 당시 우리나라는 '코티나' 승용차를 조립 생산 중이었는데 우리나라도 이런 방향으로 출발하였다고 생각되었다.

이어서 독일이 세계에 자랑하는 철강회사 'Krupp'을 방문하였는데 거대함과 웅장함 그리고 품질에 대한 자랑은 들어줄만 하였다. 여기에서 2차 대전 시 각종 포화기의 포신을 제작하였는데, 지금은 군수물자 생산을 금지당하고 독일제 'Panzer' 탱크조차 그 포신은 NATO 회원국인 영국제라며, 비판하면서 옛 포신 제품을 자랑해 보이며 아쉬워하고 있었다. 견학 때마다 당시 군사 정부에 의해 천지 개벽 중인 우리나라의 국가 발전 방향을 예견할 수 있는 가운데 국가 부흥 속도와 함께 중공업화를 위한 자동차 생산 체제를 또한 갖추어 가고 있던 중이라 모든 것이 관심거리였다.

도중에 통신학교를 방문하여 우리보다 반 발자국 앞서가는 서독군 통신 시스템인 'DDD'—우리는 제5공화국 시절에 완성—를 살펴보고 저녁에는 때마침 개최 중인 '가장무도회'에 참가하여, 연령과 얼굴 모양새를 재밌는 탈로 감춘 지역 여자들, 아마도 군인 가족들을 상대로(우리는 뱃사람으로 가장) 즐거운 몇 시간을 보내기도 하였다.

4. 사단 단위 참모 현지 참관—제5기갑사단(Frankfurt am Main)

함부르크 소재 '지휘참모대학'의 10개월 과정(1969.10.1.~70.6.30)을 이수하고, 바로 이어서 1970년 7월에, 사단 단위 참모 업무에 대한 실습 참관을 1개월간 실시하였다. 독일에는 '프랑크푸르트'라는 이름의 도시가 2개 있는데 그중 하나가 서독의 '마인'강 유역에 있는 '프랑크푸르트 암 마인'인데, 오늘날 독일로 가는 한국 항공기들의 대부분이 이 도시의 공항으로 향하고 있다.

서독군 유학의 마지막 과정으로 제5기갑사단으로 갈 수 있게 되어, 독일군의 상징인 기갑부대를 관찰할 수 있는 기회를 갖게 되어 정말 다행이었다. 그리하여 기대를 안고 도착해 보니 사단장을 비롯하여 관계 사단 참모들이 반갑고 친절하게 맞아 주었다.

그리하여 사단 내 각 참모부를 둘러보고 참모 회의에 참석해 보기도 하면서 사단사령부 내에서 일과를 주로 진행하기도 하였으나 어느 때는 근접 여단을 방문도 하면서 독일 기갑사단의 전후 기세를 탐구해 보았다. 다만 아쉬웠던 것은 그동안 기동훈련이나 대부대 연습훈련 등이 없어서 야전훈련의 진 모습을 관찰하지 못해 유감스러웠다. 하루는 사단 참모들과 함께 근방 야산으로 등산 겸 훈련을 겸하여 등정하고 정상 공원에서 맥주도 마셨는데, 독일군 동료가 권하기를 '등산하여 땀 흘리며 휴식 때는 과실주가 좋다면서 함께 맛보기도 하였다.

과정이 끝나갈 때쯤 부대 참모장이 물었다, "곧 한국 육군참모총장이 한국 국회의원과 우리 부대를 방문하는데 접대 준비를 해야겠다, 혹시 참모총장의 식성과 취미를 아느냐?"고. 당시 육군 소령인 내가 어찌 참모총장의 그것들을 알 수는 없었으나 그들의 성의를 보아서 일반적인 한국인 식성을 말해주었다. 그런데 국회의원도 함께 온다는데 전혀 신경 쓰지 않은 눈치였는데, 역시나 독일 사회의 국회의원 위치는 한국 사회에서와 달리, 공무원 사회에서 국장급 정도로 인식되어 있었기 때문으로 보였다.

5. 독일 유학 여담 ; 1970년대 초 서독, 유럽, 일본 견문록

◇ 프랑스 파리 탐방 여행(1970.5)

이제 그 지루하고 향수에 차기도 했던 겨울도 가고, 활동하기 좋은 봄이 되었다. 그래서 함부르크 '지참대' 수료 전 어느 날을 이용하여 시내 여행사를 통해 일반 독일인과 같이 버스를 이용하여 프랑스 파리 여행을 다녀온 기억을 더듬어 여기에 그 견문록을 옮겨 보고자 한다.

독일 함부르크를 출발하여 독일 북부 쾰른을 지나 벨기에의 '리에주(Liege)'와 '나무르(Namur)'를 통과하여 '디넝(Dinant)'을 지나 프랑스의 '아르덴네' 산맥(지금은 아르덴네 국립공원)속 의 '세당(Sedan)'에 들어왔다. 유럽 전사를 연구한 육사 출신 장교로서 이 길은 참으로 감개무량한 바 있었는데, 특히 세계 제1차 대전에서 독일군의 'Schlieffen 전략계획'에 따라 독일군이 프랑스를 노도와 같이 침략한 길이었고, 제2차 대전 시에도 독일 기갑군이 프랑스 '마지노' 장벽을 우회 돌파하여 프랑스 파리로 전격전을 감행한 길이었기 때문이다.

그러기에 지나가는 길목마다 무명용사비들이 줄지어 있는가 하면, 특히 '디넝'에는 과거 격전장을 기념하여, 프랑스, 벨기에, 독일, 영국, 미국 국기들이 4철 내내 높은 언덕 위에 휘날리고, 그 아래에 거대한 십자가 밑에는, 희생된 무명용사들의 공동묘지가 있었으며, 듣기로는 해마다 때가 되면 참전 국가 대표들이 피아 구분 없이 모여 크게 위령 행사를 집행한다는 것이었다.

파리에 들어가기 앞서 '렘스 시(Reims)'에 도착하여 세계에 잘 알려진 '램(REIM)' 샴페인 주조장을 방문하였다. 지하 50미터 한 지점을 중심으로 수백 미터가 넘는 다수의 지하 저장고가 방사선으로 연결되어 있고, 개별 병에 담긴 샴페인이 끝 안 보이게 저장되어 있었는데, 여러 명의 기술자들이 그 병들을 적당한 기간으로 세웠다 눕혔다 하면서 손보며 저장하다가 햇빛을 보게 하는데 한 10년 묵은 것이 제일 맛이 좋다고 했다. 안내자 무작위로 병을 하나 들어 콜크 마개를 딴 뒤 젓가락 같은 걸로 가볍게 병을 치자 곧바로 거품이 되어 한 방을 남김없이 솟아올랐다. 샴페인의 진미였다. 농담으로는, 독일군이 파리로 진격해 오다 여기서 돈이 들게 된 것은, 이 샴페인을 마실려고, 그래서 마시고 또 마시고 취해서 그만 주저앉았기 때문이라 했다.

파리에 들어와서는 피와 희망 그리고 아프리카 침략의 역사 전통이 아울러져 있는 넓은 콩코드광장의 한편에 있는 관광객용 어느 호텔에 자리 잡았다. 식후 해 질 무렵, 밖에 나와 광장 가운데 서서 저 멀리 개선문을 향해 샹제리제 야경을 보니 절로, 전 세계에서 흔하게 볼 수 있는 그림, 비오는 샹제리제 거리의 꼬리를 문 자동차들과 그 테일라잇의 붉은빛 색감이 때마침 내리는 보슬비와 어울려 만들어내는 아름다운 야경이 내 앞에 그대로 그려지고 있음을 보았다.

오늘은 늦었기에 일단 돌아와 잠자리에 들기 전에 화장실에 들렀더니, 변기와 비슷한 것이 또 있어, 손도 씻고 발도 씻고 양말도 빨래하면서 과연 예술의 나라답게 희한한 가재도구도 있구나 했는데, 다음 날 여자용 그런 것이라 듣고는 과연 프랑스하고도 파리로구나 했다. 우리나라에서는 그 후 40년 뒤 2010년경에 '비대'로 이름으로 유행하였다.

다음 날 나와본 광장에는 구석마다 농촌 이농자들과 해외 구 식민지에서 돌아온 귀환동포들이 벌여놓은 오락 난장판과 고물 장사와 채소 장수들이 혼잡한 가운데 사람 사는 냄새가 물씬 나기도 하였다. 다시 걸음을 옮겨 개선문을 향해 폭 100여미터로 마로니에 가로수와 양편으로 넓은 보도가 시원하면서도 멋들어진 샹젤리제 거리를, 두리번거리며 감탄하면서 천천히 우편 보도를 따라 걸어서 올라가 보았다. 특히 인상적인 것은 거리 양편과 한가운데로 조성되어 있는 '마로니에' 가로수—잊을 수 없어 그러부터 8년 뒤인 1978년 연대장 때 논산훈련소 26연대본부 앞과 옆으로 7그루를 심었는데, 어언 50년도 더 넘었으니 그대로 있다면 거목이 되었으리라.—와 그 돌봄이었는데, 간격과 크기와 모양도 모두가 비슷하며 정연한 것은 물론 매 그루마다 그 바닥에는 멋지게 디자인된 쇠판이, 깨끗하게 닦여진 대로 깔려 있어서, 프랑스의 '질서와 돌봄과 아름다움'을 그대로 느낄 수 있었다.

또한, 50년이 지난 지금에서 우리네 대도시에서 유행을 시작하는 가로 풍경, 울긋불긋 상점들로 줄이어진 보도 옆 가게들은 상점에서 내놓은 의자와 테이블들로 분위기가 평화롭고 사람 사는 곳 다웠다. 드디어 나폴레옹의 세계 제패를 기념하여 세운 개선문에 도착해 보니, 소문대로 30년의 대공사로, 파리를 대표하는 12개의 방사선 도로가 모인 한가운데에 거대한 대문 모양의 석조 구조물이 세계 대표적인 개선문답게 장중함을 자랑하고 있었다. 내용을 보기 위해 가까이 가서 사면의 벽을 둘러보았는데, 4면의 큰 벽면에 'La Marseillaise(진군)', 'La Triomphe(승리)', 'La Resistance(저항)', 'La paix(평화)'를 의미하는 군상들이 조각되어 있었다. 대한민국 우리는 언제 이러한 개선문을 광화문에 세울 수 있을까. 어느 땐가는 반듯이 이 꿈이 이루워지기를 바란다.

다음에 찾은 곳은 바로 세계 최초이며 세계 최대 규모인 '군사(軍史, Military History) 박물관'이었는데, 전쟁 역사를 통해서 수많은 전장과 전투에서 사용되었거나 탈취한 무기, 장비, 군기, 군복 그리고 군사 회화들이 진열되어 있어서 비록 나폴레옹 시대 뿐만 아니라 군사(軍史) 전반에 걸친 이해를 도와주고 있었다. 그 수는 상당하여 아마도 일반 관광객으로 무심하게 지나가기만 해도 2시간여는 걸릴 정도였다.

다음 전사(戰史, War History) 건물에는, 프랑스 군대의 정승과 패배 역사는 물론 세계 전쟁사를 눈으로 볼수 있었다. 특히 거대한 메인홀에는 찬란하고도 엄숙한 나폴레옹의

'대리석관'이 천정 높이로 높은 곳에 안치되어 있는 것으로 보아 프랑스 사람들의 나폴레옹에 대한 존중심이 대단하다는 것을 새삼 느끼게 하였다. 우리 군인으로서도 그의 공적과 위훈을 높이 평가하는 것은 말할 나위도 없다 하겠다.

파리를 소개할 때 빠질 수 없는 '에펠탑(아이펠 타워)'은 거대한 대포 분수를 배경으로, 320미터 높이의 철강탑으로 제1회 세계박람회를 기념하여 독일 기술자에 의해 제작되었다. 에스카레이터를 타고 상층부 전망대 올라가 보면 360도 파리 시내 전체와 저 멀리 교외까지도 보이는데, 원형의 방향판에는 12방향 세계 유명 도시를 표기해 두었는데, 극동 방향에 도쿄만 있었다. 그래서 섭섭하여 내려와서는, 탑 관리 당국에 서울도 병기해 달라고 관광객 민원을 제기하기도 하였다.

파리에는 세계에 알려진 수많은 이름의 거리, 교회, 공원, 극장, 궁전, 조각 등이 있는데, 특히 '후렌치캉캉' 춤으로 유명한 '무랑루즈(붉은 풍차)'와 술과 여자의 거리 '피가레', 그리고 거리 미술가들의 작업터요 시장터인 '몽마르트르', 그리고 역사와 전통, 예술을 자랑하는 '벨사이유' 궁전과 그 정원, 세계적 미술품 전시장 '루부루 미술관', 파리 로멘스를 상징하는 '세느강의 뱃노리'와 고풍 창연한 '노틀담' 등등이 있다.

그러나 그중에서도 놀라운 것은 '파리 메트로' 즉 지히철이었다. 당시로는 세계 어느 도시 전철보다 거대하고 방대하게 발달되어 있었다. 대충 30킬로미터가 넘는 지하 노선 15개가 지하 1, 2, 3층으로 구성되어 파리 시가지 밑으로 거미줄같이 얽혀 있어서, 마치 관광객은 지상으로 다니고, '파리쟌느'들은 지하로 통행하는 듯 보였고, 파리 시가지는 허공에 떠 있는 것이 아닌가 생각될 정도로 엄청난 규모로 보였다.

'세계를 관광하는 사람은 마지막으로 파리를 보라'는 말이 있다. 결코 과장이 아니었다. 유럽의 수많은 아름답고 전통적인 도시들도 스스로 '소 파리' 또는 제2의 파리라고 불리어지기를 원하고 있을 정도였다. 파리 주택은 거의 전체가 나폴레옹 시대 도시 계획에 의해 건축된 5층 아파트로 아래층은 상가와 사무실, 위층은 주거층이었는데, 지금까지 그대로이며, 앞으로도 변화할 전망은 없어 보였다. 신천지 미국의 '업타운, 다운 타운' 개념과는 확연히 다른 유럽식 역사와 전통이 들어 보였다.

보충하건대, 오늘날 2021년에 한국 서울에는 길이 60여킬로미터가 넘는 지하철이 10개 이상으로 서울 지하를 거미줄같이 얽혀서 경기도 심지어는 충청도와 강원도 멀리까지 연결하며 발전해 나가고 있다. 그러나 1970년 당시 우리나라는 꿈도 꾸지 못할 때였고, 또 프랑스 하면 그저 향수와 향락이 연상되는 때라 내겐 더욱 인상 깊었다.

지금까지 유럽 탐방의 결론으로 말하자면, 유럽에서 성당(교회) 빼고, 프랑스에서 '나폴레옹'과 '드골' 빼고, 영국에서 '넬슨'과 '처칠'을 빼고 나면 유럽의 역사책은 헐값이 되어 휴지통에 들어가도 돌아보는 사람이 별로 없으리라.

◇ 서 베를린시 초청, 방문 여행(1970.5.19~21)

1970년 5월 19~20일에, 강좌장과 학생 그리고 그 가족들과 함께, 졸업여행을 겸하여,

당시는 동독 장벽 속에 있으면서 그 도시 절반 이상을 연합군이 점령하여 그나마 그 보호 하에 서독 시민들이 영위하고 있는 도시, 구 독일 수도였고, 당연히 미래에 통일 독일의 수도가 될 '베를린'으로, 정부 계획에 의한 선전 목적의 일환을 겸한 'VIP' 초청 단체 여행을 하게 되었다.

당시 서독은 전 세계인들의 공분을 사고 있던 '히틀러의 만행'에 대해서 국가적 수치로 단정하고 특히 서방 국가들애 대해 계속적으로 사죄하면서 여러 방면으로 그 진지성을 보이려고 애쓰고 있었다. 즉 세계대전 전범 국가의 오명으로부터 도덕적으로 복원하고자 노력하고 있었다. 1970년 막 당선된 서독 수상 '빌리 브란트'는 폴란드에 가서 바르샤바의 전쟁 희생자 묘비 앞에 꿇어앉아 사죄하기도 하였다. 그런 정책 중의 하나로, 세계 여론 조성 유력자나 집단을 초청하여, 독일 내부에서는 다수의 군관민에 의한, 특히 엘리트 시민에 의한 '반 히틀러 운동'도 극렬하게 전개되기도 하였다는 증거를 보여주기도 하였다. 동시에 전쟁 후유증으로 폐허되었던 베를린과 현재 '베를린 장벽'으로 분단된 베를린을 현장을 보여주면서 '전범 독일의 이미지를 바꾸어 달라'고 호소하는 의미의 노력도 하고 있었다.

우리 일행은 군용기로 베를린에 도착하여 시내 중심가에 있는 '유럽 센터'의 종합빌딩 속의 'Hotel Palace'에 안내되어 일단 여장을 풀었다. 다음날 베를린 시장이 직접 환영하며 접대해 주었고, 이어 안내한 곳이, 한 옛 형무소였는데, 그곳에서 '반 히틀러 세력'— 특히 독일 항복의 날이 가까웠던 1944년 7월에 있었던 독일 육군(핵심 장교단)의 '히틀러 암살과 쿠데타 미수사건' 가담자—에 대한 고문(각종 형틀과 함께)과 처형 현장을 보여주었는데, 특히 연합군이 두려워했던 용감한 장군으로, 독일 국민들이 존경했던 '롬멜 장군'을 반 히틀러 반란 음모 세력으로 몰아 처형(자살로 가장)했다는 사실을 열심히 설명도 해 주었다. 그런가 하면 그와 함께 특히 독일 국민에게 독일 군대를 대표하여 존경받았던 'General Stab(핵심참모단)' 요원들 다수를 또한 '반 히틀러 엘리트 세력'으로 의심하여 잔인한 형벌을 가하고 처형도 불사하였다고 하는 설명을 들을 때는 과연 소문대로 독일군의 '게너럴 스탑'이 국내외로 유명하고도 존경받았던 '핵심 군인'들이었구나 하는 생각이 절로 들었다.

그럼에도 불구하고 전후 '뉴른베르그 전범 재판에서 개인이 아닌 집단의 이름으로 단죄받은 '게너럴 스탑'의 존재감은 가히 독일군의 핵심이었음을 군인이라면 아무도 부정할 수 없었다.

다음으로 안내된 곳은 당시로 보아서는 동서냉전의 현장이며, 분단 독일의 긴장 지대였던 '베를린 장벽(Berlin Mauer)'의 상징 지점인 '브란덴브르크 문(Brandenburg Tor)'— 프로이센 왕국 시대 고전주의 양식으로 지어진 개선문의 하나—앞이였다. 그 문 앞을 연하여 북에서 남으로 시멘트로 된 장벽이 설치되어 독일의 심장부요 수도였던 베를린을 동서로 분단해 놓았으며, 동시에 이를 남북으로 이어서 철조망과 초소들로 조성되어 독일 전체가 동서독으로 나뉘어져 국경으로 마주하게 되어 있는 것이다. 광복 후는 38선으로 '6·25 남침적란' 후는 휴전선으로 남북이 분단되어 있는 한국의 우리 현실과 닮은 독일의 현실을 상징하는 이곳에서 그 현상을 보며 설명을 들으니 정말 감개가 무량하였다.

일행은 그 앞, 냉전의 상징 앞에서 기념사진을 찍었는데, 그 후 50여 년이 지난 2021년에 다시 그 사진을 들여다보며 역사의 흐름을 새삼 느끼게 되는 것은 물론이거니와, 북의 공산주의 3대 김씨 왕조의 불장난 때문에 아직도 통일되지 못한 내 조국 한국의 현실이 새삼 안타깝기만 하다.

개선문에서 조금 옆으로 운동 경기장 관람대와 같은 구조물을 조성하여 관광객들이 올라가 장벽 저쪽 동 베를린을 구경할 수 있었는데, 대체로 적막과 긴장감이 역력하였다. 그리고 장벽을 따라 조금더 이동하면 장벽에 원형 꽃다발이 몇군데 놓여 있었는데, 이는 동 베를린 시민과 동독 경비 군인이 탈출하면서 사살되거나 불행을 당한 그 자리를 표시하며 희생자들을 추모하기 위한 것이었다. 현재도 끊이지 않는 우리의 탈북민들을 새삼 생각하게 하였다.

다음은 시내로 돌아 들어가서 폭격 맞아 파괴되어 뼈대만 남은 '카이저 빌헬름 기념 교회'와 그 바로 옆에 붙여 세운 8각형의 새 교회를 둘러 보면서 또 하나의 베를린 전후 복구 기념 교회가 건축되었음을 보았다. 동독으로 포위 즉 동독 안에 포위되어 있으면서도 또 베를린 자체도 동독이 세운 장벽으로 분단 되어 있는 서 베를린이지만, 좀전에 장벽 넘어 바라본 동독과 지금 돌아보고 있는 서 베를린은 분명 별천지로 확연하게 구별되고 있었다. 한눈으로도 구분되는 이 광경, 이는 분명 공산주의와 민주주의의 구분법이기도 하였다.

마지막 날은 자유 시간이 주어졌다. 다만 '지하철 잘못 타면 동베를린으로 넘어갈 수도 있으니 조심하라는 주의'가 있는 것으로 보아 동서 베를린이 한국과 같이 완전히 분단되어 있지는 않은 것 같아 우리와의 차이점을 느끼기도 하였다. 낮 관광을 끝낼 지음에, 한반 독일 장교를 만나 함께 저 골목 안길에 있는 '킹 조지 5세'라는 간판이 붙은 3층 규모 미복구 빌딩에 들어가 보니 바야흐로, 선전물에 적힌 그대로 'Ganz Akt Show Striptease'였다. 구경하면서, 좀 머석 해서 옆을 보니 웬걸, 한 할아버지가 어린 초등학교 아동 손자와 함께 열심히 보고 있었다. 사실 독일은 전국 곳곳에 'Ero Centrum'이 다 있고 그런 물건들을 길거리에서 여자들이 팔고 있는 것을 흔히 볼 수 있었다.

◇ 서독 생활 체험 속의 견문록

1969~1970년대의 서독 견문을 여기서 다 말하기에는 역부족이기에 그저 잊을 수 없는 몇 가지만 반추해 보기로한다.

◦ 독일다운 '도이취 풍크트!(Deutsch Punkt)'

독일은 매사가 실질적이고 강건하며 정확하다는 사실을 들어나게 체감되었다. 알프스 산악여단 참모 참관 실습 당시 2개월간 '바드 라이헨할' 시내 어느 호텔에 기거하였는데, 내게는 필요 시 독일군 소위 한 명이 수행하였다. 어느 휴일 날 아침 9시에 호텔에서 출발하자고 약속한 그날 아침, 준비를 마치고 실내에서 기대리고 있다가, 1초도 안 틀리게 그 시간에 내가 문을 열려고 문고리를 잡았는데, 동시에 그 수행 장교가 문을 노크하였다. 문을 열고 나가니 이 친구 경례하며 왈, "도이취 풍크트!(Deutsch Punkt)"라 강조하며 웃으며 인사하였다. '풍크트'는 바로 문장 끝에 찍는 점을 말한다. '독일은 끝내준다, 즉 정확하고 믿을 수 있다'라는 의미를 강조한 것이다. 과연 독일 군인은 그러하거니와 독일인 전부가 그런 생각으로, 그런 자존심을 가지고 살고 있었다.

하루는 편지를 붙이기 위해 우체국에 갔는데 줄 선 사람들이 많아 시간이 걸렸다. 보아하니 담당 직원은 차례대로 한 사람씩 완전하게 볼일을 봐주고 있었다. 그러는 동안 점심시간이 되자, 지금까지 그렇게 성의껏 친절하게 일보던 직원은 벌떡 일어나 줄 선 사람들 아랑곳하지 않고 식사하러 나갔다. 그런데 줄 섰던 사람들은 또 헤어지지도 않고 아무 일 없다는 듯 그냥 기다리고 있을 자세였다. 나도 그렇게 그 자리에 줄 서 있을 수밖에 없었다.

독일인들은 그런 것으로 자존심에 차 있으며(미국인과는 좀 달리) 자랑한다. 독일의 제조물, 특히 군대에서 본 그들의 소총에서부터 중화기에 이르기까지의 무기들은, 미국 무기의 매끈한 디자인과는 달리 외모는 어딘가 무디고 어색해 보이나 실질 강건하면서도 기능면에서는 오히려 우수한 면도 가지고 있었다.

◦ 독일(중부 유럽) 날씨와 생활(공간), 소망(탈출 확장)과 철학

사관학교 생도 시절 철학 과목 시간에 우리 반 철학 교수는 강의를 시작할 때면 으레, "키에케고르가……" 하고는 그 자리에 서서 아마도 3분 정도(그러나 느끼기에는 10분 정도?)는 천정을 쳐다보며 행동 정지 상태가 되곤 했다. 그러면 교실은 문자 그대로 쥐 죽은 듯이 고요해지고 철학의 기운이 교실의 공기를 엄숙하게 바꾸어 놓은 듯하였다. 다음 독일의 철학자 '니체'를 말할 때도 역시나, "니체가 말하기를 '신은 죽었다.'"고 하고는 또 한 10분간 천정을 쳐다보곤 하였다.

그런데 그때부터 그 독일 철학자가 '신은 죽었다'고 하는 이유가 무엇일까. 도대체 독일이란 나라가 어떠하기에 그런 철학(형이하학적)이 나올까 하는 의문을 품고 있었다. 그런데 독일 현지에 와서 그 의문을 풀게 되었다. 지리 지정학적 원인과 날씨가 그(들)를 그렇게 생각하게 만든 것이라고.

그가 살았던 19세기 중~말엽 시대 독일은, 여전히 40여 개 공국이 뭉친 연방 국가로 약소 민족국가여서 나폴레옹과 또 러시아와의 전쟁을 겪으며 지배당한 데다 혁명 내란도 겹친 고난의 역사로 이어져 왔다. 말엽에 가서야 철혈재상 비스마르크와 대(大) 모르트케 장군에 의한 통일이 이루어 지긴 하였으나 여전히 사방으로 강대국에 포위되고 위협받는, 고난과 격동과 미래 불확실 시대요 국가였다. 그래서 '신은 죽었다'고 생각할 수도 있었으리라.

거기에다 독일(중부 유럽)은 예나 지금이나 4계절 내내 매일 같이 흐리며 때때로 가랑비가 계속 내리며 음산하여 하루 햇빛 30분이면 그날은 날씨 좋은 날로, 특히 여자들은 톱리스로 밖에 나와 누워서 햇빛을 쪼이는 자연 환경 속에 살고 있었다. 계절적으로도 그들은 4월을 일컬어 '잔인한 4월'이라 부르는데, 봄은 봄이건만 피고 있는 꽃들이 얼음에 쌓이는 싸늘하고 찬바람 여전하고 실망적인 날씨 때문이다.—한국의 멋없는 정치적 헛소리 '잔인한 4월'이 아니다.

그래서 그들은 그렇게 열심히 일하고 돈벌이하는 이유가 뭣이냐고 물으면, 특히 일반인들은 하나같이 "돈 벌어서 여름 휴가 겨울 휴가를, 그리고 시간이 나면, 햇빛 좋고 물 맑고 건강에 좋으며, 대우해 주는 이탈리아, 스페인, 아프리카 등지로 휴양 가려고"라고 말한다. 아마도 그곳 철학가와 일반인이나 정치가는 물론 현지에 살고 있는 독일인이라면 누구나 현실과 현장을 탈출하고 싶은 생각을 가지고 있기에 역사에서 보아 오듯 독일은, 어느 때는 좌충우돌 몸부림치는 역사를 만들기도 하는 것이리라.

◦ 일반민들의 일상(가정, 경제, 사회)생활

당시 서독 경제는, 아직도 열심히 발전 중에 있었지만, 이미 상당한 수준으로 전후 회복이 되어 있었다. 미국 달러 대 서독 마르크는 1:4였고 은행이자는 8%였다. 그러나 불과 몇 년 뒤에는 반대로 1마르크당 4달러가 되었다. 당시 독일의 경제 형편은 계속적으로 발전하여 경제 지표는 가파르게 오르고 있었으며, 외국인 고용—특히 남부 이탈리아—은 100만여 명에 이르러 2000년대 한국 수준에 이미 올라있었다. 당시 우리는 여전히 인플레 시대라 은행 이자는 20% 내외였기에 기업들 대부분은 기업 활동 이득보다 토지 확보로 영업손실을 보충하고 있었다.

독일인들의 일상생활은 여전히 검소하였고 준비성이 강하였으며 사회 전체 통일적, 획일적(통제) 시스템도 여전하였다. 미국에 가면 지인들이 집으로 초청할 경우에는 통상 '만찬 초청(Dinner Party)'이었고 풍성하였다. 그런데 서독에서도 지인들이 초청을 하되, 주로 오후 시간에 하는데, 처음엔 '아하, 얘기 먼저하고 그리고 식사 대접하는가 보다' 하며 갔는데 기대와는 달리 '차 한 잔'으로 얘기하다가 저녁때면 헤어지는 초청이었다.

군부대 식당이나 일반 민간 집 식사 메뉴는 1주일 기준으로 거의 같다. 아침은 물론 간단한 빵(검은 보리빵)과 우유, 소세지가 주 메뉴이고, 점심 또는 저녁 한 끼만 끓여서 먹고 저녁은 아침과 같이 식은 음식 즉 만들어져 있는 음식이다. 하루 한 끼 더운 음식 주재료는, 월요일 소고기, 화요일 양고기, 수요일 그동안 먹다 남은 것 잡탕밥(처리탕), 목요일은 생선, 금요일은 기타 육류, 토요일은 양과자, 주일은 주로 외식 등이었다.

군대 식당에서는 퇴근할 때 시커먼 보리빵을 포함 소시지 등으로 된 '도시락'을 받아 숙소에서 맥주 또는 우유와 함께 식사(혼밥)했다. 계란은 1주일에 삶은 것 3개뿐,—미군 장교 식당에서는 매일 2개씩 즉석에서 취향대로 요리(삶은 것, 스크램블, 반숙 등)해 주었다.— 독일에서는 흰 밀 생산이 안 되기에 경제 여유가 있는 집에서는 프랑스 수입 흰 빵을 먹기도 하는데 독일 장교 식당에서도 아침 한 개의 바겟빵은 프랑스 수입으로 공급되었다.

목요일 점심때 처음 받아 본 어른 주먹만 한 그냥 삶은 생선 한 덩이와 찍어 먹는 밋밋한 맛의 소스가 주어져서 먹어보니 싱겁고 비린내 나고 해서 먹기 힘들기에, 우리 한국 입맛대로 좀 구어줄 수 없느냐 했더니 왈, "호텔에서나 할 수 있는 일"이라 했다. 참고 먹기엔 도저히 안 되어 이후 못 먹고 남길 수밖에 없었다. 우리 앞 어느 기엔가 유학 온 선배 중에는 이 독일 식사가 입맛에 맞지 않아 중도 학업을 포기했다는 얘기도 들었다.

식당에서 식사법 중에 미국과 같은 것은 그 자리에서 마음 놓고 '헹~'하며 전혀 절제되지 않은 큰소리로 '코를 푸는 소리'였고,—아마도 동양 사람들에게는 질색하고 밥맛 떨어지는 소리와 모습—틀리는 것은 미국인들은 주로 빵은 손으로 잘게 뜯어 먹는데, 독일인들은 반듯이 나이프로 잘게 짤라서 먹는다. 양손은 손목 위 부분만이 식탁 위에 움직여야 한다는 것 등이었다. 그럼에도 불구하고 밤에는 TV를 보며 반듯하다 할 정도로 '와인' 또는 맥주를 마시며 즐긴다.

서양인들의 '더치페이'는 일상적이라는 것을 알고는 있었지만 독일에서는 이런 경우도 있었다. 하루는 우리 반 학생 모두가 학교 근처에 있는 같은 반 독일 군 소령 집으로 낮에 초청받아 가서 마당에서 식사하고 담소하고 있었는데, 한 장교의 의자가 망가졌다. 이웃집 의자라 물어주어야 한다면서, 공동 부담이니 당장 모두 얼마씩 내라였다. 더치페이 세상에서는 이치가 맞다, 그러나 우리는 아직도 인정—당시 우리는 '더치페이'를 몰랐고 물론 익숙하지 않았다.—에 익숙해 있던 터라 이 경우가 좀 생소하였다.

◦ 애국, 자존심과 향수병을 실감하다

유럽에 도착한 첫날 첫 시간에 만난 독일 사람이 묻기를, "중국 사람이냐? 일본 사람이냐?"고. "한국 사람인데…" 했더니, 그제야 "아, 그 축구 잘하는 나라 코리아"라고 말하면서 반가워했다. 당시 북한 축구팀이 막강 이탈리아를 이기고 8강까지 진출했던 기억을 살려낸 것이다. 당시 우리 한국과 한국 사람의 존재는 특히 유럽인들에게는 금시 초문이라는 사람들이 많았다. 그나마 북한의 축구 실력으로 그 정도나마 알려지고 있었던 때였다.

어느 나라 국민이나 다 외국 나가면 애국자 되지만 특히 당시 우리 한국 사람들은 외국 나가면 대단한 애국자가 되었다. 어떤이는 외국(서양) 나가기 전에 서울 덕수궁 대한문 앞에서 찍은 사진을 보이며, "이거 우리 집 대문이고 많은 한국 사람들이 이런 집에 산다", 고 하기도 하고 남자들은, "너희와 달리 우리는 집에서 왕이다, 여자에게 의자 빼준다던가하는 일 없다"고도.

그런데 '향수병'이란 게 있다는 걸 그때 실감하였다. 한때 가족을 남기고 월남전쟁에 서 있었을 때도 좀 느끼긴 했지만 역시나 24시간 막중한 임무와 생명의 위협이 항상 함께 하였기에 크게 느끼지는 못하였다. 그런데 독일에 와서 독일어학학교 생활 6개월과 알프스 산악부대 참모 실습 생활 시간에도 느끼지 못했으나 막상 함부르크 '지참대' 'VOQ' 생활에서는 이상하게도 정서적으로 상당히 '향수(병)'를 느끼게 되었다.

지금 생각하면 여러 가지 이유가 생각나나 당시는 몰랐다. 아마도 그 이유는 첫째로, 뭐니 뭐니 해도 고국에 남겨둔 사랑하는 가족들에 대한 그리움인데, 특히나 같은 반 외국군 동료 가족들의 즐거운 모습을 가까이서 자주 대하다 보니 그러하였고, 둘째는 비록 어른이고 객지 생활에 충분히 익숙한 군인이긴 하지만 그래도 음식과 잠자리 그리고 주변 생활 환경이 낯설어 일상에 스트레스를 받기에 우리 한국 생활이 그리워지고, 셋째로 일과 이후나 주말 휴일에 그 조용한 학교 숲속의 숙소에서 별일 없이 혼자 남아 있자니, 또 휴일 학교 식당에 가서 온 가족 함께 둘러앉아 식사하는 모습을 보다 보면 뭔가 그리움이 온몸을 휘감는 듯 하였던 것이다. 그래서 독일제 레코드 녹음 겸용 플레이어를 일찍 구입하여 특히 이미자 노래집을 틀고 또 반복 틀면서 많은 날의 마음을 달래었고, 그렇지 않아도 외국 탐사를 원했던 바였기에 여가만 나면 길고 짧은 외국 탐방 여행으로 마음을 달래며 향수(병)을 극복하였다.

∘ **사랑하는 아내 '수연이'에게**

좀 전에 한 육군 소위가 곱고도 예쁘고 우아한 한 여자 대학생 '수연이'를. 전방의 어느 고지에서 서울의 어느 빌딩에서 그리고 미국에서 마음속 깊이, 정열 가득하게 그리고 밤새워 사랑하였다. 5년의 세월은 아름답게 흘러, 광주에서 오순도순, 그러나 셋방살이도 했다. 큰놈을 났을 땐 더더욱 보람과 환희에 쌓였다. 허나 나의 시련으로 고행도 있었지. 작은 녀석이 났을 때는 화곡동 250호가 인연이었다. 그리고는 또 한 번 파월로 인한 고행이었다.

오늘도 사랑하는 연이는 참는 공부를 하고. 허나 세상 그 무엇과도 견줄 수 있을 만큼 '수연이' 그리고 그의 사랑만 한 것이 있을까. 나는 사랑 수연이에게 '행복'과 '보람'과 내일의 아름다움을 바치리.—사랑의 7돌을 마지하여. 1969년 4월 22일, 서독에서 아빠.

◇ 서독 '지참대'가 있었던 '함부르크'

1970년대 당시 '함부르크' 시는 서독 제1 도시요. 전체 독일의 최대 무역 항구 도시로 경제 사회와 세계 최신 문물의 최상 유행지였다. 그래서 전통적으로 '베를린'에 있던 '지참대'를 여기에 임시로 피난시켜 운영하였던 것이다. 사실 이 항구는 흥미롭게도 바닷가에 있지 않고 북해에 종착하는 '엘베' 큰 강의 종점 근처 내륙에 위치해 있다. 그래서 우리 한국군 동기생들은 때로는 조금 더 북쪽에 있는 '킬(Kiel)'이라고 하는 진짜 해변 도시에 가서 모래사장에서 회포도 풀었으나 이 함부르크 항구에는 자주 나가서 수변 카페에 앉아, 좁은 해로를 드나드는 외국 선박들과 항구 출입국 관리소와의 상호 신호 인사하는 모습 등을 흥미롭게 보며 이 항구의 정서를 맞보기도 하였다.

시내는 자주 나가지 않았으나, 한번은 같은 반 동료 모두와 함께 독일군 동료의 안내로 함부르크 관광에 빠질 수 없는 곳, 즉 유명한 '레파반(Reeperbahn)'을 탐방 겸 관광한 적이 있었다. 그곳은 제법 큰 구역으로 댄스홀, 카지노, 특별한 레스토랑, 맥주 바, 재즈 무대, 포도주 시음장, 서커스, 영화관, 거시기 클럽, 거시기 캬바레 등이 있는가 하면 양 길옆으로 길게 통판 쇼윈도 안에 나체 또는 반나체 여인들이 앉아 지나가는 손님들에게 아양을 떨고 있었는데 아마도 200여 미터 거리로 기억된다.

또한 이어서 '에로센트룸'이란 곳이 있었는데, 사방이 3층 오피스텔 같은 건물로 둘러쌓인 곳에, 안뜰로 들어서면 건물 아래 바깥쪽에 베란다 지붕으로 덥힌 전시장이 있는데, 거기에 수십 명의 아가씨들이 옷 벗고 서 있으면서 바로 앞을 지나가는 고객에게 윙크하며 자기를 고르라는 신호를 보내고 있었다.

이 동네에 들어서는 수많은 사람들 중에는 실제로 볼일을 보러오는 사람들—특히나 '마도로스(뱃사람, 제만—See Man)'—도 있거니와 대부분은 눈요기 겸 '관광꾼들(보는 사람, 제만-See Man)'이었다. 그런데 독일군 동료가 자유 시간을 갖기 전에 단단히 주의를 주었다, 특히 나체쇼 클럽에 들어가면 테이블에서 술(보통 독일산 고급 '젝트'나 양주) 한 잔 안 할 수 없는데 비싸거니와, 여자가 옆에 앉아 술 권해 한두잔 더하면 그대로 바가지를 쓰게 되고, 항의했다간 덩치(깡패)들에게 창피만 당하게 되니, 볼일 있으면 자기들 독일군 동료들과 가능한 같이 가야만 한다고 충고했다. 이런 곳은 독일이라고 별다른 정직성이 있지 않다는 것이다.

◇ 1970년 '오사카 만국박람회(EXPO70)와 일본

서독 '지참대' 한국군 동반생들은 앞 장에서 이미 소개한 바와 같이 해병대 강 모 소령과 육군의 기갑병과 구 문모 중령이었다. 그런데 '구 중령'은 형제가 3명으로 두 형들은 일본 '오사카'에서 '오토파트' 생산/판매 사업자로 자신만만한 생활을 하고 있었고, 막내동생인 구 중령은 가문을 대표하여 한국 군인으로 '가문의 명예'를 쌓고 있었다.

당시 그 형들은 자동차의 차바퀴와 기타 회전 부분에 들어가는 '베아링(Bearing)'을 위탁 생산하여 세계 독보적 명차, 독일 벤츠 회사에 전량 납품하고 있었다. 그런데 이제 전후 복구 과정에서 인정된 기술을 바탕으로 일본 전체 분위기도 그러하였거니와 본인들의 의기(意氣)도 투합되어, 자기 이름으로 된 베어링을 벤츠 회사에 납품하려고 노력하여 드디어 초기 불이익을 감수하면서도 벤츠 회사와 막 '새 계약'을 맺고 있는 상태였다. 정말 자랑스러운 재일 한국 사업가였다.—물론 당시 한국도 5·16 혁명 이후 중화학 공업화 정책으로 '한강의 기적'을 이루면서, 앞으로 15년 뒤면 '일본을 따라 잡는다'고 하는 자부심으로 또 의기로 가득 차 있을 때였다. 2023년 현재 드디어 일본을 제치고 세계 6대 강국이 되었다.

그래서 독일에 유학 중이던 동생이 영광스럽기도 하여, 우리 일행을 귀국 시에 일본으로 초청—마침 일본 오사카 박람회(Expo 70)가 열리고 있었다.—해 주었다. 그리하여 독일에서 귀국 시에 우리는 즐거운 마음으로 함께 일본에 들리게 되었다(70.8.2~5)

8월 초 일본 오사카의 더위는 같은 해양성 지대인데도 불구하고 북위 35도 상의 부산과는 달리 아주 습하고 더워서 숨이 막힐 지경이었다. 다행히도 당시 일본은 막 개인 집까지도 에어컨이 발전되어 집안에서 겨우 몸을 식힐 수 있었다. 그 더운 날임에도 불구하고 구 중령의 형 두 분과 그 가족들은 우리를 위해 더움을 마다하고 정성껏 봉사해 주었다. 하루는 근처에 있는 옛 도시(우리의 경주와 같은) '교토'와 '나라'를 관광하였는데, 나라 공원에 이제 막 사슴을 울타리 속에 방사하며 자랑하였다.—2015년경 관광차 들렸을 때는 2,000여 마리도 더 되어 울타리 없이 방사하여 관광객이 귀찮아할 정도가 되고 있었다.

다음 날은 때마침 일본이 야심적으로 재활하는 일본의 국력을 과시하기 위해 개최한 '일본만국박람회(EXPO 70)'가 오사카에서 개최(70.5.15~9.13)되어 있어서 구경을 갔다. 더위가 심해서 주로 몇 군데 실내 관람하고 '나라'에 설치된 미국 '디즈니랜드(Dream Land)'를 잠깐 들려서 구경도 하였다. 지금도 기억되는 것 중 하나는 가족과 아이들이 모두가 '서울 사람들(깨끗하고 잘 사는 집 사람들)' 같이 보였는데, '아 우리는 언제 이런 수준이 될까, 서둘러야지'하는 생각이 들었다.

좀 시원해진 밤에 밖에 나가니 동네 사람들이 모두 밖에 나와 집앞 골목길에 '평상'을 내놓고 남자들은 훈도시—일본 남자들이 긴 천으로 삼각팬티처럼 만들어 맨 야만인 시대 전통 팬티—바람으로 다수가 부인네들과도 함께 둘러앉아 부채를 부치며 웃고 담소하고 있는 모습이 우리네와 닮긴 했으나, 다만 우리가 '상놈 짓'이라고 얕보는 '훈도시' 모습들을 보며 야만적 습관은 여전하구나 하는 생각도 들었다.

그다음 날은 '구 중령네' 형이 직접 운전하여 동경으로 가는 길에, 친절하고 극진하게 대접해 준 가족들에게 고마운 인사를 하고, 떠나면서 사업장 즉 '오토파트' 공장에 들렸다. 별로 크진 않았으나 마치 차돌멩이를 보듯 아주 탄탄하고 뭔가 빛나는 모습을 볼 수 있었다. 물론 공장 운영 얘기도 들었지만 특히 일본 사람들을 많이 쓴다고 하면서 '신용 있고 의리 있고 회사 발전을 자기 일로 알고 일해 준다고 했다.

오후에 도착하여 우리를 여기까지 데려다주고 그동안 지성으로 대접해 준 구 중령네 형들과 헤어져 더위를 피하느라 호텔에 들어가 낮 시간을 보내고 밤이 되어 전철을 타고 가서 'Tokyo Tower'를 구경하였다. 이 타워는 일종의 전파탑으로 333미터 높이로 프랑스 '에펠탑'보다 9미터 높다고 구구절절 선전하고 있었다. 이때 기억나는 것은 전철에 서서 보면 일본 노인들은 우리보다 훨씬 작은 키로 그들 머리 넘어 저 전철 끝까지 보이는데, 젊은이들은 우리 젊은이들보다 더 크기 시작한 느낌이 들었다. 어서어서 우리도 군사 정권의 '밀어부침'으로 부흥과 발전을 서둘러야겠다고 생각했다.

◦ 그리웠던 고국과 가족에게 돌아오다(1970. 8. 5)

김포 공항에 도착하여 마중 나온 내 사랑 가족과 만나 새삼 내 가족과 사랑이 여기에 있음을 느꼈다. 약혼과 결혼 이후 장기 체류 외국에서 돌아와 만나는 경우가 미국 유학, 파월 귀국 그리고 이번까지 세 번째이나 그리웠고 반갑기는 이 경우가 더욱 절실하였다.

6. 육군대학 교관, 게릴라전 연구와 관사 생활

'외국 유학 귀국자는 해당 교육기관 교관에 보임한다'는 규정에 따라 육군대학교관 명을 받고, 가족 4명(나와 아내 그리고 두 아들)이 서울 화곡동 국민주택에서 진해에 있는 육군대학 관사로 결혼 후 3번째로 '가족 대이동'을 실시하였다. 학교 구내 관사에서 70년 9월에서 72년 4월, 대대장 명을 받아 전방부대로 전출할 때까지, 낯설지만 당분간 가족 함께 안정된 가정생활을 할 수 있게 되었다.

◇ 교관 자격과 교관 생활

◦ 교관 선발과 교관 자격 강의

육대 교관단에는 나름대로의 규정(SOP)이 있었다. 때마침 교관단 주류는 '69학년도'를 이수한 우리 육사 동기생들이었는데, 그들은 졸업생 중에서 성적 우수하고 교육자 자질을 갖춘 자 중에 병과 별 균형을 유지하여 선발되었다.

내게 배정된 과목은 엉뚱하게도, 내가 돈과 공들여 받아온 기계화/기갑부대 전술 과목 연구와는 달리 '게릴라 전술'이었다. 사실 당시까지 우리 군에는 군단에 1개 기갑연대, 사단에 1개전차대대가 존재하여 기갑병과 전담 분야였으나 기갑사단이나 기계화사단 등이 존재하지 않아 내가 이수해온 공부는 사실 적용될 수 있는 시기가 아직은 아니었다. 그렇다고 해서 산악부대 또한 없었다. 그리고 내게는 '게릴라전' 유학 경력과 파월 맹호부대 전투 경력, 거기에 육군본부 특전감실 근무 경력이 있어 이 과목이 배정된 것으로 생각되었다.

◦ 교육과 교관 생활

독일과는 달리 여전히 주입식이고 강의식이라, 본인의 과목은 '게릴라전'이기에 30~45분 강의에 길게는 20분에서 5분 정도에 이르기까지 피교육자로부터 질문을 받고 60분 교시를 마감하는데, 통상은 오전 또는 오후 교시를 계속할 수도 있었다. 학점제도도 아니어서 학교교육 계획에 따라 과목교육 시간을 배정받았는데, 아마 10시간 정도로 기억된다. 2~3개 과정에 강의하기 때문에 시간적으로 구애받은 적은 없으나 과목 내용 자체를 한국 전사와 세계 전사를 통해 발전시키려 하다 보니 연구 시간이 필요하여 일과 시간이 여유롭지는 못했다.

그동안 게릴라전 연구에서 주로 모택동이나 '체 게바라'의 남미 전례를 주제로 해 왔으나 이제 '한국 유격전' 특히 '6·25 남침적란(赤亂)' 당시 서해 5도와 황해도 지역 일대에서 전개된 유격전에 대한 연구는 전임자가 남겨둔 자료를 비롯하여 광범위하게 본격적인 연구를 시도하였다.

◦ 신교리 전파 전 육군부대 순회 강의

교수부에서는 해마다 발전되는 신교리를 전파하기 위해서 교리 발전 해당 과목 교관 2명이 짝을 지어 1년에 1회 1개월 기간으로 전후방 부대(사단급)를 순회하며 강의한다. 부대마다 사정이 다르기는 하나 그래도 대부분 부대는 사단장 이하 전 간부가 참여하여 경청하며 관심을 보였다. 당시에 육대교관과 교육내용은 상당히 존중되고 있었다. 부대 방문 강의가 끝나면 함께 교관으로 근무했던 동기생이나 교리 발전에 관심을 가진 부대장들은 우리 순회 교관들을 성의껏 대접해 주기도 하였다. 덕분에 우리 교관들은 국내 지방 곳곳을 잠자고 지나가며 지방 사정과 지리 그리고 풍습 등을 체험할 수 있었다.

◇ 가족과 함께 관사 생활, 진해 생활

◦ 학교 주변 지리 환경

진해시 여좌동, 해발 600여 미터의 '장복산' 아래 진해 시내는 물론 진해만을 내려다보며 한국 육군대학은 자리 한번 잘 잡고 있었다. 나로서는 1954년 봄, 육군사관학교 최종(2차) 선발 시험(신체검사와 면접)을 보기 위해 갔던 추억으로 옛날 그 모습 그대로였으나, 앞으로는 가족과 함께 거주하며 교관 생활을 한다고 생각하니 감개무량하였다.

지리적 환경을 보면, 학교본부에 서서 양편으로 벚꽃나무가 울창한 학교 중앙로를 따라 200여 미터 내려가면 학교 정문이 있고 바로 앞으로 동서로 연결되는 2번 국도(부산-목포)가 가로지르고, 그 너머로 진해선 기차길 건널목이 있으며, 그걸 건너면 진해(해군통제부가 있는) 시내에 들어가게 된다. 시내 중심 시장까지는 약 1.5킬로미터고 해군사관학교(진해만 해안가)까지는 약 2.5킬로미터 정도였다. 그 근처에 해군 통제부가 있고, 거기서 '행암만' 맞은편에는 진해 해군 간이 비행장이 있고, 그 안에는 해군용 간이 골프장이 있었다. 특히 봄이 되면 통제부 내 벚꽃길이 볼만하였고, 3월 하순에 열리는 벚꽃장은 그때도 전국적으로 유명하였다.

◦ 가족 텃밭 재미와 시장 보기 얘기

당시 한국 가정 모습은, 남자는 밖에서 일(직장) 다녀서 돈 벌어오고, 여자는 집안에서 집 돌보고 애 키우고 남편 시중들고 하는 것이 정상이었다. 그래서 교관들 가족은 전부가 관사에 입주하여, 각 집 간격 좌우 5~6미터 앞뒤 길을 끼고 10미터 정도로 앞뒤 옆집 모두가 울타리도 없으니 서로 훤히 드려다 보며 살고 있었다. 거기에다 연령도 아주 비슷하여 아주 이상적인 공동체 생활이 이루어지고 있었다.

그런데, 학교 안에는 교수부 구 역내 다방 하나뿐 아무 복지시설도 없었다. 그래서 매일매일의 생활 필수 식료품조차 시장에 가거나 그리고 각자 두어 평 되는 부엌 앞 집뜰에 야채를 심어 심심풀이를 겸한 텃밭 재미를 보기도 하였다. 그래도 그 텃밭에는 상추를 비롯하여 고추, 오이, 심지어는 호박까지도 심었고, 부지런한 교관은 아예 관사 바로 뒤 언덕을 개간하여 제법 10평 정도에 본격적으로 건강 단련 소일 재미까지 보는 사람도 있었다.

그래도 그것은 한정된 일부이고, 당시는 아직도 냉장고가 없던 때라 매일같이 시장에 나가 장을 보아야 했다. 그래서 하루 두어 번 시장 버스가 운영되었는데 시간 맞추어서 주부들이 동행하여 시장에 나가 장도 보고 바깥 구경도 겸하였다.

◦ 아이들 교육과 가족들 취미 활동(수영 테니스 등)

교관들의 자녀들 또한 대부분이 유치원생이나 초등학교 1~3학년 정도였다. 그래서 대한민국 군대에서는 드물게 학교 안에 공립유치원을 설치하여 운영하였다. 그런데 그때만 해도 국민 전체 수준으로 보아 유치원 또한 드물어서 이건 교관 가정에 주는 혜택이었다. 우리 둘째(성언)는 유치원생이라 근 1년 반 재밌게 그리고 유익하게 '육대유치원' 생활을 보낼 수 있었다.

첫째 아이(정언)는 서울 화곡동에서 유치원을 다녔기에 진해에서는 바로 후문 밖에 있는 대야초등학교에 다녔다. 물론 군인 가족 자녀 교육은 크나큰 문제로 군인 가정 발전에 영향을 미치고 있었다. 예를 들어 여기 초등학교에서 2년여 공부하다가 다시 다른 지역 부대로 전근해가는 아빠 따라 가서 거기 학교에 또 한 2년 다니다가 또 낯설은 곳으로 가게 되는, 군대 생활 중 어느 한곳에 마음먹고 정착하지(사실은 그러기 어렵다.) 못하고, 그때마다 아빠 따라 다닌다면 10번도 훨씬 넘게 이사와 전학을 반복해야 했다. 이 점에 아이들의 정서상 학업 성적 상 그리고 학생 장래 학업 문제까지 참 희생 많은 군대 가정이었다. 우리 집 둘째는 유치원 하루 일과를 일찍이 마치고 또래 친구들과 함께 한 집에 모여앉아 좀 어려운 책을 모두에게 읽어주거나,—아주 일찍부터 스스로 한글을 깨우쳤다.—학교 안을 마음대로 돌아다니며 놀다가 형이 돌아올 때쯤 되면 후문에 가 후문 보초(군인 아저씨)와 얘기를 나누며 형을 기다리다가, 후문을 열고 들어오면 형이 쥐고 오는(동생 주려고) 빵 등 간식을 받아먹으며 함께 집으로 왔다. 그러다가 둘은, 우리가 퇴근할 때면 교수부 가까운 길로 마중 나와 있다가 나와 함께 우리 관사로 돌아 갔다.

당시까지는 영내에 장교 클럽은 물론 가족을 위한 그 어떠한 사교장이나 식당 등은 없었다. 다만 가족들 취미 활동(운동)으로는 학교 내에 테니스 코트가 몇 개 있어서 생각이 있는 가정은 근무 기간 상당한 수준의 실력을 쌓을 수 있었다. 동시에 당시는 진해는 물론 서울 지역에도 드문 공중(公衆) '수영 풀장'—25미터 규격 풀장으로 지방 수영대회를 개최도 하였다.—이 학교 내에 설치되어 있어서 거의 전 가족과 주부들이(처음 배우기도 하여) 여름 한 철 밤낮으로 아주 즐겁고 보람 있게 지낼 수 있었다. 이때까지도 육군 장교 교관들은 '골프'는 엄두도 내지 못했으나 그 후 1979년 내가 참모장 시기부터 우연한 기회로 교관들의 골프 여가 선용이 시작될 수 있었다. 그 얘기는 다음 기회에 하겠다.

제7장

제102기계화보병대대(1972.10.24)와 수도기계화사단(1973.3.22) 창설

1. 전방 군단 예비사단대대장(1972.4)으로 가다

당시 전방 대대장 자격으로는 육군대학교관 출신이 최우선 순위—전술 이론 일가견을 갖춘 육대 출신이 귀해 사단장 등 지휘관의 선호 순위 우선—였다. 거기에 때마침 군단 예비사단격인 제32사단이 기계화보병사단으로 개편될 계획이어서, 더구나 전차 또는 기계화 군대로 유명했던 서독군 유학 출신이라면 1등 대대장감이었다. 그래서 사단장의 요청으로 제32사단 제28연대 제1대대장으로 부임하게 되었다.

◇ 부대 환경과 부대 실정

◦ 부대 환경과 사단장

한국군이 월남에 파병되면서 미국과의 합의로 파월 조건부 국군 증강과 현대화가 약속되었다. 그 일환으로 2개 전방사단이 파월됨으로 전방 전투력 유지 및 보완을 위해 2개 예비사단을 전투사단으로 증편하여 전방으로 이동 배치하였는데 그중 한 사단이 바로 충남에서 이곳 경기도 '현리'로 올라온 제32사단이었다.

◇ 대대 Test와 특공소대 운영, 국망봉 진지 보수 공사

군단 예비사단대대장은 임기 중에 1회, 대대 야외 전투 훈련 결과를 시험받게 되어 있다. 우리 대대는 기계화대대 창설 직전에 보병대대 마지막으로 시험받게 되었다. 시험 내용은, 행군 이동, 방어 편성 및 실시, 역습, 공격(반격)이었다. 장소는 만세교와 일동 사이 지역 일대였다. 나는 소대장 시절, 여우고개에 있는 '연합훈련장(Nightmare)'에서 실탄 사격을 하며 시험을 받아 본 경험이 있고, 또한 타 대대 시험관으로 경험한 바 있어서 별문제 없이 최우수 성과를 거두었다.

특히 유격전과 특공전의 교관 출신이라 '특공소대'를 편성해 운영해 보았는데 성공적이었다. 대대 소대장 중 용감한 소대장을 '특공소대장'으로 임명하고 소대원 30명을 선발 편성하여, 명찰과 표찰을 붉게 해서 붙여주고 임무를 부여했더니 예상외로 아주 사기 충천한 모습과 긍지에 찬 모습으로 원기 왕성하게 임무(적진 침투, 정찰, 반격시 선도 등)를 달성해 주었다.

소대장 심판 때 개탄해 마지않았던 '전시 식사 보급 문제' 즉, 소대장 당시는 대대본대 이동 후 그 뒤를 취사용 화목을 실은 차가 서너대(상황 외 조건으로) 따라 갔다. 식사 시간이 되면 대대 야외 취사장은 마치 시장같이 북적거렸다. 그리고 작전(시험) 중 식사 시간에는 분대당 3~4명이 식사(밥과 국을 담은 개별 반합)를 운반하기 위해 방어진지를 이탈하지 않으면 안 되었다. 그런데 대대장 당시는 화목 대신 무연탄, 현지 흙주방 대신 '주방 셑'으로 대신 되었을 뿐 식사 시간 혼잡은 여전하고 그 시간 전투력은 여전히 반감(정도)되었다.

2. 제102기계화보병대대(육군 제1660부대) 창설(1972.10.24)
— 수도사단 제1연대 제1대대 전통을 이어받다

◇ 장갑차 인수와 '무지개부대' 창설 준비

보병대대 시험을 마치자 바로 다음 날(1972년 10월 초)부터, 한국군 창군 이후 2번째 기계화보병대대를 창설(부대개편)하기 위해 '이동'에서 '현리' 사단사령부 인근으로 대대가 이동하였다. 그날부터 매일같이, 전군 사단 전차중대 소속 'APC소대'를 'APC'와 함께 인수하였다. 방법은, 우리 대대 인수 요원이 그 부대 그 소대로 가서 검사하고 인수한 뒤 고유부대에서 우리 대대로 수십 또는 100여킬로도 넘게 제발(궤도차량)로 이동해 왔다.

그런데 당시, 사단이나 대대나 APC에 대해 아는 사람은—나 또한 생도 때 병기공학 시간에 엔진 분해 결합은 해 보았어도, 소대장 때 작전 이동을 위해 미군이 운용하던 APC에 1시간 가량 전투 승차한 경험이 있을 뿐—아무도 없었다. 그래서 이공계 대학 출신으로 자가용 운전 경험자를 책임자로 하고, ROTC 장교 몇 명으로 'APC인수검수반'을 편성하여 해당 사단별로 순차적으로 파견하였다. 파견에 앞서 내가 지시한 유일한 검사 지침은, 기갑장교의 조언에 따라, "'머플러'에서 흰 연기 나오고 엔진 소리가 셍~셍~ 하는 것"으로 선별하라는 것이었다. 그때는 모두가 그랬다. 실제는 선별 하나마나 부대가 그대로 이동해 들어왔다. '서파' 검문소 더 아래까지 내려가, 그래도 자기 능력으로 이동해 오고 있는 무리들을 보고 장하다, 고맙다를 몇 번이고 되뇌이며 환영하였다.

그래서 800여 명의 대대 정원이 갑자기 1,026명이 되고, 160명 정원 중대가 260명이 되어, 밤에 취침 시에는 서로 껴안고 자기도 하고, 답답증을 느낀 병사들은 일찍 관물대 위로 올라가, 마치 옛날 야간 완행열차의 수하물칸에 올라가듯, 침상으로 생각하고 대용하기도 하는 등 대대는 당분간 대만원이 되어, 축차적으로 제대해 나갈 때까지 그 상황을 모두가 참고 견딜 수밖에 없었다. 우리 병사들은 이 실정을 알고 잘도 견디어 주었다.

◇ 보병대대에서 장갑보병부대로 전투력 증강, 재편성

한편 보병대대가 하루아침에 그 자리에서 그 시설 범위 내에서 보병연대급 수준의 무장과 장비를 보유하게 되었다. 당장 M113 보병장갑차+M112 대대장 지휘용장갑차+ 앰뷸런스장갑차 도합 60대에 정비 반장 중사와 정비 대장 대위 1명, 차륜 차량은 행정용+전투용+통신차 등 소형 중형 대형 포함 20여 대에 정비반장 중사에 정비 대장 상사 1명 등으로 증편되었고, 81미리 박격포 대신 연대급 무장인 장갑차화 4.2인치 박격포포대(포대장은 여전히 보병 대위)가 편제되고, 통신소대가 중대가 되어 통신병과 대위가 편제되어 왔다.

뿐만 아니라 육군 2번째 기계화보병대대 즉, 제102기보대로 시작했으나 곧바로 연대 단위 부대와 같은 행정 및 보급 자급부대인 '육군 제1660부대'로 명명되었다. 자체가 행정 명령을 하고 사단 보급소를 넘어 보급창으로 직거래를 하게 되었다. 실로 중차대한 증편이었다. 대대장의 책임감이 무거워진 대신 긍지와 명예 또한 충만하였다.

◇ 제102기계화보병대대(육군 제1660부대), '무지개부대' 창설 및 발전

그래서 일단 제반 사항을 점검하고 질서를 잡으면서 부대 상징 마크를 '무지개'로, 모든 장갑차 앞머리에 페인팅했으며, 그리고 스스로 '무지개부대'로 호칭—미국 멕카더 장군이 제1차 세계대전에 출전하면서 자기 사단을 '무지개사단'이라 호칭한 것을 참고하여—하였다. 그리하여 서둘러 신고하고, 이 기념일에는 휴무하며 기억하고 휴식할 수 있도록 생각하여, 당시 휴무일로 잘 알려져 있던 'U.N-day'인 10월 24일을 기해 '무지개부대' 즉, '육군 제1660부대' 창설식을 거행하였다.

창설 이후 최우선 모토는 '장비 100% 가동'으로 하였다. 함께 온 부속품이나 장비 정비 기술병—단 한 사람 유능한 중사가 있었는데 이는 개인이 자습으로 터득한 기술자—도 없었다. 그나마 우리 부대까지 쉬고 쉬면서 고치고 또 고치고 하면서 온 것만으로도 다행한 일이었으나 지금부터 정비와 운용 책임은 나와 우리 부대에 있는 것이다.

그리하여 연대 창고를 인수해 차륜차량 및 장갑차량 정비소로 정리하고, 계속 제대해 나가는 특히 장갑차 조종병을 양성하기 위해 인근 야산에 주야간 조종 면허 훈련 및 시험장을 만들고 운영하였고, 동시에 인근 지역에 주차 및 대피호를 조성하여 안전 주차 및 집중 경계가 가능하도록 조치하였다. 그리고 이어서 내가 다녀온 서독의 작전훈련 교리를 상기하며 우리 현지 지형과 작전 계획에 맞는 작전교리 개발에 착수하였다. 그러나 이 문제는 쉽지 않았다.

3. 수도기계화보병사단(首機師) 창설(1973.3.22)

◇ 32보병사단에서 수도기계화보병사단으로

제32보병사단은 1972년 10월 이후 기계화사단으로 개편 명을 받고, 철수하는 미 제7사단의 장비 등을 인수하는 등, 제반 준비를 해오다가, 드디어 73년 초에 파월 국군의 중추였던 '맹호부대' 즉 수도사단이 본국으로 귀환함에 따라, 그 오래고도 영광된 전통과 역사 즉, 맹호부대 군기(사단, 연대, 대대 중대기까지)와 맹호 마크 그리고 모든 사단 기록물 등을 그대로 물려받아, 드디어 '수도기계화보병사단, 수기사(首機師)'으로 1973년 3월 22일에 창설되었다. 창설식은 현리에 있는 사단사령부 연병장에서 당시 국방장관을 모시고 진행되었다. 그리하여 군기와 사단 칭호 명명과 동시에, 32사단의 군기와 역사와 부대 호칭은 다시 원고지인 충남으로 돌아갔다.

◇ 영광의 '수도사단 제1연대 제1대대'의 전통을 이어받다

우리 대대는 영광스럽고 중차대하게도 대한민국 최초 창설 대대인 수도사단 제1연대 제1대대기를 수여받았다. 그 천하 제1의 대대기를 받아 들 때 그 순간 참으로 일생일대 또 한 순간의 감개무량함을 느낄 수 있었다. 대대기에 많은 전공 하사 수치—대통령 하사 수치를 포함—가 매여 있어 명실공히 대한민국 국군 최고 대대임을 과시하고도 남음이 있었다.

우리 수도기계화보병사단은 우리 대대가 소속한 전통과 영광의 역사를 자랑하는 제1기계화보병여단(구 수도사단 제1연대), 제1'기갑'기계보병화여단, 제26기계화보병여단, 포병여단 그리고 새롭게 대령이 지휘하는 보급지원단으로 구성되었고, 기계화보병여단은 1개 기계화보병대대, 1개 차량화보병대대, 1개 전차대대, 1개 포병대대로 구성된 참으로 막강한 전투부대가 되었다.

◇ 군 전투지휘 검열과 그 결과에 대한 '일희일비(一喜一悲)'

수도기계화사단 창설 이후 6개월 정도 지나자 제1야전군의 '사단단위전투지휘 검열'이 있었다. 우리 대대는 새롭게 증강 편성된 4.2인치 박격포에 대하여 그동안 특별한 관심을 가지고 훈련—포 사격과 같은 방법임으로 포병부대에 요청하여 지도를 받는 등—을 해 왔으나 이번 전투 검열을 기해서 100% 실탄 사격 성과를 내기 위해 부득이 대대 전투예비탄인 'BL탄'을 일단 사용하고 신형 교탄으로 교체 저장하기로 하였다. 내가 '한미권총사격대회'에서 경험한바, 신 탄약에 LOT 넘버가 같은 것들을 사용하면, 탄약 성격 파악에 용이하고 그걸로 훈련하면 정확도가 확실히 보장될 수 있었음을 상기하였던 것이다. 그리하여 '주야간 10발 사격'에 100% 명중하여 우수성과를 냄으로서 사단장의 즉석 호평을 받기도 하였다.

그런데, 이번에는 그 성과로 인하여 중대 전원 소총 사격을 지명받아 사격한 결과 주간 40%, 야간 38%라는 그냥 듣기에는 황당한 정도의 성적을 기록하여 이번에는 사단장으로부터 즉석 실망평을 받음으로써 '아침에 만점을 오후에는 낙제점을 기록하게 된 에피소드를 남기게 되었다. 그러나 그것은 더구나 이제 막 재편성된 부대로서 지극히 정상적인 결과—서독에서 일반 중대 소총 사격 결과도 그 정도가 정상이었다.—로 나는 평가하고자 했다.

당시 검열 과정에서 타부대 실정을 보면, 흔히 지명받은 중대는 연대 내 고참 사수들로 대체 보충하여, 시험 사격장에서 심지어 90% 내외 성적을 얻기도 하였는데, 나는 그럴 수 없었다. 노력한 대로의 성과를 가지고 더욱 훈련하여 발전하려고 하는 곳에 실질 군사력이 있고, 그래야 적은 실질 강건한 아군을 두려워하고 국민은 군을 신뢰할 수 있는 것이 아니겠는가.

4. 사단군수참모 근무, 제1차 유류 파동과 영향

신현수 사단장으로부터(대대장 임무를 성공적으로 마치고) 군수참모 임명을 받고 부임(1973.10)은 하였으나 별로 원하지 않던 직책이라 초기는 불편했으나 일단은 정황을 이해하기로 하였다. 사단장은 그의 동생 신현배 중위(육사 후배)를 내게 보내어 함께 근무하게 하였는데, 신 중위는 시간이 갈수록 신뢰와 함께 우선 인정스러워 또 한 사람의 멤버인 '김 대위'와 함께 업무 분위기는 만족스러웠다.—그는 후에 9사단장을 거쳐 군단장(중장)이 되었다.

◇ 제1차 세계 유류 파동, 절약 절제와 고난

신임 '김 사단장'은 안정되어가고 있는 기계화보병사단을 발전시키기 위해 부대 안정과 교육훈련에 노력하였다. 그런데 1973년 10월경(~1974.2)에, 'OPEC'이 제4차 중동전쟁 시, 이스라엘 지원국들에 대한 보복으로 석유 수출 금지 조치를 단행함으로서 야기된 '급 감산'과 '석유가 급등'—72년의 5배—으로 세계 경제가 요동쳤으며, 한국도 그 영향을 크게 받았다. 이 석유 파동은 그 후에도 2차, 3차로 계속되어 한때 세계 경제는 물론 한국 경제가 큰 고난을 면치 못하였다.

따라서 국제 유류 파동 속에 군대 유류 예산도 크게 삭감되었는데 우리는 총력으로 지키며 노력한 결과 전년도 비 1/2삭감으로, 그나마 다행으로 생각하며 부대 내 절약과 절제 그리고 통제로 고난을 극복할 수밖에 없었다. 그러나 교육훈련용은 전 년비 큰 변동 없이 보장하고, 각종 기동장비는 비상 대비 '만탱크'를 유지하면서, 선 동계 한냉 극복 엔진 시

동용 유류 확보, 후 행정 소요를 책정하게 되었다. 특히 전차(당시 M48계열)는 한번 시동에 3 겔런(약 10리터)이 소모되는 기름 킬러였다. 그래서 예전 한때와 같이 다시 한번 기름 가진 전차대대장의 인기가 상승하기도 했었다.

그런데 사단장은 유류 절약을 위해 사단 참모장과 참모들의 합동 통근차—참모 관사와 사단사령부 연병장까지 약 3.5킬로미터—조차도 중단함으로써 걸어서 출근하였다. 그 11월부터 다음 해 2월까지 한겨울의 현리 계곡 겨울은 유난히도 추워서 영하 20~25도를 오르내리는 가운데, 두꺼운 내복 2벌에다 군복 상하의, 거기에 두꺼운 미제 야전 점퍼에, 울로 된 목도리까지 완전무장하고 빠른 걸음으로 숨을 좀 헐떡이면서 약 35분정도 걸렸다. 도중 10분 정도쯤부터 속으로 땀이 나기 시작하여 연병장에 도착하면(7시 30분경) 속 상의 런닝은 거의 젖은 상태인데, 연병장에서는 상의 벗고 맨손 체조를, 반듯이 사령부 근무 전 장병이 함께 실시하였다. 끝난 뒤 옷 입고 사무실로 들어가면 바로 무연탄 난로를 껴안다시피 난로 앞에 바싹 다가앉아서 한동안 몸을 말리며, 데우기를 겸한다. 그래도 나이가 막 40대라 참아낼 수는 있었으나 체력 손실과 업무능력 저하를 면할 수는 없었다.

◇ 근무 중 A형간염 통과

전방사단 모든 장병들의 모든 분야 근무가 참으로 힘들고 어렵지만 유류 파동 당시 수기사 군수 업무는 절약 절제 일도변이라 더욱 어려웠다고 기억된다. 위에서 말한바 군수 지침 준수 점검을 위해 주 1회 이상 사단의 전 대대—전부가 차량화, 기계화, 전차였기에—를 현장 점검, 유류 탱크 뚜껑 열고 눈으로 확인하고 시동 걸어보기 등을 하다 보면 저녁 식사는 밤 10~11시에 하기 일수였다. 그 밥은 물론 아무것도 모르는 사무실 병사 한 명을 관사에 때때로 보내서—아이들 교육 문제도 있고 하여 관사 가족 살림은 생각지도 못했고, 사단참모는 관사에 당번(연락병)이 없다.—시켜놓은 것이니 마땅할 리 없었다. 그렇게 해서 두어 달 지나자 지독한 몸살감기가 와서 꼼짝 못 하고 한 열흘 들어누웠다. 한 1주일 지나자 사단장이 찾아와 머리맡에 앉아 위로해 주기도 하였다. 그 후 몇 달간 허약해져서 춘천 가도를 달리는 버스만 타도 어지러웠다. 대령이 되어 정밀 신체검사를 했을 때야 비로소 A형 간염을 앓고 지나갔다는 사실을 알게 되었다. 참으로 힘겹게 일했던 시간이다.

◇ Defcon—3발령, 전군 전투 준비 태세 완비 점검

◦ 전군 전투 준비 태세 완비 점검(1973.10)

1972년 '남북 7·4공동성명' 이후 월남이 패망해 가고, 파월 국군이 원복과 동시에 국군은 정비 기간에 들어갔는데, 북은 공동 성명을 이행하지 않음과 동시에 남북대화를 일방적으로 중단하고 오히려 사면으로 무장 도발—어청도 침투, 백령도 어선 공격, 연천 무장 공비 침투, 전남 완도와 금난도에 무장 간첩 침투 등등—을 자행하고 정치적 모략 공세를 가열하였다. 이에 국방부는 1973년 10월을 기하여 전군 전투 준비 태세를 강화하고 '전투 준비 태세 완비'에 대한 전군 일제 점검을 실시하였다.

그 결과 평균 80%라는 결론을 도출하고 모든 분야에서 100%가 될 때까지 최대한의 노력을 경주하기로 하였다. 특히 중요한 화기 분야에서 BL탄이 1기수(基數. 통상 3일분)밖에 없는 무기도 있어서 시급한 조치가 필요한 경우도 있었다.

ㅇ 실상황, 'Defcon—3' 발령

73년 3월 즈음에 잘못된 휴전 조약으로 미군과 한국군이 월남에서 철수함에 따라 자유월남의 패망이 가속화되었고, '7·4 남북공동성명'이 발효 중임에도 불구하고 위에서 말한 바와 같이, 마치 월남과 같은 상황을 연출하고자 또는 전면전도 불사하겠다는 의도로 바다와 전선 전 지역을 통해 간첩을 대량으로 침투시키면서 다방면으로 도발해 왔다.

그러던 중 1974년 3월, 판문점 공동 경비 구역 내에서 북 괴뢰군 120명이 U.N군에게 집단으로 행패(장교 1명 사망, 5명 부상, 세단차 4대 피해)를 가하며 도발하였다. 그로 인하여 전군에 'Defcon—3'가 발령되었다. 이는 전투 개시(Defcon-1) 직전에 실탄을 분배받고 진지 투입(Defcon—2)하는 단계의 이전 단계로, 사실상 한반도 전선은 휴전 상태라 평소 그 자체가 'Defcon—3'에 준하는 전투 준비 태세를 유지하며 생활하고 있었는데 이때 진짜 'Defcon—3'가 발령된 것이다.

그래서 작전 예규(SOP)에 의한 절차—전 장비 및 전 투원 출동 준비 및 무장대기, 전병력 부대 복귀—를 이행해 나갔으나 동요되지는 않았다. 다만 휴가 장병에 대한 즉각 귀대 조치가 시행되야하는데, 하루 이틀 실상황으로 긴장된 가운데 상황 진전을 주시하며 판단을 미루다가 3일째 결심 시점에, 다행히도 상황이 종료되어 한시름 놓기도 하였다.

제8장

대령 시절, 후방부대장과 참모, 교수, 대외 시찰 및 군사협력조사단장(1975.3~ 1981.5)

1. 오랜만의 후방 근무, 특전사 정보처장

◇ 특전사령부 정보처장

◦ 대령 진급과 새 보직 추천

중령에서 대령 진급은, 정규 육사 출신이라면 대부분 연차별로 가능하였다. 다만 다음 장군 진출을 위해 조기 진급이 중요하였다. 통상의 경우 대령 진급 자격은, 전방부대로 예를 들면, 대대장을 마치고 사단급 이상 부대참모를 역임하고 있거나 한 후에 가능하며, 기회는 몇 단계(연차)로 나누어 주어진다. 1차 진급자는 전적으로 진급 본위 경력 관리를 하는 자에게 가능하다. 다음은 그런 자격에 충실하려고 노력하는 자—표현이 좀 어폐가 있으나—, 예를 들면, 1차 진급자는 주로 육군대학을 졸업과 동시에 즉시 대대장 경력을 이수하고 이어서 부대참모를 이수하는 자들이고, 2차 진급자는 주로 육대를 우수하게 졸업함으로써 육대 필수 교관 요원으로 발탁(강제)됨으로, 1차 진급자보다 한발작 늦게 대대장을 마치고 참모 경력을 갖게 되기 때문이다.

육대 교관 근무로 한발 늦었던 나는 당시 제5군단장 류병현 장군에 의해 추천되어 동기생 2차로 진급되었다.(75.1) 진급과 동시 대령 보직으로 옮겨가야 하기에, 고심하고 있던 중, 고맙게도 과거 보병학교 동복유격학교에서 인연을 맺은바 있는, 당시 특전사 인사참모 '장기오 선배'의 추천으로 특전사 정보참모로 가게 되었다.

◦ 특전사령부와 정보처

그리하여 한국특수전(特殊戰, Special Warfare) 사령부 정보처장에 보임되었고 검은 베레모를 쓰고 처음으로 자랑스러운 한국 특전 요원이 되었다. 동시에 오랜만에 가족과 함께 생활하며 근무할 수 있는 후방부대에서 '서울 근무'를 할 수 있게 되었다.

한국특전사령부는 기성 제1공수특전단을 모체로 제3, 5여단을 예하부대로, 육군 특수

작전부대를 통합지휘하는 '육군 특전사령부'로 창설(1969.8)되었다. 그 후 계속 증편되었는데, 1974년에 7, 9여단 창설 증편, 1977년에 11, 13여단 창설 증편, 81년에 707 특수임무부대(대테러부대)도 창설되었다. 예하 각 부대의 임무는—조금 뒤 7공수여단장 편에서 상세하게 기록하겠다.—간단히 말해서, '적지 게릴라전 준비', '반 게릴라전(예상 적 근거지 선점 활동)', '도시 폭동 진압작전', '훈련시 정규전부대 대항군 활동'에 있다.

특히 그동안 후방 운용 가능 유일한 실병력부대—1군예하 전 부대(예비사단 포함)는 연합사령부 소속으로 연합사 승인 없이 후방 차출 불가—로, 68년에 울진삼척지구 대규모 침투 대간첨작전과 서귀포 침투 대간첩작전 등을 실시하였고, 단위 부대로 월남전에 중대 규모로 각 사단에 배속 운용되기도 하였으며, 76년에는 판문점 경비 구역에서 북괴가 도발한 '도끼만행 사건'을 응징하기 위해 '미루나무 절단 및 북괴군 4개 초소 파괴 작전'에 투입되기도 하였다.

어디 그뿐이랴, '5·16 군사혁명' 때는 실병력으로 한강을 도강하여 서울 중심부로 출격, 혁명의 선봉에 섰고, 도시 요소 점령 즉시 소위 '정치 깡패' 와 '사회 깡패'들을 하루아침에 소탕하는데 크게 기여하였다. 그리하여 이때부터 특전부대는 고유의 임무 외에 후방 사회 질서 유지에 필수 불가결한 요소가 되어 군사는 물론 정치적으로도 중요시되어 계속 증편해 나감과 동시에 특히 수도 서울 치안 유지에 큰 배경이 되었다. 그리하여 드디어는 '5·18 광주항쟁'(민주화운동) 진압에 주력으로 투입되기도 하였던 것이다.

특전사 정보처는 적 지역(휴전선 이북 각 도별 지역) 분석과 표적 정보를 발췌하여 예하부대에 제공하는 것이 중요 임무이고, 그리고 병행해서 일반부대 정보참모 임무도 겸하고 있었다. 그래서 수시로 예하부대 정보참모 업무를 감독하였고, 예하부대 참모방문도 개별적으로 또는 전 참모가 동시에 실시하기도 했는데, 특히 예하부대 천리행군일 경우 야간에 훈련 상태를 분담하여 점검 및 감독도 나갔다.

후방 생활을 새로 시작한 나는 우선 오후 5시 '칼퇴근'에 정신적 육체적 적응 시간이 오래 걸렸다. 퇴근하다가도 지금 전방 장병들은 '지금 한창 근무 중일텐데…', 휴일이 되어도 '지금 전방은 무슨 공사 중일텐데…', 오후 퇴근 시간에 처음으로 테니스 운동을 익히면서도 '지금 전방은 무슨 훈련 중일텐데 미안해…' 등등.

◇ 연례 아세아 특전부대장 회의, 참모로 수행

◦ 제8차 연례 아세아 특전부대 지휘관 회의

미국이 월남전쟁에 본격적으로 개입(1963)하면서. 일찍이 케네디 시대에 확립해둔 특수전(Special Warfare)이라는 개념의 전쟁으로 국제공산주의 세력의 침투를 막는 간접전략 작전과, 동시에 후방으로 침투하여 암암리에 모략작전을 통해 적후방을 교란하고 무장 세력으로 근거지를 확보하면서 게릴라전을 전개하였다. 그런 환경하에 중공의 간접침략(한국은 북괴의 침략)에 직면한 아시아 제국에 대해서 '특수전' 전쟁을 위한 지원을 제공하려는 의도에서 미국의 특전 센터 주관으로 연례 아시아 특전부대장 회의를 개최하고 있었다.

그래서 제8차 회의(1975.11)에는, 정병주 사령관(소장)을 정보참모였던 내가 수행하게 되었다. 1962년 봄에 'Counter Insurgency' 과정 유학으로 방문했던 바로 거기, 미국 '노스케로라이너' 주에 있는 'J.F.Kennedy Center'를 다시 방문하였는데 정말 감회가 깊었다. 그런데 그동안 미국은 거의 변하지 않고 있는 것처럼 보였다. 첫날은 환영 행사와 저녁 만찬 파티가 있었고, 다음 날에는 근처에 있는 전통과 승전의 역사에 기록되어 있는 유명한, 이른바 '미 공수부대의 원조'인 제82공수사단을 시찰하고 이어서 제7특전부대의 한 팀의 작전 시범을 보게되었다. 인상 깊었던 것은 이 12명 한 팀의 실력과 능력이 완전하게 특전개념을 만족시키고 있었다는 것이다.

당시 특히 우리 팀과 비교되었던 것은, 군의관이었다. 2명의 완전한 외과전문의로 어느 지역 어느 곳에 가더라도 장비만 가지면, 외과 수술은 물론 웬만한 소규모 야전병원을 운영할 수 있는 실력을 보여주었다. 2명의 정보팀은 '폴란드'어로 기억되는데, 완벽하게 구사한다고 하였다. 당시는 우리 팀의 자격과 실력이 아직 거기까지는 미치지 못하고 북한 언어도 지방별로 구분해서 구사하지도 못하던 때였다. 돌아가면 정보 부서의 할 일을 다시 한번 검토하고 발전시키려고 마음 다짐하였다. 그리고 신형 침투 장비들이 전시되고 설명되었는데, 특히 수중 침투 장비가 인상적이었다.

◦ 뉴욕 방문에서 고등학교 절친 '이인길'을 만나다

귀국 전 뉴욕으로도 행차했는데 뜻밖에도 마중 나온 동래고등학교 절친 '이인길 사장'을 만났다. 아마도 그 형—6·25 당시 우리 동래에 거주하며 미국 유학을 다녀와서 내게 '엠파이어스테이트 빌딩 모형'을 준 장교—이 당시 특전사 부사령관이라, 형의 지시로 안내지시를 받은 것 같았다. 우리끼리는 정말 반가웠다. 도중 도중을 이용하여 우리끼리 그간의 얘기를 나누면서 회포를 풀었다.

그는 이미 저 앞에서 얘기한 바대로 서울대 법대에 입학하고, 내가 육사에 들어갔을 때 종종 육사로 면회 오기도 하였고, 외출 시에 가끔 서울 시내에서 만나기도 했다. 그는 법대 졸업 후, 우리 동래고 동기생 서울 법대 합격자 8명—모두 전쟁 중이라 고등고시를 못 하고 사업가로 진출했다.—그중 한 명으로, 당시 한국 최고 기업이며 막 성장 중이던 '럭키치약(후에 금성사, 지금의 LG기업)'의 대외 무역 담당으로 미국 뉴욕 파견원이었다가 독립을 위해 퇴사하여 뉴저지주에 정착하고 뉴욕에서 단독 무역 상사를 운영하고 있었다. 그의 형 안부도 전하면서 그가 안내해 준대로 1박 2일간 뉴욕 거리를 다시 한번 구경 잘하였다. — 그 이후 그를 또 만나지 못했다. 그러나 남은 인생 행운을 빈다.

중립국 외교, 모로코 군사지원조사단장(1976년 4월)

2. 중립국 외교, 모로코 군사 지원 조사단장

◇ 중립국 외교와 모로코의 군사원조 요청

◦ 군사원조 검토 당시 국내외 정세

1975년도에는 자유 월남의 패망과 함께 도미노 현상으로 인도지나반도 3개국이 공산화되고, 그 영향이 특히 동아시아 전체에 미치고 있었다. 한편 새로 취임한 미국 '카터' 대통령이 주한 미군 철수를 공약하자 이에 더욱 고무된 북괴 김일성이 동유럽과 아프리카 동조 국가들을 돌면서 전쟁 지원을 부탁하고 돌아와서는 '7·4 남북공동선언'도 무시한 채 후방 간첩 침략과 전선 지역의 직접 도발을 적극적으로 자행하면서 한반도 전쟁 위기를 고조시켰다. 이후 북괴는 7월 '전쟁 임박' 성명 발표하고, 8월에 판문점 공동 경비 구역 내에서 도끼로 미군 장교 2명을 참살 만행함으로 'Defcon—3'가 발령되고, 어선과 유명 인사 등을 납치하는 등 마치 전면전 직전 강도의 도발을 강행하였다.

그러나 그럼에도 불구하고 미국은 '키신저'의 소위 '데탕테' 외교와 함께 미국 조야의 동향으로 판단하건데, 한국쯤이야 '미국 국가 이익'에 별무 가치로 판단되면 언제든지 포기할 수도 있을 것이라는 생각이, 박 대통령과 애국 시민들로 하여금 '자주국방의 길'과 '생존 외교의 길'로 떠밀고 있었다.

그리하여 한국도 미국에만 의존 말고 당시 상당한 외교력을 구사하고 있는 '중립국' 즉 제3 세력권 외교의 폭을 넓히는 의미에서, 그리고 김일성의 제3 세력권 지도력에 대응하는 의미에서도 '중립국 외교'를 강화하게 되었는데, 특히 우선은 친서방 중립국, 북아프리카 '마그레브' 지역의 모로코, 알제리, 튀니지, 리비아 등에 외교를 치중하였다. 정부는 5·16 군사혁명 이후 일찍이 '중앙정보부'가 이들 국가에 태권도 등 왕실 경호 요원들의 양성에 기여하는 등 왕실 중심으로 친선을 도모하면서 친선 외교를 다지고 있었다.

◦ 모로코의 군사 지원 요청

1975년에 스페인이 아프리카 '서부 사하라' 지역에서 철수하면서 3국(스페인+모로코+모리타니아)과 협상하였다. 이를 기회로 모로코는 이 '서부사하라' 지역을 선점하고 합병을 선언하였다. 그러자 지역 민족이 독립 단체 '폴리사리오(Polisario)'를 결성하고 'Arab Sahara'라는 국가 수립—국제 미 승인 국가—을 선포하고, 모로코에 대항하여 '사막 게릴리라전'을 통한 독립전쟁을 전개하였다. 이에 모로코는 대 게릴라전 부대 20개대대 창설을 목표로, 일단 2개특전대대 창설 상태에서 대게릴라전에 유능하다고 알려진 한국군에 군사지원(특히 대게릴라전 교육훈련을 위한 교관단)을 요청하게 된 것이다. 특히 이웃 알제리가 막혀버린 대서양 방면 출구를 확보하기 위해서라도, 친서방 모로코와 적대 행위를 전개하며 이 '폴리사리오'를 적극적으로 지원하고 있었다.

그 당시 중립국 외교를 위해 순방 중이던 '김종필' 총리가 지원을 약속하였고, '심흥선' 장관이 유엔에서 모로코에게 한국 지지를 요청할 때 모로코가 동의하면서 거듭 한국의 군사 지원을 요청해 왔다. 그래서 그동안 이미, 그동안 개발된 한국산 전투복과 개인 장비 등을 지원하고 있었다.

◇ 조사단의 임무와 구성

◦ '4.24 조사단'의 구성

조사단 구성의 날을 기해서 그리고 비밀을 유지하기 위해서 '4.24 조사단'으로 명명하고, 조사단장은 특전사의 정보처장인 나를, 단원은 외교부의 '노영찬' 아 중동국장—후에 외교부 장관—, 보좌관으로 '조 중령(후에 대장으로 보안사령관)' 그리고 통역관(현지에서는 공사관 직원이 담당)으로 당시 육사 프랑스어 교수였던 '한 대령'으로 구성하였다.

신분은 '대우(大宇) 회사 실업인(상인)'으로 위장하였고, 모든 비용과 일정은 외무부 즉 노영찬 국장이 준비하였다.

◦ 조사단의 임무

외무부 의견(박동진 외무장관, 방문 시) ; 당시 북한의 '짐바브에' 군사 지원 등으로 국제여론 악화 중이고—『뉴스위크』 주간지 보도—, 반 모로코의 '알제리'를 또한 회유해야 하는 등으로 모로코 요구에 따른 적극적인 군사 지원은 곤란하다. 따라서 모로코의 지원 요청에 외교적 응대로 '일단 조사 방문'하는 목적이기에, 일단 방문해서, 그들이 요청하는 '아군 교관 파견 요청'을 경청하되, 그들 교관 요원들이 한국에 와서 교육받게 하도록 유도해 달라, 이것이 박정희 대통령의 의향—사실은 자기가 건의한 것—이라고 하였다.

- 중앙정보부 의견(홍능 정보차장보 방문) ; 당시 '친서방 비동맹외교'와 '비동맹 외교'의 선봉에서 각국 대사관에 공사(公使) 외교를 적극 전개 중— 왕이나 고위층에 안마사, 태권도 사범, 경호책임자 훈련 활동 등—이던 터에, 특히 모로코가 한국에 '군사 구매단'을 파견, 한국군 무기 및 장비(M-16소총, 군복 개인장구 등)를 구입하면서 군사교관단 파견을 요청해 오고 있음으로, 이 기회에 '교관단을 파견하여 모로코를 군사 지원하고 비동맹 외교를 완성하여야겠다'고 강조하였다.
- 국방부 의견(합참본부장 유병현 장군 방문) ; "군은 국가 정책 방향대로 행동하는 것이 옳다고 생각한다"고 하였고, 정보국장은 '한국 교관 모로코 파견 교육안'과 '모로코 교관 한국 파견 교육안'을 조사 후 건의 함이 좋겠다고 권고하였다.
- 육군본부 의견(참모총장 이세호 장군) ; "우리 육군에서 파견 군사 지원 실현되도록 노력할 것"을 강조하며 지시하였다.
- 임무 종합 판단 및 결심 ; 위와 같이 관계 당국들을 방문하여 의견을 청취하고 결론을 내려고 하면서 생각난 것은,—비록 그 사건과 비교할 만한 대사(大事)는 아니나 그래도 —'임진왜란 전 파견된 조사단이 상충된 조사 결과를 보고하게 된 경우가 이런 상황이었을 수도 있겠구나' 하는 것이었다.

나는 결심하였다, '우리 한국군도 이제 '교육훈련' 등의 군사 지원을 요청하는 국가 현지에 파견되어 이를 감당할 수 있는 수준에 이르러 있기에, 기회가 주어지면 이를 실행하면서, 월남전 참전과는 또 다른, 대외 진출을 시도하여야 한다'고. 그리하여 나는, '가능한 한 한국군 교관단을 모로코에 파견하는 것이 가하다'고 건의하리라고 일단 출국 전에 결심하였다. 그런데 출발 전부터 '노영찬 국장은 외교부 지령대로 임무를 수행할 것'으로 판단되었다.

◇ 모로코 현지 조사 경과

◦ 브리핑 회의, 대사관 대책 회의, '서부사하라' 현장 방문 등

일행은 우선 '파리'로 가서 한국대사관에 들러 외교와 군사가 따로 협력하였다. 나는 당시 주프랑스대사관 무관 '윤억섭 대령(육사 12기)'—후에 주프랑스 한국대사—과 함께 '베르사이유'궁전 공원을 산책하면서, 목적과 방법 그리고 연락사항 등 차후 대책을 상의하였다. 당시는 서유럽과 아프리카 공관에 대한 통제와 연락 사무 등 본국과의 중계기지역을 주프랑스대사관에서 담당하고 있었다.

모로코에 도착해서는 수도 '라바트(Rabat)'에 있는 주 모로코 한국대사관에서 대사, 공사, 무관 등의 참여로 일단 최초 전략 회의를 열었는데, 모두가 한결같이 반기며 우리 과업이 곧 대사관 과업으로 인지하고 관계자 모두가 자기 일처럼 열의를 다하여 협조해 주려는 모습이었다. 그리하여 '주 모로코 한국대사관'이 현지 활동 거점이 되었다. 이들 요원들의 얘기를 종합하면, 그동안 중립국 외교 중에서도 가장 친서방 중립국인 모로코를 거점으로 특히 '마그레브'지역 중립 국가들을 친한 국가로 리드하기 위해 여러 가지 수단, 특히 태권도와 안마 그리고 경호 요원 교육 및 지원 등의 공작으로, 특히 사하라사막 남부 제 국가에 침투한 북한의 영향력과 비교해서 상대적으로 상당한 영향력을 유지하고 있음을 알 수 있었다.

일단 한국대사관에서, 대사와 관계관과 우리 조사단 전원이 참여하는 '일일결산회의'를 하고 파리를 경유하여 일일 보고를 외무부로 하기로 결정을 보았다.

다음 날 모로코 국방장관과 차관을 차례로 예방하고, 이어서 이 군원 사업 담당 부서인 통합사령부로 가서 '모로코군의 본 건에 대한 브리핑과 질의응답 등의 1차 회의'가 있었다. 그런데 이날 우리를 안내하고 상대한 모로코군 간부는, 바로 본인과 함께 독일군 '지휘참모대학'에서 함께 수학한 동문 동기생이어서 반가웠는데 이 문제를 담당하여 처음부터 끝에 비행장 환송장까지 우리를 안내하고 그들의 뜻을 전해왔었다. 이날 국장장관 초대로 'Red Labster tail 오찬'이 있었는데, 장관은 수시로 사탕 과자와 갈색 설탕물을 즐겨 마시기도 했는데, 이곳이 바로 사막 지대 근접 지역이라 주민들의 생존형 생활 습관으로 보였다.

다음 날 저녁에는 통합사령부 요원들의 초대로 '구운 통 양고기' 파티에 참가하였다. 귀한 손님에게 베푸는 최고의 대접이라하였다. 그들 3명 우리 4명 도합 7인데, 주식만 보드레도, 통째로 구운 큼직하고 통통한 양 한 마리와 각자 통닭 한 마리와 그 달걀 여러 개가 차려져 있었다. 우선 통닭으로 시작하여 계란을 먹고, 그리고 통 양으로 이어갔다. 통닭만 먹어도 배가 찼는데, 그 위에 거대한 양이라, 머뭇거리는데, 그들은 맨손으로 고기를 덥석 집어 입에 넣어주기까지 하였는데, 이것이 친구에 대한 대접이라고 하면서. 흥미도 있어 먹어보니 고기는 연하고, 옛날 우리네 보신탕 맛 이상이었다. 이렇게 하루 저녁 대접을 성의껏 잘 받기도 하였다.

다만 독일 '지참대' 동기는, 자기 집에 초대 못하는 것을 미안해하는 눈치였다. 아랍권의 여자들은 처녀 때는 그렇게도 날씬하고 예쁘나 일단 결혼하고 나면 몸이 불고 조로한다고 한다. 그녀들은 결혼하면서 남편 허가 없이 밖에 나가지 못하고—남편은 출근 시에 심지어 대문을 자물쇠를 잠구어 두기도 한다는데 설마?—집안에서만 지내는 것이 풍습이라 하였다.

다음 날은 모로코 육사를 방문하고 생도들의 사열과 분열을 받아보면서, 이 나라에서 우리에게 거는 기대가 대단한 것임을 새삼 느끼기도 하였다. 다음 날은 회의와 회의 사이의 시간 공간대에, '라바트' 바로 아래 '휴양도시'로 세계에 유명한 '카사블랑카'와 라바트 내 구시가지를 관광도 하였다. '카사블랑카'에서는 때마침 세계적 미국 외교가 '키신저'가 로비에 와 있어서 우리 노영찬 국장이 다가가 다정하게 대화를 나누었는데, 인생도 외교도 '우연한 기회'라는 것이 있다는 사실을 알게 되었다.

다음날은 지금 사막 작전지대 내에서 창설 중에 있다는 특공대대와 신설기지 그리고 작전 지역 현장을 시찰하였다. 우선, 병합 전 '모로코' 국가의 남단에 위치한 '이프니, Sidi—ifni'의 신설 훈련기지를 방문 시찰하면서 환경은 물론 교육훈련 실정도 파악하였고, 그다음 날은 새롭게 점령한 '서부사하라'의 작전기지 '엘아이운(El Aiun)'과 주변을 시찰하고, 말하자면 적진 속에서 경계병에 호위를 받으며 거기서 하룻밤을 지났는데, 밤새 잠깐 밖에서 총성이 들렸다. 아침에 들으니 게릴라 침투 징후 지점에 예방 사격을 실시했다고 한다. 여하간에 모로코군과 이곳 서부사하라 지역에서 '폴리사리오' 게릴라와의 전투 분위기가 고조되고 있음은 확실하였다. 라바트로 돌아올 때는 서부사하라 국경지대 내 '사하라사막' 위를 비행하였는데, 대서양 가까운 지대라 그러한지 전적으로 모래밭은 아니었으나 그래도 삭막하기 그지없었다. 과연 이런 곳에서도 영토 쟁탈전이 전개될 수 있을까 하는 생각도 들었다.

◦ 모로코 군 당국의 열의, 조사단의 최종 결론

조사를 매듭지으려 할 때 모로코 측에서 한국교관단에 대한 대우와 교육대 위치 피교육 준비 시항 등에 대해 협의하자고 하였으나, 우선 과제는 일단 귀국해서 조사 결과를 보고하는 것이라면서 피했다. 그리하여 한국대사관에서 모두—대사, 공사(중정대표), 무관 그리고 우리 조사단 전원—모여 결론을 도출하는 회의, 사실은 (CIA)공사와 무관 측의 요구는 한국교관단이 모로코로 파견와 주는 것이고, 대사는 외교부 지령대로 모로코 교관단을 한국으로 파견해 가는 것이었다. 물론 노영찬 국장은 지령받은 사실에 대한 변심이 있을 것 같지 않았다.

그런데 모로코가 좀 강력하게, 비용이 들더라도, 한국교관단의 초빙을 원하는 이유 중 하나가, 알려진 바로는, 자국군 엘리트 장교단이 외국 다녀오면 흔히 '쿠데타' 위험성이 높아지고, 또는 외국에서 귀국하지 않은 경우도 있고 하여, 자국군의 대외 파견을 꺼린다는 것이었다.

그래서 그 모든 정황을 고려하여, 다음 날 모로코 국방부 최종 회의에서, 나는 우리 조사단을 대표하여, 말하였다. 그동안 베풀어 준 환대를 고맙게 생각한다, 모로코의 안보 환경에 대한 이해는 물론 요청 사항에 대하여도 잘 이해하였고, 만일에 교관단이 오게 되는 경우 물심양면의 준비 상태도 잘 확인하였다. 더구나 위험을 무릅쓰고 조사에 필요한 모든 편의를 도모해 주어서 만족한 조사가 될 수 있었다. 이제 돌아가서 이 모든 사실을, 특히 모로코군 당국이, 자국교관단의 한국 파견보다 한국교관단의 모로코 파견을 강력히 요청하고 있다는 사실을 상세하게 보고드리고 가까운 시일 내에 결과를 알려드리도록 하겠다. 그간의 협조에 거듭 감사드린다"고 하고, 최종 회의를 결정적 결론을 주지 못한 채 그들에게는 초조한 기대만을 남긴체 조사단의 현지 조사를 마무리하였다.

◇ 귀국 보고, 결과

귀국 비행기 내에서 거듭 생각하며 보고서 초안을 작성하였다. 그 모든 사실을 확인하고 인지한 가운데, 그래도 나는 '우리 군사 지원 교관단을 모로코로 파견하는 것이 최선'이라고 건의안을 완성하였다.

그리하여 귀국 즉시 국방부와 육군참모총장에게 직접 대면 보고를 하였는데, 국방부는 '알겠다, 수고했다'였고, 육군참모총장은 내 보고서를 지지하였다.

그러나 외교부 장관에게 보고하자 장관은, '수고했다, 그러나 대통령께는 자기가 직접 보고하겠다'고 했다.

'결과',—이미 장관과 대통령이 인식하고 있었던 대로—일단 모로코에 성의는 베풀었고, 중립국 외교에 모난 것은 없을 것 같고, 북한의 아프리카 군사 지원에 대한 국제적 비난도 피할 수 있고, 그래서 모로코가 원한다면 '모로코 교관단의 한국 초청을 언제든지 환영한다'로 '4.24 조사단'의 과업에 결론을 내렸다. 그 이후 듣기로는, '1977년도'에 모로코 교관단이 초청되어 왔다는 사실을 소문으로 들은 바 있다.

3. 국방대학원 수학—핵무장 여론, 미국 시찰, 졸업 논문

◇ 국방대학원 수학 과정

한국군의 전략, 전술학 최고 과정은 합동참모대학이 담당하고 있고, 국대원은 국방부가 설립하여 운영하는 한국 국가안보 최고 교육기관으로, 매년 1개기 즉 10개월 과정의 '안보과정'이 있고, 부설기관으로 '안보연구소'가 있다. 안보 과정에는 군(육해공군 대령급 이상), 관(치안감급 경찰과 검찰 그리고 국장급 공무원), 민(신문 기자 등)에서 선발된 자가 입학하는데, 제도는 좀 어설픈 점이 있으나 수업 내용은 국가 고급 요인에게는 필수적인 것으로, 국가기관 간 안보 협조 면에서 특히 중요하고, 국가기관 간 개인적 발전 및 소통 관계 면에서도 중요한 값을 가지고 있다. 거기에다 80년도부터는 국가 정규 '군사학 석사 과정'을 개설하여 운영하고 있다.

다만 아쉬웠던 것은, 군인에게는 장군이 되기 위한 필수 과정으로, 공무원에게는 1급 또는 정무관(장관 포함)급이 되기 위한 필수과정으로 운영되는 것이 바람직하였으나 그러지 못하고, 공무원이나 군인에게 한때의 한직을 경과하는 정도의 인식이 지배하고 있었음을 유감스럽게 생각하였다. 그러나 뜻이 있는 많은 대령급 군인들은 스팩과 실제 학문 충일을 위해, 자원해서 수학하는 경우가 흔하였다.

◇ 졸업여행, 미국(인권 문제 토의)과 케나다

이미 말한 바와 같이 내 어릴 때 귀중한 소원은 '서울 가서 공부하는 것'과 '미국 유학 가는 것'이었다. 그렇게 마음먹었던 소원 즉 꿈은, 하나님의 말씀 '구하라 그러면 주실 것이다' 하고 일치하여 이때도 미국 시찰을 가게되는 행운을 갖게 되었다. 이번으로 3번째 도미인 것이다. 대위 때 미 특수전학교 유학, 작년에 제8차 아세아 태평양 특전지휘관 회의 수행 그리고 이번의 기회이다.

이번에는 안보 과정 졸업여행—영어시험 성적순으로 졸업생 1/3은 미국, 유럽, 아세아 중동으로, 2/3는 국내 전국 순회 군부대 및 지방 관청 방문—으로, 우리 팀은 미국과 케나다의 안보 관계 연구소와 기관 그리고 의회 등을 방문하게 되었던 것이다. 그래서 먼저 미국 국회의사당과 국방부를 방문하였다. 과거 워싱턴을 방문할 때마다 그저 멀리서 소개받고만 말았는데 이번 미국 국회의원 안내로 여기저기 둘러보기도 하였다. 역시나 신천지 미국 것이라 영국 의사당의 규모와 내부 시설과는 비교할 바 못되었다.

특히 기억나는 것은, 'Rand', 'Brookings' 연구소 방문 시 그쪽에서 한국의 현 인권상황에 대한 지적을 자주 듣게 되었는데, 귀에 거슬려 나는, 다른 이들 만류에도 기어이, 한국 실정과 현 정권의 정책 불가피성을 좀 강한 항의 톤으로 주장하기도 하였다. 사실상 그만큼 당시에 그들 외국인 안중에는 '그저 한국 인권이 우선적 논의 과제'로 정해져 있었던 것이다.

캐나다에 가서는 국방부 주최로 만찬 파티에 '리셉션' 등에도 초청되었는데 특히 기억되는 것은 '벤쿠버'를 방문하여 아름다운 해변 도시가 마음에 들어 다음에 다시 한번 방문하기로 마음을 두었었다. 그런데 그 소원은 은퇴 후 몇몇 동기생 내외가 케나다 여행의 기회를 가졌을 때 이루어졌거니와 그 이후 우리 가족들, 손자며느리, 아들과 우리 내외가 '알라스카 크르즈' 갈 때 다시 한번 그곳에 들려 아름다운 풍경은 물론 옛날을 가리키며 감개무량하기도 하였다.

◇ 졸업 논문, '환태평양집단안보, 한미일 삼각안보'

1977년도를 전후하여 한국 정부 즉 박정희 대통령은 북의 적화남침 위협의 고조와 세계적 정치 경향이던 미국의 국익 우선 전략정책—80년도까지 주한미군 철수는 이미 선언되 있고, 그래서 세 불리하면 한국도 포기할 수 있다는 등—에 대응하여 소신대로 핵무기를 포함하는 모든 무기의 국산화, 그리하여 자주국방론의 깃발을 높이 들어 올리고 강행군을 주도하고 있었다. 그런 한국적 국가안보 정세 하에서 국가 안보전략을 수학하였던 우리는 졸업 논문을 남기게 되었는데 나는, '아세아·태평양 집단 안보 체제 구상'을 논제로, 제1장에서 국내외 안보 정세 분석을, 제2장에서 한국안보 체제 분석을, 제3장에서는 문제점 및 대책을 논하고 그리고 결론하였다.

결론으로는, 1980년대까지 즉 북괴보다 우위가 명확히 입증될 때까지 '한미일 3각안보 체제를 확고히 하고 주변국과 쌍무 또는 집단 안보 체제를 구축하여 전쟁을 억제하고 평화를 쟁취하여 오늘을 극복하고 내일에 승공 통일을 기약하며 나아가서는 멀지 않은 장래에 북방 세력 즉 대륙 세력과 해양 세력을 밀어제치고 민족 중흥의 창업을 이룩하여야 한다'고 맺었다.

◇ 1977년 박 대통령의 핵무장 결의와 국대원학생여론

고위공무원 친목, 대통령 포함 귀빈 강연 등, 학교는 서울 중앙에서 그리 멀지 않았기 때문에 그리고 또 최고의 국가 안보 기관 중의 하나였기에 통상 국방장관을 비롯한 장관들과 주용 국가기관장들이 그때마다 주요 이슈를 초청 강의 해 왔다. 뿐만 아니라 방문 중인 외국 귀빈들도 초청되어 강연 시간을 갖기도 했다. 특히 박정희 대통령 시절에는 학생 졸업식 때마다 한해도 빠자지 않고 임석하였다. 그런가하면, 좌경 정권 시절에는 이상하게도 대통령들이 참석을 기피하였는데, 이를 두고 학생들, 즉 국가 간부될 인재들은 '역시나 좌경 정권은 안보에 의문을 품게 하는구나'라고 이구동성으로 성토하기도 하였다.

특히 잊을 수 없는 기억은, 박 대통령은 북괴의 침략성에 대하여 철저히 대비한다는 관점에서 또 미국의 안보 신뢰 불충분성에서 '자주국방'을 추진하였다. 그중 종결 편이 '핵무장'이었다. 물론 미국이 자국 이익 우선의 전략으로 주한미군을 철수해 간다고 선언했기에 더욱 굳게 결심하려하였다. 그래서 우리 학생에게 질문 즉 여론 조사를 하였다. '핵무장을 할 것인가, 말 것인가, 그 장단점은?'이었다. 학생들은 전원— 확인은 못했다, 짐작하건데—이 핵무장을 찬성한다고 답하였다.

4. 논산훈련소 연대장(1977.8~1979.5)

◇ 군계일확(群鷄一鶴)의 각오

육군본부는 안타깝게도 국방대학원을 졸업하는 인재를 논산훈련소 연대장으로 가게 하였다. 그래서 인사 명령에 따라 임지에 부임하기 앞서 유병현 장군(당시 합참의장)께 인사차 방문하였는데, 그는 그 자리에서 바로 이세호 육군참모총장에게 전화했다, "수도기계화사단 출신은 그 부대로 보직하여야 한다고 강조하였는데 왜 약속을 안 지키느냐?"고 항의성 문의를 하였으나 육참총장은 변명만 하는 것으로 들렸다. 다음엔 이세직 장군—부산사범 선배로 후에 서울시장과 88올림픽위원장—을 방문하고 인사하였는데, 크게 실망하는 모습으로, "일단 연대장 마칠 때 보자"고 위로해 주었다. 이렇듯 주변의 관심 있는 상급자들의 한결같은 실망스런 표정들로 보아 장래가 어려운 보직으로 평가받고 있음을 다시 한번 확인할 수 있었다.

그러나 나는 실망하지 않았다. 전에 읽었던 미국 군사 리더쉽을 다룬 명저 『19 Stars』에서, 미국 '마샬 원수'가 대령 때 어느 학교 부교장으로 한직 근무도 했다는 얘기가 상기되기도 하면서, 나는 생각하기를, 대한민국 국군 어느 부대에 일(임무) 없는 군대가 어디 있겠는가. 후순위 부대일수록 찾아 할 일은 많을 것이고 부대 요원들은 협조적일 테니, 심기일전하여 심신의 노력을 다하여 '군계일확'(群鷄一鶴)' 되겠다고 결심하였다. 그래서 논산훈련소 제26연대장으로 보임되어 갔다.

논산훈련소는 그동안 세간에 알려진 바와 같이 '돈산훈련소'로 알려져 있었으나, 1960년경 육사 출신 1~2기생(5·16 후 11~12기로 개칭됨)—그 후 대통령이 된 전두환 중위도 포함—이 대량으로 훈련소 중대장으로 보임되어 가서, 그야말로 천지개벽시켜 놓았고, 그 위에 최근(1976년경)에 미국식 P.X제도가 도입되어 있어서, 1978년경에는 경제, 인사 문제를 비롯하여 훈련 제도 등이 거의 정상화 되어 있었다. 또한 부대 시설들도 이제 막 현대화되어가고 있었으나 아직은 모든 면에서 완성되었다고는 평가할 수 없었다.

연대는 본부에 연대장 외 부연대장(중령)과 연대참모로 인사(소령), 교육 겸 작전(대위), 군수(중위), 군의관, 그리고 예하 12개중대(중대장 대위)로 구성되어 있었다.

◇ 신병훈련과 부대 생활 이모저모

훈련소 각 연대는 대략 분기에, 1개기 1개월 2,000명의 보병 신병훈련을 담당하였다. 연대는 신병의 내무 생활과 군기 그리고 훈련장으로 인솔 및 귀대 그리고 입소 및 퇴소식을 담당하였고, 과목 훈련과 교육은 훈련소 교도대가 담당하였다. 훈련시 1개중대는 180명 이상으로 12개중대 2,000여 명이 동시에 기상하여 화장실과 세수 그리고 식사 등을 동시에 실시하니 그 가운데 무리한 일도 우스운 일도 어려운 일도 따르게 마련이었다.

◦ **2년 연속 '선봉(先鋒)연대'**

공한기(훈련병 미 입소 시기)에는 훈련소에도 연대대항 훈련소 전술실기대회가 있다. 각 중대 조교가 내무반에서 훈련병에게 직접 교육시켜야 하는 과목들, 소총 분해결합, 사격술, 제식훈련 등인데 중점은 역시 10킬로미터 단독 군장 구보—전방부대는 통상 무장 구보—였다. 연대 내 조교 30여 명이 장교 인솔하에 훈련소에서 출발하여 논산역 근방까지 돌아오는 코스였다. 각 연대의 환경 조건은 동일한데도 승부는 성립되었다. 지휘관 즉 연대장의 관심과 성의(사기앙양)에 달렸다고 해도 과언이 아니었다. 훈련소 연대가 물질적으로 풍부하지 못한 것은 말할 필요도 없으나 가진 것으로 성의를 다하면 되었다. 무엇보다 첫째는 연대장의 관심 즉 정신적 동기부여로 "야 우리가 말이야, 남자가 말이야, 한번 해보자!"고 위로 격려하면서 준비 기간 중 매일 훈련 시간에 함께 지내고, 밤에는 잠자기 전에 그들을 돌아보고 위로 격려해 주었고, 무엇이든지 우리 범위 내에서 줄 수 있는 건 구해서 주었다. 보급 건빵을 2배 정도(모으기도 얻기도 하여)는 물론 주보의 빵 과자—해 보았자 간식거리도 못 되지만, 연대장이 사다 준 맛과 성의로—도 주고, 휴식 때 "수고한다"고 격려하면서도, 연습은 엄격하게 최고 성적을 목표로 하여 달성할 때까지 연습하고 또 연습하였다.

그리고 시합 당일은 전 장교가 시험장에 가서 전 종목 현장에 지켜서서 직/간접적으로 응원하고 후원함으로써, 그때마다 과목 실력 성적은 물론 심판관들의 마음까지도 얻어서 8개연대 중 최우수 성적으로 '선봉연대'가 되었고, 이 명예를 2년 연속으로 달성하였다.

5. 국대원 관리 교수부장, 사우디 군협 조사단장, 국대원 석사과정 창립

◇ 국대원 안보교수부 제2처(경제, 관리)장, 국대원 석사과정 창립

그동안 군계일학의 뜻을 이루고 부여된 임무에 대한 책임은 완수하였으나 육군본부의 인사정책(적재적소, 인사심의)의 혼미로 다시 한번 좌절의 맛을 보았다. 그래서 그래도 희망을 가지고 또 취향도 살릴 겸 국방대학원 군인 교수를 지망하게 되었다.

그리하여 때마침 동고(東高) 동기생으로 미국 콜럼비아대학 박사학위로 국방대학원에 와있던 '권문술' 교수와 미국 예일대 박사인 15기 후배 '이한종' 교수가 추천해 주고 또 그들이 소개해 준 미국 모대학 출신의 안보연구소장 '김종휘' 교수—후에 청와대 외교안보특보 —를 만나 추천받아서 국대원 군인 교수로 보임하게 되었고 자동적으로 안보 교수부 2처(경제, 관리처 후에 관리교수부)장이 되었으며, 이후 이들과 친하게 지내면서 부여된 과업을 협조적으로 무난히 수행해 낼 수 있었다.

당시 관리과정 교수부에는 미국 '인디아나 주'에 있는 유명한 '퍼듀대학'에 유학하여 '컴퓨터' 과정 석사학위를 이수한 육사 11기 선배 교수가 재직해 있었는데, 물론 그 당시 미국도 막 컴퓨터를 시작 중이었지만, 우리는 소위 '486' 이전 시대로, 손으로 쓰던 월급봉투를 컴퓨터로 인쇄해 내고 월급 계산을 주판 대신 컴퓨터로 해서 기록해 내는 정도였는데, 그래도 미국 수준 정도는 가려고 컴퓨터 활용에 관한 미래 설계와 학생교육 계획을 세우고 있었다.

그동안 매사에 열정적이었던 조문환 대학원장(중장)은 대학원에 '안보 석사 과정' 설립을 위해 문교부 장관을 초청한다던가 국회에 협조를 구하는 등, 노력 끝에 12월 28일에 드디어 '국대원 설립법 개정(석서 과정 설치)'을 통해 결실을 맺고 81년 2월 교육 개시를 목표로 모든 준비를 하게 되었다.

내가 석사 과정 교육 준비위원회 위원장이 되어 기성 교수들과 숙의 및 논의하면서 일단 주공 과정을 '국제 문제', '국방 관리', '군사전략 전공' 과정으로 정하였다. 그리고 이어서 세부 사항으로 각 교수들의 전공 교수 과목과 시간 및 학점 배당 등에 대해서 심의하면서 타협시키면서 희망에 찬 한때를 보내었다. 바로 지금 국방대학교가 자랑하는 '석사 과정'의 기반이 그렇게 자리를 잡았던 갓이다.

이와는 별도로 내 개인적으로는, 독일 유학 시절 마지막 단계에서 실시했던 '종합훈련'을 참고하여 안보 과정(정치, 군사 , 외교, 경제) 마감 시, 과정 종합훈련 즉 '국가통합안보전략의 종합 작성'과정을 한 1주일간 기간으로 실습 위주로 실행에 옮겨보기도 하였다. 물론 그 때는 미국 레이건 대통령 때부터 정의된 '국가안보전략'과 이를 기반으로 대통령 임기 중 두 번 정도로 미국 국회에 보고를 겸해 발행하는 「The National Strategy of U.S.A」도 아직 발행 이전이었다.

◇ 10·26 사태와, 직결된 12·12 사태

◦ 10·26 대통령 시해 사태

북한의 극렬한 '베트남식 도전'을 '자주국방' 정책으로 극복하기 위해 72년의 유신 체제를 출범시키면서, 박정희 대통령은 여전히 민주화라는 국내 정치 욕구를 억지하며 오로지 중화학 공업화에 박차를 가하였다. 그러나 78년 말의 제2차 국제 유가 파동 등 내외적 요인으로 18%가 넘어서는 국내 인플레가 조성되어 경제가 악화 되고, 점증하는 좌익 운동을 민주화운동으로 착각한—좌익 운동과 민주화운동은 크게 보아 둘이 아니고 하나였음에도 —미국 카터의 노골적인 압박(주한 미군 철수) 등으로, 1979년도의 한국은 정치 경제적으로 위기를 맞이하고 있었다. 이 와중에 부산과 경상남도에서 소위 '부마항쟁'이 일어나 그 일대에 비상계엄령이 선포되고 위수령이 발표되면서 군(해병대와 공수부대)에 의한 진압 작전도 실시됨으로써 사회적 긴장과 위기감이 고조되었다.

그리하여 대통령의 막역한 친구로 가장 신임을 받고 있던 중앙정보부장 김재규는 자의건 타의건 간에 이런 상황에 대한 대응책에 대해 자천 타천(미국 측 포함?)의 방책으로 '배은망덕하고 반역적인 거사'를 미리부터 준비하고 있었던 것으로 보였다. 그는 소위 '3단계 혁명 계획'—1. 육참총장 정승화를 사건 현장에 입회시켜 공범화하고, 2. 대통령 시해 후 정승화로 하여금 계엄령을 선포하고 제반 조치를 실행하고, 3. 군 주도로 혁명위원회를 구성하여 국가를 통치한다.—을 가지고 있었다. 이를 위해 사전에 3군사령관, 최기 군단장, 최기 사단장, 특전사령관, 수경사령관 등을 친 세력으로 배비해 두었던 것이다. 이와 같은 치밀한 사전 계획을 가지고 벼루어서 '10·26 국가 반역 사태'를 야기하였던 것이다.

그리하여 때마침 사단장에서 국군 보안사령관으로 보직되어 있던 전두환 장군이 법에 의해 자동적으로 계엄사령부 '합동수사본부장' 되어 국가 전 수사기관을 총괄 지휘하여 사건을 수사하였는데, 사건 다음 다음날 28일에 일차적으로 발표하기를, '김재규 일당과 비서실장 김계원이 주범이고, 배후는 없다, 미 CIA 등 관련 조직은 전혀 없다고 강조하여 발표함으로써 '대통령 시해 사건' 자체 내용은 군대식으로 간단하게 마무리된 것으로 보였다.

◦ 12·12 정승화 참모총장 연행 사태

그러나 김재규 반역 사건의 법적 처리를 위해 수사는 계속되었다. 주범들에 대한 조사에 따라, 당시 일국의 참모총장이 KCIA 김재규의 지시를 받아, 대통령의 술자리 바로 문밖 50미터 지근 거리에서 수십 발의 총성을 들어가며 김재규의 차후 지령을 대기하다가, 피투성이로 뛰어나온 김재규와 함께 차에 동승하여 한때나마 김재규의 명령대로 실행하였다는 사실이 확인되었다. 바로 공범으로 의심되고도 남는 사실이었다. 정말 있을 수 없는 군 통수권자에 대한 반역과 군에 대한 배반이며 적에 대한 이적 행위였다.

그런데, 발표된 계엄령에 의하여 계엄사령관이 된 정승화는 김재규의 범행을 옹호하면서 서둘러 11월에, 만일(연행 조사 등)에 대비해, 군 내부 기존 김재규 세력에 자기 추종 세력을 추가하여 군의 주요직 인사 이동—장군 진급 심사 포함—을 단행하였다. 뿐만 아니라 당시 자기 입장을 옹호(변명)하는 한편, 문자 그대로 누가 봐도 의심되는 자기를 수사하려는 전두환 합수부장을 '적반하장'으로 오히려 제거—보직 이동, 해임—하려 하였다. 이에 '합수부'는 요령을 다해, 희생을 무릅쓰고, 당시 최고 군의 실세요 상사인 계엄사령관이기는 하나 엄연히 '대통령 시해 사건'의 피의자요, 증거 인멸을 기도하고 있음이 확실한 정승화를, 부득이 연행하게 되었는데, 이를 두고 세간에서는 소위 '12·12 사건'이라고 한다.

◇ '유류 파동' 대책, '사우디 군사협력조사단장'

◦ 유류 파동과 '사우디 군사협력조사단장'

인륜과 도덕 가치를 중요시하는 한국 사회에서 있을 수 없는 '10·26 대통령 시해 사태'가 발생하자 즉시 최규하 대통령이 수반이 된 위기 관리 정부가 성립되었다. 동시에 그동안 정치 활동에 통제를 받아왔던 정치꾼들의 대표격인 소위 '3김씨 시대'가 되었으나 사회가 혼돈의 소용돌이에 말려드는 한편, 국외로부터는 제2의 석유 파동이 밀려와, 그러지 않아도 어려워진 경제에 기름을 부어 인플레가 천정 부지로 솟아올라 한국 경제 사상 최악의 위기가 도래하고 있었다.

이에 절호의 기회를 맞이한 북의 김일성은 전후방 간첩 침투를 통한 대남 적화 공작을 강화하는 한편 10월 27일에 '전군 전투태새 강화'(폭풍 5호)를 하달하면서 제2의 남한 '4·19 정국'을 기대하며 예의 주시하였다.—그리하여 곧이어 서울 지역 좌익 대학생들의 격렬 시위와 그를 이은 5·18 광주항쟁사태(민주화)'가 발발하였다.

이제 전두환 합수부장과 그 기구는 김재규에 대한 조사와 법적 조치를 취하는 과정에서 국가안보에 대해서도 자동적으로 최규하 대통령을 보좌하게 되었다. 그리하여 그중에서도 당장 국가 경제에 사활이 달린 유류 파동 문제를 극복하기 위해—외교부와 산자부가 사우디 '야마니 석유장관'과 면접 일정조차 정하지를 못하는 가운데—대통령이 직접 방문해서 해결해 보고자 하는 계획 즉 '무궁화 계획'을 세우고, 이를 위해 사전에 현지 조사단을 비밀리에 파견하여 '야마니' 석유상을 직접 접촉해 보려 하였다.

* 무궁화계획 ; 제2차 유류 파동 돌파(극복) 방책으로 전두환의 보안사가 주도하여 '대통령이 직접 방문하여, 사우디가 요구해온 군사 지원 문제와 유류의 안정적인 공급 문제를 담판하려는 계획이었다.

◦ 사우디 '군사협력조사단장'

당시 상당수(60여 개) 건설 회사가 소위 '중동 붐'을 타고, 특히 '사우디아라비아'을 비롯하여 열사의 중동에 진출, 건설 물건을 경쟁적으로 수주하면서 '달러 벌이'는 물론 국제적 건설 기술과 설계 경험을 쌓아가고 있었다. 그중에서도 '한일개발(韓逸開發, 아리카타 한일) 사우디 본부'가 중견 회사가 되어 있었는데, 일찍부터 진출하여 사우디 왕가의 신용을 바탕으로 성장 중에 있었다. 당시 이 회사는 막 사우디의 한 실권 왕자로부터 '특수전 훈련 시설'을 수주하여 비밀리에 공사 중이었다. 특수전에 정통한 전두환 장군이 이런 상황을 포착하고 현 시국 돌파에 호기로 활용해 보려고 결심하였다.

그리하여 국대원 교수이던 본인을—아마도 전두환 장군은 제1공수여단장, 나는 사령부 정보처장으로 함께 근무 중 '모로코 군사지원 조사단장'의 경험을 가진 나를 기억?—'사우디 군사협력방책조사단 단장'으로 기용하여 사우디로 파견하였는데, 이때도 '아리카타 한일(한일개발) 직원'으로 위장하여 '사우디'에 비밀리에 침투(?)해 들어가게 되었다. 1980년. 3월, 목적은 '사우디 군사협력 방안 도출 보고'였다.

그리하여 전두환 합수부장(동시에 보안사사령관, 동시에 당시는 중앙정보부장 겸무)에게 신고하기 전에 우선 보안사 정보처장으로부터 사전 설명을 들었다.

* 요지 ; 그동안 사우디가 외교 통로를 통해 우리에게, 1. 남 예멘 폭격을 위한 조종사 교육교관 및 정비 요원, 2. 병원 간호원, 3. Turnkey base Hospita 과 간호원 등을 요청해 왔으나 거절해 왔는데 지금 상황은 긴박하다, 그래서 이런 요구 조건이 지금도 유효한 것인지(들어 줄 수도 있다는 뉘앙스)를 확인이 필요하다.

그리고 '한일개발 사장 '조중훈'과 인연이 있다는 실권 왕자로부터 수주한 '턴키 베이스'의 '특수전 훈련 시설' 공사에 대해 '지원 가능한지'를 확인하고 필요하다면 지원을 위한 조사도 요망한다는 내용을 전두환 합수부장에게 신고하였다. 그는 원래가 자상하고 긍정적이고 적극적이라, 더 상세하게 현재 상황과 그의 의도를 설명해 주었다. 특히 그는 자기가 열정적으로 지휘하며 근무했던 한국 특전부대와 대통령 경호실 요원들에 대한 특수 교육훈련을 사우디 왕실 경호부대에도 지원할 수 있기를 열망하였다.

따라서 그는,

1. 사우디 왕실/일반 특전학교 설립을 위해 어떤 종류의 전문교관이 요구되는지?
2. 교관 파견 여부를 결심하기 위한 필요 정보(교육 내용, 지원 문제 등), 특히 현 안보 측면(안정적 유류 확보)을 고려 지원 가능 여부를 검토할 수 있도록.
3. 필요 시/요구 시는 당국 책임자—사우디는 실권 왕자도, 야마니 석유상도 좋고—간 상호 초청 상호협조 문제 조사 등. 추가한다면, 현 사우디 체제를 지지, 그리고 지원용의 등을 표명하라고. 그리고 강조하기를 그들보다 나은 수준의 우리가 군사적, 보안적, 안보적으로 지원할 수 있고 용의도 있음을 설득하는 것도 임무에 포함된다 하였다.

◦ 결론 및 보고(건의)

그리하여 조사단은 결론을 내고 귀국하여 전두환 합수부장에게 다음과 같이 직접 대면 보고하였다(3월 25일). 그는 과중한 업무로 피곤함을 무릅쓰고 졸림을 참으면서 끝까지 장시간(1시간 이상) 들었으며, 위로 격려는 물론 "그대로 반영하도록 하겠다"고 약속하였다.

* '사우디 군사협력방책 건의' 보고 내용 요약
1. 군병원 운용 의료팀(군의관, 간호장교) 지원
2. 사우디 자체 대외원조용 군장비(북예멘, 아프카니스탄) 지원
3. 군 정보학교신설(예정) 교육(계획요원, 교관요원 등) 지원
4. 2개 Airborne 대대의 SWF(Special Warfare Forces)화 권유 및 지원
5. Special Security School의 규모 증가에 따른 교육지원
6. 사우디 자체 대외지원용 전투기와 수송기 조종사 교관요원 및 정비요원 등 지원

나는 보고를 마치고 나오면서 비서실장이던 허화평 후배—이미 생도 시절 2중대본부에서 함께 근무해서 친숙하고 월남 갈 때 편의를 도모해 준바 있으며 하나회 아우이기도 한— 에게 말했다, "이미 국가 정책에 깊이 개입되었다, 이대로 가야할 것 같다"고 했다. 그러자 즉시 비서실장 허화평이 "이미 뺀 칼, 일없이 다시 집어넣을 수는 없지 않습니까"라고 했다. 때는 이미 군심(軍心)이 국정 참여에 깊이 들어가고 있었던 상황이었다.

◦ 결과 실행

그 후 역사는, 5월 중순에 최 대통령이 사우디에 가서 담판하여 어느 정도 안정된 유류 공급을 보장받았으나 그것으로 부족하였는데, 때마침 인도네시아가 'LNG 가스'전을 개발하여 한국에 보급해줌으로써, 이후 한국 유류 정책은 새로운 방향으로 전환해 가며 발전해 갔다. 이 역사적 사실 또한 잘 알려져 있지 않은 전두환 장군의 업적 중 하나였다.

6. 육대참모장/교수부장(1980.7~1981.11), 장군이 되다(1981.1.1)

◇ 육군대학 참모장

5·18광주사태'의 수습을 겸하여 국가비상사태수습을 위한 기구로 '국가보위비상대책위원회" 구성(5.31)하고, 전두환 장군의 신군부 세력—'하나회'가 아닌—과 이에 동조하는 친군 정치 세력이 일대 국정 쇄신의 길로 정진하였다. 그리하여 과감하게 부정부패를 척결하고, 과외를 금지시키고, 사회 불량배를 소탕하여 군부대에서 순화교육 즉 '삼청교육'을 실시하는 등 '구세대 개혁'과 '파사현정(破邪顯正)'이 이루어지는 역사를 창조해 나갔다. 그런데 이 시기에 나는, 육군본부명에 의해 육군대학 참모장으로 보임되었고, 근무 중에 장군으로 승진되었다.

◇ 장군이 되어(1981.1.1) 전장의 장수(將帥)와 영웅되기를 바라다

육군사관학교 졸업과 동시 육군 소위로 임관하면서 '나는 장군이 되어야겠다'고 마음먹거나 선언하는 사람은 없다. 그러나 군대 간부로 멸사봉공하며 상위 계급으로 진출할수록 장군 지향적인 생각이 짙어간다. 그러나 구조적으로, 유감스럽게도, 같은 자격을 가졌음에도 동기생 모두가 장군이 될 수는 없고, 각 기별로 대략 30여 명이 장군(준장)으로 진출하게 된다. 그러하기에, 전시가 아닌 평화 시에는, 이를 두고 '운5 + 기5의 행운의 수'로 읽을 수밖에 달리 생각할 수가 없는 것이리라.

가장 먼저 생각나는 것은 부모님께 신고하고 이 내 장군의 모습을 보여드려야겠는데, 유감스럽게도 저승에 가신 지 오래되고 묘소도 없어 부득이 크게 크게 마음속으로만 자랑해 보여드리고 베풀어주신 부모님 은혜에 새삼 감사드렸다. 특히 4월 초파일, 바로 앞날 밤에 나를 낳으실 때 "벼슬도 큰 장닭이 우리 집 지붕 위에 올라가 크게 소리쳐 울었다"는 꿈을 꾸셨다는 우리 어머니 말씀을 생각하며 그동안 이에 보답하고자 그동안 노력해 왔었다.

그리고 동시에 이 기쁨과 영광을 내 생의 영원한 동반자요 내조자인 아내에게 돌려 마땅하다고 생각했다. 앞으로 남은 인생 부모님 특히 어머니의 그 꿈을 마음에 되새이며, 그리고 내 사랑하는 아내와 가족을 위해 또다시 최선을 다해 살아갈 것이다.

81년 1월 1일, 그해 그날은 유난히도 눈이 많이 왔다. 신고를 마치고 현충원으로 향해 가는 길이 대설로 덥혀 느렸으나 세상은 밝고도 밝아 첫해 첫날의 상서러운 눈과 함께 우리를 그리고 우리 국군의 앞날을 함께 축복해 주는 광경이어서 감개무량하였다. 저녁에는 그 어려웠던 세월을 참고 넘기며 함께 살아왔던 사랑하는 아내와 함께 육군회관에서, 군과 국가에서 베풀어 준 축하연에 참가하여 그동안의 고되었던 '나라에 바친 삶'의 회포를 잠시나마 풀어보기도 하였다.

장군이 되면 흔히 30여 가지의 대우가 바뀐다고 한다. 당장 장군의 깃발을 수여받고 승용차(군용차)에 별판을 달게 된다. 그러나 그 모든 것보다 앞서 장군이 되면 내 뜻을 펼 수가 있다. 그것이 참모 부서든 부대 지휘관이던 내 뜻이 반영될 수 있는 규모와 수준의 직위에서 근무할 수 있게 되는 것이다. 예부터 역사에는 전쟁이 있었고 거기에는 그 전쟁에서 승리로 이끈 '장수(將帥)'의 이야기가 있어 왔다. 을지문덕과 강감찬 그리고 이순신을 우리는 장군 또는 장수라고 하며 받든다. 그렇다, 이제 앞으로 전쟁이 나면 이름을 남길 수 있는 장수, 곧 전쟁 승리의 영웅이 되기 위해 위국헌신과 파사현정의 정신으로 정진하고 또 정진할 것이다.

◇ 육대 교수부장, 교육제도 쇄신의 기회

◦ 독일식 교육제도 쇄신 시도

5월이 되자 육대 교수부장으로 보직 명을 받았다. 실로 원하는 바였다. 드디어 장군이 뜻을 펼 수 있는 기회 즉, 한국 육군대학 교육 쇄신의 기회가 왔다고 생각했다. 그래서 바로 재직 교관 중 독일, 영국, 프랑스 육대(지참대) 유학 출신자들로 '교육발전위원회'를 구성하여, 1단계 6개월 기한으로 자료 수집과 기본 조사, 2단계 3개월 예정으로 신 커리큘럼(Curriculum) 작성하기로 정하고 추진하였다.

* 그러나 유감스럽게도 그 끝을 보지 못하고 일선 부대로 전출하였으나 그 뒤에, 다행하게도 내 뒤를 이어 독일 '지참대'를 다녀온 친한 동기생 '홍성태 장군'이 교수부장이 되어, 그때 나는 작전참모부장이 되어 뜻을 같이하여 결실을 맺을 수 있었다.

◦ 전방 작전계획실습 인솔

해마다 하는 행사로 정규 과정 학생들과 함께 교수부장은 전방부대(사단)로 가서 그 부대 작전 계획을 가지고 실습한다. 81년에도 7월 중에 10일간, 정규 29기생을 인솔하여 중동부 전선의 화천에 있는 제7사단과 사창리에 있는 제15사단으로 학습 출장하였다. 학습 내용은, 먼저 사단 사령부 현지에 도착하여 사단 현황에 대한 '브리핑'을 청취하고, 과업(숙제)을 수령한 뒤에, 조별 편성 단위로 연대 이하 전방(GOP—COP—FEBA)부대와 지역을 정찰한 뒤에 학교에서 익힌 야전교범원리와 현장 현지 지형과 부대 임무에 따라 자체 작전계획을 수립한다. 그동안 2박 3일간 전방 지역에서 조별로 자유 시간(원하는 지역, 상황 파악하며)을 가지면서 작전 구상을 한 뒤에 사령부로 돌아와 학생단의 종합안을 완성한다.

그리하여 그 결과를 실습부대 사단장과 예하 지휘관 및 참모 배석하에 발표함으로써 기존 사단 계획과 비교가 됨으로서 학생은 현지 실습의 성과를 이루고 현지 부대는 자체 작전계획을 육대학생들이 검토해주는 바 되어 서로 작전계획 발전의 계기가 되었다.

제3부

장수(將帥), 영웅(英雄)의 꿈 II

제9장

육군 상급부대 지휘관, 육본 작전참모부장 (1981~1988)

1. 제7공수여단장(1981.11~1983.1)

◇ 부대 임무와 구성, 능력

1981년 11월에 육군본부 인사 명령에 의해 나는 전라북도 전주 근방 금마에 있는 제7공수특전여단장으로 부임하였다. 한국 공수특전사령부 예하 공수특전여단은 모두가 같은 임무와 구성 그리고 능력을 가지고 있다. 부대 편성 즉 구성은 4개대대+본부대+낙하산정비대로 약 2,000여 실병력이고, 대대는 4개지역대+본부중대로 대대장은 중령이고 약 300명 실병력이다. 지역대는 5개중대(팀)+본부대로 지역 대장은 소령이고 약 70명 실병력로 중대(팀)는 중대장 대위 1+부중대장 중위 1+의무특기 2명+폭파특기 2명+통신 특기 2명+정작 특기 2명+병기 특기 2명, 계 12명으로 구성되어 있다. 특기병들은 주로 장기 복무하사관과 중고 졸업자 중 지원자—주로 지방 출장으로 모병—들인데 때로는 신병훈련소에서 선발도 하였다.

특전여단의 본 임무는, 적 후방에(육해공) 침투하여 토착 반정권 주민을 훈련시키고 필요한 요구를 지원하여 게릴라전을 실시하는 것이다. 거기에는 암살, 유괴, 음모 등도 포함되며, 때로는 특공전, 정보전, 아군 유도전 등도 포함된다.

위와 같은 임무 수행을 준비하면서 현재 평상시 임무는, 반(反) 게릴라전(Counter Guerrilla OP), 적의 게릴라전 거부작전 즉, 예상 거점(예, 운장산, 지리산 등) 선점 또는 소탕작전(대대별 년 3주)이다.

반 폭동작전(Counter Incergency OP)은 국가 후방 가용부대로. 기타 작전(평상시 대민 안정작전)은 대민봉사, 대민재해지원, 대항군 활동 지원으로 부대 능력, 즉 전투력은 1개여단이 약 2,000여명으로 후방 유일의 실 병력 단위 부대이고, 막강한 실력을 가진 후방전투역량부대이다.

◇ 부대 교육훈련 및 작전

◦ 반(反) 게릴라작전과 천리행군

부대원들은 장사병 불문하고 일단 특전사 교육대에서 공중낙하(점프)훈련—3주간 지상훈련, 1주간 실제 주간 점프 4회 야간 점프 1회 계 5회로 기본 윙 자격 획득—과 특기훈련과 특전기본훈련을 수려한 병사들을 전입 받아 각 팀으로 바로 배치한다. 부대원은 의무적으로 매 3개월마다 1회 이상 공중낙하하여 자격을 유지하며, 낙하 수당으로 훈련 중 못쓰게 되는 런닝이나 팬티 보충 정도 값을 받는다.

대체로 봄과 가을에는 작전 겸 훈련으로, 대대 단위로 적 침투 및 활동 근거지로 예상되는 산악 지역—우리 부대 책임 지역은 태백산, 운장산, 지리산의 요지요부—을 선점하여 3주간에 걸친 두더지와 유사한 순 땅굴 속의 야전 활동을 적 점령 거부작전 겸 적 지역 작전 활동을 겸한 훈련을 실시한다.

작전훈련 후 귀대시는 악명 높은 '천리행군'을 실시하는데, 이는 '도피 및 도망', 또는 적 지역 신속 탈출훈련의 하나로, 밤에만 그리고 기성 도로를 피해서, 감독관이 부여하는 각종 상황 처리를 수행해 가며, 7일만에 귀대하는 문자 그대로 고강도 훈련이다. 특히 이 훈련에서 '참기 힘든 수면 문제'를 극복하면서, 그리고 발가락과 발바닥의 물집을 참고 극복해 가며—출발 전 발바닥 발가락에 바늘 실을 넣어 두었다가 물집이 생길 때마다 실을 뽑아 터트리면서, 그리고 미리 구두 바닥에 솔잎도 넣어보고 비누와 약도 발라보고 하면서—하루 행군 70여킬로미터를 완전 무장으로 '전술 강행군'해서 임무를 수행해 가며 귀대한다. 이는 위국헌신의 정신 무장 아니면 할 수 없는 오로지 우리 특전부대 용사만이 해낼 수 있는 훈련임을 자부한다.

◦ 특수 침투 수단훈련

여름이 되면 여단 전체가 하계 수영훈련을 실시하는데, 우리 부대는 '부안 벽산 해변가'에서 1개월간 야영하며 단독 군장 및 완전 군장 전투 수영훈련을 실시한다. 이 훈련도 고강도 훈련이라 때로는 안타깝게도 훈련 중 순직 용사가 발생하기도 한다. 해마다 더욱 조심하면서도 이 훈련은 계속됨으로서 점차 세련되고 있다.

겨울이 되면 동계훈련으로 특정 지역대 또는 순환으로 '설한지 특별훈련' 즉 스키 전술훈련을 실시한다. 전에는 설악산에서 실시하였으나 지금 우리 부대는 무주구천동 스키 훈련장이 새로 조성되어 그곳을 이용하고 있다. 실제 우리나라 기후와 자연 환경에서 스키 작전 기술은 실용성이 낮으나 그래도 모든 상황에 대비해야 하는 특수부대로서는 준비가 필요하다.

하계 적지 해상 침투훈련 또한 중요 훈련 과목이다. 해군과 협조하여 해군 함정/잠수함 등으로 우리 특전 적지 침투 요원을 적 지역 연안 3킬로미터 근접 해역에 침투 보트와 함께 하선시켜주면 거기서부터 적 해안까지 보트와 수중침투(수영) 기술로 침투해 가는 훈련이다. 미군 특수부대는 이미 수중 침투 장비로 큰 고통이나 애로 없이 침투하는 훈련을 하나 그때까지 우리는 오로지 수영 기술을 이용하였는데, 아마도 지금쯤은 크게 개선되었을 것으로 생각한다.

◦ 무등산에서 을지 포커스(乙支—Focus)훈련, 기타훈련

매년 정부와 군 그리고 연합사와 함께 실시하는 '을지—Focus훈련'에 여단 본부가 FTX 및 CPX로 참가한다. 그해 늦여름에 우리 여단 본부는 무등산 산정 북단 부분에 위치하여 첫째는, 예하 부대가 북한 지역에서 게릴라전을 수행하고 있음을 가상하여 통신 지휘가 가능한지를 특히 점검하고 둘째는, 대통령 훈령 제28호, 후방 지역 적 게릴라 소탕작전 지휘, 셋째는 전군 독수리훈련(대 게릴라전)에 대한 대항군 운용훈련 등도 겸하여 약 1주일 이상의 야전 지휘소를 운영하면서 작전 요소를 점검하였다. 참으로 좋은 유익한 경험이었다.

다음 해 늦여름에는 지리산에서 시작하여 섬진강에서 뗏목작전을 구상하여 실시하던 중, 한 대대장이 도중에 뗏목에서 내려 건너편 하동 지역 가상 적진을 향해 급속 강습 도하(완전 무장) 작전훈련을 착안하여 시도하다가 예상외의 섬진강 조조의 수중 온도(18도)로 3 사람의 순직자가 발생하였다. 이들에게 지금에도 거듭 위국헌신의 넋을 위로하며 명복을 빌어 마지않는다.

◇ 임무형 부대 발전 창조적 노력

◦ 여단대항 특전사전술전기대회 우승

그해 특전사령부 주체 각 여단 특전술 및 기술대회가 개최되었는데, 그 정도의 우리 여단 기술—그동안 관계 부대원을 국가 공인 지역 민간 기술자 양성 기관에 파견하여 국가 자격을 확득하였다.—로도 단연코 1위 우승을 거두었다. 그런데 그 과정에서 에피소드가 있었다. 예를 들어 심판관이 1, 2위를 놓고 어물거릴 때면 우리 여단 선수가 "교관님 저는 국가 공인 자격증을 가지고 있습니다, 다른 사람은 자격증 안 가졌습니다!"라고 하면서 당당히 주장해, 교관조차 인정해 주었다고 한다.

7개여단 대항 시합에서, 이 전라도 시골에 있는 7여단이 우승할 수 있었던 것은 물론 부지런히 노력하여 갖게 된 연마된 기술과 실력이었지만, 보다도 우리 선수들이 가졌던 그 자신감과 자부심, 남이 안 가진 그것, "나 자격증 가진 사람이야"였다.

그래서 그 깃발 들고 책임 장교와 함께 그팀 20여 명, 모두 대전 유성 온천에 있는 계룡호텔로 위로 휴양을 보내기도 하였다. 지금 생각해도 그것은 투자할 가치가 있는 과업이었다. 그런데 웃을 수도 웃지도 못할 부작용—사실은 예상도 했으나—이 생겼다. 아, 이 국가 공인 기술 자격증을 취득하고 경연대회 등에서 입선하면서 기술에 자신이 생기자, 어서 사회로 돌아가고 싶은 생각을 하게 되었다는 것이다. 나는, 그 얼마나 좋은 일인가, 개인이건 사회일이건 우리 부대서 당당한 기술 일꾼들이 배출되어 나간다는데 대해서 기쁨이고 자랑일 수 있기 때문에, 부대 능력 손실은 다시 양성하면 되는 일이기에, 물론 개의치 않고 허락해 줄 용의가 있었다.

◦ 야전 식량 발전 노력

또 하나 나의 군대 생활 내내 관심사였던 야전 식사 문제다. 물론 보병부대에서도 그러하였지만 특전사에서는 더욱 그러하였다. 당장 우리 부대는 연 3개월 이상 야외 비상 전투 작전훈련+천리행군(도피 및 도망작전훈련)을 실시하고 대항군작전도 실시하고 실제 후방 침투 대간첩작전도 실시한다. 그때마다 우리 부대는 본대를 떠나 대대 단위 또는 지역 대단위로 독립 행동을 실시함으로서 야외 식사가 큰 문제였다.

그래서 일단 경험을 통해 연구해 보기로 하고, 야외 훈련과 야외 이동 식사는 가능한 휴대 가능한 음식으로, 대간첩작전 시 은거 진지에서 또는 이동하며 식사해야 하는 경우는 빵과 캔 음식을 제공해 보았다. 물론 그 비용은 그때마다 현금으로 나왔고 필요할 때는 대대 단위까지 현금으로 지급되었다. 다만 캔 음식은 육군군수참모부 승인을 받아 캔 음식 공장을, 당시는 아주 열악하였으나 그래도 대구 등, 찾으면 있었다.

시행착오도 있었다. 아침 식사 한 끼는 빵과 우유 소시지—예산 가능 범위—로 하려고 지방 제과점에서 납품받았으나, 빵을 처음 대하는 병사들이 많아, 물렁한 빵을 한 손으로 꽉 쥐어 먹으니 맛도 없고 배도 차지 않고, 하는 등 애로가 여러 가지 있었다. 그래서 임기 중에 완성하지는 못하였다. 그러나 장군이기에 부하 복지 발전을 위해, 전투 준비 발전을 위해 내 뜻을 그렇게 펴보려고 애를 써 보기도 한 것이었다.

2. 육군 보병 제8사단장(1983.1~1984.7)

◇ 육군 제8사단의 임무와 사단장의 권위

◦ 사단장의 권위와 책임

사단장은 문자 그대로 중책이었다. 우선 3권(지휘, 행정, 사법) 즉 지휘 통솔에 필요한 3권 전권을 독립적으로 행사한다. 지휘 즉 작전에서도 배속 또는 예속된 상급부대(군단)의 지시를 받아 작전하나 독자적인 독립작전을 할 수 있도록 전투부대와 화력지원 포병부대 그리고 군수지원부대를 아예 편제부대로 가지고 있다. 그래서 필요시는 해외 파견도 가능한 적절한 단위부대이다.

따라서 사단장은 전권을 행사하는 최고 단위 부대장으로서 실제 면에서는 군단장보다 권위가 있을 수 있다. 그래서 흔히들 '사단장은 군인, 군대 생활의 꽃'이라고도 말해지고 있다. 이는 군단장을 거치면서 알게 된 사실이다. 그러기 때문에 사실상 그 책임은 어느 단위 부대장보다 크고 무겁다.

◦ 제8사단의 임무와 사단장 복무 신조

사단의 임무는, 수도기계화사단과 함께(당시) 군단 예비사단으로, 작전 계획상의 주 임무는 철원 문혜리 일대 적 포위 섬멸 후(전술핵 등 사용) 주력으로 반격하는 것이었다. 평상시는 훈련을 주 일과로 하는 사단, 육군 또는 군 범위 시범사단, 군단 예비진지/후방진지 공사사단, 군단 후방 대간첩작전사단, 그리고 후방(정권)안보 비상대비사단 등이었다. 그래서 병사들은 전방에서 제일 훈련이 강한 사단이라 배치를 꺼려하는 부대로 소문나 있었다.

본인은 사단장 부임과 동시 복무 신조로, '절대 책임 완수', '초전 3일 돌격결전', '의식 개혁'을 내 걸고 강조하고 또 강조하였다. 내가 지금까지의 군대 생활에서 특히 명심하고 있는 것은, 개인이든 부대든 부여된 임무를 완수해야 한다는 기본 원칙이다. 그를 위해서 각 장병 개개인은 부여된 임무를 절대(희생 불사)로 책임지고 완수해야 한다는 것이다. 당시 북괴가 강조하는 '초전 3일 전쟁'을, 개전 이후 최고 최악의 상황에서(가능한 한 현장에서) 방어에 성공하는 즉시 반격—당시 미군의 1주일여 예상을 앞당겨서—하겠다는 당시 박정희 대통령과 전두환 대통령의 비장한 전투 지침에 따라 시행하면서, 방어 성공을 '돌격 정신'으로 완수하고 나아가 즉시 돌격 정신으로 반격해 나가자는 작전, 전술 사상과 각오를 의미하였다. 그리고 당시 국내외 정세에 따라 전 국민—우리는 장병과 가족 및 근무 지역 내 주민도—에게 필요불가결한 '의식 개혁' 문제 특히 인프레와 마이너스 성장과 연관된 경제재건을 위한 의식 개혁과 정의 구현을 위한 의식 개혁 운동이 중요하다고 강조하였다.

◇ 부대 야외기동훈련 및 시범 ; 1984 T/S 연습과 1983 T/S(CP, FTX) 참여 등

◦ 1983 Team Spirit-CPX, FTX 연습 참여(1983.11)

나는 육군 대위 시절에 제5사단 작전참모부 작전 장교(대간첩작전 장교)로 근무하였는데, 당시 3박 4일간의 CPX훈련이 있어서 그대로 밤새워가며 훈련에 임하였다. 그런데 작전상황 처리는 작전 장교(대위)가 혼자서, 사단장도 참모도 필요 없이 그때 그때마다 기계적으로 자동적으로 종이 한 장에 '예 처리하였음'으로 기간 중 모든 상황 조치를 끝낼 수 있었고, 그렇게 지나가는 것이 'CPX'로 인식되었다. 그래서 그 이후 상급부대 지휘관이 되어서도 'CPX'에는 별로 흥미도 없었기에 관심도 두지 않았다. 다만 'FTX' 'Team Spirit' 야외 기동연습은 흥미 있었으나 이 또한 시나리오를 따라 자동적으로 기계적으로 움직이는 연습이었음으로 크게 열의를 다하지는 않았다. 다만 야전에서 작전 변화와 환경 변화에 대한 적응 문제에 관심을 가지고 경험을 쌓아 나갔다.

그런데 1983년 11월에, 내년도 봄에 실시할 정식 야외기동연습(演習) 'T/S 84'훈련' 참가를 위한 예비훈련으로, 사단사령부 요원만 7군단 배속부대로 야외 'FTX'(지휘소 기동훈련)를 실시하였다. 한국군(미군 포함) 유일한 대부대 춘계 야외기동연습 훈련장인 '안성—이천—(도하)—지평리—횡성 지역 간'에서 시나리오에 의해 실제로 이동하며 시행되었다. 특히 사단 'TAC—CP'(전술 지휘소) 운용에 대한 경험을 얻어 차후 훈련에 크게 도움이 되었다.

◦ 사단 동계 '작계 5027훈련'과 '초전 3일 돌격 결전훈련'(1984.1~4박 5일간)

당시 우리 사단은 육군 제3야전군 예하 한미야전군단(의정부)에 속해 있어서 매년 겨울이면 연례적인 '동계 작계 5027훈련'을 실시(참가)한다. 원래 우리 부대는 군단 예비부대이기에 통상의 경우 유사시에도 진지 점령은 하지 않고 대기하다가 의명 반격이나 부대 교대에 투입되게끔 교범에 규정되어 있다. 그러나 당시는 문혜리 신철원 지역 작전 형태는 전술핵 상황을 고려한 작전 계획이었음으로 FEBA의 안쪽 끝이 운천 직북 방선으로 U자형으로 내려와 있었다. 그래서 우리 부대는 유사시 군단 최후 저지선인 U자의 아래 부분을 일부 부대가 일단 점령하게 되어 있었다. 그러기에 그선에 교통호를 구축하고 겨울에는 취침호와 같은 지하 공간에서 방어 태세를 유지하도록 되어 있었다.

금번 훈련은 2개 단계화하여 1단계는 기계획훈련으로 군단 명에 의거 1개 연대를 군단 좌일선 돌파 지역에 급파하여 적 공격을 저지하는 훈련을 하였고, 2단계는 연례 동계훈련 상황은 종결된 가운데, 그 연장 선상에서 사단 자체 훈련 계획으로, 운천 직북방 동계 진지방어와 반격훈련을 실시하였다. 당시 날씨는 맑았으나 통상의 경우 즉 대한이 지나면 기온이 하강함에도 그해는 더욱 올라 야간엔 영하 21도의 악천후가 계속되었다. 그럼에도 불구하고 나는 덮개를 벗긴 찦차로 지휘하며 주야간 훈련을 강행하였다.

밤에는 교통호에서 극한지 극복훈련을 겸하고, 다음날 주간에는 지포리 신철원 방향으로 반격전 즉 '초전 3일 돌격전'을 실시하였다. 이때 당시 한미야전군사령관이었던 'Menetry 장군'도 와서 참관하였다. 옛날 소대장 시절 문산 지역에서 소한 대한 때 야외기동훈련하던 때를 생각해 가며 이 극한 상황훈련을 지휘해 나갈 수가 있었다.

◦ 84' T/S 연습 참여, 대통령과 미육군 참모총장 참관

전년의 예비적인 사단 '83' T/S, CPX-FTX'' 훈련에 이어 그 해(1984.3)는 '84' T/S, Team Spirit 연습'에 사단사령부와 1개 연대가 연대전투단을 구성하여 참가하였다. 연초에 명령을 하달받고, 사전 현지 지형 정찰과 협조 그리고 훈련 계획을 수립(3.1~9)하였고, 실제 참가 도보부대는 14일에, 차량 및 지휘부는 15일에 현지로 이동하였다.

사령부는 일찍부터 야전 장비 및 도구들을 준비하고,—아직도 제식화된 야전 사무용 보급 세트가 없어서—연병장에서 출동을 위한 무기 장비 점검과 제반 준비 사항을 최종 점검하고, 군목의 '성공적인 책임/임무 완수와 안전 귀환'을 위한 기도를 마치고, 사령부 앞 '삼팔교(三八橋)' 교차 지점에서 사단 군악대의 사단가 연주를 들으며 사기를 올리면서, 참가부대는 모두 동시에 출진하였다. 도보부대는 전곡(30킬로미터)으로 가서 기차를 이용하여 안성 훈련장으로 이동하였고, 사단 지휘부와 차량부대는 바로 방어 전선인 안성 첫 기지로 직접 이동하여 전개하였다.

날씨는 이제 막 봄기운이 도는 3월 하순의 시작 시점이고 첫 주둔 지역은 강원도 아닌 경기도 지대요, 때마침 봄 가리가 아직 시작되지 않은 시점이라 논밭을 보병도 차량도 이용할 수 있는 즉, 야외 가동훈련에 적절한 시기요 장소였다. 사단은 도착 즉시 이제 막 편성된 한국군 '제7기계화군단'에 배속되었다.

연습(야외대부대기동훈련)은 3월 20일에 개시되었는데, 일단 남한강 선에서 방어하다가 작전상 안성 방면으로 후퇴 이동(예하부대와 지휘부) 하였다가, 23일에 반격작전을 개시하였다. 여주—이천을 거쳐, 남한강을 임시 교량을 이용해 도강하고, 남원주 문막으로 진격하고, 최종 목표 횡성비행장 탈환을 위해 도보부대와 헬기 강습작전으로 적을 포위 섬멸전을 완수(3.26)하였다. 그리고 다음 날 27일에 현지 강평(겸 종료 파티)을 마지막으로 연습훈련은 종료하였다.

마지막 단계에서 우리 사단은 미제1군단에 배속되어 횡성비행장을 육로와 헬기 강습으로 포위 공격하게 되었는데, 미제1군단장이 내게 물었다, "3. 26 날씨가 좋아야할 텐데?" 내가 자신 있게 말하기를 "그날은 '이승만 대통령의 날'로 분명히 좋아진다, 내기해도 좋다"고 옛 얘기를 곁들여 설명하고 확인해 주었다. 아니나 다를까 정말 신기하게도 포격과 헬기 출동 시점에 비도 구름도 걷히고 작전계획이 무난히 실행될 수가 있었다.

훈련 기간 중에 전두환 대통령이 7군단과 가상 적 군단도 방문(22일)하여 한미연합연습 장병들을 위로해 주었다. 전두환 대통령은 재임 중 빠짐없이 해마다 참관하고 위로 격려 행사를 잊지 않았다. 다음 날에 '정호용 참모총장'과 '미육군참모총장 워커 장군' 그리고 연합사 사령관 세네월드 장군'이 우리 사단 전방 지휘소(TCP)를 방문하였기에 내가 상황도와 함께 현지형과 현 상황을 간단하게 브리핑하였는데, 만족해 하였으며 노고를 치하해 주었다.

한국에 온 미제1군단은 미국 북서부 '워싱턴 주'에 주둔해 있는 예비군단으로 유사시 한국전 참전을 위해 예비역 장병을 소집하여 완편되는 군단으로 기간 중 군단장과 참모(예비역)들과 교류하였으며, 훈련 종료 즉시 군단을 친선 방문하여 한국 훈련 참여와 노고 그리고 친선에 감사하고, '먹는 배'와 특별히 주문한 '도자기 그릇'을 참모들에게 증정하기도 하였다.

◦ 한국군과 미군의 전기 전술 여건 차이

부대가 일선 전개를 준비 중에 미군 병사 3명—2명의 남군과 1명의 여군—이 사단사령부에 파견되어 왔다. 위성 통신 지원이 그들의 임무였다. 귀한 작전 요원이라 생각하면서 특히 여군병사에게 우리 장교 숙소 한편을 준비해주기로 하였는데, 그 여군은 사양하면서 밤에는 'A tent'(보병 3인용 야영텐트)에서 남군 2명 사이에서 취침한다고 했다. 물론 미국 여군은 이미 'Woman's Corps' 소속이 아니고 그냥 부대원의 1명으로 부대에서나 전선에서 남녀가 함께 딩구르며 생활해 가고 있다는 사실을 알고 있긴 하였으나 이제 바로 실감하게 되었다.

그런가 하면 사단 TCP를 구성하여 위치하자마자 미군 인접 사단과 상급부대에서 데이터베이스에 입력할 자료들을 요청하였는데, 당시 우리 군에서는 미쳐 준비하고 있지 않은 자료여서 제공해 주지 못한 채 작전에 들어갔는데 한국군으로서는 별 지장 없이 어려움 없이 임무를 수행하였으나 미군은 이미 컴퓨터를 사용하고 데이터화하고 시뮬레이션하고 워게임하는 것이 군작전 분야에도 이미 일상사가 되고 있었던 같이 보였다.

그런데 이렇게 상호 협조해야 하는 분야에서 또 선진 기술을 지원해 주겠다고 요원을 파견해 주는데도 불구하고, 내용이 뭔지도 잘 이해하지 못하였기에 그들의 기술을 전혀 이용해 보지 못하였는데, 한국군의 당시 과학화 수준이 그러하였다.

3. 육군 작전참모부장(1984.7~1986.7)

◇ 작전참모부장의 임무와 책임 및 권한

◦ 임무, 책임 및 권한

한국 육군의 작전참모부장(Deputy Chief of Staff, G-3)이란, 육군 장군이라면 누구라도 선망하는 직책이다. 그만큼 중요하면서 영광된 자리이기에, 많은 유자격자 가운데서 내가 선발되었다는 것을 생각하면, 영광인 동시에 중차대한 책임감을 느끼지 않을 수 없었다.

일반적으로, 지휘관이나 참모 생활을 수행해야 하는 군인에게는, 주어진 임무를 책임지고 완수할 수 있도록 일정한 권한이 부여되는데, 특히 육군 최상위 참모요 핵심참모인 작전참모에게도 통상의 권한이 부여됨은 물론, 그 권한의 재량권 범위 내에서 어느 때는 독단 전횡도 불사할 수가 있다.

한국 육군 작전참모부장의 임무 및 책임은, 육군 참모총장을 보좌하면서 부여받은 권한으로, 전시와 평시에 육군의 교육, 훈련을 '기획·계획'하고 실시하며 장비와 무기를 발전시켜 무장해 나가면서, 평시 국내 비상시 작전을 실시하는 것이다. 다만 전시작전 지휘 권한은 한미연합사에게 주어져 '합동참모본부'를 통해 행사됨으로 유감스러우며, 가능한 한 조속한 시일 내에 '진정한 의미의 자주국방'—한미동맹강화적 발전—이 이루어지기를 바란다.

◇ 육군 전략·작전 대비

◦ 전략작전 대비—1 ; 'Binary' 준비

특히 북의 소위 '3.5(7) 남침 전략작전'—당시는 생물 및 화학전을 포함한 기습적 전면전 개시, 3일에 수원/오산, 5~7일 만에 전국 점령 작전계획—에 대비하여 육군은 이미 80년부터 후방 각도에 있던 동원사단(몇몇)을 한수 이북으로 이동시켜 전개하였다. 그리고 ABC전(력) 중에 상대적인 화학전에 대비하여 수차에 걸친 '워게임'을 실시한 결론은, 화학전 방어(특히 경고시)는 비치명적이긴 하나 유사시 대응을 위해서는, 미국 본토 저장고에서 긴급 수송해 와야하는 문제(2~3일 소요)가 있음으로, 자체 개발(Binary)로 대치해야겠다는 결론이었고, 생물학전에 대비하기 위해서는 조속히 공격 및 방어전에 대한 연구를 실시하도록 결론 내었다.

◦ 전략작전 대비—2 ; '현무(玄武) 미사일' 실전화

6·25 전쟁 이후 이때까지 남쪽 기지에 주둔하여 180킬로미터 사정의 고고도 중고도 '지대공 미사일'로 우리의 영공을 지켜준 '나이키 허큘리스, SAM—N-25'가 퇴역하게 되었다. 이에 조속한 시일 내 자체 개발을 서두르는 한편 미군 미사일부대인 'Lants 대대'의 한국 전개를 요청하였고, 'Pershing I'의 한국 전개를 교섭하려고 고려하였다. 그러는 가운데 다

행이도, 이 상황을 일단 모면할 수 있는 동종의 한국군 미사일, 현무가 개발 완료되고 이를 실전에 배치하기 위해 주둔지를 모색하였다.

일단은 지대지용으로 하되 평양을 타격할 수 있는 위치를 선정하기로 하였다. 여러 가지 검토 끝에 최대 사거리와 음밀한 장소로 용문산 아래를 선정하고 토지 매수를 서둘렀는데, 토지 주인(군과도 관계 있었으나)이 반대함으로 은밀성을 유지하기 위해 포기하고, 남한강 바로 남쪽 어느 계곡 고지를 선정하고 진지를 구축하였다. 그리하여 드디어 200미터 직경 산탄과 HEAT탄을 장비하여 유사시 평양에 포격할 수 있게 되었다.

그러나 그동안에도 과학자들은 현무를 발전시켜 240킬러미터 순항미사일도 개발했으니 한시바삐 '미국의 제한'이 풀리도록—미국은 그동안 한국의 이승만 대통령 이래 '북진 주장'을 경계하여 제한했으며, 이제 2021년에 완전히 풀림—건의를 해왔으나 당시는 방법이 없었다. 그동안 이웃 대만과 북한이 우리를 앞서 미사일 기술을 발전시켰고, 특히 북한은 우리를 위협하였는데, 이제(2021)는 한국이 곧, 몇 달 뒤면 그 'Gap'을 넘어서 북을 리드할 것으로 예상되고 있다.

◦ 전략작전 대비—3 ; 철조망 비무장지대 내 추진

당시 비무장지대에는 임진강 어구에서 동해안까지 이은 240킬로미터—흔히 155마일로 표기한다.—남북 4킬로미터 한가운데로 1292개의 휴전선 표시 말뚝(표식목(標識木))이 이어져 있고, 북은 바로 그 말뚝에 근접하여 일찍부터 전기 철조망을 가설해 외부 침입 또는 남으로의 도망을 막고 있다. 아군은 그동안 남방한계선을 연하여 적의 기습 공격이나 무장 정찰병 남침 방지를 위해 일반 철조망을 가설하여 운용하고 있었다.

그러다가 육군은, 이 북괴의 '3.5(7)작전'에 대비하기 위한 전략작전의 대비책의 하나로, 북괴의 현재 상황과 같이 우리도 휴전선 가까이에 상당히 강성의 철조망을 설치하여 적의 기습공격(보전포 합동)을 일차적으로 방어 또는 조기 경보용으로 활용하기로 결정하였다. 그래서 전방 모사단에서 일단 가설 및 목적 시범을 보이고 전방 전 전선에 연결 가설하도록 조치하였다. 그 작업은 축차적으로 진행되어서, 내가 군단장으로 부임했을 때 우리 군단 전방은 이제 가설에 착수하고 있었다. 이렇게 또 한 겹의 장벽을 쌓아 북괴의 기습공격을 예방하려하였다.

◦ 전략작전 대비—4 ; 후방 대침투작전 계획 및 훈련

특히 80년대에 우심했던 북괴의 대남도발에 대응하여, 전방 침투나 전면 전쟁에 대한 대비를 강화하는 한편으로, 후방에 대한 적의 공수부대 침투작전 또는 해상을 통한 해안 침투작전에 대비하여서도,'3.25 작계'(후방 대침투작전 계획)를 후방 군관민 관계 기관에 이미 선포(1983)해 두었었다. 이제 더욱이 '86아세안게임', '88서울올림픽'을 앞두고 북괴의 방해작전까지도 대비하여, '적 침투 후방 대응훈련'을 전두환 대통령의 임석하에 충청남도 호남고속도로 변 중심 지역에서 실시하였다.

물론 유사시 군경이 출동하겠지만, 후방 지역에서는 적출현 신고 즉시 일차적으로 지역 주민이 낫이나 곡갱이 등으로 이들에 대응하고 그리고 출동한 군경과 함께 이들을 진압한다는 시나리오에 따른 것이었다. 이러한 시범훈련은, 실제로 그런 경우 지방민들도 분연히 일어나 신속하게, 침투한 북괴군에 맞서야 되겠다는 각오를 할 수 있게 강조하는 의미가 포함되었었다. 그후 후방사단은 이 계획을 '정규작전계획'에 포함시키게 되었다.

ㅇ 전략작전 대비—5 ; 적 도발시 즉각 응징 보복

그동안에 전방에서 적이 도발할 때는 즉각 대응하여 가차 없이 보복하기로 되어 있었다. 그러나 그런 사태가 드문 경우라 전방부대와 지휘관들은 가끔 대응 매뉴얼에 대해 문의하는 경우가 있었다. 그리고 정세의 흐름 등에 비추어 과잉 대응할까 염려하는 연합사와 절충해서 새로 수정한 'SOP'를 하달하였다. 이제부터는, 그동안 지켜왔던 적의 도발 종류와 범위 불문하고 일단 즉각 실시했던(하려했던) '적진 대응 보복(습격)계획'—소대 단위로 적 원점 진지 침투 습격 파괴—은 일단 보류(소멸)하고, 즉각 응징 보복 사격은 1~2배로 하기로 결정하여 시행하도록 하였다.

◇ 육군 교육훈련 및 편제 발전, 학생중앙군사학교 창설(1985.11)

그동안 전국 학군단(ROTC)의 하계 군사훈련을 각 지방별로 실시함으로서 수준의 차이라던가 통일성 문제가 있어 왔는데 이를 해소하기 위해 대통령의 지시 사항—규모가 국방예산을 초과하는 등으로 국방부로는 고려하기 어려웠던 문제—으로, 하계 군사훈련을 전담할 수 있는 '학생중앙군사학교' 창설하게 되었다.

리 참모부 학교교육 담당 부서에서 연구를 시작하여 육군참모총장(정호용 대장)의 결재에 이르기까지 상당 기간 토론과 검토를 거쳐 계획을 완성하였다. 그리하여 담당 학교장은 학군단 출신 장군으로 보임하고, 위치는 남한산성 밑 군 행정교육 기관의 통합 지역 일부를 할애해 시설을 구비하고 창설식(1985.11)을 가졌다. 그리하여 전국 학군단 후보생들을 하계훈련 기간 중에 전원 합숙하여 통제된 교육훈련을 실시함으로써, 일반적인 군 내무 생활을 경험도 하면서, 학군단 출신 장교들의 통일되고 일치된 소부대 지휘자 자질을 구비하는 성과를 거둘 수 있었다.

◇ 육군 장비, 무기 발전

ㅇ 장비, 무기 발전—1 ; K—1 155미리 자주포

1980년대에는 박정희 대통령의 자주국방 노력에 의하여 소총으로부터 야포에 이르기까지 역설계를 통해서 또는 조건부원 설계도면 인수 등을 통해서 국산화를 착착 진행 중에 있었다. 그중에서도 오늘날의 K—9자주포의 원조가 되는 K—155미리 자주포는 1980년 초반에 '삼성항공'에서 미제 M109A2자주포를 라이센스 생산하여 전군에 보급하기로 하였다. 그런데 바로 그 과정을 내가 지켜보게 되었다.

삼성은 이 자주포를 라이센스 생산하기로 하고 도입하면서 자체 포탄 운반차(괘도장갑차)를 한 세트로 도입하여 같이 생산하려 하였다. 이 당시 막 각종 군용 장갑차를 개발 중이던 대우중공업이 개입하여 이 탄약 운반차 조차 독점하려 하였다. 나는 애초 육군의 ROC대로 삼성이 생산하도록 해 주었다.

◦ 무기 발전—2 ; MD—500의 정비 실패와 원인 불명

전방에서 사용 중인 MD—500은 조종사 1명과 이용자 1명용인 최소형 군용 헬기이다. 그런데 정기 정비를 위해 후방 정비창에서 들어갔다가 나와서 전방 소속부대로 복귀할 때마다(본인 근무 이전 2회) 도중에 추락하여 그때마다 인명과 장비 손실이 발생하기에 본인 근무 유의 사항 중 하나였는데, 역시나 들던 대로 또 같은 사고가 발생하였다. 그래서 즉각 전군의 동 기종 헬기 비행을 금지—작전 비행은 작전참모부 책임—시키고 정비 창의 기술 점검 및 사고 원인을 조사 지시하였다. 당시 기술 담당은 교육 파견되어 온 미국인 기술자와 한국 정비 및 도입 및 개발(미래) 기업인 '대한항공'이 책임이었는데, 2개월여가 되어도 원인을 찾지 못하고 있다는 보고만 있을 뿐이었다. 무엇을 숨기는 것일까

물론 정비 책임은 군수 계통이기에 직접 책임 추궁이나 독려할 수 없는 동안 실무 비행부대에서는 더 이상 비행 지체는 작전상 불리함으로 비행 재개를 건의해 왔기에 부득이 군수 계통에 '반듯이 원인을 찾아내어 안전이 보장되어야 한다'는 조건부로 허락한 바 있었다. 그와 같이 기술자와 돈벌이 기업 그리고 사업 승인자들의 참으로 무책임한 일이 무고한 조종사의 희생과 장비 및 국고의 낭비를 초래하는 일이 있기도 하였다.

◦ 무기 발전—3 ; 미래형(ECCM) 통신 장비 도입 검토

통신감실에서 장차 전 특히 전자전을 대비해 전투부대 통신장비를 미래형 장비(ECCM, Electronic-Counter-Counter-Measures)로 발전시키려고 노력하던 중, 미국에서 발명된 신제품(16번 재밍 돌파 가능)을 도입하기로 생각하고 실무자간 협상을 진행하면서 수요자 시험을 실시하였다. 그런데 당시 한국 통신 기술 수준은 이제 막 상승하고는 있었으나 선진국 수준에는 아직 미달하였다. 그래서 미래형 통신장비 도입을 위해 일단 미국이 개발한 최신형 통신기의 선전 내용을 보면서 'ROC(Required Operational Capability, 작전 요구 성능)'를 작성하고 바로 그 통신 장비를 가지고 요구 성능 시험을 하였는데, 미안하게도 최신 통신용어도 잘 몰라 상대 미국 기술자에게 묻고 물어서 시험을 진행하였다. 결과적으로 지나친 가격 요구로, 비교해 볼 타의 방법이 없어 무산되고 말았다.

◦ 무기발전—4 ; 한국 최초 K—1전차와 155미리 견인포 개발 및 양산화

한국 최초 국산화 전차가, 85년 최초 양산 부대 배치 직전, 몸체 주철이 포탑(미국형 새 발명 복합철강제)을 적재하고 주행하자 금이 갔다. 그 때문에 긴급 외제 몸체를 도입하여 수요와 전개 계획을 겨우 충족시킨 일이 있었다. 당시만 해도 의욕적으로 발돋움하고 있었으나 능력은 그 정도여서 첫해는 역시 외국산이 되고 말았다. 그러나 다음 해부터는 주철 시험과 시험 끝에 국산화에 성공하였다.

그런데 155미리 견인포 국산화도 서둘러서 완성하였으나 역시나, 시험 중에 몇 번이고 포신이 파열하고 발사 속도가 충족되지 못하는 경위를 겪었으나 그래도 끝내 외제 말고 국산으로 연구 개발에 성공한 바 있었다.

◦ 무기 장비 발전 결심 사항 ; 미군 사용 무기 도입이 최선

한국군이 그 수 많은 장비와 무기를 국산화하려고 노력하여 오늘날 대부분은 그 뜻을 이루게 되어 감히 자주국방을 앞당길 수 있게 되었다. 그러나 무기 장비는 과학 발전에 따라 계속해서 개선시켜 나가거나 새롭게 발명해 나가야 한다. 그러기에 경우에 따라서는 그 시점의 소요에 따라 외국 제품을 도입해 사용할 수도 있고, 일단 도입한 그 제품을 참고로 우리 제품을 개발해 낼 수도 있다. 그런 이유 등으로 외국제 무기 장비 도입 협상은 계속되고 있다.

그런데 한국은 두말할 나위 없이 미국과 군사 동맹국으로 미국과 합동 및 연합작전을 실시해야 하기에 무기 체계가 동일한 것이 가장 바람직하다. 한 예를 들면, 레이다 망에서 유사 항공기를 식별하였으나 피아 구별을 못 하면 안 되는데, 만일에 어느 타국의 항공기를 구입해서 동시에 작전에 투입되었을 때 순간 식별 불가면 작전에 지장을 초래한다.

그럼에도 개발 조건이나 가격 조건 등이 맞지 않으면 가끔 기타 외국제에 관심을 가지고 흥정을 하게 되는데 그래도 가능한 한 그러지 않기를 바란다. 나의 장기간 군사 경험에 의하면, 오늘까지도 세계에서 제일가는 무기 장비는 물론 미국 제품이고, 그중에서도 미국 군대에 의해 채택되고 사용 중인 것 즉, 요구 성능이 완전히 증명된 것으로 도입하는 것이 최상의 방책이라고 믿는다.

4. 육군 제1군단장(1986.7~1988.1)

작전참모 임기가 다 되어갈 때, 군단장 명령을 받고 청와대에 들어가 전두환 대통령께 신고하고, 내 가문의 가보 1호가 되는 영광의 '삼정도(三精刀)'에 군단장 '수 띠'를 증정받았다. 전 대통령은 내게 그리고 모두에게 굳은 신뢰의 마음을 눈빛으로 보이며 행사를 진행했고 말씀도 하였다. 나는 그의 신뢰와 기대에 책임 완수로 부응하리라고 마음으로 다짐하였다. 돌아오는 차 속에서 정호용 참모총장은 내게 "특전사령관으로 추천하려했는데…"라고 짧게 한마디로 말하며 거듭 축하해 주었다. 정말 믿고 일할 수 있는 전두환 대통령과 정호용 참모총장 두 분이었다. 그런데 그때 만일에 '특전사령관이 되었다면' 그 후는…. 이런 걸 두고 '운명'이라고 하는 것이지.

◇ 제1군단 전통과 현 상황 하의 군단장의 당면 임무

◦ 국군 최정예부대 전통

'6·25 남침적란' 발발 직후, 최초 군단으로 편성된 한국군 제1군단은 미 주력에게 서부 전선을 맞기고 주로, 중부(충북) 지역을 담당하여 지연전을 계속하다가 낙동강 전선이 형성되자 자동적으로 한국군 주류부대를 지휘하여 중, 동부 전선을 방어하였다.

반격 당시는 한국군 제2군단(6사단, 8사단 예속)이 편성되어 중동부 전선을 담당하였고, 1군단은 3사단과 수도사단을 예하부대로 태백산맥 동부에서 동해안까지의 동부 전선을 담당하여 이승만 대통령의 명령으로 10월 1일—이후 '국군의 날'로 국경일이 되었다.—정오에 38선을 돌파 북진을 개시하였다. 그리하여 북한의 길주와 한만 국경 혜산진까지 진격 후 다시 후퇴하였는데, 이후 재 반격하여 현 휴전선—최북단 고성 간성에까지 진출—으로 고착하였다. 이후 가평(60년~70년대 초)에 잠시 주둔했다가 72년에 현 위치(고양 벽제)로 미 제1군단과 교대하여 주둔하게 되었다.

그래서 육군 제1군단은 한국군 제1의 가장 오랜 전통과 6·25 전사에 빛나는 공훈 군단으로, 현재도 '정예 제1군단'으로 그 위명(偉名)을 드날리고 있다.

◦ 부대 작전 환경(지리 환경적, 인적)과 범위

그런데 부대 전략 및 작전 환경은 결코 만만찮은 특징을 가지고 있었다. 군단 작전 종심은 통상 60여 킬로미터이나 여기는 휴전선에서 서울까지 40여 킬로미터로 부대 배치 즉 지면 편성이 비좁게 되어 충분한 완충 경계 지대가 편성될 수 없었다. 그러기에 방어에 불리한 여건이다. 그러나 다만 피아간 작전 장애물인 임진강이 있어서 공격에는 불리하나 방어에는 도움이 될 수 있었다.

한편 방어 정면은 통상 30~40여 킬로미터(장단반도~고랑포 동북방)이나 평상시 대간첩작전이나 후방 지역 대침투작전 지대로 30여 킬로미터(통일전만대~행주산성)가 추가되어 있었다. 그래서 1개여단이 증강되어 한강 내선 방어를 담당하고 있었다. 또한 정상적인 군단이 갖는 27킬러미터 정도의 민간 출입 통제구역도 갖지 못하면서 COP(전투전초)나 GOP(일반전초) 편성이 어려워, 적 기습작전대비에 상당한 주의를 요하였다.

그러다 보니, 예를 들어, 주저 항선(당시 FEBA선과 전투 지대)을 연한 최후 저지 사격 선상의 철조망과 이를 통합한 화망 구성을 각종 장애물 시설들이 민간 사용물에 혼합(논밭)되어 평소 관리가 곤란하여 상당한 주의가 필요하기에 주민과의 적극적인 협조가 또한 필요한 실정이었다.

군단은 북한이 전면 남침해 내려올 때 접근로로 이용하게 되는 3개의 큰 축선(의정부→서울, 춘천→서울, 문산/고랑포→서울) 중에서도 가장 단거리인 동시에 시시각각 그 작전 영향력이 지대한 접근로 방어책임을 부여받고 있었다.

그러기에 일단 유사시 상황이 전개되면, CPX를 통해서 아는 바와 같이, 상당수의 포병부대와 동원사단 그리고 새로 배속되는 전투사단과 여단 등을 도합하며 최소 30만 이상의 대군—현 야전군보다 더한 세력—이 군단작전 공간 지대에 집결하여 군단장 본인 책임

(명령)으로 방어전을 전개하게 되어 있었다.

◦ 군단(장)의 전시, 평상시, 그리고 당면 임무

위와 같은 전략 및 작전 환경에서 군단(장)은, 전시에는 '작전계획 5027'에 의한 방어전과 반격전을 주로, 평시에는 대간첩작전과 전선 경계 임무를 실행해야 한다. 동시에 당면 과제로는 '86아세안게임'과 '88서울올림픽'을 지원하면서 '시국 안정(자유민주주의 가치 확립, 멸공 통일 사상 확립, 경제 안정 문제에 대한 국민 계도 교관화 등)'에 대한 노력이 기본 임무에 추가되었다고 판단하였다. 그리고 지역 내(고양, 문산, 파주) 예비군에 대한 훈련도 담당하였다.

한편 당시의 한국 군의 대간첩작전에서 동해안과 한강 연안 대침투작전이 중요시되었는데, 특히나 한강 하류 작전에서는, 현 '통일전망대'에서 행주산성 유수지까지 30여 킬로미터에 걸쳐, 강남은 수도군단에서 강북은 우리 군단 책임이었는데, 무장 간첩들은 거의 대부분이 임진강 하류에서 수로를 이용, 물 흐름대로 주로 한강 북변으로 침투하여, 그 즉시 서울 시민 속에 살아지는 전술을 사용하였다. 그래서 한강변에는 지금까지도 민간인 통제 경계용 철조망이 설치되어 있고, 주야불문 철저하게 간첩 침투를 경계하고 있다.

그리고 잘 알려진 대로 '1. 21사태(김신조 사건, 1968.1.21)' 또한 적지에서 청와대가 근접해 있기에 가능하였는데, 이를 사전에 차단하고 유사시는 지체 없이 소탕해야 하는 작전이 군단의 또 하나 평상시 임무에 추가되어 있었다.

군단(장) 예하사단(장)과의 관계는 4개 전투사단 중, 1, 25사단은 전방에 배치되어 있고, 9, 30사단은 예비 사단인데 이 2개사단은 '12.12 사태' 이후 평상시 '충정작전'을 위해서는 군단장의 사전 승인이나 심지어는 통보 없이도 출동해 나갈 수 있도록 전통화되어 있었다. 그래서 이들 사단장들은 군단장 경유 없이 청와대로부터 명령을 바로 수령하는 경우가 종종 있었다. 그러나 사후 보고는 준수되었는데, 다만 '충정작전' 외 대통령 암행 예하부대 방문 시는 불편한 점이 있었다.

군단내 관민(官民)과의 관계는, 서울 시장은 말할 것도 없거니와 경기도 지사와도 별 관계가 없었으나 다만, 군단이 '팀 스프리트 훈련' 시 경기도지사가 찾아와 위문해 주었으며, 연말에도 경기지사가 찾아와 위문해 주는 정도였다.

군단 전 지역의 1차적인 대민 관계나 접촉은 사단(장)과의 관계였고, 군단(장)은 군단 사령부 지역 반상회에 친선차 방문한 바 있었다. 다만 1사단 관할 지역이긴 하지만 '광탄' 지역 주민이 식수가 부족하다는 민원에 따라, 때마침 육군 공병부에서 전방 땅굴 시추 작업을 일단 완료하고 철수하는 공병시추부대를 잔류시켜 관정을 3군대 시추해 성공하여 크게 도움을 준 적이 있었다. 행정적으로는 주로 문산시와 파주시가 해당되어 가끔 민관군 회의 시 시장들과 만나 당면 정부 과제를 논의하고 강조한 바 있었다.

◇ 나의 군단 지휘 통솔 방침과 실행

◦ 지휘 통솔 방침

나는 32대 군단장으로 취임함과 동시에 군단장 '지휘 통솔 방침'을 하달하였다. 그것은, '절대 책임 완수', '승리를 믿는자 승리한다', '국가 시책 옹호'였다. 그동안 소대장에서부터 오늘에 이르기까지 대소부대 부대장과 참모 생활의 원칙과 체험을 통하여, 특히 부대 구성원의 한 군인으로서 가장 중요하고도 근본적인 덕목은 '개인에게 부여된 임무를 절대로 책임지고 완수해야 한다'는 것이고 그것이야말로 '승리'의 핵심 요소이라고 믿기 때문이다.

그리고 예하지휘관은 물론 장병 개개인 모두는 각자 나름대로의 '이 전투에서 이긴다, 이겨야 한다는 승리에 대한 확신'을 승리할 때까지 가지고 전투에 임함으로써 그 전투에서 '승리할 수 있다'는 신념을 강조하였다. 그리고 당시는 군대가 애국에 대해서 국가 및 국민에 시범적 존재였음으로, 전 장병에게 '국가 시책에 대한 이해와 실천'을 강조하였다.

◦ 지대 내 주요 관심 요소와 신장 상황

제1사단 전술작전 전방 지역에는 민간 출입이 허용되어 '안보관광' 명소가 되어 있는 '도라산 전망대'와 그 앞의 제3땅굴이 관심사가 되었다. 전망대 아래층에는 일반 전초부대 관측소와 전투지휘소가 있었는데, 그곳에서 개성으로부터 남을 향한 접근로가 아주 명확하게 관측될 수 있었고, 개성 '송악산'까지(약 12킬로미터) 지대 내 주간 군사 동향은 육안으로도 관측 가능할 정도였다. 제3땅굴은—74년, 귀순자 제보로 시추공을 설치, 1978에 발견하였는데, 지하 73미터에 위치하고, 길이 1635미터(분계선 북1200, 남435미터), 높이와 폭 각 2미터의 아치형으로, 시간당 완전 군장 장병 3만 명이 침투 이동 가능하고, 그 길로 차량을 이용 급행한다면 서울에 45분이면 도달할 수 있다고 판단되었다. 실체 확인을 위해 일단 300미터 도보 하강 후, 땅굴을 만나 북으로 분계선(시멘트 차단벽 설치해 놓았음)까지 진입하였는데, 땅굴 경사도는 북으로 3도 경사되어 지히수를 북으로 흘러나가게 되어 있었다.

그런가 하면 전두환 대통령이 사단장이었던 시절, 그는 당시 적전차 성능과 특성을 고려하여 1킬로미터 이상 길이—폭 20미터 깊이 10미터—의 대전차호구(壕溝)를 '장단' 지역에 구축하여 적전차의 급습을 저지할 수 있는 장애물로 활용하고 있었다. 아주 좋은 착안이었다. 그런데 이 장단반도 지역은 이미 민간인들이 남방 한계선에서 임진강까지 점유하여 거주함으로써 민간 관광에는 유리하나 군사작전을 위해서는 애로사항이 많았다.

◦ 한강변 대간첩 경계작전

1주일간의 최전선(남방 한계선, 주저항선, GP) 순시 후 이어서 제2전선인 한강변 대간첩 침투작전 지역 현황 파악을 시작하였다. 통일동산 동편 아래에서 행주산성 '창릉천' 중계 펌프장(수문)—서울 경기 경계선은 가양대교까지—대략 55킬로미터로 군단 방어 정면의 2배 길이, 즉 군단의 좌종심 선단 그대로가 바로 한강 하류 대간첩작전경계선이었다. 물론 임진강 상의 대간첩침투작전 외에 또 겹친 임무이다.

이미 수차례 언급한 바와 같이 1959년, 중부 전선에 있던 수도사단 제1연대는 제1연대 전투단(RCT)을 편성하여 이 지역을 한국군 해병 제1여단으로부터 인수하여 방어 임무를 수행하였다. 당시 나는 통일동산 좌일선 소대장이 되었고, 동기생 이승주 소위는 통일동산 좌일선 소대장이 되었다. 그런데 '이 소위' 소대는 그해 가을 입수된 정보에 의거, 공릉천 최하류에 매복하였다가 배구공 튜브를 끌어안고 조류길 따라 침투해 온 무장 간첩 3명을 사살하고 무공훈장을 받았다. 그 후도 끊임없이 한강 하구에서 행주산성에 이르기까지 한강 북변 즉 서울로 간첩 및 무장 공비가 알게 모르게 침투해 왔다.

다음날은 한강 북편 강둑—일반적으로 위는 소달구지 1대 지날 만큼의 넓이, 높이는 14미터 전후로 홍수 때는 종종 넘치며, 두께는 가끔 대홍수로 일부 뚝이 무너져 일산이 물바다가 되기도 하였다.—을 따라 행주산성 방향으로 이동하면서 요소요소에서 중, 소대장의 보고와 현 상황을 확인하였다. 특히 '장항' 근처(지금의 일산대교와 장항인터체인지 어간과 그아레 '신평' 배수펌프장 근처에는 대형 갈대숲이 우거져 있고 지반도 단단하여 궤도형 장갑차로 한강 중심부까지 순찰하기도 하였는데, 지도나 또는 현지에서도 밖에서 보는 것과 달리, 드넓고 깊으며 무성한 갈대밭은 북괴 무장공비나 간첩의 서울 침투 루트가 되고도 남을 것이라고 판단되었다.

신평동의 '신평배수펌프장' 둑에 올라서 보면 저 건너편 김포 방향에 '신곡 양수장'이 보였다. 그런데 그곳에는 둑 북쪽 신평마을에서 뚝을 넘어 강변으로 내려오는 트럭의 길 —강변 생상 농산물 수송용—이 있었다. 때마침 한강 개발사업에 '신곡수중보' 공사가 포함되었기에, 건너편 군단장(17기 김 중장, 육사 후배)과 상의하여, 1. 수중보 윗면에 최소 폭 7미터 이상의 수중 차량 도로를 만들고, 2. 도로 하류 쪽 끝단을 둘굴게 하여 간첩들이 손을 얹으면 미끌어지도록 굴곡지게 하여 보 위로 올라오지 못하게 할 것, 3. 이 지역 즉 한강 수면부터 이남은 반대편(남쪽)에 있는 수도군단 경계 책임 지역이라 권하건데, 촘촘히 수상경계초소를 세워 간첩 침투를 감시하자고 제의하여 그렇게 하였는데, 수중 도로는—유사시 지연 작전의 일환으로 준비—그 후 한 번도 시험해보지 못했으나, (수중으로는 완벽하게 차단되어) 여기를 통한 간첩침투사건은 듣지를 못했다.

행주대교를 지나 행주산성에 이르면, 바로 강가에 강둑 겸 도로가 있고 이어 민간 가옥이 죽 전개되어 있고, 그 끝으로는 다시 남한산성 와지선이 한강 물에 닿아 있었으며, 그 끝은 바로 '창릉천' 중계펌프장인데, 군단 책임 지역은 여기까지였다. 9사단의 엄중한 후방 경계 임무 중의 하나였다.

◇ 86아세안게임 지원과 88서울올림픽 준비

취임 후 군단에 부여된 첫 국가적 임무는 '86아시안게임(9.20~10.5, 15일간)'에 대한 대비였다. 첫째는 이 기간을 전후한 북괴의 군사적 도발에 대한 대응이고, 둘째는 기간 중 대회 방해를 목적으로한 북괴의 작란이나 기 침투 요원에 의한 게임 현장 훼방 방지책이고, 다음이 지역 내 게임 전체에 대한 완전한 경계대책(군관민 합작)이었다.

군단 책임 지역 내 아시안 게임의 현장—골프 한양컨트리클럽(고양시), 사이클(통일로 일대), 승마(원당종합마술경기장)—지원작전으로는, 게임 준비 기간과 실시 기간 중 군단 전 요원을 총동원하여, 게임 지역을 중점으로하는 전 지역 완벽한 수색작전을 실시하고 유지하며, 지속적으로 확보된 상태를 유지하도록 하였다. 게임 실시 중인 전 지역과 지대에는 사전 정찰 후 현장을 확보하고 감시하면서, 준비 시간대부터 행사 종료시까지 주로 영외 거주 간부들을 최대한 편의대(便衣隊)로 활용하였다.

특히 게임 실시 지역은 여전히 시골이라 예를 들어, 경주 자전거가 지나가는 통일로 상에 행여나 간첩이나 제5열에 의한 직접 도발 행패 또는 모래를 뿌리는 등의 방해 행위를 예방하고, 승마경기장 근처에는 '닭 울음소리와 닭의 돌출 및 비상(飛上)' 등등을 예방하고 방지하기 위해 철저하게 닭, 개 등 동물들의 접근과 돌발 상황 등의 감시를 실시하였다. 그 결과 지역 내 모든 게임은 무사하게 성공적으로 끝나게 되었고, 따라서 우리의 노력과 정성은 행사 성공에 크게 기여하였음을 크게 자랑할 수 있게 되었다. 그리고 이 경험은 곧 2년 뒤에 시행될 진짜 '88서울올림픽' 준비에 큰 도움이 될 것으로 믿었다.

◇ 군단전술 토의와 '초전 3일 섬멸전' 지침

전방부대(사단이나 군단)에서 전술 토의는 흔히 과제를 안고 있는 현지에서 지휘관들과 관계참모들을 소집하여 부대 지휘관 주재하에 실시한다. 주로 지휘관의 의도를 강조하거나 새로운 지침 변화에 대한 통일된 이해를 돕기 위해 실시된다. 전후방 순시와 현장 파악을 끝낼 무렵 제1차 군단전술 토의를 개최하였다. 비무장지대 남단 야외 유개교육장에서 바로 앞 비무장지대 내 GP를 바라보며 실시하였다. 토의 요지는, GP의 전술적 운용 문제로 고수방어냐, 적 공격 경고 후 즉시 철수냐였다.

특히 바로 앞에 보이는 GP는 인공보다 자연 동굴 형태로 조성되어 있어 그러한지, 관할 지휘관이나 참모들은 대부분은 포위되어도 고수 방어를 논하였는데, 분위기를 보니 대부분이 찬성하는 듯하였다. 열띤 토의 후 나는 강평 겸 군단장 전술 지침으로 강조하였다. "GP는 전투전초와 같이 적 발견 경고 후 적과 접촉을 유지하며 아군의 지원 사격 엄호를 받으면서 신속히 철수해야 한다, 그래야 초전에 병력 절약은 물론 초전 필승의 사기 진작에 기여한다"고 하였다.

다음은 25사단의 전술 토의에 참여하였는데, 고랑포 임진강 장애물의 수제 선방어냐, 적을 안으로 유인하여 감악산을 핵심 거점으로 적을 포위 섬멸할 것이냐였는데, 후자가 지금까지의 사단 방어 지침이었다고 했다. 나는 권고했다, "임진강 장애물을 중시하여 일단 수제선 방어에 충실하였다가, 유인 섬멸전은 다음 단계로 고려하는 방법이 유리하다고 판단된다"고 하였다.

여하간에 임진강 하구에서 고랑포에 이르기까지 '임진강'이라는 대 자연 장애물을 완벽하게 활용하는 방안에, '초전 3일 섬멸전'의 핵심을 두고, 임진강 선을 넘는 적은 그때마다 반격에 반격 즉 '돌격'과 '돌격'으로 섬멸하는 방어계획이 군단 최선의 방어지침(방책)이라 판단하고 실행하려 하였다.

◇ 김일성의 사망 오보 사건

1986년 11월 16일과 17일 어간에, 비무장지대 내 우리 측 '대성동 자유의 마을'을 상대하여 조성한 북측의 비무장지대 내 '기정리 평화마을'에 있는 인공기가 반기(半旗)로 게양되었고, 개성 시내에 있는 김일성 동상이 흰 천으로 가려져 있다는 군단 관측 보고가 상부에 보고되자 북한 정세에 민감한 군과 정부 당국이 예의 주시하는 가운데, 전 전선 북괴 대남선전 방송에서 '장송곡'과 함께 '김일성 총격 사망' 방송을 잇달아 청취하고 상부에 보고되었다.

그런 가운데 미8군 정보 보고서—북한 김일성 신변 변고 추정 정보—가 군단까지도 배포되었다. 그러자 국방부(장관)도 이 정보를 믿고 국회 대정부 질문 답변에서 김 국방장관이 김일성 사망설을 답변하기도 하였다. 그런데 그다음 날인 18일에 김일성이 평양비행장에 나타남으로써 한국민의 기대가 그만 무산되고 말았다. 그동안 진행된 사실은 분명하기에 북괴군의 기대적 과잉 행위였는지 또는 고의적인 대남 음모였는지 지금도 밝혀지지 않고 있다.

◇ '1987 TeamSpirit 연습', 미제1군단과 어깨를 나란히 하다

나는 군인으로서 영광스럽게도 한미연합군 야전기동훈련인 팀스리트연습을 1984년에는 8사단장으로, 이 해(1987.3.28~4.10)는 군단장으로 미제1군단—군단장은 후에 이라크 침공군 지휘관으로 승리의 영웅이 된 '스워즈코프(Swartzkopf)' 중장—과 어깨를 나란히 하여 한미연합군(급) 야외기동연습에 참가하였다. 예하 주력 배속부대는 수도기계화사단+제8사단+미 제25사단(동원)이었다.

팀스리트연습의 목적, 역사, 훈련 내용 그리고 정치, 군사적 의미는 이미 널리 알려져 있기에 생략하고, 당시에 있었던 한두 가지 잊지 못할 얘기를 적어보기로 한다. 내가 지휘하는 한국군 제1군단과 옆으로 나란히 지연전, 방어, 반격전을 협조하며 연습을 함께한 미제1군단은 미국 서부 '워싱턴 주'에 주둔해 있으며, 한반도 유사시 예비군을 소집하여 가장 먼저 한국 전선으로 투입되는 부대이기에 해마다 이 훈련에 참여하고 있다. 이 해에도 참여한 이 군단의 지휘관은 '엘리트 과정'을 밟은 '슈발츠코프' 장군이었다.

연합군사령부 작전 회의에서 만난 그는 내게 말하기를, '자기는 귀국하면 육군본부 작전참모—한국은 작전참모 후 군단장—로 보임될 예정이고 그 후는 세계 어느 전구(Theater) 사령관(대장)을 희망하고 있다'고 했다. 그는 내 나이보다 한 살 위이고 미국 육군사관학교는 2년 앞서 졸업하며 임관하였다. 그의 아버지도 장군이라 특히 중동 전장에서 함께 전전하였기에 외모로 보나 그간의 활동 모습으로 보아 아주 유능하며 능동적이고 적극적인 장군으로 보였다. 아니나 다를까, 1990년에 있었던 '걸프전쟁'의 '사막의 방패작전'에서부터 미군사령관 즉 다국적군 총사령관이 되어 '사막의 폭풍작전'에서 이라크 침략군을 반격하여 불과 100여 시간 만에 대승하여 명실공히 '사막의 영웅'이 되었다. 흔히 '시대가 영웅을 낳고 그 영웅이 시대를 낳는다'는 말을 이 때에 실감하면서, 그러나 아무에게나 그런 기회가 주어지는 것이 아닌 것은 유감스러웠다.

◇ 한 군인의 주장 ; 군사가 정치에 통상적(일상적) 종속은 안 된다

생도 때 '클라우제빗츠'의 『전쟁론』에 몰입하였던 때가 있었다. 그는 말하기를, 전쟁은 정치의 도구이다, 그래서 전쟁은 정치적 성격을 띠며, 군사적 관점을 정치적 관점으로 종속시킨다. 그러기에 군 지도자는 시국 정치를 알아야 하고 적어도 당대 몇 정치가의 이름 성격 신념 정치 성향을 알아야 한다고 했다. 그러나 나는 감히 그의 '정치와 군사' 관계 이론과 군사 철학을 수정하면서 이해하려 하였다.

그는 주로 구중 궁궐에서 왕자를 지도하면서 '전쟁론'을 연구하였다. 다시 말하면, 그는 정치 분위기 속에서 군사학(또는 이론)을 지도하며 그 속에서 추가로 생성된 군사 철학은 아무래도 정치에 치우쳤을 것으로 추리하였다. 그래서 '정치인은 군사를 알아야 하고 군 지도자 또한 정치를 알아야 하나, 군사는 반듯이 정치에 종속되는 것이라고 당연시하는 것은 잘못이라 생각하였고, 지금도 그 생각은 변함없다.

즉, 때로는 군사가 정치에 종속될 수도 있는가 하면, 또한 때로는 군사적 승리를 위해 정치가 군사에 속할 수도 있다고 생각한다. 최근의 역사 즉 '6·25 남침적란' 때 유엔군 총사령관 '맥아더 장군'이 트루먼 대통령에게 전쟁과 연관된 만주 내 시설 일부를 폭격해야 한다고 건의하고 주장하였다. 트루먼 대통령은 중공과의 정치적인 고려로 이를 허락지 않고 오히려 '맥아더 장군'을 파직하였다. 결과적으로 중공은 만주를 근거지로 대규모로 전쟁에 투입되었고, 그로 인하여 연합군은 후퇴하고 한국(이승만)의 자유민주주의 통일 전략은 물거품이 되고 말았던 것이다. 이런 경우는 정치가 군사적 승리를 위해 군사에 종속되어야 함에도 불구하고 '군사가 정치의 도구'만을 내세워 정치가들이 실수함으로써 한국 역사에 천추의 한을 남기게 되었던 것이다.

더구나 군단장 당시 한국 정치와 군사 관계는 아예 군사가 정치와 사회를 지배하고 있었던 반면 군사 또한 정치(정치 군인)에 의해 지배되고 있었다. 따라서 나는 군사를 지배하는 정치 군인을 지지하고 싶지 않았다.

제4부

노병은 끝까지 국가에 봉사한다

제10장

'전장의 장수, 영웅의 꿈'을 접고 노병으로 용퇴하다

1. 제13대 대통령 선거, 군의 정치적 중립과 자유 투표권 고수

◇ 전두환 대통령의 호출, 청와대 독대

11월 중순 경, 전두환 대통령께서 단독으로 들어오라는 청와대 전달이 왔다. 대통령이 된 이후 단독 면담은 드물었기에, 더구나 청와대에서 대통령을 단독으로 만난다는 것은 영광으로 생각되었다. 그러면서 내심, 공직을 마치면서 요직에 있는 부하들에게 '수고했다'는 위로와 격려 인사를 해주려고 부르는 줄 알았다. 그래서 가벼운 마음으로 들어갔는데, 반갑게 예의 정스러운 마음의 웃음으로 맞이해 주었다. 그래서 가까이 옆으로 마주 앉았다.

그러자 수고했다는 덕담과 함께 봉투를 들면서 물었다, "선거 준비는 어때 잘 되어 가는가? 어떻게 준비하고 있지?" 나는 순간 당황하였고 참으로 난감하였다. "아, 예 그것이~"말을 흐렸다, 거짓말은 말할 것도 없거니와 참말도 하기가 지난하였다. 사실은 '그런 준비'는 전혀 하지 않았고, 오히려 군단 내 전 대대장들을 군단 휴양소로 불러, 군대의 정치적 중립과 개인적인 헌법이 보증하는 4대 투표의 자유권을 역설하고, 본인의 소대장 때 부정 선거 반대의 역사를 자세히 교육도 하였던 터였다.

그러자 이미 보고를 받고 다 알고 있는 듯(?), "아 알았다, 그런데 이번 선거는 참 중요하다 철저하게 준비 잘해주기 바란다, 이건 '금일봉'인데 개인용으로도 좀 써도 좋고, 그런 준비를 위한 부대 운용 비용에 보태쓰도록 하라", 하면서 내게 그 봉투를 건네주고는, 더 이상 선거 얘기는 없었다. 그래서 나는, 평소 마음에 두었던 생각대로 "앞으로 10여 년 뒤면 공산당의 의회 정당 활동도 예상됩니다, 그러나 지금 시점에는 이들 주사파를 일단 다스려 주시기 바랍니다"고 진언했다. "응 음…" 하면서도 약간의 침묵이 흐른 뒤, 대통령은 긍정도 부정도 아닌 다만 약간은 덜 정스러운 표정으로 나를 배웅했다.

◇ **군의 중립과 개인의 투표 자유권을 보장하는 것(헌법 5조2항, 67조 1항)이 참 군인의 도리요 의무라 믿는다**

청와대에서 나와 돌아오는 길에 생각나기를, 내 생각과 내 행위를 이미 알고 있다고 보이기에, 나의 선거관, 투표관, 정치와 군사관 그리고 참된 군인관에 대해 설명을 드리지 못해 유감스러웠다.

1987년 12월 16일에 선거 투표가 있었다. 나는 군단 본부대로 가서 일반 병사와 함께 줄 서서 기다렸다가 차례가 왔을 때 한 표를 행사하였다. 그리고 그 자리에서 병사들에게 강조하였다. "투표는 보장되어 있다. 자기 뜻대로 투표하라"고.

전국적 선거 결과는 근소한 차이로나마 노태우 후보가 대통령에 당선되었다. 결과적으로 보아 사실상 군인의 한 표가 그렇게도 중요함이 여실하였다. 그러하였기에 그 세밀하고 완벽한 마음씨의 전두환 대통령이 직접 나서서 군대 투표를 그렇게도 중요하게 생각하여 필요 요원들에게 종용하였던 것이리라.

2. '장수·영웅의 뜻'을 접고, 노병으로 용퇴하다

◇ **군단장직을 떠나 제1야전군 부사령관으로 가다**

선거 결과 발표 이후 불과 열흘 뒤인 12월 27일에 연말 군 고위직 인사 이동이 단행되었다. 그 발표에 의하여 나는 현직(제1군단장)을 떠나 강원도 원주에 있는 제1야전군 부사령관으로 전보되었다. 크게 말하면 정치가 군사를 종속시킨 것이요, 적게 말해도 정치적 중립의 헌법을 지키고 부정 선거를 거부하려는 정의로운 (참) 군인을 정치적으로 지배한 것이다.

그 이후 위와 같은 정치적 논란을 감안하여, 노태우 정부는 발족 이후 즉시 선거법을 개정하여, 군 영내 투표를 영외 민간 투표소에서 실시하도록 하였다. 그러나 내가 보기에 문제의 본질은 선거(투표) 당시 '대통령의 결심'에 있는 것이지 형식적인 투표소 민간화에 있는 것이 아닌 것이 확실하다고 믿는다. 때문에 정치가인 동시에 국군통수권자인 대통령은, 앞으로는 부디 군대의 정치적 중립을 보장하기 위해, 군대의 한 표를 더 이상 위법 강요하지 말고 헌법 정신에 맡겨 주기를 간곡히 당부해 두고자 한다. 그래야 국군의 각급 지휘관이 거짓 없는 올바른 지휘 권위를 보존할 수 있을 것이라고 믿는다.

◇ **"나는, 나의 임무를 다하였다"**

나는 소시 적부터 역사 공부가 특별히 재밌었다. 그래서 어릴 적부터 조선 시대 9명의 '충무공' 중 한 무장이던 '남이 장군'을 흠모했는데, 그가 일찍부터 무과 급제하고 국경 지대에서 적국을 정벌하며 위국헌신의 영웅으로 읊었다는 〈북정가(北征歌)〉—두산석마도진(白頭山石磨刀盡) 두만강수음마무(豆滿江水飮馬無) 남아이십미평국(南兒二十未平國) 후세수칭대장부(後世誰稱大丈夫)—를 특별히 좋아하며 그 의기를 평생 마음에 새겨두고 있었다.

또한 한국의 영원한 영웅 이순신 장수와 영국 트라파르갈 승전(해전)의 영국 영웅 '넬슨 제독'의 "나는 나의 임무를 다하였다!"라는 마지막 대사(臺詞)를 항상 마음에 두고 있어서 때가 되면 나도 그렇게 독백하려 하였다.

또한 제2차 세계대전의 미국 전쟁 영웅 중 한 장군인 '패튼 장군'은 미군을 지휘하여 북아프리카에서 독일의 유명한 '롬멜 군단'을 격파하고 이탈리아 '시실리'섬에 상륙하여 북상, 프랑스와 독일—특히 '발지전투'—에서 혁혁한 전공을 세운 전쟁 영웅이기에 나도 그런 기회에 그런 승전 장군 즉 전쟁의 영웅이 되고 싶었다. 또한 특히 태평양전쟁과 한국전쟁의 영웅인 '맥아더 장군'의 그 신념, '군사적 승리를 위해 군사에 대한 정치적 종속'까지도 주장하였으나 끝내는 "노병은 죽지 않고 다만 살아져갈 뿐이다"라고 한 의기(義氣)를 담고 군인 생활을 다했다.

자, 이제 '시대가 영웅을 만들고 영웅이 시대를 만든다'는 역사적 시대 운명을 만나지 못한 노병은 미련 없이 사라져 가는 것, 이 또한 (참) 군인의 도리 아니겠는가.

더 이상 '전장의 장수와 전쟁 영웅의 꿈'을 이룰 기회는 올 것 같지 않았다. 용퇴하기로 결심하였다. 전장에서 장수의 깃발을 날리는 꿈, 전쟁으로 승전의 영웅이 되는 꿈을 잊고 이제 이 노병은 한국군에서 살아져 간다.

군단장 이취임식에서 나는 간명하게 그러나 힘주어 말했다, "나는 나의 임무를 다하였다"고, 그리하여 '나는 나의 임무를 다하였다' 고 마음속으로 거듭 외치면서 더는 말없이 군단을 떠나갔다.

그래서 잠시나마 제1야전군사령부 부사령관(1987.12~88.6)으로 재임하였는데, 사령관 '정호근 장군' 부부는 우리 부부를 극진히 대해줘서 고마웠다. 그는 지난 한 해 동안 나와 대통령과의 관계를 알지 못하기에, 그동안의 여러 가지 인과관계로 보아, 잠시나마 자기를 이을 후계자로, 미리 여기에 오게 된 것이라고 생각하였던 것으로 보였다. 그도 나도 한때 수도기계화사단에서, 진정을 서로 느낄 수 있는 기회, 즉 사단참모와 연대장, 참모장과 사단참모로 고락을 공유한 때가 있었기도 하였다.

◇ 현충문을 나오면서 국군이여 안녕!, 군대여 안녕!

용퇴 신고를 마치고 그 길로 바로 동작동 국군묘지로 가서, 특히 그동안 나와 함께 위국헌신하다가 운명을 달리한 나의 옛 전우들에게 거듭 명복을 빌었다. 그리하여 전장에서 쓰러지지 않고 살아남은 한 늙은 군인으로서, 나는 조용히 군을 떠났다. 대한민국 국군이여, 안녕! 군대여 안녕!

제11장

노병, 국가안보에 전념하며 봉사하다

1. 국가안보회의 겸 비상기획위원회 부위원장(1988.10~1993.3)

◇ 나라에서 이 노병을 다시 부르다

바로 다음 날부터, 집(성북구 자양동)에서 가까운 육사 도서관에 가서 그동안 생각해 왔던 '안보학(安保學)' 연구의 일환으로, 또 당시 미소간의 냉전 시대 마지막 고비를 넘기 위한 '군비관리·군비축소 회담'의 연장 선상에서 '한국의 군비관리(통제) 군비축소'에 대한 연구와 저술에 몰두하였다. 마침 육군사관학교 교장에는 후배 절친이요 하나회 아우인 '민병돈 장군'이 있었는데, 잠시 신세를 지면서도 가급적 폐가 안되도록 유의하였다. 당시 민 장군은 특히 노태우 대통령이 전두환 전 대통령에 대한 비정한 예우(?)와 불안한 시국처리에 대한 불편함을, 나와 공감하고 있었다.—그 이후 이미 알려진 바와 같이 그해 생도 졸업 및 임관식장에서 불편한 모습을 보여, 그 직에서 해임되고 예편되는 안타까운 일이 있었다.

'88서울올림픽'이 대 성공리에 끝난 10월 초순 어느 날, 나는 당시 '김종휘' 청와대 외교안보수석으로부터, 만나자는 연락이 왔기에 가 만났더니, '국가비상기획위원회 부위원장'으로 천거됐으니 그리 알라 하였다. 직접 만나 얘기를 듣고 나는 생각하고 결심하였다. '국가안전보장회의'라면, 곧 국방 즉 군사를 한 축으로 경제외교 등의 분야를 통합하는 국가안보전략 최고봉의 국가기관 아닌가.

이제 군문을 나와 살아져 가던 노병이 다시 국가안보기관에 봉사할 수 있는 기회를 갖게 된다는 것은 또 한 번의 기회요 영광의 길이 될 것으로 생각하고 부름에 쾌히 응하기로 하였다.

'김종휘' 외교안보수석은 내가 국방대학원 관리 교수부장으로 갈 때 적극 추천해 주었고, 근무 중 친하게 지냈으며, 그동안의 내 사정도 이해하고 있었던 걸로 짐작이 되며, 이번 일도 그의 추천으로 되었다고 믿어진다. 다만 임명권자인 노태우 대통령은 어떤 입장을 보였는지 알 수 없으나, 김 수석의 제의는 나로서 잊을 수 없는 친절이었다.

◇ 우리 위원회의 역사, 임무, 구성

'국가안전보장회의 겸 비상기획위원회'라는 긴 간판 명칭을 가졌으나 정부 조직법 상의 부처가 아니고 국무총리 직속 위원회였다. 그래도 엄연히 위원장은 '장관급'이고 부위원장인 나는 '차관급'으로 차관 배지를 달고 국무회의와 차관 회의에 정식 멤버로 매주 참석하여 정부 전 부처 차관들과, 때로는 위원장을 대리하여 전 국무위원들과 국책을 최종적으로 논하고 심의하는데 참석하였다. 그러나 서열은 법제처 차관 다음으로 말석 차관이었다.

위원회 역사를 보면, 그동안 국가안보에 대한 관민의 인식이 파란만장하였음을 엿볼 수 있다. 미국에서도 '국가안보 또는 안보전략'이라는 논리가 명확하게 성립(1987년경) 되기 이전인 1962년, 제3공화국 헌법에 '국가안전보장회의' 설치를 규정하여 63년에 '안보회의'가 설치되었다. 1968년의 '김신조 사태'로 정부는 대오각성하여 '비상기획위원회'를 그 소속으로 추가 설치하였다. 이때 야당의 반대로 그 작명에 상처를 입기도 하였으나 내가 근무할 당시까지 우여곡절을 겪으며 유지되어 왔었다.

위원회의 기능 즉 임무로는, '안전보장회의'를 준비(주관)하고, 매년 실시하는 '을지-FOCUS 연습'의 정부 연습(을지)을 주관하고 감독하며 발전시킨다. 그래서 이에 따르는 정부 '전쟁지도 벙커의 상황실'을 관리유지, 운용하며, 유사시 전시 통제하게 되는 필수 국가기관과 동원 유관 민간 기업에 설치된 '비상계획관'의 인사, 운영, 관리를 담당하고 있다.

위원회 구성은, 위원장, 부위원장, 그 아래로 기획통제실, 동원기획실, 조사연구실로 구성되어 있다. 기획과 동원 실장은 군 예비역 장군이고 조사 실장은 주로 서울대 출신 1급/정무급이었고 약 100여 명의 직원으로 구성되었다. 부위원장은 중장급 장군 출신으로 일반 정부 차관의 임무(역할)와 같이, 그러나 군부의 '부'(副) 지휘관과는 다르게, 실제 부서 부책임자로서 결제 선상에 있고, 하부 부처의 업무 조정은 물론 그 부를 대표하여 '차관회의'에 참석 책임을 진다. 때문에 마치 한 부대의 참모장과 같은 역할도 담당한다. 다만 우리 위원회에서는 '국가비상기획위원회'에만 부위원장의 임무를 당당하게 되어 있다.

그냥 보기에는, 미국의 '연방비상관리처(FEMA, Federal Emergency Management Agency)'와 닮았으나 미국에는 평상시 '국가재해대책'까지도 포함하고 있으나 한국은 오로지 전시 동원 업무에 국한하고 있었다.

◇ 당시의 '국가안전보장회의'를 주관

한국과 같이 국가안보와 국가안보전략의 중요성을 인식할 수밖에 없는 나라들은 '국가안전보장회의(NSC, National Security Council)'라는 정부 기구를 대통령 가까이에 두고 운용한다. 그동안 우리나라도 안보 문제 논의와 심의의 중요성이 점증하는 가운데, 변화와 수정을 거쳐 비정기적으로 국가적 이슈가 있을 때 우리 위원회가 준비하고 대통령이 주관하여 국가안보회의를 개최해 왔다.

그런데 이상하게도 직계상 차관인 부위원장은 이 업무밖에 있도록 돼 있었다. 그래서 중차대한 국가안보문제를 생각하면 반듯이 관여—발언과 제도발전 등—하고 싶었으나 법률상 월권이 될 수 있음으로 안타깝지만 직접 관여하지 못했다. 그러나 보아 오건대, 청와대 외교안보실에서 개최 준비 통보가 오면, 참석 부처에 통보하여 준비시키고, 사전에 그 준비물을 모아 청와대에 제출하고, 회의 장소를 준비하는 즉 행정 사무처 역할을 담당하고 있었다. 자체 정책이나 전략 개발 또는 국내외 책임 안보담당(비서)관이 없었다. 즉 진짜 국가안보문제를 담당하고 있지를 않았고, 말로만 '국가안전보장회의'였으며 실제는 청와대 외교안보실이 역할을 하고, 그 사무를 담당하는 사무국 정도 역할이었다.

◇ 충무계획(忠武計劃)의 유지, 집행, 발전

위원회의 핵심 업무로, 전시 또는 국가 비상시 준비된 '충무 계획'을 발동하여 정부 기관 및 국가 기간 업체를 통제하면서, 국가 (총)동원을 집행하는데, 평상시 이를 위한 준비와 연 1회 국가적 연습훈련(乙支鍊習)—'을지-포커스 연습' 중 정부 분야 연습—을 담당하여 실시한다.

'데프콘-3'—(DEFCON, Defense Condition)—가 발령(국방부)됨과 동시 위원회는 전 정부 기관에 일제히 경보를 발령한다. 그러면 위원회는 '국가전쟁지휘소 벙커'를, 전 부처는 현지 지하벙커 개소를 준비하며 전 부처 상황실을 연결—당시는 비상 전화망—한다. 이어서 '데프콘-2'가 발령되면, 위원회는 즉시 '국가 전쟁지휘소 벙커'로 이동하고, 5개 안보관계 부처 지휘부는 벙커로 들어오고 잔여 모든 부처는 의명 서울에서 지방으로 이동을 대기한다. '데프콘-1'이 발령되면 대통령과 지휘부가 한강 이남 벙커에 정좌하고, 남은 부처들은 상황에 따라 대처하며 전국 동원령 즉 충무 계획이 집행된다. 이와 같은 절차훈련을 매년 1회, 8월에 실시하는데, 그 주관 부서가 바로 우리 위원회이다.

◇ '비상계획관'의 인사, 관리, 운용

'김신조 사태' 이후 정부는 대오각성하여 군비를 증강하면서 자주국방에 심혈을 기울이는 한편, 민방위 문제와 국가동원 문제에도 역량을 집중하였다. 그래서 69년도부터는 정부 각급 기관(투지 기관 포함)과 주요 동원 업체에 '비상계획관'을 임명하고, 전시 정부의 제 기능을 유지하고 국민 생활의 안정을 도모하는 '전시 대비 계획'을 수립하여 유지 보완하고, 기업체의 전시 전환 계획 즉 동원 계획을 평시부터 수립하여 유지 보완하도록 하였다.

정부 각급 기관(각 시도 밑 투자기관 포함)에는 예비역 대령을, 주요(대형) 기업체에도 예비역 대령을, 단 기관과 업체의 규모에 예비역 중령과 소령도 선발하여 배치하고 운용하였다.

◇ 박정희 대통령의 '서울 고수 전략작전 계획' 유지

지금은 모든 것이 시대 변화에 따라 발전하였겠지만, 당시는 박정희 대통령이 수립하였던 '서울 고수 전략작전 계획'이, 변화가 필요하였음에도 여전히 유효하였다. 그래서 북괴가 전면 재남침 시 서울 결사 고수 방어로 고립되었을 때 서울과 주민의 생활을 안정적으로 유지하기 위해 몇 가지 대책이 준비되어 있었다.

예를 들면, 서울 시내 비상용 전기 수요를 16만 킬로와트로 상정하고 비상 발전기를 시내에 준비하였고, 시내 아파트단지는 그 규모에 맞게 우물(물)을 준비하였고, 주요 건물마다 자체 비상 발전기를 준비하였고, 서울 시민 비상용은 물론 겸해서 전국 민용(군사용 포함) 국가 비상 물자 비축—식량 최대 3년분, 유류(서울, 거제도 등), 의약품(약효 초과품 수시 교체) 등—을 엄수하였다. 때문에 위원회가 특히 '을지훈련' 때 직접 점검하는 업무 감독이 필수 사항이었다.

◇ 차관 회의와 국무 회의

매주 1회 차관 회의는 목요일, 장관 회의는 금요일로 기억한다. 회의가 있는 날은 평소보다 약간 일찍이 과천청사로 출근해서 아침 업무를 마무리하고, 서울 시내 교통 사정을 고려하여 늦지 않기 위해 일찍 출발한다. 어느 때 2~30분 여유가 생기면 또는 어느 때 일부러 일찍 출발하여 여유 시간에 삼청공원에 들려서 입구 안쪽에서 산책 겸 머리를 식혔다. 군인 출신 차관으로는 국방 차관, 통일부 차관 그리고 위원회 차관인 내가 있었다. 위원회 차관은 평소 여타 차관들과 업무 협조 관계가 거의 없어 언제나 그들과 만나면 생소하였다. 다만 내가 4년 이상 오래 근무하다 보니 고참이 되어 낯이 익어지면서 그냥 동료로 친하게 지나게 되었다.

차관 회의는 주로 선임 차관 주재하에 개최되는데, 장관 회의 회부에 앞선 정책 사항을 최종 협조하고 조율하는 기회이다. 그런데 대부분의 경우는 일반 정책 사항이라 발언할 기회나 경우가 없으나 평균 1개월에 2~3건 정도가 안보와 비상 기획 업무에 능동적으로 관계됨으로 발언을 하고 주장도 하였다. 위원장이 휴가나 어떤 사정으로 불참 시 대리하여, 주로 국무총리가 주재하는 '국무 회의'에 참석하였는데, 거의 참석에 의의를 두는 정도였다.

청와대 초청 연회에 차관급까지 참석하는 경우는 연 2~3회 정도였는데, 주로 연말 또는 어떤 경축 행사에 부부간에 초대되어 갔다. 그러나 대통령 부부와의 직접 접촉과 담화 기회는 거의 없었던 걸로 생각된다. 오히려 전두환 대통령 당시 군 장성으로 청와대 연회나 회의에 초대되어 참석하던 경우가 더 생각나고 있다.

2. 미국 'BALL주립대학교' 군사학(ROTC) 방문 교수(1994.5~1996.8)

◇ 인디아나 주립 'BALL대학교' 방문 교수로 가다

1993년 봄, 노태우 정권이 김영삼 정권으로 교체됨에 따라 자동으로 부위원장직을 떠나게 되면서 정부 공직에서 국가안보에 대한 봉사는 일단 끝을 맺게 되었다. 도리켜 보니 육사생도 생활과 월남전쟁 기간의 가산을 포함하여 군대 생활은 37년, 정부 공무원 생활은 4년 반, 그래서 만 41년 이상을 국가공무원으로 공직 생활을 한 것이다.— 물론 그 이후 다시 2년을 더 공직 생활을 하였다.—이미 군대 생활을 마치면서 더 없는 감회를 느낀 바 있었기에 별도의 감상은 없었으나 그래도 국가에 대한 직접적인 봉사를 이제 더 할 수 없게 되었다고 생각하니 한 인생 다 간 것 같은 허전함이 앞섰다.

그런데, 그대로 은퇴하기에는 나이도 경력도 주변 환경도 이르다는 생각도 들었거니와 군대 생활을 하면서 생각해 두었던 '나의 소명' 즉 '군사학'의 국가공인 학문화와 개인적으로는 '국가안보전략사상'에 대한 연구를 내 마음대로 본격적으로 시작해 보기로 결심하였다. 그래서 잠깐이나마 수색에 있는 국방대학원의 예비역 장군 지원실과 도서관을 드나들면서 10여 개 미국 유수 대학교 대학원에 요구서(Requirement)를 보내 보았다. 그랬더니 역시나 세계 최강국이요 민주주의를 주도하는 선진 국가답게 즉시—편지 보낸 대학 하나도 빠짐없이—회답이 왔다.

'예일대학'의 유명 역사학 교수 'Paul Kennedy' 교수로부터는, '역사에 관심이 있다니 환영한다, 숙소를 제공할 테니 오시라'였고, '스텐포드대학'에서는 '금년은 이미 늦었으니 내년에는 준비해 드리겠다'였고, '하버드대학의 케네디 행정학부'에서는 '언제든지 환영한다'고 하였다. 그래서 한동안 미국 '국가안보전략' 연구에 적절한 그리고 내 환경 조건에 맞는 대학교를 선택하려고 검토 중에 있었다.

그런데 갑자기 가정 통사를 만나 다음 기회로 미루고 당분간, 미국에서 공부하고 있는 아들네 가까이 가보기로 하였다. 물론 아들네 학업에 지장이 없는 조건에서였다. 때마침 아들의 장인 '장주호 박사'의 주선과 현지 'BALL대학교' 교수인 '박성재 교수'의 친절한 도움을 받게 되었다. 그래서 그 대학의 'Military Science Department' 즉 ROTC의 방문교수(Visiting Scholar)로 초대되었고, 가서는 미국 '인디아나' 주의 전통 깊은 주립 '볼 대학'이 있는 인구 8만 명 정도의 소도시 'Muncie'의 대학 동네 한 아파트에 자리 잡았다.—2 bath, 2 bed에 월 350달러.

◇ 학교 내외 초청·방문 및 연구 저술 활동, 단 조심 생활

∘ 대학교 군사학부(ROTC)에서 강의 및 연구 생활

대학에서는 고맙게도 총장 관사에서 학교 간부들과 함께 만찬하며 환영해 주었고, 월 700여 달러의 의료보험을 넣어주고, '군사학부(ROTC)'에 소속—현역 중령이 부장, 현역 여자 대위가 교관, 중사 한 명이 조교, 민간 여자 행정 사무원, 소형 도서실과 각자 사무실 보유—으로 해 주었다.

군사학부에서는 내게 환경 좋은 방을 개인 사무실로 제공해 주고 10시간 이상의 '북핵 문제'에 대한 강의 겸 토론을 할 수 있도록 배려해 주었다. 거기에다 마침 한국 ROTC 여학생이 있어서 통역까지도 배려해 주었다. 미국으로 가기 전에 '북핵 문제'—93년도라 6자회담에서 소위 '94년 경수로 합의'가 도출되어 가던 시점—에 대해 강의 및 토의 준비를 하고 이 원고를 번역해 갔었다. 그래서 우선 학생(후보생 30여 명)들에게 통역을 통해 강의하고 토론도 하였다.

◦ 국가안보전략(사상사)에 흥미, 연구와 저술 활동

그 뒤부터는 사무실과 도서관—한 방을 신청하여 정식으로 빌려서—을 왕래하며 연구하면서 '미국 역사와 함께 미국 국가안보전략사상사'를 연구하며 저술에 열중하였다. 미국 현지에서 관찰되는 것은, 불과 몇 년 전에 '공산주의에 마지막 일격을 가하여 승리한' '레이건' 대통령에 의해 미국 안보 역사상 처음으로 '87년도 미국국가안보전략' 문서가 발간되어 국방과 안보 관계 인사들에게 큰 관심이 되어 있었던 가운데, '걸프전쟁'에 승리한 부시(아버지 부시) 대통령은 '신세계 질서'를 정의하는 '미국 국가안보전략, 1991'을 발표하였다.

이제 지구상에는 큰 전쟁이 없을 것으로 기대되는, 초강대국 미국의 시대가 되었을 때 새로 선출된 클린턴 대통령은 '미국 국가안보전략, 1994'를 발표하였다. 그는 대외 정책면에서 세계적 역사가 '토인비'가 말한바, '도전과 응전 그리고 융합(Engagement, 합(合), 융합, 포용)'를 표방하여, 크게는 'Win-Win전략'을 표방하고, 일종의 '전후복원(戰後復員)' 형식으로, 국가안보전략면에서, '버텀업 리뷰(BUR, Bottom Up Review, 1993)' 정책—군사전략의 전환과 함께 군사력 복원 및 적응 검토—을 추구하고 있었다. 특히 북핵 문제에 대해서는 공화당과 상당수 국민들의 반대 여론에도 불구하고 94년 '미북제네바합의'를 앞두고 있었다.

그래서 대폭 축소되는 군대는 나름대로 적응하기 위해 간부 위주 조직 개편과 동시에 '군사혁명(Military Affairs)', 심지어는 이를 '군사혁명(Military Revolution)'이라고도 칭하면서 그로부터 20/30년 후의 '극초현대화' 를 시도하고 있었다. 이는 '로봇전쟁'도 지나 '레이저전쟁' 또는 '인마살상 아닌 무력화(無力化)전쟁' 시대로 직행해 가는 이른바 '판도라의 상자'를 열려고 시도하고 있었다.

◦ 한인 교회가 한인 사회와 유학생들의 안식처

여기 '먼시'라는 소도시는 1800년대 초기 '볼대학'이 창립됨으로써 대학 도시로 태어났다. 그래서 특히 지역 커뮤니티 광범위하게 '볼대학'의 영향력이 미치고 있었다. 그중 하나가 볼대학이 운영하는 '방송국'이 있다. 이 방송국은 학교와 그 지역 사회가 필요로 하는 학교 교육 방송국인 동시에 지역 방송국이다. '볼대학' 즉 '교육재단'은 이뿐만 아니라 상당히 아름답고 유서 깊은 장로교계 교회를 가지고 있어서 이 또한 지역 종교 생활의 중심 역할을 하고 있었다.

그런데 이 교회 본 건물의 한켠, 처음 시작했던 교회당과 그 부속방 몇 개를 우리 열렬한 한국 유학생 교인들에게 제공해서 '한인 교회'로 운영되고 있었다. 얘기를 듣고 반가워서 가보니 정말 훌륭한 시설이요 훌륭한 학생들의 교회요 안식처요 집회소였다. 이 학교 한국 유학생은 30여 명, 그중 대부분이 이 교회—김 아무개 유학생 신도가 인도하는 주일 예배—에 나오고 있었고, 아직도 한국 교포가 '먼시'에는 3~4집 정도인데 그래도 모두 나와 주도적인 일을 하며 이들을 돕고 있었다.

우리 부부가 주일에 나가자 좀 먼 거리의 '카운티(County)'에 살고 있는 한인들이 둘, 셋에서 나중에는 10여 명 정도로 교인이 늘어났다. 애초에는 유학생 스스로 모여 주말에 점심 한 끼 해결하면서 한두 가지 한국교회에서 하는 교회 활동을 시작해서 서로 위로하고 돕다가, 조금씩 학생과 지역 한인들이—주말 예배에 30~40명—늘어나자 젊지만 많이 알고 의욕에 찬 목사까지 더 모시게 되었다. 그런데 이 목사는 많지는 않지만 미국인 본교회—한국인 교회 활동을 지원해주는 일환으로—에서 매월 생활 및 활동비를 보장해 주었다.

우리도 이 교회의 내력과 목사 그리고 학생을 비롯한 구성인들의 교인다운 마음씨에 끌려 미국에 있는 동안 내내 일상의 한 주요 부분이 되었다. 좀 먼 동네(1시간 정도 이상)에서도 왔는데, 5·16 때 이민 왔다는 '닥터 김' 부부, 그 이웃에 한국 택사스촌에서 미군과 결혼해 와서 미국 부모들의 마음을 거슬려도 지금도 함께 살고 있는 부인, 그러나 같은 경우이면서도 이미 헤어진 부인 등, 언제나 한인 사회가 그리운 사람들이었다.

우리는 가을에는 인디아나 주립대학이 있는 'Bloomington'공원에 가서 거대한 단풍 숲속에서 '바베큐 잔치'를 벌리기도 하였고, 크리스마스 때는 '닥터 김' 동네에 가서 거리의 크리스마스 츄리에 푹 빠지고, '닥터 김'네 집으로 와서는 푸짐한 한식 뷔페를 먹으며 담소하는 등 미국 소도시 한인 사회의 행복을 함께 누려보기도 하였다.— 지금은 그 목사와 가족이 영주하고 있다고 들었다.—'먼시' 도시의 한인 사회와 유학생 그리고 교회와 그 목사에게 하늘의 가호 있기를 기원한다.

◇ 미국서 새삼 많은 장점을 발견하다

나는 소시적 일찍부터 미국 유학을 꿈꾸었고, 사관학교도 유학할 수 있다는 말에 끌리기도 하여 지원하였다. 직업 군인으로 성장하면서 미군과의 접촉과 실제 미국 유학을 통해 미국을 겉핥기로 견문하면서도 생각보다 아주 다른 신세계 신천지임을 실감한 바였다. 이제 실제 공동체 일원으로—비록 짧은 2년 여였지만—살며 경험하며 견문해 보니, 민주주의 국가로서 인류의 이상향을 지향하는 나라, 자체 자원이 풍부하여 명실공히 부강한 나라임을 확인하게 되었다. 물론 인류 사회의 근본 악과 미국 자본주의 사회 자체의 단점도 있기는 하나, 오히려 그 시절(1990년대) 내가 느꼈던 더 많은 미국의 장점, 배울 점을 몇 가지만이라도 기억해 보고자 한다.

◦ **부지런(Protestant diligent)함과 절약 정신**

나는 일찍부터 '국민성이 틀린다'라는 말을 부정하며 주장하였다. 어느 국가 국민이건 경제 사회적으로 발전하고 문명화하면 선진국 국민들과 같은 성격 즉 국민성을 가질 수 있을 것으로 생각하였다. 예를 들어 독일 국민성은 '밤에 누가 보지 않아도 빨간불이면 멈춰 서 있다'던가, '미국 가면 어제 본 시계가 오늘도 그 자리에 있다' 던가 하며, 미국과 독일의 국민성이라 하였다. 그런데 몇십 년이 지나자 우리 국민도 그렇게 되었다. 따라서 국민성이 따로 있는 것이 아니고 그 나라가 발전함에 따르는 것이다. 그런 뜻에서도 미국이 우리 앞서가고 있음을, 다시 말하면 우리도 발전하면 언젠가는 그렇게 될 수 있다는 걸 일게 되었다.

미국 아파트—단층 연립주택도 월세인 경우는 그렇게 부른다.—는 앞 주인이 떠나면 짐을 다 가져가든지 넘기든지 하고, 일단 싹 비워서 내부 청소와 보수와 페인팅 등 전체 정비를 하고 새 주인에게 내준다. 미국은 뜨내기들(새로 온 이주자, 직업을 바꾸면서 옮겨 온 이들) 천국이라 그게 편리하고, 거기에 맞추어 사회가 돌아가고 있다. 그래서 새 세입자는 자기 가구를 가져오던지 들여놓아야 한다.

특히 외국에서 맨손으로 들어온 가족은 새로 장만해야 하는데 자기 격에 또는 필요에 맞게 비품들을 구입할 수 있다. 겉으로 보기에 미국 사회는 호화 사치스럽게 보이나 알고 보면 미국 사회 이상 검소하고 절약적이고 부지런하고 건전한 사회는 보기 드물 것이다. 미국에는 물론 신 상품과 사치품을 파는 백화점도, 전문점도 있고, 생필품을 파는 마트도 다 있다.

그런가 하면 이러한 실수요자를 위해 또 부지런하고 절약 정신에 가득찬 사람들을 위해 동네 한 단위에 Flea market(도떼기, 고물, 벼룩시장—실내 상시시장)도 있고, Free Market(정기적, 노천, 난전)도 있고, Antique라는, 남이 쓰던 헌 물건을 기부받아 정비해서 내놓은 아주 싸게 파는 사회 봉사 상점, 일종의 자선사업 점포도 있다. 호기심이 있어 가보았더니, 많은 사람들이 이용하고 있었는데, 비록 헌 것이지만 사용 가능한 손질을 다해 둔 것들로 침대 침구, 바로 입을 수 있는 새 옷과 헌 옷, 헌책, 문구, 카제트 등 온갖 것이 멀지 않은 곳에 진열되어 있었다.

그런가 하면 지역별로 다른 날을 잡아 매주 1회 개인 집집마다 '가라지 세일(Garage Sale)'이라 하여, 문자 그대로 집 자동차 차고 등에, 자기 집에서 쓰다가 버리는 것을 전시해 놓고, 그저 주다시피 그러나 공짜는 안 된다는 개념으로 판매한다. 생각해 보시라 오늘날 우리 동네 아파트 물건 버리는 모양새가 어떠한지? 배워서 남주지 않을 것이라 생각된다.

그리고 '기회 잡화상'이라고 할, 백화점과 도매상의 중간 점포로 잡화 잡동산이 상점(도매+소매)—예, TJ.Max—도 있는데, 일반 주민들에게 인기였다. 주로 새 상품 중에 손님은 잘 모르나 어딘가 아주 조금 하자가 있는 것, 또는 약간 유행이 지난 것들 그러나 멀쩡한 신품들을 시세보다 싸게 파는데, 많은 사람들이 구경도 하고 사 가기도 한다.

살아가며 의자가 더 필요했는데, 마침 '볼대학' 창고에서 사용 후 물건들을 경매도 하고 그냥 팔기도 한다기에 가보았다. 아니나 다를까, 학교 창고에서 실제로 좀 닳은 카펫을 경매로 내놓았고, 아직 쓸만한 의자도, 찌그러진 의자도—아마도 고쳐서 쓸 수 있다고 판단한 듯—있었는데, 나도 두어 개 샀지만 여러 사람들도 구경하고 사 가기도 하였다. 아니, 동네 부자 대학에서 닳은 카펫이나 찌그러진 의자도 버리지 않고 돈 받고 팔고 있다니, 야 신기하다는 느낌 마저 들었다.

그런가 하면 어느 날 여학생 기숙사 앞에도 장이 열렸는데, 허허, 여대생이 쓰다 내 놓은 '브래지어'도 나와 있었는데, 누가 사갈까 하는데 그래도 누군가가 사 간다는 것이다. 그들 사회에는 이런 말이 있었다. '일찍 일어난 새는 지렁이(새벽에 밖으로 나옴)를 먹을 수 있다' 즉, 부지런한 새는 양질의 음식을 먹을 수 있다는 금언이다. 사실인즉, 일찍 일어나 '가라지 세일' 등을 돌아다 보면 상당히 값지고 귀중한 물건을 발견할 수도 있다는 얘기다. 사실이었다.

한편 우습지만은 않은 사회 질서 얘기도 있다. 1960년대에 '미국의 꿈'을 안고 한국 사람들도 미국에 많이 이민 갔었다. 그 부모들 노인네들도 따라 갔었다. 어떤 노인네는 하도 동네 미국 아이들이 예쁘고 좋게 생겼기에, 당시 한국 풍습 식으로, 아이 자지를 만지거나 머리를 쓰다듬으며 "야 잘생겼다"고 했는데, 금방 경찰이 와서 격노하기에 도저히 미국을 이해할 수 없었다고 했다. 그런가 하면 미국 길거리 동전 넣는 주차장에 차를 세우고 시간이 지나도 '조금이야 봐주겠지 하고는 돈을 더 넣지 않아 경찰에 적발되어 벌금을 6달러 내게 되었는데, '그까짓 것' 하다가 곱으로 오르자 가서 사정하였는데 안 들어주자 또 좀 미루었더니 제곱으로 올라 혼나고, 그때부터 미국 사회 질서가 어떻다는 걸, 그래서 유지된다는 걸 실감했다는 것이다.

◦ 진심으로 친절하고 남을 돕고 동정하는 인심

청년 장교 때 미국 유학 가서 동기 요르단 장교와 '미국 사람 뭐주고도 뺨 맞는다'면서 이심전심 불평도 하였으나 그것은 긴급 구호 원조 정책—단기적 생필품만 원조—에 대한 것이었다. 그러나 미국 와서 깊이 속을 들여다보면, 수정자본주의 개념이 확실한 미국식 민주주의를 체험으로 감지하게 된다.

남 도우기, 이웃 돕기는 사회 습관화 되어 있는데 사회적 약자 특히 초입 외국인에 친절하여, 길거리에서 조금만 두리번거려도 남녀노소 가리지 않고 다가와서는 "May I help you?" 한다. 마켓 또는 몰에서 물건을 가지고 계산대 오면 계산해 주고는 물건이 많아 보이면 계산원이 얼른 친절하게 장바구니 넣기를 도와준다. 미국에서 세일 종류도 많으니까 모르고 가도, 계산원이 친절하게 알려주어 가며, 마치 손님을 위해 일하는 사람처럼, 손님이 모르는 할인 티켓도 주어 가며 손님에게 유리하게 계산해 준다. 알고 보면 그것이 바로 그 점포의 장기 이익을 위한 상도인 것임에도 손님이 느끼기에는 '친절'이 바로 그것으로 기분 좋게 해준다고 느끼게 된다. 그렇다고 해서 일본에서 느껴지는 '로봇의 친절'과는 달리, 특히 시골에서는 그런 친절이 진정으로 보였다.

◦ 지방민의 사교와 골프 운동

지방 즉 시골은 부자 나라의 시골답게 나름대로 즐겁게 살게 되어 있었다. 예를 들면 지방민 전부가 남녀노소 할 것 없이 골프 회원이 되어 값싸게 신체 단련—시골에는 케디 도움이는 물론 없고, 자기 운동 기구 혼자서 끌거나 메고 다니고, 혼자도 좋고 함께도 좋고,

사전 예약 없이 어느 때던 가서 운동할 수 있을 만큼 적절한 골프장이 준비되어 있고, 값은 7달러에서 비싼 곳이 10~15달러 정도라—하면서도 운동을 즐기고, 그리고 끝나면 샤워만 간단히 하고, 그때마다 클럽에서 간단한 식사(참으로 간단하게)나 차 한 잔하면서 즐긴다. 물론 시골이라도 공식 모임이나 큰 모임은 교회도 공회당도 있어서 그건 그것대로 모이고 즐겁게 지날 수 있게 되어 있었다. 물론 도회지 변두리에는 우리와 같은 '멤버십 골프장'도 있어서 그건 그것대로 그런 멤버들의 편리를 위해 존재하였다.

3. 한국 국대원 초빙 교수, 한국국가안보전략사상사(학) 연구회 설립

◇ 전문 경력 인사 국대원 초빙 교수(제1기)

약속된 비자 기간이 끝나 우리 부부는 공부하는 아들과 며느리를 두고, 그리고 그동안 고마웠고 신세 진 미국 현지 한국 사람들, 특히 먼시대학의 한국인 교수 박성제 교수 내외와 교회를 함께 관리했던 이웃 카운티의 닥터 김 내외 분 그리고 교회 목사 내외, 또한 같은 아파트 구내에서 친했던 이웃 한국 사람과 미국 사람들, 그리고 특히 군사학부 ROTC 단장 이하 요원들에게 고맙다고 인사하고 헤어져 한국 내 나라로 돌아왔다.

들어올 때, 셋째 처제 윤정이네(박진희)의 청에 따라, 둘째 처남 집에 의탁하고 있는 장모님을 모시고 세 집이 서로 가까운 거리에서 함께 살기로 하고, 자양동 집을 처분하여, 경기도 고양시의 신일산 마두동으로 이사해 왔다.(1996년 6월경) 그리하여 지금 이날까지(2025년) 29여 년간 은퇴 생활을 별다른 변화 없이 계속 중이다.

돌아오자 말자 여기서 가까운 수색 국방대학원 도서관으로 매일 출퇴근하다시피 다니면서, 미국에서 가져온 숙제, '미국국가안보전략사상사'에 대한 연구와 집필을 계속하였다.

그런데 좀 지나자 문체부 산하 '한국과학재단'에서 '전문 경력 인사 초빙 활용 지원사업'으로 '전문 경력 인사 대학 초빙 교수 제도'가 생겼다. 그 목적으로는, 우리 같은 인사—공무원 정무직과 1급 이상, 군인은 장관 경력 소지자—들이 가능한 한 출신 고향의 대학이나 수도권 외 대학에 가서 전문 경험과 지식을 후진들에게 전함으로서, 고위 인적 자원의 활용과 함께 지방과의 학문적이나 기타 격차와 소외 문제 해소를 목적으로 하는 것이었다. 기간은 도심지는 2~3년, 고향 지역은 3~5년 기한이고 전액(월 250만 원) 국고 지원이었다. 그래서 지원했더니 제1기는 거의 우리 함께 근무했던 차관들과 일부 장관들도 포함되었었다.

국대원에 출근해서 우선 안보 교수부에 소속하고, 무엇을 교육해 볼 것인가를 교수들과 상의 해 보았으나 신통한 과목이 나오지를 않았다. 교수들은 그렇지 않아도 최근에 구조 조정 즉 학과목 축소와 교수 조정 단계에 들어가려는 때라 어떤 과목도 어떤 시간도 여유를 내 줄 수 있는 입장이 아니었다. 이제 처음으로 이런 제도를 도입하는 것이라 교수들 모두가 긴장하고 있었다. 그래서 나는, 교수들에게 내 경험이 필요할 때 언제든지 초청하라 하고,

일단은 '국가 비상 기획'과 관련된 과제를 가지고 제공되는 시간—학점이 없는 여가 시간—에 한해서 그것도 전원 강당에서 한, 두 교시를 사용하도록 배정받아 활용해 보았다.

그리고 주로 석사과정 학생들을 상대로, '한미전략의 실제', '한국안전보장회의와 전쟁 지휘의 실제', '국가안보전략사상사(미국편)', '한국군비통제의 실제'라는 과목으로 준비되는대로 실전 경험을 토대로 연구한 이론을 강의해 보기도 했다. 물론 시험이 없으니 눈에 보이는 성과는 알 수 없었으나 소기의 성과는 거두었으리라 생각된다.

그런데 이제 막 은퇴한 장군이—중, 대령 정도의 전문 교관이 아닌, 야전군 출신의—피교육자를 상대로 특별 강연 등이 아닌, 정식 교과목 교육을 한다는 것은 역시나 번지수가 좀 다른 것 같았다. 그래서 시간이 흐름에 따라 나는 미국서 가져온 숙제로, 나의 취미요 해야만 할 일, '미국의 국가안보전략사상사'를 집필하는데 전념하였다.

◇『미국의 국가안보전략사상사』 발간

이전에는 잡지나 언론에 발표할 내용은 원고지나 또는 A4용지에 직접 글을 써서 송고 했었다. 그러나 94년 이후부터는 미제 'GATEWAY(14인치)' 노트북에 직접 타자하고 보관하였다가 탈고가 되면 그걸 그대로 출판사에 보내주면, 출판사에서 정리 보정하여 인쇄 즉 출판해 주었다. 그래서 1999년에 『미국의 국가안보전략사상사』라는 이름의 책을, 육사 후배 그것도 잠깐이나마 육사 학교 대표 럭비부에서 잠깐이나마 함께 뛰었던 18기 후배 '방용남 사장'—당시 유수한 출판사요 을지로 입구 큰 책방이었던 '을지서적'을 운영—에게 부탁해 양질의 책으로 500권 출판하였다. 후배 방용남 사장에게 거듭 감사한다. 이 책은 특히 국방대학원 도서관에 다수 비치되어, 어느 때는 전권(10여 권)이 동시에 대출되는 등 빛을 발하기도 하였다.

이 책을 발간한 동기와 의미 그리고 개요에 대해, 책 머리말을 인용하여 대신하고자 한다.

1960년대 초, 필자는 단기간이나마 수학을 위해 미국을 방문한 적이 있다. 기간 중 워싱턴시(D.C.) 소재 '워싱턴 기념 첨탑'과 '링컨 기념관' 그리고 '알링턴 국립묘지'를 찾았었다. 필자는 그곳에서 '미국 형성의 역사' 즉, 13개 주로부터 시작한 미국이 300여 년 만에 50개 주로 팽창되는 과정의 역사 기록을 보았고, 노예 해방의 역사적 사건은 물론 '시민(국민)' 자신에 의한 '자치 사상'(Civilian Control)을 체득할 수 있었으며,…

그 후 1990년대 후반에 미국 전쟁사학회(戰爭史學會) 모임 차 워싱턴을 재차 방문한 적이 있다. 주최 측의 안내로 미 의회, 화이트 하우스, CIA본부 등을 둘러볼 수 있었다. 이때는 미국이 동서 냉전에서 최종 승리하고, 걸프전에서도 환상의 승리를 달성한 직후라 미국의 안보전략 결심권자들은 '신세계 질서를 미국 주도'로 정의하고 있었으며, 21세기 미래 전망을 '팍스 아메리카나(Pax-Americana)'로 확신하고 있었다.

오늘날 미국은 세계 유일 초강대국으로 존재하고 있다. 또한 그들의 '국가안보전략사상'은 곧 세계 안보전략사상이 되고 있다. 세계화 경제 시대에 들어서고 있는 현실에서 한국의 국가 이익이 미국과의 경제·군사적 안보 관계 유지 발전에 있음을 상기한다면 우리는 그들의 국가안보전략사상사를 심도 있게 연구해야 할 것이다. 이 책은 이러한 목적에 기여했으면 하는 바램에서 쓰여졌다. 이 책이 완성되기까지 도움을 주신 분들게 감사의 뜻을 전하고자 한다.

우선 이 책을 쓰기 위해 미국에 가야 했을 때 제반 절차와 편의를 제공해 준 '볼대학'의 박성재 교수님, 아울러 동 대학의 총장이신 Dr. John E. Worthen과 관계 교수님들께 감사드린다. 특히 미국 ROTC 후보생들에게 강의할 수 있는 기회를 준 군사학부(Department of Military Science)의 책임자 Col. Foley와 직원 일동에게도 감사드린다, 끝으로 이 책이 미국의 국가안보전략사상사를 이해하고, 한국의 국가안보전략사상의 발전에 조금이나마 도움이 된다면 큰 보람으로 생각하겠다.

◇ '한국국가안보전략사상사(학)연구회(사이버)' 설립

◦ 국가안보전략에 대한 연구

미국의 '국가안보전략'에 대해 관심을 가지고 연구하고 책을 써내면서 자연히 우리 '한국의 국가안보전략'에 관심을 갖게 되었다. 이미 말한 바와 같이, 미국 최초로 발간된 「The National Security Strategy of U.S.A. 1987」이라는 문서는 미국 의회의 요구에 따라, 레이건 대통령 정부에 의해 발간되었는데, '소련과 공산권에 대한 최후의 일격'을 가하려는 결심을 나타낸 것이었다. 그동안 미국은 국가안보에 대해 주로 'National Deffence, 국방'이라는 개념을 사용해 오다가 이때부터 '국가안보전략'이라는 개념을 정립하고 용어를 사용하기 시작하였다.

이후 한국에서도 '전략문제연구소' 등이 여러 곳 생겨나 그동안 '국방 문제'라는 과제에서 '세계화한 전략 문제'를 연구하기 시작하였다. 이때부터, 이미 말한 바 있는, 내가 친하게 지내온 '홍성태 장군'이 '한국전략문제연구소' 설립하여 국내 전략 문제 연구를 선도해 나갔다.

◦ '한국국가안보전략사상사(학)'에 대한 연구회 설립

나는 생각했다. 아직도 취약한 '한국의 국가 안보 전략'을 발전 격상시키기 위해서는 한국다운 국가안보전략이 확립되어야겠고, 그러려면 전통 있는 '한국적 국가안보전략사상'이 토대가 되어야 한다고 생각했다. 그러려면 역대 정부, 특히 그를 지도한 역대 대통령과 왕들의 국가안보전략사상연구와 이를 역사와 함께 연계된 '국가안보전략사상사' 연구가 필수적이며 바른 길이라고 믿게 되었다. 그러면서도 야심차게 이를 학문화하려는—한국에는 30여 종류의 사상사가 있고, 여성 사상사도 있다.—시도로 '한국국가안보전략사상사(학)연구회'를 설립하여 당분간은 'Cyber' 공간에서 개인적으로 운영하기로 하였다.

그 공식 명칭은 'The Institute of Korea National Security Strategy Thought History', IKONSSTORY,라 하고, 앱은, 'www.ikonsstory.com'로 정하였다. 동시에 동기

생 홈페이지에 한자리 잡아 한국의 국가안보전략발전에 기여할 수 있도록 노력하였다. 그래서 미국서 가져온 자료와 각종 기초 자료들을 'e-book'으로 제작하여 열거해 두기도 하였다. 그러나 자본이 없어 대외 활동은 처음부터 제한되었으나 그래도 육군대학에는 몇 번 초빙되어 가서 강의도 하였다.

그러다가 2010년대에 들어와 동기생의 동기회 활동도 문을 닫고, 사이버 활동도 위축되기에 나의 욕망도 여기에서 반은 접고—ikonsstory.com도 문 닫고, 대외 활동 자연 소멸—, 내 개인적인 연구 활동은 더 활발하게 계속하고 있다. 곧 2026년경에는 『한국국가안보전략사상사』의 '하권'을 출판할 예정으로 지금도 연구에 연구를 충실하게 노력하고 있다. 그래서 내가 남길 비명에 '여기 '한국국가안보전략사상사(학)을 창시한 사람이 누워 있노라'라고 새겨넣으라고 유언할 생각이다.

마무리 말

우리 손자 준호와 그 후손들에게

1. 우리 자식들의 결혼과 출세 그리고 현재

우리에게는 일찍이 복 받은 두 아들이 있었다. 큰애는 이름이 정언(廷彦)이고 둘째는 성언(盛彦)이다. 정언이는 경희대학교 ROTC에서 졸업과 동시 장교로 임관하여 한강 하류 김포 최전선에서 소대장으로 근무하였고, 둘째는 중앙대학교 ROTC를 졸업하고 장교로 임관하여 동부 최전선 사단의 고성군 통일전망대 인접에서 소대장으로 근무하였다.

큰아이는 출신학교 추천에 따라 전역과 동시 미국 '인디아나주'에 있는 BALL주립대학교 대학원에서 '체육교육학' 석사학위를 받았다. 그동안 그곳 같은 학교에서 수업 중에 양가 집 여학생 '장영미'하고 사귀어서, 양가 부모의 허락을 받아 한국에 나와서 결혼하고 다시 복학하여 학업을 계속하였다. 우리 복된 며느리도 같은 학교에서 같은 해 '아동교육학' 석사학위를 마치고 둘이 함께 '인디아나'주 안에 있는 'Purdue' 주립대학교 대학원으로 가서, 조교 생활을 하는 등 학비를 보태가며 노력해서 둘 다 같은 해에, 같은 학교 같은 학위수여식장(졸업식장)에서 아들은 'Biomechanics', 며느리는 '아동교육학' 전공으로 박사학위를 취득하였다.

그러자 때마침 모교 'BALL주립대학교'에서 기회가 주어져 둘 다 거의 같은 시기에 각각의 전공으로 교수로 취직되었다. 그런데 그동안 학업 때문에 미루어 오던—우리 내외가 많이 기다리던—아기, 정말로 반갑고 귀엽고 든든하고 고마운 손자 '준호'를 낳았다. 이때 사부인이 6개월여, 우리 내외가 6개월여 가서 손자를 봐 주었으나 며느리는 일단 학교를 쉬면서 수고를 많이 했다.

우리 며느리는 어려운 가운데도 교육열이 대단하여 아이가 조금 자라자, 앞으로 아이의 교육 발전을 위해 시골 'Muncie'를 떠나 이웃 '오하이오'주의 교육 도시—우리식의 8학군 동네—'New Albany'로 이주해 가서, 동시에 'OHIO Dominican University'에 교수로 초빙 받아 그곳에 영주하게 되었다. 아범은 'Ball State University'에서 '멀티미디어그룹' 리더, 화상강의 스페시얼리스트로, 또한 동 대학교 'Faculty'로 활동하고 있다. 그리하여 그들은 미국서 공부하며 가정을 이루고, 동시에 교수로 학생 수업을 지도하면서도 아주 스마트한 손자를 잘 키웠다.

이렇게 잘 자란 손자 준호는, 그동안 중고등학교 때부터 대학까지 함께 알고 지내던 동급생 미국 아이로 예쁘고 참한 'Kate'와 결혼하고, 'J.P. Morgan의 Chase 은행' 계열의 같은 직장에서 직장 생활하면서 가정을 잘 리드해 나가고 있다. 우리에게는 정말 복받은 아범 어멈이고, 손자며느리가 되어 있다.

그런데 아범과 어멈은 주말부부—미국에서는 흔하기는 하지만—가 되어 보기에 딱하나 그들은 아주 행복하게 잘 지내고 있는데, 다만 그동안 거의 혼자서(라고 보일 정도로) 준호를 데리고 교수 생활을 해낸 수고 많은 어멈이 참으로 안쓰럽기는 하였으나 기특하기 그지없고 고마울 뿐이다.

◇ **'천재와 바보는 종이 한 장 차이'**

그런데, 둘째인 성언이는 어릴 때부터 천재성을 나타내었는데 특히 소리(음정)에 밝았다. 물론 대중 매체에서 보여주는 그런 천재성은 아니고, 그저 가족들이 신기해하고 놀랄 정도, 한동안 함께 집에서 지내던 (수재형) 외삼촌 형제들—서울 유명 고등학교로, 그리고 이미 거기를 졸업하고 서울공대에 통학 중인 서울 유학생들—이 아주 귀여워하고 놀라워했다. 세상에는 '천재와 바보는 종이 한 장 차이'라는 말이 있다. 바로 생각의 차이이다. 천재로 보이는 사람들도 '천재같이 생각하면 천재가 되고 바보같이 생각하면 바보가 된다'고.

그 우리 집 둘째는, 겨우 일어나 앉을 즈음에 혼자서 한글을 깨우쳐 티비 자막을 읽었고, 초등학교 가기 전 또래들을 모아놓고 동화와 만화책을 읽어주었다. 그런데 한편으로는, 방안에서 무얼 나무라서 우는 걸 멈추라 하면, 방문밖에 나가 앉아 "나는 여기서 울래" 하며 기어이 운다. 커가며 무엇이든 깊이 생각하고 많이 생각하는 듯 흔히 일반 상식과는 대조적인 말을 하기도. 예를 들면, '대붕은 높이 떠 멀리 본다'면, '작은 새는 낮게 떠서 더 확실하게 본다' 던가, '일찍 일어나는 새가 벌레를 잡는다' 하면 '일찍 일어난 벌레 잡아 먹힌다'고 하였다.

가까운 친척 특히 외삼촌들의 기대와 사랑을 받으며 성장하였는데, 별로 원하지는 않았으나 그래도 순순히 ROTC 과정을 마치고 대한민국 강원도 고성의 최북단 최전선에서 소대장으로 소대원과 잘 어울리고 존경받으며 근무하고 전역하였다. 전역과 동시 직업의 안전성과 장래성 그리고 전역 장교 집단 취업 등의 매력에 끌려 주력 은행에 취업하였으며, 근무 중 은행 자체 엘리트 과정도 우수하게 수습하였다. 그러나 시간이 가면서 그는 'IT' 분야에 깊은 관심을 가지고 여유 시간과 금전을 투자하며 나날을 보냈다.

그러나 당시—1990년대 초 즉 이제 막 컴퓨터와 전자 분야에 눈을 떠가던 486 시대—그가 가고 싶은 곳을 발견하지 못하자, 그는 점차 직장이 싫어지고 장래 희망이 보이지 않는데다, 이 애비조차 그런 줄도 모르고 '근면·자립·자조'만 강조하다 보니, 세상살이에 실망하였다고 보여진다. 그래서 '천재와 바보는 종이 한 장 차이'로, 아마도, 그가 가보고 싶은 세상이 문밖 어디에 있을 것으로 생각하고, 어느 날 그리로 떠나고 말았다. 나이 26세……, 더 이상 이 애비가 무슨 말을 할 수 있겠느냐. 오로지 세상 고민 없는 하나님의 나라에서 편히 그리고 마음에 맞는 일을 하며 지내기를 기도하고 또 기도한다.

2. 우리 사랑하는 손자 '준호'가 태어나다

아들 문정언(文廷彦)과 며느리 장영미(張英美)가 미국 인디아나 주립대학 'Purdue'에서 함께 한날한시에 성공적으로 각각의 '박사학위'를 취득하고 일단 석사학위의 모교인 '먼시' 동네로 돌아와 교편을 잡으면서 정착하였다. 그들이 원해서, 또 당시는 그것이 그들의 삶에 좋을 것 같아서 미국 정착을 허락하였다.

그리하여 교수 생활을 하던 그들로부터, 단기 4331년(서기 1998년) 5월 27일 18:00에, 미국 'Indiana 주' 'Muncie'에서, 드디어 우리가 기다리고 기다리던 손자가 태어났다. 무게 3.3kg, 당당하고 씩씩한 '고추 달린 녀석'이었다. 경사스럽게도 지 아버지하고 같은 5월 달 같은 27일에 태어났다. 우리 가족 5명 중 이 할아버지와 할머니, 아범 그리고 손자가 모두 5월생이 되었다.

이 할아버지는 기꺼이 우리 손자에게 기대와 미래 행복을 기원하며 이름을 지어주었다.

한글 : 문준호
영어 : MOON JUN HO ; JUN HO MOON
한문 : 文俊浩
띠 : 호랑이 띠(Tiger Year)

* 이름의 뜻 ; 사람이 뛰어나고, 큰물이 깊고 넓게 흐르듯 큰마음 큰 뜻을 가지고, 만인을 이롭게 하는 큰 인물이 되리라.(俊—뛰어나다, 크다. 浩—크다, 물이 넓고 넓게 흐르는 모양, 광대한 모양)

3. 한국의 5000년 역사와 전통 그리고 미국과의 관계

이미 이 할아버지의 군대와 군인 생활을 통해서 내 시대 한국과 미국과의 관계를 잘 이해할 수 있었겠지만은 그래도 내 깊은 뜻을 이해하는데 도움이 되도록, 너희들 할아버지의 조국이요 너희들의 원 고향인 한국의 5000년 역사와 전통 그리고 미국과의 관계를 간단히 개관해 두고자 한다. 역사 연구를 즐겨했던 이 할아버지가 연구(종합)한 우리나라는, 5000년의 뿌리 깊은 역사와 전통을 자랑하는바, 흔히 '한국(韓國)'이라고 한다. 이는 '대한민국'(大韓民國)을 줄인 말이기도 하나 원래는 전체 역사에서 통하는 우리나라 고유의 이름이기도 하다.

우리의 옛 나라는 5000여 년 전 '단군왕검'이 개천(開天, 건국)하여 '단군왕검 시대'를 열었고, 우리 민족이 살았던 지역은, 지금의 중국 화남 화중 회북과 동북성 그리고 한반도와 일본열도 그리고 사람이 살 수 있었던 당시 황해(지금은 바다)에 걸친, 마치 '바람풍자 풍(風)' 모양의 평지 평원 지대였다. 그러하기에 이 할아버지는 주장하고 있다, "지금의 중국 역사와 일본의 역사는 한국 역사의 일부라고". 이때부터 공동체의 지도 이념으로 '홍익인간(弘益人間) 사상, 즉, '인간 상호간에 '상부상조(相扶相助), '유무상통(有無相通)' 하면서 '널리 인간세계를 이롭게 한다'는 사상을 표방하였다. 이는 오늘날 미국이 주도하며 인류가 지향해 가고 있는 바로 그 'U.N'의 사상 즉, 자유 민주주의(Democracy) 사상과 뜻을 같이한다.

일찍부터 우리 종족은 '하늘과 사람과 땅'이라는 인류의 3대 기본 사상을 정의함으로써, 오늘날의 민주주의 기본 정신 즉, 자연과 사람을 기본으로 하여 우리 한국을 개천(開天) 하였던 것이다. 그 표현으로 '3'이라는 숫자는 한국인의 기본 사상이 되어서, 고대로부터, 그 상징으로 우리의 (특히) 각종 제기(祭器)는 '삼각(三脚, Tripod)' 받침으로 만들어 사용해 왔다.

단군왕검의 자손들(부여계)에 의해 나라가 발전되어 오다가, BC 1000년경에 이르러 단군왕조가 잠시 열국(列國)화 하였고, BC 200년경에는 북방에서 강력한 '고구려' 탄생하고, AD 직전에 중 남부에서 신라와 백제가 나타나 고대 한국은 삼국시대가 되었다. 이후 AD 500년경에 신라가 통일 전쟁을 이르켜 삼국통일을 이루었으나, 신라와 연합을 이루었던 '지나(支那), China'의 '당나라'의 역습으로 '나당전쟁'이 되고, 그 결과 신라는 현재의 중국 대륙 영토를 잃고 한반도로 축소되어 들어오게 되었다.

이후 북방의 '발해'와 남북국(南北國)을 이루며 천년의 왕조를 누렸던 '신라' 또한, 10세기경에는 대륙에서 한반도에 정착하려는 같은 민족인 '고려(高麗, Korea)' 세력에게 패망하였는데, 이때부터 고려 역사가는 고려의 정통성을 부각하기 위해 한국 역사를 한반도 역사로 축소 변질시켰다. 그러나 그래도 현재 차이나 땅이 우리 고유의 땅임을 잊지 않으려고, 한반도 지명들을 옛 고토(현 차이나)의 지명으로 변조시켜 한국의 지리와 역사를 차이나 옛땅 환경으로 고착시키게 되었다. 예를 들어, '백제', '호남' 등이 중국에 있고 한국에도 있다.

14세기경에 고려 장군이었던 '이성계'가 군민 쿠테타에 성공하여 완전하게 한반도에 축소된 '이씨 조선'을 세우고, 한양(서울)에 정도하여 600여 년을 한반도 통일국가로 유지하여 왔다. 이 역사를 통하여 우리나라 우리 민족은 동아시아의 반만년 역사를 자랑하는 '평지평원 지대 원주 종족'의 종주 민족으로서, '차이나'(支那)' 역사가 곧 우리 민족사의 일부요,—중원(中原)이 곧 우리의 옛 땅이요.—일본사는 곧 우리 아우 형제(열도로 이주한 동족)의 역사로서 이 또한 우리 한국사의 일부임을 잘 알 수가 있는 것이다.

이후 이씨 조선의 말년에 이르러 제국주의 서세동점(西勢東占)과 일제(日帝)의 망동으로 '고종'의 '이씨 조선'은 망국지경에 이르렀다. 이 시대 미국이 '셔먼호 사건(1866)'을 계기로 '이조선'(李氏朝鮮)에 '포함 외교'를 강요하였으나 1871년 '신미양요(辛未洋擾)'를 계기로 오히려 한—미가 소통하게 되었다. 그래서 1882년에 '조미수호통상조약'을 체결하고 '미국식 사관학교'—'연무공원(鍊武公院)'을 창설(1888)하여 미군 교관단이 도착하였으나 일제의 압력으로 폐교되었다. 1904년, 일제가 '러일전쟁'을 일으키고, 서울로 들어와 고종황제와 제 각료들을 협박하여 '한일의정서'를 강제로 체결하고 '이조선의 주권'을 강탈하였다.

이에 고종은 이승만을 미국에 급파하여 미국 대통령 '루즈벨트'를 만나 지원을 요청하였으나 '이미 늦었다'는 대답만 들었다. 이후 이승만은 미국에 남아 공부하고, 한국 독립운동을 지도하였는데 미국의 배려덕이었다. 특히 이승만을 수제자로 두었던 미국 '죠지워싱턴 대학교' 총장이던 '윌슨 대통령'이, 미국이 참전하여 세계 제1차 제국주의 전쟁에서 승리하고, 전후 신질서 즉 제국주의 식민지주의를 타파할 목적으로 '민족자결의 원칙'을 선포하자 우리 한국 민족 전체는 이에 용기를 얻어 망명정부를 세우고 국내외적으로 '3·1만세 운동〉과 함께 '광복 운동'을 본격적으로 전개하였다.

그런 가운데 한국은 1945년 미국이 주력이던 연합군의 제2차 세계대전 승리로 광복은 되었으나 무일푼이 된 한국을 미국은 한때, 전적으로 먹여 살려주고 구호해 주면서 새 삶의 길을 열어주었다. 1950년의 6·25 남침적란 때에 미국은 즉각 개입하여, 국제 공산주의 세력을 제압하고 동시에 '한미방위조약' 체결과 '한미연합사' 창설로 오늘에 이르기까지, 대한민국 군사적 방어와 전방위적 민주주의 발전에 크게 기여하고 있다. 그리하여 미국은 미래에도 우리의 동맹국이요. 최선의 우방국으로 우리와 함께 세계와 인류의 민주주의화의 길로 매진해 갈 것이라고 믿는다.

4. 사랑하는 우리 손자 '준호'와 그 후손들에게 할아버지가 당부한다

너희들이 일생을 살아가는 동안 직업이 무엇이건 또 어느 때건 간에 한국과의 상부상조 관계를 항시 염두에 두고, 너희 미국 것과 한국 것 간의 가교 역할을 꼭 다해주기 바란다.

그리고 너희 한국 조상, 이 할아버지 할머니의 나라를 잊지 말기를 바라며, 동시에 이 나의 자서전에 쓰여 있는 대로, 이 할아버지 할머니의 너희들에 대한 간절한 사랑 또한 잊지 말기를 바란다. 그래서 말인데, 가능한한 대대(代代)로 우리 한글을 익혀서 알도록 하고, 한국을 의미하는 밥과 김치, 치마저고리와 노리개를 잊지 말고, 그리고 설날과 추석에는 가족 모두 한자리에 모여 조상을 기리며 즐거운 한때 지내는 인정이 넘쳐나는 한국 풍속도 잊지 말기를 바란다.

행여나 군인 되는 후손 있다면, 특히나 이 군인 할버지가 바라는 바지만, 가능한 주한 미군 부대로 와서 우리 한국군과 함께 한국과 미국 최전선을 지킴과 동시에 아름다운 금수강산을 두루 다니며 구경하고, 한국과 이 할아버지 할머니와 그리고 한국 조상들의 정취를 느껴 보기 바란다.

나아가서 운이 닿는다면, 이 할아버지가 못다 한 그것, 전선의 장군이 되어 정의의 깃발 아래 인류를 위한 승전의 영웅이 되어주기를 바란다. 그 뜻이 이루어지면 반듯이 내게 와서 "할아버지 소망도 이루었노라"고 고해야 하느니라. 그러면 우리는 기뻐할 것이며 축복해 주리라.

나와 할머니가 하나님을 모시고 항상 너희들의 행운을 반드시 지켜줄 것이다. 아범, 어멈 그리고 준호와 손자며느리 Kate 그리고 그 후손들, 곧 나의 자손들이여, 만대(萬代)로 영원히 번창할지어다.

5. 2023년 12월 30일, 손자 준호와 Kate 결혼, 축하 또 축하

2023년 12월 30일, 미국 오하이오 주의 훌륭한 천주교회당에서 아주 멋지고 뜻깊은, 우리 손자 준호와 Kate의 행복한 결혼식이 거행되었다. 이 할머니와 할아버지는 멀리서나마 세상에 더 없는 가장 큰 축하를 보낸다. 그와 동시에 몇 줄 당부의 말을 보내니 명심하여 행하기를 바란다.

우리 손자 준호와 Kate의 결혼을 지성을 다하여 축하한다!
We (grand pa and ma) congratulate with all our heart to our loveliest grandson Jun Ho and Kate for Wedding!

할아버지와 할머니가 너희 결혼식에 마땅히 참석해 직접 축하하고 기념선물도 주어야 하는데, 건강상 여의치 못해 참석하지 못하지만 마음은 더 뜨겁게 너희들의 오늘 결혼식을 축하해 마지 않는다.
We have to participate and congratulate and give you souvenir present on face to face, but could not by health. But with our heartful congratulation give you from here our home, Korea.

특히 너희 둘이 동기동창으로 오래전부터 약혼하여 그 약속대로 그날에 결혼식을 올리게 된 것을 높이 평가하고 축하한다. 그러하기에 두 사람의 이 약속 지킴이는 이후 100년 가약 또한 지켜 저서 평생을 함께하는 행복한 가정이 되리라고 믿는다.
Specially, we appreciate highly you(schoolmate) keep your promise of wedding day on the day. Because of keeping promise, You couple will be 'hundred years couple' and happy as the day is long family.

이제 결혼식을 통해서 미국 땅에서 새로운 한 문씨 가문(Munchi/Albany MOON Family)을 창조해 낸 우리 자랑스러운 문준호—케이트 커플에게 이 할아버지와 할머니가 깊고 큰 사랑을 담아 몇 가지 당부하려고 한다.
Now as this wedding, a new MOON's family(J MOON's) in U.S.A is create. With this honorable and proudful chance, We would like say to you(couple) some requests with deep love.

첫째는, 둘이가 서로 믿고, 존경하고, 사랑하여 평화의 가정을 이루고, 이 가정 평화를 바탕으로 직장 평화, 커뮤니티 평화, 사회 평화 그리고 나아가 인류 평화에 기여해 주기 바란다.
Firstly, you make basically peaceful home with love, respect and believe in

each other. Then, we hope, on this basic home peace you contribute job peace, community peace, society peace and by extension, peace for mankind.

둘째는, 가능한 한 아이들을 많이 가져서 복 많고 웃음이 많고 정이 넘쳐나는 가정을 이루고, 그리하여 새로운 J MOON의 가문이 하나님의 축복을 받으면서 영원무궁하도록 번성해 갈 수 있기를 바란다.

Secondly, we wish that you have your sufficiently children, and so you will be get good luck, laugh a lot, and affectionate family home.

셋째는, Wealthy 보다 Healthy다, 주어진 일은 기어이 완수해야 한다, 그러나 일방적으로 무리하지는 말라. 그리고 너가 본 바와 가능한 한 할아버지가 매일 아침에 하던 간단한 기초 체조를 평생 일상생활화 해보라. 그러면 지금 이 할아버지같이 90세는 넘길 수 있으리라

Thirdly, it is Healthy than Wealthy. You shall complete your duty but don't push yourself too hard. And, as you saw grandpa every morning soft physical exercise, you make it activities of daily living, then you will be over 90 years old.

넷째로, 준호 너는 너 스스로 이미 크리에이터이다, 그대로 능동적이고 적극적이고 창조적인 길로 가라, 또한 너희들은 Taker 아닌 Giver인 것으로 믿는다. 그러하기에 Giver로서 이웃과 남에게도 항상 친절하고 너희보다 못한 사람들, 길거리 beggar에게도 동정심을 갖고 적선하여야 한다. 그래서 항상 상부상조하는 마음으로 사회에 기여해 주기를 바란다.

Fourth, Jun Ho, you are Creator already. As it is, you go ahead the way of active, positive, and creative all life. We believe You couple are not Taker but Giver. And so, you keep your very good kind mind always, you sympathize your poor neighbor and give money to beggar and amass alms giving. And so Always, with a spirit of mutual help you serve your society.

다섯째로, 살아가면서 남과 이웃 그리고 누구에게도 원수지는 일이 없도록 하라. 그래야 평생을 편안한 마음으로, 특히 은퇴 후에도 편안한 마음과 건강을 유지하며 살아갈 수가 있다.

Fifth, while your life time you don't hold back with neighborhood and everybody. And then you can get peaceful mind all days, specially after retire, you will be get peaceful mind and healthy life.

끝으로, 내 유일한 손자 준호와 그 사랑하는 동반자 케이트가 이루는 이 가정에 만복이

깃들고 하나님의 축복이 있으시기를 기원한다.

Finally, we pray "God bless you (Jun Ho and Kate MOON) and God be with Jun Ho family with full luck !" On the day beautiful Wedding, 2023.12.30, by Grand Pa & Ma.

아울러, 너희 둘과 앞으로 가지게 될 여러 자손들 모두에게 하나님의 축복과 가호가 함께 하기를 거듭 기원하면서, 이로서 이 자서전을 마무리 하련다.

단기4358년, 2025년 5월
한국 경기도 일산에서, 군인 할아버지가

작가 연보

1935. 5. 9	부산 동래에서 태어나다.
1935. 5. 9 ~ 1954. 6	동래 내성초등학교, 부산사범학교(병설중학교), 동래고등학교.
1954. 6 ~ 1958. 6	육군사관학교(화랑대-태능) 사관생도 졸업, 육군소위 임관(1958. 6. 16), 이학사(理學사).
1958. 6 ~ 1962. 1	수도사단 제1연대 소대장, 대대작전 과장, 중대장, 육군보병학교 장교초등군사반(OBC) 수료.
1962. 1 ~ 1962 . 4	비정규전 과정, 미국 특수전학교(J. F Kennedy Center, Ft. Bragg, NC).
1962. 4 ~ 1964. 10	보병학교 유격학부 교관—동복 올빼미 유격교육대, 결혼(1962. 4. 22)하고 광주에서 첫 살림, 첫아들 정언이 탄생(1963. 5. 27), 보병학교전술학부 교관 겸 학생대 중대장—ROTC 2기생 훈육 중대장, 수도육군병원 입원
1964. 10 ~ 1966. 10	연세대학 ROTC교관, 육군보병학교 고등군사반 (OAC) 수료, 제5사단 작전참모부 대간첩작전 장교, 보병연대 중대장, 파월지원.
1966. 10 ~ 1967. 10	파월 맹호부대사령부 전사(戰史) 과장.
1967. 10 ~ 1969.	육군본부 특전감실 특수전 담당 장교.
1969. 1 ~ 1970. 9	서독군 지휘참모대학(함부르그) 유학, 군사어학학교(6개월)-Euskirchen, 알프스 산악여단(2개월)-Bad Reichenhal Alps, 프랑크푸르트 제5기갑사단(1개월)-Frankfurt am mine.
1970. 9 ~ 1972. 1	육군대학 특수전학부 유격과목 교관(진해, 관사 생활).
1972. 1 ~ 1975. 9	수도기계화사단 근무, 제106부대(제2기계화보병대대-1972. 10. 24) 창설, 수도기계화사단창설(1973. 3), 수도기계화사단 군수참모(1974 ~ 1975).
1975. 9 ~ 1977. 2	공수특전사령부 정보참모, 모로코 군사지원 조사단장, 제8차 아태지역특전사령관회의(미국, 1975. 11)수행.
1977. 2 ~ 1980. 5	국방대학원 안보과정(~ 1977. 10), 논산훈련소 연대장(~ 1978. 11), 국방대학원 군인교수 겸 관리과정 교수부장, 외교안보 무궁화계획(사우디아라비아 군사지원) 조사단장, 사우디아라비아 파견.
1980. 5 ~ 1981. 5	육군대학 참모장, 육군대학 교수부장.
1981. 5 ~ 1983. 1	제7공수특전여단장.

1983. 1 ~ 1984. 6 육군 제8사단장.
1984. 6 ~ 1986. 7 육군본부 작전참모부장.
1986. 7 ~ 1088. 10 육군 제 1군단장(~ 1987. 12), 육군 제1야전군사령부 부사령관,
1988. 10 ~ 1993. 3 국가안전보장위원회 겸 비상기획위원회 부위원장(차관급).
1994. 5 ~ 1996. 8 미국 '볼'인디아나주립대학 군사학부(ROTC) 방문 교수, 귀국.
1997. 3 ~ 1999. 2 국방대학원 초빙 교수—전문 경력 인사 활용 제도.
1999. 2 ~ 현재 한국전략문제연구소(KRIS) 자문위원.

학 력

석사 : 인력자원관리(인사관리), 국립 전북대학교(1983).
학사 : 이학사, 육군사관학교(1958).

상 훈

보국훈장 국선장 : 국가안전보장위원회 겸 비상기획위원회 부위원장, 1993.
보국훈장 천수장 : 육군 제1군단장(육군중장), 1988.
미국 보국훈장 : Legion of Merit(Degree of Officer) 육군 제1군단장, 1988
미국명예시민권 : Fayetteville. NC, U.S.A.
육군 최고 권총 사수(45구경) : 1960년도 육군사격대회(제5군단주최).

출 간

미국국가안보전략사상사 : 을지서적, 1999. 5, 582쪽.
한국국가안보전략사상사(상·고대. 중세편) : 21세기군사연구소, 2007. 5, 791쪽.
한국국가안보전략사상사(중·근현대편) : 좋은옥토, 2018. 5, 703쪽.
한국국가안보전략사상사(하·현대편) : 집필 중, 2026년 발간 예정.
한국미래국가안보전략사상 : 집필 예정(구상 중).

논문·논설·에세이

아세아—태평양 집단안보조약기구 구상 : 국방대학원 졸업논문, 1977.
군비통제·군축·안전보장 : 1990, 국가안보총서, 국가안전보장위원회.
한반도 군비축소·군비통제에 대한 포괄적인 제안 : 1994. 2, 한국전략문제연구소 세미나 발표.
기타 국가안보전략 및 군사전략문제 에세이 등 다수

Grandpa was a Soldier

2025년 10월 30일 초판 1쇄 펴냄

지은이 _ 문영일
펴낸이 _ 양문규
펴낸곳 _ 詩와에세이
디자인 - 장영도, 안소라

신고번호 _ 제319-2005-000014호
주　　소 _ (30021) 세종특별자치시 조치원읍 충현로 159,
상가동 107-1호
대표전화 _ (044)863-7652
팩시밀리 _ 0505-116-7653
휴대전화 _ 010-5355-7565
전자우편 _ sie2005@naver.com
공 급 처 _ 한국출판협동조합
주문전화 _ (02)716-5616
팩시밀리 _ (031)944-8234~6

ISBN 979-11-91914-93-1 (03810)